International Politics on the World Stage

EVOLUTION OF THE WORLD POLITICAL SYSTEM

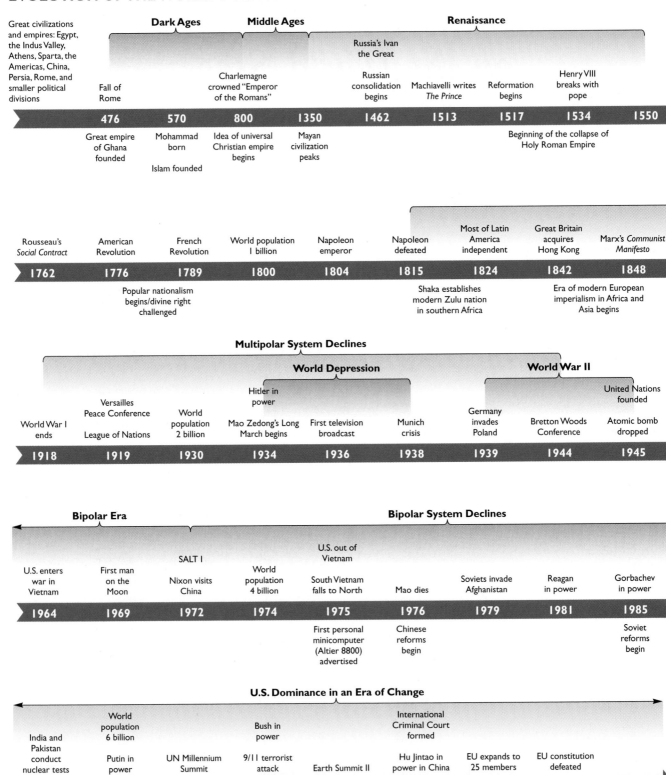

Thirty Years' War

Treaty of Augsburg	Spanish Armada defeated		Grotius publishes first book on international law	Treaty of Westphalia	Hobbes publishes *Leviathan*	Louis XIV begins to govern	Industrial Revolution under way
1555	**1588**	**1618**	**1625**	**1648**	**1651**	**1661**	**1750**
		Tokugawa Era of premodern Japan begins		Manchu dynasty founded in China			

Multipolar Balance of Power

U.S. naval squadron in Tokyo Bay demands U.S.–Japan trade	Charles Darwin's *The Origin of Species*	Dominion of Canada established		Spanish-American War	First manned flight		World War I begins	Russian Revolution
1853	**1859**	**1867**	**1868**	**1898**	**1903**	**1911**	**1914**	**1917**
			Meiji restoration begins modern era in Japan	U.S. imperialist period			Chinese Manchu emperor deposed	

Bipolar Era

U.S.–USSR Peaceful Coexistence

India and Pakistan independent / Cold war / Containment	Israel independent	NATO established / Chinese Communists take power	Stalin dies	Vietnam independent and divided	Ghana independent	European Common Market formed	World population 3 billion	Cuban missile crisis
1947	**1948**	**1949**	**1953**	**1954**	**1957**	**1958**	**1960**	**1962**
				Beginning of African independence				

Bipolar Era Ends   U.S. Dominance in an Era of Change

World population 5 billion	Berlin Wall opened	Germany reunites	War in Persian Gulf	Clinton in power / Yeltsin in power	NAFTA ratified / European Union begins	Cairo Population Conference / Genocide in Rwanda	4th World Conference on Women / UN's 50th anniversary	Kyoto Global Warming Conference
1987	**1989**	**1990**	**1991**	**1992**	**1993**	**1994**	**1995**	**1997**
	Tiananmen Square massacre		Soviet Union collapses	Earth Summit / Chaos in Bosnia	START II	Summit of the Americas	World Trade Organization begins	Kofi Annan becomes UN secretary-general

JOHN T. ROURKE, Ph.D., professor emeritus, is former head of the Department of Political Science at The University of Connecticut. He is a coauthor with Mark A. Boyer of *International Politics on the World Stage, Brief,* Sixth Edition (McGraw-Hill, 2006); the author of *Presidential Wars and American Democracy: Rally 'round the Chief* (Paragon House, 1993); a coauthor of *Direct Democracy and International Politics: Deciding International Issues through Referendums* (Lynne Rienner, 1992); the editor of *Taking Sides: Clashing Views on Controversial Issues in World Politics,* Eleventh Edition, expanded (McGraw-Hill/Dushkin, 2005) and *You Decide 2005: Current Debates in American Politics* (Longman, 2005); the author of *Making Foreign Policy: United States, Soviet Union, China* (Brooks/Cole, 1990), *Congress and the Presidency in U.S. Foreign Policymaking* (Westview, 1985), and numerous articles and papers. He continues to teach and especially enjoys introductory classes. His regard for students has molded his approach to writing—he conveys scholarship in a language and within a frame of reference that undergraduates can appreciate. Rourke believes, as the theme of this book reflects, that politics affects us all and we can affect politics. Rourke practices what he propounds. His career long involved the university's internship program and advising one of its political clubs. Additionally, he has served as a staff member of Connecticut's legislature and has been involved in political campaigns on the local, state, and national levels.

International Politics on the World Stage

ELEVENTH EDITION

John T. Rourke
University of Connecticut

Boston   Burr Ridge, IL   Dubuque, IA   Madison, WI   New York   San Francisco   St. Louis
Bangkok   Bogotá   Caracas   Kuala Lumpur   Lisbon   London   Madrid   Mexico City
Milan   Montreal   New Delhi   Santiago   Seoul   Singapore   Sydney   Taipei   Toronto

The McGraw·Hill Companies

Higher Education

Published by McGraw-Hill, an imprint of The McGraw-Hill Companies, Inc., 1221 Avenue of the Americas, New York, NY 10020. Copyright © 2007. All rights reserved. No part of this publication may be reproduced or distributed in any form or by any means, or stored in a database or retrieval system, without the prior written consent of The McGraw-Hill Companies, Inc., including, but not limited to, in any network or other electronic storage or transmission, or broadcast for distance learning.

This book is printed on acid-free paper.

1 2 3 4 5 6 7 8 9 0 CCI/CCI 0 9 8 7 6

ISBN-13   978-0-07-310355-6
ISBN-10   0-07-310355-1

Editor in Chief: *Emily Barrosse*
Publisher: *Lyn Uhl*
Sponsoring Editor: *Monica Eckman*
Marketing Manager: *Katherine Bates*
Director of Development: *Lisa Pinto*
Developmental Editor: *Ava Suntoke*
Production Editor: *Brett Coker*
Manuscript Editor: *Sheryl Rose*
Art Director: *Jeanne M. Schreiber*
Text Designers: *Glenda King and Preston Thomas*

Cover Designer: *Jane Hambleton*
Art Editor: *Emma Ghiselli*
Illustrator: *Rennie Evans*
Photo Researcher: *Pamela Carley*
Production Supervisor: *Randy Hurst*
Media Producer: *Ginger Bunn*
Media Project Manager: *Kathleen Boylan*
Composition: *10/12 Berkeley by Thompson Type*
Printing: *45# Pub Matte by Courier*

Cover Credit (clockwise): © Matthew Polak/Corbis Sygma; © AP/Wide World Photos; © Reuters/Corbis; © AP/Wide World Photos; © Getty Images News by Scott Nelson

Credits: The credits section for this book begins on page C-1 and is considered an extension of the copyright page.

Library of Congress Cataloging-in-Publication Data
Rourke, John T., 1945–
    International politics on the world stage / John T. Rourke.—11th ed.
        p. cm.
    Includes bibliographical references and index.
    ISBN 978-0-07-310355-6   ISBN 0-07-310355-1 (alk. paper)
    1. International relations.   2. World politics—1989– I. Title.

JZ1305.R68 2006
327.1'01—dc22

The Internet addresses listed in the text were accurate at the time of publication. The inclusion of a Web site does not indicate an endorsement by the authors or McGraw-Hill, and McGraw-Hill does not guarantee the accuracy of the information presented at these sites.

www.mhhe.com

Preface

This Edition: Changes and Organization

Taking the view that our lives are inescapably affected by world politics, *International Politics on the World Stage,* Eleventh Edition, stresses the impact that world events and global interdependence have on your students' lives. In addition to highlighting this interconnection, the text points out how the events of current history relate to the theories of international politics that have been formulated by political scientists.

Each time I revise this text I think to myself, "The world will settle down and the next edition will be easier." Wrong! This edition proved to be a major challenge and effort. You will see that there is a continued emphasis on being current in order to engage the students without being journalistic. The struggle of the United States in Iraq to achieve political victory by helping Iraqis build a democratic, unified country; the ongoing threat of terrorism; the looming threat of avian influenza; the genocidal horror in the Darfur region of Sudan; corruption in the UN's oil-for-food program; tensions with both Iran and North Korea over their alleged nuclear weapons programs; the increasing presence of China as a political, economic, and even military power; the impact on U.S. foreign policy of Condoleezza Rice, the first African American woman to serve as U.S. secretary of state; the defeat of the proposed European Union constitution by voters in both France and the Netherlands; and other recent events are all extensively detailed. It is also important to be as current as possible with the massive amount of changing data on economic performance and capacity, weapons levels and transfers, and other statistical aspects of world politics. I have used original sources for my data when possible so that students will have the most recent information available.

The more I study global politics, the more I am impressed with the idea that the world is a primitive political society. It is a political system that is marked by little organization, frequent violence, and a limited sense of global responsibility. It is a world of conflict. But there is also a world of cooperation, a countertheme, based on a desire among states and their people to work together globally. Although it is still only a nascent desire, people have begun to realize that their fates are inextricably entwined with one another and with the political, economic, social, and environmental future of our planet. The organization of the text flows from this conception of the world as a primitive, but developing, political system. Therefore, the chapters not only analyze world division and conflict but also focus on cooperation both as a goal and in practice. Indeed, the organizational scheme reflects this text's view that the world is at a juncture echoing Robert Frost's poem, "Two Roads Diverged in a Wood." One road is the traditional way of sovereign states pursuing their self-interests in an often inequitable and conflict-filled world. The alternative, less-traveled-by path is the way of cooperation in a system in which states are less sovereign and international organizations play a wider and more authoritative role.

The introduction to the text discusses the importance of world politics and the methods, theories, and purposes of political science (chapter 1), the evolution of the world political system and its current instability (chapter 2), and the three levels of analysis that need to be studied simultaneously—the system, state, and individual levels (chapter 3).

Instructors who have used this text before will undoubtedly notice that what had been three chapters on the economic aspects of world politics in earlier editions has been consolidated here into two chapters (12 and 13). This change came about as a result of outside reviews of the text that McGraw-Hill and I sought. Most of the comments were gratifying and confirmed the strengths that distinguish this book since the first edition was published in 1986. But a number of reviewers commented that it was a bit long and had more chapters (16) than the usual academic semester had weeks (14 or 15). As far as where to tighten up, the consensus was that the three economic chapters (12, 13, and 14 of the tenth edition) provided greater detail than needed for a one-semester introductory course. I was not sure I agreed, and so I sent e-mail inquiries to a dozen or so instructors who were using the text at other colleges and universities. I asked them whether they favored keeping the three chapters as is or consolidating them. To my surprise, frankly, their overwhelming response was the same as that of the first set of reviewers. So, bowing to the greater wisdom, I consolidated the three chapters into two (12 and 13).

The remaining chapter organization of the book remains the same as in the tenth edition, although, again accepting suggestions of some reviewers, I moved material from one chapter to another to consolidate and avoid overlaps. For example, some material on human rights was moved from chapter 9 on international law, to the main chapter on human rights (chapter 14).

Beginning with chapter 4, the two roads theme organizes the remaining chapters of this edition, with usually alternating discussions of national conflict and international cooperation in successive chapters. In this way, equal attention can be given to the two roads without losing sight of the fact that they lead in divergent directions.

Chapters 4 and 5 deal with two divergent political orientations. The traditional orientation is nationalism (chapter 4); the alternative orientation comprises transnational ideas, identifications, and processes (chapter 5). Alternative ways of organizing the world politically are the subject of the next two chapters, with chapter 6 focusing on the traditional political unit, the state, and chapter 7 taking up international organizations, with particular emphases on the European Union and the United Nations.

Then chapters 8 and 9 explore divergent approaches to the conduct of world politics. Chapter 8 covers the traditional approach, national diplomacy; chapter 9 examines the alternative road of international law and morality. This pair of chapters is followed by another pair that introduce two approaches to physical security in the world political system: national security (chapter 10) and international security and other alternative approaches (chapter 11).

The text then turns to international political economy. The commentary begins in chapter 12 with an overview of IPE theory and of global economic conditions and trends. The main thrust of chapter 12, however, is economic nationalism, the traditional approach to the international political economy. By contrast, chapter 13 focuses on an alternative approach, economic liberalism, as part of the greater phenomenon of globalization. Chapter 13 concludes by reviewing the arguments for and against economic nationalism and economic liberalism and asking its readers to evaluate the two approaches. The final two chapters look into the traditional and alternative approaches to global human rights and dignity (chapter 14) and the environment (chapter 15).

Writing Style and General Approach

The single greatest factor that prompted me over two decades ago to begin to write my own introductory text was the desire to use one that, in today's jargon, was "user friendly." Over the years, I have tried to accomplish that in a number of ways. One is to make my theoretical points in straightforward, "plain language," and then to illustrate them with an interesting and usually current example. Being up-to-date is a major goal of this book. Sometimes, heeding the advice of Mary Poppins that "a spoonful of sugar makes the medicine go down," I even take time to include a joke or tell a "story" (such as the travails of presidential foreign travel in chapter 8) that make a point in a light way. This is meant to show the student readers that international relations can be fascinating, even fun. A third thing that makes this book user friendly for students is the "road signs" to provide reference points and guidance during the journey through the text and semester. These road signs include an outline (a map, so to speak) to begin each chapter, lots of headings; an array of boldface glossary words, and judicious use of italicized phrases to highlight concepts and points. I am pleased to report that the feedback from instructors and from the occasional student who writes or e-mails me is that most students are delighted with the book's accessibility and readability.

Data and Graphics

This text presents students with an extensive array of tables, figures, photographs, maps, and other graphics to emphasize, expand, and give visual life to ideas. Each photograph is picked personally by me, and I have designed almost all the figures and tables, often making my own calculations to create them from the data. Another part of my approach is to present a significant amount of data to students so that they can see for themselves what the statistics indicate rather than accept my interpretations or those of any other scholar.

Research, Citations, Bibliography, and Suggested Readings

One of the aims of this text is to bring together a representative sampling of the latest research in international relations. Scholarly articles, so often ignored in survey texts, are particularly emphasized. This research is documented by extensive references using the "in-text" style and by a significant reference list/bibliography. In addition to recognizing my intellectual debt to a host of scholars, the references and bibliography also serve as a reading list for students, as explained to them in the "To the Student" section following this preface. As such, references are often meant to serve as suggestions for further reading and do not necessarily mean that the cited author(s) propounded what is being said at the point of reference. Using this approach instead of the end-of-chapter placement gives inquisitive students immediate thoughts for additional reading. For those instructors whose organization differs from mine, I have taken care to provide a detailed table of contents and index in order to facilitate the integration of this text with your syllabus. You will find, for example, that:

> **Economics** is discussed, among other places, in chapters 1 (how it affects students), 2 (globalization), 12 (theory, general global conditions, and economic nationalism), 13 (economic liberalism), and 15 (sustainable development).

> **Terrorism** is addressed in chapters 1, 5, 9, and 10.

Moral and humanitarian issues are taken up extensively in chapters 9 and 15 and also form an important part of the discussions of national interest, coercion, and economic challenges in, respectively, chapters 4, 10, and 13.

Supplements

Several supplements are available to assist both instructors and students in the use of this text. For instructors, the Instructor's Testing and Resource CD-ROM to accompany *International Politics on the World Stage* contains chapter outlines and objectives, sample lectures, discussion questions, and analytical exercises. The Test Bank provides approximately 1,500 multiple-choice and essay questions organized by chapter and degree of difficulty. A computerized version of the Test Bank and a PowerPoint slide presentation are also included. To get a copy of the Instructor's Testing and Resource CD-ROM, contact your local McGraw-Hill representative or McGraw-Hill Customer Service (1-800-338-3987) for details concerning availability.

Online Learning Center

Students and instructors will find additional resources at www.mhhe.com/rourke11. For students, the site offers free access to current course-specific articles by leading authorities in the field, daily news feeds from a variety of media outlets including the *New York Times,* interactive exercises including simulations, debates, research links, and chapter quizzes, and interactive maps to enhance the classroom and learning experience. The password-protected instructor's edition of the site also contains the Instructor's Manual and PowerPoint slides available for easy download. Contact your local McGraw-Hill representative or McGraw-Hill Customer Service (1-800-338-3987) for a username and password.

John T. Rourke

To the Student

The world, familiar to us and unknown.
—William Shakespeare, *Henry V*

The world is changing at breathtaking speed! That reality is one of the most important things for you to understand about international politics. Yet I have found that most undergraduate students, having been born into this era of warp-speed change, consider it normal. It is not. Recorded history dates back over 30 centuries. A great deal of what we will discuss in this text has happened in the last century, even within your lifetime. But truly understanding this rate of change—maybe feeling the rate of change is a better way to put it—is hard without perspective.

As a way of trying to convey the dramatic pace of change, I will introduce you to Maria Olivia da Silva of Astorga, Brazil, the world's oldest person. When she was born on February 28, 1880, Brazil was still ruled by an emperor, Pedro II, and Rutherford B. Hayes was the U.S. president. An emperor also ruled in China and a sultan headed the Ottoman Empire. Russia's czar, Germany's kaiser, and Austria-Hungary's emperor ruled much of Central Europe, and Queen Victoria reigned over the British Empire. Most of Africa and Asia were still colonies of European powers. The communist revolution in Russia occurred when she was 37; the Soviet Union disappeared when she was 111. For me, communism and the cold war were the totality of my historical experience; for da Silva they were mere interludes. For many who read this book they are not even memories, only matter learned about in history books.

If you think about events, trends, and technology in this way—in terms of what one person has seen and experienced—you can begin to grasp how fast they are moving. When da Silva was born people were basically earthbound. She was 23 when the first airplane flew, 62 when the first jet plane took off, 81 when Soviet cosmonaut Yuri Gagarin became the first human in space, and 89 when Neil Armstrong stepped on the Moon's surface. There are many other things to consider. Ms. da Silva is more than twice as old as atomic weapons; the world's population has quadrupled during her life; she is older than three-quarters of the countries that exist today. Radios, televisions, computers, and some of the other technological innovations that affect us so profoundly now did not exist when da Silva was born.

One of the strong themes in this book is the challenges that face the world and the alternative approaches to addressing those challenges. Use da Silva to help you think about these issues. If, for example, it took all of human history—tens of thousands of years—to reach a world population of less than 1.5 billion in 1880, when she was born, and if, during her life, we have added another 4.5 billion people, then how much time do we have to get the world population under control? If you live as long as da Silva has (and you might, given modern medical technology), then what will the world population be when you are 125 years old?

In this sense of contemplating the future by pondering the past, thinking about Maria Olivia da Silva is really more about tomorrow than about yesterday or even today. When I talk about her, my thoughts are on our 21st century more than on her 19th and 20th centuries.

Using This Text

The text that follows is my attempt to introduce you to the complex and compelling study of international politics. Prefaces are often given scant attention, but they can be a valuable learning tool for you. They let you in on the author's conceptions, the mental pictures behind a text. What is the author's approach? What are the author's orientations and biases? Does the text have one or more basic themes? How is the text organized? In this preface I have addressed these issues. I hope you'll read it.

In writing this text I have tried to use straightforward prose and have assumed that students who take this course know little about international politics. To help you further, I have included an outline at the beginning of each chapter. Before you read the chapter, pay attention to its outline. It is axiomatic that if you know where you are going, you will find it a lot easier to get there! Additionally, I have written a numbered summary at the end of each chapter to help you quickly review the scope of the chapter. This, of course, is no substitute for carefully studying the chapter.

There are many figures, tables, maps, and photographs in this book. Pay close attention to them. You will find that they graphically represent many of the ideas presented in the text and will help you understand them. But if you really want to know all about something, you will have to read a lot more than just this book and to involve yourself in more than just the course for which it has been assigned. To make it easier for you to do this, I have chosen an "in-text" reference system that gives you citations as you read. Thus (Tickner, 2005:6) refers to page 6 of the book or article written by (in this case, Professor J. Ann) Tickner in 2005, which is listed alphabetically in the references at the end of the book.

I have also noted studies that helped me think about and organize various topics and those that might be informative to you. I encourage you to utilize the references to advance your knowledge beyond the boundaries of this text. Explanations for terms set in **boldface** will be found in the glossary at the end of the text.

Some note should be made of this book's title, *International Politics on the World Stage,* and the Shakespearean quotations that begin each chapter and are used from time to time to highlight a point. The idea behind this motif is to convey some of the sweep and complexity of the world drama. No one who has ever read William Shakespeare can dismiss his masterpieces as easily understood or inconsequential. The events on the world stage are similar—complex, full of drama, sometimes hopeful, often tragic, and always riveting. But you, the reader, would be mistaken to assume that the play analogy means that, as a member of the audience, you can be content to sit back and watch the plot unfold. Quite the contrary—part of what makes the world drama so compelling is that the audience is seated onstage and is part of, as well as witness to, the action that is unfolding. And that is one reason why I have also quoted more recent world players. Shakespeare's plays are of the past; the world drama is ongoing. Furthermore, as in an improvisational play, you in the audience can become involved, and, given the consequences of a potentially tragic rather than a happy ending, you ought to become involved. If there is anything that this text proposes, it is that each of us is intimately affected by international politics and that we all have a responsibility and an ability to become shapers of the script. As we shall see, our play has alternative scripts, and what the next scene brings depends in part on us. There is wisdom, then, in Shakespeare's advice in *All's Well that Ends Well* that "Our remedies oft in ourselves do lie."

I am sincerely interested in getting feedback from the faculty members and students who use this text. My pretensions to perfection have long since been dashed, and your recommendations for additions, deletions, and changes in future editions will be appreciated and seriously considered. People do write me, and I write or call them back! You are encouraged to join this correspondence by writing to me at the Department of Political Science U1024, University of Connecticut, Storrs, CT 06269-1024 or sending me an e-mail at John.Rourke@uconn.edu. This book, just like the world, can be made better, but its improvement depends heavily on whether or not you are concerned enough to think and act.

John T. Rourke

Acknowledgments

It is a difficult task to keep this acknowledgment of those who have contributed to the text down to a reasonable length. There are many who have played an important part, and my debt to each of them is great. I have tried to make adjustments wherever possible. Some contributors have pointed out specific concerns about matters of fact or interpretation, and a number of corrections were made. On a larger scale, this edition's organizational changes; its greater coverage of constructivism, postmodernism, and other critical approaches; and several other shifts in coverage are responses in part to suggestions. Adding to the long list of those who have reviewed earlier editions and made this text better, I would like to also thank those who contributed to this edition:

Karen Adams	*Louisiana State University*
Desmond Arias	*John Jay College of Criminal Justice, City University of New York*
Dlynn Armstrong-Williams	*North Georgia College & State University*
Gawdat Bahgat	*Indiana University of Pennsylvania*
Mary Jane Burns	*Idaho State University*
Richard Byrne	*Kirkwood Community College*
Sophie Clavie	*San Francisco State University*
John A. C. Conybeare	*University of Iowa*
Katy Crossley-Frolick	*DePaul University*
Claire Cutler	*University of Victoria*
Robert Denemark	*University of Delaware*
Roxanne Doty	*Arizona State University*
Dennis Driggers	*California State University, Fresno*
Douglas Durasoff	*Seattle Pacific University*
David Frolick	*North Central College*
Vilma Elisa Fuentes	*Santa Fe Community College*
Clifford Griffin	*North Carolina State University*
Gregory Hall	*St. Mary's College of Maryland*
Elizabeth Crump Hanson	*University of Connecticut*
Clinton Hewan	*Northern Kentucky University*
George Kent	*University of Hawaii*
Kent Kille	*The College of Wooster*
Jeffrey P. Krans	*Keuka College*

Marwan Kreidie	*Villanova University*
Timothy C. Lim	*California State University, Los Angeles*
Paul McCartney	*Rutgers University*
Rajan Menon	*Lehigh University*
Allen Meyer	*Mesa Community College*
Mark J. Mullenbach	*University of Central Arkansas*
John Queen	*Glendale Community College*
G. Hossein Razi	*University of Houston*
Steve Owen	*Kirkwood Community College*
Karl Schonberg	*St. Lawrence University*
Wayne A. Selcher	*Elizabethtown College*
Rosemary Shinko	*University of Connecticut, Stamford*
Christopher D. Skubby	*Lakeland Community College*
Michael W. Sonnleitner	*Portland Community College*
Stacy VanDeveer	*University of New Hampshire*
Kimberly Weir	*University of Northern Kentucky*
John Allen Williams	*Loyola University*
Robert E. Williams	*Pepperdine University*
Michele Zebich-Knos	*Kennesaw State University*

I also owe a debt to each author listed in the references of this and the previous editions. The work that these scholars have done on specific subjects forms the intellectual building blocks that are a significant part of the final structure of this, or any, worthwhile introductory textbook. This text is also evolutionary, and I want to continue to express my appreciation to all those who read and commented on the previous editions. Additionally, I also want to thank the colleagues who have taken the time at International Studies Association meetings or other conferences to give me the benefit of their views. I have even, on occasion, taken off my name tag and helped the staff at the publisher's booth at professional meetings. The comments I have received in this anonymity have been sometimes encouraging, sometimes humbling, but always helpful.

Best of all, I have received many good suggestions from students. My own students have had to both read the text and listen to me, and their often obviously candid comments have helped the generations of students who will follow. My favorite was a sophomore who did not do well on his first exam and came to my office to lay blame at the door of the blankety-blank textbook. As we talked, he made some interesting, if pointed observations. It was also clear that he had not connected the author's name on the front of the book with his professor. Boy, was he surprised when it finally dawned on him that he was grumping about the book to its author!

I owe special thanks to Brian Urlacher of the University of Connecticut, who is responsible for revising the Instructor's Manual and Test Bank to accompany *International Politics on the World Stage*. Brian shouldered the task of preparing, revising, and updating this instructor's tool for the eleventh edition with the utmost care and good nature. Another exciting feature of this text is the supplementary material and exercises that can be found on the Online Learning Center. For this I thank Natalie Hudson of the University of Connecticut for her meticulous updates and polish.

Then there is the staff of McGraw-Hill. McGraw-Hill's political science editor, Monica Eckman, and director of development, Lisa Pinto, have encouraged me and supported me. More of a day–to–day mainstay is my general editor, Ava Suntoke. She has gently and expertly guided me through several editions, and I am continually delighted with her unusual combination of substantive expertise and editing expertise. Sheryl Rose, copyeditor, with her amazing eye for technical detail and substantive consistency, added to the process of ensuring accuracy. I also want to thank Brett Coker and the rest of the McGraw-Hill production staff and Thompson Type for their diligence and for not threatening my life through innumerable changes.

One of the things I like best about this edition is "its look." Pamela Carley has assembled photographs and editorial cartoons that bring powerful visual life to the concepts I express in words. Glenda King was the interior designer for the eleventh edition. Preston Thomas designed its striking cover. Thompson Type performed the difficult but crucial task of layout, arranging text and illustrations. Charles Vitelli drew the original cartoons in this book. He took my raw mental images and turned them into wonderful representations of the issues being discussed in the text. In the same area, Emma Ghiselli and Rennie Evans did an extraordinary job with the exacting art of creating the text's many figures and maps. Thanks are also due to Alice and Will Thiede of Carto-Graphics in Eau Claire, Wisconsin, for their standard of excellence in producing the maps in the book. I owe a great debt to those who have created such a visually attractive, educationally effective package for my words.

To all of you:

I can no other answer make but thanks, thanks, and ever thanks.
—William Shakespeare, *Twelfth Night*

Contents in Brief

Contents

PART II   Two Roads: Divergent Political Orientations

PART III   Two Roads: Divergent Organizational Structures

CHAPTER 6   National States: The Traditional Structure   163

CHAPTER 7   Intergovernmental Organizations: Alternative Governance   190

PART IV   Two Roads: Divergent Approaches to Conduct

PART V Two Roads: Divergent Approaches to Pursuing Peace

**PART VI   Two Roads: Divergent Approaches
                to Pursuing Prosperity**

**PART VII   Two Roads: Divergent Approaches
to Pursuing Preservation**

MAPS

BOXES

A Brief Walkthrough of the Features in Each Chapter

JOHN ROURKE'S *International Politics on the World Stage* has long been known for an abundance of learning aids that help to enrich student understanding while enlivening the study of international relations. Engaging graphics and features prompt students to think critically about world events and concepts in international relations.

Chapter Opener Page

Shakespearean quotes and a photo set the stage by presenting the theme of the chapter. The chapter structure is outlined on the chapter-opener page, providing an overview of the chapter coverage for the student.

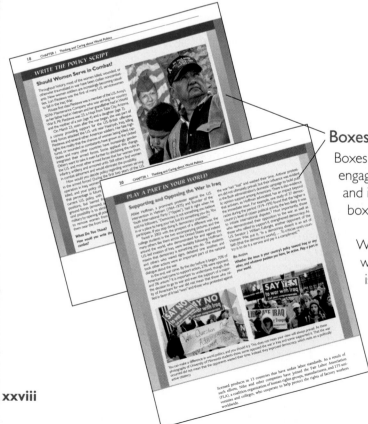

Boxes

Boxes provide students with opportunities to engage with the concepts in the text in a lively and interactive way. There are two types of boxes.

Write the Policy Script boxes present students with the main points of a thought-provoking issue and ask them to decide on a course of action and to support their decision.

Play a Part in Your World boxes focus on student activism. They invite students to take action and become engaged with world issues.

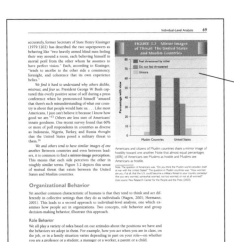

Figures

Exceptionally clear graphics with detailed captions encourage students to gain an understanding of world events and trends by analyzing data.

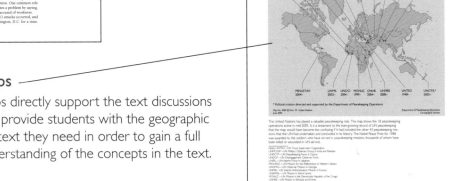

Maps

Maps directly support the text discussions and provide students with the geographic context they need in order to gain a full understanding of the concepts in the text.

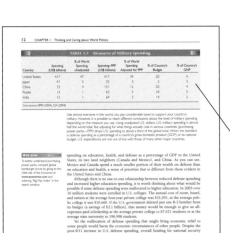

Tables

Up-to-date tables provide students with data that can be noted at a glance. The tables provide an excellent summary of complex topics.

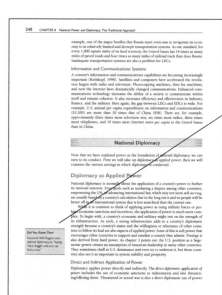

DYK

Did You Know clips provide a moment of diversion, giving students facts about the world today that are surprising, amusing, or informative.

Glossary

It is important for students to master the terminology of international relations, and this text helps them do so. Key terms are boldfaced in the text, listed at the end of the chapter to provide a review, and defined in the glossary at the end of the book. The Online Learning Center has an interactive list of key terms for each chapter.

Chapter Summary

An excellent tool for chapter review is the numbered summary of main points at the end of the chapter.

Web Links

Web links to the Internet connect students to sites that are chosen to engage students in addition to containing more information on the topic being presented in the text.

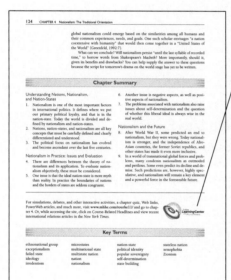

OLC

Each chapter of the book has an Online Learning Center (OLC) organized by chapter. Each chapter contains an abundance of learning tools, including quizzes.

Web Site Icon

The interactive exercises on the OLC are tightly integrated with the text. Icons in the margins show students where there is a relevant activity on the OLC.

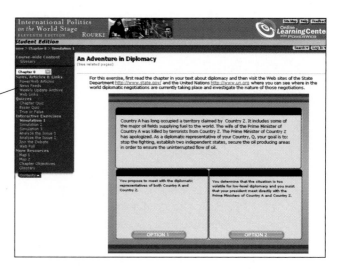

Web Site Exercise

Interactive simulations on the OLC allow students to step into a decision-making role using the concepts they learn in the text.

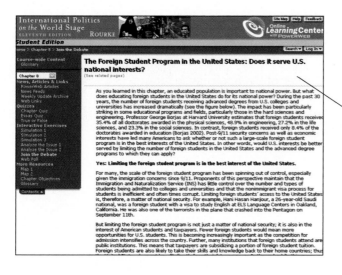

Web Site Exercise

Debate exercises on the OLC invite students to join the debate on controversial political, economic, and social topics.

Web Site Exercise

Maps reinforce the geography students need to know in order to understand world politics.

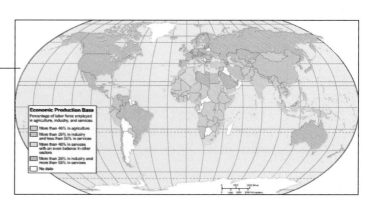

Thinking and Caring about World Politics

An honest tale speeds best being plainly told.
—William Shakespeare, *Richard III*

Be not too tame neither, but let your own discretion be your tutor; suit the action to the word, the word to the action.
—William Shakespeare, *Hamlet*

This chapter stresses that world politics is important to you and that whatever your opinions, you, like actress Christine Lahti at the forefront of this photo, should be active in trying to shape world events.

"ALL THE WORLD'S A STAGE, and all the men and women merely players," William Shakespeare (1564–1616) wrote in *As You Like It*. The Bard of Avon's words highlight the remarkable parallels between international relations and his masterful plays. Both have epic and complex plots. Their characters range from heroic to evil. The action is always dramatic and sometimes tragic. Justice sometimes prevails, but not always. Yet for all its complexity, the one constant in the action on the world stage is that it is riveting and a tale worth telling. It is to this epic story that we should now turn our attention.

Previewing the Global Drama

Whether you are going to a play or a movie or watching television, it helps you to get into the action if you have some sense of what you will be seeing from a playbill, movie review, or synopsis on the cable television guide. Similarly, your journey through this book will be easier if you have some idea of the cast of characters you will meet and the basic outline of the script. So, before the curtain rises, here is a preview of the global drama that introduces you to the cast and to the theme around which this text is organized.

Global Actors: Meet the Cast

Unlike cast members in a play, most of the actors in the world drama are organizations, not people. States (countries) are one such type of organizational actor, and they undoubtedly have the starring role (Wendt, 2004). There are nearly 200 countries in the international system today. Just like some theatrical stars, they can be self-absorbed and jealously guard their claim to fame, which for states is their independence (sovereignty). It is this sovereign status that separates states from the other actors. Of course, sovereignty also means that the world drama has no director who can bring order to the interaction among the stars. This lack of central authority often leaves the actors in conflict with one another. Also, while all the states are legally equal, the reality is that some are bigger stars than others. The United States would certainly head the "A list" of top stars, with China, Japan, and a few other countries also major players. Andorra, Mauritius, Vanuatu, and many other countries, despite their equal billing in the UN General Assembly and elsewhere, are usually consigned to bit parts.

Joining the states onstage is a host of international organizations. Perhaps the most prominent of these are the 300 or so **international governmental organizations (IGOs)** whose membership is made up of states. Some are global (the United Nations); others are regional (the European Union). Even more numerous are the transnational organizations. One type, **nongovernmental organizations (NGOs)**, has individuals as members. These NGOs range in character from the laudable (Human Rights Watch) to the villainous (al Qaeda). They also extend from the ancient (the Roman Catholic Church) to the nearly new (Families of Victims of Involuntary Disappearance—FIND). Multinational corporations (MNCs) are another type of transnational actor. The annual earnings of some of these companies rival the economic output of midsize states and dwarf most of the smaller ones. In a largely unregulated drama where money is an important source of power, MNCs can be important cast members.

Finally, some people are also important actors on the world stage. Usually the roles they play are as decision makers, protesters, voters, or other types of political

Web Link

For regularly updated information about countries and related data, access the CIA's *World Factbook* at www.cia.gov/cia/publications/factbook/.

participants in a state or international organization. Sometimes, however, individuals play roles that transcend national and other institutional boundaries. Later in the book you will meet Jody Williams, a native of Putney, Vermont, who decided that land mines are evil. She joined with others who felt the same, established an IGO to campaign against land mines, was responsible for an international treaty to ban them, and won the 1997 Nobel Peace Prize for her efforts. For a political actor, it is like getting a Tony, Emmy, and Oscar all rolled into one.

How This Text Is Structured

This book is structured around the conviction that the world is at something of a crossroads in the way we organize and conduct our global politics. Contemplation of that junction brings to mind Robert Frost's famous poem, "The Road Not Taken" (1916). Frost concluded his poem with this thought:

> I shall be telling this with a sigh
> Somewhere ages and ages hence:
> Two roads diverged in a wood, and I—
> I took the one less traveled by,
> And that has made all the difference.

Traditionally, world politics has followed a path centered on countries pursuing their self-interests in a largely anarchical world as far as their power would let them. This is still the main thrust of world politics, but increasingly there is an alternative route that many people advocate and that many countries are cautiously trying, at least sometimes. This other way somewhat resembles how individuals fit within countries. Certainly, individuals pursue their own interests in domestic systems and have considerable freedom to do so. But in domestic systems, individuals also recognize rules, are held accountable for obeying them, and have some sense of shared responsibility to the common good. The alternative path for world politics would have states act more like citizens in a society and be willing to approach politics with a bit less sense of "I" and a bit more sense of "we." That would involve, among other things, working cooperatively through, and at least sometimes even following the directions of, international organizations to improve global security, economic welfare, human rights, and environmental conditions.

Like the works of Shakespeare, Frost's lines have implications that challenge the reader's intellect. He leaves his reader with the thought that choosing the less familiar road "made all the difference." But we do not know whether Frost was content with his choice or regretted it. He wisely left that to the reader's imagination and judgment. Similarly, a major challenge that this text presents is for you to decide which road you think the world should travel by.

Exploring these two paths, the traditional route of competition and conflict and the alternative root of cooperation, drives the structure of this text, as visualized in Figure 1.1 on page 6. To begin, the first three chapters set the stage, so to speak, by discussing the importance of world politics and some basic theories of global politics (chapter 1), the evolution of and current instability in the world political system (chapter 2), and how foreign policy is made from the perspective of three levels of analysis—the system, state, and human levels (chapter 3).

After chapter 3, the two roads theme runs through the remaining chapters. Chapters 4 and 5 deal with divergent ways we define ourselves politically. The traditional

States: The Principal Actors on the World Stage

The international system includes many types of actors. Of these, states (or countries) are the most important. National boundaries are the most important source of political division in the world, and for most people nationalism is the strongest source of political identification.

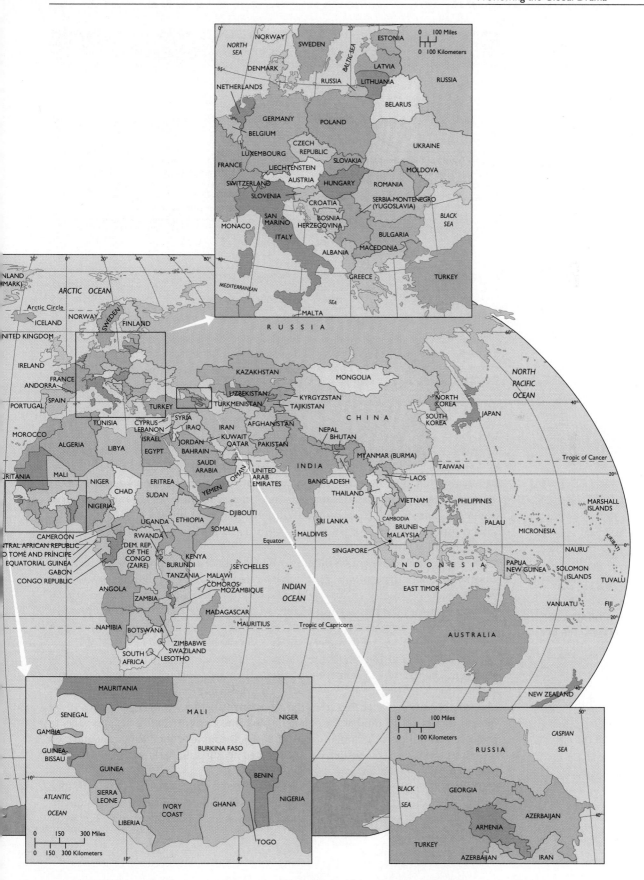

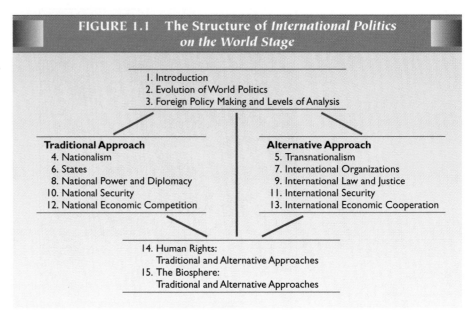

FIGURE 1.1   The Structure of *International Politics on the World Stage*

1. Introduction
2. Evolution of World Politics
3. Foreign Policy Making and Levels of Analysis

Traditional Approach
4. Nationalism
6. States
8. National Power and Diplomacy
10. National Security
12. National Economic Competition

Alternative Approach
5. Transnationalism
7. International Organizations
9. International Law and Justice
11. International Security
13. International Economic Cooperation

14. Human Rights:
Traditional and Alternative Approaches
15. The Biosphere:
Traditional and Alternative Approaches

This text is structured around the theme that the world is facing an important choice. It can follow the competitive traditional path of world politics or an alternative path of greater cooperation. This outline of the book offers something of a road map, allowing you to understand where you are during your reading.

MAP
World Countries

orientation is nationalism (chapter 4), which focuses on the individual nation (such as Americans) and its self-governance in a state (such as the United States). Transnationalism (chapter 5), seeing yourself politically connected to others across borders is the alternative approach. Chapters 6 and 7 deal with how we organize ourselves politically. Chapter 6 focuses on the traditional political unit, the state, and chapter 7 takes up international organizations, with particular emphasis on the European Union and the United Nations.

Chapters 8 and 9 explore different ways to conduct world politics. Chapter 8 covers the "might makes right" traditional approach to national diplomacy based on power; chapter 9 examines the "right makes right" alternative road of international law and morality. The next pair of chapters take up physical security. One approach is the traditional emphasis on national security discussed in chapter 10. The other path, international security cooperation, is addressed in chapter 11.

Chapters 12 and 13 turn to international political economy. The commentary be gins with chapter 12's examination of the traditional approach, national economic competition. Then chapter 13 offers the contrasting alternative, international economic cooperation. Departing from the alternative chapters scheme, chapters 14 on human rights and 15 on the environment look into current conditions and ways to preserve and improve the human condition. Each chapter contains commentary on the interplay and even tension between states acting singularly and the drive for international cooperation.

The text's organizing theme of a crossroads and the paths the world can take brings us back to you, global politics, and the future. Tomorrow's course is not determined. It is for you to decide what should happen and, as best you can, to convert that conviction into what will happen.

This book's central theme is that the world is at a fork in the road. One choice is to continue the traditional approach to world politics. This is based on sovereign states pursuing their self-interests in a conflict-prone, largely unregulated international system. The other option is for countries to work more cooperatively toward a common good and to surrender some of their sovereignty to international organizations, so that they can effectively address the global issues that face humankind.

The Importance of World Politics to Each of Us

When Shakespeare wrote that we are all players on the world stage, he meant that in an active sense. Underlining that reality in *The Merchant of Venice,* he has Antonio exclaim, "I hold the world [to be] . . . a stage where every man must play a part." If Americans did not know it already, they learned on September 11, 2001, that world politics can dramatically impact them. That morning terrorists turned four commercial airliners into weapons and shattered Americans' sense of security. Two planes demolished the twin towers of the World Trade Center in Manhattan; another plummeted into the Pentagon just outside Washington, D.C.; the fourth crashed into a field near Pittsburgh despite the heroic efforts of the passengers to retake control of the aircraft. Aboard the airliners, 33 crew members, 214 innocent passengers, and 19 terrorists died. More than 3,000 others on the ground perished, many before the horrified, almost disbelieving eyes of Americans who had turned on their televisions as news of the attacks spread. When they had awakened that morning, most Americans had never heard of Osama bin Laden or al Qaeda; by noon those names were seared in the American psyche.

The trauma of 9/11, the fear of further terrorist attacks, the U.S.-led retaliation against Afghanistan, the invasion of Iraq 18 months later, and the troubled occupation of that country all worked to focus Americans' interest on foreign affairs. A high level of concern with the world has not been the norm, however, and it is not clear whether in the long run Americans will sustain their interest in the world around

Web Link

Lest any of us forget, view accounts and images of the 9/11 attack at www.september11news.com/.

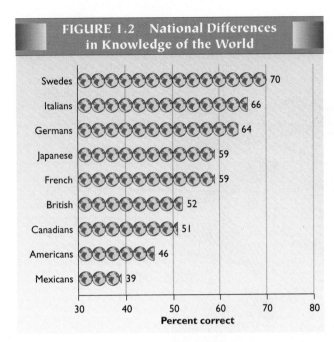

FIGURE 1.2　National Differences in Knowledge of the World

		Percent correct
Swedes		70
Italians		66
Germans		64
Japanese		59
French		59
British		52
Canadians		51
Americans		46
Mexicans		39

How much people know about the world around them varies from country to country. This figure shows the average percentage of correct answers given by people aged 18 to 24 in nine countries about world geography and affairs. Note that Americans finished next to last, only somewhat ahead of Mexicans, who live in a poor country in which only about half of all youths finish high school (compared to 90% in the United States).

Note: The data are based on the average of the scores on two questionnaires: one with 10 questions on world affairs and another with 56 questions on geography. On the world affairs questionnaire, two questions (one on the world's largest religion, the other on the euro) were factored out by the author for methodological reasons. *Data source:* National Geographic—Roper 2002 Global Geographic Literacy Survey, November 2002, available on the Web at http://www.nationalgeographic.com/geosurvey/. Calculations by author.

them (Mindich, 2004). Studies before 9/11 found that only about 20% of Americans followed foreign news and that most Americans knew little about global politics or world geography.[1] Even after 9/11, knowledge seems woefully limited, as evident in a study conducted a year after the attack that tested 18–24-year-olds in nine countries with 56 questions about world geography and 8 questions about world affairs. As Figure 1.2 details, the study found that the percentage of correct responses by Americans was next to last. On the geography questions, 62% of the Americans got more than half wrong. Unbelievably, only 13% of American young adults could point to Iraq on a blank world map, even though war was brewing with that country. On a multiple-choice question about the size of the U.S. population, not only did a scant 25% of Americans select the correct answer, but their score was lower than that of the respondents in any of the other eight countries.[2]

Is this widespread lack of information about or interest in world events justifiable? The answer is no! This text does not often try to tell you what to think or do. But one message is stressed: The world drama is important and deserves our careful attention. Even more importantly, we do not have to content ourselves with being passive observers. Do not stand idly by, especially if you agree with the wry observation of Irish literary lion Oscar Wilde (1854–1900), "The world is a stage, but the play is badly cast." You can play an active part; you can make a difference! The script is not set. It is an improvisational play with lots of room for ad-libbing and even for changing the story line. To help you think about whether you agree with Wilde, you will find a number of "Write the Policy Script" boxes in this text. Each asks you to formulate a view on an important policy issue. To further highlight the importance of the world to you, let us turn to a number of ways, some dramatic, some mundane, in which international politics affects your economic well-being, your living space, and your very life.

World Politics and Your Finances

World politics affects each of our personal economic conditions in many ways. The human toll of the attacks of September 11, 2001, on those who died, their families, and their friends was, of course, the most devastating impact. But the economic impact was also staggering. Just in the first four months, the 9/11 attacks cost the United States at least $81 billion in destroyed property, lost business earnings, lost wages, increased security expenditures, and other costs.

More routinely, the impact of international economics on individuals continues to expand as world industrial and financial structures become increasingly intertwined. Indeed, as we shall see, the ties between national and international affairs are

Did You Know That:

During 2003, the 586,323 foreign students enrolled in U.S. colleges contributed $12 billion to the U.S. economy. Foreign student expenditures are considered a U.S. service export.

The cost of gasoline is just one of the many ways that each of us is affected daily by the world around us. Increasing demand for oil worldwide has outstripped the supply, more than doubling the price of imported oil between 2003 and 2005 and driving up the price of gasoline to over $3 a gallon in some places, as shown in this San Francisco gas station.

so close that many social scientists now use the term **intermestic** to symbolize the merger of *inter*national and do*mestic* concerns. To illustrate the increasingly ubiquitous connections between your own personal financial condition and world politics, we will briefly explore how international trade, the flow of international capital, and defense spending affect your finances.

International Trade and Your Finances

The global flow of goods (tangible items) and services (intangible items such as revenues from tourism, insurance, and banking) is important to your financial circumstances. One example is U.S. dependence on foreign sources for vital resources. That reality was brought sharply into focus as crude oil prices rose more than 540%, from $12 a barrel in January 2002 to $65 a barrel in September 2005, driving up the prices of gasoline, heating oil, and other petroleum products to record highs in the United States. Thus, every time you pumped gas, you paid more thanks to the realities of the international system.

Trade also wins and loses jobs. There is a steadily increasing likelihood that international trade and your job are related. Exports create jobs. The United States is the world's largest exporter, providing other countries with $1.1 trillion worth of U.S. goods and services in 2004. Creating these exports employed some 16 million Americans, about 13% of the total U.S. workforce.

While exports create jobs, other jobs are lost to imports. Americans imported $1.8 trillion in goods and services in 2004. Many of the clothes, toys, electronics, and other items they bought were once produced extensively in the United States by

Web Link

The U.S. Energy Information Administration has good material about supply, demand, and prices for gasoline and other fuels at **www.eia.doe.gov/**.

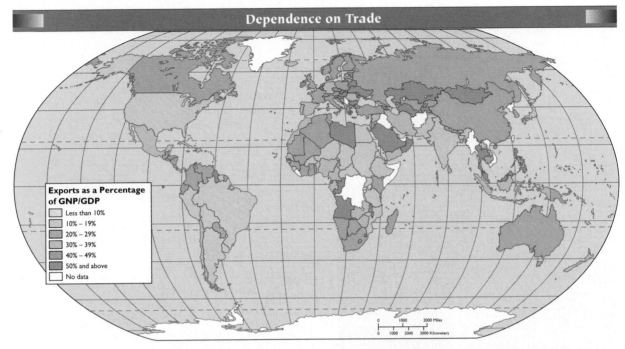

Dependence on Trade

Exports as a Percentage of GNP/GDP
- Less than 10%
- 10% – 19%
- 20% – 29%
- 30% – 39%
- 40% – 49%
- 50% and above
- No data

All countries, even the most economically powerful ones, are becoming increasingly dependent on trade for their economic health. Whether you are American or Zimbabwean, there is a good chance that your job, the price you pay for the goods you buy, and other factors in your economic well-being are dependent on global trade.

MAP
Dependence on Trade

American workers. Now most of these items are produced overseas by workers whose wages are substantially lower. Jobs are also lost to service imports through the "outsourcing" or "offshoring" of jobs. For example, software programmers in India, who earn 75% less than American programmers, provide about $60 billion annually in services to Microsoft, IBM, and other software giants in the United States and elsewhere. According to one analysis, Americans lost an aggregate 155,000 to 215,000 business, professional, and technical jobs to outsourcing during the two-year period 2002–2003 (Schultze, 2004).

Lost jobs are a serious matter, but before you cry "Buy American!" and demand barriers to limit foreign goods, it is important to realize that inexpensive foreign products improve your standard of living. For example, the United States annually imports more than $85 billion worth of clothes and footwear. What Americans pay for shirts, sneakers, and other things they wear would be much higher if the items were all made by American workers earning American wages.

The Flow of International Capital and Your Finances

The global flow of international finance affects you in more ways than you probably imagine. These are covered in detail in chapter 12, but to begin to see the impact of international capital we can look at two examples.

International Investment Capital   Each year, individuals and companies invest many billions of dollars abroad in business and real estate. For Americans, one thing this means is that many familiar U.S. companies have foreign owners. For example, the British firm Pearson P.L.C. owns Addison-Wesley, Longman, Prentice Hall, and other American publishers that produce many of the textbooks American college students read. Check the texts you have purchased this semester. It would not be surprising to find one or more of these imprints among them. Such investment from overseas arguably creates a degree of foreign control over the U.S. economy and how Americans live, but foreign capital also provides jobs and other benefits. This is true, for example, for American workers who make Nissan automobiles in Tennessee, Hondas in Ohio, Toyotas in Kentucky, and Mitsubishis in Illinois.

International Financial Markets   Yet another of the multitudinous connections between your pocketbook and the global economy stems from the huge sums that are invested across national borders in stocks and in private and government bonds each year. One way that affects Americans relates to the U.S. government estimates that the national debt will increase by $2.4 trillion between **fiscal year (FY)** 2002 and FY2009 due to annual federal budget deficits. In 2004, foreign investors owned one-third of the $4.4 trillion U.S. debt, and Americans need them to buy at least as high a percentage of the new bonds that the federal government will sell to finance its soaring debt. If foreigners do not invest in U.S. bonds, then the law of supply and demand will drive up the interest rates on those bonds. Since they compete for dollars, rising U.S. bond rates will result in higher interest rates, meaning that Americans will pay more each month on new mortgages, car loan payments, college tuition loans, and other forms of borrowing.

ANALYZE THE ISSUE
Finance

Defense Spending and Your Finances

The budget of your national government and the taxes to fund it are yet another way that world politics affects you economically. At the very least, you pay taxes to support your country's involvement in world affairs. In FY2004 the U.S. government spent $2.3 trillion (that's right, trillion, not billion). Spending on general foreign affairs (such as foreign aid) was minor, accounting for only about 1% of the budget. Defense spending was considerably more important. It amounted to $453 billion, approximately 20% of the U.S. budget. This equals over $1,400 per American for national defense.

As more of a country's wealth is devoted to military spending, less is available for private use and for domestic government spending. Of course, safety is important, and this leads to an ongoing debate over whether defense spending is too high, about right, or too low. Here the numbers can be tricky, and Table 1.1 on page 12 portrays a number of ways of evaluating defense expenditures by comparing them in several important countries. The easiest way to show expenditures is in U.S. dollars, with the expenditures of other countries calculated according to the exchange rate between their currencies and the dollar. By that standard, U.S. defense spending in 2003, at $417 billion, equaled a breathtaking 47% of all world arms spending. However, the cost of many things is cheaper in other countries than in the United States. This has led economists to calculate **purchasing power parity (PPP)** to adjust comparative spending among countries. Using the PPP standard, U.S. defense spending equals 34% of global spending. Other measures include defense spending as a share of a country's national budget and defense spending as a percentage of a country's wealth, or **gross domestic product (GDP)**, the value of all goods and services produced within a country. By these two measures, as Table 1.1 shows, U.S. military spending is not extraordinary. Which standard do you find most valid?

Another way to think about defense spending and how it relates to you is to compare it with domestic spending in areas that affect you, such as education and health. Figure 1.3 on page 13 compares public

Did You Know That:		
Even limited military operations are very costly. Recent U.S. interventions and their costs are:		
Grenada	1983	$76 million
Panama	1989	$164 million
Persian Gulf	1990–1991	$61 billion
Somalia	1992–1994	$675 million*
Haiti	1994–1995	$427 million
Bosnia	1996–	$1.3 billion*
Kosovo	1999–2000	$5.2 billion*
Afghanistan	2001–	$10 billion*
Iraq	2003–	$85 billion*

*first year of multiyear operation

		% of World		% of World		
Country	Spending (US$ billions)	Spending Unadjusted	Spending–PPP (US$ billions)	Spending Adjusted for PPP	% of Country's Budget	% of Country's GNP
United States	417	47	417	34	20	4
Japan	47	5	33	3	3	3
China	33	4	151	12	20	4
Russia	13	1	63	5	18	5
India	12	1	64	5	14	2

TABLE 1.1   Measures of Military Spending

Data sources: SIPRI (2004), CIA (2004).

Like almost everyone in the world, you pay considerable taxes to support your country's military. However, it is possible to reach different conclusions about the level of military spending depending on the measure you use. Using unadjusted U.S. dollars, U.S. military spending is almost half the world total. But adjusting for what things actually cost in various countries (purchasing power parity—PPP) drops U.S. spending to about a third of the global total. When the standard is defense spending as a percentage of a country's gross domestic product (GDP) or its national budget, U.S. expenditures are not out of line with those of many other major countries.

Web Link

To better understand purchasing power parity, compare global hamburger prices by going to the Web site of the *Economist* at **www.economist.com** and entering "Big Mac Index" in the search window.

spending on education, health, and defense as a percentage of GDP in the United States, its two land neighbors (Canada and Mexico), and China. As you can see, Mexico and Canada spend a much smaller portion of their wealth on defense than on education and health, a sense of priorities that is different from those evident in the United States and China.

Although there is no one-to-one relationship between reduced defense spending and increased higher education spending, it is worth thinking about what would be possible if some defense spending were reallocated to higher education. In 2003 over 16 million students were enrolled in U.S. colleges. The annual cost of room, board, and tuition at the average four-year private college was $31,051; at the average public college it was $10,660. If the U.S. government deleted just one B-2 bomber from its budget (a savings of $2.1 billion), that money would be enough to give an all-expenses-paid scholarship at the average private college to 67,631 students or at the average state university to 196,998 students.

Yet the reallocation of defense spending that might bring economic relief to some people would harm the economic circumstances of other people. Despite the post-9/11 increase in U.S. defense spending, overall funding for national security declined from 6.2% of the GDP in 1985 to 4% in 2004. One impact has been a decline in defense-related employment during that period, from 8 million to 4.9 million civilian and military workers. Therefore, the many individuals, communities, and states that benefit from defense spending view it as a domestic economic issue as well as a national security issue. This was aptly illustrated by the coverage of President Bush's FY2006 budget proposal by the *Hartford Courant* in Connecticut, a state with such key defense manufacturers as Electric Boat (submarines), Sikorsky (helicopters), and Pratt Whitney (jet engines). The newspaper covered the president's overall budget message in its main section, but the defense budget was analyzed on page 1 of the Business section under the headline, "Defense Budget 2-Sided: State Would Gain in the Short Term, Worry Down the Road."[3] The economic impact of jobs gained or lost on individuals and their communities also influences the views of

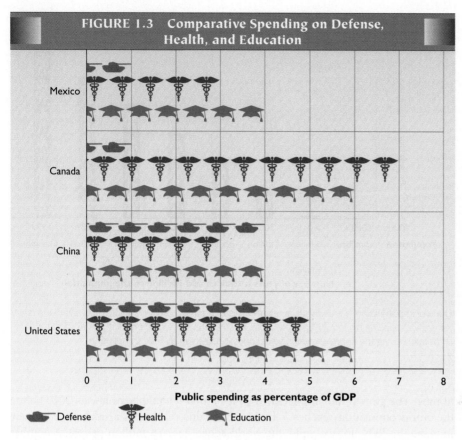

FIGURE 1.3   Comparative Spending on Defense, Health, and Education

Public spending as percentage of GDP

Defense   Health   Education

To some extent, government spending on national security and other aspects of world affairs involves a trade-off with domestic spending. This figure compares how much four countries spend in public funds on defense, health, and education as a percentage of their respective GDPs. As evident, U.S. spending on the three is somewhat evenly distributed and resembles the pattern for China. This pattern differs from Canada and Mexico, the U.S. neighbors to the north and south. Those countries devote much higher percentages of their wealth to education and to health than to defense.

Source: IMF (2004).

the elected officials who represent them. To a degree, a former Defense Department official explains, "Both the administration and Congress . . . view defense as a federal jobs program."[4]

World Politics and Your Living Space

International politics affects far more than your pocketbook. It also helps determine the quality of the air you breathe, the water you drink, and other aspects of the globe you inhabit.

The growth of the world's population and its pressure on resources threaten to change the quality of life as we know it. It took 100,000 years of human existence for the world population to reach 6 billion, a dubious mark that the UN calculates occurred on October 12, 1999. What is worrisome, as Figure 1.4 on page 14 depicts, is that each additional billion people have been added in shorter and shorter periods

ANALYZE THE ISSUE
The UN Population Fund

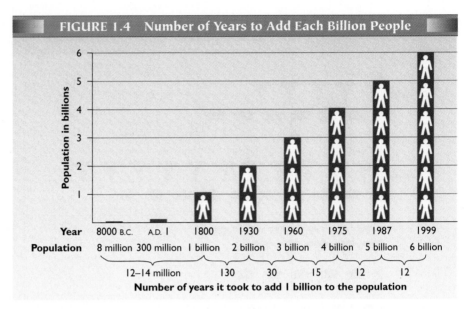

FIGURE 1.4 Number of Years to Add Each Billion People

Year	8000 B.C.	A.D. 1	1800	1930	1960	1975	1987	1999
Population	8 million	300 million	1 billion	2 billion	3 billion	4 billion	5 billion	6 billion

12–14 million 130 30 15 12 12

Number of years it took to add 1 billion to the population

The world population is growing at an alarming rate. It passed 6 billion in October 1999 and is currently expanding by 199,790 people a day. At this rate, the world population will increase by 10 people during the approximately five seconds it takes you to read this caption.

Data sources: U.S. Census Bureau; United Nations Population Fund.

Web Link

The world population site of the U.S. Census Bureau at **www.census.gov/main/www/ popclock.html** has links that lead to a wealth of valuable information.

of time. The growth rate has declined a bit, so that it could be as late as 2015 before the world population reaches 7 billion. Still, this represents a tidal wave of new humans. In 2004, for example, the world added over 76 million people, a number about equal to the population of Egypt.

Among other concerns, Earth's expanding population presents serious environmental dangers. Burning oil and other fossil fuels to warm, transport, and otherwise provide for this mass of people annually creates more than 6 billion tons of carbon dioxide and other gas emissions. These, most scientists believe, are causing global warming. Nine of the ten warmest years since records were first kept in 1856 occurred between 1995 and 2004. The warmest year on record was 1998; 2004 ranked fourth; and the first decade of the new century is on track to replace the last decade of the 1900s as history's hottest.

Warmer temperatures may be welcome to some, but the overall ramifications are worrisome. Among other things, many scientists claim that global warming is melting the polar ice caps, thereby raising sea levels and threatening to flood coastal areas of the world. Some Pacific island countries could even disappear under the rising seas. Additionally, according to the director of the UN Environment Programme (UNEP), "Climate scientists anticipate an increase and intensity of extreme weather events" such as heat waves, droughts, hurricanes, and other forms of destructive weather.[5] For examples, some scientists saw a connection between the near-record warmth of 2004 and record-setting heat waves in Japan and southern Europe and the large number of especially powerful hurricanes that pummeled Florida and other parts of the southeastern United States. Highlighting the view that such cataclysmic climate events were tied in with politics, the group Scientists and Engineers for Change and Environment 2004 sponsored billboards in Florida during the presidential campaign faulting President George W. Bush's environmental policy. One such billboard showed a photograph of a hurricane swirling toward Florida accompanied by the words, "Global warming equals worse hurricanes. George Bush just doesn't get it."[6]

Many scientists believe that global warming, caused by the increased discharge of carbon dioxide and other greenhouse gases, is increasing the frequency and intensity of destructive weather patterns. Among these are storms such as Hurricane Katrina, seen here in a satellite infrared image as it moves menacingly toward the Louisiana-Mississippi coast on August 29, 2005. Hurricanes, typhoons, and other types of powerful storms pose a serious threat to the lives and property of people in many parts of the world.

An important factor in the weather changes that many people are having to endure are the El Niño/La Niña (unusual warming/cooling) conditions that have been occurring with increasing frequency and intensity in the equatorial Pacific Ocean. Among other impacts in the last decade, scientists say, these conditions caused the torrential rains and horrendous flooding in Central and South America in 1999, which cost billions of dollars in damage and killed thousands, followed in 2001 by a prolonged drought in Central America that caused further economic ruin by severely damaging the region's crops. These El Niño/La Niña conditions also affect areas beyond the Pacific Rim. On the U.S. east coast, for example, years in which El Niño predominates can be drought prone, but they have fewer, milder hurricanes. La Niña can bring flooding and is likely to foster more frequent and violent hurricanes.

There are numerous other proven or suspected deleterious environmental trends that are also despoiling our living space. UNEP reports that in addition to the perils already mentioned, erosion destroys 25 billion tons of topsoil each year, 900 million urban dwellers breathe dangerous levels of sulfur dioxide, and more than half the world's population could be facing critical water shortages by midcentury. "Our world is characterized by . . . the accelerating loss of the environmental capital that underpins life on Earth," warns UNEP's director Klaus Toepfer.[7]

Certainly, world politics has not caused most environmental problems. However, we are unlikely to be able to stem, much less reverse, the degradation of the biosphere without global cooperation. As Toepfer put it, "We suffer from problems of planetary dimensions. They require global responses." These are being initiated, but only slowly and somewhat uncertainly, as detailed in chapter 15.

Web Link

Information and graphics on El Niño/La Niña are available from the National Oceanic and Atmospheric Administration at **www.elnino.noaa.gov/**.

World Politics and Your Life

Not only our lives are affected by world politics, so too in some cases is whether we live at all. Disease control and political violence are just two events that intertwine your very life with world politics.

Transnational Diseases

Politics may not directly cause diseases, but we are increasingly in need of global responses to counter health threats that ignore national borders. One example relates to the environment. Chlorofluorocarbons (CFCs) and other chemicals we have spewed into the air have significantly depleted Earth's ozone layer, which helps shield us from the sun's deadly ultraviolet rays. Because higher exposure to ultraviolet rays increases the risk of developing melanoma, the deadliest form of skin cancer, the rate of new melanoma cases has skyrocketed. For Americans, this means that more than 54,000 of them will be diagnosed with melanoma each year, and almost 8,000 will die of the disease. Certainly there are things that you can do, like wearing sunscreen, to reduce the chances of becoming a skin cancer victim. But achieving that goal can also be greatly helped by international agreements, such as the UN-sponsored Montreal Protocol (1987) to phase out the use of CFCs and other ozone-attacking chemicals that were once used in such common items as air conditioners and deodorant sprays.

We also increasingly rely on global cooperation to prevent the spread of infectious diseases. Such diseases have always been international travelers. Italian sailors carried bubonic plague (the Black Death) to Europe in 1347 after contracting it during a voyage to the Black Sea region from people who, in turn, had been infected through their trade contacts with people in China. During the next three years, the Black Death killed between a third and one-half of the people in Europe. Diseases still travel today, but they do so in part by high-speed airliners rather than by sedate sailing ships. The Black Death took years to spread; the "Spanish flu" spread around the world in months, killing more than 500,000 Americans and 20 million to 50 million people worldwide during 1918–1919. The spread of AIDS globally is an epic pandemic, but other comparatively less deadly diseases have also spread transnationally and often very rapidly. For instance, severe acute respiratory syndrome (SARS) spread around the world in weeks during 2003. It is just one of several many "new" diseases that travel far from their epidemiological origins to assail Americans and others. Figure 1.5 illustrates this point by tracing the increased incidence of West Nile virus in the United States. According to a top epidemiologist, the new number of infectious diseases and their ability to spread rapidly has made the period since "the 1970s without precedent in the history of the annals of medicine."[8] Of course each country acts to contain transnational diseases and treat their victims. However, it is far more effective to counter diseases where they first begin to appear than after they cross national borders, and it falls to the World Health Organization (WHO) to coordinate the global effort.

FIGURE 1.5 U.S. Cases of West Nile Virus

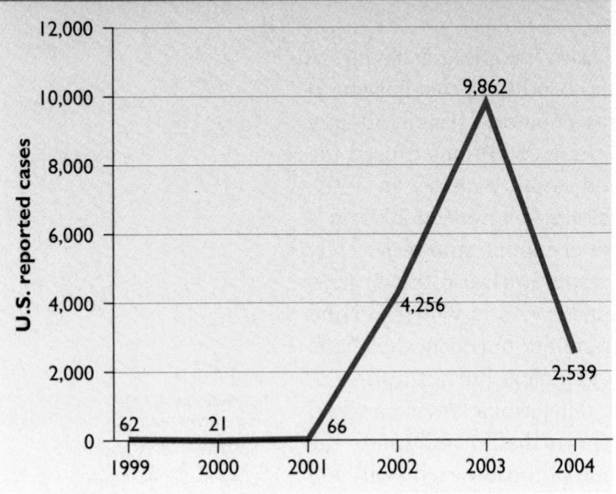

West Nile virus is one of several diseases that have come to the United States in recent years from abroad. The disease, which is carried by birds and transmitted by mosquitoes, was first identified in the West Nile district of Uganda in 1937 and has since spread to the rest of Africa, Europe, the Middle East, west and central Asia, Oceania, and most recently (1999) to North America. There is about a 4% mortality rate in the United States. The data presented here is from July 2005, and the total for 2004 may increase as data is finalized.

Data source: U.S. Centers for Disease Control.

Transnational Political Violence

War, terrorism, and other forms of transnational political violence are in many ways more threatening today than ever before (Horne, 2002). Until the 20th century, the vast majority of war deaths were soldiers. Civilian casualties began to rise drastically as noncombatants increasingly became a target of military operations. Nearly as many civilians as soldiers were killed during World War II. Now more civilians than soldiers are killed. According to the UN, civilians accounted for more than 85% of everyone killed during wars in the 1980s and 1990s. Most tragically, these casualties included 2 million children, who died from wounds and other war-related causes. In a nuclear war, military casualties would be a mere footnote to the overall death toll. And terrorists almost exclusively target civilians.

The attacks of September 11, 2001, also brought into sharp focus the reality that violent international attacks are not confined to those launched by countries using their military forces. Americans found that they were vulnerable to terrorism anywhere and at any moment in their daily lives. It must also be said that this unsettling reality has long been felt more acutely in other parts of the world that have been subjected to more frequent acts of international terrorism (Laquer, 2004; Heymann, 2002).

War is a special concern for college-age adults because they are of prime military age. An examination of the ages of U.S. troops killed during the Vietnam War shows that of those who died, 84% were aged 18 to 22. For this age group in the Iraq war and occupation, the percentage is much lower (44%). One reason is that U.S. forces in Iraq were part of an all-volunteer military, whereas many U.S. soldiers in Vietnam were draftees. Still, as Figure 1.6 shows, it was young adults who bore the overwhelming brunt of American casualties in Iraq.

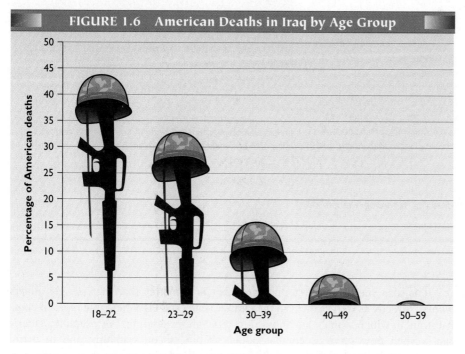

FIGURE 1.6   American Deaths in Iraq by Age Group

As in other wars, young adults bore the overwhelming percentage of U.S. military deaths in Iraq. American servicemen and servicewomen ages 18–22 accounted for 44% of the dead, and those ages 23–29 made up an additional 33% of the Americans who died in the war.

Note: The data is as of February 2005 and includes over 1,400 fatalities.
Data source: U.S. Department of Defense.

WRITE THE POLICY SCRIPT

Should Women Serve in Combat?

Throughout history, most of the women killed, wounded, or otherwise traumatized in war have been civilian noncombatants. Now women soldiers are increasingly becoming casualties. Lori Piestewa was the first of many U.S. servicewomen to fall in the Iraq War.

Private first class Piestewa was a member of the U.S. Army's 507th Maintenance Company who was serving her country as her father had in Vietnam and her grandfather had in World War II. Pfc Piestewa was 23, a Hopi from Tuba City, Arizona, and the mother of a son (age 4) and a daughter (age 3).

On March 23, soon after the war began, she was part of a convoy providing support for the U.S.-British offensive. Iraqi forces attacked the U.S. unit near Nasiriyah, Iraq, killing Piestewa and several other American soldiers. Her fate highlights the reality that the chances of women being killed, captured, or wounded as combatants have grown as the United States and many other countries have increasingly gender-integrated their armed forces. Some applaud this change. Others want to take it even further by abolishing the rules in the U.S. and most other armed forces that bar women from infantry, artillery, and armored units. Still others find women in combat abhorrent and would eliminate the possibility.

How would you decide policy regarding women serving in the armed forces? During the first two years of the U.S. operation in Iraq, women constituted 2% of the Americans killed, and your policy choice will almost certainly impact that percentage in future wars. One option is to maintain current U.S. policy, with women serving in most military positions, but barred from being in the most perilous ground forces (amored, artillery, and infantry units). A second possibility is to eliminate all barriers to women in the military by opening all positions to them. Your third choice is to remove women from all military jobs that might take them near the front lines.

What Do You Think?

How would you write the policy script regarding women in combat?

American women have increasingly served in military positions that have exposed them to enemy fire. Private first class Lori Piestewa, a Hopi, was killed when her combat maintenance unit was attacked by Iraqi forces in March 2003. She is shown here behind her father and her son, Brandon, at a 2005 memorial service. She also had a daughter, Carla. In 2005, Congress debated and rejected a proposal to end the prohibition on women serving in infantry, armor, and artillery units. Should women, including mothers of small children, serve in all military units?

It is also the case that military combat is a matter that increasingly affects women directly as well as men. In the United States and elsewhere, the types of combat units in which women are allowed to serve are expanding. For example, American women now serve as combat pilots, as officers on warships, and in many positions in the ground forces that subject them to enemy action. Also, changes in tactics mean that more lightly armed opponents often try to attack support units, ones in which more women serve. As a result of these changes, many more women may fight and die in future wars. As of early 2005, 29 American servicewomen had lost their lives in Iraq. Moreover, public attitudes are moving slowly toward accepting the idea of women in units that are even more dangerous. One poll of Americans found that 52% were willing to see women serve in ground forces such as the infantry. When asked if women should be subject to the draft, 46% of Americans said yes, 50% said no, and 4% were undecided.[9] How do you feel about this issue? That question is taken up in the box, "Should Women Serve in Combat?"

More than anything, the lesson that you should draw here is that world politics plays a role in your everyday life and sometimes can also have a dramatic, very individual impact on you. We are all involved economically and environmentally. Furthermore, world politics can threaten our very lives. Wars will continue to be fought. Young men—and increasingly young women—will be called upon to fight them. Some will die. In the worst possible circumstance, nuclear war, it will not matter whether you are in the military or not. Furthermore, terrorism is no longer a remote event for Americans, as those unfortunate souls in the twin towers found out as they stared in stunned horror at an airliner hurtling toward them.

You Can Make a Difference

The next logical question is, "Can I make a difference?" Yes, you can! It is true that we cannot all be president or secretary of state, but we can take action and we can make our views known.

Taking Direct Action

One way to influence global relations is through various forms of direct action. This happens more frequently than you might think (Sharp, 2001). Among the activists, students have often been important agents of political change. Also note that fruitful student activism is not limited to Americans. For instance, Ukrainian students recently played an important role in their country's future after Prime Minister Viktor Yanukovych used blatant fraud to defeat opposition leader Viktor Yushchenko. Students were at the forefront of the massive protests, and their role in preserving democracy in Ukraine and forcing a new election in 2005 (which reversed the earlier one) was captured in one news headline: "The Students Who Shook Ukraine—Peacefully."[10]

In the United States, millions of individual student actions, ranging from burning draft cards, to massive and sometimes violent demonstrations, helped end American involvement in Vietnam. College students also were often at the forefront of both the protests against and the rallies for the war with Iraq in 2003, as related in the box, "Supporting and Opposing the War in Iraq" on page 20. It is the first of a number of "Play a Part in Your World" boxes meant to encourage participating in world politics rather than being merely an armchair critic. In this case, those who demonstrated against the war with Iraq were able only to delay it, not prevent it (Foyle, 2004). But the more important point is that they and those who rallied in support of action against Iraq did more than sit passively in the political audience.

Consumer boycotts and other forms of pressure can also be effective. Individuals have made a difference by refusing to eat tuna fish that does not bear the "dolphin safe" label. More recently, students on U.S. college campuses have participated in protests and brought consumer pressure to bear on clothing and footwear companies that sell products manufactured in so-called sweatshops in Asia and elsewhere. These factories pay little, require employees to work long hours, and have poor safety records. Adding to the pressure, colleges began to follow the lead of their students. The University of Notre Dame, for one, banned the manufacture of its

Web Link

You can find out if your school is a member of the Fair Labor Association by going to the FLA Web site at **www.fairlabor.org/**.

PLAY A PART IN YOUR WORLD

Supporting and Opposing the War in Iraq

Abbie Hoffman, a prominent protester against the U.S. intervention in Vietnam (1964–1975) and founder of the Youth International Party ("Yippies"), had it right when he told his followers, "Democracy is not something you believe in or a place to hang your hat, but it's something you do. You participate. If you stop doing it, democracy crumbles."[1]

Faced in 2003 with the prospect of a different war, the college students in the two accompanying pictures and the many others like them across the United States and indeed around the world, who demonstrated for and against the U.S.-led invasion of Iraq, were laudably following Hoffman's maxim that democracy is something you do. The students and others who waved signs, debated one another, and took other actions were an important part of the national dialogue about the war.

In the end, war came. By the day before it began, 70% of Americans had come to support action, 27% were opposed, and 3% unsure.[2] It is important to understand, though, that the decision to go to war and even the support of a majority of Americans for war did not mean that those who rallied in favor of it had "won" and those who protested against

the war had "lost" and wasted their time. Antiwar protesters did not ultimately prevail, but their influence was evident in the Bush administration's domestic campaign to build public opinion support among Americans. There is also evidence that activism, as Hoffman advocated, has an impact beyond the immediate issue. For example, one study of 37 democracies during the period 1919–1992 found that the higher a country's level of citizen political activity, the less likely it was to initiate international disputes.[3] Most importantly, those who demonstrated their opposition to the war, as well as those who rallied to support it, strengthened democracy. As U.S. Senator J. William Fulbright, another opponent of the Vietnam War, put it, "In a democracy, dissent is an act of faith [that the democracy works]. . . . To criticize one's country is to do it a service and pay it a compliment."[4]

Be Active

Whether the issue is your country's policy toward Iraq or any other, and whatever position you have, be active. Play a part in your world.

You can make a difference in world politics, and you should try. This does not mean your view will always prevail. As these photographs of University of Minnesota students show, some opposed the war in Iraq and some supported it. That the war occurred did not mean that the opponents wasted their time. Instead, they improved democracy, which rests on a politically active citizenry.

licensed products in 13 countries that have unfair labor standards. As a result of such efforts, Nike and other companies have joined the Fair Labor Association (FLA), a coalition organization of human rights groups, manufacturers, and 175 universities and colleges, who cooperate to help protect the rights of factory workers worldwide.

Voting

Democracies provide opportunities to affect world politics through the ballot box. Voting for candidates is one of these. Leaders do not always follow campaign promises, but who gets elected usually does influence policy. During the 2004 U.S. presidential election, George Bush and John Kerry disagreed sharply over the degree to which the United States should act unilaterally in its foreign policy, on whether the war against Iraq was justified, on whether the U.S. should join global negotiations to reduce the emission of global warming gases, and on a range of other issues. The voters determined that it would be George Bush and not John Kerry who would guide U.S. foreign policy during 2005–2008.

In the United States and most other countries, however, all age groups do not vote in equal percentages (Patterson, 2005; Phelps, 2004). Therefore some age groups have a greater say than others. Among Americans, for example, voter turnout among adults age 25 and older is almost 50% higher than among college-age (18–24) adults. This voting gap makes a difference. Voters under age 24 were more likely than those over that age to favor the Democratic presidential candidate in both 2000 and 2004, as shown in Figure 1.7. The upshot of the voting gap is evident if you project what would have occurred in 2000 and 2004 if college-age adults had voted at the same rate as older adults. During the exceptionally close 2000 election, Al Gore, not George W. Bush, would have clearly carried Florida and won the election. Under the same conditions in 2004, the vote would have narrowed to the point where, because of sampling error, it is not possible to conclude definitively who would have prevailed. John Kerry would almost surely have carried more states, including Iowa and New Mexico. He might also have won the election by capturing the 20 pivotal electoral votes of Ohio. Younger voters there favored him by a 14% margin, compared to the state's older voters, who favored Bush by a 9% margin. Especially if you are a young adult, as most of those reading this book are, the point is that if you and others your age exercise your democratic rights as fully as do other Americans, then you can change who leads the world's most important national actor, the United States.

Direct voting on international questions is also possible in some countries (Rourke, Hiskes, & Zirakzadeh, 1992). In 2004 the European Union (EU) created a new constitution that will have to be ratified by the EU member-states. Of the 25 EU countries, at least 10 scheduled referendums during 2005 and 2006 allowing the people to decide whether or not their country will ratify the EU constitution. French and Dutch voters rejected it. In other recent instances of direct democracy, voters in Hungary, Lithuania, Malta, and Slovenia consented to their country's membership in the EU; the people of Gibraltar opted to remain a British dependency, voters in East

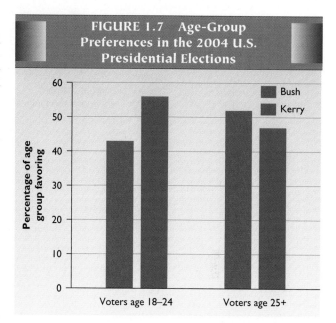

FIGURE 1.7   Age-Group Preferences in the 2004 U.S. Presidential Elections

American college-age adults (age 18–24) were more likely in 2004 to favor the Democratic Party presidential candidate than the Republican Party candidate, as this figure shows. The same pattern existed during the 2000 presidential election. It was also the case in both elections that older adults (age 25 and up) were more likely to vote than were college-age adults. In 2004, for example, 62% of older adults, but only 42% of college-age adults, voted. These gaps in voting percentage and candidate preferences are important. Had college-age adults voted in 2000 and 2004 at the same rate as older adults, Al Gore would have won the 2000 election, and the 2004 race would have narrowed to the point where it is arguable that John Kerry would have been elected.

Note: The outcome in 2004 cannot be precisely calculated because of sampling error in the exit polls on which the data is based and other factors. Percentages do not add to 100 because of voter support of third-party candidates.

Data sources: Exit polls conducted for the Associated Press by Edison Media Research and Mitofsky International.

Some students of political science go on to practice world politics. Before joining the Bush administration in 2001, Secretary of State Condoleezza Rice was provost at Stanford University, where she also taught political science.

Timor chose independence from Indonesia, Swiss citizens voted to join the United Nations, and Swedes rejected adopting the new EU currency, the euro. The ability of citizens to make direct decisions about foreign policy is still not common, but it is becoming more so, and there is strong support in the United States, the countries of Europe, and other democracies for greater use of referendums and other such **direct democracy** techniques (Dalton, Burklin, & Drummond, 2001; Qvortrup, 2002).

Becoming a Policy Maker

It is also possible to become a policy maker by running for elective office or securing an appointment in such areas as foreign policy, national security policy, intelligence operations, the military, and international trade in your country. You can also work for the United Nations or one of the other important international organizations. It may take some time to work your way up through the ranks to a key position, but it is possible.

Studying political science can be a start on the path to becoming a policy maker. Secretary of State Condoleezza Rice holds both undergraduate and graduate degrees in political science. Other recent top U.S. policy makers with degrees in political science include President Bill Clinton, Vice President Al Gore, Secretary of State Madeleine Albright, and Secretary of Defense Donald Rumsfeld.

The point is that you count—by voting, protesting, joining issue-oriented groups, donating money to causes you support, or even by having your thoughts recorded in a political poll. Few individual actions are dramatic, and by themselves few significantly change world politics, but the sum of many smaller actions can and does make a difference. Do not consider politics a spectator sport. It is more important than that. Treat politics as a participant—even a contact—sport.

Web Link

You can learn about becoming a diplomat and about other careers in the U.S. State Department at its Web site, **www.careers.state.gov/.**

Putting World Events in Context

It is important to bring some order to our thinking about world events given their importance in each of our lives. The day this is being written the *New York Times* is carrying news items related to such happenings as Palestinian and Israeli leaders meeting for the first time in four years; U.S. Secretary of State Condoleezza Rice conferring with European leaders on strains in transatlantic relations; the impact of the election in Iraq on the insurgency; North and South Korea opening a joint economic zone; Spain changing policy about illegal immigrants; and President Bush proposing increases in defense spending and foreign aid. Each of these stories has unique elements. Yet each is also part of the pattern of global politics and is best understood within that context.

One way to begin to see the context is to "catch up" on the story if you have not been following global events. To help you do that, chapter 2 provides a base for understanding world politics by laying out a brief history of the world system and its current trends. If you do not do so already, you should also take up reading the newspaper daily.

Thinking theoretically is a second way to put things in context. Knowing about theories—generalizations—about politics is necessary to identify patterns of action and reaction. Theory allows us to think systematically. You will encounter extended discussions of various political theories at several points in this text. The first of these, discussed just below, are realism and liberalism, two fundamentally different ways of looking at the world. Chapter 3 introduces you to levels of analysis, a set of theories about whether humans, countries, or the international system is the best unit of analysis to study in order to understand world politics. Chapter 5 takes up feminism, postmodernism, and constructivism. Whereas realism and idealism are classic theoretical approaches, the concepts in chapter 5 represent more recent contributions to a general understanding of world politics. Yet another important set of theories is discussed in chapter 12. These are international political economy (IPE) theories, including economic nationalism, economic internationalism, and economic structuralism. You will see that these various theoretical approaches modify rather than replace the basic notions of realism and idealism.

Also note the many smaller points of theory you will find in this text's scheme of making a general statement about how politics works (theory) and giving an example. When you study, the general point is almost always more important than the example. Also, do not be surprised to find disagreements among scholars about which theories are valid. We have learned much, but it is only a small fraction of what there is to know (Chernoff, 2004).

Introducing Realism and Liberalism

Your eventual choice about which of the two divergent roads you think world politics should follow in the future is likely to be influenced by your views about the basic nature of humankind. Those who believe that the world is and/or should continue on the traditional road are often associated with a theory called realism (associated terms: realpolitik, balance of power, nationalism, conservative, and state-centric). Those who believe that the world is beginning to chart a new course are frequently identified with another theory, liberalism (associated terms: liberal institutionalism, globalism, idealist, cosmopolitan, and internationalist). You will also find the prefix "neo" attached to some of these words (as in neorealism or neoliberalism) to designate recent variations on the classic concepts (Schmidt, 2004).

Web Link

Two great sources for international news are the *New York Times* at http://www.nytimes.com/ and the *Washington Post* at www.washingtonpost.com.

Web Link

For many political science resources and also a few good jokes, go to the Ultimate Political Science Links maintained by Professor P. S. Ruckman of Rock Valley College at www.rvc.cc.il.us/faclink/pruckman/PSLinks.htm.

Some comments on the terms are appropriate. First, do not be fooled by the connotations of realism and liberalism. One school of theorists labeled their position "realism" and the sobriquet stuck, but they do not necessarily see things as they "really" are. It would also be an error to equate the use of "liberal" here with its application in domestic politics to describe left of center political parties, like Democrats in the United States. For example, President George W. Bush is a conservative in terms of American domestic politics, yet he exhibits some distinctly liberal tendencies in the international relations theory use of the term. Given the sometimes confusing use and implications of the terms, it is best, perhaps, to think of realists as "pessimists." Conversely, "optimists" is probably a more descriptive label for liberals.

Second, the effort to group theories together is merely a helpful vehicle to introduce them to beginning students of international relations. Table 1.2 summarizes the main points of realism, liberalism, and their two "neo" offshoots. Still, putting theories into neat categories partly obscures their range and subtleties. As one study noted, "If you put four IR theorists in a room you will easily get ten different ways of organizing theory, and there will also be disagreement about which theories are relevant in the first place" (Jackson & Sørenson, 2003:34). Thus, if you delve into theory you will find many nuances in the writings of the leading realist and liberal scholars as they try to describe how the world works politically.

Third, most people's political views are a mixture of realism and liberalism. For example, we shall see that in many ways President George W. Bush fits the realist mode in his willingness to use preemptive war to smite those whom he considers an enemy and to do so against the majority of world opinion. Yet Bush's strong belief in spreading democracy in order to create a more peaceful world is classic liberalism. So if you find yourself less than a consistent realist or liberal, do not worry. Most other people are divided too.

The Nature of Politics: Realism and Liberalism

The disagreement between realists and liberals about the nature of politics is perhaps the most fundamental division in all of political discourse. The two schools of thought disagree over the very nature of *Homo politicus* (political humankind).

Realism and the Nature of Politics

At root, **realists** are pessimistic and liberals are optimistic about human nature. Realists believe that political struggle among humans is probably inevitable because people have an inherent dark side (Donnelly, 2000; Sayer, 2000). Therefore realists have little political trust, and that extends to other countries and their people (Brewer, Gross, Aday, & Willnat, 2004). As one realist puts it, "The sad fact is that international politics has always been a ruthless and dangerous business and it is likely to remain that way" (Mearsheimer, 2001:2). Many realists would trace their intellectual heritage to such political philosophers as Thomas Hobbes (1588–1679), who believed that humans possess an inherent urge to dominate, an *animus dominandi*. In his book *Leviathan* (1651), Hobbes argued that "if any two men desire the same thing, which nevertheless they cannot both enjoy, they become enemies and . . . endeavor to destroy or subdue one another." Taking the same point of view, one leading realist scholar, Hans Morgenthau, wrote that an "ubiquity of evil in human actions" inevitably turns "churches into political organizations . . . revolutions into dictatorships . . . and love of country into imperialism" (Zakaria, 1993:22).

A relatively recent variation on realism is the neorealist (or structural realist) school of thought (James, 2002). **Neorealists** focus on the anarchic nature of a world

JOIN THE DEBATE
The Human Nature Divide

Realism and the Competitive Future

There are many implications to the realist view that the drive for power and resulting conflict are at the heart of politics and that there is "little hope for progress in international relations" (Brooks, 1997:473). Based on this view, realists advocate a relatively pragmatic, realpolitik approach to world politics. One principle of realpolitik is to secure your own country's interests first and worry about the welfare of other countries second, if at all, on the assumption that other countries will not help you unless it is in their own interest. This makes realists wary of what they see as the self-sacrificing policies advocated by liberals. Such policies are not just foolish but dangerous, according to Morgenthau (1986:38), because countries that shun realpolitik will "fall victim to the power of others."

A second tenet of realpolitik holds that countries should practice balance-of-power politics. This standard counsels diplomats to strive to achieve an equilibrium of power in the world in order to prevent any other country or coalition of countries from dominating the system. This can be done through a variety of methods, including building up your own strength, allying yourself with others, or dividing your opponents.

A third realist policy prescription is that the best way to maintain the peace is to be powerful: "Peace through strength," as President Ronald Reagan was fond of saying. Showing his realist side, President George W. Bush takes a similar line, arguing, "We will build our defenses beyond challenge, lest weakness invite challenge."[16] Thus, realists believe that it is necessary for a country to be armed because the world is dangerous. Liberals would reply that the world is dangerous because so many countries are so heavily armed.

It is important to say that this does not cast realists as warmongers. Instead, a fourth realist tenet is that you should neither waste power on peripheral goals nor pursue goals that you do not have the power to achieve. This frequently makes realists reluctant warriors.

It is worth noting, for instance, that Morgenthau was an early critic of U.S. involvement in the war in Vietnam as a waste of resources in a tangential area. More recently, two leading realist scholars opposed the invasion of Iraq in 2003 on the grounds that Saddam Hussein had been successfully contained and that ousting him would require an unsupportable expenditure of U.S. power (Mearsheimer & Walt, 2003). In sum, they wrote, "Saddam Hussein needs to remain in his box—but we don't need a war to keep him there."[17] Prudence, then, is a watchword for realists, and some even tend toward isolationism.

Liberalism and the Cooperative Future

Liberals believe that humanity can and must successfully seek a new system of world order. They have never been comfortable with a world system based on sovereignty, but they now argue that it is imperative to find new organizational paths to cooperation. Liberals are convinced that the spread of nuclear weapons, the increase in economic interdependence among countries, the decline of world resources, the daunting gap between rich and poor, and the mounting damage to our ecosphere mean that humans must learn to cooperate more fully because they are in grave danger of suffering a catastrophe of unparalleled proportions.

Liberals are divided, however, over how far cooperation can and should go. Classic liberals believe that just as humans learned to form cooperative societies without giving up their individuality, so too can states learn to cooperate without surrendering their independence. These liberals believe that the growth of international economic interdependence and the spread of global culture will create a much greater spirit of cooperation among the world countries. Neoliberals are more dubious about a world in which countries retain full sovereignty. These analysts believe that countries will have to surrender some of their sovereignty to international organizations in order to promote greater cooperation and, if necessary, to enforce good behavior. "The fundamental right of existence," Pope John Paul II told the UN General Assembly, "does not necessarily call for sovereignty as a state." Instead, the pontiff said, "There can be historical circumstances in which aggregations different from single state sovereignty can . . . prove advisable."[18]

As for the future, liberals are encouraged by some recent trends. One of these is the growth of interdependence. Liberals also support their case by pointing to the willingness of countries to surrender some of their sovereignty to improve themselves. The EU, for instance, now exercises considerable economic and even political authority over its member-countries, and it has even drafted an EU constitution. Member-countries were not forced into the EU; they joined it freely. This and other indications that sovereignty is weakening will be discussed at length later in the text. Liberals are also buoyed by the spread of democracy and interdependence. They believe that both tend to lessen the chances of conflict among states, and research shows that there is substantial validity to this notion (Kinsella & Russett, 2002).

Liberals also condemn the practice of realpolitik. They charge that power politics leads to an unending cycle of conflict and misery in which safety is temporary at best. They look at the last century with its more than 111 million deaths during two world wars and innumerable other conflicts and deride realists for suggesting that humanity should continue to rely on a self-help system that has failed to provide safety so often and so cataclysmically. Liberals further assert that the pursuit of power in the nuclear age may one day lead to ultimate destruction.

This does not mean that liberals are unwilling to use military force, economic sanctions, and other forms of coercion. Almost all liberals are willing to use force in self-defense or to prevent overt international aggression, such as Iraq's invasion of Kuwait and threat to Saudi Arabia in 1990. Many liberals would intervene militarily to prevent or halt genocide and other gross violations of human rights. Such interventions are especially acceptable to liberals if they are undertaken through such cooperative efforts as UN peacekeeping. Beyond such cases, liberals are at odds over whether such goals as expanding human rights and democracy should be pursued using military force and economic sanction as well as moral suasion and the power of example. Assertive liberalism is the kind of impulse exhibited by Woodrow Wilson's assertion that the bayonets of American doughboys could help make the world safe for democracy and George W. Bush's belief that toppling Saddam Hussein and fostering democracy in Iraq justified the U.S. invasion of the country. Proponents of a more passive liberalism argue that using force is often counterproductive and that it also often leads to imperial domination even if the initial intentions were lofty (Morefield, 2004).

Assessing Reality: Realism and Liberalism

Before we leave our discussion of realism and liberalism, it is worth pausing to ask which theory better explains how the world has operated and how it operates now. On balance, it is safe to say that throughout history competition, not cooperation, has dominated international relations. Not being at war is not necessarily the same as being at peace in a cooperative way, and suspicion, tension, and rivalry, rather than cooperation, have been the most common traits of what we euphemistically call international peace. Thus, realpolitik is still usually the order of the day, especially where important national interests are involved. Most political leaders tend toward realism in their policies, and even those who lean toward liberalism often take the realpolitik road.

Does this mean that liberalism is a sterile theory confined largely to the halls of academia and the utopian dreams of those without power? It does not. While realpolitik self-interest has been the dominant impulse of countries, it is also true that countries can be cooperative and even altruistic at times. Moreover, it may well be that the liberal approach is gaining ground as states recognize that competition and conflict are increasingly dangerous and destructive and that peaceful cooperation is in everyone's self-interest. It would be naive to argue that the world is anywhere near the point of concluding that self-interest and global interests are usually synonymous. But it is not fatuous to say that an increasing number of people have decided that working toward the long-term goal of a safe and prosperous world is preferable to seeking short-term national advantage. Thus, while the question "what is" should engage our attention, the far more important questions are "what should be" and "what will be." What should be is for you to decide after reading this book and consulting other sources of information. What will be is for all of us to see and experience.

Chapter Summary

Previewing the Global Drama

1. This book's primary message is captured by Shakespeare's line, "All the world's a stage, and all the men and women merely players." This means that we are all part of the world drama and are affected by it. It also means that we should try to play a role in determining the course of the dramatic events that affect our lives.

2. This text is organized to reflect the theme that that world is at a crossroads. One option is to continue on the traditional path of countries pursuing their national interests as far as their power permits within a largely anarchical international system. The alternative path would have states abandon their pursuit of short-term self-interest and take a more cooperative, globalist approach to world politics.

The Importance of World Politics to Each of Us

3. Economics is one way that we are all affected. The word *intermestic* has been coined to symbolize the merging of *inter*national and d*omestic* concerns, especially in the area of economics. Countries and their citizens have become increasingly interdependent.

4. Economically, trade both creates and causes the loss of jobs. International investment practices may affect your standard of living in such diverse ways as determining how much college tuition costs, what your income is, what interest rate you pay for auto loans and mortgages, and how much you can look forward to in retirement. The global economy also supplies vital resources, such as oil. Exchange rates between different currencies affect the prices we pay for imported goods, the general rate of inflation, and our country's international trade balance.

5. Our country's role in the world also affects decisions about the allocation of budget funds. Some countries spend a great deal on military functions. Other countries spend relatively little on the military and devote almost all of their budget resources to domestic spending.

6. World politics also plays an important role in determining the condition of your living space. Politics, for the most part, has not created environmental degradation, but political cooperation almost certainly will be needed to halt and reverse the despoiling of the biosphere.

7. Your life may also be affected by world politics. You may be called on to serve in the military. Whether or not you are in the military, war can cost you your life.

8. There are many things any one of us can do, individually or in cooperation with others, to play a

part in shaping the future of our world. Think, vote, protest, support, write letters, join organizations, make speeches, run for office—do something!

Putting World Events in Context

9. We improve our understanding of world politics by putting events within the context of theory to see patterns and make generalizations about the conduct of international affairs.
10. Two theories, realism and liberalism (and their variations neorealist and neoliberal), give important insights into the traditional and alternative paths world politics can take.
11. The traditionalist approach is associated with a theory called realism. It focuses on the self-interested promotion of the state and nation. Realists believe that power politics is the driving force behind international relations. Therefore, realists believe that both safety and wisdom lie in promoting the national interest through the preservation and, if necessary, the application of the state's power.
12. The second, alternative road is advocated by those who stress the need for significant change, including both a restructuring of power within states and international cooperation and global interests. One term associated with this approach is "liberalism." Liberals believe that realpolitik is dangerous and outmoded. They believe that idealpolitik should be given greater emphasis and that everyone's "real" interest lies in a more orderly, humane, and egalitarian world.

For simulations, debates, and other interactive activities, a chapter quiz, Web links, PowerWeb articles, and much more, visit **www.mhhe.com/rourke11/** and go to chapter 1. Or, while accessing the site, click on Course-Wide Content and view recent international relations articles in the *New York Times*.

Key Terms

direct democracy	international governmental	neoliberal	purchasing power parity
fiscal year (FY)	organizations (IGOs)	neorealist	(PPP)
gross domestic product	intermestic	nongovernmental	realist
(GDP)	liberal	organizations (NGOs)	

CHAPTER 2

The Evolution of World Politics

I am amazed, methinks, and lose my way
Among the thorns and dangers of the world.
　　　　　—William Shakespeare, *King John*

Whereof what's past is prologue, what to come,
In yours and my discharge.
　　　　　—William Shakespeare, *The Tempest*

UN Secretary-General Kofi Annan and President George Bush disagree strongly over whether the preemptive war against Iraq violated U.S. obligations under the UN Charter. This chapter's opinion box, "Is Preemptive War Good Policy?" asks what you think.

THIS CHAPTER HAS TWO PURPOSES. One is to establish a historical foundation for our analysis of international relations that emphasizes the themes and events you will encounter repeatedly in this book. Second, this chapter sketches the evolution of the current, rapidly evolving world political system. The concept of an **international system** represents the notion that (1) the world is more than just the sum of its parts, such as countries, (2) that world politics is more than just the sum of the individual interactions among those parts, and (3) that there are general patterns of interactions among the system's actors. The nature of the international system and its impact on world politics are further explored in chapter 3.

Be patient as you read this chapter. You will find that it often introduces a topic briefly and then hurries on to another point. "Wait a minute," you may think, "slow down and explain this better." Hang in there! Other chapters fill in the details.

The Evolving World System: Early Development

There have been numerous global and regional international systems, with some scholars dating them back to the southern Mesopotamian region of Babylon (in what is now Iraq) some 7,500 years ago (Cioffi-Revilla, 2000). Modern politics is vastly different than it was, but that change has, for the most part, evolved slowly.

Ancient Greece and Rome

We can begin tracking the international system with a brief exploration of the era that included the Greek city-states (about 700 B.C. to 300 B.C.) and the rise of Rome in about 500 B.C. to its fall in A.D. 453. It was during this period that four of today's important political characteristics were first seen. Each of them subsequently almost disappeared, only to flourish more than a thousand years in the future.

Territorial State: Before the city-states, political organization was based on a ruler or on a cultural group, such as a tribe. Each controlled territory, but the political connection of those who lived in that territory was to the ruler or group, not to the territory itself. Other than the rulers, people had no sense of "owning" the territory. With the rise of the Greek city-states, territory as such defined a political entity, its people felt some permanent ownership of the land, and that connection became part of their political identity. As a result, the concept of citizenship first developed. After 450 B.C. Athenian citizens included only those born of two citizens or approved through what may have been the world's first naturalization process. Athenians, then, were not those living in Athens, only those legally accorded citizenship (membership) in the territorially defined unit.

Sovereignty: Aristotle (384–322 B.C.), in his epic work, *Politics,* argued that supreme authority stemmed from a political unit's law and system of government, not just from its rulers or religion. Therefore, each Greek city-state *(polis)* considered itself to have **sovereignty** under its own law. This meant that it recognized no legitimate higher authority, either secular or religious.

Nationalism: The citizens of the Greek city-states identified strongly with the polis, making it "a state of mind," as well as the place they lived (Sherman & Salisbury, 2004:56). Or, as Aristotle commented, "Man is an animal of the polis." This state of mind was a precursor of nationalism, today's most important sense of political identity and one that interconnects people, government, and territory.

Democracy: Also in the Greek city-states, the people became the source of political authority for the first time in history. Athenians and others "did not think of themselves as subjects of a king. . . . Instead they were 'citizens' who were actively responsible for guiding their polis" (Sherman & Salisbury, 2004:56). This idea of citizen participation reached its zenith in Athens, where a democracy existed for approximately 150 years beginning about 500 B.C. Just about the time Athens was at its height, Rome was beginning to grow far to the west. Like Athens, it was a city-state that expanded into an empire, and then itself was eventually invaded and conquered. Also like the Athenians, the Romans had a democracy until it was throttled by military dictatorship. It would be incorrect to try to closely correlate the Greek and Roman political systems with modern ones. For example, Athenian democracy was limited to the small percentage of people in the city who were male citizens, while women, slaves, and foreigners were excluded from participation. Still, the outlines of things to come can be traced to these ancient times.

After the Fall of Rome, A.D. 476 to 1700

Five centuries of Roman tyranny and empire obliterated most notions of democracy and nationalism, and what little remained disappeared after Rome fell in 476. These ideas did not die, though. They merely lay moribund for a millennium awaiting the right historical circumstances to reemerge. During this extended period called the Middle Ages (to about 1500), political power in the West was wielded at two levels of authority—one universal, the other local.

Universal Authority in the Middle Ages

Governance during the Middle Ages rested in part on overarching authority that controlled territory and people but was defined by neither. There were religious and secular aspects to this universalistic authority.

Religious Authority   The Roman Catholic Church was one source of universalistic authority. It served as the integrating force in several ways. The Church provided a common language among intellectuals by keeping Latin alive. Christian doctrine underlay the developing concepts of rights, justice, and other political norms. Even kings were theoretically (and often substantially) subordinate to papal authority. To extend that, the pope in concert with various powerful monarchs sought to promote the idea of a universal Roman-Christian state. This goal led Pope Leo III to crown one Germanic king, Charlemagne, as "Emperor of the Romans" in 800. Similarly, Pope John XII bestowed Charlemagne's old title on another German king, Otto I, in 962, thereby legitimizing his control over what became known as the **Holy Roman Empire.**

Political authority in the international system was once organized quite differently than it is now. One difference was the overarching secular as well as religious authority of the Roman Catholic Church and the pope. An echo of this earlier status is captured here by the member of the Vatican's Swiss Guard standing behind Pope Benedict XVI. The now largely ceremonial unit was once a true fighting force and dates back to the sixteenth century.

Secular Authority   As the Middle Ages proceeded, the overarching authority of the Catholic Church was supplemented, and sometimes supplanted, by great multi-ethnic empires. Most of the people under the control of the Austro-Hungarian, British, Chinese, Dutch, French, German, Ottoman, Russian, Spanish, and other empires were not culturally related to the emperors and felt little loyalty to them. As for the monarchs, they claimed their authority came from God, and most of them did not feel a strong political identification with or an emotional attachment to the commoners. Many of these empires lasted into the 20th century, but they and the degree of macrolevel integration they provided were all eventually swept away by the rising tide of nationalism.

Local Authority in the Middle Ages

The local, microlevel of authority was called the **feudal system.** It was organized around principalities, dukedoms, baronies, and other such fiefdoms. Nobles ruled these, exercising near complete sovereignty over them. In theory, these nobles were vassals of a king or an emperor, but in fact they were usually autonomous and sometimes even more powerful than the monarch they supposedly served.

It is important to understand that the concepts of territory and political authority during the medieval period were much different from what they are now. Fiefdoms and other political units "were nonterritorial, and sovereignty was, at best, disputed" (Spruyt, 1994:35). Certainly monarchs and nobles controlled specific territories, but in theory they did not exercise sovereignty over them. Instead, God and God's Church gave monarchs the right to rule over certain lands, and the kings subdivided their territory by granting nobles dominion over parts of it. Thus the very nature of the feudal system, in which vassals were theoretically subservient to kings and kings were theoretically subservient to emperors and popes, meant that sovereignty did not exist legally and often did not exist in fact. Commoners had little or no authority and were considered subjects, a concept closer to the status of property than to citizen.

By the 13th century the fabric of universalism and feudalism had begun to fray. During the next few centuries, "the international system went through a dramatic transformation in which the crosscutting jurisdictions of feudal lords, emperors, kings, and popes started to give way to territorially defined authorities" (Spruyt, 1994:1). The existing nonterritorially defined, hierarchical system was replaced by a system based on territorially defined states whose sovereignty made them equals legally.

The Decline of the Feudal System

Many forces of change in the Middle Ages eroded the feudal system. Of these, two stand out—military technology and economic expansion.

Military Technology   The introduction of gunpowder to European warfare in the mid-1300s and other changes in military capabilities diminished the ability of the smaller feudal fiefdoms to defend themselves. Inexpensive, little-trained commoners armed with rudimentary rifles could shoot highly trained, expensively armored knights, the epitome of the feudal warrior elite, off their horses. Relatively inexpensive cannons could readily demolish expensive castles, the centerpiece of feudal defense. These and other realities meant that static defenses of small territories needed to be replaced by a defense based on maneuver, which was best provided by a territorially larger unit, the state.

Economic Expansion   Europe's growing economy also undermined the feudal system. *Improved trade* was one factor that contributed to the economic expansion. The Mongol Empire's control of much of Asia and the Middle East in the late 13th century fostered the stability that trade needs to flourish. Expanded trade with Asia led Europeans to build larger ships, which, in turn, created even greater possibilities for trade. The journeys of Marco Polo of Venice to China and other lands between 1271 and 1295 were related to this new commercial activity. Later search for new trade and trade routes led, among other things, to the journey of Christopher Columbus in 1492.

The beginning of *mass production* was a second factor driving economic expansion. Individual craftsmen began to give way to primitive factories. Full-scale industrialization did not take place for another 500 years, but the early stages of the industrial revolution were in place by the 1200s.

The growth of trade and manufacturing had important political consequences. First, it created a wealthy and powerful commercial class, the burghers, who increasingly dominated the expanding urban centers of trade and manufacturing. Second, the burghers became dissatisfied with the prevailing political system because they needed greater access to raw materials for their factories and markets for their products. This access was hampered by the impediments to commerce inherent in the maze of feudal entities. Third, the desire to create larger political units to facilitate their commercial ventures made the burghers natural allies with kings, who were constantly striving to increase their control over their feudal lords. The burghers and the kings each had something the other needed. The kings could legitimately destroy the fiefdoms; the burghers could supply the kings with the money to pay for the soldiers and arms needed to overcome the nobles. The resulting alliance helped to create the modern state.

In sum, changes in military technology rendered the feudal fiefdoms obsolete as a defensive unit, and changes in manufacturing and commerce rendered the fiefdom obsolete as an economic unit. Safety and prosperity required larger units. States provided those.

The Decline of Universalistic Authority

At the same time that the micropolitical feudal system was decaying, the macropolitical claims of universalistic authority by the pope and the Holy Roman Emperor were being challenged by the growing power of the kings. This decline of papal authority and increase in royal power were reinforced by a period of cultural and intellectual rebirth and reform called the **Renaissance** (about 1350–1650). Many of the concepts that emerged, including scientific inquiry and personal freedom, undermined the authority of the Church.

One significant outcome was the **Protestant Reformation**. Influenced by Renaissance thinking, Martin Luther rejected the Catholic Church as the necessary intermediary between people and God. In 1517 Luther proclaimed his belief that anyone could have an individual relationship with God. Within a few decades, nearly a quarter of the people of Western Europe became Protestants. The first great secular break with the Catholic Church occurred in England, where King Henry VIII (r. 1509–1547) rejected papal authority and established the Anglican Church. The Reformation also touched off political-religious struggles elsewhere in Europe. The ostensible issue was religious freedom, but there were also important political causes and consequences. When the century-long struggle between the imperial and Catholic Holy Roman Empire and the nationalist and Protestant ethnic groups ended with the **Treaty of Westphalia** (1648), centralized political power in Europe was over. The Holy Roman Empire had splintered into two rival Catholic monarchies (Austria and Spain); a number of Protestant entities (such as Holland and many German states) gained independence or autonomy. Yet other countries, such as Catholic France and

Web Link

The text of the Treaty of Westphalia is available at **www.yale.edu/lawweb/avalon/ westphal.htm**.

Protestant England, were more secure in their independence. Therefore, many scholars regard 1648 as marking the births of the modern national state and of the world political system based on sovereign states as the primary political actors.

The Victory of the Sovereign State

The breakdown of the feudal-universalistic system of governance did not, however, lead immediately to the uncontested role of the **state** as the dominant political actor. Instead, the people of the Middle Ages experimented with several types of political organizations to see how well they would meet the security and economic needs of the time.

The Early State and Its Competitors   The revival of city-states, such as Venice, was one alternative scheme of political organization. Another was the formation of loosely confederated city-leagues based on common economic interests. The most famous of these mercantile alliances, the Hanseatic League, was founded in 1358 to protect commerce against piracy. It eventually included 70 northern European cities stretching from Bruges (in modern Belgium) to Novograd (in modern Russia) and became a major economic force.

What is important is that states, not city-states or city-leagues, became the new focus of political organization. The Hanseatic League ended in 1667. The fortunes of Venice and other city-states ebbed more slowly, but they eventually faded also. The failure of these experiments and the survival of the state occurred for identifiable, pragmatic reasons. Those are beyond our telling here, but the essential point is that in time "sovereign states displaced city-leagues and city-states . . . because their institutional logic gave them an advantage in mobilizing their societies' resources" (Spruyt, 1994:185). States were best equipped to conduct commerce, provide defense, and meet other needs.

Consequences of the Victory of the State   The triumph of the state as the dominant mode of governance had profound consequences for the international system. One of these was that states became the primary actors in the post-Westphalia international system. They continue in that starring role today. Therefore, much of the action on the world stage is about states and groups of states interacting with one another.

More subtly, the fact that states recognize no higher authority necessarily means that the international system has no central authority to maintain order and dispense justice. Therefore, international relations occur in an **anarchical political system.** This does not mean that the international system is a scene of unchecked chaos. There is an informal hierarchy based on power, with more powerful states often maintaining some semblance of order (Hobson, 2005). Moreover, the international system usually operates in a reasonable way. This occurs, however, mostly because countries find it in their interests to act according to expectations. When a state decides that it is in its interests to break the largely informal rules of the system, as Iraq did in 1990 when it invaded Kuwait, there is little to stop it except countervailing power.

The Eighteenth and Nineteenth Centuries

The emergence of the sovereign state as the primary actor marked a major shift in the nature of international system. Following the Peace of Westphalia, national states continued to gather strength as monarchs such as Louis XIV of France (r. 1643–1715), Frederick II of Prussia (r. 1740–1786), and Peter the Great of Russia (r. 1682–1725) consolidated their kingdoms and even expanded them into empires. If anything, the pace of change quickened in the 18th and 19th centuries. Three themes stand out:

the advent of popular sovereignty, the Westernization of the international system, and the zenith of the multipolar system.

Popular Sovereignty

In the early 18th century, most kings claimed to rule their realms by "divine right." *"L'état, c'est moi"* (I am the state), France's Louis XIV proclaimed. Perhaps, but in 1793 another French king, Louis XVI, lost his head over this presumption, and the people claimed the state for themselves under the doctrine of **popular sovereignty.**

The revival of popular sovereignty, which had lain dormant since the demise of Athenian democracy and the Roman republic, marked a major change in the notion of who owned the state and how it should be governed. Until this time, the prevailing belief was that kings ruled by divine right over both territory and people, who were subjects, not citizens. Understandably, the people had limited attachment to the state, since it was the king's, not theirs. The American (1776) and French (1789) revolutions challenged this philosophy. *Democracies* were established on the principle that ultimate political power rests with the people, not the monarch. Popular sovereignty also expanded the concept of *nationalism* to include mass identification with and participation in the affairs of the state. If the people owned the state, then they had both a greater emotional attachment to it and a greater responsibility to support it. One symbol of this change was that Napoleonic France (1799–1815) was the first country to have a true patriotic draft that raised an army of a million strong.

From its beginnings in America and, particularly, in France, democratic nationalism spread throughout Europe and steadily undermined monarchical government and its concept of divine right. The collapse of the dynasties in China, Germany, Austria-Hungary, Russia, the Ottoman Empire, and elsewhere early in the 20th century marked the real end of strong monarchical government. Nationalism and popular sovereignty were also antithetical to empire. The large multiethnic and in some cases colonial empires that were prevalent in the early 1900s began to unravel in World War I. Then the British and French colonial empires fell apart in the mid-twentieth century, and the last great multiethnic empire imploded in 1991 when the Soviet Union fragmented into 15 independent countries.

Westernization of the International System

The domination and shaping of the international system by the **West** was a second important characteristic of the 18th and 19th centuries. Somewhat earlier, the growth of European power had enabled Great Britain, France, and other European countries to thrust outward and take control of North and South America and some parts of Asia. The Arab, Aztec, Chinese, Incan, Mogul (Indian), Persian, and other non-European empires or dynasties began to decline and fall. The process accelerated in the 19th century, and Europeans came to dominate the globe and to see themselves "as forming an exclusive club enjoying rights superior to those of other

These fighter aircraft over the Arc de Triomphe in Paris are trailing blue, white, and red smoke to represent the colors of the French flag during the annual celebration of Bastille Day, the anniversary of the fall of the Bastille prison on July 14, 1789, and the beginning of the French Revolution. That uprising was a key event in the growth of popular sovereignty, the idea that political authority ultimately rests with the people, not with the monarch.

political communities" (Bull & Watson, 1982:425). One reason for the **westernization of the international system** was the scientific and technological advances that sprang from the Renaissance in Europe. This sparked the **industrial revolution**, which began in the mid-1700s in Great Britain. During the next 150 years, industrialization spread rapidly but not globally. Instead, it was mostly a Western phenomenon, with the notable exception of Japan.

Industrialization and associated advances in weaponry and other technology had a profound impact on world politics. Europe gained strength compared with nonindustrialized Asia and Africa. Industrialization also promoted colonialism, because the manufacturing countries needed to expand resources and markets to fuel and fund their economies. Many industrialized countries also coveted colonies as a matter of prestige. The result was an era of Euro-American **imperialism**. The fate of Africa is graphically displayed in the map on page 41. **Eurowhites** similarly subjugated most Asian cultures. China, it should be noted, was never colonized, but after the 1840s it was divided into spheres of influence among the Western powers. Only Japan and Siam (now Thailand) remained truly sovereign. Joining the scramble for possession, Americans acquired Hawaii and Samoa in the 1890s. Victory in the Spanish-American War (1898) added Guam, Puerto Rico, and the Philippines. Additionally, U.S. military interventions in the Caribbean–Central American region became so frequent in following decades that the true sovereignty of those countries was questionable.

Even though these colonial empires were, for the most part, not long-lived, they still had a major and deleterious impact that continues to affect world politics. The imperialist subjugation of Asians, Africans, and others by Europeans and Americans set the stage for what became the division of the world into two spheres—one wealthy, one poor— that continue to exist.

The Growth of the Multipolar System

The 1700s and 1800s also saw the zenith of the **multipolar system**, which governed political relations among the globally dominant major European powers from the Treaty of Westphalia in 1648 through the mid-twentieth century. In the century between the final defeat of Napoleon (1815) and the outbreak of World War I (1914), the major powers, or **power poles**, were Great Britain, France, Prussia/Germany, Austria-Hungary, Russia, and to a lesser extent Italy and the Ottoman Empire/Turkey.

The multipolar system was marked by shifting alliances designed to preserve the **balance of power** by preventing any single power or alliance from dominating Europe and, by extension, the world. Prime Minister Winston Churchill clearly enunciated Great Britain's balance-of-power politics when he explained that "for four hundred years the foreign policy of England has been to oppose the strongest, most aggressive, most dominating power on the Continent" (Walt, 1996:109).

The Evolving World System: The Twentieth Century

The 20th century witnessed momentous and rapid global change. The *rapid pace of change* that continues today is an important theme to keep in mind. When the 20th century began monarchs ruled most countries; there were no important global organizations; and there were about 1.5 billion people in the world. By the time the century ended, elected officials governed most countries; the UN and other international

Web Link

More on the industrial revolution including some interactive activities are available from the BBC at www.bbc.co.uk/history/society_culture/industrialisation/.

MAP
The Colonization and Decolonization of Africa, 1878, 1914, 2005.

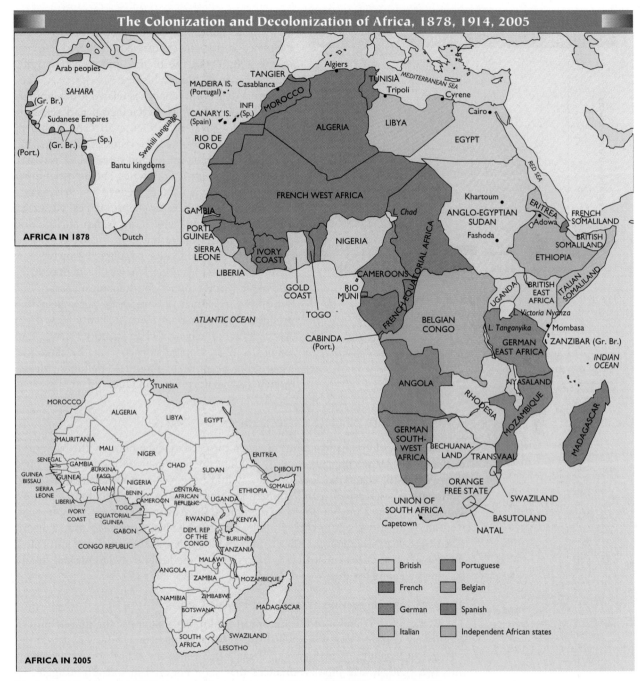

The Colonization and Decolonization of Africa, 1878, 1914, 2005

Map legend:

- British
- French
- German
- Italian
- Portuguese
- Belgian
- Spanish
- Independent African states

The industrialization of the West was one factor that caused the colonization of Asia and Africa in the late 1800s and early 1900s. This map and its insets show that Africa was largely controlled by its indigenous peoples in 1878 (inset) but had by 1914 (larger map) become almost totally subjugated and divided into colonies by the European powers. Then, after World War II, the momentum shifted. Independence movements led to decolonization. Now there are no colonies left in Africa. Thus the West's domination of the world has weakened.

Source: Perry Marvin, Myra Chase, James R. Jacob, Margaret C. Jacob, and Theodore H. Von Laue. *Western Civilization: Ideas, Politics and Society,* Fourth Edition. Copyright 1992 by Houghton Mifflin Company. Adapted with permission.

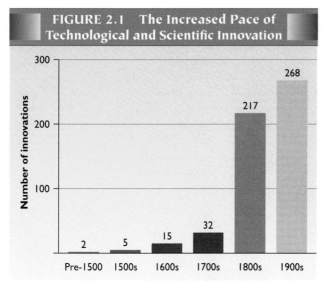

FIGURE 2.1   The Increased Pace of Technological and Scientific Innovation

The escalating pace of technological and scientific change has had a major impact on human beings in general and on world politics in particular. This figure depicts important innovations whose dates of discovery or invention are known. As you can see, only about 10% of these occurred before 1800. Another 40% occurred in the 1800s, and about 50% during the 1900s.

Data source: World Almanac (2005).

organizations were prominent; and the world population had quadrupled to 6 billion people. All this happened in just one century, a time period that represents only about 3% of the approximately 3,500 years of recorded human history.

A great deal of this change is related to a seemingly ever-increasing pace of technological and scientific innovation, as evident in Figure 2.1. The 20th century saw the creation of television, computers, the Internet, nuclear energy, air and space travel, missiles, effective birth control, antibiotics, and a host of other innovations that benefit or bedevil us. Technology both creates and solves problems. Medical advances, for one, mean that many more babies survive and people live much longer, but those changes have also contributed to an explosive population growth. New technologies have also been a key factor in the expansion of the world economy by dramatically improving our ability to extract raw materials, turn them into products, and transport them to consumers. Here again, though, the benefit of an improved standard of living for most people has been offset by economic expansion's negative by-products: pollution, deforestation, global warming, and other ills.

The Eclipse of the Multipolar System

The pace of world political evolution began to speed up even more by the beginning of the 1900s. Democracy was rapidly eroding the legitimacy of monarchs. In 1900 there were still czars and kaisers; they would be gone in less than two decades. **Nationalism** increasingly undermined the foundations of multiethnic empires. World War I was a pivotal point. Two empires, the Austro-Hungarian and Ottoman, were among the losers. From their rubble, countries such as Czechoslovakia, Poland, and Yugoslavia (re)emerged. Other countries like Jordan, Lebanon, Syria, and Palestine/Israel came under the mandate (oversight) of the League of Nations and finally became independent after World War II.

The Collapse of Europe as a Global Power Center

The causes of the demise of the European multipolar system by the mid-twentieth century are complex and subject to dispute. What is important, however, is that the system lost its ability to maintain a balance of power as the major powers coalesced into two rigid, nearly bipolar alliances that soon engaged in a death struggle. In World War I (1914–1918) the Central Powers included Germany, Austria-Hungary, and Turkey. The Allied Powers consisted of France, Russia, Great Britain, and Italy. After its defeat in the war, Germany was at first treated severely, but the **realpolitik** logic of a multipolar system led the British and French to let Germany rebuild its strength in the 1930s. That suited the British, who worried that France might once again dominate Europe and threaten them as it had under Napoleon. The seizure of power in Russia by Lenin's Bolsheviks in 1918 also prompted London and Paris to tolerate German revitalization. France was especially alarmed by the specter of Communist ideology combined with Russian military might and saw a rearmed Germany

Did You Know That:

The rapid pace of world change is evident in the life of the world's oldest person, Maria Olivia da Silva of Astorga, Brazil. When she was born on February 28, 1880, Brazil was still ruled by an emperor, Pedro II, and Rutherford B. Hayes was the U.S. president. She was 23 years old when the Wright brothers first flew and 89 when Neil Armstrong stepped on the moon. Ms. da Silva is older than 75% of the world's countries.

as a bulwark against the "Red menace." For the British and French, these balance-of-power maneuvers constituted a near-fatal mistake.

The grotesqueness of World War I was another reason why Great Britain and France did not seriously try to restrain resurgent Germany. The two victors had each lost almost an entire generation of young men. When Adolf Hitler came to power (1933) and rearmed his country, Great Britain and France vacillated timorously. The **Munich Conference** (1938) became synonymous with this lack of will. In that conference, Great Britain and France gave way to Hitler's demands for the annexation of part of Czechoslovakia based on the mistaken belief of British Prime Minister Neville Chamberlain and other leaders that an **appeasement policy** toward Germany would satisfy it and maintain the peace.

The Rise of Non-European Powers

Although Europe was center stage, important changes were occurring elsewhere. Almost all of the Western Hemisphere was made up of independent countries by 1900, and a few states in other areas also gained independence. Other existing states, especially Japan and the United States, began to play a more significant role and to undercut European domination of the international system. China began the century saddled with a decaying imperial government and foreign domination, but it overthrew its emperor in 1911 and started a long struggle to rid itself of foreign domination and to reestablish its role as a major power. Also during the first part of the century, the League of Nations was established, and many non-European countries became active in world diplomacy through membership in it. Thus, a shift was under way. The voices of Africa, Asia, and Latin America became stronger, and two non-European powers, the United States and Japan, readied themselves to take a starring role.

The Cold War and the Bipolar System

World War II (1939–1945) was a tragedy of huge proportions. It also finally destroyed the European-based multipolar structure. In its aftermath, a **bipolar system** dominated by the Union of Soviet Socialist Republics (USSR, Soviet Union) and the United States soon formed. To those who experienced its intensity, the hostility between the two superpowers seemed to augur an unending future of bipolar confrontation and peril. As is often true, the view that the present will also be the future proved shortsighted. The bipolar era was brief. It began to gradually weaken in little more than a decade; by 1992 it was history.

The Rise and Decline of the Bipolar System

World War II devastated most of the existing major actors. In their place, the United States emerged as a military and economic **superpower** and the leader of one power pole. Even though incredibly damaged, the Soviet Union emerged as the superpower leader of the other pole. The USSR never matched the United States economically, but the Soviets possessed a huge conventional armed force, a seemingly threatening ideology, and, by 1949, atomic weapons. The uneasy alliance that had existed between Washington and Moscow during World War II was soon replaced by overt hostility. Indeed, their rivalry divided much of the world into two antagonistic spheres in what became known as the **cold war**, a conflict with all but the shooting of a "hot war."

Historians still debate the causes of the cold war, but it is safe to say that varying economic and political interests and the power vacuum created by the collapse of the old balance-of-power structure created a bipolar system in which a great deal of world politics was centered on the confrontation between the two superpowers along

Web Link

For a flavor of the Munich crisis in 1938, you can hear radio programming from the day that Neville Chamberlain explained to a happy British crowd his decision to appease Adolf Hitler at http://archives.cbc.ca/IDD-1 -109-1257/1930s/1938/.

Web Link

A site that focuses on the cold war with audio, video, and interactive elements is offered by CNN at www.cnn.com/specials/cold.war/.

It is hard for those not old enough to have experienced the intensity of the cold war in the decades immediately after World War II to understand how scary a time it was. The fear among Americans about the threat posed by communism in general and the nuclear-armed Soviet Union in particular is captured here by these Newark, New Jersey, children and their teacher taking cover under the classroom's desks in 1952 during an air raid drill, while sirens wail a warning of impending atomic attack. Such "duck and cover" drills were common.

the so-called **East-West axis**. The United States reacted to what it saw as a Soviet/communist threat with the **containment doctrine**, a policy of global opposition to the Soviet Union and other communist countries. To that end, Washington sponsored a number of regional alliances, most notably the **North Atlantic Treaty Organization** (**NATO**, established in 1949). The Soviets responded in 1955 with the Warsaw Treaty Organization (or Warsaw Pact). Both sides also vied for power in the developing countries (known then as the **Third World**), and Soviet and American arms and money flowed to various governments and rebel groups in the ongoing communist-anticommunist contest. Yet despite the intense rivalry, a mutual fear of nuclear war deterred the superpowers from direct confrontations. The wisdom of avoiding eyeball-to-eyeball crises was evident in one of the few times the superpowers did not. Perhaps the scariest event of the cold war was the Cuban missile crisis of 1962 that occurred when the Soviets had begun building nuclear missile sites in Cuba, and President John F. Kennedy risked nuclear war to force them out.

One outgrowth of the containment doctrine was the U.S. involvement in Vietnam. Vietnamese forces led by nationalist/communist Ho Chi Minh defeated France's colonial army in 1954 and achieved independence. But the country was divided between Ho's forces in the north and a nondemocratic, pro-Western government in the south. The struggle for a unified Vietnam soon resumed, and the United States intervened militarily in 1964. The war quickly became a trauma for Americans. Perhaps the most poignant domestic tragedy was the death in 1970 of four students at Kent State University during clashes between antiwar demonstrators and the Ohio National Guard. War-weariness finally led to a complete U.S. disengagement. Within a short time Ho's forces triumphed and Vietnam was unified in 1975.

Vietnam caused a number of important changes in American attitudes. One was increased resistance to the cold war urge to fight communism everywhere. Second, Americans saw more clearly that the bipolar system was crumbling, especially as

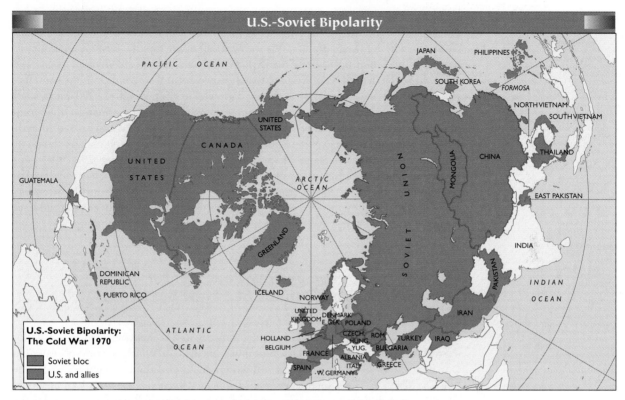

The bipolar era was marked by mutual hostility and fear between the United States and its allies and the Soviet Union and other communist countries. Americans perceived Soviet-led communism to be threatening everywhere, and adopted the containment doctrine to counter it. The Soviets were equally alarmed by what seemed an encircling set of U.S.-led allies. This polar projection map depicts the world as something like the way Moscow saw it, with the communists (in red) alarmingly surrounded by the Western allies (in blue).

relations between the Soviet Union and China deteriorated. Beginning approximately with the administrations of Soviet leader Leonid I. Brezhnev (1964–1982) and American President Richard M. Nixon (1969–1974), U.S.-Soviet relations began to improve, albeit fitfully. Nixon accurately assessed the changing balance of power, especially the rise of China, and he moved to improve relations through a policy of **détente** with Moscow and Beijing. They came to similar realpolitik conclusions about the changing power configuration of the international system and sought improved relations with Washington.

The End of the Bipolar System

During the 1970s and early 1980s, relations between Moscow and Washington continued to warm, fitfully at first, then more rapidly. Mikhail S. Gorbachev became the Soviet leader in 1985 and instituted a range of reforms designed to ease the Soviet Union's oppressive political system and to restructure its cumbersome bureaucratic and economic systems. While Gorbachev's goals were limited, he opened a Pandora's box for the communist Soviet Union and unleashed forces that were beyond his control.

Gorbachev also sought better relations with the West in an effort to reduce the USSR's burdensome military spending, to improve trade, and to accrue other economic benefits. Among other things, Gorbachev announced that the USSR would let

Eastern Europeans follow their own domestic policies. They responded by moving quickly to escape Moscow's orbit. This was symbolized most dramatically in East Germany, where the communist government fell apart rapidly. East German guards withdrew from their posts along the Berlin Wall, which physically divided its city and symbolized the overall East-West split, and protesters and souvenir hunters soon tore most of the barrier down. East Germany dissolved itself in October 1990, and its territory was absorbed by West Germany into a newly reunified Germany. Other communist governments in the region also fell, and the Warsaw Pact dissolved in early 1991. It was hard to believe then, but the Soviet Union was next. It collapsed, and its constituent republics declared their independence. On December 25, 1991, Gorbachev resigned as president of a country that no longer existed. That evening, the red hammer-and-sickle Soviet flag was lowered for the last time from the Kremlin's spires and replaced by the red, white, and blue Russian flag. Few novelists could have created a story of such sweep and drama. The Soviet Union was no more.

The Twenty-First Century: The Genesis of a New System

"What's past is prologue," Shakespeare comments in *The Tempest*. That is as true for the real world of today and tomorrow as it was for the Bard's literary world of yesterday. One hopes that no future historian will write a history of the 21st century under the title *The Tempest*. Titles such as *As You Like It* or *All's Well That Ends Well* are more appealing possibilities for histories yet to be. It is we who will write the script for the history to come. As Shakespeare tells us in *Julius Caesar*, "It is not in the stars to hold our destiny but in ourselves." The sections that follow are meant to help you determine your preferences for the future by examining the factors and trends that will benefit or beset the world "tomorrow, and tomorrow, and tomorrow," as Macbeth put it.

The Structure of Power in the Twenty-First Century

There are numerous important changes occurring in the international system. A new polar structure is emerging, the Western orientation of the system is weakening, and the authority of the state is being challenged from without and from within.

The Polar Structure

Clearly the bipolar system is gone. What is not certain is how to characterize the current, still evolving system. Although not all scholars would agree, the view here is that what exists in the first decade of the 21st century is best described as a limited unipolar system that is struggling to become a multipolar system.

A Unipolar Moment   Just before the Soviet Union's final collapse, analyst Charles Krauthammer (1991:23) wrote an article entitled "The Unipolar Moment." It disagreed with the widespread assumption that a multipolar system was forming to replace the anticipated end of bipolarity. "The immediate post–cold war world is not multipolar," he observed. "It is unipolar. The center of world power is the unchallenged superpower, the United States."

Many analysts scoffed at Krauthammer's view and some still do, but he had a point. Since then, U.S. global economic dominance has grown further, especially as Japan and Europe have struggled. Militarily, U.S. arms with some allied support twice defeated

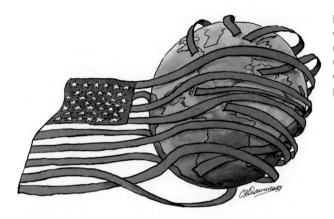

Many analysts believe that world politics is currently a unipolar or perhaps limited unipolar system, in which the dominant, or hegemonic, power is the United States.

Iraq (1991, 2003) and overwhelmed Yugoslavia (1999) in wars that were wildly one-sided, mostly because of the vast and growing lead of U.S. military technology.

Others concur with Krauthammer's view. "For the first time in the modern era, the world's most powerful state can operate on the global stage without the counterbalancing constraints of other great powers. We have entered the American unipolar age," one scholar believes (Ikenberry, 2004: 609). Similarly, another writes, "Not since Rome has one nation loomed so large above the others" (Nye, 2002:545). Certainly U.S. military power is a key factor supporting the U.S. status as the **hegemonic power.** But U.S. dominance is not just based on military might. Instead, according to France's foreign minister, "U.S. supremacy today extends to the economy, currency, military areas, lifestyle, language, and the products of mass culture that inundate the world, forming thought and fascinating even the enemies of the United States."[1]

The Multipolar Urge In his poem, "Mending Wall," Robert Frost wrote about the seemingly inexorable forces of nature that topple stone walls. Wisely he observed:

> Something there is that doesn't love a wall,
> That wants it down.

Similarly, there is something in the balance-of-power nature of the international system that does not like unipolarity. U.S. dominance rankles many countries, whether they were allies, enemies, or neutrals in the cold war era (Malone & Khong, 2003). In 2005 after a group of U.S. senators met in Paris with President Jacques Chirac, they told reporters that he had stressed his belief that the international system was multipolar and implied that France was one of the multiple power centers. Chirac "still doesn't like the idea of the unipolar world with the United States as top dog," Senator Joseph R. Biden, Jr. (D-DE) noted astutely.[2] Other country's leaders have also noted their opposition to unipolarity. Among them, Russia's President Vladimir Putin has argued, "The world order can and should be multipolar," and Prime Minister Atal Behari Vajpayee of India spoke favorably of a "cooperative multipolar world order."[3]

These expressions of support for a multipolar world by the leaders of France, India, and Russia do not mean that they are anti-American, merely anti-unipolarity. The reason is that a world in which there is one dominant power, the United States in this case, is an international system in which all other countries are at least partly subordinate. We will see in chapter 3 that unipolarity arguably has some benefits, but it is a difficult state of affairs for any sovereign country (other than the hegemon, of course) to accept. In addition to this resistance, some critics charge that the United

MAP
The Geopolitical World
at the Beginning of
the 21st Century

States is wandering into "hegemonic quicksand" by stubborn unilateralism and by squandering its power in Iraq and elsewhere in an ill-conceived pursuit of empire (Brzezinski, 2004:16). This view leads critics of U.S. policy to argue that to the extent that U.S. hegemonic power exists, the unipolar moment will soon pass (Cockburn & St. Clair, 2004; Mann, 2004).

Limited Unipolarity   There is no precise line where unipolarity begins and ends. This vague boundary is one reason why all analysts do not agree that the world is unipolar. Although unipolarity does not imply absolute power, the important challenges that exist to U.S. power lead some analysts to depict the current state of affairs as a **limited unipolar system** (Huntington, 1999). The most important of the restraints on U.S. power result from the extensive degree to which the United States, like all countries, is intertwined with and reliant on other countries. For example, the U.S. war on terrorism will make little progress unless other countries cooperate in identifying and arresting terrorists within their borders and dismantling the financial networks on which terrorists often rely. Similarly, the U.S. economy may be the world's most powerful, but it depends heavily on favorable trade relationships with other countries for its prosperity. A third example involves the frequent U.S. need for diplomatic support. The simmering crisis with North Korea is likely to be resolved much more easily if the region's countries, especially China, cooperate with Washington in persuading Pyongyang to give up its nuclear weapons program. The point is that because the United States frequently benefits from the cooperation of others, it can only go so far in riding roughshod over their preferences on a range of issues. Currently, there are probably not too many issues on which a determined Washington cannot get its way. Yet there is a price to pay for exercising power, as Americans have learned anew in the aftermath of their invasion of Iraq (Patrick & Forman, 2002). The unipolar role of the United States is also limited by what the American public will tolerate. As evident in Figure 2.2, a majority of Americans support playing an active role in world politics, but less than 20% want to play the part of the hegemonic power. Therefore, presidents risk a politically dangerous backlash if they follow a policy that Americans feel overextends their country's involvement (Sobel, 2001).

Future Polarity   Forecasting the future configuration of world power is difficult, beyond Krauthammer's safe-bet prediction that, "No doubt, multipolarity will come in time. . . . [when] there will be great powers coequal with the United States" (Krauthammer, 1991:23). Certainly, as the statements by Chirac and others demonstrate, a great deal of the diplomatic strategy of many countries seeks to hasten the arrival of that multipolarity. For example, many observers expressed the arguably reasonable suspicion that the German and French opposition in 2003 to war with Iraq, which prevented the United States from getting UN Security Council support of the invasion, was based in part on a desire to assert their own authority in the system.

FIGURE 2.2   American Opinion on the U.S. Global Role

Unsure
6%

Play no leadership role
9%

Be single world leader
11%

Share leadership
74%

Americans overwhelmingly favor playing a leadership role in the world, with only small minorities wanting to either abandon leadership or try to be the dominant world power.

Note: The question was: "What kind of leadership role should the United States play in the world? Should it be the single world leader, or should it play a shared leadership role, or should it play any leadership role?"
Data source: Survey by Pew Research Center and Chicago Council on Foreign Relations, July 2004. Data provided by The Roper Center for Public Opinion Research, University of Connecticut.

Particularly if U.S. policy is overly aggressive and unilateral, it could drive the next tier of powers, such as Russia and China, into alliance with one another and opposition to the United States. At the opposite extreme, if the United States drastically reduces its leadership role, then a multipolar system could quickly reemerge by default (Ikenberry, 2002, 2001; Bender, 2003). One view is that such a system will be state-centric and look and function much like the *traditional multipolar system* that existed in the 19th century (Mearsheimer, 2001). Another view is that the system is evolving toward becoming a *modified multipolar system.* Such a system would not look or operate like a traditional multipolar system because states and alliances are now being joined as important actors by regional and global international organizations, such as the European Union (EU) and the United Nations (UN). These new types of major actors could well change the dynamics of the international system in ways that are discussed in chapters 3 and 7.

WEB POLL
What Does the Future Hold
for World Politics?

The Weakening Western Orientation of the International System

Another ongoing change is the weakening of the dominant Western orientation of the international system as a result of the expansion of the number and power of non-Western states. The colonial empires established by the imperial Western powers collapsed after World War II, and in the ensuing years over 100 new countries have gained independence. The vast majority of these new countries are located in Africa, Asia, and other non-Western regions. A few, especially China, have achieved enough power to command center stage. Even the smaller non-Western countries have gained a stronger voice through their membership in international organizations. For example, non-Western countries now command a majority in the UN General Assembly, and in the Security Council the U.S. attempt in 2003 to gain support for war with Iraq failed because Washington was unable to persuade such Council members as Angola, Mexico, and Pakistan to support the U.S. position.

While the non-Western countries have many differences, they share several commonalities. Most struggle economically, are ethnically/racially not Eurowhite, and share a history of being colonies of or being dominated by Eurowhites. Furthermore, the value systems of many of these countries differ from Western values. Just one reason is that Eurowhite countries tend to base their values in major part on Judeo-Christian tradition, while other countries draw on the values of Islam, Confucianism, Hinduism, and other non-Western religions and philosophies.

It should not be surprising, then, that many of these new or newly empowered countries support changes in the international system. The result of all this is that the perspectives and demands of these countries are considerably changing the focus and tone of world political and economic debate.

The international system has become less Westernized in the last several decades. More and more African, Asian, and other countries have gained independence and strength, and they and their leaders have taken on increasingly important roles on the world stage. This shift is represented by this photo of President George Bush wearing a traditional Chinese coat while talking with Chinese President Jiang Zemin of China in Shanghai during the annual summit meeting of the leaders of the Asia-Pacific Economic Cooperation organization.

The Common Colonial Experience of Non-Western Countries

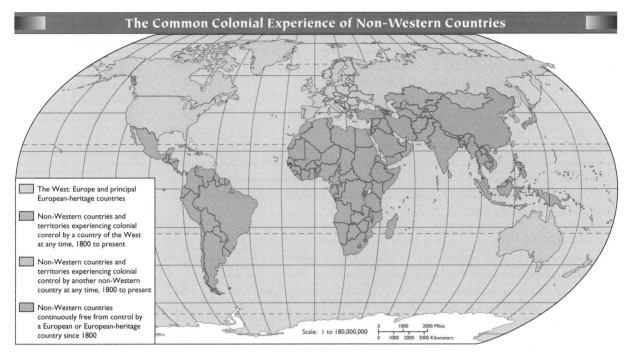

The West: Europe and principal European-heritage countries

Non-Western countries and territories experiencing colonial control by a country of the West at any time, 1800 to present

Non-Western countries and territories experiencing colonial control by another non-Western country at any time, 1800 to present

Non-Western countries continuously free from control by a European or European-heritage country since 1800

Scale: 1 to 180,000,000

Most countries of the South share a past of having been direct or de facto colonies. With a few exceptions, the colonial power was a European country or the United States. There is a very short list of non-Western countries that did not come under control, and even most of them experienced outside domination. Much of China, for example, was divided into spheres of influence among European countries and Japan.

Challenges to the Authority of the State

Along with the changing polar configuration and the rise of non-Western states, the 21st-century system is also being affected by the fact that states' starring role in the world drama has become somewhat less secure. This idea is captured by Benjamin Barber (1996) in his book, *Jihad vs. McWorld: How Globalism and Tribalism Are Reshaping the World*. He contends that the authority of states is being eroded by antithetical forces. Pushing in one direction, some forces (jihad or tribalism) are fragmenting states. Pushing in the other direction are forces on states to merge into an integrated world (McWorld, globalism). Barber (p. 4) worries that the first direction leads to the "grim prospect of a retribalization of large swaths of humankind by war and bloodshed: a threatened balkanization of nation-states in which culture is pitted against culture, people against people, tribe against tribe, a Jihad in the name of a hundred narrowly conceived [identifications and loyalties]." The other direction, Barber predicts, will meld "nations into one homogeneous global theme park, one McWorld tied together by communications, information, entertainment, and commerce." For now, Barber believes, "Caught between Babel and Disneyland, the planet is falling precipitously apart and coming reluctantly together at the very same moment." If this depiction is correct, it means that the world is moving back to something resembling the pre-Westphalian system of macroauthority and microauthority. Whereas that system's collapse resulted in the ascendancy of the middle level of authority (state power), the current system is being challenged by a reverse process of disintegration of the state into smaller units, and integration of states into more regional or universalistic wholes.

The Forces of McWorld   Many analysts believe that the political, economic, and social pressures that constitute the forces of **McWorld** are breaking down the importance and authority of states and moving the world toward a much higher degree of political, economic, and social integration.

Political integration, for example, is evident in the increasing number and importance of international organizations such as the World Trade Organization (WTO). When there are trade disputes, countries are no longer free to impose unilateral decisions. Instead, they are under heavy pressure to submit disputes to the WTO and to abide by its decisions.

Economic interdependence, the intertwining of national economies in the global economy, means that countries are increasingly less self-sufficient. This loss of economic control diminishes the general authority of a state. There is a lively debate over what this means for the future of states. One likely scenario is that "globalization will markedly constrain the autonomy and effectiveness of states and, at a minimum, raise serious questions about the meaning of internal and external sovereignty" (Korbin, 1996:26).

Social integration is also well under way, in the view of many scholars. They believe that the world is being integrated—even homogenized—by rapid travel and communication and by the increased interchange of goods and services. People of different countries buy and sell each other's products at an ever-increasing rate; Cable News Network (CNN) is watched worldwide; the Internet provides almost instant global information and interpersonal interaction; English is becoming something of a lingua franca. At a less august level, it is possible to travel around the world dining only on Big Macs, fries, and shakes at the more than 31,000 McDonald's outlets in 118 countries that serve fast food to about 17 billion customers each year. In sum, there are indications that the world's people are moving toward living in a more culturally homogenized global village. This outward trend works to weaken inward-looking nationalism, the primary basis of identification with and loyalty to one's country.

Popular reactions to globalization are mixed and cautious. A survey of 44 countries found that 58% of the respondents favored globalization, but a mere 16% of them thought it was very good. A small minority (17%) declared globalization to be somewhat or very bad, and another 25% were unsure, for a total of 42% unwilling to endorse globalization. Also evident were major regional variations. Africans supported globalization most enthusiastically (68%), while people in the Near/Middle East were least supportive (35%). Figure 2.3 on page 52 details these opinions.

The Forces of Tribalism   States are also being tested by and sometimes collapsing because of such pressures as erosive ethnic rivalries. Barber's main title refers to this as *jihad* (an Arabic word that means struggling to spread or defend the faith), but his other term, **tribalism**, better captures the process of disintegration.

Whatever the term, there has been an upsurge of states splintering and collapsing under the pressure of secessionist **ethnonational groups.** Most momentously, the Soviet Union dissolved into 15 independent countries in 1991, and some of them are ethnically unstable. The Chechen people, for instance, are engaged in a frequently bloody struggle to carve an independent Chechnya out of Russia. Similarly, Yugoslavia broke apart, and one of its new republics, Bosnia, itself collapsed in ethnic warfare. In 1998 an already diminished Yugoslavia further convulsed when ethnic Albanians, who are a majority in Kosovo Province, rebelled. Elsewhere, Somalia in the early 1990s fell into chaos among warring clans, and it remains a shell; Czechoslovakia split into two countries; East Timor declared its independence from Indonesia; Afghanistan struggles for stability among the rivalries of its numerous ethnonational

Web Link

A short version of Benjamin Barber's "Jihad vs. McWorld" can be read in article form online at: www.globalissues.org/ Geopolitics/WarOnTerror/ McWorld.asp.

Did You Know That:

Television is a major transnational force. One common reference point is CNN, which is now available in virtually every country on the world's 1.7 billion television sets.

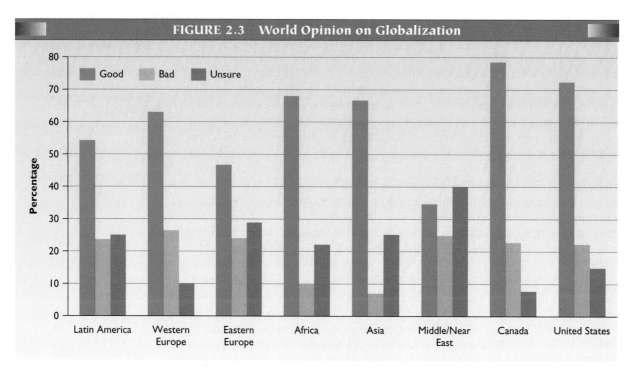

FIGURE 2.3   World Opinion on Globalization

Most people (58%) worldwide favor globalization, but the endorsement is less than ringing. Only 16% believe it is very good; the rest of its supporters give it a qualified "somewhat good" evaluation. Moreover, a sizeable minority of people (42%) either feel globalization is bad or are unsure. There are also wide regional variations in support. Africans are quite enthusiastic about globalization, but it draws less than majority support in Eastern Europe and the Middle/Near East.

Note: Countries in the Middle/Near East stretch from Egypt to Pakistan.
Data source: Pew Research Center for the People and the Press (2002).

groups; the Hutu massacre in 1994 of hundreds of thousands of Tutsis exposed the myth of a single Rwandan people; there is a sometimes violent Basque separatist movement in Spain, and, in an informal referendum among Kurds during the 2005 Iraqi national elections, 95% voted for an independent Kurdistan by circling the Kurdish flag on the ballot rather than the Iraqi one. Perhaps most distressingly, in 2005, Sudan continues to be wracked by violence between the country's Arab Muslims, who control the government, and two groups: Christian and animist black Africans who live in southern Sudan, and black Muslims who live in the western area of Darfur. The violence in Darfur is especially grotesque, with at least 70,000 dead from attacks by a government-backed militia called the Janjaweed. The list could go on, but that is not necessary to stress the point that many states are troubled by ethnonational tensions.

Security in the Twenty-First Century

On the traditional path the world still follows, each state is responsible for its own protection and tries to maintain a military capable of defending its national interests. Other countries may aid a country that has been attacked but only if they find doing so is in their national interest. For example, the United States came to Kuwait's aid in 1991, but did so mostly because of oil. If Kuwait produced tropical fruit, it is unlikely that a half-million U.S. troops would have rushed to defend the world's banana supply from Iraqi aggression.

The international system is experiencing cross-pressures from the centripetal forces of globalization working toward McWorld and the centrifugal forces, or tribalism, creating disunity in existing countries. This picture of an elderly and suffering woman from the Darfur region of Sudan captures the agony that country has experienced in its civil war. Central government forces, dominated by Arab-Muslims, are fighting black non-Muslims in the south and black Muslims in Darfur.

Self-reliance has its advantages, but there are also disadvantages. *Cost* is one. Even with the cold war over, cumulative world military expenditures between 1992 and 2004 came to nearly $10.5 trillion. Of these, the U.S. share was $4.3 trillion.

Uncertain effectiveness is the second drawback to the traditional approach to national security. Critics charge that "national security" is an oxymoron, given the fact that over 111 million people were killed in wars during the 20th century alone. This staggering total is almost 6 times more people than were killed in the 19th century and 16 times the number of people slain during the 18th century. Thus, even taking population growth into account, war is killing a greater percentage of humans each successive century. Most ominously, the advent of nuclear weapons means that the next major war could be humankind's final performance. Moreover, the possibility of such an apocalyptic scene being played out has been increased by the proliferation of **weapons of mass destruction (WMDs)** in the form of biological, chemical, nuclear, and radiological weapons, and by the spread of the missile technology to rapidly deliver these WMDs over long distances (Brown, 2003).

The limited ability of national forces alone to provide security was also highlighted by the terrorist attacks of September 11, 2001. The devastation raised global awareness of what has been termed **asymmetrical warfare**. As one analyst explained, "The notion of 'asymmetrical warfare' [involves] using unconventional tactics in combat rather than using forces of comparable size and employing similar tactics in battle. Terrorism takes the concept of asymmetrical warfare to another level by not even engaging military forces in battle."[4] And if terrorists with conventional explosives and even airliners transformed into missiles were not scary enough, there is increasing concern about the possibility of terrorists acquiring WMDs.

Given the limited ability of the traditional approach to provide effective security, the world is beginning to try new paths toward safety, which chapter 11 details. *Arms control* is one approach by which the world is trying to limit weapons, war, and perhaps avert Armageddon. During the last decade alone, new or revised treaties have been concluded to deal with strategic nuclear weapons, chemical weapons, land mines, nuclear weapons proliferation, and several other weapons issues.

International security forces are another part of the alternative approach. UN peacekeeping forces provide the most prominent example. Prior to 1948 there had never been a peacekeeping force fielded by an international organization. In 2005 there were 16 under way, with over 64,000 military and police personnel from 102 countries deployed. Such forces still have limited utility, but under different conditions they might offer an alternative to nationally based security.

> **Did You Know That:**
> At $879 billion, world military spending in 2003 was 250% more than the combined gross national products of the 47 poverty-stricken countries in sub-Saharan Africa and their 705 million people.

SIMULATION
You Be the Policy Maker:
Who Should Be in Charge
of Peacekeeping?

The possibility of biological attack is one of the security challenges facing the world in the 21st century. One threat that worries experts is the spread of the smallpox virus as a bioterrorism weapon. The U.S. government is striving to create a large enough supply of smallpox vaccine, including this 100-dose bottle, to treat all Americans in the event of an attack.

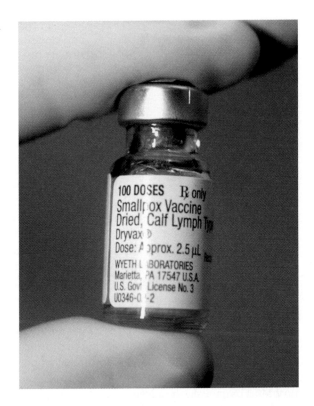

The Bush administration came to office in 2001 with a skeptical view of international security cooperation, and that attitude was enhanced in 2003 when the Security Council refused to support the American and British resolution authorizing immediate force against Iraq. At least part of the inability of Washington to win support for action against Iraq was the disagreement of many countries and even many Americans with the idea of striking first. Where do you stand on this issue after considering the points raised in the decision box, "Is Preemptive War Good Policy?"

Global Economics in the Twenty-First Century

There are a number of trends since World War II that will continue to affect the international system as this century evolves. Economic interdependence and economic disparity between the few wealthy countries and the many relatively poor ones are of particular note.

Economic Interdependence

One trend that has gained considerable momentum since World War II is the growth of **economic interdependence**. The trade in goods and services during 2004 exceeded $9.2 trillion; Americans alone own more than $7.2 trillion in assets (companies, property, stock, bonds) located in other countries, and foreigners own more than $9.6 trillion in U.S. assets; the flow of currencies among countries now exceeds $1.5 trillion every day. The impact of this increasingly free flow of trade, investment capital, and currencies across national borders is that countries have become so mutually dependent on one another for their prosperity that it is arguably misleading to talk of national economies in a singular sense.

WRITE THE POLICY SCRIPT

Is Preemptive War Good Policy?

In "The National Security Strategy of the United States of America," a 2002 report to Congress, President George W. Bush argued that Americans were increasingly threatened by terrorism and weapons of mass destruction. To address these dangers, he announced that, "As a matter of common sense and self-defense, America will act against such emerging threats before they are fully formed. . . . [T]he only path to peace and security is the path of action." In essence, the president declared that the United States reserved the right to strike enemies before they attacked Americans.

Theory became reality when the United States invaded Iraq in 2003. Speaking to the nation, Bush argued that Iraq "threatens the peace with weapons of mass murder" and declared, "We will meet that threat now, with our [military forces] so that we do not have to meet it later with armies of firefighters and police and doctors on the streets of our cities."[1]

UN Secretary-General Kofi Annan is among those who disagree with President Bush. Annan told the General Assembly that the idea of preemptive war "represents a fundamental challenge to the principles on which, however imperfectly, world peace and stability have rested for the last 58 years. My concern is that, if it were to be adopted, it could set precedents that resulted in a proliferation of the unilateral and lawless use of force, with or without justification."[2]

Preemptive war, hitting before you get hit, is controversial at both the practical and legal levels (Walzer, 2004). Pragmatically, striking enemies before they attack has clear benefits. However, liabilities also exist. What if you are wrong, and people die because of that? Another worry is that if you claim the right to preemptive war, others also have that right. It is important to ask yourself if world stability and security are enhanced or lessened by the universal application of the principle of legitimate preemptive war.

Legal controversy about preemptive war theory centers on the obligations of the United States and every other country that has signed the UN Charter, which is a binding treaty. Two articles in the Charter are especially relevant. Article 51 says that "nothing in the Charter" should be interpreted as denying a country "the inherent right of individual or collective self-defense if an armed attack occurs." Article 39 stipulates that except in self-defense, it is the UN Security Council that "shall determine the existence of any threat to the peace, breach of the peace, or act of aggression and . . . decide what measures shall be taken . . . to maintain or restore international peace and security."

Deciding about the wisdom of preemptive war is more than a "for-or-against" choice. Instead, you can be categorically for it, categorically against it, or favor preemptive war only in limited circumstances. If you favor the limited use option, then you also have to specify when preventive war is permissible and when it is not. Remember, the standard that you adopt as legitimate for your country also applies to every other country.

What Do You Think?

When, if ever, do threats justify war?

To deal with interdependence, the world has created and strengthened a host of global and regional economic organizations. The leading global economic organizations are the World Bank, the International Monetary Fund (IMF), and the World Trade Organization (WTO). Among the numerous regional economic organizations are the Association of Southeast Asian Nations (ASEAN), the European Union (EU), and the Southern Common Market (Mercosur) in South America.

Before leaving our discussion of economic interdependence, we should note that the course of economic globalization is not smooth nor is its future certain. Trade and monetary tensions exist among countries. Many people oppose surrendering any of their country's sovereignty to the UN, the WTO, or any other international organization. Other people worry that free trade has allowed multinational corporations to escape effective regulation to the detriment of workers' rights, product safety, and the environment. As one analyst puts it, the move to create an unfettered global economy "pulls capital into corners of the globe where there is less regulation, which in turn makes it harder for advanced nations to police their capital markets and social standards" (Kuttner, 1998:6). Indeed, these and other worries have sparked an upsurge of opposition to further interdependence and occasionally violent protests against it. There are, in short, significant choices to be made in how to order financial relations among countries.

Economic Disparity Between North and South

A wide gulf in economic circumstances separates the small percentage of the world population who live in the few wealthy countries and the large majority of humanity that lives in the many much poorer countries. The terms *North* and *South* are used to designate the two economic spheres that divide the world. The **North** represents the wealthy and industrialized **economically developed countries (EDCs)**, which lie mainly in the Northern Hemisphere. By contrast, the **South** is composed of the **less developed countries (LDCs)**, the majority of which are near or in the Southern Hemisphere. This categorization does not mean that the world is divided precisely between wealthy and poor countries. Instead their economic circumstances range from general opulence (the United States) to unbelievable poverty (Bangladesh). There are a few countries, such as Portugal, grouped with the North that are far from rich. And there are some countries of the South, such as South Korea, that are now industrialized and whose standard of living even exceeds a few EDCs. These countries are called **newly industrializing countries (NICs)**. Moreover, there are some wealthy people in LDCs and numerous poor people in EDCs.

SIMULATION
Systems of Political Power

Nevertheless, the core reality is that there is a huge economic disparity between North and South. In 2003, the per capita **gross national product (GNP)** of the North was $28,603, which is 22 times as much as the per capita wealth of the South, $1,280. Calculating the figures in purchasing power parity (PPP) to adjust for costs of living, narrows the spread, with the North's per capita GNP-PPP at $29,450 and the South's at $4,320. But this is still a 7-to-1 (7:1) ratio.

What makes these dry statistics important is that the yawning wealth gap, whether 22:1 or 7:1, has devastating implications for the LDCs. Their children, for instance, suffer an unconscionable mortality rate that is almost 13 times greater than the infant mortality rate in the North. As Figure 2.4 shows, the people in countries of the North and those in the South live in virtually different worlds. The North is predominantly a place of reasonable economic security, literacy, and adequate health care. By contrast, the lives of the people of the South are often marked by poverty, illiteracy, rampant disease, and early death. One ramification of the weakening Western orientation of the international system discussed earlier is that this economic inequity is causing increased tension between the North and South. The LDCs are no longer willing to accept a world system in which wealth is so unevenly distributed.

ANALYZE THE ISSUE
The Group of 77

Many people in the South blame much of their poverty on past colonial suppression and on what they believe to be continuing efforts by the EDCs to dominate the LDCs by keeping them economically and politically weak. Some in the North agree with this analysis. While such feelings do not justify terrorism, it is important to understand that the widespread grinding poverty among the LDCs is one of the factors that led to the rage behind the September 11, 2001, attacks on the United States. President Bush later indirectly acknowledged that by pledging to take such actions as doubling the size of the Peace Corps so that it could "join a new effort to encourage development and education and opportunity in the Islamic world," with the goal of "eliminating threats and containing resentment" in order to "seek a just and peaceful world beyond the war on terror."[5]

The point, whether or not you believe that the EDCs oppress the LDCs, is that choices must be made. One option for the wealthy countries is to ignore the vast difference in economic circumstances between themselves and the LDCs. The other option is to do more, much more, to help. Both options carry substantial costs.

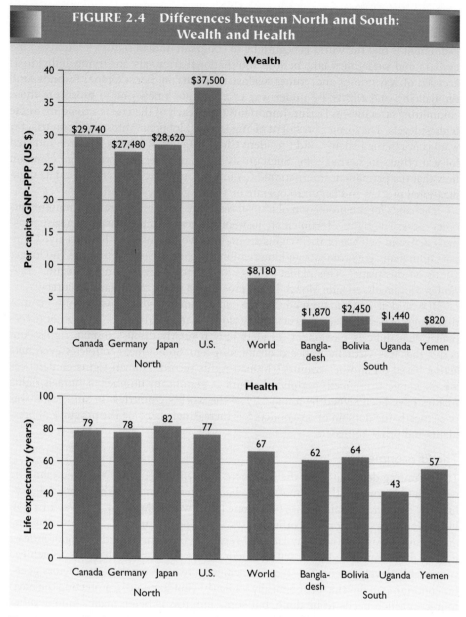

FIGURE 2.4   Differences between North and South: Wealth and Health

The difference between the lives of people in the North and those in the South is measured by per capita GNP wealth and life expectancy. By these, and many other standards, the people of the South are severely disadvantaged compared to those who live in the North.

Data source: World Bank (2004).

Quality of Life in the Twenty-First Century

The last few decades have spawned several changes involving the quality of human life that will continue to affect world politics in the new century and the choices we must face. Preserving human rights and the environment are two matters of particular note.

Human Rights

Violations of human rights have existed as far back into history as we can see. What is different is that the world is beginning to condemn human rights violations across borders and sometimes take action. International tribunals are trying individuals accused of war crimes and crimes against humanity in Sierra Leone, Rwanda, and the Balkans, and efforts are under way to constitute a new one to prosecute those committing atrocities in Darfur. Importantly, the reach of the law is extending to the highest levels. The former president of Yugoslavia, Slobodan Milosevic, is on trial for war crimes in the Balkans, and President Charles Taylor of Liberia has been indicted for war crimes in Sierra Leone. Such prosecutions may become even more common now that the permanent International Criminal Court (ICC) has completed its organizational process and begun to operate in The Hague, the Netherlands.

Demands for the protection of human rights are louder and stronger in numerous other areas. The rights of women are just one of these. Women have become increasingly active in defense of their rights around the world, and they have received support from many governments and international organizations. Women are "no longer guests on this planet. This planet belongs to us, too. A revolution has begun," Tanzanian diplomat Gertrude Mongella has proclaimed with considerable accuracy.[6]

It would be naive to pretend that the end of human rights abuses is imminent or that progress has not been excruciatingly slow. Yet it would also be wrong not to recognize that there is movement. Leaders now regularly discuss human rights concerns; that was virtually unheard of not long ago. Sometimes, countries even take action based on another country's human rights record. Human rights conferences are no longer unnoticed, peripheral affairs. A significant number of human rights treaties have been signed by a majority of the world's countries. In sum, what was once mostly the domain of do-gooders has increasingly become the province of presidents and prime ministers.

The Environment

The mounting degradation of the biosphere is a byproduct of the rapidly expanding world population and the technological changes that began with the industrial revolution. Considerable damage has been done to the world's land, air, and water by pollution, forest destruction, and other abuses. Additionally, many natural resources are disappearing. Among the many facets of repairing the damage and easing or at least halting these continued destructive practices, the greatest challenge is to achieve **sustainable development.** This requires achieving two seemingly contradictory goals: (a) continuing to develop economically while (b) simultaneously protecting the environment. Much needs to be done, but some progress is being made. Among other advances, the subject has shifted from the political periphery to presidential palaces. Many leaders now realize that their national interests are endangered by environmental degradation, as well as by military and economic threats. For example, a U.S. national security report concluded that environmental problems "compromise our national security," and warned of potentially "devastating threats if we fail to avert irreparable damage to regional ecosystems and the global environment. Other environmental issues, such as competition over scarce fresh water resources, are a potential threat to stability in several regions."[7]

The need to balance economic development and environmental protection is recognized by almost everyone, yet achieving sustainable development will not be easy. Among other challenges, the LDCs need extensive assistance to develop in an environmentally responsible way. UN officials have placed that cost as high as $125 billion a year, and the financial weakness of the South means that the only source for much of this funding is the North. One reason for the North to help, some observers

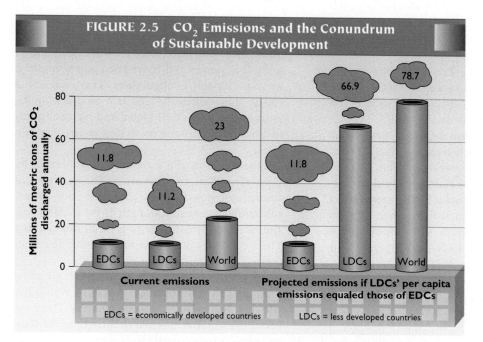

FIGURE 2.5 CO_2 Emissions and the Conundrum of Sustainable Development

The 15% of the world's population who live in EDCs currently produce 52% of the carbon dioxide (CO_2) emissions. If the LDCs were to reach the same level of economic development as the EDCs, the emissions of the LDCs would increase 597%, and total world emissions would grow 342%, thereby hyperaccelerating global warming. The conundrum of sustainable development is to help the LDCs develop economically in an environmentally acceptable way.

Data source: World Bank (2004).

argue, is because over the last 250 years it was and remains the source of a substantial majority of most pollutants, despite having less than one-fifth of the world population. "You can't have an environmentally healthy planet in a world that is socially unjust," Brazil's president noted.[8]

Even if you do not agree with the social justice view, self-interest is a second arguable reason for the North to help the South. Pollution and the problems it spawns, like acid rain and global warming, do not recognize national borders. To better understand the North's stake in LDC development and its impact on the environment, consider Figure 2.5. On the left you can see that with about 85% of the world population, the LDCs still emit slightly less carbon dioxide (CO_2) than the EDCs. On the right you can see that if the LDCs produced the same amount of per capita CO_2 as the EDCs, then the LDC's annual discharges would soar to 66.9 billion tons, increasing the world total by 342% from an already too high 23 billion tons to an astronomical 78.7 billion tons.

Chapter Summary

The Evolving World System: Early Development

1. This chapter has two primary goals. One is to establish a reference framework from which the historical examples used in this book can be understood in context. The second goal is to

sketch the evolution of the current world political system.

2. The genesis of the modern world system can be traced to the classical civilizations of ancient Greece and Rome. Four important political concepts—

the territorial state, sovereignty, nationalism, and democracy—have evolved from these ancient states.

3. Following the fall of the Roman Empire, governance during the Middle Ages until 1500 rested in a universalistic authority on the one hand and a local, microlevel authority on the other.

4. The current world system began to develop in about the 15th century, when modern states started to form due to a process marked by both integration and disintegration of earlier political authority. The Treaty of Westphalia (1648), more than any other event, demarcated the change between the old and the new systems. With the sovereign state at its center, the newly evolving system is anarchical.

5. Several changes occurred during the 1700s and 1800s that had an important impact on the international system. The emergence of the concept of popular sovereignty involved a shift in the idea of who legitimately controls the state. The divine right of kings gave way to the notion that political power does, or ought to, come from the people. During these two centuries, the system also became Westernized and the multipolar configuration reached its apogee.

The Evolving World System: The Twentieth Century

6. The 20th century witnessed the most rapid evolution of the system. The multipolar system tottered, then fell. The bipolar system declined as other countries and transnational actors became more important, as the expense of continuing confrontation strained American and Soviet budget resources, and as the relative power of the two superpowers declined. The bipolar system ended in 1991 when the Soviet Union collapsed.

7. During the 20th century, nationalism also undermined the foundations of multiethnic empires. European contiguous empires, such as the Austro-Hungarian Empire, disintegrated. The colonial empires dominated by Great Britain, France, and other Eurowhite countries also dissolved.

The Twenty-First Century: The Genesis of a New System

8. There are numerous new trends, uncertainties, and choices to make as we enter the 21st century. One significant question is what will follow the bipolar system. For now a limited unipolar system exists, with the United States as the dominant power, but numerous forces are working to undermine U.S. power and move the system toward a more multipolar configuration. That could be a classic state-centric system or a modified multipolar system, in which global and regional international organizations, as well as states, play key roles.

9. Another shift in the international system is its weakening Western orientation. The number and strength of non-Western countries have grown substantially, and the strength of these states will almost certainly continue to grow in this century. These countries often have values that differ from those of the Western countries.

10. Challenges to the authority of the state represent a third shift in the international system, which has strong implications for the 21st century. There are both disintegrative internal challenges to the state and integrative external challenges.

11. The pursuit of peace is also at something of a crossroads. The destructiveness of modern weaponry has made the quest for peace even more imperative. There are two overriding issues. One is how to respond to the challenge that asymmetrical warfare presents to traditional national defense strategies. The second is whether to seek overall security through the traditional approach of self-reliance or to place greater emphasis on international peacekeeping, arms control, and other alternative international security approaches.

12. The international economy is also changing in ways that have important implications for the 21st century. Economic interdependence has progressed rapidly. The transnational flow of trade, investment capital, and currencies has economically entwined all countries. There are, however, counterpressures, and countries have important choices to make in the near future. One is whether to continue down the newer path to economic integration or to halt that process and follow more traditional national economic policies. If the decision is to continue toward greater economic integration, then a second choice is how to regulate the global economy to deal with the legitimate concerns of those who are suspicious of or even outright opposed to greater globalization.

13. The effort to resolve the wide, and in many ways growing, gulf between the economic circumstances of the countries of the economically developed

North and the less economically developed South is also a mounting issue in the new century.

14. A final set of issues that must be addressed in the new century involves the quality of life: human rights and the environment. Both issues have become the subject of much greater international awareness, action, progress, and interaction. Yet ending the abuses of human rights and protecting the environment are still distant goals.

For simulations, debates, and other interactive activities, a chapter quiz, Web links, PowerWeb articles, and much more, visit **www.mhhe.com/rourke11/** and go to chapter 2. Or, while accessing the site, click on Course-Wide Content and view recent international relations articles in the *New York Times*.

Key Terms

anarchical political system
appeasement policy
asymmetrical warfare
balance of power
bipolar system
cold war
containment doctrine
détente
East-West axis
economic interdependence
economically developed countries (EDCs)

ethnonational groups
Eurowhite
feudal system
gross national product (GNP)
hegemonic power
Holy Roman Empire
imperialism
industrial revolution
international system
less developed countries (LDCs)
limited unipolar system
McWorld

multipolar system
Munich Conference
nationalism
newly industrializing countries (NICs)
North
North Atlantic Treaty Organization (NATO)
popular sovereignty
power poles
Protestant Reformation
realpolitik
Renaissance
South

sovereignty
state
superpower
sustainable development
Third World
Treaty of Westphalia
tribalism
weapons of mass destruction (WMDs)
West
westernization of the international system

Levels of Analysis and Foreign Policy

Search, seek, find out; I'll warrant we'll unkennel the fox.
—William Shakespeare, *The Merry Wives of Windsor*

Dazzle mine eyes, or do I see three suns?
—William Shakespeare, *King Henry VI, Part 3*

Women are playing an increasing political role on the world stage. The women here demonstrating in Istanbul, Turkey, carrying a sign, WE ARE WOMEN, WE ARE AGAINST VIOLENCE! represents the fact that, overall, women are less bellicose than men. This chapter asks you to consider whether warfare will decline as women assume more and more leadership positions.

HAVING INTRODUCED THE GLOBAL DRAMA in chapter 1 and reviewed its history in chapter 2, it is time to turn our attention to what drives the action on the world stage. Much like the plot of a play, the course of world politics is the story of the motivations and calculations of the actors and how they put those into action. Because states have long been and remain the most powerful actors on the world stage, our focus here will be on how they make and carry out foreign policy. Therefore, most of what occurs in world politics is a dynamic story of states taking actions and other states reacting to them, either directly or indirectly through international organizations. States are certainly not the only global actors, though, and the roles and decision-making processes of individuals (such as Osama bin Laden), transitional groups (such as Greenpeace), and international organizations (such as the UN) are taken up in other chapters.

As the following pages will detail, the **foreign policy process** is very complex. Analysts untangle the intricacies by studying foreign policy making from three perspectives termed **levels of analysis.** These include: (1) individual-level analysis—the impact of people as individuals or as a species on policy; (2) state-level analysis—how the organization and operation of a government affect policy; and (3) system-level analysis—the external realities and pressures that influence a country's policy.

Individual-Level Analysis

Individual-level analysis begins with the view that at the root it is people who make policy. Therefore, individual-level analysis involves understanding how the human **decision-making process**—people (as a species, in groups, and idiosyncratically) making decisions—leads to policy making.

Humans as a Species

The central question is this: How do basic human traits influence policy? To answer that, a first step is understanding that humans seldom if ever make a purely rational decision. For example, think about how you decided which college to attend. Surely you did not just flip a coin. But neither did you make a fully rational decision by considering all colleges worldwide and analyzing each according to cost, location, social atmosphere, class size, faculty qualifications, program requirements, job placement record, and other core considerations. Furthermore, and making your choice even less rational, it was almost certainly influenced by a range of emotions, such as how far away from home the school was and whether you wanted to be near, or perhaps far away from, your family, friends, or romantic partner. To make things even less rational, you probably had to make a decision without knowing some key factors of your college experience, such as whom your dorm roommate would be.

It may be comforting to imagine that foreign policy decision making is fully rational, but the truth is that in many ways it does not differ greatly from your process in deciding which college to attend and many of the other important choices you make in life. They, like foreign policy decisions, are influenced by cognitive, emotional, psychological, and sometimes even biological factors, as well as by rational calculations.

Cognitive Factors

What you did in choosing your college and what national leaders do when deciding foreign policy is to engage in **cognitive decision making.** This means making decisions within the constraints of "bounded rationality." *External boundaries* include missing, erroneous, or unknowable information. To cite an example, President Bush and Prime Minister Blair had to decide whether to invade Iraq in March 2003 without knowing whether Saddam Hussein would respond with chemical or biological attacks on U.S. and British forces. *Internal boundaries* on rational decision making are the result of our human frailties—the limited physical stamina and intellectual capacity to study exceptionally complex issues. Whatever the "realities" were during the crisis leading up to the Iraq War in 2003, the universe of information available was far more than President Bush, Prime Minister Blair, President Saddam Hussein, or any human could absorb.

Needless to say, none of us likes to think that we are not fully rational, so we are apt to adopt one of a range of mental strategies for coping with our cognitive limits. As illustrations, three such strategies are seeking cognitive consistency, wishful thinking, and using heuristic devices.

Seeking Cognitive Consistency   Decision makers tend to seek cognitive consistency by discounting ideas and information that contradict their existing views. The controversy about the snarl of information and misinformation about Iraq's abilities and intentions will continue for years, but it is informative to ask why top decision makers in London and Washington were willing to accept British intelligence that Baghdad was attempting to buy uranium from Africa and to ignore the substantial doubts expressed by the CIA. One reason is that the British finding "fit" with the existing negative images of Saddam Hussein and his intentions, whereas believing information that there was no nuclear program would have created uncomfortable cognitive inconsistency.

Web Link

Excerpts from captured Iraqis about Saddam Hussein and Iraqi thinking before the Iraq War are included in a CIA report, *Comprehensive Report of the Special Advisor to the DCI on Iraq's WMD*, 30 September 2004, located at **www.cia.gov/cia/reports/iraq_wmd_2004/**.

Wishful Thinking   To self-justify our decisions, we humans often convince ourselves that our choice will succeed (Johnson, 2004). Given the overwhelming forces he faced, it is hard to understand why Saddam Hussein chose to fight rather than go safely into exile. The reason, according to some of his former aides, is that he believed he would survive in power. In the Iraqi dictator's mind, his military defeat in 1991 was only a tactical retreat. This wishful thinking was evident just before the 2003 war when a reporter pointed out that the forces facing him were even more powerful than those that had routed Iraq's army in the Persian Gulf War and asked, "Why would you think that you could prevail this time on the battlefield?" The Iraqi leader replied, "In 1991 Iraq was not defeated. In fact, our army withdrew from Kuwait according to a decision taken by us. . . . We withdrew our forces inside Iraq in order that we may be able to continue fighting inside our country." Extending his wishful thinking, Saddam Hussein assured the reporter, "If war is forced upon us, then Iraq will continue to be here. . . . [We] will not finish just like that, even though a huge power may want it to be like that."[1]

Using Heuristic Devices   A third way humans deal with their cognitive limitations is by using **heuristic devices**. These are mental shortcuts that help us make decisions more easily by allowing us to skip the effort of gathering considerable information and analyzing it thoroughly.

Stereotypes are one type of heuristic device. For example, the willingness of the U.S. Department of Justice to countenance at least the limited torture of Muslim prisoners suspected of terrorism was arguably voiced in Attorney General John Ashcroft's stereotypic comment that "Islam is a religion in which God requires you to send your son to die for him. Christianity is a faith in which God sends His son to die for you."[2]

SIMULATION
Heuristic Devices

Analogies are another heuristic shortcut (Breuning, 2003). We make comparisons between new situations or people and situations or people that we have earlier experienced or otherwise have learned about. One such mental connection that frequently figures in policy debates is the **Munich analogy.** This refers to the decision of France and Great Britain to appease Nazi Germany in 1938 when it threatened Czechoslovakia. World War II signified the failure of appeasement, and the "lesson" later leaders drew was that compromise with dictators only encourages them. The Munich analogy was clearly in the mind of President George W. Bush during his 2002 State of the Union address when he charged that three countries (Iraq, Iran, and North Korea) "constitute an axis of evil," as did the Axis powers (Germany, Italy, and Japan) during World War II. Secretary of Defense Rumsfeld was even more explicit. He urged action against Iraq despite the lack of definitive evidence of Iraqi WMDs, by arguing, "Think of the prelude to World War II . . . [and] all the countries that said, 'Well, we don't have enough evidence.'. . . There were millions of people dead because of the miscalculations."[3]

Wishful thinking is common in human decision making. Statements by Saddam Hussein and postwar comments by his top subordinates indicate that he believed that he would politically survive a war with the United States in 2003 just as he had in 1991. This may have increased his willingness to risk war. Wishful thinking cannot change reality, though, as indicated in this photograph of the disheveled dictator soon after his capture in December 2003.

Emotional Factors

Although it is comforting to imagine that decision makers are coolly rational, the reality is that they get depressed, sad, angry, and experience all the other human emotions. For example, President Jimmy Carter was irate when Iranian students studying in U.S. colleges picketed the White House in 1980 during the hostage crisis with Iran over its seizure of the U.S. embassy and its staff in Tehran. An incensed Carter growled that he would like to "go out on the streets myself and take a swing at . . . those bastards" (Vandenbroucke, 1991:364). Carter could not go out on Pennsylvania Avenue and beat up protesters, but his anger and desperation to do something arguably led to his ill-advised and ill-fated attempt to rescue the hostages. Similarly, President Bush was outraged by the 9/11 terrorist attacks. "We're going to find out who did this," he told Vice President Cheney, "and we're going to kick their asses."[4]

Psychological Factors

Humans share a number of common psychological traits that also help explain why their feelings and decisions are usually less than fully rational. One such approach is **frustration-aggression theory**, which argues that individuals and even societies that are frustrated sometimes become aggressive.

"Why do they hate us?" President Bush rhetorically asked Congress soon after the 9/11 attacks.[5] "They hate our freedoms," was the answer the president supplied to his own question. Perhaps, but others put the source of rage in a very different light. Instead of a hatred for freedom, one analyst suggests that "the disproportionate feelings of grievance directed at America have to be placed in the overall context of the sense of humiliation, decline, and despair that sweeps the Arab world."[6] Polls confirm the analyst's view of widespread negative feeling among Muslims toward the United

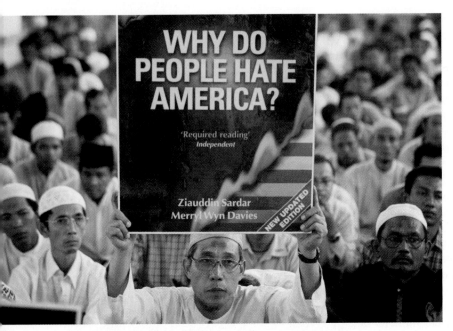

The poster being held aloft by these Indonesian Muslims in 2004 protesting the U.S. occupation of Iraq echoes the question, "Why do they hate us?" that President Bush rhetorically asked soon after the 9/11 attacks. He said that the reason was that the United States represented freedom. Another of many explanations is that frustration with U.S. policy has fostered aggression among some Muslims. The poster references the book *Why Do People Hate America?* (2002) by Ziauddin Sardar and Merryl Wyn Davies in which the authors place the blame on American attitudes and U.S. policy.

States (Zunes, 2005). One Gallup Poll conducted in nine Muslim countries in January 2002 revealed that 53% of the respondents had an unfavorable opinion of the United States, compared to only 22% with a favorable view, and 25% undecided. These results, argued the editor-in-chief at Gallup, indicated that "The people of Islamic countries have significant grievance with the West and the United States in particular" based on their view that the United States is "ruthless, aggressive, conceited, arrogant, easily provoked, [and biased against Muslims]."[7]

It is not necessary to agree with Muslims, especially Arabs, to understand their sense of frustration over the lack of a Palestinian homeland, the underdevelopment that characterizes most of the Muslim countries, or the sense of being dominated and sometimes subjugated by the Christian-led West. Nor does one have to agree that Muslims' anger justifies the violence that has sometimes occurred to pay heed to the old maxim that an "ounce of prevention is worth a pound of cure." Preventing terrorism surely includes building defenses and bringing terrorists to justice. Those are half-measures, though, and they will be much enhanced by addressing the root causes of terrorism rather than by simply waging war on the terrorists themselves.

Biological Factors

Although they are highly controversial, various biological theories provide yet another way to explain why human decisions fall short of being fully rational. One of the most important issues in human behavior is the degree to which human actions are based on animal instinct and other innate emotional and physical drives or based on socialization and intellect. With specific regard to politics, **biopolitics** examines the relationship between the physical nature and political behavior of humans. Biopolitics can be illustrated by examining two approaches: ethology and gender.

Ethology   The comparison of animal and human behavior is called **ethology**. Konrad Lorenz (*On Aggression,* 1969), Desmond Morris (*The Naked Ape,* 1967), Robert Ardrey (*The Territorial Imperative,* 1961), and some other ethologists argue that like animals, humans behave in a way that is based partly on innate characteristics. Ardrey (pp. 12–14), for example, has written that "territoriality—the drive to gain, maintain, and defend the exclusive right to a piece of property—is an animal instinct" and that "if man is a part of the natural world, then he possesses as do all other species a genetic . . . territorial drive as one ancient animal foundation for that human conduct known as war."

It is clear that territorial disputes between neighboring countries are a common cause of war. As one study puts it, "empirical analyses consistently show that territorial issues . . . are more likely to escalate to war than would be expected by chance"(Vasquez & Henehan, 2001:123). To an outsider, some of these territorial clashes may seem rational, but others defy rational explanation. One inexplicable war was the 1998–2000 conflict between two desperately poor countries, Ethiopia and Eritrea, over tiny bits of territory along their border. The land was described in one press report as "a dusty terrain of termite mounds, goatherds, and bushes just tall enough for a camel to graze upon comfortably." It was, said one observer, "like two bald men fighting over a comb."[8] Even the leaders of the two countries could not explain why war was waged. "It's very difficult to easily find an answer," Eritrea's president admitted. "I was surprised, shocked, and puzzled," added Ethiopia's perplexed prime minister.[9]

Gender   A second biopolitical factor is the possibility that some differences in political behavior are related to gender. An adviser to President Lyndon Johnson has recalled that once when reporters asked him why the United States was waging war in Vietnam, the president "unzipped his fly, drew out his substantial organ, and declared, 'That is why.'"[10] Such earthy explanations by male leaders are far from rare in private, and they lead some scholars to wonder whether they represent a gender-based approach to politics or are merely gauche.

Political scientists are just beginning to examine whether gender makes a difference in political attitudes and actions. It is clear that a **gender opinion gap** exists between men and women on a range of issues. War is one of those. Polls going back as far as World War II have almost always found women less ready than men to resort to war or to continue war. For example, a survey taken just before the Persian Gulf War in 1991 found 62% of American men compared to 41% of American women favoring military action. This gender opinion gap also existed in other countries, as evident in Figure 3.1 on page 68. Similarly, a poll of Americans conducted in 2003 just before the war with Iraq found two-thirds of American men compared to half of American women supporting military action.[11] This gender gap was again found internationally with, for instance, men in Australia, Canada, Great Britain, and Italy 10% to 15% more favorable toward war than their female counterparts.

Why do gender gaps exist? Are they inherently rooted in differences in male/female biological traits, or are they produced by differences in male and female socialization? Perhaps even more intriguing is whether an equal representation (or perhaps dominance) of women in foreign and defense policy making would change global politics. Taking the view that it would and, moreover, would do so for the better, Francis Fukuyama (1998:33) contends that "statistically speaking it is primarily men who enjoy the experience of aggression and the camaraderie it brings and who revel in the reutilization of war." This leads Fukuyama to speculate that a world led by women "would be less prone to conflict and more conciliatory and cooperative than the one we inhabit now." Supporting this view, one recent study found that women tend to adopt more collaborative approaches to negotiation and conflict resolution, while men pursue more conflictual ones (Florea et al., 2003). Other studies, however, have found more mixed results about the potential impact of women decision makers and contend that a future world dominated by women "would not be as rosy as Fukuyama suggests" (Caprioli, 2000:271; Caprioli & Boyer, 2001).

What do you think? Would the U.S. invasion of Iraq have occurred if Laura Bush, not her husband, George W., had been president of the United States; if the long-time head of Iraq had been Sajida Khairallah Telfah, not her husband, Saddam Hussein; and if most of the other top diplomatic and national security posts in the United States and Iraq had been held by women, not men?

Web Link

To learn more about the parallels between the behavior of primates and humans, click the "Chimpanzee Central" link on the home page of the Jane Goodall Institute at **www.janegoodall.org/**.

JOIN THE DEBATE
Do Women Speak with
a Different Voice?

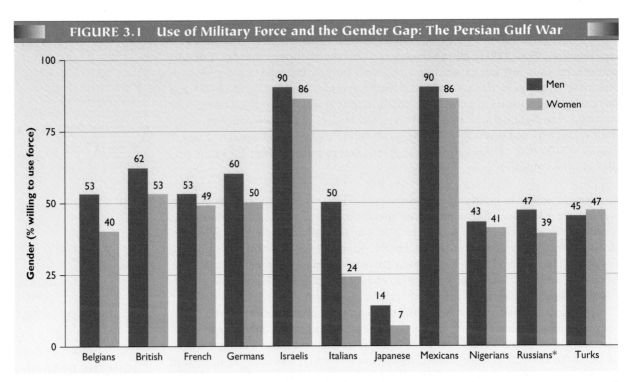

FIGURE 3.1 Use of Military Force and the Gender Gap: The Persian Gulf War

Take note of several things in this figure. One is the gender opinion gap. The men in all but one of the countries, Turkey, were more likely to favor war than were the women. Second, notice the variations between countries. Women, on average, cannot be described as antiwar, nor can men be characterized as pro-war because both men and women in some countries favored war and opposed it in others. Americans were not included in this poll, but the gap existed for them also. One representative poll taken in January 1991 just before the U.S. counteroffensive began found 62% of men in favor of military action, compared with only 41% of women.

Note: The question was: Should UN soldiers fight if the [economic] embargo [on Iraq] fails?
*The Soviet Union still existed, but the survey was taken in Moscow. Respondents were almost certainly Russians.
Data source: Wilcox, Hewitt, & Allsop (1996).

Perceptions

There is an ancient philosophical debate over whether there is an objective world or whether everything is only what we perceive it to be. Whatever the answer to that debate may be, it is clear that we all view the world through perceptual lenses that distort reality at least to some degree. All the elements of individual-level analysis that we have been discussing, and others, help shape perceptions. Whatever their source, though, perceptions have a number of characteristics that influence global politics. To demonstrate this, we can take a look at four common characteristics of perceptions.

We tend to see opponents as more threatening than they may actually be. The nuclear programs of North Korea and Iran have alarmed many Americans. A survey in 2003 found that 71% of Americans considered Iran a threat to regional stability and 77% saw North Korea in the same way. By contrast, in the other 20 countries surveyed, only 40% believed Iran to be a force for instability and just 47% perceived North Korea in that light.[12]

We tend to see the behavior of others as more planned and coordinated than our own. During the cold war, Americans and Soviets were mutually convinced that the other side was orchestrating a coordinated global campaign to subvert them. Perhaps more accurately, former Secretary of State Henry Kissinger (1979:1202) has described the two superpowers as behaving like "two heavily armed blind men feeling their way around a room, each believing himself in mortal peril from the other whom he assumes to have perfect vision." Each, according to Kissinger, "tends to ascribe to the other side a consistency, foresight, and coherence that its own experience belies."

We find it hard to understand why others dislike, mistrust, and fear us. President George W. Bush captured this overly positive sense of self during a press conference when he pronounced himself "amazed that there's such misunderstanding of what our country is about that people would hate us. . . . Like most Americans, I just can't believe it because I know how good we are."[13] Others are less sure of Americans' innate goodness. One recent survey found that 60% or more of poll respondents in countries as diverse as Indonesia, Nigeria, Turkey, and Russia thought that the United States posed a military threat to them.[14]

We and others tend to have similar images of one another. Between countries and even between leaders, it is common to find a **mirror-image perception**. This means that each side perceives the other in roughly similar terms. Figure 3.2 depicts this sense of mutual threat that exists between the United States and Muslim countries.

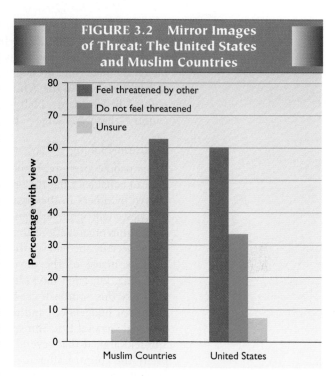

FIGURE 3.2   Mirror Images of Threat: The United States and Muslim Countries

Americans and citizens of Muslim countries share a mirror image of hostility toward one another. Note that almost equal percentages (60%) of Americans see Muslims as hostile and Muslims see Americans as hostile.

Note: The question of Americans was, "Do you think the Muslim world considers itself at war with the United States?" The question in Muslim countries was, "How worried are you, if at all, that the U.S. could become a military threat to your country someday? Are you very worried, somewhat worried, not too worried, or not at all worried?"
Data source: Pew Research Center for the People and the Press (2003).

Organizational Behavior

Yet another common characteristic of humans is that they tend to think and act differently in collective settings than they do as individuals (Hagen, 2001; Hermann, 2001). This leads to a second approach to individual-level analysis, one which examines how people act in organizations. Two concepts, role behavior and group decision-making behavior, illustrate this approach.

Role Behavior

We all play a variety of **roles** based on our attitudes about the positions we have and the behaviors we adopt in them. For example, how you act when you are in class, on the job, or in a family situation varies depending in part on your role—on whether you are a professor or a student, a manager or a worker, a parent or a child.

Presidents and other policy makers also play roles. The script for a role is derived from a combination of *self-expectations* (how we expect ourselves to act) and *external expectations* (how others expect us to behave). For leaders, these latter expectations are transmitted by cues from advisers, critics, and public opinion. One common role expectation is that leaders be decisive. A leader who approaches a problem by saying, "I don't know what to do" or "We can't do anything" will be accused of weakness.

For example, President Bush was in Florida when the 9/11 attacks occurred, and the Secret Service wanted him to remain safely out of Washington, D.C. for a time.

However, Bush's sense of his role as president soon prevailed, and he irritably told his chief of staff, "I want to go back [to Washington] ASAP." By 7:00 P.M. that evening he was back in the White House, and 90 minutes later he addressed the nation from the Oval Office. The president felt it was important to reassure the public by being visible at his post in the White House. "One of the things I wanted to do was to calm nerves," he later said. "I felt like I had a job as the commander in chief" to show the country "that I was safe . . . not me, George W., but me the president."[15]

Decision-Making Behavior Within Organizations

When people give advice and make decisions within an organization, they not only have to consider what they think but also how their opinions and decisions will be viewed by others in the organization, especially its leaders. The calculation of how our views will "go over" tends to promote **groupthink.** This concept denotes pressure within organizations to achieve consensus by agreeing with the prevailing opinion, especially the view of the leader (Schafer & Crichlow, 2002).

The image of the devil's advocate pressing principled, unpopular views is appealing, but such individuals are rarities in organizations, in part because those who take this approach get forced out. Similarly, agencies that dissent can wind up with their budgets cut and their areas of responsibility diminished. A case in point involved General Eric Shinseki, head of the U.S. Army. Prior to the invasion of Iraq, Shinseki argued that several hundred thousand troops would be needed in Iraq to pacify the country after the war ended. His boss, Secretary of Defense Rumsfeld, favored a much smaller force. As it turned out, General Shinseki was right, but long before that was known, Rumsfeld had pushed him into retirement. Secretary of the Army Thomas White, who supported Shinseki, was outright fired. Other potential dissenters learned that, as one retired four-star general put it, "Rumsfeld is not a good guy to cross. . . . The message is 'Do it my way or leave.'"[16]

In some cases, not giving a leader unpleasant advice may even involve physical survival. One reason that Saddam Hussein miscalculated his chances of success was that his generals misled him about their ability to repel U.S. and British forces. The officers knew they could not withstand the allied onslaught, but they feared telling Saddam Hussein the truth. As one Iraqi general later explained, "We never provided true information as it is here on planet Earth. . . . Any commander who spoke the truth would lose his head."[17]

Even if a leader wants broad advice, getting it is sometimes difficult because groupthink tends to screen out those who "think outside the box." Anthony Lake, who served as national security adviser to President Clinton, recognized that "there is a danger that when people work well together" and are of the same mind, it can lead to "groupthink . . . [with] not enough options reaching the president."[18] That concern continues. As one adviser has commented about the flow of information in the Bush White House, "The president finds out what he wants to know, but he does not necessarily find out what he might need to know."[19]

Poor decisions are frequently the end result of groupthink. This characteristic is evident in Figure 3.3. Thus developing strategies to avoid such decision-making pathologies should improve the quality of the output.

Leaders and Their Individual Traits

Foreign policy making is much more likely than domestic policy making to be centered on a country's top leadership. Therefore, a third approach to individual-level analysis focuses on **idiosyncratic analysis.** This is the study of humans as individuals and how each leader's personal (idiosyncratic) characteristics help shape his or

---

Did You Know That:

When Iraq's Minister of Health, Riyad al-Ani, suggested to Saddam Hussein that he might be able to end the war with Iran (1980–1988) by resigning, then resuming the presidency after the peace, the Iraqi dictator was so outraged that he had the hapless minister executed, his body dismembered, and the parts sent to his wife.

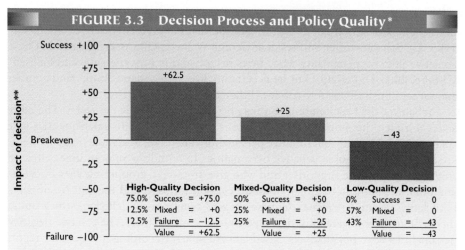

FIGURE 3.3   Decision Process and Policy Quality*

	High-Quality Decision		Mixed-Quality Decision		Low-Quality Decision	
75.0%	Success = +75.0	50%	Success = +50	0%	Success = 0
12.5%	Mixed = +0	25%	Mixed = +0	57%	Mixed = 0
12.5%	Failure = −12.5	25%	Failure = −25	43%	Failure = −43
	Value = +62.5		Value = +25		Value = −43

* **Quality:** The quality of the decisions (based on the number of symptoms of groupthink) were high (0–1 symptoms), medium (2 or 3 symptoms) and low (4 or more symptoms).

** **Outcome:** The outcome of policy (based on later evaluations by a balanced team of experts assigning +1 for a success, 0 for a mixed outcome, and −1 for a failure).

Decisions characterized by a lack of groupthink tend to result in better policy than decisions with medium or high instances of groupthink. The research represented in this figure examined the decision making of various policies for evidence of groupthink and then asked experts to evaluate the success or failure of the resulting policy. As this figure indicates, decisions with little or no evidence of groupthink worked well in the estimate of 75% of the experts, with another 12.5% each adjudging the policy a mixed outcome or a failure. By contrast, decisions with significant examples of groupthink were evaluated to be a failure by 43% of the experts, to have only mixed results by the other 57%, with none of the analysts seeing the policy as a success.

Data sources: Herek, Janis & Huth (1987:217). Also see Purkitt (1990) and Welch (1989).

her decisions (Renshon & Larson, 2002; Hermann et al., 2001). As one study puts it, "The goals, abilities, and foibles of individuals are crucial to the intentions, capabilities, and strategies of a state" (Byman & Pollack, 2001:111).

The fundamental question idiosyncratic analysis asks is how the personal traits of leaders affect their decisions. Five of the many possible factors to consider are personality, physical and mental health, ego and ambition, political history and personal experiences, and perceptions and operational reality.

Personality

When studying personality types and their impact on policy, scholars examine a leader's basic orientations toward self and toward others, behavioral patterns, and attitudes about such politically relevant concepts as authority. There are numerous categorization schemes. The most well known places political personality along an active-passive scale and a positive-negative scale (Barber, 1985). Active leaders are policy innovators; passive leaders are reactors. Positive personalities have egos strong enough to enjoy (or at least accept) the contentious political environment; negative personalities are apt to feel burdened, even abused, by political criticism. Many scholars favor active-positive presidents, but all four types have drawbacks. Activists, for example, may take action in a situation when waiting or even doing nothing would be preferable. Reflecting on this, former Secretary of State Dean Rusk (1990:137) recalled, "We tended then—and now—to exaggerate the necessity to take action. Given time, many problems work themselves out or disappear."

ANALYZE THE ISSUE
The Cuban Missile Crisis

Of recent U.S. presidents, Clinton has an active-positive personality. He reveled in the job and admitted to being "almost compulsively overactive" (Renshon, 1995:59). Scholars differ on President George W. Bush. One assessment is that he is an active-positive personality who "loves his job and is very energetic and focused" (DiIulio, 2003:3). Perhaps, but he is certainly less active than Clinton, and another analyst sees Bush as positive-passive (Etheredge, 2001).

Whatever the best combination may be, active-negative is the worst. The more active a leader, the more criticism he or she encounters. Positive personalities take such criticism in stride, but negative personalities are prone to assume that opponents are enemies. This causes negative personalities to withdraw into an inner circle of subordinates who are supportive and who give an unreal, groupthink view of events and domestic and international opinion. Lyndon Johnson and Richard Nixon were both active-negative personalities who showed symptoms of delusion, struck out at their enemies, and generally developed bunker mentalities. Their active-negative personalities were but shadows of Saddam Hussein's. According to a postwar report to the CIA, Saddam's psychology was shaped powerfully by a deprived and violent childhood.[20] Reflecting that, he changed his original name, Hussein al-Takrit, by dropping al-Takrit (his birthplace) and adding Saddam, an Arabic word that means "one who confronts."

Physical and Mental Health

A leader's physical and mental health can be important factors in decision making. For example, Franklin Delano Roosevelt was so ill from hypertension toward the end of World War II that one historian concludes that he was "in no condition to govern the republic" (Farrell, 1998:xi). Among other impacts, some analysts believe that Roosevelt's weakness left him unable to resist Stalin's demands for Soviet domination of Eastern Europe when the two, along with British Prime Minister Winston Churchill, met at Yalta in February 1945, just two months before Roosevelt died from a massive stroke.

Occasionally leaders also suffer from psychological problems. Adolf Hitler was arguably unbalanced as a result of ailments that may have included advanced syphilis and by his huge intake of such medically prescribed drugs as barbiturates, cardiac stimulants, opiates, steroids, methamphetamine, and cocaine (Hayden, 2003). According to one analysis, "The precise effects of this pharmaceutical cocktail on Hitler's mental state [are] difficult to gauge. Suffice it to say, in the jargon of the street, Hitler was simultaneously taking coke and speed."[21] The drug combinations Hitler used offer one explanation for the bizarre manic-depressive cycle of his decision making late in the war.

Alcohol abuse can also lead to problems. Secretary of State Henry Kissinger once referred to President Richard Nixon as "my drunken friend," who among other events was once reportedly incapacitated during an international crisis with the Soviet Union (Schulzinger, 1989:178). And Nixon was a virtual temperance leader compared to Russia's President Boris Yeltsin. A top foreign policy official in the Clinton administration has recalled that Yeltsin was often inebriated. Indeed, during the first summit meeting of the two presidents in 1994, Yeltsin arrived so drunk that he "could barely get off the plane." He continued to get "pretty roaring" at other times during the summit, the adviser remembers, and at one point was "staggering around in his underpants shouting for pizza." As for Yeltsin's decisions, the U.S. official terms them "sometimes . . . just wacko." As an illustration, the adviser relates that during the U.S.-led bombing campaign against Serbia in 1999, "Yeltsin, who was clearly in his cups, suggested that he and Clinton had to get together on an emer-

A leader's ego can impact foreign policy. At times, Saddam Hussein depicted himself as an epic leader in the tradition of King Nebuchadnezzar of ancient Babylonia, and Sultan Saladin, who defeated the Christians during the Crusades. This self-image is captured in this prewar mural in Baghdad depicting the Iraqi president heroically astride a white charger fighting a winged serpent, whose three heads are U.S. President George Bush (center), Israeli Prime Minister Ariel Sharon (bottom), and British Prime Minister Tony Blair. Saddam Hussein's ego may have led him to try to assume the mantle of a great Muslim leader defying Western force.

gency basis, and . . . should meet on a submarine." Such images might have been grotesquely amusing had not the besotted Russian president controlled a huge nuclear arsenal.[22]

Ego and Ambition

A leader's ego and personal ambitions can also influence policy. One thing that arguably drove Saddam Hussein was his grandiose vision of himself. According to one report issued after the 2003 war, the Iraqi leader saw himself in "larger than life terms comparable to Nebuchadnezzar [the great Babylonian king, 605–563 B.C.] and Salah-al-Din [Saladin, the Sultan of Egypt who defeated the Christians in 1189, ending the Third Crusade]."

The ego of the first President Bush also may have influenced policy. He came to office in 1989 with a reputation for being wishy-washy, and *Newsweek* even ran a picture of him with a banner, "The Wimp Factor," on its cover. Arguably an ego-wounded Bush responded by being too tough. He soon invaded Panama, and the following year in the Persian Gulf crisis his fierce determination not to negotiate with Iraq left it little choice but to fight or capitulate. Certainly, it would be outrageous to claim that Bush decided on war only to assuage his ego. But it would be naïve to ignore the possible role of this factor. In fact, after defeating Panama and Iraq, the president displayed a prickly pride when he told reporters, "You're talking to the wimp . . . to the guy that had a cover of a national magazine . . . put that label on me. And now some that saw that we can react when the going gets tough maybe have withdrawn that allegation."[23]

Political History and Personal Experiences

Decision makers are also affected by their personal experiences. It is worth speculating how much the personal experiences of President Bush influenced his determination in 2003 to drive Saddam Hussein from power. It is clear that Bush is very close to his family (Greenstein, 2003; Helco, 2003). That connection, in the view of some, made him especially sensitive to the criticism of his father for not toppling the Iraqi dictator in 1991, and may have created in the younger Bush an urge to complete the business of his father (Wead, 2003).[24] Moreover, it is widely believed that Saddam Hussein tried to have the first President Bush assassinated when he visited Kuwait in 1993. Nine years later, his son told a gathering, "There's no doubt [that Saddam Hussein] can't stand us. After all, this is the guy that tried to kill my dad at one time." White House officials quickly issued assurances that the president did not mean "to personalize" his campaign to depose the Iraqi dictator, but it is hard to totally discount the antipathy of a devoted son toward a man who "tried to kill my dad."[25]

Perceptions and Operational Reality

Decision makers' images of reality constitute a fifth idiosyncratic element that influences their approach to foreign policy. Although we have already examined human perceptions in this chapter, it is worth separately considering the perception of leaders here because of the central role they play in making policy. Whatever their source, the sum of a leader's perceptions creates his or her worldview (Hermann & Keller, 2004). One scholar who served on the staff of President George W. Bush has written, "By the time I left the White House . . . I was convinced . . . [that] the sitting president's 'world view'—'his primary, politically relevant beliefs, particularly his conceptions of social causality, human nature, and the central moral conflicts of the time'—probably explain as much or more about . . . foreign policy than any other single variable" (DiIulio, 2003:3).

Perceptions play a key role in policy because they form an **operational reality**. That is, policy makers tend to act based on perceptions, whether they are accurate or not. For example, the operational reality of perceptions among most ranking officials in the Bush administration that Iraq had WMD capabilities and intended to develop them more fully was a key factor in the U.S.-led intervention. That those perceptions were wrong is an important question in its own right. But as far as the causes of the war itself are concerned, the operational reality (even though it differed from the objective reality) was determined by the belief of President Bush, Prime Minister Blair, and others that Saddam Hussein did have such weapons and that they presented a long-term threat.

A related perceptual phenomenon is called an **operational code**. This idea describes how any given leader's worldview and "philosophical propensities for diagnosing" how world politics operates influence the "leader's . . . propensities for choosing" rewards, threats, force, and other methods of diplomacy as the best way to be successful (Walker, Schafer, & Young, 1998:176).

President Bill Clinton's worldview saw the United States as operating in a complex, technology-driven, interconnected world, in which conflict was more likely to result from countries' internal conditions (such as poverty) than from traditional power rivalries between states. Among other things, this led Clinton to favor a multilateral approach to diplomacy, to often view the motives and actions of other countries in nuanced shades of gray, and to delve deeply into the intricacies of policy (Harnisch, 2001).

George W. Bush's operational code is very different. Whereas Clinton took a cerebral approach to policy, Bush has described himself as more a "gut" player than an intellectual (Daalder & Lindsay, 2003:7). Perhaps stemming from his profound reli-

A leader's sense of self can impact foreign policy. President George W. Bush arguably has a strong sense of obligation to reshape the United States and the world drawn from his family's tradition of public service. This 1950 photo shows Bush's grandfather, Senator Prescott Bush of Connecticut, as well as his father and future president, George H.W. Bush, who is holding the younger President Bush. Also shown are the senator's wife, Dorothy, and Barbara Bush, the current president's mother. Younger brother Jeb, now the governor of Florida, had not yet been born.

gious convictions, Bush, more than Clinton, is apt to see the world in right-versus-wrong terms.[26] For him, not only were the terrorists who launched the 9/11 attacks analogous to the fascists of the 1930s, but countries suspected of abetting terrorism were part of an axis of evil. Compared to Clinton, this belief also makes Bush more disposed to see the world as a more inescapably dangerous place and to follow a unilateralist path in pursuit of what he believes to be right. Just as Woodrow Wilson's strong religious convictions helped shape his crusading desire to make the world safe for democracy, so too may Bush's religious fervor be an element in his missionary-like urge to make the world into a better place by promoting democracy, free enterprise, and generally what he might term the "American way" (Rhodes, 2003). As one analyst notes, "it is impossible to understand Bush's presidential character without fully appreciating his profoundly small 'd' democratic beliefs" (DiIulio, 2003:3).

Finally, some analysts believe that Bush draws a strong sense of duty to lead and sacrifice from the history of the Bush family's public service dating back several generations. For the president this sense of personal leadership translates into feeling responsible to use his position as the leader of what he sees as a great and good country to reshape the world. As one scholar has noted, for Bush, "With 9/11, the long-hidden mission, the purpose for everything that had gone before [in becoming president], seemed to snap into place. In the political ethos of the Bush family, the charge to keep was to behave with responsibility. The terrorist attack filled in the blank space as to what responsibility required in the new post–Cold War era. . . . The Bush Doctrine . . . was born" (Helco, 2003:20).

Policy as a Mix of Rational and Irrational Factors

After spending considerable time on the myriad emotional, perceptual, and other factors that detract from rationality, a balanced discussion requires us to stress here that while decisions are rarely fully rational, they are seldom totally irrational. Instead, it is best to see human decisions as a mix of rational and irrational inputs. This view of how individuals and groups make policy choices is called **poliheuristic theory**. This theory depicts decision making as a two-stage process (Kinne, 2005;

Redd, 2005; Dacey & Carlson, 2004). During the first stage, decision makers use shortcuts to eliminate policy options that are unacceptable for irrational personal reasons. Poliheuristic theorists especially focus on reelection hopes and other domestic political considerations, but the shortcuts could include any of the other irrational factors we have been discussing. With the unacceptable choices discarded, "the process moves to a second stage, during which the decision maker uses more analytic processing in an attempt to minimize risks and maximize benefits" in a more rational way (Mintz, 2004:3). It is at this second stage that decision makers tend to set aside domestic politics and personal factors and concentrate on strategic, realpolitik considerations (DeRouen Jr. & Sprecher, 2004).

For example, one recent study using poliheuristic theory looked at U.S. decision making during the hostage crisis with Iran. As noted above, there is ample evidence of nonrational factors in the decisions of President Carter and other top administration officials. The study concluded that "Carter ruled out alternatives" that had negative domestic political consequences, then "selected from the remaining alternatives according to its ability to simultaneously maximize net benefits with respect to military and strategic concerns" (Brulé, 2005:99).

State-Level Analysis

For all the importance of the human input, policy making is significantly influenced by the fact that it occurs within the context of a political structure. Countries are the most important of these structures. By analyzing the impact of structures on policymaking, **state-level analysis** improves our understanding of policy. This level of analysis emphasizes the characteristics of states and how they make foreign policy choices and implement them (Bueno de Mesquita, 2002). What is important from this perspective, then, is how a country's political structure and the political forces and subnational actors within the country cause its government to decide to adopt one or another foreign policy (Chittick & Pingel, 2002).

Making Foreign Policy: Type of Government, Situation, and Policy

Those who study how foreign policy is made over time in one country or comparatively in several countries soon realize there is no such thing as a single foreign policy process. Instead, how policy is made varies considerably.

Type of Government and the Foreign Policy Process

One variable that affects the foreign policy process is the type of government a country has. These types range along a scale that has absolute **authoritarian governments** on one end and unfettered **democratic governments** on the other. The more authoritarian a government is, the more likely it is that foreign policy will be centered in a narrow segment of the government, even in the hands of the president or whatever the leader is called. It is important to realize, though, that no government is absolutely under the thumb of any individual. States are too big and too complex for that to happen, and thus secondary leaders (such as foreign ministers), bureaucrats, interest groups, and other domestic elements play a role in even very authoritarian political systems.

At the other end of the scale, foreign policy making in democracies is much more open with inputs from legislators, the media, public opinion, and opposition parties, as well as those foreign policy–making actors that influence authoritarian government policy. President Bill Clinton signed the Comprehensive Test Ban Treaty on behalf of the United States, for example, but the Senate disagreed with his view and in 1999 refused to ratify it. Yet even in the most democratic state, foreign policy tends to be dominated by the country's top leadership.

Type of Situation and the Foreign Policy Process

The policy-making process also varies within countries. Situation is one variable. For example, policy is made differently during crisis and noncrisis situations. A **crisis situation** occurs when decision makers are (1) surprised by an event, (2) feel threatened (especially militarily), and (3) believe that they have only a short time to react (Brecher & Wilkenfeld, 1997). The more intense each of the three factors is, the more acute the sense of crisis.

Whereas noncrisis situations often involve a broad array of domestic actors trying to shape policy, crisis policy making is likely to be dominated by the political leader and a small group of advisers. One reason this occurs involves the **rally effect**. This is the propensity of the public and other domestic political actors to support the leader during time of crisis. Figure 3.4 shows the impact of the rally effect on the popularity of President Bush at the time of the 9/11 attack and also at the onset of the Iraq War in 2003 (Hetherington & Nelson, 2003). A similar pattern was evident in Great Britain, the only major U.S. ally. There, support for the way Prime Minister Tony Blair was handling the crisis with Iraq rose from 48% before the war to 63% after it began.[27]

Type of Policy and the Foreign Policy Process

How foreign policy is decided also varies according to the nature of the **issue area** involved. Issues that have little immediate or obvious impact on Americans can be termed pure foreign policy. A narrow range of decision makers usually makes such decisions in the executive branch with little or no domestic opposition or even notice. For instance, President Bush consented to expanding the North Atlantic Treaty Organization (NATO) by adding seven new members (Bulgaria, Romania, Estonia, Latvia, Lithuania, Slovakia, and Slovenia) in 2004. Even though this substantially added to U.S. defense commitments by including countries that border Russia, the move was nearly invisible within the United States. The media made little mention of it, and pollsters did not even bother to ask the public what it thought. Neither did the expansion arouse much interest in the Senate, which ratified it unanimously.

By contrast, foreign policy that has an immediate and obvious domestic impact on Americans is called **intermestic policy**. This type of policy is apt to foster substantial activity by legislators, interest groups, and other foreign policy–making actors and thereby diminish the ability of the executive leaders to fashion policy to their liking. Foreign trade is a classic example of an intermestic issue because it affects both international relations and the domestic economy in terms of jobs, prices, and other factors.

FIGURE 3.4 Public Opinion and the Rally Effect

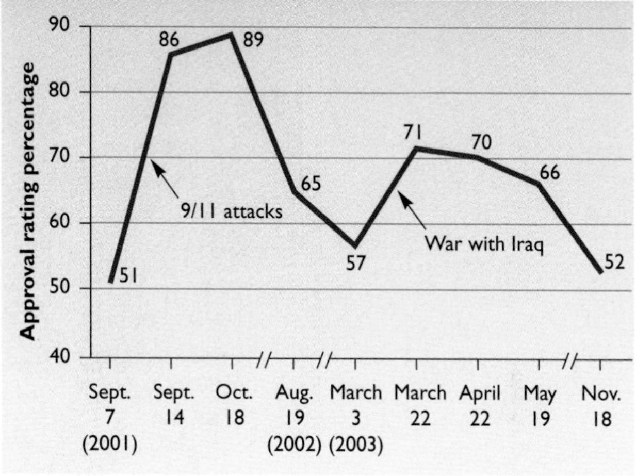

The public tends to rally behind the leader during times of crisis. Public approval of President Bush's performance in office skyrocketed 34 points after the 9/11 attacks and rose 14 points after the onset of war with Iraq on March 19, 2003. As you can see, support tends to drop off markedly after the crisis subsides.

Note: The poll date reflects the first day the poll was being taken. All polls took two or three days to complete.
Data source: CNN/USA Today/Gallup Polls found on the Web site of Polling Report.com at www.pollingreport.com/BushJob.htm.

The expansion of the North Atlantic Treaty Organization (NATO) eastward to the very borders of Russia has potentially great stakes for Americans because it pledges them to defend numerous small states that were once in the orbit of Moscow and even part of the former USSR. Yet as pure foreign policy issues, the rounds of expansion in 1999 and 2004 drew almost no notice and less dissent among the American people and members of Congress. By contrast, intermestic issues, such as trade, draw much greater public and legislative interest and activity.

This domestic connection activates business, labor, and consumer groups who, in turn, bring Congress into the fray (Grossman & Helpma, 2002). Therefore national leaders, such as presidents, usually have much greater say over pure foreign policy than they do over intermestic policy. For example, in stark contrast to Bush's easy success in getting the NATO expansion ratified, he had to struggle mightily to persuade Congress to give him greater latitude (called *fast-track authority*) in negotiating trade treaties. Although his party controlled both houses of Congress, the president was only successful after a concerted effort that included personally going to Capitol Hill to lobby legislators and to offer inducements to gain support. Even then, the final vote in the House of Representatives was a razor-thin 215 to 212.

Making Foreign Policy: Political Culture

Each country's foreign policy tends to reflect its **political culture**. This concept represents a society's widely held, traditional values and its fundamental practices that are slow to change (Paquette, 2003; Jung, 2002). Leaders tend to formulate policies that are compatible with their society's political culture because the leaders share many or all of those values. Also, even if they do not share a particular value, leaders want to avoid the backlash that adopting policies counter to the political culture might cause. To analyze any country's political culture, you would look into such things as how a people feel about themselves and their country, how they view others, what role they think their country should play in the world, and what they see as moral behavior.

How Americans and Chinese feel about themselves and about projecting their values to others provide examples. Both Americans and Chinese are persuaded that their own cultures are superior. In Americans, this is called *American exceptionalism,* an attitude that, for instance, led 81% of Americans in a recent poll to say that the spread of their values would have a positive effect on other parts of the world.[28] A similar sense of superiority among the Chinese is called *Sinocentrism.* This tendency of the Chinese to see themselves as the political and cultural center of the world is expressed, among other ways, in their word for their country: "Zhong Guó" means "middle place" and symbolizes the Chinese image of themselves.

Where American and Chinese differ based on their respective political cultures is in their beliefs about trying to impose it on others. Americans are sometimes described as having a *missionary impulse,* that is, possessing a zeal to reshape the world in the American image. For example, it is this aspect of American political culture that has led the United States to try not only to defeat hostile regimes in Afghanistan, Iraq, and elsewhere, but additionally, to replace them with democratic governments. There is also evidence that the United States makes other decisions, such as foreign aid allocations, based in part on how closely countries adhere to American conceptions of human rights.

Chinese attitudes about projecting values are very different. Despite China's immense pride in its culture, there is no history of trying to impose it on others, even when China dominated much of the world that it knew. The orientation is based in part on Confucianism's tenet of leading by example rather than by forceful conversion. It also has to do with the Sinocentric attitude that the "barbarians" are not well suited to aspire to the heights of Chinese culture and are best left to themselves as much as possible. Among other current ramifications, this *nonmissionary attitude* makes it very hard for the Chinese to understand why Americans and some others try to insist that China adopt what it sees as foreign values and standards of behavior on human rights and other issues. Instead of taking these pressures at face value, the Chinese see them as interference or, worse, as part of a campaign to subvert them.

One aspect of political culture that affects China's foreign policy is Sinocentrism, the tendency of the Chinese to see themselves and their country as the center of the political and cultural world. This self-image is represented by these Chinese characters. They are Zhong Guó, the Chinese name for their country, which translates as middle (Zhong, on the left) place (Guó, on the right).

Foreign Policy–Making Actors

"Washington is like a Roman arena [in which] gladiators do battle," Secretary of State Henry Kissinger (1982:421) wrote. As his analogy implies, foreign policy making is not a calm, cerebral process. Instead it is a clash of ideas and a test of political power and skills to determine which of many policy proposals will prevail. The combatants of which Kissinger wrote are the **foreign policy–making actors,** including political executives, bureaucracies, legislatures, political opponents, interest groups, and the people.

Heads of Government and Other Political Executives

President Harry S. Truman once remarked that he possessed foreign and defense policy-making authority that would make "Caesar, Genghis Khan or Napoleon bite his nails with envy" (Rossiter, 1960:9). That was an overstatement, but it does highlight the fact that the most important actor in virtually every country's foreign policy process is its **head of government** (most commonly titled president, prime minister, or premier). A step below, but still of note, are the leader's cast of other **political executives,** such as ministers of foreign affairs (secretary of state) and ministers of defense (secretary of defense).

In almost every country, the head of government has important **formal powers** granted by statutory law or the constitution. Most chief executives, for example, are

WEB POLL
Attitudes in Foreign Policy
Decision-making

WRITE THE POLICY SCRIPT

Who Should Decide on War?

Deciding for war is the most important decision a country makes. The question is, who should decide? Article I of the Constitution empowers Congress "to declare war." Article II designates the president as "commander in chief" of the military. These clauses reflect the belief of those who wrote the Constitution that presidents should "be able to repel [but] not commence war," as delegate Roger Sherman put it. The problem is where the line is between repelling an attack and commencing a war. President George W. Bush, for example, portrayed U.S. action again Iraq in 2003 as preemptively repelling the threat of Iraqi weapons of mass destruction.

Historically, presidents sometimes used limited force without a congressional declaration of war or other resolution of support. But the frequency of such use and the size of the conflicts grew after World War II. Beginning with Harry S. Truman, presidents began to argue that they have almost limitless authority as commander in chief to use military force as they see fit. Signifying that, Truman waged the Korean War on his own authority.

Reacting to the unpopular war in Vietnam (which ironically Congress had authorized), legislators tried to rein in the president's self-claimed war power by enacting the War Powers Resolution (WPR, 1973). It specified limited circumstances when the president could use force unilaterally and required congressional consent in all other instances. For the most part, the WPR has been ineffective. One reason is that Congress has never refused a presidential request that it authorize military action. Second, Congress has been unwilling to challenge presidents when they ignored the WPR and used the military unilaterally. Third, all presidents have explicitly or implicitly rejected the WPR as an unconstitutional restraint on their authority as commander in chief. For example, President George W. Bush welcomed resolutions of congressional support for action against Afghanistan in 2001 and Iraq in 2003 as nice but not necessary, claiming that he was taking action solely "pursuant to my constitutional authority to conduct U.S. foreign relations as commander in chief and chief executive."[1] Fourth, the Supreme Court considers the issue a political one and has refused to hear challenges to the president's use of the military.

Think about amending the Constitution to clear up its intent about who should be able to make the decision to go to war. One option is a clause supporting current practice by explicitly giving the war power to the president. The second option is to explicitly bar presidents from using military force without congressional authorization except in cases of a significant and sustained attack on the United States, its territories, or its armed forces. A third option is specifying that except in the case of a significant and sustained attack, the

In a democracy, who should have the authority to commit the country to war? The protesters who are being arrested in this photograph are urging Congress not to issue President Bush a blank check to wage war against Iraq. Congress did authorize action, though. Presidents often order military action without asking for congressional support. But when they do ask for it, Congress has always complied. Should Congress play a stronger role? It might even be that the decision on war in most cases should be made by the public in a referendum.

president and Congress could only send U.S. forces into combat after approval by a majority of Americans voting in a national referendum. That way the most important decision a country can make would be made by its owners, the people.

What Do You Think?
How should the United States decide to wage war?

the commander in chief of their country's armed forces. This gives them broad, often unilateral authority to use the military. Congress passed resolutions supporting President Bush's planned actions against Afghanistan in 2001 and Iraq in 2003, but he claimed the right to act without legislative support. Instead, the president claimed the authority to go to war "pursuant to my constitutional authority to conduct U.S. foreign relations as commander in chief and chief executive."[29] Such an assertion of unilateral authority dismays many Americans as undemocratic, and it is an issue for you to consider in the decision box, "Who Should Decide on War?"

Political executives also frequently possess important **informal powers**. Their prestige as national leader is often immense, and skillful leaders can use that status to win political support for their policies. This is especially true in world affairs and doubly so in crises where a president is the chief "we" in dealings with "them." Chief executives understand this advantage and use it. "The way to do that," former U.S. Secretary of State Dean Acheson once admitted, "is to say politics stops at the seaboard—and anyone who denies that postulate is a son-of-a-bitch or a crook and not a true patriot. Now, if the people will swallow that, then you're off to the races" (Rourke, 1983:81).

Fortunately, people do not always swallow that, and in democracies at least, chief executives do not exercise unlimited foreign policy power. Indeed, the spread of democracy and the increasingly intermestic nature of policy in an interdependent world mean that political leaders must often engage in a **two-level game** in which "each national leader plays both the international and domestic games simultaneously" (Trumbore, 1998:546). The strategy of a two-level game is based on the reality that to be successful, diplomats have to negotiate at the international level with representatives of other countries and at the domestic level with legislators, bureaucrats, interest groups, and the public in the diplomat's own country. The object is to produce a "win-win" agreement that satisfies both the international counterparts and the powerful domestic actors so that both are willing to support the accord. Reflecting this reality, one former U.S. official has recalled that "during my tenure as Special Trade Representative, I spent as much time negotiating with domestic constituents (both industry and labor) and members of the U.S. Congress as I did negotiating with our foreign trading partners" (Lindsay, 1994:292).

Bureaucracies

Every state, whatever its strength or type of government, is heavily influenced by its **bureaucracy**. The dividing line between decision makers and bureaucrats is often hazy, but we can say that bureaucrats are career governmental personnel, as distinguished from those who are political appointees or elected officials.

Although political leaders legally command the bureaucracy, they find it difficult to control the vast understructures of their governments. President Vladimir Putin of Russia and President George W. Bush candidly conceded that gap between legal and real authority during a joint press conference. The two presidents were optimistically expounding on a new spirit of U.S.-Russian cooperation when a reporter asked them if they could "say with certainty that your teams will act in the same spirit?" Amid knowing laughter, Bush replied, "It's a very good question you ask, because sometimes the intended [policy] doesn't necessarily get translated throughout the levels of government [because of] bureaucratic intransigence." President Putin agreed. "Of course, there is always a bureaucratic threat," he conceded.[30]

Bureaucrats sometimes do not agree with their country's foreign policy. Instead they may favor another policy option based on their general sense of their unit's mission. How any given policy will affect the organization is also an important factor in

SIMULATION
Utilizing Levels of Analysis

Web Link

To learn what presidents say privately, listen to and read the transcripts of recorded conversations archived by the Presidential Recordings Program at the University of Virginia's Miller Center of Public Affairs at **www.whitehousetapes.org/**.

creating bureaucratic perspective. Often what a given bureaucracy will or will not favor makes intuitive sense. The military of any country will almost certainly oppose arms reductions or defense spending cuts because such policies reduce its resources and influence. But the stereotypical view of the military as always gung ho for war is not accurate (Gelpi & Feaver, 2002). Whether the area was Kosovo, Bosnia, Haiti, or elsewhere, the U.S. military has often been a reluctant warrior within the council of government, especially regarding the use of ground forces. A common view, expressed by then Chairman of the Joint Chiefs of Staff, General Colin Powell, is that "politicians start wars. Soldiers fight and die in them."[31]

Filtering information is one way that bureaucracies influence policy. Decision makers depend on staff for information, and what they are told depends on what subordinates choose, consciously or not, to pass on. This was illustrated after the Iraq War by the uproar over President Bush's assertion in his 2003 State of the Union message that Iraq "recently sought significant quantities of uranium from Africa." In reality, the statement was based on shaky British sources that the CIA doubted. Yet it wound up in the president's speech when his speechwriters used information from an intelligence report that cited the British report but buried the CIA's objections in a footnote.

ANALYZE THE ISSUE
Applying Levels of Analysis in the Wake of September 11 and the War in Iraq— The Bush Doctrine

This occurred in part because groupthink seemed to intimidate the CIA and prevent it from pushing more strongly a view that it assumed would not please the president. As Senator Pat Roberts (R-KS), chairman of the Senate Intelligence Committee, noted after hearings and reports on how the Iraq War began, "Groupthink caused the [intelligence] community to interpret ambiguous evidence such as the procurement of dual use technology" to mean Iraq had an active weapons program. It is clear that this groupthink also extended to our allies.[32] Additionally, the dubious assertion about Iraq seeking uranium went unchallenged by the National Security Council (NSC) staff member who reviewed the speech despite an earlier telephone conversation with the CIA director, who said that the agency doubted that Iraq had sought uranium from Africa. The NSC official, who favored action against Iraq, later conceded, "I should have recalled . . . that there was controversy associated with the uranium issue," but many observers doubted that it was a mere oversight.[33]

Recommendations are another source of bureaucratic influence on foreign policy. Bureaucracies are the source of considerable expertise, which they use to push the agency's preferred position. One scholar, after analyzing bureaucratic recommendations in several countries, concluded that leaders often faced an "option funnel." This means that advisers narrow the range of options available to leaders by presenting to them only those options that the adviser's bureaucratic organization favors. This recommendation strategy, the analyst continued, "often decided what national leaders would do even before they considered a situation" (Legro, 1996:133).

Implementation is another powerful bureaucratic tool. There are a variety of ways that bureaucrats can influence policy by the way they carry it out (McKeown, 2001). As the investigations into the 9/11 attacks have proceeded, it has become clear that the terrorists were able to carry them off in part because of flaws in the implementation of U.S. antiterrorist policy. Evidence shows that government agencies often failed to share information or otherwise cooperate, that they discounted the terrorist threat, and that they ignored information that pointed to an impending attack. For example, a congressional report indicates that an FBI agent warned in July 2001 that "an inordinate number of individuals of investigative interest" were taking flight training. Yet, the report noted, this alert "generated little or no interest" among FBI officials and was not passed on to the CIA or other relevant agencies. The following month the CIA's Counter-Terrorism Center warned in a report that "for every [al Qaeda operative] that we stop, an estimated 50 . . . slip through . . . undetected. . . . It is clear that [al Qaeda] is building up a worldwide infrastructure which will allow

Critics of the failures of the CIA and other U.S. intelligence agencies prior to the 9/11 attack and the war with Iraq believe that a major house cleaning is order. This view is symbolized by the janitor cleaning up at CIA headquarters in Virginia.

[it] to launch multiple and simultaneous attacks with little or no warning." The agency also predicted, "The attack will be spectacular and designed to inflict mass casualties against U.S. facilities or interests." These and numerous other signals went unheeded, however, leading the congressional committee to conclude that because government agencies "failed to capitalize" on available information, they had "missed opportunities to disrupt the September 11 plot and . . . to generate a heightened state of alert and thus harden the homeland against attack."[34]

Legislatures

In all countries, the foreign policy role of legislatures is less than that of executive-branch decision makers and bureaucrats. This does not mean that all legislatures are powerless (Howell & Pevehouse, 2005; Scott & Carter, 2002; Leogrande, 2002). They are not, but their exact influence varies greatly among countries. Legislatures in nondemocratic systems generally rubber-stamp the decisions of the political leadership. China's National People's Congress, for example, does not play a significant role in foreign policy making.

Legislatures play a larger foreign policy role in democratic countries, but even in these states legislative authority is constrained by many factors. One of these is that chief executives usually have *extensive legal powers* in the realm of foreign policy. American presidents, for instance, are empowered by the U.S. Constitution to negotiate treaties, to extend diplomatic recognition to other countries, to appoint diplomatic and military personnel, to use U.S. forces as commander in chief, and to take numerous other actions with few or no checks by Congress or the courts. *Tradition* is a second factor that works to the advantage of chief executives in foreign policy making. The leadership has historically run foreign policy in virtually all countries, especially in time of war or other crises.

Third is the *belief that a unified national voice is important to a successful foreign policy*. This is particularly true during a crisis, when Congress, just like the public, tends to rally behind the president (Baker & O'Neal, 2001). This emotional response helped win support for a congressional resolution in late 2001 giving the president almost unchecked authority to use military forces against terrorism by votes of

98 to 0 in the Senate and 420 to 1 in the House of Representatives. Just 13 months later, by votes of 77 to 23 in the Senate and 296 to 133 in the House, Congress authorized military action against Iraq. Surely, many members agreed with the war, but at least some voted "aye" despite their misgivings because they agreed, as Senate Democratic leader Tom Daschle explained, commenting on his vote, that "it is important for America to speak with one voice."[35]

Fourth, *legislators tend to focus on domestic policy* because, accurately or not, most voters perceive it to be more important than foreign policy and make voting decisions based on this sense of priority. For this reason, legislators are apt to try to influence intermestic policy issues, such as trade, and are apt to be much less concerned with pure foreign policy issues, such as the membership of the NATO alliance.

By this logic, though, legislative activity is especially likely and important when a high-profile issue captures public attention and public opinion opposes the president's policy. Even more commonly, intermestic issues such as trade that directly affect constituents and interest groups spark legislative activity (Marshall & Prins, 2002). For instance, a study of 25 developed countries found that right-of-center parties, which are aligned with business, usually favor free trade, while left-of-center parties, which are supported by labor unions, lean toward protectionism (Milner & Judkins, 2004). Moreover, globalization is increasingly blurring the line between foreign and domestic affairs. As one member of the U.S. Congress put it, "Increasingly all foreign policy issues are becoming domestic issues. . . . [and] Congress is demanding to play a greater role."[36]

Interest Groups

Interest groups are private associations of people who have similar policy views and who pressure the government to adopt those views as policy. Traditionally, interest groups were generally considered to be less active and influential on foreign policy than on domestic policy issues. The increasingly intermestic nature of policy is changing that, and interest groups are becoming a more important part of the foreign policy–making process. We can see this by looking at several types of interest groups.

Cultural groups are one type. Many countries have ethnic, racial, religious, or other cultural groups that have emotional or political ties to another country. For instance, as a country made up mostly of immigrants, the United States is populated by many who maintain a level of identification with their African, Cuban, Irish, Mexican, Polish, and other heritages and who are active on behalf of policies that favor their ancestral homes (Saideman, 2001; de la Garza & Pinchon, 2000; Henry, 2000). Religious groups are one type of cultural group that exercises influence in many countries. Conservative Protestant groups, for one, are influential in the administration of President George W. Bush because of his personal religious convictions and the important political support he receives from them. This connection helps explain some of the president's unilateralist tendencies and reluctance to rely on the UN and other international organizations. As Bush told a friend after a meeting with the Christian Coalition, "Sovereignty. The issue is huge. The mere mention of [Secretary-General] Kofi Annan in the UN caused the crowd [the audience at the Christian Coalition meeting] to go into a veritable fit. The coalition wants America strong and wants the American flag flying overseas, not the pale blue of the UN."[37]

Economic groups are another prominent form of interest activity. As international trade increases, both sales overseas and competition from other countries are vital matters to many companies, their workers, and the communities in which they live. They lobby their governments for favorable legislation and for support of their interests in other countries. President George W. Bush advocates free trade, but that did not prevent him in 2002 from increasing tariff barriers on imported steel. Republican control of Congress hinged in part on several electoral races in Pennsylvania, Ohio, and elsewhere in districts with steel companies and unions pressing for protection from what they argued was unfair competition.

Issue-oriented groups make up another category of interest group. Groups of this type are not based on any narrow socioeconomic category such as ethnicity or economics. Instead they draw their membership from people who have a common policy goal. The concerns of issue-oriented groups run the gamut from the very general to the specific and from liberal to conservative. Just one of the multitude of groups, the neoconservative Project for the New American Century, is an organization that during the later Clinton years included in its membership such soon-to-be Bush administration appointees as Secretary of Defense Rumsfeld and Deputy Secretary of Defense Paul Wolfowitz. It was this neoconservative (neocon) group that was the driving force behind the Bush Doctrine of preemptive war and its use in Iraq (Benn, 2004).

Transnational interest groups also deserve mention. Growing interdependence has increased the frequency of countries, international organizations, and private interest groups lobbying across borders. In 2004, there were 823 foreign interest groups registered with the U.S. government. Other national governments are not required to register, and they lobby through their diplomats. But subnational units such as the Province of Quebec in Canada were registered. So too were some hoping to become national governments, including Tibet's exiled Dalai Lama, the Kurdish Regional Government of Iraq, and the Palestinian Authority. Other foreign registrants, reflecting a panoply of interests, included the Icelandic Tourist Board, Petroleos Mexicanos, the Euro-Asian Jewish Congress of Russia, and Volkswagen of Germany. Canadian interests (94 registrants) were the most heavily represented in Washington, followed by the British (65), Japanese (50), and Mexicans (32).

The People

Like legislatures, the public plays a highly variable role in foreign policy. Public opinion is a marginal factor in authoritarian governments. In democracies, the role of the people is more complex (Everts & Isernia, 2001). On occasion, public opinion plays a key role. The United States got out of Vietnam in the 1970s in significant part because of the determined opposition of many Americans to continued involvement in that war. Yet even in democracies, the public usually plays only a limited role in determining foreign policy.

Public Interest in World Affairs   One reason for the public's limited role is that few citizens ordinarily pay much attention to international issues. During the 2004 U.S. presidential election, terrorism and Iraq were prominent issues. That was unusual, though. Normally, the public's political interest focuses on domestic issues. Reflecting that were the responses to a poll during the 2000 election that asked Americans about the importance to their voting decision of the candidates' views on four domestic issues (education, health care, Social Security and Medicare, and the economy and jobs) and one foreign issue (America's role overseas). More than 75% of the respondents said that each of the four domestic issues would be very important; only 43% said that the U.S. global role would be very important.

This is not to say that all of the public pays little heed to foreign policy all of the time. First, there is a segment of the public, the "attentive public," that regularly pays attention to world events. Second, crisis issues, such as the war with Iraq, and intermestic issues, such as trade, are apt to draw significantly greater public attention. Third, studies show that although the public is not versed in the details of policies,

One way the public can affect foreign policy is through the ballot box. Especially because the United States is the world's most powerful country, it made a difference whether Americans elected George Bush or John Kerry as president in 2004.

its basic instincts are neither disconnected from events nor unstable (Witko, 2003; Isernia, Juhasz, & Rattinger, 2002).

Channels of Public Opinion Influence on Foreign Policy
There are a few countries in which the public occasionally gets to decide a foreign policy issue directly through a national referendum (Dalton, Burklin, & Drummond, 2001). However, all democracies are basically republican forms of government in which policies and laws are made by elected officials and their appointees. Therefore, it is more common for public opinion to have an indirect democratic influence on policy through voting for officials and through the sensitivity of those officials to public attitudes.

Even if they cannot usually decide policy directly, voters do sometimes have a choice of candidates for national leadership positions who have different foreign policy goals and priorities (Fordham, 2002). The change of Spain's prime ministers from conservative José Maria Aznar to liberal José Luis Rodríguez-Zapatero in 2004 distinctly changed that country's policy toward keeping its troops in Iraq, and it is probable that the foreign policy of a President John Kerry would have differed in important ways from that of President George Bush.

Additionally, research shows that both elected and appointed officials are concerned with public opinion and that it often influences policy (Burstein, 2003; Heith, 2003; Reiter & Tillman, 2002). One reason is that most decision makers in a democracy believe that public opinion is a legitimate factor that should be considered when determining which policy is to be adopted. Second, leaders also believe that policy is more apt to be successful if it is backed by public opinion. Third, decision makers are wary of public retribution in the next election if they ignore majority opinion. "I knew full well that if we could rally the American people behind a long and difficult chore, that our job would be easier," President Bush commented about ordering military action against Afghanistan in 2001. "I am a product of the Vietnam era," the president explained. "I remember presidents trying to wage wars that were very unpopular, and the nation split."[38]

Bush also followed this philosophy in the movement to war with Iraq. There was strong momentum within the Bush administration to go to war over a year before action commenced in March 2003. One important obstacle, though, was U.S. public opinion. Most polls found that a majority of Americans wanted Saddam Hussein removed, and they tentatively supported military action. But the surveys also showed that Americans wanted the president to present a stronger case for action, to give UN inspectors more opportunities, and to try to build an international coalition to participate in the invasion. These "conditions" for public support were important factors that explain the efforts of the Bush administration to meet the public's demands during the latter part of 2002 and early 2003.

Dimensions of Foreign Policy Opinion   Most polls only report overall public opinion on a topic, but it is important to realize that opinion is not split evenly across all segments of the public. One of these opinion splits, the gender gap, is discussed earlier in this chapter. Additionally, there is a **leader-citizen opinion gap** on some issues in the United States and other countries. This term represents the difference in the

Web Link

The full range of the opinions of U.S. leaders and citizens is in "Global Views 2004: American Public Opinion and Foreign Policy" on the site of the Chicago Council on Foreign Relations at **www.ccfr.org/globalviews2004/sub/usa.htm.**

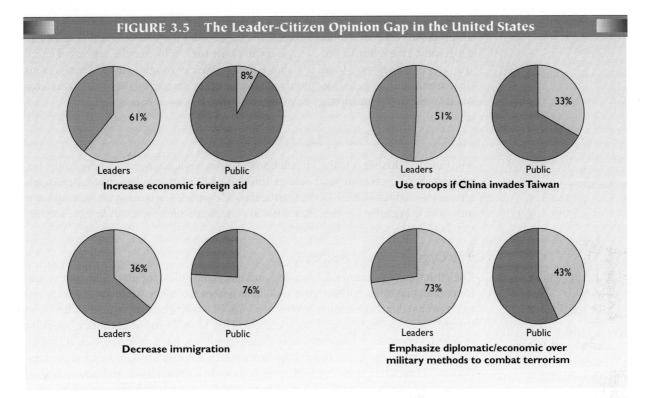

FIGURE 3.5   The Leader-Citizen Opinion Gap in the United States

Increase economic foreign aid

Leaders — 61%
Public — 8%

Use troops if China invades Taiwan

Leaders — 51%
Public — 33%

Decrease immigration

Leaders — 36%
Public — 76%

Emphasize diplomatic/economic over military methods to combat terrorism

Leaders — 73%
Public — 43%

A gap exists between the aggregate opinion of a society's leaders and its public on many issues. Leaders and citizens agree on most issues, although usually in different percentages, but there are issues on which leaders and citizens disagree. As you can see here, U.S. leaders and the American public differ on foreign economic aid, what to do if China invades Taiwan, the level of immigration, and how to best combat terrorism.

Note: Percentages indicate those in favor.
Data source: Chicago Council on Foreign Relations (2004).

average opinions of those who are the leaders of government, business, the media, and other areas in a society and the general public. Figure 3.5 depicts this gap between U.S. leaders and the American public on several issues.

System-Level Analysis

Countries may be theoretically free to make any foreign policy decision they want, but as a practical matter, achieving a successful foreign policy requires that they make choices that are reasonable within the context of the realities of the international system. For example, Mexico could exercise its sovereign authority and declare war on the United States over its overuse of water from the Colorado River and the damage that has done downstream in Mexico. However, doing so would be foolhardy because one fact of life in the international system is that the U.S. military power is vastly greater than that of Mexico. Thus, power realities in the international system dictate that Mexico would be wiser to attempt to use more moderate means in its effort to persuade the United States to be a more considerate neighbor.

MAP
The Geopolitical World
at the Beginning of
the 21st Century

System-level analysis focuses on the external restraints on foreign policy. This is a "top-down" approach to world politics that examines the social-economic-political-geographic characteristics of the system and how they influence the actions of countries and other actors (Moore & Lanoue, 2003). We can roughly divide the restraints on reasonable state behavior into those related to the system's structural characteristic, its power relationships, its economic realities, and its norms.

Structural Characteristics

All systems, whether it is the international system, your country's system, or the immediate, local system in your college international relations class, have identifiable structural characteristics. Two of particular relevance to our analysis here are how authority is organized in the international system and the scope and level of interaction among the actors in the system.

The Organization of Authority

WEB POLL
System-Level Analysis

The structure of authority for making and enforcing rules, for allocating assets, and for conducting other authoritative tasks in a system can range from hierarchical (vertical) to anarchical (horizontal). Most systems, like your class and your country, tend toward the hierarchical end of the spectrum. They have a **vertical authority structure** in which subordinate units are substantially regulated by higher levels of authority. Other systems are situated toward the **horizontal authority structure** end of the continuum. There are few, if any, higher authorities in such systems, and power is fragmented. The international system is a mostly horizontal authority structure. It is based on the sovereignty of states. *Sovereignty* means that countries are not legally answerable to any higher authority for their international or domestic conduct (Jackson, 1999). As such, the international system is a **state-centric system** that is largely anarchic; it has no overarching authority to make rules, settle disputes, and provide protection.

The anarchical nature of the international system has numerous impacts on national policy. Consider defense spending, for instance. We debate whether it is too high, too low, or about right; but almost nobody suggests that we spend zero and eliminate our country's military entirely. To see why the anarchical international system pressures countries to have an army, ask yourself why all countries are armed and why few, if any, students bring guns to class. One reason is that states in the international system (unlike students in your college) depend on themselves for protection. If a state is threatened, there is no international 911 to call for help. Given this anarchical self-help system, it is predictable that states will be armed.

While the authority structure in the international system remains decidedly horizontal, change is under way. Many analysts believe that sovereignty is declining and that even the most powerful states are subject to an increasing number of authoritative rules made by international organizations and by international law. In 2003, for example, the World Trade Organization (WTO) ruled in favor of a U.S. charge that Canada was violating trade rules by subsidizing its dairy industry, thereby allowing Canadian exports to undercut U.S. producers. But in another case that year, the United States lost when the WTO found the European Union (EU) justified in its complaint that "emergency" U.S. tariffs placed on steel imports were a violation of world trade rules. Canada changed policy immediately, announcing, "By moving quickly on compliance . . . we have demonstrated our commitment to respecting our trade obligations."[39] On the other side of the border, President Bush soon withdrew the special steel tariff, although he made no mention of the WTO's role in his decision.

Countries still resist and often even reject IGO governance, but more often than not they also comply with it. Moreover, Americans and others are increasingly willing to accept the idea that their country should abide by IGO decisions, as Figure 3.6 indicates.

Scope, Level, and Intensity of Interactions

Another structural characteristic of any political system is the scope (range), frequency, and intensity (level) of interactions among the actors. In your class, for example, the scope of interactions between you and both your professor and most of your classmates (1) is probably limited to what happens in the course; (2) is not very intense; and (3) is confined to two or three hours of class time each week over a single semester.

At the international system level, the scope, frequency, and level of interaction among the actors is not only often much higher than in your class but has grown extensively during the last half century. Economic interdependence provides the most obvious example. Countries trade more products more often than they did not long ago, and each of them, even the powerful United States, is heavily dependent on others for sources of products that it needs and as markets for products that it sells. Without foreign oil, to pick one obvious illustration, U.S. transportation and industry would literally come to a halt. Without extensive exports, the U.S. economy would stagger because exported goods and services account for about 15% of the U.S. GNP.

Data about expanding trade does not, however, fully capture the degree to which the widening scope and intensifying level of global financial interactions are increasing transnational contacts at every level. For individuals, modern telecommunications and travel have made once relatively rare personal international interactions commonplace. For example, between 1990 and 2000 the number of foreign visitors to the United States jumped 29% from 39.4 million to 50.9 million. During the same period, the number of Americans traveling overseas increased 35% from 44.6 million to 60.2 million. Trillions of phone calls, letters, and e-mail messages add to the globalization of human interactions.

How does this affect foreign policy? One way is that it makes isolationism irrational. All countries, even one as powerful and geographically isolated as the United States, are thoroughly and inextricably involved in the world. There are certainly times when the entanglements of world politics make it appealing to echo the title of the 1960s play and movie and shout, *Stop the World—I Want to Get Off.* That is not possible, though, and imagining that it is recalls the musical's best-known song, "What Kind of Fool Am I?" In fact, ignoring the world has never been possible. Early in American history, President Thomas Jefferson tried to avoid dealing with the power politics of Europe by persuading Congress to enact the Embargo Act of 1807. By barring all trade with the countries of Europe and their possessions, the act banned

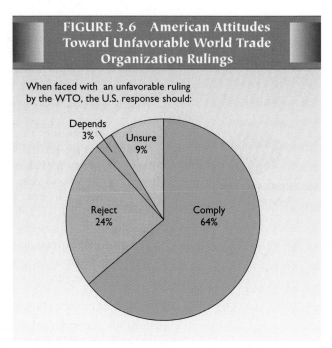

FIGURE 3.6   American Attitudes Toward Unfavorable World Trade Organization Rulings

When faced with an unfavorable ruling by the WTO, the U.S. response should:

Depends 3%
Unsure 9%
Reject 24%
Comply 64%

People are increasingly willing to accept some restrictions on their country's sovereignty. When asked what the United States should do when the World Trade Organization ruled against the U.S. position in trade disputes with other countries, almost two-thirds of Americans said their country should comply. Less than a quarter of Americans wanted Washington to reject the WTO decision.

Note: The question was: The World Trade Organization was established to rule on disputes over trade treaties. If another country files a complaint with the World Trade Organization and it rules against the U.S., as a general rule, should the U.S. comply with that decision or not?
Data source: Survey by Chicago Council on Foreign Relations and German Marshall Fund, June 2003. Data provided by The Roper Center for Public Opinion Research, University of Connecticut.

virtually all foreign commerce. The embargo had little impact on the European powers, but U.S. exports plummeted 80%, inflicting economic devastation on Americans, who did and still do rely heavily on foreign trade for their prosperity. After two dismal years, Congress repealed the act in 1809.

Power Relationships

SIMULATION
Rules of the Game

Countries are restrained by the realities of power in the international system, much like individuals are limited by the distribution of power in more local systems. For instance, it is very probable that the distribution of power in your class is narrow. There is apt to be one major power, the professor, who decides on the class work, schedules exams, controls the discussion, and issues rewards or sanctions (grades). Sometimes students grumble about one or another aspect of a class, and they might even be right. But the power disparity between students and their professor makes open defiance exceptionally rare. Similarly, the conduct of the international system is heavily influenced by power considerations such as the number of powerful actors and the context of power.

The Number of Powerful Actors

Historically, international systems have been defined in part by how many powerful actors each has (Wilkinson, 2004). Such an actor, called a **power pole,** can be (1) a single country or empire, (2) an alliance, or could be (3) a global IGO, such as the UN, or (4) a regional IGO, such as the EU.

Some scholars believe that the number of power poles in existence at any one time helps determine how countries are likely to act. According to this view, it is possible to identify patterns or rules of the game for systems. Figure 3.7 displays four power configurations (unipolar, bipolar, tripolar, and multipolar) and ways in which the patterns of interaction arguably differ across them. Bear in mind that these rules indicate what actors are apt to try to do. The rules are neither ironclad nor do actors always succeed in implementing them.

As a sample of how these rules work, note that in a **unipolar system,** which exists in many ways today with the United States as the single pole, the **hegemonic power** tries to maintain control. From a system-level perspective, this impulse to power is not so much caused by the preexisting desires of the dominant power as by the pressure in the system to maintain stability and order. The argument is that "a unipolar system will be peaceful," but only so long as the hegemonic power acts like one (Wohlforth, 1999:23). This leads some scholars to worry that if the United States refuses to play the leading role in the world drama, then the system becomes unstable, leading to greater violence and other negative consequences (Lal, 2004). Advocates of this view warn, "Critics of U.S. global dominance should pause and consider the alternative. If the United States retreats from its hegemonic role, who would supplant it? . . . Unfortunately, the alternative to a single superpower is not a multilateral utopia." What will occur, the argument continues, is a "power vacuum . . . an era of 'apolarity'," leading to "an anarchic new Dark Age: an era of waning empires and religious fanaticism; of endemic plunder and pillage in the world's forgotten regions; of economic stagnation and civilization's retreat into a few fortified enclaves" (Ferguson, 2004:32). This view is akin to Barber's (1996) image of tribalism, as discussed in chapter 2.

Needless to say, there is considerable debate over such views. Some scholars contend that a reduced U.S. presence in the world would not destabilize the system (Bobrow & Boyer, 1998). Yet other analysts debate the motives behind and the implications of

FIGURE 3.7 Models and Rules of the Game of Various International System Structures

Unipolar System

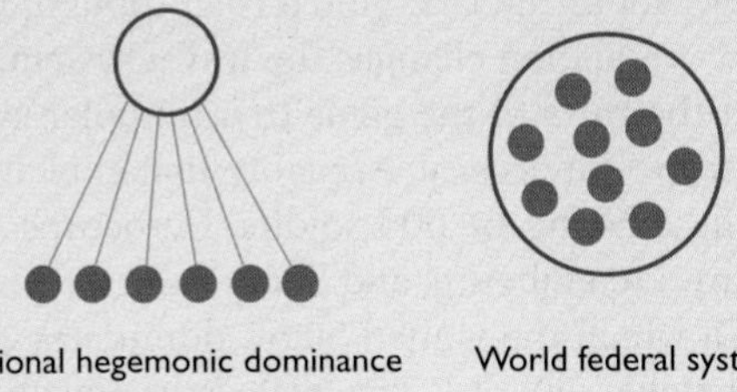

Traditional hegemonic dominance   World federal system

One pole

Rules of the game are: (1) The central power establishes and enforces rules and dominates military and economic instruments. (2) The central power settles disputes between subordinate units. (3) The central power resists attempts by subordinate units to achieve independence or greater autonomy and may gradually attempt to lessen or eliminate the autonomy of subordinate units.

Bipolar System

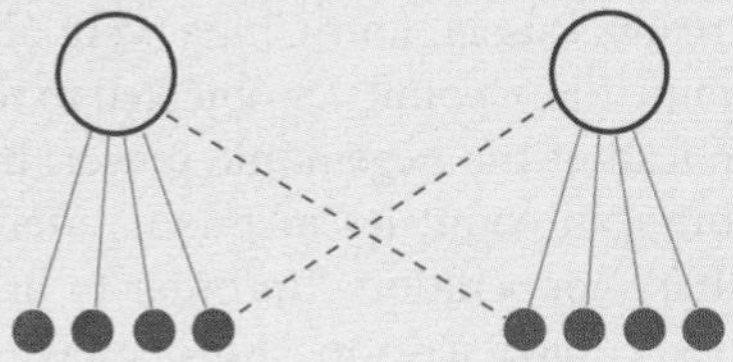

Two poles

Acute hostility between the two poles is the central feature of a bipolar system. Thus primary rules are: (1) Try to eliminate the other bloc by undermining it if possible and by fighting it if necessary and if the risks are acceptable. (2) Increase power relative to the other bloc by such techniques as attempting to bring new members into your bloc and by attempting to prevent others from joining the rival bloc.

Tripolar System

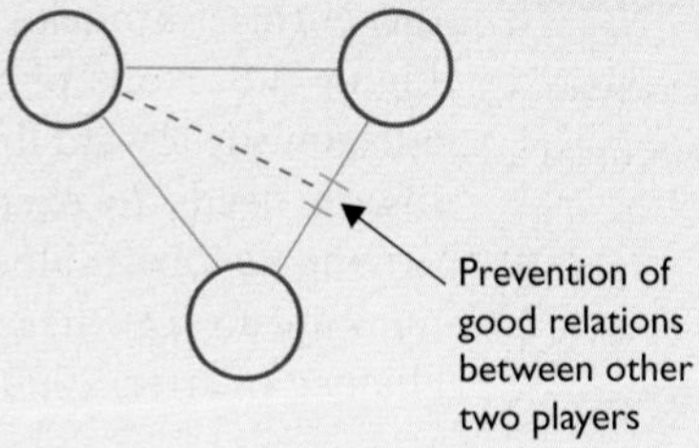

Prevention of good relations between other two players

Three poles

The rules of play in a triangular relationship are: (1) Optimally, try to have good relations with both other players or, minimally, try to avoid having hostile relations with both other players. (2) Try to prevent close cooperation between the other two players.

Multipolar System

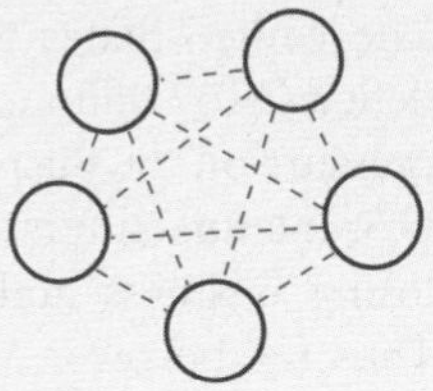

Four or more poles

Rules of the game are: (1) Oppose any actor or alliance that threatens to become hegemonic. This is also the central principle of balance-of-power politics. (2) Optimally increase power and minimally preserve your power. Do so by negotiating if possible, by fighting if necessary. (3) Even if fighting, do not destabilize the system by destroying another major actor.

● Small power   - - - - - - - Short-term or potential link

○ Large power   ———— Dominant and lasting link

The relationships that exist among the actors in a particular type of international system structure vary because of the number of powerful actors, the relative power of each, and the permitted interactions within the system. This figure displays potential international system structures and the basic rules that govern relationships within each system. After looking at these models, which one, if any, do you think best describes the contemporary international system?

the United States conducting itself as the hegemonic power. Some condemn it as a destructive imperialistic impulse (Gitlin, 2003; Lobell, 2004). Others argue that U.S. power is not only necessary for stability, but will also have other positive impacts such as spreading democracy (Kaplan 2004; Krauthammer, 2004). Amid all these sharply divergent views about the U.S. global role, though, there can be little doubt that changing the power equation changes the way a system operates.

The theory about the rules of the game in a unipolar system also suggests that lesser powers try to escape dominance. Arguably, that explains why many Europeans favor transforming the existing 60,000-soldier Eurocorps (with troops from Belgium, France, Germany, Luxembourg, and Spain) into a de facto EU army to rival or even to replace NATO, which the United States dominates. As former British Prime Minister Margaret Thatcher put it, "The real drive towards a separate European defense" is based on the unstated goal of "creating a single European superstate to rival America on the world stage."[40] The urge to escape the U.S. orbit also may help explain why France, Germany, Russia, and China were all opposed to U.S. action against Iraq in 2003. Certainly those countries objected to the war as such, but it was also a chance to resist the lead of the hegemonic power. In this context, it was not surprising that several European countries met soon after the Iraq War to discuss how to increase their military cooperation. "In order to have a balance, we have to have a strong Europe, as well as a strong U.S.," is how French President Jacques Chirac explained the purpose of the conference.[41] Moreover, surveys indicate that Europeans agree with him, as evident in Figure 3.8. None of this means that Europe will be antagonistic toward the United States, only that Washington needs to exercise power carefully to avoid driving its former allies together with its former enemies in an anti-hegemony, not an anti-American, alliance (Carter, 2003; Owen, 2001).

The Context of Power

The United States is troubled by its massive trade deficit ($162 billion in 2004) with China, and there is pressure on the Bush administration to react strongly. U.S. manufacturers and unions assert that they are losing business and jobs to the flood of imports. Thus far, however, Washington has not pressed Beijing hard on the issue. The reason is that raising tariffs on Chinese goods and other decisive actions, which the United States has the power to do, would dramatically decrease China's willingness to cooperate with the United States in other key areas. One of these is North Korea's nuclear weapons program, a situation that could lead to the spread of nuclear weapons beyond North Korea to South Korea and Japan and even to war on the Korean Peninsula. China is one of the few countries with any influence in Pyongyang, and Beijing might respond to U.S. pressure to reduce the trade deficit by refusing to cooperate with Washington's efforts to persuade North Korea to end its nuclear program.

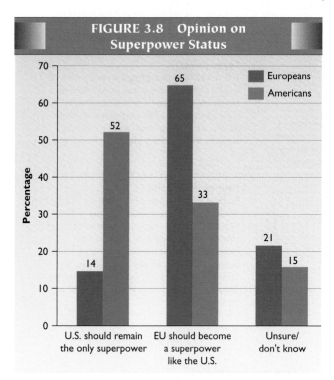

FIGURE 3.8   Opinion on Superpower Status

"Uneasy lies the head that wears a crown," Shakespeare tells us in *Henry I, Part II*. This advice may be appropriate for the United States, which, at least for now, is the world's dominant country. Dominance by one means being dominated for others, however, and as this figure shows, Europeans are much less likely than Americans to approve of the current balance of power (or lack thereof) in the international system.

Data source: The German Marshall Fund of the United States and the Chicago Council on Foreign Relations Poll, 2002, available on the Web at www.worldviews.org/.

Economic Realities

System-level analysts contend that the economic realities of the international system help shape the choices that countries make. Again, this is the same in systems from the global to your local level. For example, a safe prediction is that after finishing your education you will get a job and spend most of the rest of your life working instead of pursuing whatever leisure activities you enjoy the most. You will almost certainly do that because the economic realities of your local system require money to get many of the things you want, and most of us need a job to get money. Similarly, the international system has economic facts of life that help shape behavior.

At the international level, interdependence is one of the economic facts of life that influences states' behavior (Gartzke, Li, & Boehmer, 2001; Mansfield & Pollins, 2001). For example, many studies conclude that increasing economic interdependence promotes peace as countries become more familiar with one another and need each other for their mutual prosperity (Schneider, Barbieri, & Gleditsch, 2003). The ramifications of this on policy are evident by again turning to U.S.-China relations. It is tempting to advocate imposing tariff hikes and other sanctions on Beijing, and certainly that would stagger China's economy. But it would also damage Americans economically. Equivalent U.S.-made products would be much more expensive, thereby increasing the cost of living for the American consumer. Toys, electronic products, and many other things that Americans import from China might be in short supply or not available, at least until substitute sources could come on line. Many U.S. businesses and their stock- and bondholders might also suffer because they have invested heavily in setting up manufacturing plants in China that produce goods for the U.S. market. In short, the United States could decide to impose sanctions on China, but doing so would at least partly be the equivalent of Americans shooting themselves in their own economic foot.

Natural resource production and consumption patterns also influence the operation of the system. From this perspective, the U.S. military reaction to Iraq's attack on Kuwait in 1990 and its threat to the rest of the oil-rich Persian Gulf region was virtually foreordained by the importance of petroleum to the prosperity of the United States and its economic partners. As U.S. Secretary of State James A. Baker III explained to reporters, "The economic lifeline of the industrial world runs from the Gulf, and we cannot permit a dictator . . . to sit astride that economic lifeline."[42]

By contrast, U.S. officials repeatedly denied that petroleum was connected to the war in 2003. Secretary of Defense Rumsfeld, for one, asserted that the U.S. campaign against Iraq "has . . . literally nothing to do with oil."[43] Nevertheless, numerous analysts believe that it was an underlying factor. Some contend that Washington sought to ensure continued supplies at a stable price by adding control of Iraq to its already strong influence over Saudi Arabia, Kuwait, Qatar, and other oil-rich states in the region. The administration "believes you have to control resources in order to have access to them," argues Chas Freeman, a former U.S. ambassador to Saudi Arabia.[44] Other analysts believe that the motive behind U.S. policy was a power play. As one scholar put it, "Controlling Iraq is about oil as power, rather than oil as fuel. Control over the Persian Gulf translates into control over Europe, Japan, and China. It's having our hand on the spigot."[45]

There has also been speculation that the opposition of France, Russia, and some other countries to the U.S.-led invasion and their support for easing sanctions on Iraqi oil exports were in part oil related. The contention is that these countries were concerned with the contracts their oil companies had with Iraq to develop its oil production once sanctions were lifted, and they feared that those agreements would be

> **Did You Know That:**
> Iraq contains about 11% of the world's proven oil reserves.

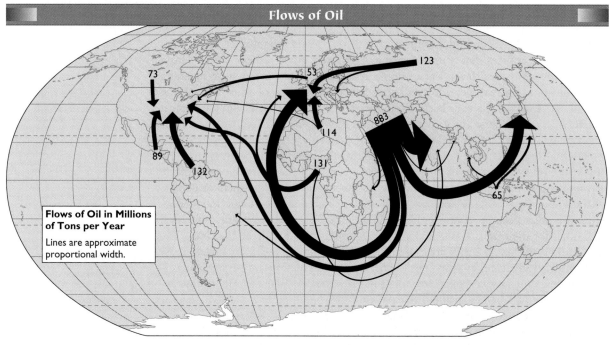

Flows of Oil

Flows of Oil in Millions of Tons per Year

Lines are approximate proportional width.

World politics is strongly influenced by the reality in the international system that much of the world's petroleum is produced in the Middle East and consumed in North America, Europe, and Japan.

MAP
Flows of Oil

abrogated and given to U.S. firms in the wake of a U.S. occupation of the country. As one U.S. oil expert put it before the war, "Most of these governments . . . have [a financial] interest in the current Iraqi government surviving. It's not trivial. . . . Once it's developed, the oil will be 2.5 million barrels [worth about $70 million] per day."[46]

Norms

Like all the other factors we have been discussing, norms influence the actors in systems from the global level to the local level. Norms are one of the reasons that even on a very warm day you will almost certainly come to class wearing clothes rather than *au naturel*. In fact, norms make it reasonably predictable that most students will come to class not only dressed, but dressed similarly. Jeans, sweatshirts, sneakers or work boots, and baseball caps (often worn backwards) seem the most common "uniform."

So too do norms play a part in determining actions within the international system. In a world in which absolutely horrendous things sometimes happen, it is hard for some to accept that norms exist, but they do. Certainly it would be far too strong to say there is anything near a universally accepted standard of behavior, but it is the case that values are a more important part of international conduct and are becoming more globally uniform.

For example, one hypothetical option for U.S. foreign policy in 2003 was "nuking" Iraq's main cities and military sites and killing most Iraqis. It surely would have ended the regime of Saddam Hussein, it would have been quick, and it would have cost many fewer American lives and dollars than the conventional attack and subsequent occupation. Yet the U.S. decision was to send troops to Iraq at great expense and at great risk, especially given the perceived threat of a chemical or biological attack on them. Why?

Norms were one reason for not choosing the nuclear course. The global population would have been horrified, and Americans themselves might have risen up and removed President Bush from office. Indeed, the norm against using nuclear weapons, especially against a non-nuclear power, is so strong that only massive Iraqi use of chemical or biological weapons might have prompted such a response.

Moreover, even within the parameters of a conventional invasion, it is noteworthy that U.S. and U.K. military forces generally conducted operations in a way to keep civilian casualties much lower than they might otherwise have been. That reflected the growing norms in the world, including those of Americans, 75% of whom, according to one poll, believed there should be a "very high" or "high" priority on minimizing civilian casualties.[47]

It is easy to lose track of the main message in this long section on system-level analysis. So to recap our focus, system-level analysis looks for the way that the structure, power distribution, economic realities, and norms of the international system influence foreign policy. Indeed, we have seen that foreign policy–making is much more complex than merely "what the president decides." Instead, foreign policy and by extension world politics are heavily influenced by numerous factors related to the traits of humans as individuals and as a species, to the complicated structure of government with its many important subnational actors, and to the context of the international system in which all countries operate.

Chapter Summary

Individual-Level Analysis

1. Individual-level analysis is based on the view that it is people who make policy. It analyzes the policy-making process by examining how people (as a species, in groups, and individually) make decisions.

2. Individual-level analysis can be approached from three different perspectives. One is to examine fundamental human nature. The second is to study how people act in organizations. The third is to examine the motivations and actions of specific persons.

3. The human nature approach examines basic human characteristics, including the cognitive, psychological, emotional, and biological factors that influence decision making.

4. The organizational behavior approach studies such factors as role (how people act in their professional position) and group decision-making behavior, including groupthink.

5. The idiosyncratic behavior approach explores the factors that determine the perceptions, decisions, and actions of specific leaders. A leader's personality, physical and mental health, ego and ambitions, understanding of history, personal experiences, and perceptions are all factors.

6. The application of perceptions to policy can be explained by exploring operational reality and operational codes.

State-Level Analysis

7. State-level analysis assumes that since states are the most important international actors, world politics can be best understood by focusing on how foreign policy is influenced by the political structure of states, the policy-making actors within them, and the interactions among the policy actors.

8. Foreign policy is not formulated by a single decision-making process. Instead, the exact nature of that process changes according to a number of variables, including the type of political system, the type of situation, the type of issue, and the internal factors involved.

9. States are complex organizations, and their internal, or domestic, dynamics influence their international actions.

10. One set of internal factors centers on political culture: the fundamental, long-held beliefs of a nation.

11. Another set of internal factors centers on the policy-making impact of various foreign policy–making actors. These include political leaders, bureaucratic organizations, legislatures, political parties and opposition, interest groups, and the public. Each of these influences foreign policy, but their influence varies according to the type of government, the situation, and the policy at issue.

12. Usually, heads of government are the most powerful foreign policy–making actors. Bureaucratic

organizations are normally the second most powerful actors.

System-Level Analysis

13. To be successful, countries usually must make policy choices within the context of the realities of the international system. Therefore, system-level analysis examines how the realities of the international system influence foreign policy.
14. Many factors determine the nature of any given system. Systemic factors include its structural characteristics, power relationships, economic realities, and norms of behavior.
15. One structural characteristic is how authority is organized. The international system is horizontal, based on state sovereignty, and therefore it is anarchical. There are, however, relatively new centralizing forces that are changing the system toward a more vertical structure.
16. Another structural characteristic is a system's frequency, scope, and level of interaction. The current system is becoming increasingly interdependent, with a rising number of interactions across an expanding range of issues. Economic interdependence is especially significant.

17. When analyzing power relationships, an important factor is the number of poles in a system and how the pattern of international relations varies depending on how many power centers, or poles, a system has.
18. The current system most closely resembles either a unipolar system or limited unipolar system dominated by the United States.
19. The context of power is another system characteristic. One contextual factor is the applicability of power in a given situation.
20. Another aspect of the context is the intricate interrelationships among almost 200 countries and the need of even powerful countries for diplomatic reciprocity, the cooperation of others on a range of issues. It is therefore wise, before using power, to calculate the long-term impact of the attitudes of other countries.
21. Norms are the values that help determine patterns of behavior and create some degree of predictability in the system. The norms of the system are changing. Many newer countries, for instance, are challenging some of the current norms of the system, most of which are rooted in Western culture.

For simulations, debates, and other interactive activities, a chapter quiz, Web links, PowerWeb articles, and much more, visit **www.mhhe.com/rourke11/** and go to chapter 3. Or, while accessing the site, click on Course-Related Headlines and view recent international relations articles in the *New York Times*.

Key Terms

authoritarian governments
biopolitics
bureaucracy
cognitive decision making
crisis situation
decision-making process
democratic governments
ethology
foreign policy process
foreign policy–making actors

formal powers
frustration-aggression theory
gender opinion gap
groupthink
head of government
hegemonic power
heuristic devices
horizontal authority structure
idiosyncratic analysis
individual-level analysis

informal powers
interest groups
intermestic policy
issue area
leader-citizen opinion gap
levels of analysis
mirror-image perception
Munich analogy
operational code
operational reality
poliheuristic theory
political culture

political executives
power pole
rally effect
roles
state-centric system
state-level analysis
system-level analysis
two-level game
unipolar system
vertical authority structure

Nationalism: The Traditional Orientation

Who is here so vile
that will not love his country?
—William Shakespeare, *Julius Caesar*

If he govern the country, you are bound to him indeed;
but how honourable he is in that, I know not.
—William Shakespeare, *Pericles, Prince of Tyre*

Like almost everyone, you probably have a strong sense of nationalism, the topic of this chapter. The power of nationalism was evident in Lebanon in 2005 after Syrian agents assassinated a Lebanese leader. Outraged Lebanese protesters forced Damascus to withdraw its forces that had been in Lebanon for 30 years.

ALIENS FASCINATE US. NOT THE ALIENS that immigration officials worry about, but the ones that come from other planets. Whether it is movies such as the 2005 release, *Star Wars: Revenge of the Sith,* television such as the numerous Star Trek series, sci-fi novels, or comics, our entertainment media are filled with "others." These aliens can do more than amuse or scare us; they can teach us something. For instance, take E.T., the extraterrestrial being. Now, there was one strange-looking character. He—she?—had a squat body, no legs to speak of, a large shriveled head, saucer eyes, and a telescopic neck. And the color! Yes, E.T. was definitely weird. Not only that; there was presumably a whole planet full of E.T.s—all looking alike, waddling along, with their necks going up and down.

Or did they all look alike? They might have to us, but probably not to one another. Perhaps their planet had different countries, ethnic groups, and races of E.T.s. Maybe they had different-length necks, were varied shades of greenish-brown, and squeaked and hummed with different tonal qualities. It could even be that darker-green E.T.s with longer necks from the country of Urghor felt superior to lighter-green, short-necked E.T.s from faraway and little-known Sytica across the red Barovian Sea. If E.T. were a Sytican, would the Urghorans have responded to the plaintive call, "E.T. phone home"?

We can also wonder whether E.T. could tell Earthlings apart. Was he aware that some of his human protectors were boys and some were girls and that a racial and ethnic cross section of Americans chased him with equal-opportunity abandon? Maybe we all looked pretty much the same to E.T. If he had been on a biological specimen–gathering expedition, would he have collected a Canadian, a Nigerian, and a Laotian, or would he have considered them duplicates?

The point of this whimsy is to get us thinking about our world, how we group ourselves, and how we distinguish our group from others. This sense of how you are connected politically to others is called **political identity**. What we humans mostly do is to ignore our many and manifest similarities and perceptually divide ourselves into Americans, Chinese, Irish, Poles, and a host of other national "we-groups."

Web Link

You can participate in the Search for Extraterrestrial Intelligence (SETI) program at the University of California at Berkeley through its Web site at: **http://setiathome .ssl.berkeley.edu/.**

Nationalism is a learned form of political identity. None of these babies has any sense of loyalty to any of the countries represented by the flags on their blanket, but they soon will. As a result, even though they seem pretty much the same in this photo, each baby will come to see the others as different and perhaps even hostile.

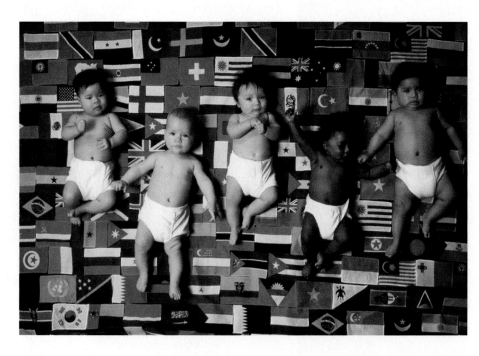

Understanding Nations, Nationalism, and Nation-States

This chapter explores nationalism, the most important way we group ourselves politically. For more than five centuries it has been, and remains, the world's "most powerful political idea" (Taras & Ganguly, 1998:xi). As such, nationalism is a key characteristic of traditional global politics. Despite its strength, however, nationalism is not as dominant a political identity as it once was. Indeed, some even doubt whether it will or should continue and predict or advocate various transnational alternative orientations. These alternatives are taken up in chapter 5, and their juxtaposition with the traditional nationalist orientation in this chapter represents one of this book's main themes: that the world is at a critical juncture where two roads diverge in the political woods. The two paths to the political future—traditional and alternative—are mapped out briefly in chapter 1.

Nations, Nationalism, and Nation-States Defined

The world's political divisions rest in great part on three concepts: nation, nation-state, and nationalism. Understanding both the theory and reality of what they are and how they relate to one another is central to our analysis of international politics.

Nations

A **nation** is a people who (a) share demographic and cultural similarities, (b) possess a feeling of community (mutually identify as a group distinct from other groups), and (c) want to control themselves politically. As such, a nation is intangible; it exists because its members think it does. A state (country) is a tangible institution, but a nation is "a soul, a spiritual quality" (Renan, 1995:7). Americans, for one, are a nation; the institutional vehicle of their self-governance is their state, the United States.

Demographic and Cultural Similarities   The similarities that a people share are one element that helps make them a nation. These similarities may be demographic characteristics (such as language, race, and religion), or they may be a common culture or shared historical experiences. It could be said that the American nation is the outcome of Valley Forge, Martin Luther King, the interstate highway system, McDonald's, MTV, the Super Bowl, Jennifer Lopez, the 9/11 terrorist attacks, and a host of other people, events, and processes that make up the American experience. Symbols such as the American flag, Uncle Sam, and the bald eagle reinforce the feeling of nationalism (Geisler, 2005).

Feeling of Community   A second thing that helps define a nation is its feeling of community. Perception is the key here. Whatever its objective similarities, a group is not a nation unless it subjectively feels like one. Those within a group must perceive that they share similarities and are bound together by them. Thus a nation is an "imagined political community." As one scholar explains, "It is imagined because the members of even the smallest nation will never know most of their fellow-members, meet them, or even hear of them, yet in the minds of each lives the image of their communion" (Anderson, 1991:5).

The central role of perceptions in defining a nation leads, perhaps inevitably, to a "we-group" defining itself not only by the similarities of its members but also in

MAP
World Languages

Nationalism is a feeling of community based in part on shared experiences. The Mexican boys in this photo are rooting for their country's team during a World Cup Soccer match against the Caribbean island country of St. Kitts and Nevis. They are also bonding with the Mexican nation, as evident in the Mexican flag they are displaying, the flag's colors in their shirts, and the traditional Mexican hat one is wearing.

terms of how the members of the nation differ from others, the "they-groups." The group members' sense of feeling akin to one another and their sense of being different from others are highly subjective.

Desire to Be Politically Separate   The third element that defines a nation is its desire to be politically separate. What distinguishes a nation from an ethnic group is that a nation, unlike an ethnic group, desires to be self-governing or at least autonomous. In the United States there are many groups, such as Italian Americans, who share a common culture and have a sense of identification. They are ethnic groups, not nations, however, because they are not separatists. In nationally divided states (like Cyprus, with its majority Greek and minority Turkish communities), the minority nationalities refuse to concede the legitimacy of their being governed by the majority nationality.

It should be noted that the line between ethnic groups and nations is not always clear. In many countries there are ethnic groups that either teeter on the edge of having true nationalist (separatist) sentiments or that have some members who are nationalists and others who are not. In Canada, for instance, there is an ongoing dissatisfaction among many French Canadians in the province of Quebec about their status in the Canadian state. Some Québécois favor separation; others do not. Once the prevailing opinion of the ethnic group perceives it to be distinct politically as well as culturally, then it becomes an **ethnonational group** (Conversi, 2002 & 2004).

Nationalism

The second aspect of the traditional political orientation is **nationalism**. It is the sense of political self that makes people feel patriotic about their country, connected to a we-group, and different from they-groups. It is hard to overstate the importance of nationalism to the structure and conduct of world politics. Nationalism is an **ideology**. Like all ideologies, nationalism is a set of related ideas that (1) establish values about what is good and bad, (2) direct adherents on how to act (patriotism), (3) link together those who adhere to the ideology, and (4) distinguish them from those who do not.

Specifically, nationalism connects individuals through links that are forged when people (1) "become sentimentally attached to the homeland," (2) "gain a sense of identity and self-esteem through their national identification," and (3) are "motivated to help their country" (Druckman, 1994:44). As such, nationalism is an ideology that holds that the nation should be the primary political identity of individuals. Furthermore, nationalist ideology maintains that the paramount political loyalty of individuals should be patriotically extended to the nation-state, the political vehicle of the nation's self-governance. While most people have more than one political identity, nationalism almost always is their primary political orientation. For example, President Lyndon B. Johnson once said, "I am an American, a Texan, and a Democrat—in that order." Like Johnson, we emotionally rank our identities, and also like LBJ, most of us put our country first. Thus you probably see yourself first and foremost politically as a citizen of the United States or some other country. You might even be willing to fight and die for your country. Would you do the same for your hometown? Or Earth?

Nation-States

A third element of our traditional way of defining and organizing ourselves politically is the **nation-state**. This combines the idea of a nation with that of a state. A state, about which much more is said in chapter 6, is a country, a sovereign (independent) political organization with certain characteristics, such as territory, a population, and a government. Canada and China, for example, are states. Ideally, a nation-state is one in which virtually all of a nation is united within the boundaries of its own state, and the people of that state overwhelmingly identify with the nation. Few states even approach this ideal, as we shall see, but the image is a powerful force for both those nations seeking to found their own states and those states seeking national unity.

The Rise and Ascendancy of Nationalism

Nationalism is such a pervasive mindset in the world today that it is difficult to believe that it has not always existed. But it has not. Indeed, most scholars contend that nationalism is a relatively modern phenomenon. Certainly, as one scholar notes, "there have always . . . been distinctive cultures." It is also the case that in some very old societies the "upper classes have had some sense of shared ethnic solidarity." What is modern, the scholar continues, is the "nationalist idea," the belief that people who share a culture should "be ruled only by someone co-cultural with themselves" (Hall, 1995:10).

This reality that nationalism has not always existed is important because if something has not always been, it will not necessarily continue to be. As we shall see later in the chapter, nationalism has its pluses and minuses, and numerous observers believe that it is an outmoded, even dangerous, orientation that should be abandoned. Understanding that nationalism is not an absolute also leads to a discussion of how it has evolved over time.

Early Nationalism

It is impossible to establish precisely when nationalism began to evolve (Smith, 2004). In the West, though, the fall of the universalistic Roman Empire set the stage. Under Rome something of common culture, language (Latin), and law prevailed, at least among the elite in the various parts of the empire. After Rome's collapse these common cultural and political ties deteriorated. Some sense of universality (such as the authority of the pope over kings and the use of Latin) survived in the Roman Catholic Church.

There were also various attempts to reestablish a Western empire. For example, the king of the Franks, Charlemagne (742–814), gained control over most of western and central Europe and in 800 was proclaimed by Pope Leo III to be *Imperatori Augustus,* a symbolic title reminiscent of the Roman emperors. This led to the concept of the Holy Roman Empire (HRE), which lasted in theory until 1806. Yet despite its pretentious title, the HRE never wielded the power of Rome and sometimes had little power at all.

Web Link

A good source of additional information about nationalism is the Nationalism Project at www.nationalismproject.org/.

As a result, the universality that had existed under Rome, and which the Church and the HRE tried to maintain, fragmented into different cultures. The use of Latin, a language spoken by all elites across Europe, declined, and the local languages that supplanted Latin divided the elites. This was but the first step in a process that eventually created a sense of divergent national identities among the upper classes. By dividing Western Christendom beginning in 1517, the Protestant Reformation further fragmented European culture.

The growth of nationalism became gradually intertwined with the development of states and with their synthesis, the nation-state. The history of states is reviewed in chapter 2, but we can say here that some of the earliest evidence of broad-based nationalism occurred in England at the time of King Henry VIII (1491–1547). His break with the centralizing authority of the Roman Catholic Church and his establishment of a national Anglican Church headed by the king were pivotal events. The conversion of English commoners to Anglicanism helped spread nationalism to the masses, as did the nationalist sentiments in popular literature. In an age when most people could not read, plays were an important vehicle of culture, and one scholar has characterized the works of William Shakespeare (1564–1616) as "propagandist plays about English history" (Hobsbawm, 1990:75). "This blessed plot, this earth, this realm, this England," Shakespeare has his King Richard II exult. In another play, *Henry VI,* Shakespeare notes the end of the authority of the pope in Rome over the king in London by having Queen Margaret proclaim, "God and King Henry govern England." This sounds commonplace today, but omitting mention of the authority of the papacy was radical stuff 450 years ago (Maley, 2003).

Ascendant Modern Nationalism

Modern nationalism began to emerge in the 1700s. Until that time, the link between the states and their inhabitants was very different than it is today. Most people were not emotionally connected to the state in which they lived. Instead, people were subjects who were ruled by a monarch anointed by God to govern (the divine right theory). This changed under the doctrine of **popular sovereignty**. It holds that people are not subjects, but citizens who have a stake in and are even owners (no matter how tangentially) of the state. Moreover, rulers governed by the consent of the people, at least in theory if often not in fact (Heater, 2004).

Until the late 1700s, popular sovereignty had been evolving slowly in Switzerland, England, and a few other places. Then it accelerated with the American Revolution (1776) and the French Revolution (1789). They dramatically advanced popular sovereignty by doing away with kings altogether and in their place proclaiming, in the words of the American Declaration of Independence, that governments derive their "just powers from the consent of the governed."

From these beginnings, the idea of popular sovereignty began to spread around the globe. Within 200 years of the American and French Revolutions, absolute monarchism, the most common form of governance from time immemorial, had virtually disappeared. Transnational ties among the elites also waned. When Great Britain's royal house of Stuart died out in 1714, it was still possible for the British to import a German nobleman to become King George I. Such a transplanted monarch or president would be virtually unthinkable today.

Nationalism's spread also dramatically changed the political map. An important factor was the associated concept of **self-determination**. This is the idea that every nation should be able to govern itself as it chooses. Following this notion, some nations that were divided among two or more political entities coalesced to create a single state. The formation of Germany and Italy in the 1860s and 1870s are exam-

---

Did You Know That:

National flags are relatively modern inventions that replaced flags of royal dynasties. The French tricolor, for example, dates only to 1794, when it replaced the white flag with the gold fleur-de-lis of the royal house of Bourbon.

ples. In other cases, national states were established on the ashes of empire. Indeed a key change in the last 250 years has been the decline and death of vast multiethnic empires, as one after another has sunk under its own ponderous weight like a woolly mammoth in the La Brea tar pits. First, American colonists revolted against British colonial rule. Then the urge for self-determination contributed to the decline and fall of the Spanish empire in the 1800s, followed by the Austro-Hungarian and Ottoman empires in the late 19th century and early 20th century. In each case, many of the nations that had existed within these empires established states. By the mid-twentieth century, nearly all of Europe and the Western Hemisphere had been divided into nation-states, and the colonies of Africa and Asia were beginning to demand independence. The British and French empires were similarly doomed by nationalist pressures within them and fell apart in the three decades after World War II. Finally, the last of the huge multiethnic empires, Russia/the Soviet Union, collapsed in 1991, with 15 nation-states emerging. Nationalism reigned virtually supreme around the world.

These developments were widely welcomed on two grounds. First, the idea of a nation implies equality for all members. Liberal philosophers such as Thomas Paine in *The Rights of Man* (1791) depicted the nation and democracy as inherently linked in the popularly governed nation-state. Supporters of nationalism also welcomed it as a destroyer of empires. Among other important expressions of this view is Article 55 of the United Nations Charter, which states that "the principle of . . . self-determination of peoples" is one of the "conditions of stability and well-being which are necessary for peaceful and friendly relations among nations." As we shall see later in the chapter, this support of self-determination is more controversial than it may seem.

Patterns of Nation-State Formation

As the history of nationalism suggests, nations, nationalism, and nation-states can come together in various patterns. Sometimes nations and nationalism precede states; sometimes states precede nations and nationalism; and at other times nations and nationalism evolve along with states.

Nations and Nationalism Precede Nation-States   The easiest form of **state building** occurs when a strong sense of cultural and political identity exists among a people, and the formation of the nation precedes that of the state. This process is called "unification nationalism" (Hechter, 2000:15). Europe was one place where nations generally came together first and only later coalesced into states. As noted, for example, Germans existed as a cultural people long before they established Germany in the 1860s and 1870s. In much the same way, the Italian peninsula was fragmented after the fall of the Roman Empire and remained that way until a resurgent sense of Italian cultural unity and its accompanying political movement unified most of the peninsula in a new country, Italy, in 1861. Similarly, on the other side of the world in Japan, increased nationalism helped end the political division of the Japanese islands among the *daimyo* (feudal nobles) during the Tokugawa Shogunate (1603–1867), and restored real power to what had been a figurehead emperor.

Nation-States Precede Nations and Nationalism   Another scenario is when the state is created first and then has to try to forge a sense of common national identity among the people and between them and the state. This state-building process is very difficult. Colonialism is one common cause of states coming into existence without a national core. For example, European powers artificially included people of different tribal and ethnic backgrounds within the borders of their African colonies (Larémont, 2005). When those colonies later became states, most lacked a single, cohesive nation

Sometimes a country's political identity predates a sense of unity among its people. In such cases, it is a hard task to create a unified nation. Shiite, Sunni, and Kurdish Iraqis managed a degree of unity after the war in 2003 because, like the man in this photo, many had a common goal: reclaiming control of their country from the U.S.-led occupying force. Maintaining that unity once the Americans are gone will be difficult.

on which to forge unity once independence had been achieved. Numerous problems resulted and persist. For example, Rwanda and Burundi are neighboring states in which Hutu and Tutsi people were thrown together by colonial boundaries that, with independence, became national boundaries, as depicted in the map of Africa on page 41. The difficulty is that the primary political identifications of these people have not become Rwandan or Burundian. They have remained Hutu or Tutsi, and that has led to repeated, sometimes horrific, violence.

The difficulties of building national identities and a stabilizing state have also beset the United States, and to a degree other involved countries, the UN, and regional organizations, in the aftermath of interventions in such places as Somalia and the Balkans in the 1990s and Afghanistan and Iraq more recently. Outside powers can find themselves "stuck" because they are neither able to create stable political situations that will allow them to withdraw nor willing to withdraw and permit a violent struggle for power to ensue (Etzioni, 2004; Fukuyama, 2004; Migdal, 2004).

Nations, Nationalism, and Nation-States Evolve Together
Frequently nation-building and state-building are not locked in a strict sequential interaction, when one fully precedes the other. Sometimes they evolve together. This approximates what occurred in the United States, where the idea of being American and the unity of the state began in the 1700s and grew, despite a civil war, immigration inflows, racial and ethnic diversity, and other potentially divisive factors. Still, as late as 1861, the limitations of nationalism could be seen when Colonel Robert E. Lee declined President Abraham Lincoln's offer of the command of the United States Army and accepted command of the militia of his seceding home state, Virginia.

The point is that American nationalism was not an instant phenomenon in 1776. As has happened elsewhere, living within a state over time allowed a demographically diverse people to come together as a nation through a process of *e pluribus unum* (out of many, one), as the U.S. motto says.

Nationalism in Practice: Issues and Evaluation

SIMULATION
The Future of the State:
Will Nationalism Survive?

The idea of a mutually identifying people coming together as a political nation to establish their own nation-state in order to govern themselves is an attractive one. Surely, it has brought benefits, but the reality of nationalism also has its dark side. As a first step toward evaluating the pros and cons of nationalism, it is important to understand how the theory and practice of nation-states differ.

Nation-States: More Myth Than Reality

Like most ideological images, the ideal nation-state is more myth than reality (Axtmann, 2004). The reason is that the territorial boundaries of nations and states often do not coincide. Instead, most states are not ethnically unified, and many nations are split by one or more national boundaries. This lack of "fit" between nations and states is a significant source of tension and conflict (Williams, 2003). There are five basic patterns: (1) The first is the ideal model of one nation, one state. The other four are lack-of-fit patterns including (2) one state, multiple nations; (3) one nation, multiple states; (4) one nation, no state; and (5) multiple nations, multiple states.

One State, One Nation

Only about 10% of all countries approximate the ideal nation-state by both having a population that is 90% or more of one nation and also having 90% of that nation living within its borders. The United States is one such country. More than 99% of all Americans live in the United States, and there are no large ethnonational groups seeking independence or autonomy. There is some such sentiment among indigenous Americans, such as Native Hawaiians, but combined they make up only a bit more than 1% of the population. Indeed, polls show that the vast majority of U.S. residents, citizens and noncitizens alike, express considerable attachment to the United States. This was evident in a U.S. poll conducted in 2003 in which 98% of the respondents said they were "proud . . . to be an American."[1]

One State, Multiple Nations

A far greater number of countries are **multinational states**, those in which more than one nation lies within a state. In fact, 30% of all states have no nation that constitutes a majority. The map on page 106 showing the degree of demographic unity of each country indicates racial and ethnic, as well as national, diversity. Most of these minority groups do not have separatist tendencies, but many do or could acquire them.

Canada is one of the many countries where national divisions exist. About one-fourth of Canada's 32 million people are ethnically French (French Canadians) who identify French as their "mother tongue" and first language (Francophones). The majority of this group resides in the province of Quebec, a political subdivision rather like (but politically more autonomous than) an American state. Quebec is very French; of the province's 7.2 million people, more than 80% are culturally French.

Many French Canadians have felt that their distinctive culture has been eroded in predominantly English-culture Canada. There has also been a feeling of economic and other forms of discrimination. The resulting nationalist sentiment spawned the separatist *Parti Québécois* and led to a series of efforts in the 1980s and 1990s to obtain autonomy, even independence, for the province. The most recent of these was a 1995 referendum on separation. The voters in Quebec rejected independence, but did so by only a razor-thin majority, with 50.6% voting *non* to sovereignty and 49.4% voting *oui*. Since then, nationalist feelings have continued in Quebec, but they have eased because of reforms that have improved economic and cultural conditions for the Francophones (Seymour, 2000). A poll conducted in 2001 that presented *Québécois* with the same question that was on the 1995 referendum found that support for sovereignty had dropped to 42%.[2]

Canada has avoided bloodshed over its national division, but many other multinational states have not. Some have suffered extraordinary violence. Rwanda, for one, is divided between two ethnonational groups, the minority (but politically dominant) Tutsi people and the majority Hutu people. In 1994 an orgy of killing decimated Rwanda when Hutus slaughtered some 800,000 Tutsis and their sympathizers over about 100 days and well over 1 million Tutsis and moderate Hutus fled for their lives to neighboring countries. The horrific massacre was given voice by Prime Minister Agathe Uwilingiyimana: "There is shooting. People are being terrorized. People are inside their homes lying on the floor. We are suffering," she said in a

MAP
Global Distribution
of Minorities

Global Distribution of Minority Groups

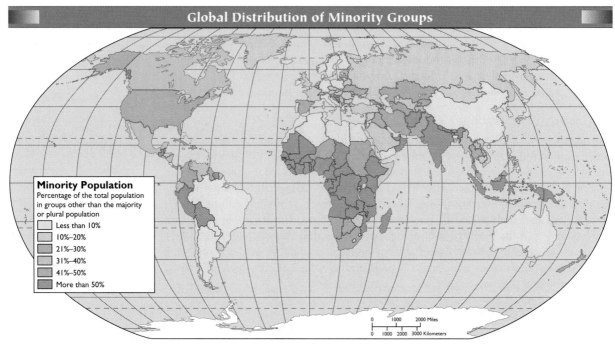

Minority Population
Percentage of the total population
in groups other than the majority
or plural population

- Less than 10%
- 10%–20%
- 21%–30%
- 31%–40%
- 41%–50%
- More than 50%

Very few states are ideal nation-states, ones where most of the people in the country are of one nation and where almost everyone of that nation lives within the country. Much more common are multinational states and multistate nations, as described in the text. Diversity within a state based on ethnicity, race, and religion is not necessarily divisive. Americans are fairly diverse, but most see themselves as Americans, whatever their demographic characteristics. In many other countries, though, diversity engenders separatist ethnonational groups and that often leads to violence.

broadcast from the capital, Kigali, appealing for help.[3] Those were her last public words. A Tutsi, she was soon dragged from her refuge in a UN compound and gunned down by Hutu militia.

One Nation, Multiple States

A **multistate nation** is another departure from the nation-state ideal. This type of mis-fit between nation and state occurs when a nation overlaps the borders of two or more states. Conflict between the states that share the nation is common (Woodwell, 2004).

One multistate nation pattern occurs when one nation dominates two or more states. The cold war created a number of such instances, including North and South Vietnam, North and South Korea, East and West Germany, and the two Yemens. The Irish in Ireland and Northern Ireland provide another possible example of a multi-state nation, although the Scottish heritage of many of the Protestants in the North makes the existence of a single Irish nationality controversial. In any case, a single nation that dominates two states has an urge to unite itself by merging the two states. Often conflict over union occurs, as it did in Vietnam, Korea, Ireland, and Yemen. Today only Korea (and arguably Ireland) remain as examples of such a division.

Another multistate nation pattern is where a nation is a majority in one state and a minority in one or more other states. The 5.7 million Albanians provide a good ex-ample of this type of multistate nation. Only 3.6 million of them live in Albania, where they are the overwhelming majority of the population. Another 1.6 million Albanians live in and make up 90% of the population in Kosovo, a province of Serbia and Montenegro (the renamed remnant of what was Yugoslavia). Fighting broke out in 1997 when Albanian Kosovars asserted their autonomy from the central government in Belgrade. The brutal campaign waged by Serbian-led forces eventually sparked a U.S.-led NATO air war against Serbia and Montenegro in 1999 and the insertion of a NATO security force, Kosovo Force (KFOR), into the province, where it remains.

A third concentration of about 500,000 Albanians live in and constitute almost 25% of the population of Macedonia. There the Albanians have clashed bloodily with the Macedonian-dominated government. "We must also fight for our freedom in Macedonia, just as Albanians are fighting for their freedom in Kosovo," proclaimed one ethnic Albanian in Macedonia.[4] Calm was restored in 2001 by another international peacekeeping force, first under NATO, then under European Union command. When tension abated, the EU troops were replaced by a small police contingent in 2004. What remains to be seen is whether the relative calm established by outside forces in Kosovo and Macedonia will persist or will sooner or later disintegrate amid the region's ancient ethnic rivalries.

To complicate matters in the region further, the Macedonians are also a multistate nation. The Macedonians in Yugoslavia declared their independence in 1991. However, about 1 million Macedonians, or 40% of that nation, live across the border to the south, in northern Greece. This leaves the Greeks understandably wary about the possibility that independent Macedonia might have designs on the Macedonians in Greece. In such situations where a nation is a majority in one state and a minority in one or more other states, "irredentist nationalism" is common (Hechter, 2000:16). **Irredentism**, a term based on the Italian word *irredenta* (unclaimed), is the drive to bring outlying members of the nation and their territory into the main nation-state.

One Nation, No State

A **stateless nation** is yet another pattern of misfit between state and nation. This occurs when a nation is a minority in one or more states, does not have a nation-state of its own, and wants one (Hossay, 2002). This drive has been termed "peripheral nationalism" (Hechter, 2000:16). Two such stateless nations that have been much in the news in recent years are the Kurds and the Palestinians.

The Kurds   The Kurds are an ancient non-Arab people who are mostly Sunni Muslims. The most famous of all Kurds was Saladin, the great defender of Islam. He captured Jerusalem from the Christians (1187) and then defended it successfully against England's King Richard I (the Lion-Heart) and the other invading Christians during the Third Crusade (1189–1192).

Estimates of the Kurdish population range between 14 million and 28 million. As the map on page 108 shows, the Kurds are spread among several states and have no country of their own. About half of them are in Turkey; Iran and Iraq each have another 20 to 25%; and smaller numbers reside in Armenia, Azerbaijan, and Syria. Sporadic and continuing attempts to establish an independent Kurdistan have caused conflicts with the countries in which the Kurds live. These disputes sometimes have involved outside countries. The United States and other countries protected the Kurds in the UN-designated Kurdish Security Zone in northern Iraq from attack by Saddam Hussein's regime in Baghdad. This arrangement lasted from soon after the Persian Gulf War in 1991 to the fall of Saddam Hussein in 2003 (Stansfield, 2005; McDowall, 2004).

Kurdish forces fought against the Iraqi army in 2003, thereby strengthening the autonomy they had enjoyed in the northern part of the country since 1991. What remains to be seen, and what worries Turkey and other neighbors of Iraq with Kurdish populations, is whether the Kurds in Iraq will be content to remain part of a reformed

Web Link

For a map showing the locations of ethnic Albanians in the Balkans and related commentary, visit the U.S. Institute for Peace site at **www.usip.org/pubs/ specialreports/early/ kosovomap.html**.

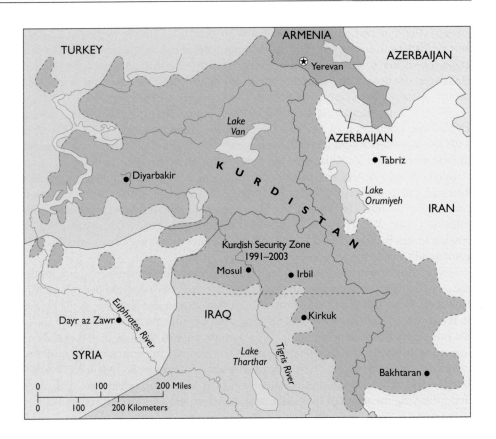

Iraq, or whether the autonomous region will serve as a base to militate for an independent Kurdistan that includes all or most of the Kurds in other countries and territories.

At least in the short term, Iraq's Kurds seem willing to join in the formulation of the postwar government of Iraq. Kurds participated fully in the legislative assembly election in early 2005 and won 28% of the seats. There was immediate tension with the majority Shiite Muslim bloc, however, over whether the Kurds would have regional autonomy or be fully subject to Baghdad's control. Perhaps the clearest sign of the Kurds' long-term aspiration was the result of an informal referendum held in conjunction with the parliamentary election. Fully 98% of all Kurds voted for eventual independence. "The fact remains that we are two different nationalities in Iraq—we are Kurds and Arabs," one Kurdish leader noted.[5]

Any attempt to establish an independent Kurdistan in northern Iraq would almost certainly have significant international ramifications. Turkey might well intervene militarily because of fears that its own sizeable Kurdish population might attempt to secede and join the new Kurdistan. Syria and other countries with Kurdish populations might also join the fighting as allies of the central government in Iraq. Yet other countries, those that have grievances with the members of a potential anti-Kurd alliance, might aid the Kurds, creating massive instability in the already-fragile region.

The Palestinians The story of the Palestinians centers on the fact that they and another nation, the Jewish people, have long existed in the same area. The Jewish nation and its state, Israel, now control most of that territory; the Palestinians intend to reclaim enough of it to create their own state. The ancient dispute dates back many millennia to Abraham and his two sons: Isaac, who founded the Jewish nation, and Ishmael, the symbolic father of all Arabs. The historical ebb and flow in the region of

Jews and Palestinians is cloudy and far too complex to unravel here, but we can pick up the story in 1920 when Palestine was governed by Great Britain. At that time, Palestinian Arabs were about 90% of the population.

In Europe, however, **Zionism** gathered strength in the 19th century. Zionism is the nationalist, not strictly religious, belief that Jews are a nation that should have an independent homeland. This belief and virulent anti-Semitism in Nazi Germany and elsewhere in Europe accelerated Jewish emigration to Palestine, swelling the Jewish population there from 56,000 in 1920 to 650,000 by 1948 (along with about 1 million Arabs). At that point, fighting for control erupted, the British withdrew, and Arab leaders rejected a UN plan to partition Palestine into a Jewish state and an Arab state. Israel won the ensuing war in 1948 and acquired some of the areas designated for the Arab state. About 500,000 Palestinians fled to refugee camps in Egyptian-controlled Gaza and elsewhere; another 400,000 came under the control of Jordan in an area called the West Bank (of the Jordan River), and 150,000 remained in the new state of Israel (Handelman, 2004).

Since then, Israel has fought and won three more wars with its Arab neighbors. In the 1967 war Israel captured considerable territory, including Gaza from Egypt and the West Bank (including East Jerusalem) from Jordan. Both these areas had major Palestinian populations. Victory, however, did not bring Israel peace or security. The key reason is the unresolved fate of the West Bank, which is central to Palestinians' quest for an independent homeland.

The struggle between Israelis and Palestinians for land, security, even survival has created an explosive situation that has defied resolution for over half a century. Surely, there have been times of progress. Most significantly, a majority of Israelis now grudgingly accept the idea that the Palestinians should have their own state. And most Palestinians, with equal reluctance, now concede the permanent existence of Israel and that a Palestinian state will be largely confined to the West Bank. However, each time of hope for resolution has been followed by renewed violence.

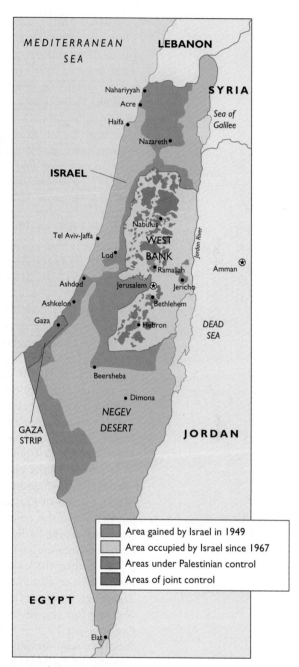

Area gained by Israel in 1949
Area occupied by Israel since 1967
Areas under Palestinian control
Areas of joint control

At this writing in 2005, the cycle of violence and hope was in a moderately positive phase after several years of ghastly terrorism in Israel, often carried out by suicide bombers, and Israeli reprisals in the West Bank and Gaza. The change came after the death of longtime Palestinian leader Yasser Arafat and his replacement in early 2005 by a new, popularly-elected leader, Mahmoud Abbas. He strongly denounced terrorist tactics and quickly took steps to try to constrain Palestinian militants. Israel responded with a number of conciliatory moves. Raising hopes further, Abbas and Prime Minister Ariel Sharon of Israel met in the first Israeli-Palestinian summit since 2000. The two agreed "to cease all violence against the Israelis and against the Palestinians, wherever they are," and encouragement poured in from around the world.[6]

Did You Know That:

A poll found that 16% of Israelis and 22% of Palestinians answered yes to the question, "Have you had a member of your immediate family killed in the fighting?"

Yet the hard lessons of history counsel caution about assuming the current upswing will last. Militants have murdered the dove of peace more than once in the Middle East. Not surprisingly then, the efforts of Abbas and Sharon to advance peace were soon beset by new terror attacks on Israel and Israeli retaliation. Moreover, even though most Palestinians and Israelis want peace, very difficult issues divide them (Nabulsi, 2004). Just a few of these are the status of Jerusalem (which both claim as their rightful capital), the Palestinians' claimed "right of return" to Israel to reclaim their land, the future of Jewish settlements in the West Bank, and the legitimacy of the security fence that Israel is building in part on lands claimed by the Palestinians. It may come to pass that Palestinians and Israelis will eventually coexist peacefully in neighboring sovereign states. But when Abbas was asked whether he expected to see that in his lifetime, he wisely was willing to say only, "I hope. I hope we will see it."

Multiple Nations, Multiple States

Still another misfit pattern that falls short of the ideal nation-state occurs when several states and several nations overlap. This complex configuration is common and is illustrated by Afghanistan, Russia, and their respective neighboring countries.

Afghanistan and Neighboring Countries   Afghanistan, the countries around it, and their ethnonational groups provide a prime example of the volatile mix created by overlapping borders among nations and states. Certainly Afghanistan exists as a legal state. Yet it is also struggling to escape its status as a **failed state**, a country so fragmented that it cannot be said to exist as a unified political or national entity. Symbolizing the ethnonational complexity within Afghanistan and the links that many of its groups have to nearby nations and countries, the word *Afghan* was coined over 1,000 years ago from an ancient Turkic word meaning "between." While there have been brief periods of some unity in the face of invaders or under strong rulers, the sense of being an Afghan has been much less central to the political identification of most people in the country than their ethnic identification. Afghanistan's ethnic groups (and their percentage of the population) include the Pashtuns (38%), Tajiks (25%), Hazaras (19%), and Uzbeks (6%), with smaller groups making up the remaining 12%. Even this diverse recounting underestimates Afghanistan's ethnic diversity. For example, the Pashtuns are divided into some 60 clans or tribes. Each has a traditional territory, and many of them have a history of armed conflict with one another.

Extending the focus outward to the neighboring countries increases the complexity of the ethnonational tangle. To begin, there are 10 million Pashtuns in Afghanistan and another 18 million in neighboring, Punjabi-dominated Pakistan. Together this stateless Pashtun nation has some aspirations to found its own state, Pashtunistan. Further to the north are the Tajiks, the Uzbeks, and a small number of Turkmen, who are linked respectively to their ethnic brethren in the neighboring countries of Tajikistan, Uzbekistan, and Turkmenistan. Then there are the Hazaras, who claim descent from Genghis Khan and the Mongols and harbor some dreams about an independent Hazarajat. These groups speak some 31 different languages and dialects. Pashto is the language of the Pashtuns. Tajiks, Hazaras, and some others groups speak variations of Dari, which is akin to Farsi, the language of Iran. The Uzbeks and Turkmen speak different, but related, Turkic dialects.

One ramification of this is that the United States has found that it was far easier to take over the country in 2001 and oust the Taliban regime than to create a viable, united Afghani state. The central problem, as one expert put it, is that "You don't have a functioning state [in Afghanistan]. There is no sense of nationhood. . . . Blood [kinship] is much more important."[7] Although Afghanistan now has an elected national government and there are no major efforts by an ethnonational group to take power or secede, this unity is partially a function of the multinational force that remains in the country. Whether the current fragile unity will survive or collapse once foreign troops depart remains to be seen.

Russia and Neighboring Countries   Czarist Russia and its successor state, the Soviet Union, were a multiethnic empire that dissolved in 1991 into Russia and 14 other former Soviet republics (FSRs). This left a hodgepodge of nations and states that frequently resembles a *matryoshka,* the classic nested Russian folk art doll in which each doll has a smaller one inside. For example, in addition to living in their own nation-state, Russians make up 10% or more of the populations of seven other FSRs (Belarus, Estonia, Kazakhstan, Kyrgyzstan, Latvia, Moldova, and Ukraine).

Russia itself is predominantly Russian, but it has some restive ethnonational groups, especially the Chechens. The approximately 1 million, mostly Muslim Chechens live in the northern Caucasus region just west of the Caspian Sea. Chechnya (or the Chechen Republic) encompasses about 6,000 square miles (a bit larger than Connecticut). Imperial Russia began a campaign in 1783 and eventually conquered the territory, but the Chechens' ongoing resistance was so strong that one Russian military governor warned there would be "no peace as long as a single Chechen remains alive."[8]

During World War II, Moscow deported the entire Chechen population to Siberia in the east because Soviet dictator Josef Stalin suspected the Chechens might assist the invading Germans in return for independence. More than one-third of all Chechens died during their time in Siberia, but they were unbowed. They were allowed to return to their native land in the mid-1950s but remained restive. Once the USSR dissolved, their quest for self-rule redoubled. Amid ferocious fighting that left 100,000 dead, the Chechens achieved autonomy in 1996, then lost it in 2000 when Russian arms again overran them. The struggle continues, however, with sporadic, often brutal fighting in Chechnya and occasional Chechen terrorist attacks in Russia. The most ghastly of these occurred in the Russian town of Beslan, where Chechen terrorists seized an elementary school in 2004. During the ensuing siege, 330 people, mostly Russian schoolchildren, died. For now, Russia maintains a tenuous hold on Chechnya, but current Russians leaders, like czars and commissars before them, are finding it daunting to subdue a people whose national anthem asserts in part:

> Never will we appear submissive before anyone,
> Death or Freedom—we can choose only one way. . . .
> We were born at night, when the she-wolf whelped.
> God, Nation, and the Native land.

Many of the other FSRs also have complicated ethnonational compositions. As noted above, Uzbeks and Tajiks

The lack of fit between nations and states often causes conflict. Most Chechens want an independent Chechnya, but Russia opposes their secession. This has led to violent, often horrific, acts by both sides. In one such incident, Chechens seized a school in Beslan, a town in a nearby province of Russia, holding hundreds of children, teachers, and others hostage. After a three-day standoff, a shootout between the Chechens and Russian security forces killed over 300 civilians, about half of them children, and wounded hundreds of others, including this boy being carried away by a rescuer.

not only live in Uzbekistan and Tajikistan respectively, they also live in Afghanistan. To complicate matters more, numerous Tajiks live in Uzbekistan, and many Uzbeks live in Tajikistan. Numerous separatist movements also exist in the European FSRs, including those in the South Ossetia and Abkhazia regions of Georgia, the so-called Transdniester Republic within Moldova, and the Nagorno-Karabakh enclave in Azerbaijan. Each has seen fighting that could spread and bring neighboring countries into conflict. This possibility led President Traian Basescu of nearby Romania to describe the tensions as "transnational threats" to European stability. "We cannot leave the countries of this region as victims of European history, as unstable borderlands outside Eastern Europe," Basescu warned.[9]

Positive and Negative Aspects of Nationalism

Nationalism has been a positive force, but it has also brought despair and destruction to the world. During an address to the UN General Assembly, Pope John Paul II spoke of these two nationalisms. One was *positive nationalism,* which the pontiff defined as the "proper love of one's country . . . [and] the respect which is due to every [other] culture and every nation."[10] The other was *negative nationalism,* "an unhealthy form of nationalism which teaches contempt for other nations or cultures . . . [and] seeks to advance the well-being of one's own nation at the expense of others."

Positive Nationalism

Most scholars agree that in its philosophical and historical genesis, nationalism was a positive force. It continues to have a number of possible beneficial effects and many defenders (Conway, 2004, Wiebe, 2002).

Nationalism promotes democracy. In the view of one scholar, "Nationalism is the major form in which democratic consciousness expresses itself in the modern world" (O'Leary, 1997:222). The logic is that nationalism, at least in so far as it is rooted in the notion of popular sovereignty, promotes the idea that political power legitimately resides with the people and that governors exercise that power only as the agents of the people. The democratic nationalism that helped spur the American Revolution has spread globally, especially since World War II, increasing the proportion of the world's countries that are fully democratic from 28% in 1950 to 46% in 2005.

Nationalism discourages imperialism. During the past 100 years alone, nationalism has played a key role in the demise of the contiguous Austro-Hungarian, Ottoman, and Russian empires and of all or most of the colonial empires controlled by Belgium, France, Great Britain, Italy, the Netherlands, Portugal, and the United States. More recently, nationalism was the driving force behind the birth of the newest state, East Timor. It was one of the last remnants of the moribund Portuguese empire when its people declared independence in 1975. Freedom was stillborn, however, when Indonesia annexed it in a bloody takeover that cost some 60,000 East Timorese lives. For the East Timorese, Indonesian overlords were no more acceptable than European ones, and their campaign for self-determination continued. This drive and considerable international pressure finally persuaded Indonesia to allow a referendum on independence in 1998. Seventy-nine percent of the East Timorese voted for independence. In a desperate effort to thwart independence, Indonesia's military armed a horde of thugs who slaughtered thousands of East Timorese and destroyed vast amounts of property. The devastation was finally stopped when Australia and the United Nations intervened militarily. The UN created a transitional administration for East Timor, then turned the government over to a fully independent East Timor on May 20, 2002.

Nationalism has also strengthened the resolve of other countries and their nation(s) to resist foreign domination. A century ago, the establishment of a colonial government controlled by the victorious power might have followed a conflict such as the Iraq war of 2003. Certainly the initial postwar government in Baghdad was heavily influenced by the Americans, but it was clear that real power soon would have to be turned over to Iraqis. Global norms would have reacted too strongly against a colonial takeover. Moreover, even if that had been the U.S. intention, it soon became clear that Iraqis, whatever their ethnic and religious internal divisions, were opposed to control of their country by any outside power. The transition to a fully sovereign Iraq took an important step forward in 2005 with the first national elections and the formation of a new government under Prime Minister Ibrahim al-Jaafari.

Nationalism allows for economic development. Colonies and minority nations within states have often been shortchanged economically. Many countries in Africa and elsewhere are still struggling to overcome a colonial legacy in which the colonial power siphoned off resources for its own betterment and did little to build the economic infrastructure of the colony. This pattern also occurred in theoretically integrated multiethnic empires, such as the Soviet Union. There, the six predominantly Muslim FSRs (Azerbaijan, Kazakhstan, Kyrgyzstan, Tajikistan, Turkmenistan, and Uzbekistan) were neglected under Russian/Soviet control and still have an average per capita gross domestic product (GDP) that is only one-third of Russia's and a child mortality rate that is more than quadruple that of Russia. It is certain that these new countries face years of economic hardship, but, from their perspective, at least their efforts will be devoted to their own betterment.

Nationalism allows diversity and experimentation. Democracy, for instance, was an experiment in America in 1776 that might not have occurred in a one-world system dominated by monarchs. Diversity also allows different cultures to maintain their own values. Some analysts argue that regional or world political organization might lead to an amalgamation of cultures or, worse, to cultural imperialism, the suppression of the cultural uniqueness of the weak by the strong. For good or ill, as chapter 5 details, the world is coming closer together culturally. However, nationalism embodied in sovereign states at least helps ensure that whatever acculturation occurs will generally be adopted willingly by the people rather than dictated by an outside power.

Negative Nationalism

For all its contributions, nationalism also has a dark side. "Militant nationalism is on the rise," Bill Clinton cautioned early in his presidency. He warned that it is "transforming the healthy pride of nations, tribes, religious, and ethnic groups into cancerous prejudice, eating away at states and leaving their people addicted to the political painkillers of violence and demagoguery."[11] Illustrating this, Figure 4.1 on page 114 shows that the number of ongoing ethnonational conflicts over self-determination rose steadily from 4 in 1956 to 41 in 1990. Then the number declined steadily to 22 in 2004. Perhaps ethnonational conflict will continue to decline, but it is too early to tell (Fearon & Laitin, 2003). Unfortunately, whatever the number of conflicts, the intensity and magnitude of ethnonational conflicts remain high. Moreover, these internal conflicts can become internationalized given the evidence that "states suffering from ethnic rebellions are more likely to use force and to use force first when involved in international disputes than states without similar insurgency problems" (Trumbore, 2003:183).

Although it has a number of aspects, the troubling face of nationalism begins with how nations relate to one another. By definition, nationalism is feeling a kinship

JOIN THE DEBATE
Can Nationalism Go Too Far?

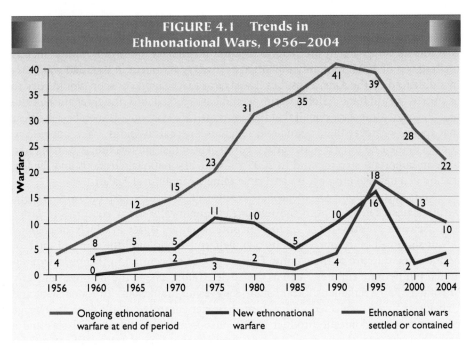

FIGURE 4.1 Trends in Ethnonational Wars, 1956–2004

Ethnonational conflict rose rapidly beginning in the 1960s and peaked in the late 1980s. It has declined since then because many conflicts have been settled and fewer new conflicts have broken out. Still, ethnonational fighting remains much more common than other forms of internal conflict or wars between countries.

Note: New wars are those beginning since the end of the previous earlier date. Completed wars are those settled or won since the previous earlier date.
Data source: Marshall & Gurr (2003); "Major Episodes of Political Violence: 1946–2004," data compiled by Monty G. Marshall, Center for Systemic Peace.

with the other "like" people who make up the nation. Differentiating ourselves from others is not intrinsically bad, but it is only a small step from the salutary effects of positively valuing our we-group to the negative effects of nationalism. Because we identify with our we-group, we tend to consider the they-group as apart from us. This lack of identification with others often leads to a reluctance to help others, exclusionism, exceptionalism and xenophobia, internal oppression, and external aggression.

Reluctance to Help Others   Our nationalist sense of difference and separateness limits our sense of responsibility—even our human caring—for the "theys." Most of us not only want to help others in our we-group, but we feel we have a duty to do so through national social welfare budgets and other methods. Internationally, most of us feel much less responsible. Horrendous conditions and events that occur in other countries often evoke little notice relative to the outraged reaction that would be forthcoming if they happened in our own country. In sub-Saharan Africa, for example, the prevalence of HIV/AIDS is 371 times higher than in the United States. Only 41% of that region's people live to age 55, compared to 80% of Americans. And the chances of an infant in sub-Saharan Africa perishing before his or her first birthday are 15 times greater than the risk to American babies.

If most Americans began dying before retirement age or if the death rate of American babies skyrocketed, there would be an outburst of national anguish in the United States, and vast financial resources would flow to increase adult longevity and

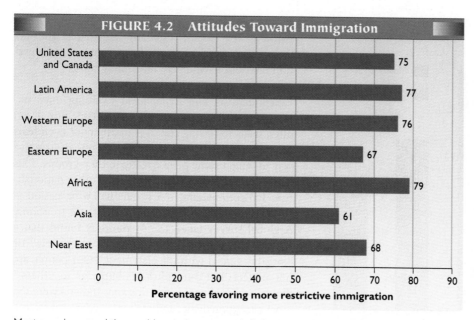

FIGURE 4.2   Attitudes Toward Immigration

United States and Canada — 75
Latin America — 77
Western Europe — 76
Eastern Europe — 67
Africa — 79
Asia — 61
Near East — 68

Percentage favoring more restrictive immigration

Most people around the world are reluctant to admit foreign immigrants to their country because of the "we-they" differentiation people make between their nation and others. Globally, 68% of those polled felt that way, as shown in a recent survey, with a majority of respondents in every region favoring tighter restrictions on immigration.

Note: The question asked people to agree or disagree with the statement, "We should restrict and control entry of people into our country more than we do now."
Data source: Pew Research Center (2002).

decrease the infant mortality rate. Yet, the U.S. response to the equivalent human tragedy in sub-Saharan Africa is largely limited to sending about $2 billion in economic and humanitarian aid—bilateral (to individual countries) and multilateral (through international organizations)—to the region. This comes to about $3 per person in sub-Saharan Africa or about $7 per American. Is this enough? Americans seem to think so. A poll found that 60% of them thought their country was spending too much on foreign aid. Only 9% thought it too little.[12] In part, that is because, on average, Americans think that 31% of the federal budget goes to foreign aid.[13] The actual percentage is about 1% for all foreign aid, with about 0.7% for economic assistance. Ironically, the average respondent thought foreign aid should be cut to 19% of the federal budget, which would actually be a monumental increase. None of this means that Americans are particularly mean spirited. They are not. It is simply that, like people in other countries, they have a sense of responsibility for citizens of their own country, but not toward those of other countries. Therefore, most people contend, government aid should go primarily toward addressing needs "at home" rather than abroad.

Exclusionism   Each year, millions of people are forced or seek to flee from their homes due to political violence, poverty, and other forces beyond their control. Indeed, as chapter 14 details, refugees are a global problem. The we-they basis of nationalism creates a near-universal resistance of "them" coming to "our" country. A survey of people in 40 countries found that on average 76% of them wanted to further their country's limits on immigration, as detailed in Figure 4.2. A strong majority of Americans (81%) and Canadians (69%) felt that way, even though most of them come from immigrant stock. Opinion in the two countries with the smallest percentage of

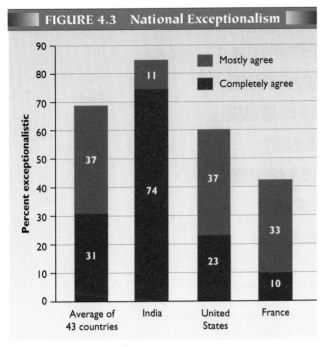

FIGURE 4.3   National Exceptionalism

Exceptionalism, feeling that your culture is superior to others, is one negative aspect of nationalism. One recent survey of 43 countries found that 68% of people "completely agree" or "mostly agree" that "our people are not perfect, but our culture is superior to others." This included majorities in all but four countries (Angola, France, Germany, and Great Britain). The people of India were the most exceptionalistic. Especially note the astounding 74% of Indians who completely agreed. The French were the least exceptionalistic, with Americans expressing that view a bit less than average.

Data source: Pew Research Center (2003).

people favoring more restrictions, Japan (43%) and South Korea (37%), ironically may reflect the fact that both countries already have stringent immigration restrictions and very few immigrants.

Exceptionalism and Xenophobia   Valuing one's nation is a positive aspect of nationalism, but it too often leads to feeling superior to others or even fearing and hating them. **Xenophobia** is one destructive way in which some people relate to they-groups. This emotion involves disliking or fearing other nationalities. **Exceptionalism**, the belief that your nation is better than others, is less virulent but still troubling. A global survey taken in 43 countries found that a majority of people in 39 of them "completely" or "mostly" agreed with the statement, "Our people are not perfect, but our culture is superior to others." Overall, 68% of people felt this way. Indians were the most exceptionalistic, and, defying a common stereotype, the French were least exceptionalistic. The view of people in these two countries and others is shown in Figure 4.3. Some critics charge that among other recent instances, the Wilsonian impulse to advance democracy in the world that helped persuade the Bush administration to invade Iraq is an example of the exceptionalist urge to reshape the world in your own image (Lieven, 2004).

Xenophobia and exceptionalism often lead to conflict (Marx, 2003; Wimmer, 2002; Kateb, 2000). This reality moved Voltaire to lament in 1764 that "it is sad that being a good patriot often means being the enemy of the rest of mankind."[14] Feelings of hatred between groups are especially powerful if there is a history of conflict or oppression. Past injuries inflicted "by another ethnic group [are] remembered mythically as though the past were the present."[15] Understanding the intensity that xenophobia can reach helps explain much of what has happened in the Balkans since the early 1990s. An emotional catalyst for Serbs centers on the Battle of Kosovo in 1389. In it, the Ottoman Turks defeated Serbia's Prince Lazar, thus beginning five centuries of Muslim domination. The battle, according to one commentary, is "venerated among the Serbs in the same way Texans remember the Alamo." Adds Serb historian Dejan Medakovic, "Our morals, ethics, mythology were created at that moment, when we were overrun by the Turks. Kosovo . . . has permeated the Serbian people."[16] The festering mythic wound of 1389 for the predominately Christian Orthodox Serbs spilled its poison through their so-called ethnic cleansing attacks on Bosnian Muslims in the early 1990s, then on Kosovar Muslims later in the decade.

Web Link

The impact of the Battle of Kosovo (1389) on the Serbs' sense of oppression is captured in the heroic painting *The Maiden of Kosovo* and the epic poem of the same title, both available at: **www.kosovo.com/sk/history/dorich_kosovo/kosovo16.htm.**

Internal Oppression   In those states with a dominant ethnonational group and one or more minority groups, the dominant group almost always has political, economic, and social advantages over the other(s). At its extreme, dominant groups sometimes violently suppress minority groups or even attempt genocide. This aptly characterizes the Serbs' ethnic cleansing frenzy in Bosnia and Kosovo, the genocidal attacks on the Tutsis by the Hutus in Rwanda, and the recent murderous campaign against black Christian and black Muslim groups by Arab Muslims in Sudan. An even more horrific example occurred in Nazi Germany, where Adolf Hitler preached in *Mein Kampf* that pure Germans were an "Aryan nation" that epitomized human development. By contrast, Russians and other Slavic people were considered marginal humans to be kept as virtual and expendable slaves in segregated and degrading conditions. Jews and Gypsies were "nonpeople" and "racial vermin" to be exterminated, along with the insane and homosexuals.

The earlier, multinational state of Yugoslavia, since renamed Serbia and Montenegro, collapsed because it did not command the internal loyalty of most of its people. Instead, Yugoslavia atomized amid deadly conflict into the states and restive provinces shown here.

Even in less dire circumstances, when the oppression of minorities is limited to economic and social deprivation, conflict often occurs. Almost inevitably, the disadvantaged groups become restive. However, their complaints often get little positive response because, as UN Secretary-General Kofi Annan has pointed out, the social and economic inequality of minority groups "tends to be reflected in unequal access to political power that too often forecloses paths to peaceful change."[17] Not surprisingly, oppressed groups then take direct action if they are unable to resolve their grievances through the legal or political processes. In more fortunate countries, these take the form of protest marches, economic boycotts, and other peaceful tactics. The strategy followed by American blacks led by the Reverend Martin Luther King during the 1960s serves as an example. Other countries are less fortunate, and many of the numerous ethnonational wars represented in Figure 4.1 have been the result of frustrated minority groups taking up arms when less violent avenues of action led nowhere.

External Aggression   Negative nationalism can lead to external aggression based on the belief that it is acceptable to conquer or otherwise incorporate other nations. Russian/Soviet history provides an example. The country was a classic multiethnic empire built on territories seized by centuries of czarist Russian expansion and furthered by Soviet arms. From its beginning 500 years ago as the 15,000-square-mile Duchy of Moscovy (half the size of Maine), Russia/the USSR grew to be the world's largest country. This expansion is shown in the map on page 118. Many of those territories were lost in 1991 when the Soviet Union fragmented, and Russia's weakened position precludes any determined attempt to reassert its earlier domination of its neighbors. Indeed, old-fashioned imperialism may have become too costly economically and diplomatically to pursue in the future.

Yet it may be well to remember the warning of Karl Marx (1818–1883) that "the policy of Russia is changeless. Its methods, its tactics, its maneuvers may change, but the polar star of its policy—world domination—is a fixed star."[18] Indications that Marx may have been right continue (Bugajski, 2004). For example, Russia's parliament, the Duma, passed a resolution asserting that the dissolution of the Soviet Union (and, by inference, the independence of the FSRs) was illegal and another in 2001 welcoming secessionist areas from other FSRs to (re)join Russia. "What Russian deputies did reveals their neo-imperialistic ambitions," a diplomat from a neighboring FSR worried.[19] An attempt in 2004 to repeal the 2001 act was overwhelmingly defeated.

Evidence of Russian ambitions were arguably once again revealed when President Putin attempted to intervene in Ukraine in December 2004 in support of the blatantly fraudulent presidential election of Russian-leaning candidate Prime Minister Viktor Yanukovych over Western-leaning Viktor Yushchenko. When Yushchenko's

500 Years of Russian Expansion

Grand Duchy of Moscovy, 1462

1462–1689

1689–1801

1801–1904

1904–1991

—— Present Boundary

Nationalism has positive and negative effects, and both are illustrated in the history of Russia. Among the negative effects, nationalism often prompts expansionism. The Grand Duchy of Moscovy was about half the size of Maine when it was founded in about 1480. It expanded under Russian czars and then Soviet commissars to become what was the world's largest country.

supporters staged massive protests demanding a new vote, and leaders from the United States, EU, and elsewhere supported them, Putin warned other countries "not to meddle and apply pressure." In the end, democracy prevailed. Yushchenko's supporters refused to be intimidated by the threat of violent reprisals, and unrelenting world pressure forced Putin to back down. A new election with international observers and a much different result was held in January 2005, and, soon thereafter President Yushchenko was inaugurated.

Self-Determination as a Goal

An additional gap between the ideal and reality of nationalism is related to the wisdom of self-determination as a goal (Danspeckgruber, 2002). As with nationalism generally, there are positive and negative aspects of self-determination.

Positive Aspects of Self-Determination

Many observers have lauded the principle of self-determination. For one, American philosopher William James (1842–1910) judged "the attempt of a people long enslaved to attain the possession of itself, to organize its laws and government, to be free to follow its internal destinies, according to its own ideals" to be "the sacredest thing in this great human world."[20] Similarly, President Woodrow Wilson believed that "self-determinism is not a mere phrase. It is an imperative principle of action."[21] Moreover, the origins of many nation-states are rooted in the demand for self-determination of their nation. For example, the Declaration of Independence begins with the proclaimed determination of Americans to "assume among the powers of the earth, the separate and equal station to which the laws of nature and of nature's God entitle them."

Certainly, there are numerous reasons to support self-determination. In addition to the benefits of nationalism noted earlier, self-determination ends many of the abuses that stem from ethnic oppression. If all ethnic groups were allowed to peacefully found their own sovereign units or join those of their ethnic brethren, then the tragedies of Bosnia, Chechnya, East Timor, Kosovo, Rwanda, Sudan, and many other strife-torn peoples and countries would not have occurred.

Concerns About Self-Determination

The principle of self-determination becomes more problematic in practice. The core problem is that there are thousands of ethnic groups worldwide. Each has the potential to develop a national consciousness and to seek independence or autonomy. If the principle of self-determination is valid, then what would the world be like if each of these groups was able to establish its own sovereign state? Before dismissing such an idea as absurd, recall that political scientists widely recognize the existence of Barber's (1996) tribalism tendency: the urge to break away from current political arrangements and, often, to form into smaller units. To do so involves several potential problems.

Untangling Groups   Untangling groups is one challenge presented by self-determination. Various nations are intermingled in many places. Bosnia is such a place; Bosnian Muslims, Croats, and Serbs often lived in the same cities, on the same streets, in the same apartment buildings. How does one disentangle these groups and assign them territory when each wants to declare its independence or to join with its ethnic kin in an existing country?

A second problem that the principle of self-determination raises is the prospect of dissolving existing states, ranging from Canada (Quebec), through Great Britain (Scotland and Wales), to Spain (Basque region and Catalonia). Americans also need to ponder this problem. They have long advocated the theory of a right of self-determination. One has to wonder, however, how Wilson would have applied this principle to national minorities in the United States. Should, for example, the principle of self-determination mean that Americans support those native Hawaiians who claim correctly that they were subjugated by Americans a century ago and who want to reestablish an independent Hawaii?

In other places, creating ethnically homogeneous states would have multiple complexities. To create nation-states out of the various ethnonational groups in Afghanistan would require disentangling many places where the groups overlap. It would also include some groups joining neighboring countries such as Tajikistan and Uzbekistan. But then what would happen to the Tajiks who live in Uzbekistan and the Uzbeks who live in Tajikistan? And in the case of the Pashtuns, a Pashtunistan would have to be created by pieces taken out of Pakistan and Iran, as well as Afghanistan.

Microstates   A third problem of self-determination relates to the rapidly growing number of independent countries, many of which have a marginal ability to survive on their own. Is it wise to allow the formation of **microstates**, countries with tiny populations, territories, and/or economies? Such countries have long existed, with Andorra, Monaco, and San Marino serving as examples. But in recent years, as colonialism has become discredited, many more of these microstates have become established. The problems microstates created are detailed in chapter 6. We can say here, though, that about one-third of the world's countries have populations smaller than

ANALYZE THE ISSUE
Taiwan

Self-determination, the idea that every nation should be free to govern itself, is a noble thought. In practice, though, it can lead to difficulties, including the creation of microstates that have little ability to defend or support themselves. The newest country, East Timor, was born on May 20, 2002, but the joy that the East Timorese felt was soon overtaken by the country's crushing problems. With an annual per capita gross domestic product of just $520, many East Timorese are as poor as this mother and child shown here in the country's capital, Dili.

that of Los Angeles, California, and about 10% have less land than that city. Such countries often cannot defend themselves, economically sustain themselves, or both. This incapacity to perform one or both of two basic obligations of a state—to provide for the security and the economic welfare of its citizens—undermines such states' reason for being, increases economic burdens on the rest of the world, and creates potentially unstable power vacuums.

International Instability   Allowing current states to fragment could also decrease regional and even world stability. The concern about microstates has already been discussed. Another type of threat to international stability related to self-determination was set in motion by the U.S. invasion of Iraq in 2003. Among other consequences, toppling Saddam Hussein increased the potential for a dismembered Iraq. It is divided among the majority Shiite Muslims, Sunni Muslims (who dominated under Saddam Hussein), and Kurds. As noted earlier, most Kurds' ultimate goal is an independent Kurdistan. If Iraq's Kurds tried to establish such a state, other countries in the region with a Kurdish population would fear destabilization as their Kurds sought to join an independent Kurdistan. Turkey would be especially likely to use military force to abort an independent Kurdistan in order to prevent its substantial Kurdish population from being draw into the nascent state. Yet another concern about a fragmented Iraq is that Shiite-dominated Iraq would gain power in the region. In part this might result from Iranian influence among Iraqi Shiites. Additionally, a weakened Iraq would no longer be an effective buffer separating Iran from Saudi Arabia and the other oil-rich Arab states that lie to the south of Iraq along the western shore of the Persian Gulf. For now, the presence of U.S. and other foreign troops will keep Iraq from atomizing, but it is unclear what will ensue once Iraq is left exclusively to the Iraqis.

Deciding About Self-Determination   Existing countries face important choices when deciding whether to recognize new countries. Among other things, as new countries come into existence, the global community, through its commitments to the United Nations and to the integrity of the international system, acquires some obligation to assist them in the face of external aggression. Similarly, new and impoverished states add pressure on already inadequate international economic assistance through donor countries and international organizations. Furthermore, recognizing secessionist movements as new states arguably encourages yet more ethnonational groups to seek independence.

Given that there is a large array of ethnonational groups with aspirations to self-determination that believe their goals are just as legitimate as were American goals in 1776, the issue is whether to support them at all, or if not, which ones and why? Some commentators advocate broad support of self-determination, which one analyst calls "the most powerful idea in the contemporary world" (Lind, 1994:88). Others reply that "self-determination movements . . . have largely exhausted their legitimacy. . . . It is time to withdraw moral approval from most of the movements and see them for what they mainly are—destructive" (Etzioni, 1993:21; Dahbour, 2003). Between these two ends of the spectrum of opinion, many seek a set of standards by which to judge whether or not a claim to the right of secession is legitimate.

One such standard is whether a minority people is being discriminated against by a majority population. Perhaps it would be wiser for the international community

WRITE THE POLICY SCRIPT

Self-Determination: Good for One, Good for All?

An old axiom tells us that "What's good for the goose, is good for the gander." It cautions against the hypocrisy of favoring one thing for ourselves (the geese) and objecting to the same thing for others (the ganders). Perhaps believing in equal treatment for geese and ganders tell us something about how we should feel about self-determination for others, as well as ourselves.

As the text notes, the United States and most other countries were born amid nationalistic assertions of a claimed right to self-determination. Since then, President Woodrow Wilson and other U.S. leaders have also lauded the importance of the principle of self-determination.

It is difficult to argue with such a lofty principle in the abstract. Harder, though, is supporting it when it threatens to dismember your own country. For instance, if you are an American, how would you feel about returning Hawaii to its original owners, Native Hawaiians, and granting it independence? Hawaii was a sovereign country until it was incorporated into the United States in 1898 against the will of its native people. An active Hawaiian independence movement exists, and when a referendum was held in 1996 among Native Hawaiians about their preferences for the future, 73% voted for independence.

There are other groups living in the United States who were also incorporated into the country without their consent. Aleuts, Alaskan Indians, and other Native Alaskans were first dominated by Russia, then sold to the United States in 1867. Mexico once held all or part of Arizona, California, Colorado, New Mexico, Nevada, Texas, and Utah until the United States seized those territories by war in 1848 and involuntarily converted the Mexicans living there into Mexican Americans. Now the ancestors of those first Mexican Americans, supplemented by more recent immigrants from Mexico, are a growing part of the populations of those states and could one day be a majority in some of them. Would they have a claim to self-determination?

What Do You Think?

Is the right to self-determination claimed by American colonial geese in 1776 equally a right for Native Hawaiian ganders today? The same question can be asked about Native Alaskans and Mexican Americans, but for now, concentrate on writing the policy script for the future of Hawaii.

to guarantee human and political rights for minority cultural groups than to support self-determination to the point of *reductio ad absurdum*. Whatever the standard, though, it is certain that applying the principle of self-determination is difficult in a complex world (Ramet, 2000; Talbott, 2000). How would you write the script for self-determination in the future? That is the question asked in the decision box, "Self-Determination: Good for One, Good for All?"

Web Link

For more information on the Native Hawaiian independence movement, visit its Web site at www.hawaii-nation.org/.

Nationalism and the Future

People have almost certainly always identified with one or another group, be it based on family, extended clan, religion, or some other basis. However, nationalism, the particular form of political identification that welds a mutually identifying people, their territory, and self-governance is much more recent. Some scholars find traces of nationalism extending back to ancient times, but there is little disagreement that nationalism has only been an important political idea for about the past 500 years and that it did not reach its current ascendancy as a source of primary political identification until the 19th and 20th centuries.

What of the future, though? Since nationalism has not always been, it is not immutable. It could weaken or even disappear as our dominant sense of political identification. In addition to recognizing this possibility, we should ask ourselves how we would evaluate the persistence or demise of nationalism. Would that be positive or negative?

The Recent Past and Present of Nationalism

Nationalism continues to thrive and dominate our political consciousness in most ways. Yet, doubts about nationalism have increased in some circles. It has weakened somewhat, and there are those who predict and/or advocate its further diminution or even its extinction as the primary focus of political identification.

The Predicted Demise of Nationalism

World War II changed the thinking of many people about nationalism. They blamed fascism and other forms of virulently aggressive nationalism for the war itself, and for the other horrors of the period. Moreover, critics argued that the second global war in 30 years demonstrated that the state system based on national antagonism was not only outdated, but dangerous. The advent of weapons of mass destruction added urgency to the case, making "the nation and the nation-state . . . anachronisms in the atomic age."[22] As a counterpoint, the establishment of the United Nations in 1945 symbolized the desire to progress from competitive, often conflictive nationalism toward cooperative globalism.

The thrust of this thinking led numerous scholars to predict the imminent demise of the national state or, at least, its gradual withering away. As it turned out, such retirement announcements and obituaries proved reminiscent of the day in 1897 when an astonished Mark Twain read in the paper that he had died. Reasonably sure that he was still alive, Twain hastened to assure the world: "The reports of my death are greatly exaggerated." Similarly, one scholar notes that contrary to predictions of nationalism's impending extinction, "this infuriatingly persistent anomaly . . . refused to go away" (Wiebe, 2001:2). Instead, nationalism gained strength as a world force.

Persistent Nationalism

The continued strength of nationalism is unquestionable. Insistence on national self-determination has almost tripled the number of states in existence since World War II. For most of this time, the primary force behind the surge of nationalism was the anti-imperialist independence movements in Africa, Asia, and elsewhere. More recently, nationalism has reasserted itself in Europe. Germany reemerged when West Germany and East Germany reunited. More commonly, existing states disintegrated. Yugoslavia dissolved into five countries and Czechoslovakia became two states. Soon another state became 15 countries when the last great multiethnic empire, the vast realm of Russia, then the USSR, atomized. Except for East Timor, Eritrea, Namibia, and Palau, all of the states that have achieved independence since 1989 are in Eastern Europe or are FSRs. There are also nationalist stirrings—in some cases demands—among the Scots, Irish, and Welsh in Great Britain; the Basques and Catalans in Spain; and among other ethnonational groups elsewhere in Europe.

Another sign of persistent nationalism is the continuing attachment of people to their countries (Gijsberts, Hagendoorn, & Scheepers, 2004). As detailed in Figure 4.4, one cross-national survey found that nearly 80% of all people polled said they would rather be a citizen of their own country than any other. Somewhat unexpectedly, the strength of nationalist sentiment was not connected to a country's economic circumstances. For example, among those in relatively poor countries, 85% of Bulgarians and 87% of Filipinos felt that way. By contrast, only 63% of those in relatively wealthy Italy shared that view (Smith & Jarkko, 1998). Asking people if they would move to another country yields similar results. One such poll found that only 18% of those in relatively poor India would do so, while 38% of those in comparatively well-off Great Britain would.[23]

The Future of Nationalism

It may seem contradictory, but the continuing strength of nationalism does not necessarily mean that those who earlier predicted its demise were wrong. Perhaps they were only premature. This possibility is raised by numerous signs that nationalism is waning and that states are weakening. Therefore, a critical question is whether nationalism will significantly weaken or even die out.

The answer is unclear. The existence of divergent political identities based on community, language, religion, and other cultural differences extend as far back into time as we can see (Smith, 2005; Smith, 2004). From a biblical perspective, there may have been a single people at the time of Adam and Eve and their immediate descendants. But later in the first book of the Bible, God divides them after they attempt to build the Tower of Babel up to the heavens. To defeat that pretentious plan, God creates different languages to complicate communication. "Behold," God commands, "the people is one, and they have all one language. . . . [L]et us go down, and there confound their language, that they may not understand one another's speech" (Genesis 11:6–7).

Whether this tale is taken literally or symbolically, the point is that diverse cultural identities are ancient and, some analysts would say, important—perhaps inherent—human traits, stemming from the urge to have the psychological security of belonging to a we-group. It may be, for example, that being a member of a nation both "enables an individual to find a place . . . in the world [in] which he or she lives" and also to find "redemption from personal oblivion" through a sense of being part of "an uninterrupted chain of being" (Tamir, 1995:432). Yet it must also be said that group identification and nationalism are not synonymous. The sense of sovereignty attached to cultural identification is relatively modern. "Nationalism and nations have not been permanent features of human history," as one scholar puts it (O'Leary, 1997:221). Therefore, nationalism, having not always existed, will not necessarily always be the world's principal form of political orientation.

What does the future hold? One view is that nationalism will continue as the main source of political identification. "Given that globalization has done little to diminish the nation's political [and] ideological . . . appeal—and in many cases has invigorated it," one scholar writes, "we are stuck with the nation—politically, academically, practically, and theoretically" (Croucher, 2003:21). Others expect nationalism to eventually cease to be an important political phenomenon. The most common view among political scientists is a middle position that holds that nationalism will persist for the foreseeable future as a key sense of the political identification of most people but that it will not enjoy the unrivaled center stage presence it has had for several hundred years.

Also unclear is what would follow if state-centric nationalism were to die out. One possibility is that it will be replaced by culture, religion, or some other demographic characteristic as the primary sense of political self. Alternatively, a sense of

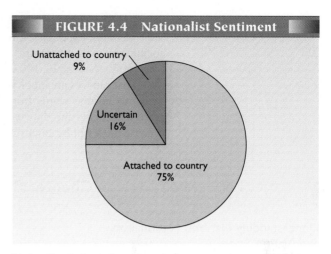

FIGURE 4.4 Nationalist Sentiment

Unattached to country
9%

Uncertain
16%

Attached to country
75%

Nationalism is the feeling that makes most people attached to their country. One survey found that three-fourths of the people polled in 22 countries worldwide felt that way. Only a small percentage were ambivalent; even fewer people were emotionally unattached to their country.

Note: The question asked people about the statement, "I would rather be a citizen of [their country] than any other in the world." "Attached" includes those who "agreed" and "strongly agreed." "Uncertain" includes those who said "neither agree nor disagree" or "can't choose." "Unattached" includes those who replied, "disagree" or "strongly disagree."
Data source: Smith & Jarkko (1998).

Did You Know That:

There are 6,809 languages spoken in the world. That is a decline of 306 since 1600, with another 500 or so currently in danger of extinction.

ANALYZE THE ISSUE
Nationalism: A Melting Pot?

global nationalism could emerge based on the similarities among all humans and their common experiences, needs, and goals. One such scholar envisages "a nation coextensive with humanity" that would then come together in a "United States of the World" (Greenfeld, 1992:7).

What can we conclude? Will nationalism persist "until the last syllable of recorded time," to borrow words from Shakespeare's *Macbeth*? More importantly, should it, given its benefits and drawbacks? You can help supply the answer to these questions because the script for tomorrow's drama on the world stage has yet to be written.

Chapter Summary

Understanding Nations, Nationalism, and Nation-States

1. Nationalism is one of the most important factors in international politics. It defines where we put our primary political loyalty, and that is in the nation-state. Today the world is divided and defined by nationalism and nation-states.

2. Nations, nation-states, and nationalism are all key concepts that must be carefully defined and clearly differentiated and understood.

3. The political focus on nationalism has evolved and become ascendant over the last five centuries.

Nationalism in Practice: Issues and Evaluation

4. There are differences between the theory of nationalism and its application. To evaluate nationalism objectively, these must be considered.

5. One issue is that the ideal nation-state is more myth than reality. In practice the boundaries of nations and the borders of states are seldom congruent.

6. Another issue is negative aspects, as well as positive aspects of nationalism.

7. The problems associated with nationalism also raise issues about self-determination and the question of whether this liberal ideal is always wise in the real world.

Nationalism and the Future

8. After World War II, some predicted an end to nationalism, but they were wrong. Today nationalism is stronger, and the independence of Afro-Asian countries, the former Soviet republics, and other states has made it even more inclusive.

9. In a world of transnational global forces and problems, many condemn nationalism as outmoded and perilous. Some even predict its decline and demise. Such predictions are, however, highly speculative, and nationalism will remain a key element and a powerful force in the foreseeable future.

For simulations, debates, and other interactive activities, a chapter quiz, Web links, PowerWeb articles, and much more, visit **www.mhhe.com/rourke11/** and go to chapter 4. Or, while accessing the site, click on Course-Related Headlines and view recent international relations articles in the *New York Times*.

Online *Learning*Center with POWERWEB

Key Terms

ethnonational group
exceptionalism
failed state
ideology
irredentism

microstates
multinational state
multistate nation
nation
nationalism

nation-state
political identity
popular sovereignty
self-determination
state building

stateless nation
xenophobia
Zionism

Globalization and Transnationalism: The Alternative Orientation

What wouldst thou do with the world,
... if it lay in thy power?
—William Shakespeare, *Timon of Athens*

Why, here's a change indeed in the commonwealth!
What shall become of me?
—William Shakespeare, *Measure for Measure*

When Rudyard Kipling predicted in 1889 that "East is East, and West is West, and never the twain shall meet," he could not have foreseen the degree to which this chapter's subject matter, globalization and transnationalism, would prove him wrong. Now you could e-mail this Cambodian Buddhist monk, swap computer files with him, or use your ability to communicate globally to form a transnational group to promote your common interests.

MOST OF US ARE COMFORTABLE with nationalism and its message of primary political loyalty to our nation and our state. Indeed, this political orientation is so familiar that most people find it difficult to imagine alternatives. This chapter challenges our traditional view by exploring such alternatives. They have long existed, but they have been gaining strength in recent decades. As such, human interaction and political identification are moving beyond traditional national boundaries and creating myriad regional and global links. Keep your mind open to the possibilities of these different ways of connecting yourself to the political world even if they seem far-fetched. Bear in mind that in Shakespeare's time people believed, as he had a character exclaim in *The Taming of the Shrew*, "He that is giddy thinks the world turns round." To simplify the complex changes that are occurring, it is possible to divide them into two related trends: globalization and transnationalism.

Globalization denotes the increasing integration of economics, communications, and culture across national boundaries. It is mostly the product of technological changes that have rapidly expanded the speed with which merchandise, money, people, information, and ideas move over long distances. Certainly people, money, culture, and knowledge have flowed across political borders since ancient times. What is different, though, is the speed at which globalization is now proceeding. As discussed in chapter 2 (see Figure 2.1), about 90% of history's significant technological advances have occurred since 1800, and the rate of discovery and invention has been accelerating during that time. Be it the Internet, jet travel, or some other advance, a great deal of this technological innovation is moving the world away from the national orientation that has dominated for several centuries and toward a growing global connectedness. "It's a Flat World, After All," the title of a recent article by a veteran journalist telling "a tale of [globalized] technology and geoeconomics that is fundamentally reshaping our lives," is a bit overdrawn, but it captures the importance of globalization.[1]

Transnationalism signifies social, economic, and political links among people and private organizations across national borders. It has both preceded and been spurred by globalization. The two terms are closely linked, but while globalization is a process and a state of affairs, transnationalism is attitudinal and includes a range of cross-border political identities and interactions. Transnationalism undermines nationalism (and its tangible manifestation, the national state) to a substantial degree by promoting cross-national political activity and even political loyalties. Like globalization, transnationalism is ancient. But also like globalization, transnationalism is growing rapidly in recent times and combining with globalization to cause "sweeping and revolutionary changes" in global politics (Klare & Chandrani, 1998:vii).

Globalization

SIMULATAION
Transnational Personal
Inventory

Ready or not, globalization has arrived! The morning activities of your author include beginning to revise the chapter you are now reading and working on lecture notes for an afternoon introduction to international relations class. Globalization permeates these activities. The computer keyboard I am working on was made in Thailand, the mouse came from China, the monitor was produced in South Korea, and the CD I use to back up my files was manufactured in Taiwan. Both my phone and desk calculator are from Malaysia. The work I have done this morning has led me to connect with Internet sites of more than a half-dozen countries, several international organizations, and English-language news sites in China, Russia, Qatar, and several other countries. Among the top news stories today are the continuing cost to

Americans in lives and money of their military presence in Iraq and the implications of the increase in the value of the dollar against the European Union euro and other major currencies for jobs and interest rates in the United States. Getting back to my immediate activities, this book will be produced in the United States, but there is a good chance the paper started as a tree in Canada, and my editor is originally from India. The shirt I am wearing is from Mauritius, my shoes were made in China, and my sweater began its existence in Ireland. The car I drove to the office today was assembled in Mexico and propelled by fuel probably imported from Venezuela, Nigeria, or another foreign source. My class this afternoon has students from a variety of countries beyond the United States, and my graduate assistant is Israeli. If you think about it, globalization is probably entwined with your daily economic, communications, and cultural existence as much as it is with mine. We all live in an increasingly interconnected and, in many ways, ever more amalgamated world.

Globalization of Transportation and Communications

Globalization could not exist to the extensive degree it does without the technological ability to transport our products and ourselves rapidly and in large numbers across great distances. Similarly, globalization is dependent on the technology that permits us to transmit images, data, the written word, and sound easily and rapidly on a global basis.

Global Transportation

Modern transportation carries people and their products across national borders in volume and at a speed unimaginable not very long ago. Oceangoing transport provides a good example. The most famous merchant vessel of the mid-1800s was the *Flying Cloud* (1851–1874), a 229-foot-long sailing ship. Now the oceans are being plied by such modern megaships as the tanker *Jahre Viking,* which at almost one-third of a mile long is so large that crew members often use bicycles on board to travel from one point to another. The immense ship carries more than a half-million tons of cargo, 900 times the capacity of the *Flying Cloud.* Yet the *Jahre Viking* is but one of the vast world merchant fleet of almost 28,000 freighters and tankers with a combined capacity of over 733 million tons of goods. These behemoths not only carry more cargo, but they have also expanded trade by reducing seagoing transportation costs to a small fraction of what they were a century ago. In 2004, for example, it cost only about three cents per gallon to transport oil from the Middle East to the United States.

WEB POLL
How Globalized Are You?

Advances in transportation have been important in moving people as well as goods. When the first English settlers traveled from the British Isles to what would be Jamestown, Virginia, in 1607, the only way to make the trip was by ship, and their three tiny ships took four-and-one-half months to carry 101 settlers to their destination. Now, air transportation has reduced the time to cross the Atlantic from months to hours. As late as 1895, Lord Kelvin, president of the Royal Society, Great Britain's leading scientific advisory organization, dismissed as "impossible" the idea of "heavier-than-air flying machines."[2] Just eight years later, in 1903, Orville and Wilbur Wright proved Lord Kelvin wrong. Now the largest airliners, such as the Boeing 747-400, can carry over 500 passengers between New York and Europe in as little as seven hours.

These advances have made international travel almost routine, with hundreds of millions of travelers flying between countries each year. For example, about 25 million Americans traveled beyond North America in 2000, and about 26 million non–North Americans came to the United States. If travel to and from Mexico and Canada is added to these numbers, they increased to over 58 million Americans traveling out of their country and more than 48 million foreign visitors coming to the United States.

Global Communications

It is almost impossible to overstate the impact that modern communications have had on international relations. In only a century and a half, communications have made spectacular advances, beginning with the telegraph, followed by photography, radio, the ability to film events, telephones, photocopying, television, satellite communications, faxes, and now computer-based Internet contacts and information through e-mail and the World Wide Web.

The Growth of Communications Capabilities   The flow of these communications is too massive to calculate precisely, but if the growth of international telephone calls are any indication, we are increasingly able to "reach out and touch someone" internationally, as the AT&T advertising slogan went. In 1985 about 425 million phone calls were made from the United States to another country. That number had shot up to over 5.9 billion calls by 2002.

The technological revolution in communications has also meant that more and more people around the globe are getting their news from the same sources. The most obvious example is CNN, which now reaches virtually every country in the world and broadcasts in nine languages. And while CNN carries something of an American perspective to the rest of the world, non-U.S. news networks are bringing foreign news perspectives to Americans. Al-Jazeera, which translates as "The (Arabian) Peninsula," is based in Qatar and began operations in 1996 as the first Arabic language television news network. Since then it has become well known around the world for its broadcasts of, among other things, video and audio tapes of Osama bin Laden from his hiding place. The news agency has also added Internet news sites in

Modern technology has made transnational communications an important factor in global politics. Among news media, CNN has the greatest global reach, but other networks are also playing a strong role. Al-Jazeera, the Qatar-based network, which broadcasts in Arabic and also has an English-language Web site, brings an Arab perspective to the news. Among other things, Al-Jazeera has been willing to air tapes, such as this one, sent by al Qaeda leader Osama bin Laden expressing his political views.

both Arabic and English, which, it claims, get more than 160 million hits a year, making Al-Jazeera "amongst the 50 most visited sites worldwide."

Not only are almost instantaneous news and information available over the Internet, but the number of people using the Internet is growing exponentially. Between 1990 and 2003, the share of the world population using the Internet soared 26 times from only 0.5% to 13%. Furthermore, today's Internet users are not only able to access the Web, they can communicate on it to one another via e-mail and create Web sites for themselves or their groups to share information and to promote their causes globally.

The Impact of Globalized Communications   The communications revolution, with its ongoing spread of global access to information and interactive communications, is of immense importance. One impact has been to facilitate the formation and growth of a multitude of transnational groups espousing causes of nearly every imaginable type. These groups, discussed in more detail later in this chapter, are flourishing and having an important impact on policy at the international level through the UN and other international organizations and on the national level through the pressure brought on governments by the groups' national chapters.

Modern communications have also enabled people to seek alternative information and opinions from what is normally available to them. For example, Arabs in the Middle East can get an American perspective on the news by watching or going to the Web site of CNN, and Americans have an Arab view of the world available on the Al-Jazeera site.

Yet another effect of global communications is to undermine authoritarian governments. The rapid mass communications that are taken for granted in the industrialized democracies are still greeted with suspicion by authoritarian governments. China tries to control the Web by using technology to monitor and block dissident communications and by imposing fines and imprisonment on those who the government claims endanger national security by transmitting information and opinions. In the end, though, Beijing's efforts are probably doomed to failure. "The more they [Chinese authorities] do to block it, the more people want to get online," says dissident Liu Xiaobo. "People in China now understand a lot more about what's going on than . . . in the '70s and '80s. Then, the only contact we had with the outside world was through meeting the very occasional foreigner or somehow getting hold of a foreign paper or magazine." According to Liu, "That's why in China these days you can see all kinds of organizations and activities springing up, moving the country towards real change."[3]

The Internet revolution has made it impossible for even authoritarian regimes to control the flow of information and ideas into and out of their country. China monitors Internet traffic and has many laws against "antirevolutionary" uses of the global communications medium. But as the image of this young man surfing the Web at an Internet café in Shanghai attests, Beijing is almost certainly fighting a losing battle against thought control and the international spread of ideas.

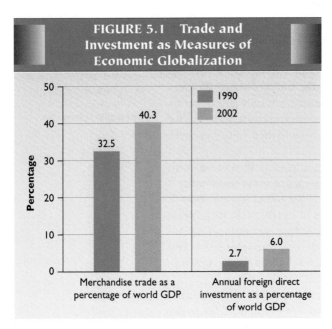

FIGURE 5.1 Trade and Investment as Measures of Economic Globalization

Economic globalization and the expanding economic interdependence of countries are evident in global merchandise (goods) trade increases between 1990 and 2002. Amounting to over 40% of the world's collective economic production (gross domestic product, GDP), exports and imports are an increasing part of overall economic activity. Much the same can be said about investments. Note that the international flow of direct investment (ownership of companies and real property) more than doubled as a percentage of GDP during the period.

Data source: World Bank (2004).

Web Link

The Campus Action Web Center at **www.campusaction .net/** is one source of links to college groups active on issues of international as well as domestic affairs.

"Democratic internationalism" is a fourth outcome of modern communications. Transnational communications have provided citizens from different countries with the ability to interact, exchange views, organize political activity, and undertake political action (Schmitz, 2004). There are now so many examples that are facilitated through modern communications, especially the Internet, that it is tempting to say that almost any cause you might think of has a transnational network. To get some sense of this, try going to a Web search engine such as Google and keyboard in "Students for a Free Tibet," "Students United for a Responsible Global Environment," "Students for Peace," "United Students Against Sweatshops," or virtually any other political cause, and you will find college student groups organizing themselves and communicating across the world on behalf of their beliefs.

Economic Globalization

Economic interchange across borders is bringing the world together in many ways. The intensifying reality of economic interchange and interdependence is detailed in chapters 1, 2, and 12, but two basic points are important here. First, the international economy affects each of us through our jobs, what we pay for the goods and services we consume, and many other economic aspects of our lives. Second, as economically intertwined as we are today, it is likely that the connections will grow even more complex and comprehensive. As just one indication, the degree to which we are absorbing one another's products and capital investments is evident in Figure 5.1, which shows that the increased amount of wealth the world produces each year is related to trade and foreign investments.

What is important to see here is that beyond merely increasing trade in terms of dollars and cents, global economic interchange is bringing people together transnationally through familiarity with one another and one another's products. Some of these contacts are interpersonal; more have to do with the role of international economics in narrowing cultural differences and creating a sense of identification with trading partners. About half of Japan's annual foreign trade is with the Western industrialized countries. The impact of this trade flow is evident in Japan's sense of affinity with others. One study found that when Japanese people were asked whether they more closely associated with Asian or Western countries, 54% of those willing to make a choice replied "Western countries." When asked why they identified with Western countries, 89% said it was because of "economic interaction" (Namkung, 1998:46).

Cultural Globalization

To an important degree, the early development of diverse languages, practices, and the other aspects of the world's diverse cultures was a product of the isolation of groups of people from one another. It is not surprising, then, that a degree of cultural amalgamation has occurred as transportation and communication have improved, thereby bringing people of various societies into ever more frequent contact. While it is far too early to speak of a world uniculture, global cultural differences have decreased substantially during the last half-century. It is also the case, though, that the drift toward cultural homogenization—McWorld in Barber's (1996) term—is meeting substantial resistance.

Discussions of the evolution of an amalgamated global culture inevitably include a great deal about fast food, basketball, rock music, e-mail, and other such aspects of pop culture. It would be an error to suppose that such examples trivialize the subject. Instead, a long line of political theory argues that the world will come together through an increasing number and range of such commonplace interactions. From this perspective, the process of intercultural familiarization and amalgamation is helping to create a global **civil society**. This concept includes all the cultural, social, economic, and other activities of individuals and groups that are beyond direct government control. Some nations emerged from civil societies and, as discussed in chapter 4, carved out their own nation-states. By the same process, if transnational civil societies develop, then regional and even global schemes of governance could conceivably form and supplement or supplant the territorial state. Scholars who examine this bottom-up process of transnational integration look for evidence in such factors as the flow of communications and commerce between countries and the spread across borders of what people wear, eat, and do for recreation.

The Spread of Common Culture

There is significant evidence of cultural amalgamation in the world. The leaders of China once wore "Mao suits"; now they wear Western-style business suits. When dressing informally, people in Shanghai, Lagos, and Mexico City are more apt to wear jeans, T-shirts, and sneakers than their country's traditional dress. Young people everywhere listen to the same music, with "Boulevard of Broken Dreams" by Green Day on the top 10 charts in Brazil, China, India, Ireland, Russia, South Africa, and many other countries in addition to the United States in 2005. And whatever it means to our gastronomic future, Big Macs, fries, and milk shakes are consumed around the world.

Before looking further at the evidence of cultural amalgamation, one caution is in order. You will see that a great deal of what is becoming world culture is Western, especially American, in its origins. That does not imply that Western culture is superior; its impact is a function of the economic and political strength of Western Europe and the United States. Nor does the preponderance of Western culture in the integration process mean that the flow is one way. American culture, for example, is influenced by many "foreign imports," ranging from fajitas, through soccer, to acupuncture.

Web Link

To find out what movies people in other countries are watching and what music they are listening to, visit the box office and music charts at http://allcharts.org/.

Globalization includes the spread of common culture. Whether they are in Boston, Berlin, Bogotá, or Beijing, young adults and others dress pretty much alike, listen to the same music, and eat fast food. This cultural amalgamation is represented in this photo of T-shirt–clad rock star Wang Leehom posing with Ronald McDonald in one of the chain's Beijing outlets.

Language   One of the most important aspects of converging culture is English, which is becoming the common language of business, diplomacy, communications, and even culture. President Hamid Karzai of Afghanistan and many other national leaders can converse in English. Indeed, a number of them, including President Jacques Chirac of France, learned or improved their English while enrolled at U.S. universities. A bit more slowly, English is spreading among common citizens. This is evident in differences among various age groups. Among Europeans, for instance, 89% of all school children now have English instruction, and 67% of those between 15 and 24 speak at least some English compared to only 18% of Europeans over age 55 who can do so.

Modern communications are one driving force in the spread of English. There are certainly sites on the World Wide Web in many languages, but most of the software, the search engines, and information on the vast majority of Web sites are all in English. One estimate is that 90% of all Internet information and traffic is in English. As the Web master at one site in Russia comments, "It is far easier for a Russian . . . to download the works of Dostoyevsky translated in English to read than it is for him to get [it] in his own language."

Business is also a significant factor in the global growth of English. The United States is the world's largest exporter and importer of goods and services, and it is far more common for foreign businesspeople to learn the language of Americans than it is for Americans to learn other languages. A report issued by the Japanese government declared that "achieving world-class excellence demands that all Japanese acquire a working knowledge of English."[4]

The use of English will probably continue to expand throughout the world. A recent survey of people in 42 countries found that 85% of them "completely" or "mostly" agreed with the statement, "Children need to learn English to succeed in the world today." Moreover, as Figure 5.2 demonstrates, an overwhelming majority of people in every region of the world held that view.[5]

Consumer Products   The interchange of popular consumer goods is another major factor in narrowing cultural gaps. American movies are popular throughout much of the world. Hollywood is pervasive, with American movies earning 50% of all film revenues in Japan, 70% in Europe, and 83% in Latin America. By contrast, foreign films account for just 3% of the U.S. market. American television programming is also widespread. For example, 62% of all television programs in Latin America originate in the United States. Jeans, logo-bearing T-shirts, and other American-style dress is also ubiquitous. Burgers, fried chicken, and other types of fast food are further spreading common culture.

China provides just one example of the degree to which diverse cultures have succumbed to many things American. Perhaps the words, "Oh, East is East, and West is West, and never the twain shall meet," seemed true when Rudyard Kipling penned them in "The Ballad of East and West" (1889), but they hardly apply anymore. Children in China successfully pester their parents to buy them Mi Loushu (Mickey Mouse) comic books, and to go to the Hong Kong Disneyland, which opened in September 2005. Kentucky Fried Chicken has also won many converts and now has over 1,200 outlets. McDonald's, with 700 outlets, is the second largest fast-food company in China, even though a Big Mac, at $1.26 in 2004, is very pricey for most Chinese workers (Watson, 2000). After fortifying themselves with a *jishi hanbao* (cheeseburger), Chinese can rock and roll (*gun shi*) at a Hard Rock Café in Beijing or Shanghai. Finally, exhausted revelers might choose to get some rest at one of the scores of hotels in China operated by Hilton, Holiday Inn, Sheraton, and other Western chains. While at the hotel relaxing, patrons can turn on the television and

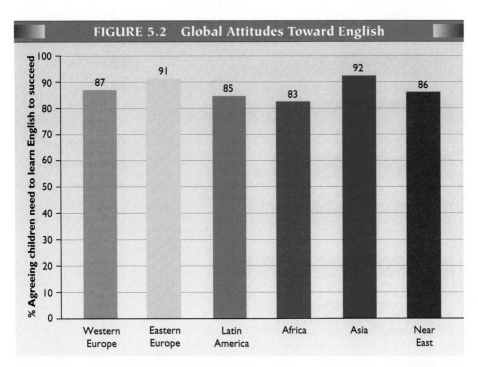

FIGURE 5.2   Global Attitudes Toward English

The growth of English as the language of business, the Internet, and other aspects of global communications is likely to spur the continued increase in the number of English speakers. Strong majorities of people worldwide believe that it is important for their children to learn English in order to succeed in the modern world.

Note: The Near East is broader than the Middle East and stretches from Egypt to Pakistan.
Data source: Pew Research Center (2003).

watch CNN in English or change channels to watch MTV-China or catch a National Basketball Association (NBA) game. Finding one will be easy, because all Chinese stations carry NBA games. Enthusiasm for basketball has grown even more now that 7′6″ Yao Ming of the Houston Rockets has become an NBA all-star noted for his awesome *kou qui* (slam dunk). A recent comment pinpoints the impact of Yao Ming and basketball on the austere culture of Chairman Mao Zedong, "China [is] a country increasingly more about Yao than Mao."[6]

To reemphasize the main point, there is a distinct and important intermingling and amalgamation of cultures under way. For good or ill, Western, particularly American, culture is at the forefront of this trend. The observation of the director-general of UNESCO, that "America's main role in the new world order is not as a military superpower, but as a multicultural superpower," is an overstatement, but it captures some of what is occurring (Iyer, 1996:263). What is most important is not the specific source of common culture. Rather, it is the important potential consequences of cultural amalgamation. As noted, some analysts welcome it as a positive force that will bring people and, eventually, political units together. Others see transnational culture as a danger to desirable diversity.

Global Reactions to Cultural Homogenization

How are people around the world reacting to the spread of English, the expansion of Western fast-food chains, and other aspects of cultural amalgamation? The answer is mixed, perhaps even contradictory.

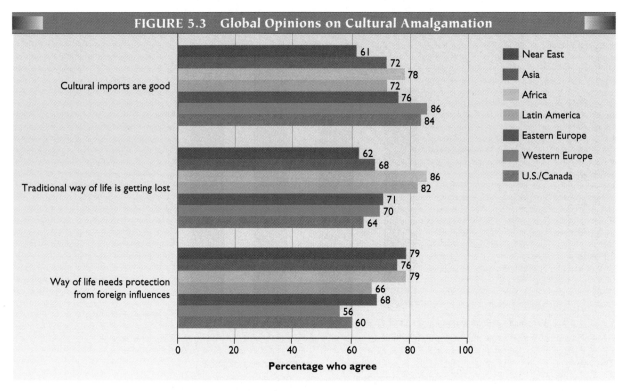

FIGURE 5.3 Global Opinions on Cultural Amalgamation

People have a degree of ambivalence about cultural amalgamation. As the top series of bars shows, most people around the world like cultural imports, such as foreign movies, television programming, and music. Yet the middle group of bars indicates that most people believe their traditional way of life is getting lost, and it is likely that they would recognize that the cultural imports they favor are playing a role in that deterioration. Therefore, as evident in the bottom group of bars, a strong majority of people in every region wants to protect their way of life from foreign influences. The reactions are reminiscent of the old saw about wanting to have your cake and eat it too.

Note: The Near East is broader than the Middle East and stretches from Egypt to Pakistan.
Data source: Pew Research Center (2003).

Reactions are quite positive about one of the strongest agents of cultural homogenization, imported entertainment media (movies, television, and music). A survey of attitudes in over 40 countries found that overall, 75% of respondents said such cultural imports are good, 21% thought they are bad, and 4% were unsure. This support of cultural homogenization appears a bit less enthusiastic when those saying "very good" (30%) and only "somewhat good" (45%) are distinguished. Also important is the fact that reactions did not differ dramatically among the world's regions. Americans and Canadians were the most likely (82%) to perceive cultural imports positively, but as Figure 5.3 shows, all the other regions but one have positive reactions above 70%. People are less happy about the spread of fast-food chains. But even on this aspect of cultural amalgamation, a plurality of people (40%) saw it as good, 30% viewed it as negative, 20% thought it made no difference, and 10% were unsure.

People globally also recognize that cultural imports and other aspects of cultural amalgamation are eroding their traditional way of life. Worldwide, 75% feel that way, and as Figure 5.3 also shows, strong majorities in every region have that view. This sense of loss causes people to favor protecting their traditional way of life against foreign influence (which contradictorily includes the movies, television, and music that they find good).

The ambivalent feelings evident in Figure 5.3 have set the stage for strong reactions against cultural amalgamation. Typical of politics, it is those who dislike something who are the most vocal. The strength of the opposition to outside cultural influences also stems from the generation gap, with older people usually more averse to cultural imports than younger people. In the West African country of Senegal, for example, 76% of young adults (age 18 to 29) favor cultural imports; only 47% of adults aged 50 and over support that view. Since it is usually older adults who occupy leadership positions in government, organized religion, and other societal structures, it is their views, rather than those of younger adults, that are most likely to influence policy.

France provides a good example of both the ambivalence about and resistance to cultural amalgamation. Among the French, 91% favor popular entertainment imports, but 55% think that foreign fast food has made life worse. This mixed reaction is evident in French attitudes toward cultural exclusion. While only a small majority (53%) thinks their way of life should be protected against foreign influences (with 46% disagreeing, and 1% uncertain), France has often been a hotbed of resistance to cultural amalgamation. For example, the French newspaper *Le Figaro* has called fast food gastronomic "new terrorism" and charged that the United States "doesn't just intend to stuff our heads with its diplomatic obsessions. It also means to cram our bellies in its own way."[7] The French also worry that their language is under siege. For one, President Jacques Chirac has warned that a "major risk for humanity" is posed by the "linguistic uniformity and thus cultural uniformity" that may result from the spread of English.[8]

Reflecting this view, France constitutionally declared French to be the national language, passed legislation requiring the exclusive use of French in teaching, business, and government, and pressed the entertainment industry to feature French-language movies and music. None of these measure has worked well. "Get Right" by Jennifer Lopez was France's best-selling single in early 2005, and *Hitch* starring Will Smith was the top box-office draw. The French are more apt to say *le e-mail* or *le laptop* than *un message electronique* or *un ordinateur portatif.* Moreover, 32% of them already speak English, and it is spreading quickly, with 90% of the French agreeing that learning English will enhance their children's chances of success. Then, to make matters worse for language purity, the European Union ruled in 2002 that France could not require labels of imported food products to be exclusively in French. Now, to the horror of some, French shoppers can buy chicken wings, not *ailes de poulet,* at the supermarket.

Transnationalism

Transnationalism springs from two sources. Globalization is one. Economic interdependence, mass communications, rapid travel, and other modern factors are fostering transnationalism by intertwining the lives of people around the world. As the world becomes ever more interconnected, people interact transnationally more often, become more interdependent on one another, and become increasingly aware of the extent to which their futures are intertwined with global forces.

Human thought is the second source of transnationalism. The philosopher René Descartes argued in *Discourse on Method* (1637) that intellect is the essence of being human. "I think, therefore I am," he wrote. People can think abstractly. This allows them to imagine—to see themselves beyond what they have experienced and to define how they wish to be connected to people, ideas, and institutions. Transnationalism, indeed any political sense, is based on this abstract self-awareness.

While globalization is something that is happening and that exists, transnationalism is a more political term that relates to how people identify, interact, and organize themselves politically. However far globalization may proceed, its political impact will be limited if people continue to have the same political identities, to interact, and to see themselves as they have traditionally. This traditional way has long been to most often identify primarily with your nation and state in a relationship called *nationalism*.

Transnationalism has both action and identification elements. On the action dimension, transnationalism is the process of people working together as individuals and collectively in private groups across borders with other individuals and groups to accomplish a common purpose. On the other dimension, transnationalism provides alternatives to nationalism as a source of **political identity.** This concept refers to connection(s) we perceive between ourselves as individuals and ideologies (such as communism), religion (such as Islam), demographic characteristics (such as ethnicity or gender), region (such as the European Union), or virtually any other perceived common bond. We will speculate on the future of transnationalism later in the chapter, but it is important to say here that most people will not abandon nationalism in the foreseeable future. It is also important to see, however, that things are changing, and that at least some people are shifting some or all of their political identification away from their nationalist identity and toward one or more other identities. Many scholars believe, in the words of one, "that we need to question today the extent to which the imagination of political identity remains territorialized—that is, whether political identity remains the exclusive reserve of a single territorial referent" and to explore "the ways in which international socio-political life manages increasingly to escape the constraints of the territorial nation-state" (Mandaville, 2000:10).

Early Transnationalism

Although the process of globalization has spurred transnationalism, it is not new. Instead, what may seem to be a very modern idea has ancient origins.

The Origins of Transnational Thought

Transnational thought in Western culture can be traced to Stoicism, a philosophy that flourished in ancient Greece and Rome from 300 B.C. to A.D. 200. The Stoics saw themselves as part of humanity, not as members of one or another smaller political community. As such, Stoics were cosmopolitan, a word derived from combining the Greek words *cosmos* (world) and *polis* (city). One of those with a sense of being a global citizen was the Roman emperor Marcus Aurelius, who wrote in *Meditations,* "my . . . country, so far as I am [the emperor], is Rome, but so far as I am a man, it is the world."

Other ancient, non-Western great philosophical traditions contain teachings that are similar to the cosmopolitan thrust of Stoicism. Philosophies such as Confucianism and religions such as Buddhism and Hinduism all contain transnational elements. For example, Siddhartha Gautama (ca. 563–483 B.C.), who became known as the Buddha, urged that we adopt a universal perspective. "Whatsoever, after due examination and analysis, you find to be conducive to the good, the benefit, the welfare of all beings," he taught, "that doctrine believe and cling to, and take it as your guide."

Later Transnational Thought

Although Stoicism declined, the concept of transcending local political identity remained alive over the centuries. During the Middle Ages, the Roman Catholic Church was a transnational force. As one study notes, "The pope's temporal rule in Vatican City reminds twenty-first century observers" of the Roman Catholic Church's early "notion of political unity" with its "roots in medieval Christendom and papal claims of universal temporal authority" (Nelsen & Guth, 2003:4). Similarly the Holy Roman Empire, the Chinese Empire, and many other empires that once held sway justified their existence in part by the universalistic claim that rulers derived their authority from God and ruled by divine right over diverse people and lands.

Still later, transnationalist thought was evident in the philosophy of Thomas Paine and other revolutionaries of the late eighteenth century. Americans remember Paine as a patriot of their revolution, but that is an ill-fitting description. Instead, he was committed to a philosophy, not to any country. Paine described himself as a "citizen of the world" and was dubious about countries because they "limited citizenship to the soil, like vegetation." Paine's writing helped galvanize Americans during their struggle for independence, but he wrote in *The Rights of Man* (1779) that he would have played "the same part in any other country [if] the same circumstances [had] arisen."[9] Putting this view into practice, Paine also supported the French Revolution, which he saw as continuing the work of its American counterpart and leading a "march [of liberty] on the horizon of the world. . . . [that nothing] can arrest" (Fitzsimons, 1995:579). That transnational march, Paine predicted, would lead to free trade and to an international congress to resolve differences among states. Thus today's globalization would have neither surprised nor dismayed Paine.

During the same era, the philosopher Immanuel Kant took the idea of international cooperation for peace even further. He wrote in *Idea for a Universal History from a Cosmopolitan Point of View* (1784) that countries should abandon their "lawless state of savagery and enter a federation of people in which every state could expect to derive its security and rights . . . from a united power and the law-governed decisions of a united will." The thinking of nineteenth-century German communist philosophers Friedrich Engels and Karl Marx also contained strong transnational elements. They believed that all human divisions were based on economic class and that the state was a tool of the wealthy bourgeoisie to oppress the proletariat. Therefore, *The Communist Manifesto* (1848) explained, "Workingmen have no country." Moreover, Engels predicted that once the proletariat prevailed, "the state would lose its purpose as the "special repressive force" of the bourgeoisie and, being "superfluous," would "die out of itself."

Contemporary Transnational Thought

After long existing on the periphery of political thought dominated by nationalism, transnational thought reemerged gradually during the 20th century. To a degree this perspective is covered in the extensive discussion of liberalism in chapter 1. As noted there, liberals contend that a transition from a conflictive, state-centric system to a cooperative, interdependent system is both under way and desirable.

Realism and liberalism are not the only theoretical approaches to international relations, and in recent decades several other ways of thinking about world politics have gained standing among scholars. Three of especial note are postmodernism, constructivism, and feminism. Analysts who take one or another of these approaches view realism and liberalism as paths that merely perpetuate the current international system and offer nothing, as one analyst put it, "to assure a day of peace for international relations" (Der Derian, 1988:191). To create change, the critics of realism and liberalism want to reinvigorate the role of individuals in politics. From this point of view, international organizations and states limit the possibilities for individual political involvement. All three critical approaches advocate changing the way we speak, the way we think, and the way we organize our society and our institutions.

Each of the three alternative approaches begins from the idea that the only truths are those we create. There is no objective political reality waiting to be discovered. Instead, we have created all political attitudes and structures. Those who follow any of these approaches would agree with Albert Einstein's observation, "Reality is merely an illusion, albeit a very persistent one." Since each of the three approaches portrays people as the creators of everything that is political, each also believes that we can change what we have constructed. Thus each approach encourages us to challenge what seem to be immutable truths, to "re-imagine" our reality and thereby recreate it. Among other things, these alternative approaches require us to think about and perhaps redefine our political identity. A brief synopsis of the core concepts of the three theories is in Table 5.1.

Postmodernism

At its core, **postmodernism** contends that reality is created by the ways that we think and by our discourse (writing, talking) about our world. Postmodernists believe that we have become trapped by stale ways of conceiving how we organize and conduct ourselves. In other words, according to one scholar, "postmodernism seeks to understand how . . . the way we think about the world and our place in it, impose[s] limits on us, and how we might be able to resist and eventually transgress those limits."

Postmodernists seek to deconstruct the discourse of world politics. For example, the meaning that most people give to the concept of "national interest" is those things that benefit the country and its people in terms of gaining, increasing, and keeping wealth, military might, and status. Postmodernists reject such a meaning because, they contend, there is no such thing as an objective national interest. If that is true, we can change what it is by conceiving of national interest differently. Although Shakespeare did not mean to, he inserted a very postmodern view in *Hamlet* when the Prince of Denmark mused, "there is nothing either good or bad, but thinking makes it so." For example, postmodernists reject the validity of the "we" and "they" discourse in international politics that distinguishes between ethnonational groups. They would also dispute the conception of progress that seeks to impose notions of scientific/technological modernity on people of traditional cultures.

Postmodernists even doubt the reality of the "metanarratives" (overarching stories) of history. The standard portrayal of the rise and fall of powerful states is based on the power struggles among them. Is that real? Perhaps the real story, as Marx and Engels suggested, has been the struggle of the propertied classes to amass more wealth and to oppress the proletariat. Or maybe politics has been driven, as some feminist postmodernists suggest, by creating structures (such as states and organized religion) that have allowed men to oppress women in the supposed interest of protecting them. Because you have not heard such alternative stories, your instinct may be to dismiss them. But do not be so sure of what is fact and what is fiction.

One of the numerous postmodernist contributions is providing an alternative way to think about how to achieve peace. For example, postmodernists view states as linked to violence in many ways and are therefore suspicious of them. One charge is that states justify their existence and power by promoting a sense of danger. Postmodernists also believe that states focus on enhancing their own security as a structure, rather than in terms of their people. Moreover, states try to harness people to

Theory	Constructivism	Postmodernism	Feminism
View of the individual	Identities and interests of agents (individuals and organizations, including states) emerge out of their interactions.	Identities are uncertain, open and unsettled. Meanings are multiple and fluid. There is no universal, abstract standard of truth.	Sex and gender are distinct. Gender is a socially created set of practices, attitudes, and ideas about biology (sex).
View of international politics	Agents create international structures (rules and images), which reciprocally impact the agents' actions. Thus agents and structures are co-constituted through reciprocal interaction.	An agonistic (ongoing struggle) process, a "will to power." Knowledge practices (our understanding of the world) determine identities and power relationships.	Unequal gender relations profoundly impact the actions states and the lives of individual women and men who live within those states.
Area of focus	The way in which agents and structures reciprocally interact.	Deconstructing the concept of sovereignty. Reinvigorating individual political practices.	Gendered social relations and how these unequal power relations adversely affect the economic, social, and political security of women, children, and men.
View of the state	The state is a social construction. A state's identity and interests emerge out of their interactions.	States are neither necessary nor inevitable. States have established themselves as the privileged center of meaning and control in order to discipline politics.	The interests and identity of states reflect patriarchal power structures.
Key concepts	Agent, Structures, Co-constitution, Intersubjective meanings (shared images)	Agonistic politics, Power/Knowledge, Resistance and/or Transgression of (going beyond) limits.	Gender, Security, Patriarchy
View of change	Agents created the structures, therefore agents can change them by changing the rules and/or their practices.	The key political activity is to resist and transgress state-imposed limits on our ways of thinking, being, and acting.	Change is contingent upon investigation of the gender biases and the gendered nature of the state.
Summary	Constructivism attempts to redescribe international politics as a social process.	Postmodernism is a radically critical approach to the practice of international politics.	Feminism focuses on socially defined relations in order to transform how we conceptualize gender and international politics.

TABLE 5.1   Contemporary Transnational Theories

Compiled and created by Rosemary E. Shinko of the University of Connecticut, Stamford Campus, to whom the author also owes a debt for her contribution to the sections on constructivism, postmodernism, and feminism.

the state's purpose by creating nationalism as the exclusive political identity and by suppressing as muddled, even treasonous, attempts to create competing political identities.[10] In short, according to one postmodernist, "It is force that holds the state together." Based on this view, to achieve peace, we must examine the relationship of violence to our current political structure and "encourage individuals to actively engage in politics" in order to change the discourse (Shinko, 2004).

If even some of the postmodernism argument is true, then it is important for transnationalism because it seeks to examine the ways we organize ourselves politically. Postmodernists believe that organizing ourselves politically around a geographically defined country is only an image in our mind reinforced by the way that we discuss politics. Postmodernists want to change political discourse so primary political identity could expand beyond nationalism to also include, for instance, being a North American, a woman, or simply a human.

Constructivism

Another group of theorists position themselves between liberalism and postmodernism and are known as constructivists (Jacobensen, 2003; Zehfuss, 2002). **Constructivism** explains the course of international relations in terms of "agents" (individuals, groups, and social structures, including states) and "structure" (treaties, laws, international organizations, and other aspects of the international system). Constructivists explore the dynamic and reciprocal process whereby agents participate in the creation of the various international structures and, in turn, are affected by those structures.

Constructivism shares with postmodernism the view that realities are socially constructed to a substantial degree. However, constructivists also accept the reality of such tangible parts of the international system as states and are even willing to concede certain existing elements of the system, such as its lack of central authority. For constructivists the key is the ways in which we communicate (speak and write) and think about the world. They believe that language calls things into existence. For them, choosing one label over another (foreigner, fellow human), then attaching certain values to that label (foreign = different, not my responsibility; fellow human = similar, my responsibility) is profoundly important politically because we act on the basis of what things mean to us (Tsygankov, 2003). Constructivists believe that we should reject traditional meanings because they have led to division and conflict. As one put it, "A path cannot be called a path without the people who walk it" (Simon, 1998:158). For example, constructivists do not believe that the anarchical condition of the international system forces states to take certain actions (like being armed). Instead, constructivists think that how we conceive of the lack of central authority is what determines interactions. In the words of one leading constructivist, "Anarchy is what states make of it" (Wendt, 1992:335). From this point of view, conflict is not the result of structural power politics. Rather, it stems from the discordant worldviews and the inability of people to communicate in ways that will allow them to construct a mutually beneficial vision and create the structure to accomplish that vision. From this perspective, according to another constructivist analyst, "Constructivism is about human consciousness and its role in international life . . . [and] rests on . . . the capacity and will of people to take a deliberate attitude towards the world and to lend it significance [by acting according to that attitude]" (Ruggie, 1998:855).

The good news is that if values and perceptions change, then so too can relations, structural realities, and other aspects of the international system. Political identification can be among these changes. How we define ourselves and the values we place on that identification in relationship to others can, according to constructivists, reshape the structures by which we organize ourselves and the interactions among those structures.

Whereas postmodernists offer more of a methodological critique than a research agenda, constructivists pursue research, particularly at the state and individual levels of analysis, that examines the use of language and symbols, communication flows, and other factors in creating the mindsets from which individuals and communities construct their social realities.

Feminism

Yet another alternative to realism and liberalism is provided by feminist theory. It is a diverse theory containing elements of liberal, postmodernist, and constructivist thought. To bridge these, we will adopt the strategy of one feminist author and use **feminism** "in its original meaning: the theory of, and the struggle for, equality for women" (Fraser, 1999:855). From this perspective, it is possible to highlight a number of common points in feminist thought about world politics. First, feminism

SIMULATION
So Say the Mamas:
A Feminist World

WRITE THE POLICY SCRIPT

Allocate the "Security" Budget

One of the objections that feminist scholars have with the way that politics and policy are construed is that terms such as *security* and, even more, *national security* are almost exclusively defined in terms of military security by male-dominated political, media, and academic centers. Feminists see this as too narrow and argue that security is much broader and includes many other aspects of societal development.

An experiment that you can do individually, or better yet, as a class is to allocate an imaginary budget among several security concerns. Consider the five programs below. People with a more traditional view are apt to heavily favor the military category. Larger amounts to health care, antipoverty, and anti–domestic violence programs would fit better with the feminist definition of security. Homeland security lies in between. It has some aspect of traditional security concern about external threats, but it is also domestically oriented.

Security Budget Category	% of Budget Allocated
Military	_____
Homeland security	_____
Health care	_____
Antipoverty	_____
Anti–domestic violence	_____

What Do You Think?

If you had $100 billion to fund the five programs, what percentage of the funds would you give to each security budget category? Once you have finished your allocation, ask yourself what it says about your view of the term security. *If you have done this exercise as a class, you could compare your allocation with the class average. Also worthwhile would be averaging the answers of men and women in the class and comparing them.*

argues that women have been left out of the process and even the conceptualization of world politics.

Feminist scholars maintain that the definition of what is relevant to the study of international relations is largely a product of the male point of view and ignores or underrepresents the role of women, their concerns, and their perspectives. Similarly, feminist scholars argue that to a significant degree male-dominated research has promoted methodologies that are not relevant to the questions posed by feminist scholars and to their perspective on knowledge (Tickner, 2005; Caprioli, 2004). In this sense, many feminists would agree with the postmodernists that mainline scholarship has presented a metanarrative of world politics that is not real. Instead it reflects just one set of perceptions (male, in this case). The overarching story from a feminist perspective would be very different.

Concepts such as peace and security are prime examples of how, according to feminists, men and women perceive issues differently. One feminist scholar suggests that "from the masculine perspective, peace for the most part has meant the absence of war" (Reardon, 1990:137). She terms this "negative peace." By contrast, Reardon (138) continues, women think more in terms of "positive peace," which includes "conditions of social justice, economic equity and ecological balance." Women, more than men, are apt to see international security as wider than just a military concept, as also including security from sexism, poverty, domestic violence, and other factors that assail women (Razavi, 1999). Women favor this more inclusive view of security because, according to another study, "the need for human security through development is critical to women whose lives often epitomize the insecurity and disparities that plague the world order" (Bunch & Carillo, 1998:230). You can explore your own views on this topic in the decision box "Allocate the 'Security' Budget."

This inclusive view of violence is supported by women's experiences. "The most painful devaluation of women," according to one UN report, "is the physical and psychological violence that stalks them from cradle to grave" (UNDP, 1995:7).

Women are gaining political strength and extending human rights around the world. This is true even in the Middle East, the region that has been the most restrictive. This Kuwaiti woman is flashing a victory sign in 2005 just after women in her country finally won the right to vote and run for public office. Unlike women in neighboring Saudi Arabia, Kuwaiti women can also get a driver's license.

Fewer women than men may die or be wounded as soldiers, but women are at least as likely to be casualties in military and terrorist attacks on economic and population centers. Many women die from the starvation and disease that frequently accompany war, and yet others fall victim to widespread sexual abuse that occurs in some wars. During the early 1990s, the campaign against the Bosnians by the Serbs included an officially orchestrated campaign of sexual attack on many thousands of women and girls as young as 13 in an effort to terrorize the Bosnians. Sometimes even the supposed peacemakers may be sexual predators. A UN report in 2005 documented many cases of UN peacekeeping troops and officials in the Congo and elsewhere sometimes raping and more often coercing destitute women and girls as young as age 12 into "survival sex," swapping sex for as little as a dollar's worth of food or other necessities.[11] Among many other signs of endemic violence against women are the facts that (1) about 80% of the world's refugees are women and their children, (2) an estimated 100 million girls suffer genital mutilation, and (3) globally, the national incidence of women who have been the victim of abuse by an intimate partner averages 25% and ranges up to 58%.

Feminism is related to political identity in two ways (Croucher, 2003a). One is to create womanhood as a focus of women's sense of who they are politically. This does not mean that women are apt to try to forge an independent feminist state somewhere in the world, but it does mean that women may view their country and its policies through a heightened feminist consciousness. Second, the political identity of some women is influenced by their suspicion that states and other political structures are designed to maintain male dominance. This view, one feminist scholar writes, "strips the [state's] security core naked so that we can see its masculine-serving guises" (Sylvester, 1994:823).

Reacting to Transnational Thought

Virtually everyone who reads this book will have been inculcated with nationalism from a very early age and will also tend to believe that the metanarrative (the portrayal of political history and reality) presented to them in school and elsewhere represents a reasonably true image of events. This background makes for great skepticism toward transnational thought. Indeed, different—perhaps seemingly radical—ideas have often alarmed those who travel the traditional path. For example, many Americans who in the 1770s welcomed Thomas Paine's revolutionary fervor later criticized him. Writing in 1807, former president John Adams doubted that "any man in the world has had more influence on its inhabitants or affairs for the last thirty years than Tom Paine." That worried Adams, who condemned Paine's efforts to revolutionize the world as "mischief" conducted by "a mongrel between pig and puppy, begotten by a wild boar and a bitch wolf" (Fitzsimons, 1995:581).

Despite such fulminations by traditionalists about the alternative path propounded by the Stoics, Immanuel Kant, Paine, and others, the ideal of transnationalism has persisted. Think about the critical approaches with an open mind; they just may offer a better path for the future and give us deeper insights into our past and present. While pondering, it would be appropriate to remember a bit of wisdom from Albert Einstein: "We can't solve problems by using the same kind of thinking we used when we created them."

Transnationalism in Action

Although nationalism still dominates how we identify and organize ourselves politically, transnationalism is making inroads. We will explore these advances by first surveying transnational organizations, then turning our attention to regional transnationalism, cultural transnationalism, religious transnationalism, and transnational movements.

One point to note in the following discussion is the potential of transnationalism to significantly restructure the international system and its conduct. Some aspects of transnationalism tend to undermine nationalism and, by extension, the state. For example, some citizens of the European Union identify as Europeans, instead of simply as French, German, or some other nationality. In other cases, transnational identification and organization help change attitudes and policies around the world related to a specific area of concern. This will be illustrated by examining the global women's movement.

You will also see that transnationalism is neither an inherent force for peace nor for discord. Some elements of transnationalism involve greater global interdependence and harmony. This impact of transnationalism is very much in accord with the vision of the liberal school of political thought discussed in chapter 1 and, in most cases, with postmodernism and the other alternative theories discussed earlier in this chapter. Ironically, globalization has also spurred a transnationalist antiglobalization movement that believes the process is destructive (O'Neill, 2004). Yet another, and in this case, dire image of transnationalism envisions a world divided and in conflict along cultural lines. Those who see transnationalism in this light tend to be realists, many of whom would strengthen the national state as a bulwark against the dangers of hostile transnational alignments.

Transnational Organizations

One indication of the increased strength of transnationalism is the phenomenal growth in the number and activities of transnational organizations called **nongovernmental organizations (NGOs)**. These are organizations that operate across national boundaries, that have a membership composed of private individuals, and that do not answer

FIGURE 5.4 Growth of International Nongovernmental Organizations

One indication of the growth of transnational activity is the sharp increase in the number of transnational nongovernmental organizations (NGOs), especially since 1975.

Data source: Union of International Associations at www.uia.org.

ANALYZE THE ISSUE
UN Conference for Nongovernmental Organizations

to any government. Two other types of transnational organizations that fall within the definitional boundaries of NGOs but are usually treated separately are terrorist groups and transnational corporations (multinational corporations). These will be treated in greater detail in chapters 10 and 12 respectively.

The Growth of NGOs

Between 1900 and 2002, the number of NGOs grew from 69 to over 10,000, as depicted in Figure 5.4. Note that by far the greatest growth spurt has occurred since 1975 in parallel to rapidly advancing globalization. Of these, more than 2,000 hold consultative status with the United Nations, up from 928 such groups in 1992 and 222 such groups in 1952. These groups have a highly diverse range of interests that include peace, human rights, the environment, and virtually every other public concern.

The increasing number of NGOs and their diverse range of interests and activities reflect globalization in several ways. First, there is a growing awareness that many issues are partly or wholly transnational, rather than just national. For instance, one country's discharge of atmospheric gases that attack the Earth's vital ozone layer increases the rate of skin cancer globally, not just in the country that emitted the gases. Similarly, many women believe that the status of women in any one country is linked to the treatment of women everywhere. For example, they see domestic violence as a global, not just a national, problem. Second, NGOs have flourished because advances in transportation and communication have made transnational contacts easy, rapid, and inexpensive. "There is no doubt the Internet is having a great, transformational impact on traditional state-to-state diplomacy," a U.S. diplomat commented. He explained that by allowing people with common interests to interact and organize to influence international politics, the Internet "is empowering civil society like never before."[12] Third, the growth of NGOs reflects disenchantment with existing political organizations based in or dominated by states in an age of globalization. "Stifled by the unwillingness of nations and international organizations to share decision making, and frustrated by the failure of political institutions to bring about reform," one study explains, "political activists began to form their own cross-border coalitions in the 1970s and 1980s" (Lopez, Smith, & Pagnucco, 1995:36).

The Activities of NGOs

In essence, NGOs are organized interest groups that operate singly or in combination with one another to promote their causes. In the realm of environmental politics, for example, there are such groups as Friends of the Earth International, headquartered in the Netherlands. It coordinates a transnational effort to protect the environment and also serves as a link among Friends of the Earth member-groups in 67 countries and 20 affiliated groups, such as Amigos de Terra in Brazil. Similarly, Greenpeace International, which is also located in the Netherlands, has regional and national offices in 41 countries. Just like more domestically oriented interest groups, NGOs promote their goals by such techniques as attempting to raise public awareness and support for their causes and by providing information, argumentation, and electoral support to policy makers in national governments and intergovernmental organizations (IGOs, international organizations in which the members are states).

One measure of the increased activity of NGOs and their presence in the international policy-making process is their participation in multinational conferences convened by the United Nations and other IGOs to address global problems. Since the early 1990s, all such conferences have two parts. One is the official conference that includes delegates from governments. The second is the parallel NGO conference.

The first major conference to follow this pattern was the UN Conference on Environment and Development (UNCED) held in Rio de Janeiro (1992). It brought not only governments together in Brazil, but also approximately 15,000 delegates representing 1,100 NGOs. Since then, conference participation has expanded, with the 2002 World Conference on Sustainable Development in Johannesburg, South Africa, drawing some 41,000 delegates from more than 6,600 NGOs to its parallel meeting.

These conferences are both the result of the work done by NGOs and a vehicle that promotes their role by enhancing their visibility and by serving as a place where they can create **transnational advocacy networks (TANs)**. These are groups of NGOs and IGOs that share an interest in a specific aspect of global society (Betsill & Bulkeley, 2004). For example, the Partnership for Principle 10 is a TAN that includes government agencies (from Africa, Europe, and Latin America), transnational groups (such as Corporación Participa in Chile), and IGOs (such as the UN and World Bank). The TAN seeks to accelerate implementation of Principle 10 of the Rio Declaration (1992). That clause expressed the view of the 178 countries attending the conference: "Environmental issues are best handled with participation of all concerned citizens" and everyone "shall have appropriate access to information concerning the environment that is held by public authorities."

Another key role for NGOs is to provide a way for individuals to become involved in and have an impact on global events. Some pointers on how you can take advantage of that opportunity are provided in the participation box, "Join an NGO" on page 146.

The Impact of NGOs

It is hard to measure the impact of NGOs or any other single factor on policy making, but there is evidence that NGOs are gaining recognition as legitimate actors and are playing an increased role in the policy process. One measure is funding. The amount of aid flowing through NGOs to economically less developed countries (LDCs) increased from $1 billion in 1970 to approaching $10 billion today. Historically, NGOs have received most of their funds from their members. More recently, some governments and IGOs have begun to channel some of their aid funds through NGOs. For example, the U.S. Agency for International Development (USAID) directs some of its funding through a number of NGOs. USAID also gives funds to strengthen NGOs themselves in order to allow them to bring about economic development, democratization, and other desired changes.

NGOs have also helped move some of their causes to the center of the political stage by increasing public information and demanding action. According to a former British diplomat, "You used to have a nice, cozy relationship [between states]. Now you have more figures on the stage. . . . This adds to the pace and complexity of diplomacy."[13] For example, fifty years ago, the environment received little political attention. Now it is an important issue that generates world conferences (such as

> **Did You Know That:**
>
> An opinion survey in 43 countries found that 74% of all respondents evaluated the role of NGOs positively. Only 13% thought poorly of NGOs, with 13% unsure.

PLAY A PART IN YOUR WORLD

Join an NGO

Are you happy with the way that everything, absolutely everything, is going in the world? If you are not, then do something about it!

Each of us has an opportunity to play a part in world affairs by joining one of the multitude of nongovernmental organizations (NGOs). There is almost certainly one and probably several of these voluntary groups that address any transnational issue that you are interested in from almost any policy perspective that you have.

Be Active!

A great way to find a group to your liking is to check the UN site that lists the more than 2,000 NGOs that have consulta-

tive status with the UN. The Web address is **www.un.org/ partners/civil_society/ngo/ngoindex.htm.** *There you will see a grid that looks very much like Table 5.2 and lists 48 interest areas. Each of these and other reference points on the page will lead you to a site that, in most cases, has yet other hyperlinks to UN agencies and to NGOs in your area of interest. A backup alphabetical listing of all NGOs that have consultative status with the UN Economic and Social Council (ECOSOC) is* **www.un.org/esa/coordination/ngo/pdf/ INF_List.pdf.**

Global Issues—UN System Partnership

Africa	Development Cooperation	Food	Labor	Statistics
Ageing	Disabilities, Persons with	Governance	Law of the Sea and Antarctica	Sustainable Development
Agriculture	Disarmament	Health	Least Developed Countries	Terrorism
AIDS	Drug Control and Crime Prevention	Human Rights	Millennium Assembly	Trade and Development
Atomic Energy	Education	Human Settlements	Question of Palestine	Volunteerism
Children	Elections	Humanitarian Affairs	Peace and Security	Water
Climate Change	Energy	Indigenous People	Population	Women
Culture	Environment	Information Communications Technology	Refugees	Youth
Decolonization	Family	Intellectual Property	Social Development	
Demining	Financing, International	International Law	Outer Space	

those in Rio in 1992 and Johannesburg in 2002), a frequent topic of conversation among heads of government, and the subject of numerous international agreements.

Transnational NGOs and their national chapters also individually and collectively bring pressure on governments. In the United States, for example, the League of Conservation Voters lobbies legislators and agency officials and takes such public relations steps as maintaining a "scorecard" that rates the voting record of members of Congress on the environment. It should also be noted that some forms of NGO activity can be destructive and, therefore, illegitimate in the view of most. For example, al Qaeda and many other terrorist groups are transnational organizations.

Regional Transnationalism

Chapter 7 on international organizations examines the European Union (EU) as an example of a regional organization. The EU has evolved since its genesis soon after World War II to the point now where there is advanced economic integration. Although at a slower rate, political integration has also proceeded. These changes are beginning to affect how Europeans define their political identity. Although there is no doubt that nationalism continues to dominate, there is also a sense of other identifications taking some hold. Among Europeans, 40% define themselves only as citizens of their country. Another 44% define themselves as citizens of their country first and Europeans second. Even more transnationally identified, 8% feel more European than national, and 4% perceive themselves as exclusively European (with 3% unsure).[14] Thus while nationalism reigns supreme, it is notable that one out of every eight people in the EU has transferred his or her traditional national identification to a primary or exclusive sense of being European and that 60% of EU citizens have some sense of political identification with it, even if it is secondary.

There are other indications that political identification with the EU may increase. One is the higher percentage of people (18%) with a primary or exclusive European identity in the six countries that in 1958 founded what became the EU than in the newer member-countries. Also, there is a stronger European identification (15%) among younger Europeans (age 15 to 24), with support dropping off with age to only 8% among Europeans aged 55 or more.

There is no other area of the globe with a regional organization that even approaches the economic, much less the political integration of the EU. Thus, to date any sense of regional political identity is almost exclusively confined to Europe. But in the 1950s, Europe's Common Market was just beginning, and it was limited to trade, much as several regional organizations such as the North American Free Trade Agreement (NAFTA, which links Canada, Mexico, and the United States) are today. What has evolved in Europe could occur elsewhere.

Although only a small minority of Europeans identify with the European Union today, that sense may increase as children who do not remember pre-EU times grow up. The EU suffered a setback when its proposed constitution was rejected by French and Dutch voters in 2005, but that may only be temporary. Perhaps when this Hungarian child holding an EU flag grows up, he and many of his contemporaries will consider themselves European first and Hungarian, British, French, or some other nationality second.

Cultural Transnationalism

There is considerable scholarship that demonstrates how greater intercultural familiarity reduces stereotyping, suspicion, fear, and other divisive factors that promote domestic and international conflict. Therefore, the familiarity with different cultures that globalization brings and even the blending of cultures holds the prospect of reducing conflict in the world. Advocates of cultural amalgamation may concede that it will lead to the "yawn of McWorld," but at least it will be a more peaceful existence.

A less sanguine view is that cultural transnationalism will lead to a "**clash of civilizations**." The best-known proponent of this view is Samuel P. Huntington's theory

(1996, 1993). Like many analysts, Huntington (1993: 22–26) believes that nationalism will "weaken . . . as a source of identity." What will happen next is the key to his controversial thesis. He believes that new cultural identifications will emerge that will "fill this gap" and countries will align themselves in "seven or eight cultural blocs," including "Western, Confucian, Japanese, Islamic, Hindu, Slavic-Orthodox, Latin American, and possibly African." These blocs, Huntington further predicts, will become "the fundamental source of conflict" as "different civilizations" engage in "prolonged and . . . violent conflicts." What should we make of this image of a future world torn asunder by the clash of civilizations?

Most scholars reject Huntington's theory (Henderson, 2004). Yet some unsettling signs suggest that it is not totally unthinkable. One example is the current conflicts that arguably could be characterized as clashes between Huntington's "Western" and "Islamic" cultures. Whatever the perspective may be from the United States or other Western, largely Christian-heritage countries, there is considerable suspicion among Muslims that a concerted campaign is under way to undermine their religion and its cultural traits. As discussed later in the chapter, there is a history of conflict between Christendom and Islam that goes back more than a millennium, and to some Muslims current policy by the U.S.-led West is an extension of that conflict. Muslims making that case might point, among other things, to their perceptions of the following U.S. and/or European policies:

- Inaction while Christian Serbs slaughtered Bosnian Muslims (1992–1995)
- Exclusion of Muslim Turkey from the mostly Christian EU
- Opposition to Iraq or Iran getting nuclear weapons while ignoring Israeli nuclear weapons
- Two invasions of Iraq and one of Afghanistan
- Sanctions on Iraq after 1991 that lasted longer than those on Germany after 1945
- Lack of sanctions on largely Christian Russia for its often brutal campaign against the Muslim Chechens
- Support of Israel

It is important to note that the view of such actions as anti-Islam or, at least, reflecting cultural insensitivity is not confined to Muslims. Just before his death, Richard Nixon wrote, "It is an awkward but unavoidable truth that had the [mostly Muslim] citizens of Sarajevo [the capital of Bosnia] been predominantly Christian or Jewish, the civilized world would not have permitted [the atrocities that occurred]."[15]

Whether such charges are true or not, it is important to see that they are perceived to be true by many Muslims. A survey taken in 2002 of Muslims in 14 countries in Africa, Asia, and the Middle East found that nearly half felt their religion to be in danger. This perception has arguably fostered the greater sense of solidarity that a strong majority of Muslims also expressed in the survey.[16] These findings are detailed in Figure 5.5.

Whether such evidence presages a future that fits with Huntington's prediction is speculative. Some analysts disagree with Huntington. Others argue that racism, ethnic and religious intolerance, and other forms of culturalism have persisted throughout human history and, thus, do not augur increased cultural clashes. Yet other scholars believe that the forces bringing the world together will overcome those that are driving it apart.

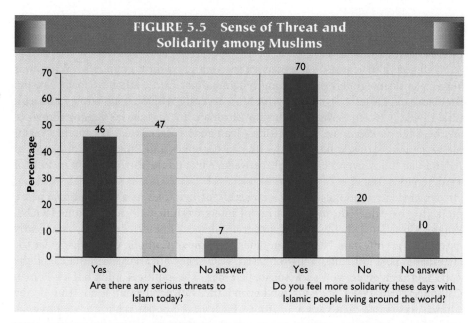

FIGURE 5.5   Sense of Threat and Solidarity among Muslims

Whatever the cause, about half of all Muslims believe that their religion is under attack. This sense of threat is especially high in the Middle East, where 78% perceived serious threats. Perhaps as part of a defensive reaction, 70% of Muslims indicated that they are currently feeling greater solidarity with other Muslims around the world.

Note: The survey was conducted in 2002 among Muslims in Jordan, Lebanon, Pakistan, Turkey, Uzbekistan, Bangladesh, Indonesia, Ghana, Ivory Coast, Mali, Nigeria, Senegal, Tanzania, and Uganda.
Data source: The Pew Research Center for People and the Press, "Views of a Changing World" (June 2003).

Transnational Religion

Most of the world's great religions have a strong transnational element. It is particularly apt to exist when a religion, which is a basis of spiritual identity, becomes a source of political identity among its members. When religion and political identities become intertwined, members of a religion may take a number of political actions. One is to try to conform the laws and the foreign policies of their country to their religious values. A second is to provide political support for the causes of co-religionists in other countries. This sense of support is why, for example, Jews from around the world are likely to support Israel and Muslims everywhere are apt to support the Palestinians. Religion also helps explain why Osama bin Laden, a Saudi, was able to recruit Muslims from Egypt, Pakistan, Chechnya, and elsewhere, including the United States and Europe, to the ranks of al Qaeda and to find a base for the organization in Afghanistan.

MAP
World Religions

Religion and World Politics

"You're constantly blindsided if you consider religion neutral or outside world politics," cautions one international relations scholar. It is "better to understand the place that religion holds in the wider international framework," he advises.[17] It is wise counsel because religion plays many roles in world politics (Fox & Sandler, 2004). Often, it is a force for peace, justice, and humanitarian concern (Johnston, 2003). It is also true, though, that religion has been and continues to be a factor in many bloody wars, conflicts, and other forms of political violence (Fox, 2004). For example, religion is an element of the conflict between mostly Jewish Israelis and the mostly Muslim Arabs. Religion is also part of what divides Pakistan and India, each of which has nuclear weapons, giving rise to what some people believe is the world's most dangerous situation.

Religion also causes or exacerbates conflict within countries. What was Yugoslavia disintegrated partly along religious lines into Catholic Croats, Muslim Bosnians, and Eastern Orthodox Serbs. More recently, religion plays a role in the cultural divide between Serbs and Muslim Albanians in Yugoslavia's Kosovo Province and between Macedonians and Muslim Albanians in Macedonia. Yet another example is the long struggle between the Roman Catholics and Protestants of Northern Ireland that killed over 3,000 people between 1969 and the establishment in 1998 of a still tenuous peace.

Organized religion also plays a range of positive roles as a transnational actor, projecting its values through an array of intergovernmental organizations (IGOs). Among Christians, the World Evangelical Alliance, founded in 1846, is an early example of a Protestant NGO. Even older, the Roman Catholic Church is by far the largest and most influential religion-based NGO. The Vatican itself is a state, and the pope is a secular as well as a spiritual leader. The political influence of Roman Catholicism, however, extends far beyond the Vatican. Under John Paul II, the Church was active on a variety of fronts. Early in the pope's reign, for example, he worked successfully to weaken communism's hold on his native Poland and other countries in Eastern Europe with a Roman Catholic heritage. One indication of his powerful influence came when he was shot in St. Peter's Square and nearly killed in 1981 by an assassin reportedly in the pay of Bulgaria's communist government. Soon after the Soviet Union collapsed a decade later, its last leader, former President Mikhail S. Gorbachev, wrote, "Everything that happened in Eastern Europe in these last few years would have been impossible without the presence of the pope and without the important role—including the political role—that he played on the world stage."[18] Later, the doctrinally conservative pontiff played a role in preventing the inclusion of language supporting abortion and other practices it opposes in the programs supported by various UN conferences on women. Additionally, John Paul II visited 129 countries outside the Vatican, and spent 10% of his time abroad. Throughout his papacy he was active on such issues as seeking an end to economic sanctions against countries, claiming that such sanctions are injurious to civilians; pressing for nuclear arms restraint; and calling on the world's wealthy countries to do more to aid the developing countries. He added moral weight to the growing chorus of voices decrying use of military force to settle disputes, opposing, among other things, every U.S. use of force during his reign. A final testament to the influence of the Roman Catholic Church and, especially, Pope John Paul II, was the impressive array of foreign leaders who attended his funeral in April 2005. Few other imaginable events could have brought together, among others, U.S. President George Bush, President Mohammad Khatami of Iran, and Israeli President Moshe Katsav to sit in silent tribute.

The Strength of Religious Fundamentalism

One aspect of religion that appears to have gained strength in many areas of the world is **fundamentalism** (religious traditionalism). As used here, a fundamentalist is someone who holds conservative religious values and wishes to incorporate those values into national law. Some fundamentalists are also transnationalists whose primary political identity is their religion, not their nation-state. This perspective promotes political cooperation among coreligionists across borders; it may also mean driving out people of another or no faith or suppressing their freedoms within borders.

There is considerable debate over whether the rise of fundamentalism is a series of isolated events or related to a larger global trend. Advocates of the latter view believe that at least part of the increase in the political stridency of religion is based on a resistance to the cultural amalgamation that fundamentalist traditionalists believe is undermining the values on which their religion is based. Religiosity is also heightened among those in "vulnerable populations" who are or who see themselves "facing personal survival-threatening risks" from war, poverty, or other causes (Norris & Inglehart, 2004:4). Whatever its source, a sense of siege increases people's awareness of their religious identity and their solidarity with their co-religionists across national borders. It is strongest in poorer countries, but also affects wealthier ones. What makes the increase in fundamentalism important to world politics is that political conservatism, religious fundamentalism, and avid nationalism often become intertwined in volatile ways.

India and Pakistan   Relations between India and Pakistan provide a prime example of the impact of religion on politics. The two countries were part of British India until 1947, when they were partitioned into Hindu-dominated India and Muslim-dominated Pakistan amid horrific religious conflict that left hundreds of thousands of people dead. Since then a volatile mix of religion and nationalism has beset relations between the two countries and led to three wars and numerous other military clashes. As it has been since 1947, the most perilous flashpoint is the border province of Kashmir, which is part of India but whose population is mostly Muslim.

Religion more than any other factor has been the source of conflict between mostly Muslim Pakistan and predominantly Hindu India. These Pakistani and Indian border guards, with headgear arrays reminiscent of the plumage displayed by avian combatants, symbolize the two countries' seeming intractable hostility and three wars.

Two things make the future of the region especially worrisome. One is that nuclear war became a horrendous possibility when India and Pakistan both tested nuclear weapons in 1998. Both countries have also developed the missile capacity to rain their weapons down on each other's cities. The second source of danger is increased religious fundamentalism in both India and Pakistan. The change in Pakistan is part of the increase in religious traditionalism throughout the Muslim world as discussed elsewhere in this chapter. India has also seen a rise of nationalist religious traditionalism, politically represented by the Bharatiya Janata Party (BJP), which first came to power in 1998. It was founded in 1980 as a Hindu nationalist party. Many members wish to create *Hindutva*, a theocratic Hindu India, or even *Akhand Bharat* (Old India), a mythical concept of a unified Indian subcontinent under Hindu Indian leadership. According to one BJP leader, "Muslims are converted Hindus, but they have forgotten their Hinduness. So we will awake them to their Hinduness."[19] Prime Minister Atal Behari Vajpayee, a moderate by BJP standards, warned that "appeasement" of Muslims and other minorities in India would "injure the Hindu psyche."[20] Vajpayee lost power in the 2004 elections and was replaced by India's first non-Hindu prime minister, Manmohan Singh, a Sikh. Still, the BJP remains the second-largest party in India's parliament. Thus it is too soon to know whether the fundamentalist appeal of the BJP has weakened among India's voters or whether the BJP will return to power.

Israel   Religious traditionalism also influences Israel's politics through the role played by orthodox Jewish groups. With respect to international affairs, Israel's religious right tends to favor a hard-line stance with the Palestinians, no compromise on the status of Jerusalem, and the continuation of Jewish settlements in the West Bank. Indeed, this political faction claims that the West Bank and the Golan Heights are part of the ancient land given in perpetuity to the Jewish nation by God. Whether the policy ramifications are domestic or international, "the issue," according to a Hebrew University scholar, "is whether Israel will shape a way of life according to Western, democratic concepts, or one infected by Middle Eastern fundamentalism and theocratic impulse." Others dismiss such concerns. "We're not going to make a second Iran in the Middle East," a rabbi who also heads a religion-oriented political party assures listeners.[21]

The United States   Whatever U.S. constitutional doctrine may be, separation of church and state in the United States has never been a complete political reality. Religion has long played a role in U.S. foreign policy. Moroever, many observers contend that religion has been an especially important factor during the presidency of George W. Bush, with traditionalist Protestants gaining a greater policy voice. Those who believe that Bush is a religious traditionalist cite his frequent invocation of God and other religious references and his repeated use of words and phrases such as "crusade" and "good versus evil" to explain his image of the world. The president also regularly expresses the belief that God should and does play a role in worldly events. For example, he once explained that his decision to run for president came because, "I believe that God wants me to run" (Mansfield, 2003:108). Others argue that Bush is not a Christian traditionalist himself but merely politically sensitive to that strong element of his constituency. "To understand this influence," once scholar writes, "it is important to recognize that the rise of the religious right as a political force in the United States is a relatively recent phenomenon that emerged as part of a . . . strategy by [leaders] in the Republican Party who—while not fundamentalist Christians themselves—recognized the need to enlist the support of this key segment of the U.S. population in order to achieve political power" (Zunes, 2004:1).

Whatever the personal beliefs of the president, there can be little doubt about the imprint of religious conservatism on U.S. policy. Many analysts point to the emphasis on spreading democracy and other aspects of the American way by word if possible and by the sword if necessary as rooted in a religious missionary impulse (Arnold, 2004). Typically, Bush declared in his 2004 State of the Union message, "The liberty we prize is not America's gift to the world, it is God's gift to humanity."[22] Washington has "exported" conservative religious "family values" as part of U.S. policy in ways such as withholding funds from international agencies that provide abortion assistance (Kline, 2004). There is also an echo of the "Protestant ethic," the "God helps those who help themselves" emphasis on hard work and self-reliance, in the Bush administration's approach to foreign aid. Bush expressed this attitude when he told the UN Conference on Financing and Development (2002) in Monterrey, Mexico, that poor countries had to try harder to improve themselves before the United States would do more to help. The president urged the delegates to "accept a higher, more difficult, more promising call" by taking a "new approach for development [that] places responsibility on developing nations." By doing so, Bush assured the delegates, "we do the work of compassion."[23]

Of course, not all the connections between religion and politics in the United States or any other country are rooted in traditionalist beliefs. Opposition to war, pressure to advance the cause of global human rights, demands that wealthy countries do more to help poorer ones, and many other examples of policy advocacy are centered in more mainline religious beliefs and organizations. That raises the question of whether religion should play a strong role in foreign policy and world politics.

For all connections between religion and global politics that we have been discussing, none has been more in the news than the role of Islam. Therefore, let us turn our attention to a detailed look at Islam because of its current importance on the world stage and because its history and tenets are too often unknown or misrepresented in the Western world.

Islam and the World

Islam is a monotheistic religion founded by Muhammad (ca. 570–632). The word *Islam* means "submission" to God (Allah), and *Muslim* means "one who submits." Muslims believe that Muhammad was a prophet who received Allah's teachings in a vision. These divine instructions constitute the Koran (or Qur'an), meaning "recitation."

It is the political application of Islam by Muslims that interests us here. A traditional Islamic concept is the *ummah,* the idea of a Muslim community that is unified spiritually, culturally, and politically. Muhammad was the first leader of the ummah. Muslims distinguish between Muslim-held lands, *dar al-Islam* (the domain of Islam), and non-Muslim lands, *dar al-harb* (the domain of unbelief). One tenet of Islam is the *jihad,* "struggle" carried on in the name of Allah by *mujahedin.* It is important to stress that jihad can mean spreading Islam or defending the faith peacefully and does not necessarily mean armed struggle any more than the noted hymn that begins "Onward, Christian Soldiers, Marching as to War" implies Christian militancy. This reality has too often been lost in false stereotypes of Islam as intrinsically violent. Certainly, there are militant Muslims. But virtually every religion is afflicted by fanatics who distort its meaning and commit unimaginable atrocities in its name.

The political ramifications of Islam are important because there are over 1 billion Muslims spread widely over the world, as demonstrated by the map on page 154 of countries in which Muslims are more than half of the population. They are a majority among the Arabs of the Middle East and also in non-Arab countries in Africa, Southwest Asia, and South Asia. Additionally, there are other countries, such as Nigeria and the Philippines, in which Muslims constitute an important political force. Overall, only about one of every four Muslims is an Arab, and the world's largest Muslim community (204 million) is in Indonesia, where it constitutes 88% of the population.

MAP
Countries with a Majority
Muslim Population

The Political Heritage of Muslims

Muslim attitudes toward the non-Muslim world are shaped by three historical elements. A *triumphant beginning* is the first. During Islam's early period, it experienced rapid religious and political expansion by peaceful conversion and violent conquest. At its farthest, Muslim domination encompassed the Middle East, North Africa, southwestern Asia to the Ganges River, Spain, and central Europe to just south of Vienna.

Conflict with Christian powers, especially those of Europe, is a second element of the Muslim political heritage. Eight crusades were launched by Europe's Catholic kings against Muslims between 1195 and 1270, and other lesser expeditions lasted into the 1400s. Muslims also clashed for hundreds of years with Christianity's Orthodox emperors of Byzantium and later with the Orthodox czars of Russia.

The domination of Muslims by others is the third key historical element of Muslims' political heritage. After about the year 1500, Muslim secular strength declined,

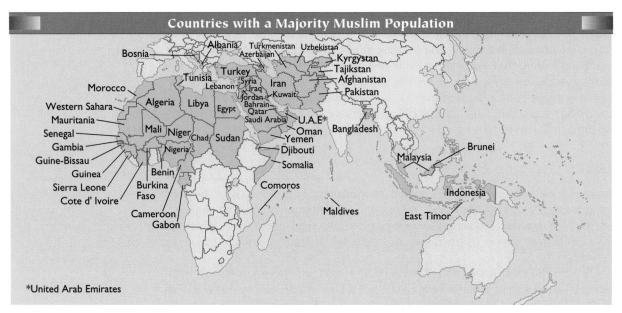

Countries with a Majority Muslim Population

*United Arab Emirates

This map of the countries in which Muslims constitute a majority of the population illustrates that Islam is not confined to the Arab states in the Middle East. In fact, most Muslims are not Arabs. The largest predominantly Muslim state is Indonesia, where 87% of the country's 238 million people are Muslims. The people of Pakistan and Iran, the second and third most populous predominantly Muslim countries, are also not Arabs.

and by the late 1800s a variety of European powers had come to dominate many Muslim areas. The last vestige of Muslim power was eclipsed when the Ottoman Empire collapsed after World War I, and the British and the French became the colonial overlords of the Middle East. As a result, most Muslim countries, whatever their location, share an experience of recent colonial domination by mostly European, Christian-heritage powers. During the last half century, direct political domination ended with the collapse of colonialism. New countries came into being; others moved from autonomy to full independence.

Yet there is a strong sense among many Muslims that Western dominance, led by the United States, has continued through alleged neocolonialist practices such as protecting authoritarian pro-Western regimes in Saudi Arabia and Kuwait and using military force to smite Muslim countries that defy U.S. demands to support its interests. For example, a 2002 poll in Turkey asking about the possible U.S. use of force to remove Saddam Hussein from power found that a majority (53%) believed that it was a part of the "U.S.'s war against Muslim countries that it sees as unfriendly." Only 34% thought Washington's policy had to do with a desire for stability in the Middle East, and 13% were unsure or refused to answer.[24]

Islam and Nationalism

JOIN THE DEBATE
Can Democracy Succeed in Islamic Countries?

There are elements of contemporary Islam that support unification by creating a true *ummah*. After centuries of outside domination, the people in the region that stretches from Gabon to Indonesia have begun to reclaim their heritage in what might be called a "Muslim pride" movement. This includes Islamic solidarity efforts, which have ranged from coordination in protecting Islamic holy places, through support of the Palestine Liberation Organization, to support of Pakistan's possession of nuclear weapons. Among Arab Muslims, the common tie of Islam has helped promote Pan-Arab sentiment. This Pan-Arab feeling has led to the establishment of some regional cooperation (the Arab League, for example) and even attempts to merge countries.

Nevertheless, it is very unlikely that Muslims will reestablish the *ummah* in the foreseeable future. Nationalism is one factor that will prevent this (Telhami & Barnett, 2002). Many Muslim countries have sharp differences and vie with one another for regional influence. Iraq and Iran, for example, fought an eight-year-long war in the 1980s that claimed at least 1 million lives. Further solidifying nationalism, there are major ethnic differences within Islam. Culturally, Indonesians are no more like Syrians than are Canadians. Even neighboring Muslim countries can be quite diverse. Iranians, for example, are ethnic Persians who speak Farsi; Iraqis are ethnic Arabs who speak Arabic. Furthermore, there is a strong sense of patriotic pride in many Muslim countries. This nationalism is particularly strong when faced by an outside influence, as the United States found out in postwar Iraq. Whatever their views of the departed Saddam Hussein, a substantial percentage of Iraqis chafed at the idea of an extended American presence in their country.

Islam and the Non-Islamic World

The political history of Muslims influences their attitudes toward the outside world, especially the West. First, many Muslims see the United States as the most recent of a long line of threatening Euro-Christian heritage powers. Americans have therefore inherited Muslim resentment of what one Arab leader describes as "Western behavior over centuries that has been unfair to Muslims."[25] Muslims also see the struggle with Israel and what they perceive as U.S. bias toward Israel as part of a long, ongoing history of attempted Western domination of their region. "There is a deep feeling that when it comes to the Arabs, it's always very harsh treatment, and when it comes to the Israelis, it's easy," notes an Egyptian analyst.[26]

The degree to which these feelings are held widely among Muslims was confirmed by a 2002 poll of nine Muslim countries. Of the Muslims surveyed, 53% had an unfavorable opinion of the United States; only 22% expressed a positive opinion. Just 12% of Muslims thought the West respects Islamic values. As for the question of Israel and the Palestinians, as few as 1% of Muslims in some countries (Kuwait and Morocco) and at most 12% of Muslims in any country (Indonesia) felt that the United States was dealing fairly with the Palestinians.[27] It is hard for most outsiders to understand how powerfully this issue affects Arab views of the United States. Some insight can be gained, however, from a poll conducted by noted Arab-American pollster James Zogby in eight Middle Eastern countries. Among its findings was that most Arabs placed the fate of the Palestinians high up on the list of issues of personal importance to them. This result led Zogby to conclude that the Palestinian question "is not a foreign policy issue [for Arabs]. It defines almost existentially their sense of who they are."[28]

Americans also held a negative mirror image of Muslims, as depicted in Figure 3.2 on page 69. Only 24% of the Americans polled in 2002 held a favorable opinion of Muslim countries, while 41% expressed an unfavorable view. The poll also found that most Americans have little respect for Muslim culture, with about two-thirds of Americans saying Muslim countries would be better off if they adopted U.S. and Western values.[29]

Islamic Sectarianism

Religion is not always a source of Islamic unity; sectarian splits within Islam have sometimes caused conflict. The most important division separates the majority Sunnis and the minority Shiites (Fuller & Francke, 2000). The issues between the two sects involve doctrinal matters beyond our scope of inquiry. What is important here is that the sometimes quiescent Sunni-Shiite rivalry was reignited in 1979 when the Ayatollah Ruhollah Khomeini led fundamentalist Shiites to power in Iran. One result was Iran's war with Iraq (1980–1988). There were territorial and other nationalistic causes behind the war, but Khomeini's determination to overthrow the Sunni-dominated regime of Saddam Hussein was also a cause of the war and the horrific casualties that occurred.

The death of Khomeini in 1989 eased, but did not end, Sunni-Shiite strife. Among other places, Muslim sectarianism has spelled continuing tragedy for Afghanistan. For example, there have been frequent charges that Iran is supporting the Shiite Hazara ethnonational group's resistance to the control of the Sunni-dominated central government in Kabul. Even more recently, events in Iraq show the interrelationship of sectarian and national forces. The downfall of Saddam Hussein, a Sunni, has opened the way for the country's majority Shiites to dominate the new government. Many Sunnis fear that change. The violence against the occupation and interim government has been centered in Sunni areas, and most Sunnis refused to participate in the January 2005 elections. There are also worries that Shiite-dominated Iran might try to gain influence in Iraq through its Shiite majority. Yet the possibility of that happening is severely constrained by the fact that Iraqis are Arab, Iranians are Persians, and historically the two groups have often clashed. Adding to the complexity, most Iraqi Kurds are Sunnis, but they have their own variations on Islam that differ from Iraq's Arab Sunnis.

Web Link

To learn more about the complex religious makeup of Iraq, visit the "Muslim, Islam, and Iraq" site created by Professor Alan Godlas of the University of Georgia at www.uga.edu/islam/iraq.html.

Islamic Traditionalism and Secularism

A second point of division within Islam separates Muslim traditionalists and secularists. Traditionalist (fundamentalist) Muslims want to preserve or, in some cases, resurrect their cultural traditions. Many of these, such as banning alcohol and having women cover their faces in public, have been weakened under the influence of Western culture. Fundamentalists also want to establish legal systems based on the *shari'ah* (the law of the Koran) rather than on Western legal precepts. The traditionalists also look forward to the reestablishment of the *ummah*. "The notion that a majority should rule and the notion of the political party are all Western notions," explains one ranking Muslim theologian. What "Islam calls for," he continues, is "obedience to the ruler, the unification of the nation, and advice by religious scholars."[30]

Secularists, by comparison, believe that within Islam there can be many Muslim states and that religious and secular law should be kept separate. A top Arab jurist argues, for example, that "politicized Islamic groups proclaim Islam to be a nation when in fact Islam is a religion."[31] Whatever may be theologically correct, the fact is that since the early 1990s traditionalist Muslim movements have gained strength in Algeria, Iran, Turkey, and several other Muslim countries.

What the average Muslim thinks is unclear, with variations in poll questions bringing very different results. For example, a recent poll that asked Muslims in 14 countries, "How much of a role do you think Islam should play in the political life of your country?" revealed that 57% (including a majority in 13 of the countries) replied a "large" role. Only 35% said a "small" role, and 8% declined to answer. Yet the same poll found that an average of 71% of the respondents in 7 overwhelmingly Muslim countries agreed with the statement, "Religion is a matter of personal faith and should be kept separate from government policy."[32]

What does all this mean about the possible existence of a "green peril," a term that relates to the traditional association of the color green with Muslims? The first answer is that it is equally wrong to ignore the role of religion in politics and to make dire and misleading predictions based on the false assumption of pan-Muslim soli-

Whether Iraqi Shiites, Sunnis, and Kurds can overcome their sectarian rivalries and cooperate in a democratic Iraq remains in doubt. The power of Iraq's religious leaders is captured in this 2005 photograph of Iraq's newly chosen prime minister, Ibrahim al-Jaafari (right), who is a Shiite, and his erstwhile rival, Ahmad Chalabi, having a press conference under a banner of Grand Ayatollah Ali al-Sistani, Iraq's most prominent Shiite religious leader, at the headquarters of the Shiite's Supreme Council of the Islamic Revolution in Baghdad.

darity. For example, it is probable that much of the strong sense of Muslim solidarity that exists is a defensive reaction prompted by the perception of many Muslims that their religion is being threatened. People who feel threatened by a common enemy often unite in opposition to that antagonist. In particular, there are numerous indications that the issue of the Palestinians and the U.S. support of Israel is a key element in the opinion of Muslims, especially Arabs, toward the United States. Given that, a peaceful solution that addresses the needs and rights of both Jews and Arabs in the region will benefit not only those two groups, but the United States and the rest of the world as well. Perhaps the best lesson to draw is that religion is a significant factor in international relations. Like any set of coherent ideas, religion helps define who is on which side and thus often plays a powerful role in shaping the perceptions of political leaders and the actions of the countries they command.

Transnational Movements

A wide range of transnational movements focus on one or another general aspect of the human condition. They can even influence people's political identity, although they do not carry the possibility of people abandoning their national loyalties in the same way that regional and some other forms of transnationalism do. Some of these movements focus on specific issues, such as the transnational environmental movement. Others are organized around demographic groups. Representing this latter type, the women's movement provides an excellent case study of the organization and operation of transnational movements.

Women in the World

It strains the obvious to point out that women globally have been and remain second-class citizens economically, politically, and socially. Historical data is scant, but current statistics show that no country has achieved socioeconomic or political gender equality. There are relative differences between countries, with the gap between men and women generally greater in less developed countries (LDCs) than in economically developed countries (EDCs). Still, the country-to-country differences are not all explained by economics. Socioeconomic gender differences are represented in the map on page 159.

The status of women is detailed in chapter 14's section on human rights, but for now consider the following barrage of facts: Women constitute 70% of the world's poor and 64% of the world's illiterate adults. They occupy only about 1 in 7 of the world's managerial and administrative jobs and constitute less than 40% of the world's professional and technical workers. Worldwide, women are much less likely to have access to paid employment, and the average woman who does have a job earns only about half of what the average man does. As noted earlier, women are much more likely than men to be refugees, the victims of domestic violence, and the targets of organized sexual assault during conflicts. A recent survey of 35 cities globally found that 2.2% of the women reported having been the victim of a sexual assault (UNDP, 2003). With such crimes often going unreported, the real percentage is almost surely substantially higher.

Such economic, social, and political deprivations of women are not new. What has changed is women's ability to see their common status in global terms through transnational communication and transportation. What is also new is the focused determination of women and the men who support the cause of gender equality to work together through transnational NGOs to address these issues. As one UNDP report (1995:1) points out, "Moving toward gender equality is not a technocratic goal—it is a political process." The global women's movement is the driving force in this political process.

Goals of the Transnational Women's Movement

Transformation is a term that captures the goals of the transnational women's movement. Chapter 6 takes up the role of women as national leaders, but we can say here that despite making up half the world population, women are only a small minority of the world's heads of government, national cabinet ministers, and national legislators. International organizations are no less gender skewed. No woman has ever headed the UN, the International Monetary Fund (IMF), the World Trade Organization (WTO), or the World Bank; and women occupy only about 15% of the senior management positions in the leading IGOs. Like male political leaders, some females have been successful in office; others have not. Yet, as the longtime (1980–1996) president of Iceland, Vigdis Finnbogadottir, has remarked, the stereotype remains that "women are not competitive enough or women do not understand economics." "If you do something wrong," she warned other women at a conference, "you will be attacked with the strongest weapon—mockery."[33]

Advocates of women's political activism see their goal as more than simply a drive for power. For them, increased power for women is also a way to change policy based on their view that, overall, women have different values than men on a variety of issues. While history demonstrates that women leaders can and have used military force, it is also the case, as discussed in chapter 3, that women have been generally less inclined to advocate force than men have been. Research also indicates that countries with higher percentages of women in their national legislatures are less likely than more male-dominated states to commit human rights abuses (Melander, 2005). Furthermore,

MAP
The Gender Gap:
Inequalities in Education
and Employment

The Gender Gap: Inequalities in Education and Employment

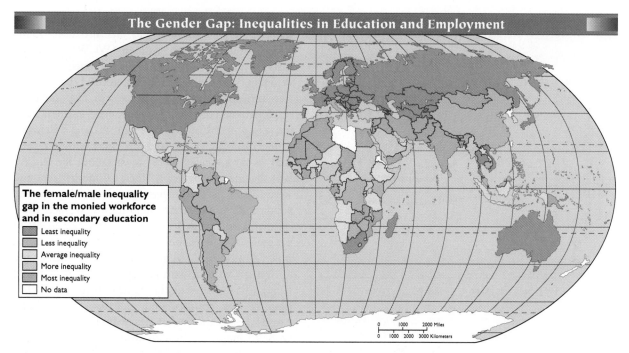

The day may come when one end of a scale of male/female equality is labeled "equal." That time has not arrived yet. This map classifies countries on a scale of relative inequality, ranging from least inequality to most inequality. All societies are held back by legally or socially restricting the educational and work opportunities of females, who make up half the population. While every country does this, the less developed countries, those that need "people power" the most, tend to be the most restrictive and to waste more of the talents of their women.

there is evidence that women place more emphasis on international social and economic programs than do men, who are apt to stress international security programs.[34]

The transnational women's movement additionally addresses the normative issue of how to improve the lot of women—and everyone else—in the international system. As such, the concern extends beyond sexism's deleterious effect on women to include the impact of discrimination on the entire society. Feminists point out correctly that keeping women illiterate retards the entire economic and social development of a society. It is not a coincidence, for example, that the percentage of women in the paid workforce is lowest in those countries where the gap between male and female literacy is the highest. Educating these illiterate women would increase the number of ways that they could contribute to their countries' economic and social growth. Beyond this, there is a correlation between the educational level of women and their percentage of the wage-earning workforce, on the one hand, and restrained population growth, on the other. In other words, one good path to population control is creating a society of fully educated men and women who are employed equally in wage-earning occupations.

Programs and Organization of the Transnational Women's Movement

Women have been and are politically active in a large number of organizations that focus all or in part on women's issues. These organizations and their members interact transnationally at many levels ranging from the Internet through global conferences. For instance, women can now find out more about their common concerns through the Internet. Collectively, women are now frequently gathering in such global

Web Link

One excellent site related to the global women's movement is the UN's "WomenWatch" at **www.un.org/womenwatch/**.

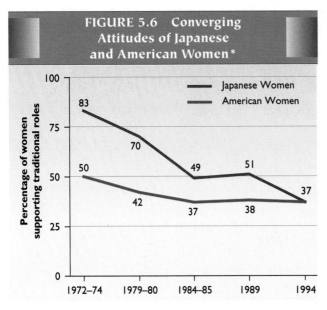

FIGURE 5.6 Converging Attitudes of Japanese and American Women*

Transnational communications help create similar values across national boundaries. Changes in attitudes about the roles played by women began earlier in the United States, Canada, and Europe than elsewhere. Feminist attitudes have, however, spread globally even to very traditional societies, such as Japan's, as this figure shows.

*This figure incorporates data from surveys that asked similar, but not always the same, questions about accepting or rejecting traditional roles for women and men. Questions were not always asked in the same year in both countries.
Data source: Ladd & Bowman (1996).

ANALYZE THE ISSUE
UN Women Watch:
Transnational Women's
Movements and the Case of
Gender Mainstreaming

forums as the UN Conference on Population and Development (UNCPD) held in Cairo (1994), the **World Conference on Women (WCW)** in Beijing (1995), and the **Beijing + 5 Conference** that convened in New York City (2000). Beyond the substantive proceedings, such conferences also facilitate transnational contacts among women. Parma Khastgir, a Supreme Court justice in India and a delegate to the 1995 WCW, stressed this contribution, noting that "what appealed to me most [about the WCW] was that people overcame their ethnic barriers and were able to discuss universal problems. They showed solidarity."[35] Even more importantly, women draw on their contacts and experiences through NGOs to promote and influence national and international policy (Jutta, 2003). A good example is Shirin Ebadi, an Iranian woman who has applied her energy and legal skills to bettering the rights of women and children in her country and globally. These efforts earned Ebadi the Nobel Peace Prize in 2003. Her work to empower Iranian women, one study concludes, has increased their "support for the international norms . . . , as well as their desire to change archaic Islamic laws, [which] will nudge . . . [Iran] along the path of globalization more so than ever before" (Monshipouri, 2004:11).

It is difficult to measure the precise impact that transnational communications among women is having through individual interactions, world and regional conferences, and the mass media (Shaheed, 1999). There is evidence, however, that cultural differences among women relating to their roles are narrowing (Inglehart & Norris, 2003). Figure 5.6 shows, for example, that the views of Japanese women, who had been very traditional compared to American women, came to parallel the attitudes of American women.

Advances of Women in Politics

Another standard by which to judge the impact of the transnational feminist movement is the advancement of women in politics. "Never before have so many women held so much power," writes one scholar. "The growing participation and representation of women in politics is one of the most remarkable developments of the late-twentieth century" (Jaquette, 1997:23).

Both these statements are certainly factual, but it is also the case that progress is slow, and that women remain a political minority part of both national and international governance. The changes within national governments, which are detailed in chapter 6, parallel the uphill climb of women to political power in international organizations. The UN Charter pledges equal opportunity for men and women. The reality a half century after the charter was adopted is that women hold only 36% of the professional staff positions and only 15% of all top UN administrative posts. Just 10% of the ambassadors to the UN are women. "We are a collection of all the world's chauvinisms," one UN staff member has commented bluntly.[36] Still, progress is being made. The secretary-general has appointed a number of women to high UN posts. Most notably, Kofi Annan in 1998 named Canadian diplomat Louise Fréchette as deputy secretary-general, the UN's second-highest post. She and six other women make up 25% of the 28 members of the UN's Senior Management Group chaired by the secretary-general. Thus, things are changing, although 25% of the senior managers is not half. Former UN executive Nafis Sadik has recalled that in the 1970s when she first came to work at the UN, "Western men saw me as an Asian woman; very decorative, but I couldn't possibly have any ideas."[37] When she retired in 2000 after 13 years as head of UNFPA, no one any longer saw Executive Director Sadik as an adornment.

The accomplishments of these women have been, of course, personal. Many of the other advances of women have been made through national efforts. It is also the case, however, that the progress of women almost everywhere has been facilitated by and, in turn, has contributed to the transnational feminist movement. Women have begun to think of themselves politically not as only American, or Canadian, or Zimbabwean women, but as women with a transnational identity and ties. This is both transforming national politics and weakening the hold of nationalism.

E Pluribus Unum?

Transnationalism Tomorrow

It is impossible to predict how far transnationalism will progress. It is not inconceivable that a century from now humans will share a common culture and perhaps even a common government. That is, however, far from certain. There are those who doubt that the trend of today toward transculturalism will continue into the future. Some analysts believe, for example, that English will cease to be the common language of the Internet as more and more non-English-speaking people gain access. "Be careful of turning astute observations about the current state of the Web into implications for the future," one observer cautions wisely.[38]

Moreover, nationalism is proving to be a very resilient barrier to globalization and to transnational movements. For example, it is true to some degree that a transnational identity has evolved among Europeans in connection with the EU. Yet those with that new political identity remain a small minority that is dwarfed by the percentage of people living in the EU countries who retain their traditional loyalty to the nation-state.

Thus we can say that the world is changing and even that it has been changing during recent decades at a rapid pace relative to the normal rate of change throughout history. If anyone 50 or 60 years ago had predicted that globalization and transnationalism would progress as far as they have by the middle of the first decade of the 21st century, critics would have called that person hopelessly befuddled. So what has occurred is remarkable. That does not mean, however, that the transnational trend will continue.

Chapter Summary

Globalization

1. The development of transnationalism springs from two sources: human thought and global interaction. Transnationalism includes a range of loyalties, activities, and other phenomena that connect humans across nations and national boundaries.

This chapter explores the bases and evidence of how globalization has furthered transnationalism in the world.

2. The world has become much more interdependent and interconnected through transportation and communications globalization, economic globalization, and cultural globalization. This globalization has spurred transnationalism.

Transnationalism

3. The lineage of transnational thought extends in Western culture back to the Stoics of ancient Greece and Rome and to Buddhism in Eastern culture. Transnational thought is evident today in many aspects of postmodernism, constructivism, and feminism.

Transnationalism in Action

4. Evidence of the recent advance of transnationalism is provided by the rapid growth, in number and range of activities, of transnational nongovernmental organizations.

5. Regional transnationalism, so far evident only in Europe, could lead to the growth of political identification with regions, rather than nation-states.

6. Many observers believe that cultural transnationalism will lead to greater harmony in the world. There are other analysts, however, who think that we are not moving toward a common culture but, instead, toward a future in which people will identify with and politically organize themselves around one or another of several antagonistic cultures or so-called civilizations.

7. Most religions have a strong transnational element. Some religions assert universalistic claims; other religions create an urge to unite all the members of that religion across countries.

8. Religion has played many roles in world politics, both positive and negative. The current rise in religious fundamentalism in many areas of the world is worrisome.

9. To understand the role of religion in world politics, a case study of Islam discusses the global impact of a transnational religion.

10. An important modern trend in international relations is the growth of transnational movements and organizations that are concerned with global issues. This includes the transnational women's movement and its associated organizations.

11. Although women's attitudes and emphases may vary, the transnational women's movement shares a similar philosophy and goals. These center on the idea that women around the world should cooperate to promote gender equality and to transform the way we think about and conduct politics at every level, including the international level.

12. Feminists, both women and the men who support gender equity, are pursuing numerous projects and making progress. The fourth World Conference on Women and its follow-up Beijing + 5 Conference are examples of activity in this area.

Transnationalism Tomorrow

13. For all the transnational change that has taken place, there is resistance to it. Nationalism remains a powerful, resilient force, and it still dominates people's political identification.

For simulations, debates, and other interactive activities, a chapter quiz, Web links, PowerWeb articles, and much more, visit **www.mhhe.com/rourke11/** and go to chapter 5. Or, while accessing the site, click on Course-Related Headlines and view recent international relations articles in the *New York Times*.

Key Terms

Beijing + 5 Conference
civil society
clash of civilizations
constructivism
feminism

fundamentalism
globalization
nongovernmental
   organizations (NGOs)

political identity
postmodernism
transnational advocacy
   networks (TANs)

transnationalism
World Conference on
   Women (WCW)

National States: The Traditional Structure

For the whole state, I would put mine armour on.
—William Shakespeare, *Coriolanus*

Something is rotten in the state of Denmark.
—William Shakespeare, *Hamlet*

This guard outside the 2005 Counter-Terrorism International Conference in Riyadh, Saudi Arabia, symbolizes one of the issues this chapter asks you to think about: Can sovereign states adequately fulfill their purpose by providing their citizens such basic services as security, including safety from terrorists?

HOW WE SHOULD GOVERN ourselves is the subject of this and the next chapter. Each examines one of the two divergent roads that we can take toward politically organizing the world stage. This chapter focuses on the traditional path that we have been following for several centuries. Organizationally, it features the state (nation-state, national state) as the core political actor. The role of the state is so important that you will find commentary on its history and operation throughout this book. Within this overarching analysis, this chapter looks at the nature of the state as a political unit, and the implications of its past, present, and possible future as the central actor in the international system.

For all their importance, states have not always existed (Opello & Rosow, 2004). Humans have organized themselves in cities, leagues, empires, and other political structures at various times in history. In fact states are actually relatively recent organizational innovations. As chapter 2 discusses, states developed late in the Middle Ages (ca. 500–1350). One part of that evolution occurred when European rulers expanded their political authority by breaking away from the secular domination of the Holy Roman Empire and the theological authority of the pope. The second phase occurred as kings subjugated feudal estates and other small entities within their realms. Indeed, as evident in the accompanying map, most current states are less than 100 years old. That makes most of them considerably younger than the world's oldest person, 125-year-old Maria Olivia da Silva of Brazil. These facts—that the state as a form of governance has a beginning and that most states are relatively young—are important because they underscore the possibility that we may not always govern ourselves exclusively through states. Hard as it is to imagine, there are other ways of politically organizing ourselves and our world.

MAP
Sovereign States:
Duration of Independence

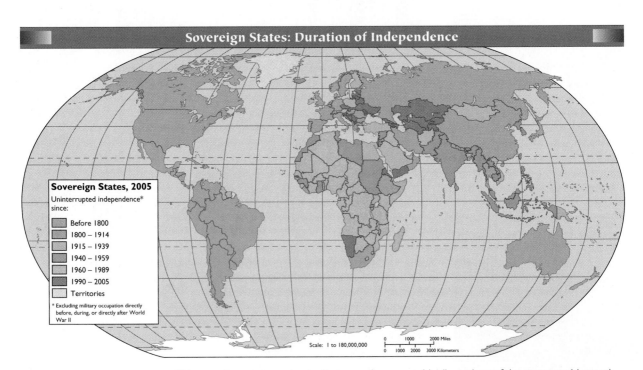

Sovereign States: Duration of Independence

Sovereign States, 2005
Uninterrupted independence*
since:

- Before 1800
- 1800 – 1914
- 1915 – 1939
- 1940 – 1959
- 1960 – 1989
- 1990 – 2005
- Territories

* Excluding military occupation directly before, during, or directly after World War II

Scale: 1 to 180,000,000

0   1000   2000 Miles
0   1000   2000   3000 Kilometers

This map gives you an opportunity to see the geographic dimensions of the recent rapid growth in the number of countries. Notice that Asia and Africa have seen the most change. Most of the countries that now exist on those continents were colonies of a European country in 1940.

If not the state, then what? Chapter 7 provides possible answers by taking up the United Nations, the European Union, and other global and regional organizations. They provide the most likely alternative path of governance in an increasingly globalized world.

The Nature and Purpose of the State

Countries are so central to our political world that we seldom question their existence and their raison d'être (reason for being). That is a mistake, because knowing what states are and what they are meant to do is important for later evaluating them and their political future.

Web Link

Maps of the world's individual countries and other territorial units are available at: **http://www .theodora.com/maps/.**

The State Defined

States are units of governance that exercise legal authority over specific territory and the people in it and that recognize no legitimate external higher authority. As chapter 4 on nationalism notes, states are also at the center of the political identity of most people. When Olympic champions step atop the ceremonial stand to receive their gold medal, their country's flag is raised and its national anthem is played. Furthermore, states are the most powerful of all political actors. Some huge companies approach or even exceed the wealth of some poorer countries, but no individual, company, group, or international organization has anywhere near the coercive power wielded by most states. Whatever their other individual differences, states share all or most of six characteristics: sovereignty, territory, population, diplomatic recognition, internal organization, and domestic support.

Sovereignty

The most important political characteristic of a state is **sovereignty**, which means having supreme legal authority. Applied to states it means that they have the exclusive legal right to govern the territory and people within their borders and do not recognize the legal legitimacy of any outside authority. Sovereignty also denotes legal equality among states. One important application of this principle is evident in the UN General Assembly and many other international assemblies, where each member-state has one vote. Are all states really equal, though? Compare San Marino and China (Table 6.1, page 166). San Marino lies entirely within Italy and is the world's oldest republic, dating back to the fourth century A.D. After years of self-imposed nonparticipation, the San Marinese in 1992 sought and were granted membership in the UN with the same representation in the General Assembly as China and every other sovereign state. "The fact of sitting around the table with the most important states in the world is a reaffirmation of sovereignty," explained the country's foreign minister.[1]

It is important to note that *sovereignty,* a legal and theoretical term, differs from *independence,* a political and applied term. Independence means freedom from outside

For several centuries the state has been and remains the primary actor on the world stage.

TABLE 6.1 San Marino and China: Sovereign Equals			
	San Marino	China	Ratio
Territory (sq. mi.)	24	3,705,400	1:154, 392
Population	28,503	1,299,000,000	1:45,579
Gross domestic product (US$ millions)	940	1,417,000	1:1,507
Military personnel	0	2,500,000	1:∞
Vote in UN General Assembly	1	1	1:1

Note: ∞ = infinity
Data sources: World Bank (2004), CIA (2005).

The legal concept of sovereign equality is evident in the equal votes of San Marino and China in the UN General Assembly. Very different are the more tangible measures of equality, such as the two countries' territories, populations, economic production, and military personnel.

control, and in an ideal, law-abiding world, sovereignty and independence would be synonymous. In the real world, however, where power is important, independence is not absolute. Sometimes a small country is so dominated by a powerful neighbor that its independence is dubious at best. Especially in terms of their foreign and defense policies, legally sovereign countries such as Bhutan (dominated by India), the Marshall Islands (dominated by the United States), and Monaco (dominated by France) can be described as having only circumscribed independence.

Territory

A second characteristic of a state is territory. It would seem obvious that a state must have physical boundaries, and most states do. On closer examination, though, the question of territory becomes more complex. There are numerous international disputes over borders; territorial boundaries can expand, contract, or shift dramatically; and it is even possible to have a state without territory. Many states recognize what they call Palestine as sovereign, yet the Palestinians are scattered across other countries such as Jordan. An accord that the Israelis and Palestinians signed in 1994 gave the Palestinians a measure of autonomy in Gaza (a region between Israel and Egypt) and in parts of the West Bank, and these areas have been expanded somewhat since then, but they can hardly be construed as territory over which the Palestinians exercise sovereign authority. Pakistan provides an example of another limit on the idea of a state's territorial authority. Northwestern Pakistan is controlled by the Pashtuns, an ethnonational group that is also the largest group in neighboring Afghanistan. Pakistan's Punjabi-dominated government exercises only limited authority over the border region and its well-armed Pashtuns, and that is one reason that Osama bin Laden has been able to hide there for all or part of the past several years.

Population

People are an obvious requirement for any state. The populations of states range from the 921 inhabitants of the Holy See (popularly referred to as the Vatican) to China's approximately 1.3 billion people, but all states count this characteristic as a minimum requirement.

What is becoming less clear in the shifting loyalties of the evolving international system is exactly where the population of a country begins and ends. Citizenship has become a bit more fluid than it was not long ago. For example, a citizen of one European Union (EU) country who resides in another EU country can now vote in local elections and even hold local office in the country in which he or she resides. Similarly, recent changes in the laws of Mexico allow Mexicans who have emigrated to the United States and become citizens to retain their Mexican citizenship, vote in that country's presidential election, and even have their children who are born in the United States claim dual citizenship.

Diplomatic Recognition

Statehood rests on both a claim to that status and its recognition by existing states. How many countries must grant recognition before statehood is achieved is a more difficult matter. When Israel declared its independence in 1948, the United States and the Soviet Union quickly recognized the country. Its Arab neighbors did not extend recognition and instead attacked what they considered to be the Zionist invaders. Was Israel a state at that point? It certainly seems so, because which countries, as well as how many of them, extend recognition is important.

Yet a lack of recognition, even by a majority of other countries, does not necessarily mean a state does not exist. Most countries' diplomatic recognition of the communist government of Mao Zedong in China came slowly after it took power in 1949. U.S. recognition was withheld until 1979. Did that mean that the rechristened People's Republic of China did not exist for a time? Clearly the answer is no because, as one scholar comments, "power capabilities are equally or more important than outside recognition" in establishing the existence of a state (Thompson, 1995:220).

The issue of recognition remains a matter of serious international concern. Taiwan is for all practical purposes an independent country, with more than two dozen countries recognizing it as such. Yet Taiwan itself does not claim independence from China, and thus is a *de facto* (in fact) but not *de jure* (in law) state. Tibet provides another example in the region of what might be called a state-in-waiting, as the participation box "The Future of Tibet" on page 168 explains.

Another contemporary issue involves the Palestinians. Many states recognize a Palestinian state and did so even before the Palestinians acquired any autonomous territory in Gaza and the West Bank beginning in the mid-1990s. Currently, according to the Palestine National Authority (PNA), almost 100 countries (including China and India) recognize an "independent State of Palestine." Moreover, the UN Security Council passed a resolution in 2002 calling for a separate Palestinian state. Somewhat less definitively, the United States and many other countries now also support the eventual creation of a Palestinian state as part of an overall Israeli-Palestinian agreement. President George W. Bush has offered a "roadmap" of guidelines and mutual steps by Israel and the PNA to reach an accord that Secretary of State Condoleezza Rice has described as " a reliable guide . . . for the Palestinian people [to] end up in an independent Palestinian state."[2] Yet amid all the diplomatic maneuvering, it is clear that an independent Palestine does not yet exist and any claim that it is a sovereign state is more a matter of legal nuance than practical reality.

While the connection between statehood and diplomatic recognition is imprecise, it is an important factor for several reasons. One is that only states can fully participate in the international system. For example, the PNA holds a seat in the UN General Assembly but cannot vote. This is roughly analogous to Puerto Rico having only a nonvoting member of the U.S. House of Representatives. External recognition is also important because states are generally the only entities that can legally do such things as sell government bonds and buy heavy weapons internationally. Israel's chances of survival in 1948 were enhanced when recognition allowed the Israelis to raise money and purchase armaments in Europe, the United States, and elsewhere. Also, it would be difficult for any aspirant to statehood to survive for long without recognition. Economic problems resulting from the inability to establish trade

PLAY A PART IN YOUR WORLD

The Future of Tibet

Tibet is almost twice the size of Texas and sits 15,000 feet high in the Himalayas. There are about 2.5 million Tibetans in their homeland, and nearly as many in adjacent areas in China and northern India. The spiritual leader of Tibetan Buddhism and the former secular leader of Tibet is the four-teenth Dalai Lama, who was born Lhamo Dhondrub and enthroned in 1940 when he was just five years old. Tibet was independent from the 800s to the 1300s. It then came under Mongol rule for over 300 years, but exercised consid-erable autonomy under its theocratic leader, who in 1577 was designated as the Dalai Lama (lama of all within the seas) by the Mongols. That autonomy ended when the Chi-nese emperor launched an invasion and in 1751 established his suzerainty over Tibet. A new era of independence began when imperial China collapsed in 1911 until Chinese forces again seized control in 1950. At first, the Dalai Lama re-mained in Tibet and exercised some authority. Then in 1959 the Tibetans revolted against China. They were crushed, and the Dalai Lama and his supporters fled south to India.

Now the status of Tibet is disputed. China claims it is a province. Most Tibetans and many others maintain that their homeland is an occupied state. The Dalai Lama is a charismatic figure who is Tibet's chief diplomat. He tirelessly campaigns for his people's political rights, while opposing violence to achieve them. These traits have earned the Dalai Lama access to world leaders and widespread sup-port by many individuals, including such celebrities as actor Richard Gere. Not even the Dalai Lama, however, has been able to win support from any of the world's governments for Tibetan autonomy, much less independence. Thus for now, China has the upper hand. Certainly the attitudes of other states reflect China's growing power, but it is also true that no country established relations with Tibet between 1911 and 1959, when China was much weaker.

Be Active

While near-term change in Tibet's status is unlikely, nothing is certain. So get involved if you support the Tibetan cause. There are numerous groups on college campuses and elsewhere that would welcome your support. A starting place is to visit the

Be active in trying to write the script of world policy to con-form more closely to your policy beliefs, whatever they may be. This woman protesting in India in 2005 believes in the cause of Tibetan independence. If you agree, find a way to support her efforts. If you disagree, be active opposing her views.

Web site of the Tibet government in exile at www.tibet.com/. There, the "How You Can Help Tibet" hyperlink offers sugges-tions and also provides further links to supportive groups such as Students for a Free Tibet (www.studentsforafreetibet.org/). No known citizen groups support Beijing's position, but you can find out more about it and establish contacts if you wish through the China Tibet Information Center at www.tibetinfor.com.cn/.

relations are just one example of the difficulties that would arise. The case of Taiwan shows that survival while in diplomatic limbo is not impossible, but it is such an oddity that it does not disprove the general rule.

Internal Organization

States must normally have some level of political and economic structure. Most states have a government, but statehood continues during periods of severe turmoil, even anarchy. Afghanistan, Liberia, Sierra Leone, Somalia, and some other existing states dissolved into chaos during the last decade or so, and none of them can be said to have reestablished a stable government with real authority over most of the country.

Yet none of these failed states has ceased to exist legally. Each, for instance, continued to sit as a sovereign equal, with an equal vote, in the UN General Assembly. For example, Somalia has not had a functioning government since the early 1990s and is effectively divided among various warring clans. As of mid-2005, a fourteenth "transitional government" had formed, but it was located in Kenya because it lacked the power to meet in safety in Mogadishu, the capital of Somalia.

Domestic Support

The final characteristic of a state is domestic support. In its most positive form, a state's population is loyal to it and grants it legitimacy: the willing acceptance of the authority to govern. At its most passive, the population grudgingly accepts the reality of a government's power to govern. For all the coercive power that states usually possess, it is difficult for any state to survive without at least the passive acquiescence of its people. The dissolution of Czechoslovakia, the Soviet Union, and Yugoslavia are illustrations of multinational states collapsing in the face of the separatist impulses of disaffected nationalities. One of the challenges facing postwar Iraq is whether it will be possible to create sufficient domestic support for any government among the badly divided Shiites, Sunnis, and Kurds, all of whom, in turn, have their own internal divisions.

As is evident from the foregoing discussion of the characteristics of a state, what is or is not a state is not an absolute. Because a state's existence is more a political than a legal matter, there is a significant gray area. No country truly imagines that the Palestinians control a sovereign state, yet many countries recognize it as such for political reasons. By the same political token, Taiwan is a functioning state, but China's power keeps it in a legal limbo. And no matter what the Tibetans and their Dalai Lama say and no matter what anyone's sympathies may be, Tibet is not and has never been recognized as a sovereign state by any government. Then there are the failed states that remain legal sovereign entities by default because there is nothing else that can be easily done with them.

Purposes of the State

Have you ever stopped to think about why we humans organize ourselves into political units with governments? After all, governments are expensive and they are telling us what we must and must not do. Yet, despite this, humans have subjected themselves to governance as far back in history as we can see.

Although political philosophers have disagreed over why humans create societies and establish governments, *individual betterment* is a common theme among them (Baradat, 2003). For example, this theme is evident in the writing of such classical theorists as Thomas Hobbes (1588–1679) and John Locke (1632–1704). Each contended that people had once lived as individuals or in family groups in a **state of nature**. Communities of unrelated individuals did not exist, and people possessed individual sovereignty, that is, they did not grant authority (legitimate power) to anyone or anything (a government) beyond their families to regulate their behavior. They also argued that people eventually found this highly decentralized existence unsatisfactory. Therefore, the theory continues, it was the desire to improve their lives that prompted individuals and families to join together in societies, to surrender much of their sovereignty, and to create governments to conduct the society's affairs. All this was based on an implicit understanding called a **social contract** that specified the purposes of governments and the limitations on them.

Hobbes and Locke disagreed about what persuaded people to abandon the state of nature and merge into societies. Hobbes said it was fear, arguing that life without government was so dangerous that people created strong governments to provide protection. Taking a more positive view, Locke contended that people joined together in societies because they realized that they could improve their lives more easily through cooperation than by individual effort alone.

Among other places, the ideas of Hobbes and Locke are clearly evident in the fundamental documents of the American Revolution and the United States. The idea in the Declaration of Independence that people had a right to "life, liberty, and the pursuit of happiness," and "that to secure these rights, governments are instituted among men," is drawn closely from Locke. And the preamble to the U.S. Constitution combines Hobbes's emphasis on protection and Locke's focus on individual advancement in its words that the purpose of the new government is to "insure domestic tranquility, provide for the common defense, [and] promote the general welfare."

The significant point about Hobbes and Locke is that they agreed that political units and their governments were not just givens. Instead, they saw them as instruments created for a utilitarian purpose. Moreover, the two philosophers believed that governments were legitimate and should survive only as long as they did what they had been created to do and did not overstep the limits placed on them by the social contract. This approach is called the **instrumental theory of government**. The idea, as President Woodrow Wilson put it, is that "government should not be made an end in itself; it is a means only—a means to be freely adapted to advance the best interest of the social organism. The state exists for the sake of society, not society for the sake of the state."[3]

A final point in this discussion of the purpose of government is to relate it to world politics. The connection is that having a sense of what states and their governments are meant to do is a necessary step to evaluating how well they are operating. Being able to judge how well states are working will help you evaluate the arguments at the end of this chapter about whether we should continue to govern ourselves principally through states. You will see that analysts disagree about whether the state can fulfill the purposes for which it was created and whether new forms of political organization will and/or should supplement or replace states as the basic unit of governance.

The State as the Core Political Organization

Having explored the nature and purpose of states, our next task is to look at the state as our primary political organization. Chapter 1 points out that the quasi-anarchical nature of the international system stems from the fact that the sovereign state is the key actor in the system. Chapter 3 examines how states make foreign policy. Here we explore differing theories of governance and discuss national interests.

MAP
Political Systems

Theories of Governance

How states are governed has a number of ramifications for world politics. These implications relate to such questions as whether some types of government are more warlike than others, whether some are more successful in their foreign policies than

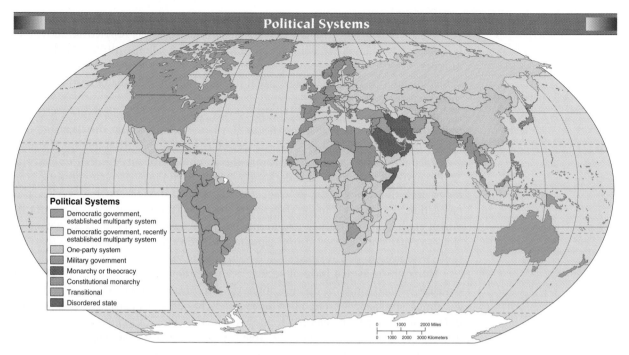

Political Systems

Political Systems
- Democratic government, established multiparty system
- Democratic government, recently established multiparty system
- One-party system
- Military government
- Monarchy or theocracy
- Constitutional monarchy
- Transitional
- Disordered state

The democratization of the world's countries, which began symbolically with the American (1776) and French (1789) Revolutions, progressed slowly for 150 years, then accelerated after World War II. Now, as this map indicates, the majority of countries are full-fledged or quasi-democracies.

others, and whether it is wise to promote a specific form of governance, much as the United States is pledged to foster democracy around the world.

We can begin to address these questions by dividing theories of governance into two broad categories. One includes types of **authoritarian government**, which allow little or no participation in decision making by individuals and groups outside the upper reaches of the government. The second category includes **democratic government**, which allows much broader and more meaningful participation. As with many things we discuss, the line between authoritarian and democratic is not precise. Instead, using broad and meaningful participation as the standard, there is a scale that runs from one-person rule to full, direct democracy (or even, according to some, to anarchism). The map above provides one way to order types of government, with the countries in shades of green being generally democratic and the countries in other colors being generally authoritarian.

ANALYZE THE ISSUE
Measuring Freedom

Authoritarian Theories

Throughout history, the most common form of governance was for an individual or group to exercise control over people with little or no concern about whether they consented to it or agreed with the ruler's policies. This approach has included many garden-variety dictatorships that sprang from an urge to power by an individual or a group rather than from any overarching theory of how societies are best governed. Yet there are a number of rationales supporting **authoritarianism**, rule from above.

One of the oldest forms of nondemocratic governance is **theocracy**, rule by spiritual leaders. Today, it has virtually disappeared, and the Holy See (the Vatican) is the world's only pure theocracy. There are, however, some elements of theocracy left in the popular, if not the legal, status of Japan's emperor, Thailand's king, and (most strongly)

Tibet's exiled Dalai Lama. Iran's government also contains an element of theocracy. So did the Taliban government of Afghanistan before it was toppled in 2001, and Islamic religious law (the *shari'ah*) plays a strong role along with secular law in a number of Muslim countries. Furthermore, the increased strength of religious fundamentalism in many places means that it is not unthinkable that a rejuvenation of theocracy might occur.

Arguments for secular authoritarianism are also ancient. For example, the Greek philosopher Plato (ca. 428 B.C.–347 B.C.), in his famous work *The Republic*, dismissed democracy as "full of . . . disorder and dispensing a sort of quality of equals and unequals alike." He contended that the common citizenry trying to direct the state would be analogous to sailors on a ship "quarrelling over the control of the helm; each thinks he ought to be steering the vessel, though he has never learned navigation . . . ; what is more, they assert that navigation is a thing that cannot be taught at all, and are ready to tear in pieces anyone who says it can." Plato's conclusion was that ships needed strong captains and crews that took orders and that "all those who need to be governed should seek out the man who can govern them."

Monarchism is one form of secular authoritarianism, although the theory that God had granted kings the divine right to govern contained a touch of theocracy. This system of governance through hereditary rulers has declined considerably. There are only a few strong monarchs (such as Saudi Arabia's king) scattered among a larger number of constitutional monarchies that severely restrict the monarch's power.

Communism as applied by Vladimir Lenin and his successors in the USSR, by Mao Zedong in China, and by other Communist leaders elsewhere, also falls squarely within the spectrum of authoritarian governance. Karl Marx expected that a "dictatorship of the proletariat" over the bourgeoisie would be necessary during a transitional socialist period between capitalism and communism. Lenin institutionalized this view by centralizing power in the hands of the Communist Party, which in turn was dominated by the Politburo and its head (Gaus, 2000). Party control over all aspects of society became so strong that its critics labeled it totalitarianism. Communism peaked in the later part of the 20th century when communist governments controlled the Soviet Union, China, the countries of Eastern Europe, and other countries whose combined populations equaled about 30% of the world population. Since then it has been swept aside in most countries, remaining the system of government only in China, Cuba, North Korea, and Vietnam. Nevertheless, Communist parties remain active in many countries and even won a majority in parliament in the 2005 elections in Moldova.

Yet another authoritarian political philosophy is **fascism.** The term is often used incorrectly to describe almost anyone far to the right. More accurately, the tenets of fascism espoused by Benito Mussolini of Italy, Adolf Hitler of Germany, and other fascists include (1) rejecting rationality and relying on emotion to govern; (2) believing (especially for Nazis) in the superiority of some groups and the inferiority of others; (3) subjugating countries of "inferior" people; (4) rejecting individual rights in favor of a "corporatist" view that people are "workers" in the state; (5) demanding that economic activity support the corporatist state; (6) viewing the state as a living thing (the organic state theory); (7) believing that the individual's highest expression is in the people (*volk* in German); and (8) believing that the highest expression of the *volk* (and, by extension, the individual) is in the leader (*führrer* in German, *duce* in Italian), who rules as a totalitarian dictator.

Fascism is of contemporary interest because it is again astir in a variety of countries (Ignazi & Kesselman, 2004). The term *fascist* is so tainted by history that few

Although fascism and other authoritarian beliefs have declined dramatically, they are not dead. Antidemocratic parties of both the left and right have recently shown some resurgence in Europe. One of those who finds dictatorship and intolerance appealing is this "skinhead" member of Germany's neofascist National Democratic Party. He is seen here taking part in a march in Berlin on May 8, 2005, decrying Nazi Germany's surrender 60 years earlier. The flag he holds depicts a World War II German soldier against a background describing them as "the best soldiers in the world."

admit to being fascist. That does not, however, diminish the worry, expressed by an official of the UN Commission on Human Rights, that "neo-fascism and neo-Nazism are gaining ground in many countries—especially in Europe."[4] There neofascist parties have won seats, sometimes several of them, in many national parliaments and in that of the European Union. No fascist has become a head of government, but in the 2002 French presidential elections, Jean-Marie Le Pen, leader of the ultra–right wing National Front Party, received 17% of the vote and finished second among 16 candidates. Le Pen advocates xenophobic, anti-immigrant policies and has dismissed the extermination of 6 million Jews and others in the Holocaust as a mere "detail of history."[5] Numerous observers also worry that Prime Minister Silvio Berlusconi of Italy is flirting with the fascism that gripped it before and during World War II. He has included numerous members of such neofascist parties as the Italian Social Movement (MSI) and the National Alliance (NA) in his government. Additionally, Berlusconi has urged Europeans to "be confident of the superiority of our civilization," has expressed the conviction that "the West will continue to conquer peoples, like it conquered communism," and claimed that "Mussolini never killed anyone."[6]

Thus, in the early 21st century, it is possible to give only a mixed report on the prospects for the end of authoritarian government. The number of authoritarian governments has declined considerably, yet retrograde political philosophies are far from extinct. As one analysis notes gloomily, "ideologies often go through a process of ebb and flow. Right-wing extremism and authoritarianism have deep roots" (Macridis & Hulliung, 1996:183).

Democratic Theory

Democracies (from the Greek word *demos,* meaning "citizenry") date back to about 500 B.C. and the ancient Greek city-states. For more than 2,000 years, however, democracy existed only sporadically and usually in isolated locations. The gradual rise of English democracy, then the American and French Revolutions in the late 18th century, changed democracy from a mere curiosity to an important national and transnational political idea. Still, the spread of democracy continued slowly. Then,

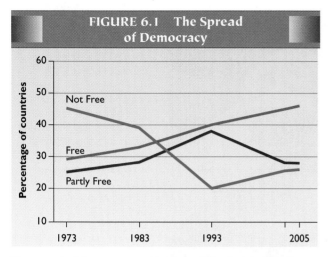

FIGURE 6.1 The Spread of Democracy

The spread of democracy worldwide is evident in the upward trend from 29% of all countries being free, as Freedom House terms it, in 1973, to 46% being free in 2005.

Data source: http://www.freedomhouse.org/.

during the past few decades, the pace of democratization picked up considerably, as Figure 6.1 shows.

Before turning to the impact of democratization on world politics, it is important to note that there are disagreements about precisely what constitutes a democracy. The most important of those is the debate over the relative importance of process versus outcome.

On one end of a scale of what is democratic, **procedural democracy** stresses process. If citizens have free speech, periodically get to choose among competing candidates, and follow other such procedures, then by this standard there is democracy. Using procedure to evaluate the extent of democracy is particularly evident in Western concepts.

At the other end of the scale, many cultures stress **substantive democracy.** They see democracy as a substantive product associated with equality. Proponents of this view contend that a country has failed democratically if, despite meeting procedural requisites, it produces a perpetual socioeconomic underclass based on race, ethnicity, gender, or some other factor. Such a system, they contend, in the end denies the most important element of democracy—the substantive human right to equality—even if the government adheres to the procedural motions of democracy. Moreover, it is arguable that any system in which citizens have vastly different economic circumstances is inherently undemocratic. The contention is that government "of the people, by the people, and for the people" is undercut by the ability of wealthy individuals, groups, and corporations to spend hugely disproportionate sums to influence the political process and to hire expert representation in the courts. This, critics say, makes the contest unfair and undemocratic, no matter what the theory may be.

Global Democratization as a Policy Goal

Many observers have heralded the steady increase in freedom as portending the coming of a democratic age (Diamond, 2003). Representing this view, Francis Fukuyama has suggested in "The End of History?" (1989:3) that we may have come to the end of political evolution, with "the universalization of Western liberal democracy as the final form of government." Others are less optimistic about democracy's strength or its continued spread (Inglehart, 2003), but Figure 6.1 makes it clear that democracy has spread rapidly in recent decades and is now the dominant form of governance. The issue here is whether the United States and other democratic countries and the UN and other international organizations should press for global democratization.

Pursuing global democracy as a policy goal presents a number of issues. One is whether democracy is always possible, at least in the short term. In most of the West, where democracy has existed the longest and seems the most stable, it has evolved slowly and often fitfully over centuries. More recently, other parts of the world have experienced increased degrees of democratization, but the likelihood that any single country will adopt democratic values and practices is at least partly linked with internal factors, such as attitudes about democracy and a country's educational and economic level.

Web Link

One place to get involved in promoting democracy is through the Carter Center, whose Web site is located at **www.cartercenter.org.**

Democracy and Economic Development

It is clear that there is a strong relationship between democracy and economic development. This is evident in Figure 6.2, which shows that the wealthier a country is, the more likely it is to be a democracy. The issue is something of a chicken-and-egg argument. If democracy promotes development, then it is wise to press poor countries to democratize. Among those who take this view, the recipient of the 1998 Nobel Prize in economics contends that democracy promotes economic growth by pressing leaders to invest their countries' capital in education, consumer products, and other areas that will build economic strength and stimulate production, instead of in military spending and other less productive economic paths (Sen, 1999).

Others believe that economic development is a necessary precursor for democracy, contending that people need to have a certain sense of economic well-being before they can spare the energy to participate in a democratic system. Leaders of economically disadvantaged countries often argue that their struggle to feed, clothe, and otherwise attend to the needs of their people does not allow the "luxury" of Western-style democracy, with its incessant political bickering and its attention to the individual.

Proponents of the development-first approach also note that educational levels parallel development and that an educated populace is necessary for a strong democracy. From this perspective, attempting to promote full-fledged democracy in countries with poor economic and educational conditions may be doomed to failure. Doing so may even prove counterproductive by destabilizing a country to the point that it collapses into violence and loses any ground it has made toward both democracy and economic development. From this perspective, in one scholar's succinct phraseology, "Democracy can be bad for you" (Hobsbawm, 2001:25).

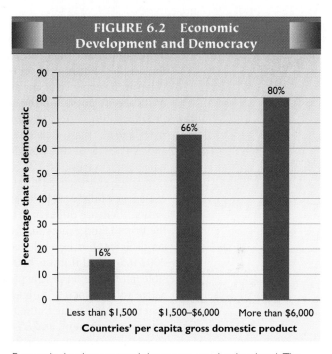

FIGURE 6.2 Economic Development and Democracy

Economic development and democracy are closely related. The poorest countries are the least likely to be democratic; the richest countries are the most likely to be democratic. What is not fully understood is whether prosperity promotes democracy, democracy promotes prosperity, or prosperity and democracy build on each other.

Data source: Freedom House (2005).

Attitudes about Democracy

It would be a mistake to assume that everyone, everywhere, is yearning to be free. A survey that asked people in 77 countries if they favored or opposed "having a strong leader who does not have to bother with parliament and elections," found that a majority of respondents in 21% of the countries approved of the idea, as did between a third and half the people in another 21% of the countries (Inglehart, 2003). Another survey asked people what they would prefer if they had to choose between democracy and a strong economy. People in a third of the countries chose a strong economy.[7] Such responses lead one scholar to conclude that while "today almost everyone gives lip service to democracy . . . when one probes deeper, one finds disturbing evidence that mass support is not as nearly solid [as one would hope]" (Inglehart, 2003:52).

As one example, 77% of Russians have more confidence in a strong leader than a democratic form of government as a way to solve their country's problems. Furthermore, 81% say they would rather have a strong economy than a democracy if

WEB POLL
McDonald's or Democracy?

they had to choose one or the other.[8] Thus President Vladimir Putin was expressing an attitude shared by most Russians when in 2005 he characterized democracy as no more "important than the aspirations for economic success or social well-being of the people." Putin went on to caution that, "Democratic procedures should not develop at the expense of law and order, or stability, which has been so hard to achieve, or the steady pursuit of the economic course we have taken." From this perspective, President Putin rejected widespread criticism that Russia is retreating from democracy, lauded "the independent character of the democratic path we have chosen," and asserted Russians would only "move forward taking into account our own internal circumstances."[9]

Another error would be to assume that the United States or any other country can successfully export its model of democracy to all other countries. As we noted earlier, there are different standards of democracy. Those emphasized by Americans, the British, and others tend to favor individualism and procedural democracy. Others disagree. For example, consider American and French responses to a survey in 2002 that asked if it was better for government to interfere in society as little as possible in order to let people pursue their goals, or better for the government to take an active role in society to guarantee that nobody was in need. A majority (58%) of Americans chose the limited government option, compared to just 34% wanting an activist government, and 8% unsure. Taking a very different view, 62% of the French chose an activist government, just 36% favored limited government, and 2% were uncertain. Yet another survey found that globally more people than not disliked "American ideas about democracy." Taken in 16 countries in 2003, the survey almost surely reflected a degree of anger at the United States over the war with Iraq, but it did reveal that 50% of all respondents did not like American-style democracy, compared to 41% who liked it and 9% uncertain.[10]

Democracy, Foreign Policy, and Security

The spread of democracy to date and the prospect of it becoming the global standard of acceptable governance lead to questions about what that does and what that would mean for world politics. To address this, we can examine the connection between democracy and foreign policy success, the impact of a greater role for women in foreign policy as a result of democratization, and what the spread of democracy portends for both international and domestic security.

Democracy and Foreign Policy Success

There is a long-standing debate over whether one form or another of government is more successful in foreign affairs, especially war. The noted French observer Alexis de Tocqueville argued in *Democracy in America* (1835) that "it is most especially in the conduct of foreign relations that democratic governments appear to me to be decidedly inferior to governments carried on upon different principles." The drawbacks, Tocqueville wrote, are that democracies tend "to obey the impulse of passion rather than the suggestions of prudence" and also that "a democratic people is less capable of sustained effort than another."

Recent scholarship disputes this view. In fact, some studies find that democracies are more successful than autocracies, at least in war (Ajin, 2004; Biddle & Long, 2004). One study found that democracies have won about 75% of the wars they have fought since 1815 and concluded, "It appears that democratic nations not only might enjoy the good life of peace, prosperity, and freedom; they can also defend themselves against outside threats from tyrants and despots" (Reiter & Stam, 2002:2). Yet other research finds that those wars that democracies do initiate are "uniformly shorter and less costly than wars initiated by nondemocracies" (Filson & Werner, 2004:296).

Democracy, Women, and Foreign Policy

Full participation for women is one aspect of democracy that has lagged during its evolution. Historically, women did not win the right to vote in national elections until 1893 in New Zealand. Other countries followed suit slowly. Switzerland in 1971 was the last economically developed country to allow female suffrage. Now, almost all countries do, although there are still some exceptions. When in 2005 women in Kuwait won the right to vote, Saudi Arabia was left as one of the few bastion of male-only voting, even in its limited elections.

Access to political office for women has come even more slowly. It has only been a century since the world's first elected female national legislators took their seats in Finland's parliament in 1907. Other than monarchs, no woman served as the head of her country until the middle of the 20th century. As former Norwegian prime minister Gro Harlem Brundtland commented dryly, "I was the first woman in 1,000 years [to head Norway's government]. Things are evolving gradually."[11] Giving truth to that observation, in early 2005 only 10 women were serving as the presidents or prime ministers of their countries. In other leadership positions, only about 8% of all cabinet ministers are women; they make up a scant 16% of the members of the world's national legislatures and 9% of the world's judiciary. Moreover, these overall figures do not reveal that women have an even smaller political presence in some regions, as Figure 6.3 indicates.

What the gradual rise in the number of women in positions of political leadership, assuming it continues, will mean for the course of international politics is

Web Link

Symbolic of women's progress in achieving leadership positions is the Council of Women World Leaders, which was established in 1996 and whose Web site is at **www.womenworldleaders.org/**.

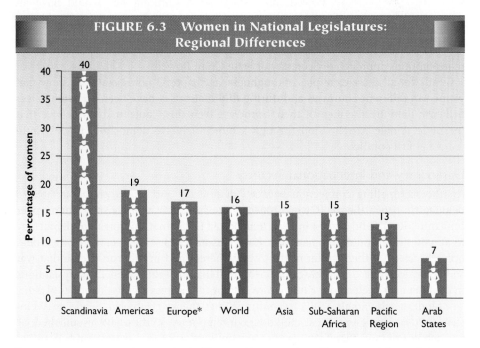

FIGURE 6.3   Women in National Legislatures: Regional Differences

By one measure, women have made significant strides toward reaching an equal share of top government positions by increasing their share of the seats in national parliaments from 3% in 1955 to 16% in 2005. But 16% is still less than one-third of 50%.

*Excluding Scandinavia

Ukrainian Prime Minister Yulia Tymoshenko seen here in 2005 speaking to reporters in Kiev about international energy supplies is one of a still small but growing number of women who are achieving positions of national and international leadership. Do you think a world in which half the leaders were women would just be more equal or would world politics also be different?

an important question. The propensity for conflict provides an interesting example. Certainly, there have been women leaders who have been determined defenders of their country when they need to be. The derogatory whisper campaign that women make weak leaders has been repeatedly disproved by the records of female leaders such as Prime Minister Indira Gandhi of India (1966–1977, 1980–1984), Prime Minister Golda Meir of Israel (1969–1974), and Prime Minister Margaret Thatcher of Great Britain (1979–1990). Each of these women led her country to victory in war. Similarly, women who have served among the ranks of such key international relations officials as foreign minister and defense minister have also proven their mettle when necessary. The first woman to serve as U.S. secretary of state, Madeleine Albright, was at times so enthusiastic about using military force that the more cautious chairman of the Joint Chiefs of Staff, Colin Powell, has remembered thinking he "would have an aneurysm."[12] Similarly, Secretary of State Condoleezza Rice has a reputation of being something of a hawk, who as national security adviser sided with Secretary of Defense Donald Rumsfeld and others who favored war with Iraq in opposition to the more cautious approach of Secretary of State Colin Powell.

Still, for all these examples of toughness, as chapter 3 notes, statistics show that women in different countries and during different crises have been on average less bellicose than are the men of their country. Given this, some analysts believe that increased female participation through a more inclusive democratic model could reduce global conflict.

Did You Know That:

U.S. Secretary of State Condoleezza Rice, an avid fan of the Cleveland Browns of the National Football League, says her "dream job" is NFL commissioner.

Democracy and International Security

Another compelling connection between democracy and world politics relates to **democratic peace theory** (Owen, 2004). It is associated with German philosopher Immanuel Kant, who argued in *Perpetual Peace* (1795) that the spread of democracy to all countries would eliminate war. Kant reasoned that a democratic peace would occur because "if the consent of the citizens is required in order to decide that war should be declared . . . , nothing is more natural than that they would be very cautious in commencing such a poor game, decreeing for themselves all the calamities of war."

Modern scholarship tends to confirm Kant's theory (Halperin, Siegle, & Weinstein, 2004). Using empirical methods, contemporary studies have established, as one scholar puts it, that "democracies are unlikely to engage in any kind of militarized disputes with each other or to let any such disputes escalate into war. They rarely even skirmish" (Russett, 2000:232). This view is accepted by many scholars "as 'the closest thing to an empirical law' in world politics" that exists (Henderson, 1999:482).

If the theory that democracies seldom, if ever, fight one another is correct, then the widespread concern that President Vladimir Putin is undermining democracy in Russia could have major implications for global peace. Representing this worry, a woman in a recent Moscow protest is carrying a placard with a photograph of the Russian president altered to make him look like Adolf Hitler. She wears a T-shirt with a crossed-out picture of Putin and the words "Down with Big Brother" (a reference to the totalitarian dictator in George Orwell's novel, *Nineteen Eighty-Four*).

Several caveats about democratic peace theory should be noted. First, democracies do go to war, although only with autocracies. The easy example is the United States, which is both a leading democracy and the country that has most often been at war since 1945. Second, not all scholars agree with democratic peace theory. For example, some analysts are skeptical that the absence of war between democracies is anything more than a historical anomaly that may not persist in the future (Henderson, 2002). Future history may prove democratic peace theory wrong. For now, though, there is broad, albeit not complete, agreement among scholars that democracies have more peaceful relations with each other than do democracies with authoritarian states or authoritarian states with one another. From this perspective, even if a world in which all countries were democratic did not produce perpetual peace, as Kant thought it would, it might produce preponderant peace and, thus, should be promoted.

This theory debate has serious implications for day-to-day world politics. President Bush has asserted, and some scholars agree, that increasing democracy in the Middle East will make that region less conflict-prone and ease terrorism (Hafez, 2004). Another matter of great current concern is whether democracy will survive in Russia. President Vladimir Putin has instituted a number of changes in recent years that have alarmed many as representing a retreat from the democratic reforms instituted in the aftermath of the USSR's collapse in 1991 (Herspring, 2004). Expressing this view, 115 U.S. and European political and cultural leaders (including several U.S. senators, former Czech President Václav Havel, and former Swedish Prime Minister Carl Bildt) signed an open letter in late 2004, which charged that Putin's government has "systematically undercut the freedom and independence of the press, destroyed the checks and balances in the Russian federal system, arbitrarily imprisoned both real and imagined political rivals, removed legitimate candidates from electoral ballots, harassed and arrested NGO leaders and weakened Russia's political parties."[13] As noted above, the Putin government rejects this view, but if Moscow does sink into authoritarianism, and if democratic peace theory is correct, then the potential for conflict between Russia and the democratic West will increase.

Democracy and Domestic Security

Some observers also contend that the transition from authoritarian to democratic government can produce very negative domestic side effects. It can unleash previously suppressed domestic intergroup hatreds (Mann, 2004). Furthermore, this domestic conflict can spill over into the international sphere. It is possible to argue, for example, that the turmoil that engulfed what was once Yugoslavia was a result of the end of the authoritarian control of the communist government. Once that control was relaxed, the multiple ethnonational rivalries that had been dormant soon erupted into bloody conflict. Similar patterns can be seen in several African countries, in the former Soviet Union, and elsewhere in cases where independence or the coming of democracy has unleashed bloody ethnic clashes.

To this contention, supporters of global democratization respond that in the long run democracies commit less violence against their citizens than do authoritarian governments (Davenport, 2004). Another counterargument is that any bloodshed that the transition to democracy brings pales when compared to the brutality inflicted by authoritarian regimes. One study of "democide," the killing of unarmed residents by governments, demonstrates that the degree to which a government is totalitarian "largely accounts for the magnitude and intensity of genocide and mass murder" committed by that government. Therefore, the study reasons, "the best assurances against democide are democratic openness, political competition, leaders responsible to their people and limited government. In other words, power kills, and absolute power kills absolutely" (Rummel, 1995:25).

States and the Future

Sovereign, territorially defined states have not always existed, as we have noted. Therefore, they will not necessarily persist in the future. The questions are, Will they? Should they? The future of the state is one of the most hotly debated topics among scholars of international relations. As one such analyst explains, "Central to [our] future is the uncertain degree to which the sovereign state can adapt its behavior and role to a series of deterritorializing forces associated with markets, transnational social forces, cyberspace, demographic and environmental pressures, and urbanism" (Falk, 1999:35). As you ponder your verdict about states, recall the discussion above about the purpose of government and apply your own conclusions about what governments should do to your evaluation of the success or failure of the state as the continued central model of governance.

The State: Changing Status

JOIN THE DEBATE
Casting the Actors for the World Stage: Has the Recent War in Iraq Reinforced the Sovereign Rights of the Nation-State?

In many ways, states remain alive and well on the world stage. One sign of health is their increasing number. As Figure 6.4 depicts, there are now more than twice as many countries as there were in the middle of the 20th century. Additionally, and as noted frequently, states remain the most important and powerful type of international actor. Some of them, especially the United States, are truly formidable. Much of what underpins states, such as nationalism, also remains strong.

Yet all is not well for the preeminent position of states. One key change is the weakening of the doctrine of state sovereignty. Ever so slowly, countries are taking on obligations to abide by the rules of the UN's International Court of Justice, the quasi-judicial trade dispute hearing panels of the World Trade Organization, and other international bodies. These trends are reviewed in other chapters.

Even what countries do within their own borders is no longer beyond international interference. For example, the world community is beginning to reject sovereignty as a defense of a government's mistreatment of its citizens. During the early

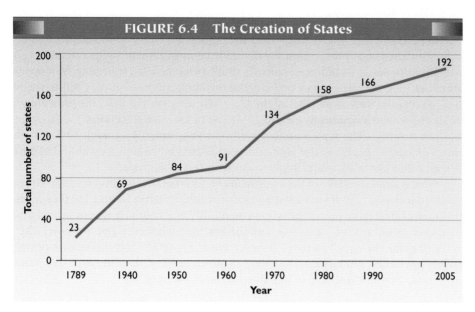

FIGURE 6.4   The Creation of States

This figure portrays the rapid growth in the number of countries in the international system. From the beginning of the sovereign states about 500 years ago, it took until 1940 for 69 states to evolve. In the intervening 60 years, that number has nearly tripled.

1990s, global condemnation coupled with economic and other forms of sanctions forced the Eurowhite-dominated government of South Africa to end the apartheid system that oppressed its non-European-heritage citizens, especially its blacks. The UN also rejected the sovereignty defense when in 1994 it condemned the military overthrow of Haiti's elected president and authorized UN members to form a multinational force to topple the military junta. Soon thereafter, a U.S.-led force sent the generals packing into exile. The international community in the late 1990s demanded that the Yugoslav government cease its brutal attacks on rebellious Albanians in Kosovo, even though that province is clearly part of Yugoslavia. When diplomacy and sanctions failed, NATO warplanes went into action. The Serbs were driven from Kosovo, and the province was occupied by a multinational force. Even more recently, the UN authorized the use of international force to topple the government of Afghanistan if it did not comply with demands that it surrender accused al Qaeda terrorists. When that did not happen, the UN supported the military overthrow of that regime. Even more recently, the UN Security Council in 2005 demanded that Sudan halt the killing of people in Darfur by Janjaweed militia and that it turn over war criminals to the International Criminal Court (ICC) in The Hague, the Netherlands. Sudan's parliament condemned the UN resolution and "call[ed] on the government and all its institutions to strongly resist this unjust resolution," which it said was devoid of "any basis for justice and objectivity and violates the principle of national sovereignty."[14] Expressing the prevailing global view, UN Secretary-General Kofi Annan praised the resolution as lifting "the veil of impunity that has allowed human rights crimes in Darfur to continue unchecked."[15]

A related and dramatic demonstration of the diminution of sovereignty is the ongoing trial of Slobodan Milosevic, the former president (1989–2000) of Yugoslavia (since renamed Serbia and Montenegro), by the ICC for war crimes he allegedly abetted during the 1990s in Bosnia, Croatia, and Kosovo. If convicted, as he almost certainly will be, Milosevic could be sentenced to life in prison.

Expressing a widespread view, one human rights advocate hailed the prosecution of Milosevic as evidence that "even the highest government officials are vulnerable to international prosecution for the most heinous human rights crimes. . . . It will begin to force would-be tyrants to think twice before replicating Milosevic's atrocities."[16] Other observers worried about the implications of putting Milosevic on trial. Taking this view, a member of the U.S. Congress asserted that "the prosecution of Milosevic, a democratically elected . . . leader of a sovereign country . . . threatens U.S. sovereignty." The representative went on to explain, "We cannot have it both ways. We cannot expect to use [war crimes tribunals] when it pleases us and oppose [them] where the rules would apply to our own acts of aggression."[17]

What should we make of these restraints on internal sovereignty in South Africa, Haiti, Yugoslavia, Afghanistan, and Sudan? It would be naive to imagine they mean that in the foreseeable future the world community will regularly ignore sovereignty to take a stand against racism or authoritarianism whenever and wherever they occur. It would be equally wrong, however, not to recognize that the actions against racial oppression, military coups, ethnic cleansing, and neofascism were important steps away from the doctrine of unlimited state sovereignty.

The State: The Indictment

How should we view the diminution of sovereignty and other indications that states are weakening? Some greet it as a good thing. They contend that states are obsolete and/or destructive. A note before we get to arguments for and against the state is to be wary of being overly influenced by your loyalty to your country and letting that lead you to reject the anti-state points out of hand. Remember that states, like all units of government, should be considered utilitarian objects meant to protect and promote the common good. If states are not doing that, it is not treason to seek change. As the Declaration of Independence counseled, "Whenever any form of government becomes destructive [or incapable] of these ends, it is the right of the people to alter or to abolish it, and to institute a new government, laying its foundations on such principles and organizing its powers in such form, as to them shall seem mostly likely to effect their safety and happiness."

States Are Obsolete

The argument that states are obsolete begins with the premise that they were created in the middle of the last millennium as utilitarian political organizations to meet security, economic, and other specific needs and to replace the feudal and other forms of political organization that no longer worked effectively. "The nation-state is a rough and ready mechanism for furnishing a set of real services," one scholar writes. The problem, he continues, is that "the relation between what a state is supposed to do and what it actually does is increasingly slack" (Dunn, 1995:9). A second line of attack is that a country's foreign policy does not reflect the interests or wishes of its citizens.

States Are No Longer Utilitarian   Those who believe that states will and/or should play a diminished role in the future point to a number of areas where they say countries are not adequately performing the tasks they were created to do. This charge is leveled against all states, but it is particularly applied to the many states created in the past half century that have some or all of the following limitations: small territories, small populations, and few prospects for economic viability. East Timor, the newest

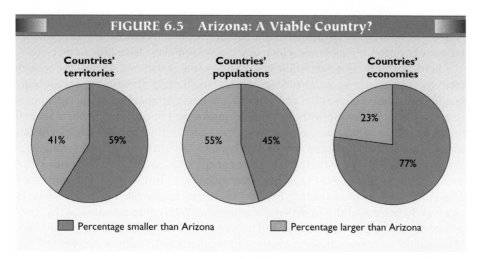

FIGURE 6.5   Arizona: A Viable Country?

Arizona's viability as an independent country would be highly questionable, yet the U.S. state has a territory that is larger than 59% of the world's countries and a population larger than 45% of them. Although not especially large by the standards of U.S. states, Arizona's gross state product if converted into GNP as an independent country would make Arizona's economy larger than 77% of all existing countries. The small size, population, and economic base (and sometimes all three) of many, even most of the world countries casts doubt on the future of the sovereign state as the central actor in the international system.

Data sources: CIA (2005), World Bank (2005), U.S. Bureau of the Census (2005).

country (independent: 2002), provides an example. It has about the same population as Delaware (approximately 1 million people), and its territory (5,794 sq. mi.) is only slightly larger than that of Connecticut, the third-smallest U.S. state. "Impoverished" would be the best word to describe East Timor economically. At $520, its per capita GNP is one of the lowest in the world, a small fraction (0.012%) of either Delaware's or Connecticut's (each with a per capita gross state product of about $43,000). Most Americans would smile with amusement at the thought of an independent Delaware or Connecticut joining the ranks of sovereign states on the world stage. Yet either of those two would make a more viable state than does East Timor. That country is something of an extreme case, but on a broader basis, an independent Arizona would be well into the middle ranks of countries in terms of population and territory and would be a leader in terms of its economic size, as Figure 6.5 shows.

Providing physical safety is one key role of the state. Yet the ability of states to protect their citizens is limited, and it has been getting worse since the signing of the Treaty of Westphalia (1648), the symbolic beginning of the state system. From then to now, almost 600 wars have occurred, killing over 140 million people. Moreover, the victim totals have risen rapidly through the centuries as humankind "improved" its killing capabilities. Indeed, 75% of all the people killed in wars during the last 500 years died in the 20th century. What is worse, science and technology have now created nuclear, chemical, and biological weapons of mass destruction, against which there is little or no defense. The question, then, is, Does the state protect people or simply define them as targets for other states in an anarchical international system?

Providing economic prosperity is a second key role of the state. The same genre of questions applies to the economic functions of a state. The tidal wave of trade and capital that moves across national borders means that states are increasingly less able to provide for the prosperity of their residents. For example, jobs are won or lost depending on a variety of factors, such as where transnational corporations decide to set up manufacturing, choices over which national governments have little or no control.

Providing for the general welfare is a third key role of the state. Health is one such concern, and states as independent entities are finding themselves increasingly unable to contain the spread of disease in an era when people and products that may carry the threat of disease with them move quickly and in massive numbers around the globe. AIDS is the most obvious example, and in the past few decades it has spread around the world and has killed about 25 million people. Other epidemics loom menacingly. Currently there is great concern that avian flu, which has killed some people in Asia, could rapidly spread globally with disastrous consequences. The World Health Organization (WHO) estimates that avian flu could infect as much as 30 percent of the world's population. One WHO official estimates that conservatively such a pandemic would kill between 2 million and 7 million people, and, "The maximum range is more . . . maybe 20 [million] to 50 million people."[18]

Whether it is AIDS, avian flu, or another microbial enemy, the reality, according to a U.S. physician, is that "today, in 30 hours, you can literally travel to the other side of the world. And likewise, while you are there, you can pick up a germ or a microorganism that may not exist on this side of the globe and within 30 hours you can have that back in the United States."[19] National borders provide increasingly scant protection against these globally transportable diseases, which, if they are to be contained, must be attacked through an international effort.

Did You Know That:

Within a few months, the Spanish flu pandemic of 1918 killed at least 20 million people worldwide, including about 600,000 Americans. Given population growth, a similar pandemic today would kill more than 60 million people globally and 1.6 million Americans.

States Do Not Pursue the Interests of Their People

Most states are huge enterprises that have authority over many millions of people and in two cases (China and India) over more than a billion of them. The issue is whether such mega-organizations are closely connected enough to their people to operate in their interests. This criticism touches on domestic as well as foreign policy, but for our purposes we will concentrate on national interest in world politics.

Critics of **national interest** as a guide for foreign policy advance a number of objections. One is that there is no such thing as an objective national interest. Critics say that what is in the national interest is totally subjective and defining it tends to be the province of every country's dominant political class, its **power elite**, rather than its citizens. This accounts for the frequent policy differences between what a country's leaders and its common citizens support, as detailed in chapter 3's discussion of the leader-citizen opinion gap.

A second objection is that using national interest as a basis of policy incorrectly assumes that there is a common interest. The contention here is that every society is a collection of diverse subgroups, many of which have differing interests. Furthermore, the concept of national interest inherently includes the assumption that if a collective interest can be determined, then that interest supersedes the interests of subgroups and individuals. Writing from the feminist perspective, for example, one scholar has noted that "the presumption of a similarity of interests between the sexes is an assumption" that cannot be taken for granted because "a growing body of scholarly work argues that . . . the political attitudes of men and women differ significantly" (Brandes, 1994:21).

Critics of the state system argue it would be far better to explore other ways of defining interests. *Global interests* are one alternative to national interest. Proponents of this standard do not reject national interest as such. Instead, they say that in the long run, a more enlightened view of interests is that all states will be more secure and more prosperous if the more fortunate ones help the others to also achieve peace and prosperity. That is essentially the point that Han Seung-soo, president of the UN General Assembly, made when he commented that particularly "in the wake of September 11" it is imperative to recognize "that development, peace, and security are inseparable," because the poorest countries are "the breeding ground for violence and despair."[20]

Individual interests are another alternative to national interest. Virtually all individuals are rightly concerned with their own welfare. In his inaugural address, President John F. Kennedy called on Americans to "ask not what your country can do for you—ask what you can do for your country." Maybe Kennedy had it backwards. Your country is arguably there to serve you, not the other way around, and what is good for your country or your nation may not be what is good for you. Considering your individual interests might seem very narrow-minded, but it also can be liberating because it can free you from attaching your policy preference to what is good for a collective (your nation) or an organization (your state). It is appropriate to ask, then, whether your individual interests, your nation's interests, your country's interests, and your world's interests are the same, mutually exclusive, or a mixed bag of congruencies and divergences. Only you, of course, can determine where your interests lie and what policies you support or oppose.

States Are Destructive

Pursuing the national interest is the essence of what a sovereign state does and what its citizens expect it to do. Critics castigate this emphasis on the national interest as inherently self-serving and inevitably leading to conflict and inequity. As France's foreign minister observed recently, the world should no longer act as if "we are . . . in prehistoric times when whoever had the biggest club would try to knock the other guy out so he could steal his mammoth skin."[21] The logic is simple. If countries pursue their national interests and those objectives are incompatible, then one likely possibility is that they will clash. Another possibility is that the interest of whichever state is the more powerful will prevail. That is, power, not justice, will win. Certainly, countries often negotiate and compromise. But in an anarchical international system that emphasizes self-interest and self-help, the chances of a peaceful and equitable resolution are less than in a hierarchical domestic system that restrains the contending actors and offers institutions (such as courts) that can decide disputes if negotiation fails.

Critics of the state system further contend that whatever the wins and losses are for states, the most likely losers are average citizens. Much more than leaders, the citizenry bear the brunt of war, economic sanctions, and other diplomatic tools states use in conflict with one another. To make matters worse, states often inflict violence and otherwise abuse the human rights of the very people they are supposed to protect. "Political regimes—governments—have probably murdered nearly 170 million of their own citizens and foreigners in this century—about four times the

National interest is a subjective standard for policy. What your country's leaders perceive as its national interests may not coincide with your view of what is good for the country, the world, and/or you personally. It is not clear whether this student protesting in Reno, Nevada, in 2005 believes that more funding for books and less for bombs would be in (a) the U.S. national interest, (b) the world's interest, (c) his individual interest. Perhaps the student would say the answer is (d) all of the above.

number killed in all international and domestic wars and revolutions," one scholar charges (Rummel, 1995:3).

A third argument is that states are destructive because they are unstable. As detailed in chapter 4, most states are a mélange of ethnonational groups rather than ideal nation-states. This ethnonational mix leads to conflict between groups that can drag outside countries into the fighting. Instability in other states comes from their grinding poverty. Whatever the cause, the result is numerous weak and even failed states, and these are the source of many of the problems the world faces (Fearon & Laitin, 2004; Fukuyama, 2004).

The State: The Defense

While those who predict or advocate the diminishment or demise of the state as a primary political organization make a strong argument, it is hardly an open-and-shut case against the state (Paul, Ikenberry, & Hall, 2004). First, as noted, nationalism has proven resilient, and its political vehicle, the state, still has many resources at its disposal. Moreover, the number of states has increased significantly. These facts undermine the assertion about the substantial weakening, much less the disappearance, of states as sovereign actors (Lentner, 2004). As two scholars write, "Reports of its demise notwithstanding, sovereignty appears to us to be prospering, not declining. . . . It still serves as an indispensable component of international politics" (Fowler & Bunck, 1995:163). Another scholar observes that while borders are becoming less and less meaningful as barriers to economic interchange, the flow of information, and some other transnational functions, "States are responding to globalization by attempting to restore meaning to national borders, not as barriers to entry, but as boundaries demarcating distinct political communities" (Goff, 2000:533).

Second, states may be able to adjust to the new realities by learning to cooperate and live in peace with other countries. Analysts who hold this view point to the increasing creation of and membership in numerous intergovernmental organizations (IGOs), like the WTO, as evidence that states are willing to give up some of their sovereignty in return for the benefits provided by free trade and other transnational interactions.

Third, states are arguably being strengthened as increasingly complex domestic and international systems create new demands for services. From this perspective, globalization and the strength of states "may be mutually reinforcing rather than antagonistic" (Weiss, 1998:204). "Empirical evidence demonstrates that the roles of the state are changing rather than diminishing," according to two scholars. "The state remains crucially involved in a wide range of problems," they continue, and "in each of these areas, specific initiatives may make state policies more efficient . . . as the roles of the nation-state continue to evolve" (Turner & Corbacho, 2000:118–119).

Fourth, sovereignty has always been a relative, not an absolute, principle and a dynamic, rather than static, concept. States and their leaders have long violated the principle when it suited their interests. Most of the examples of diminished sovereignty have occurred when stronger states or coalitions of states imposed their will on weaker states in what one scholar terms "organized hypocrisy" (Krasner, 1999). More powerful states, the contention continues, retain all their sovereignty or can and sometimes do withdraw from agreements to follow the decisions of IGOs. The United States, for instance, has refused to surrender any of its sovereign authority by joining the International Criminal Court (ICC), which would allow U.S. troops and citizens to be potentially prosecuted for war crimes by the international tribunal. This stance was also evident after the International Court of Justice (ICJ) recently ruled against the United States in a case involving its treatment of foreign nationals accused of crimes within the country. In response, the White House announced in 2005 that the United States was withdrawing from the part of the ICJ treaty giving that court jurisdiction over such disputes.

Fifth, sovereign states may prove to be better than the other forms of political organization. States do provide some level of defense, and some states have been relatively effective at shielding their citizens from the ravages of war. Sometimes that is a matter of power, as is true for the United States. But in other cases, it is related to geography, diplomatic skill, or a simple resolution not to take sides under almost any circumstances. Sweden and Switzerland, for example, managed to avoid becoming involved in any war, including either world war, during the 20th century.

Sixth, it is yet to be proven that IGOs provide an effective alternative to the state. Peacekeeping by the United Nations and other IGOs has had successes, but also notable failures. The WTO and other economic IGOs are under attack for benefiting rich countries, corporations, and individuals at the expense of less developed countries, small businesses, and workers. It may well be, as we will discuss in the next chapter, that IGOs can prove to be more effective and just instruments of governance as they evolve. That remains an open question, though.

Seventh, realists doubt that self-interest and conflict can ever be substantially eliminated from the system and support the state as a necessary guardian of the national interest. Henry Kissinger (1994:37), for one, warns against what he sees as Americans' "distrust of [U.S.] power, a preference for multilateral solutions and a reluctance to think in terms of national interest. All these impulses," Kissinger believes, "inhibit a realistic response to a world of multiple power centers and diverse conflicts."[22]

Despite criticism that they are outmoded, sovereign states remain the basic unit of governance and the focus of most people's political identity. This enduring strength is captured in this photograph of a Russian veteran of World War II talking with a young man whose T-shirt bears the Soviet-style red star. The two were at a patriotic rally held in Moscow in 2005 to celebrate the 60th anniversary of the surrender of Nazi Germany. The rally was organized by the nationalistic youth group Nashi, which translates as "Ours."

Realpolitik nationalists further contend that we live in a Darwinian political world, where people who do not promote their own interests will fall prey to those who do. Nationalists further worry about alternative schemes of global governance. One such critic of globalism notes that in intellectual circles "anyone who is skeptical about international commitments today is apt to be dismissed as an isolationist crank." Nevertheless, he continues, globalization should be approached with great caution because "it holds out the prospect of an even more chaotic set of authorities, presiding over an even more chaotic world, at a greater remove from the issues that concern us here in the United States" (Rabkin, 1994:41, 47).

The State: The Verdict

For now, the jury is still out on whether states will and should continue to dominate the political system and be the principal focus of political identity. States continue to exercise great political strength and most of them retain the loyalty of most of their citizens. Yet it is also true that the state exists in a rapidly changing political environment that is creating great pressures, whether they are those of Barber's (1995)

SIMULATION
The Future of the State:
Will Nationalism Survive?

tribalism or McWorld. The only certainty is that it would be an error to assume that the state-based system is invulnerable to change. As one scholar notes, "history sides with no one. . . . [The] lesson to be drawn [from the rise and evolution of states] is that all institutions are susceptible to challenges." Therefore, the sustainability of states depends in substantial part on whether they provide "efficient responses to such challenges" (Spruyt, 1994:185).

Where does this leave the future of sovereign states in the early 21st century? Most political scientists take a middle ground, recognizing the decline in the importance of states, but not predicting their demise in the foreseeable future (Holsti, 2004; Sørensen, 2004). As one puts it, "Although the system of sovereign states is likely to continue [in the foreseeable future] as the dominant structure in world politics, the content of world politics is changing" (Keohane & Nye, 1999:118). Those changes are well captured in the view of one scholar:

> A new epoch is evolving. It is an epoch of multiple contradictions: . . . States are changing, but they are not disappearing. State sovereignty has eroded, but it is still vigorously asserted. Governments are weaker, but they can still throw their weight around. . . . Borders still keep out intruders, but they are also more porous. Landscapes are giving way to ethnoscapes, mediascapes, ideoscapes, technoscapes, and financescapes, but territoriality is still a central preoccupation for many people. (Rosenau, 1998:18)

Chapter Summary

The Nature and Purpose of the State

1. States are the most important political actors. States as political organizations have these defining characteristics: sovereignty, territory, population, diplomatic recognition, internal organization, and domestic support.

2. There are various theories about why humans formed themselves into political units with governments. These theories give insight into what the purpose of these units is and, therefore, what people should expect from them.

The State as the Core Political Organization

3. Monarchism, theocracy, communism applied politically, and fascism are four forms of authoritarian governance. The percentage of countries ruled by authoritarian regimes has declined, but dictatorial governments are still common.

4. Democracy is a complex concept. Different sets of standards serve as a basis to determine the degree to which a political system is democratic.

5. There are disputes over when it is possible or advisable to press all countries to quickly adopt democratic forms of government.

6. There are a number of connections between democracy and domestic and international security.

7. The most important of these links, democratic peace theory, argues that democracies are unlikely to enter into conflict with one another. The reasons why democracies do not fight one another remain disputed among scholars, with explanations given from institutional, normative, and interest perspectives.

States and the Future

8. The future of the state is a hotly debated topic among scholars of international relations.

9. Some analysts predict the demise of states as principal actors, claiming that states are obsolete and destructive.

10. Other analysts of nationalism contend that the state is durable and has many resources at its disposal. These analysts doubt that states will weaken substantially or disappear as sovereign actors.

11. The final verdict among many scholars is that states will continue to exist but they will play a diminishing role in the future.

For simulations, debates, and other interactive activities, a chapter quiz, Web links, PowerWeb articles, and much more, visit **www.mhhe.com/rourke11/** and go to chapter 6. Or, while accessing the site, click on Course-Related Headlines and view recent international relations articles in the *New York Times*.

Key Terms

authoritarian government	fascism	power elite	substantive democracy
authoritarianism	instrumental theory of	procedural democracy	theocracy
communism	government	social contract	
democratic government	monarchism	sovereignty	
democratic peace theory	national interest	state of nature	

Intergovernmental Organizations: Alternative Governance

Friendly counsel cuts off many foes.
—William Shakespeare, *Henry VI, Part 1*

You peers, continue this united league.
—William Shakespeare, *King Richard III*

John Bolton, whom President Bush appointed U.S. ambassador to the UN in 2005, once said "it wouldn't make a bit of difference" if the UN's role in the world were substantially reduced. After you finish reading this chapter, ask yourself whether you agree with him, think the role of the UN is about right, or think it should be enhanced.

LTHOUGH THE STATE IS and has long been the primary actor in the international system, it is not the only one. Nor are states the only option for governance. **Intergovernmental organizations (IGOs)** are another type of international actor. This type of international organization has countries as its members. Thus IGOs are distinct from private-membership nongovernmental organizations (NGOs), as detailed in chapter 5. More importantly, IGOs provide a possible alternative to the traditional state-based system. Critics of this system say that it is inadequate to meet the challenges of a globalizing world, and it is violence-prone because of its emphasis on self-interested states operating in an anarchical international system. From this perspective, a better approach would be to pay heed to Shakespeare's counsel, in *Henry VI, Part 3,* to "Now join your hands, and with your hands your hearts" by empowering IGOs to increasingly regulate the behavior of states in an effort to reduce violence and provide a platform to address world problems. To assess this possibility, this chapter focuses on two IGOs, the United Nations (UN) and the European Union (EU). Before taking them up, though, an overview of IGOs is in order.

An Overview of Intergovernmental Organizations

There is considerable diversity among IGOs. Some of them, such as the UN, have many members; others like Africa's Economic Community of the Great Lakes Countries, with three members, are quite small. Another way to classify IGOs is by function. There are multipurpose IGOs such as the UN and EU that address a wide range of issues, and more specialized IGOs like the Arab Monetary Fund with very limited functions. Additionally, there are both global IGOs like the World Bank and regional IGOs like the African Union. Table 7.1 on page 192 presents a range of IGOs.

The Origins of IGOs

IGOs are primarily a modern phenomenon. Nearly all of them were created in the last 50 years or so. Yet the origins of IGOs extend far back in history to three main sources.

Community of Humankind

IGOs are rooted in part in a universalistic concept of humankind dating back perhaps to 300 B.C. and the Stoics, as discussed in chapter 5. As early as 478 B.C., the Greek city-states established the Delian League to create a unified response to the threat from Persia. Although mostly an alliance, it had two IGO characteristics. First, it was permanent and supposed to last until "ingots of iron, thrown into the sea, rose again." Second, the League had an assembly of representatives appointed by the city-states to decide policy. Although Athens dominated, the assembly was a precursor of such current structures as the UN General Assembly.

Such ideas began to resurface in the late Middle Ages. For example, a French official, Pierre Dubois, proposed in *The Recovery of the Holy Land* (1306) that the Christian kingdoms form "a league of universal peace" to settle disputes among members. In modern times, the first example of an IGO based on keeping peace was the **Hague system,** named for the 1899 and 1907 peace conferences held at that city in the Netherlands. The 1907 conference was more comprehensive, with 44 European, North American, and Latin American states participating. Organizationally, it

MAP
Post–Cold War
International Alliances

TABLE 7.1	Select Intergovernmental Organizations				
Organization	Mission	Members	Headquarters	Chief Officer
Arab League	Political, cultural, and economic cooperation	22	Egypt	Egyptian
Association of Southeast Asian Nations	Economic and other forms of cooperation	10	Indonesia	Singaporean
European Union	Multipurpose	25	Belgium	Portuguese
International Atomic Energy Agency	Peaceful use of nuclear energy	138	Austria	Egyptian
International Cocoa Organization	Cocoa production and trade	30	Great Britain	Dutch
International Criminal Police Organization	Investigation of global crime	182	France	American
International Monetary Fund	Currency cooperation and stability	184	United States	Spanish
International Whaling Commission	Regulation of whaling	61	Great Britain	Danish
North Atlantic Treaty Organization	Military security	26	Belgium	Dutch
Office International des Epizooties	Animal health	167	France	French
Organization of Petroleum Exporting Countries	Oil production and prices	11	Austria	Kuwaiti
United Nations	Multipurpose	191	United States	Ghanaian
World Bank	Economic development	184	United States	American
World Trade Organization	Free economic interchange	148	Switzerland	Thai

There are nearly 300 intergovernmental organizations (IGOs) and they perform a wide variety of functions. Some sense of the range of IGO activities and their global, regional, or specialized membership basis can be gained from this selection. As you can see, membership ranges from near universal to only a few countries, and the functions of IGOs range from the UN's broad range of missions to the single purpose of the International Cocoa Organization.

included a rudimentary general assembly and a judicial system. The conferences also adopted a series of standards to limit the conduct of war.

The next step on the path was the creation of the **League of Nations** after World War I. The League had a more developed organizational structure than that of the Hague system. It was intended mainly as a peacekeeping organization, although it did have some elements aimed at social and economic cooperation. Unfortunately, the League could not survive the turbulent post–World War I era that included the Great Depression and the rise of militant fascism. After only two decades of frustrated existence, the League died in the rubble of World War II.

The League may have collapsed, but the idea behind it did not. Instead, at the end of the war more than 50 countries continued to advance the idea by establishing the **United Nations (UN)**. Like the League, the UN was founded mainly to maintain peace. Nevertheless, it has increasingly become involved in a broad range of issues that encompasses almost all the world's concerns. In addition, the UN and its predecessor, the League of Nations, represent the coming together of all the root systems of international organizations. They are more properly seen as the emergent saplings of extensive cooperation and integration.

Big-Power Peacekeeping

IGOs also evolved from the idea that powerful countries have a special responsibility to cooperate and preserve peace. Hugo Grotius, the "father of international law," suggested as early as 1625 in his classic *On the Law of War and Peace* that the major Christian powers cooperate to mediate or arbitrate the disputes of others or even, if required, to compel warring parties to accept an equitable peace.

This idea first took on substance with the Concert of Europe, an informal coalition of the major European powers formed after the fall of Napoleon in 1815. Through balance-of-(big)-power diplomacy, the Concert generally managed to keep the peace until the outbreak of World War I in 1914. The philosophy of big-power responsibility then carried over to the Council of the League of Nations. Five of its nine seats were permanently assigned to the big-power victors of World War I. Additionally, the council had authority under the League's Covenant to deal "with any matter . . . affecting the peace of the world."

When the UN succeeded the League of Nations, the special status and responsibilities of the big powers were transferred to the UN Security Council (UNSC). Like the Council of the League, the UNSC is the main peacekeeping organ and includes permanent membership for five major powers (China, France, Great Britain, Russia, and the United States).

Pragmatic Cooperation

Sheer necessity has also driven the evolution of IGOs. An increasingly complex and intertwined world has created the need for specialized agencies to deal with specific economic and social problems. The six-member Central Commission for the Navigation of the Rhine, established in 1815, is the oldest surviving IGO, and the International Telegraphic (now Telecommunications) Union (1865) is the oldest surviving IGO with global membership. As detailed below, the growth of specialized IGOs has been phenomenal. This aspect of international activity is also reflected in the UN through the 22 specialized agencies (such as the World Health Organization) associated with it.

The Growth of IGOs

The 20th century saw rapid growth in the number of all types of IGOs. Just in terms of sheer quantity, the number of well-established IGOs increased sevenfold from 37 in 1909 to 251 in 2004. This expansion is depicted in Figure 7.1.

Even more important than the quantitative growth of IGOs is their expanding range of concerns and roles. Indeed, there are now few if any major political issues that are not addressed at the international level by one or more IGOs and few governmental roles that IGOs do not play. In some cases, existing IGOs take up new roles. Just as the U.S. government and other national governments have assumed new areas of responsibility over the years as problems have arisen, so too has the United Nations moved to create units to deal with terrorism, biological warfare, environmental degradation, and a range of issues that were not part of the UN's realm when it was founded. At other times, countries join to create new IGOs to address emerging areas of global concern. For example, the development of satellites and the ability to communicate through them and the need to coordinate this capability led

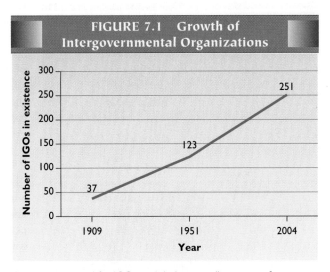

FIGURE 7.1   Growth of Intergovernmental Organizations

The growing need for IGOs and their expanding range of concerns and roles is reflected in the nearly 700% growth in their number since the early 20th century.

Note: These include only the UIA's category of "conventional IGOs," those with at least three member-countries and a permanent and functioning organizational structure.
Data source: Union of International Associations, *Yearbook of International Organizations, 2004/2005* (Brussels, 2004).

to the establishment of the International Mobile Satellite Organization (IMMARSAT) in 1979.

Theories of IGO Growth

A first step in analyzing the growth in the number of IGOs and the expansion of their roles is to look at two ideas about how IGOs develop. These two schools of thought are functionalism and neofunctionalism.

Functionalism   The term **functionalism** represents the idea that the way to global cooperation is through a "bottom-up," evolutionary approach that begins with limited, pragmatic cooperation on narrow, nonpolitical issues. One such issue was how to deliver the mail internationally. To solve that problem, countries cooperated to found the Universal Postal Union in 1874. Plato's description of "necessity" as "the mother of invention" in *The Republic* (ca. 380 B.C.) might well serve as a motto for modern functionalists.

Functionalists support their view about how global cooperation is being achieved by pointing to hundreds, even thousands of IGOs, multilateral treaties, NGOs, and other vehicles that have been pragmatically put in place to deal with specific international concerns. Functionalists further hold that by cooperating in specific, usually nonpolitical areas, countries and people can learn to trust one another. Each such instance of cooperation serves as a building block to achieve broader cooperation on more and more politically sensitive issues along the path to comprehensive cooperation or even global government.

Neofunctionalism   The "top-down" approach to solving world problems is often called **neofunctionalism.** Its advocates are skeptical about the functionalist belief that nonpolitical cooperation can, by itself, lead eventually to full political cooperation and to the elimination of international conflict and self-interested state action. Neofunctionalists also worry that the functionalists' evolutionary approach will not move quickly enough to head off many of the world's looming problems. Therefore, neofunctionalists argue for immediately establishing IGOs and giving them independence and adequate resources so that they can address political issues with an eye to fostering even greater cooperation.

Reasons for Growth

The 20th century's rapid growth of IGOs, both in number and in scope of activity, is the result of both functionalist and neofunctionalist forces. Whatever the immediate impetus for founding an IGO, they have all been created because states have realized that through IGOs, countries

Functionalism is a theory about the growth of international governmental organizations (IGOs). It argues that each successful example of international cooperation to deal with common problems serves as a building block, which gives countries the confidence to establish IGOs to address even more complex global problems.

"are able to achieve goals that they cannot accomplish [alone]" (Abbot & Snidal, 1998:29). We can note six causes for this expansion.

Increased international contact is one cause. The revolutions in communications and transportation technologies have brought the states of the world into much closer contact. These interchanges need organizational structures in order to become routine and regulated. The International Telegraphic Union, founded over a century ago, has been joined in more modern times by the IMMARSAT and many others.

Increased global interdependence, particularly in the economic sphere, has also fostered a variety of IGOs to address issues beyond the control of individual countries. The International Monetary Fund (IMF) and the World Bank are just two examples. Regional trade and monetary organizations, cartels, and, to a degree, multinational corporations are other examples.

The expansion of transnational problems that affect many states and require solutions that are beyond the resources of any single state is a third cause of the growth of international organizations. One such issue (and its associated IGO) is transnational crime (International Criminal Police Organization).

The failure of the current state-centered system to provide security is a fourth incentive for the expansion of IGOs. The agony of two world wars, for instance, convinced many that peace is not safe in the hands of nation-states. The United Nations is the latest attempt to organize for the preservation of peace. The continuing global problems in health, food, human rights, and other areas have also spurred the organization of IGOs.

The efforts of small states to gain strength through joint action is a fifth factor. The concentration of military and economic power in a handful of countries has led less powerful actors to cooperate in an attempt to influence events. For example, less developed countries (LDCs) have formed such IGOs as the 115-member Nonaligned Movement (NAM) and the Group of 77 (G-77), now with 132 member-countries, to promote economic development. One of their strategies is to use their "joint negotiating capacity" to press the economically developed countries (EDCs) to increase development aid, reduce barriers to LDC exports, and take other steps favorable to the LDCs.[1]

The successes of IGOs are a sixth reason for their expansion. As countries have learned that they can sometimes work together internationally, they have created additional IGOs to help address an ever greater range of transnational issues.

Roles That IGOs Play

Given the expanding number of IGOs, we should ask ourselves what they do and what we want them to do (Muldoon, 2003; Diehl, 2001). It is possible to arrange the current and potential future roles of IGOs along a scale that measures how close each is to the traditional road or to the alternative road of international politics. Starting at the traditional end of the scale and moving toward the alternative end, the four roles are: interactive arena, creator and center of cooperation, independent international actor, and supranational organization.

Interactive Arena

The most common function of IGOs is to provide an interactive arena in which member-states pursue their individual national interests. This approach is rarely stated openly, but it is obvious in the struggles within the UN and other IGOs, where countries and blocs of countries vigorously wage political struggles (Foot, MacFarlane, & Mastanudo, 2003; Voeten, 2000). The view that the UN should be an arena for countries

MAP
Transportation Patterns

to advance their interests was expressed during the 2005 Senate confirmation hearings of John Bolton as the new U.S. ambassador to the UN. According to one senator, Bolton's "core diplomatic mission" should be "securing greater international support for the national security and foreign policy objectives of the United States."[2]

Of course, that view is also held by other countries and can lead them to oppose U.S. initiatives for similar self-interested reasons (Voeten, 2004). One illustration was the maneuvering in the UN Security Council in 2003 over the war with Iraq and its postwar rebuilding. As war hung in the balance in early 2003, France and Russia (both of which have a veto in the Security Council) along with Germany were at the forefront of resisting the U.S. efforts to win UN support for military action against Iraq. In addition to opposing an attack for substantive reasons, there was also a palpable sense that these countries did not want to be seen as U.S. pawns. They therefore used the crisis to demonstrate their diplomatic independence and to isolate the United States. "It's better to have only a few friends than to have a lot of sycophants," French President Jacques Chirac commented at the time. "France considers itself one of the friends of the Americans," he continued, "not necessarily one of its sycophants. And when we have something to say, we say it."[3] Putting the issue in perspective, a Russian analyst noted that his country "has clearly made its choice, and it will stand with the Franco-German position on Iraq in opposition to the United States. We do not want to see the United Nations downgraded or the advent of a world order based on U.S. hegemony."[4]

In a similar way, the U.S. effort to get UN support for policing and economically rebuilding Iraq while maintaining U.S. control of the process met with staunch resistance in the Security Council. As France's deputy UN ambassador explained, "Sharing the burden and the responsibilities in a world of equal and sovereign nations means also sharing information and authority."[5] Using IGOs to gain national advantage contradicts their ostensible purpose by detracting from their ability to promote cooperation. Treating IGOs as one more field of diplomatic combat also feeds the argument within countries that they should reduce or withdraw their support from IGOs that do not serve the state's immediate national interests.

The use of IGOs as an interactive arena does, however, also have advantages. One is based on the theory that international integration can advance even when IGOs are the arena for self-interested national interaction. The reasoning is that even when realpolitik is the starting point, the process that occurs in an IGO fosters the habit of cooperation and compromise. Another advantage is that it is sometimes politically easier to take an action if an IGO has authorized it. For example, there was considerable consensus behind military action against Iraq in 1991 (unlike what occurred in 2003), and taking action under UN auspices made it easier for Muslim countries and some others to participate in an invasion conducted primarily by Christian-heritage powers (the United States, Great Britain, and France). Third, debate and diplomatic maneuvering may even provide a forum for diplomatic struggle. This role of providing an alternative to the battlefield may promote the resolution of disputes without violence. As Winston Churchill put it once, "To jaw-jaw is better than to war-war."[6]

Center of Cooperation

A second IGO role is to promote and facilitate cooperation among states and other international actors. Secretary-General Kofi Annan has observed correctly that the UN's "member-states face a wide range of new and unprecedented threats and challenges. Many of these transcend borders and are beyond the power of any single nation to address on its own."[7] Therefore, countries have found it increasingly nec-

SIMULATION
Searching for
International Organizations:
Roles and Resources

One role of the UN and other IGOs is to serve as an interactive arena in which countries promote their interests. This photograph of UN Secretary-General Kofi Annan and U.S. Secretary of State Condoleezza Rice was taken during a 2005 conference in Brussels, Belgium, to win greater global financial support for rebuilding and democratizing Iraq. Spreading the cost would be in the U.S. interest, but many other countries, and Secretary-General Annan as well, have been cautious about taking on more responsibilities unless the United States shares in the decision-making process about Iraq's future.

essary to cooperate to address physical security, the environment, the economy, and a range of other concerns. The Council of the Baltic Sea States, the International Civil Aviation Organization, and a host of other IGOs were all established to address specific needs and, through their operations, to promote further cooperation.

Regime Theory   What sometimes occurs is that narrow cooperation expands into more complex forms of interdependence. International regimes are one such development. A regime is not a single organization. Instead, **regime** is a collective noun that designates a complex of norms, rules, processes, and organizations that, in sum, have evolved to help to govern the behavior of states and other international actors in an area of international concern. One such area is the use and protection of international bodies of water (Heasley, 2003), a matter that is addressed by the regime for oceans and seas, as an example.

The Regime for Oceans and Seas   The regime that is currently evolving to govern the uses of the world's oceans and other bodies of international water is represented in Figure 7.2 on page 198. Note the regime's complex array of organizations, rules, and norms that promote international cooperation in a broad area of maritime regulation. Navigation, pollution, seabed mining, and fisheries are all areas of expanded international discussion, rule making, and cooperation. The UN Convention on the Law of the Sea (1994) proclaims that the oceans and seabed are a "common heritage of mankind," to be shared according to "a just and equitable economic order." To that end, the treaty contains provisions for increased international regulation of mining and other uses of the oceans' floors. It established (as of 1994) the International Seabed Authority, headquartered in Jamaica, to supervise the procedures and rules of the treaty.

In addition to the Convention on the Law of the Sea, the regime of the oceans and seas extends to include many other organizations and rules. The International Maritime Organization has helped create safeguards against oil spills in the seas, which declined over 80% annually between the early 1970s and the late 1990s. The International Whaling Commission, the Convention on the Preservation and Protection of Fur Seals, and other efforts have begun the process of protecting marine life and conserving resources. The Montreal Guidelines on Land-Based Pollution suggest ways to prevent fertilizer and other land-based pollutants from running off into rivers and bays and then into the oceans. Countries have expanded their conservation zones to regulate fishing. The South Pacific Forum has limited the use of drift nets that indiscriminately catch and kill marine life. NGOs such as Greenpeace have pressed to protect the world seas. Dolphins are killed less frequently because many

FIGURE 7.2 Regimes for Oceans and Seas

International laws and norms
Concept of international waters
Freedom of the seas
Maritime rules of the road
Fisheries conservation
Pollution prevention
Endangered species protection

Treaties
Convention on the Law of the Sea
Convention on Fishing and Conservation
Convention on the Continental Shelf
Anti-Dumping Convention
Convention on the Preservation
    and Protection of Fur Seals
Convention for the Prevention
    of Pollution from Ships

International organizations
International Seabed Authority
International Whaling Commission
Commission for the Conservation
    of Antarctic Marine Living Resources
International Maritime Organization
International Court of Justice (deciding cases)
International Maritime Satellite Organization
Greenpeace

Other regime contributors
Consumers demanding dolphin-safe tuna
Public outrage at the killing of whales,
    baby seals, and other marine life
National marine fisheries and wildlife laws
National laws to prevent pollution
National courts enforcing established
    international law

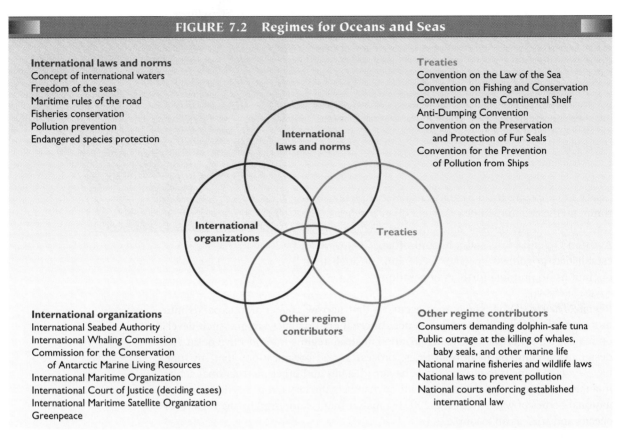

The concept of an international regime represents the nexus of a range of rules, actors, and other contributors that regulate a particular area of concern. This figure shows some of the elements of the expanding regime for oceans and seas.

Note: Entries are only a sample of all possibilities.

consumers only buy cans of tuna that display the "dolphin safe" logo. It is not necessary to extend this list of multilateral law-making treaties, IGOs, NGOs, national efforts, and other programs that regulate the use of the seas to make the point that in combination they are part of an expanding network that constitutes a developing regime of the oceans and seas.

Independent International Actor

The third IGO role is that of an independent international actor (Barnett & Finnemore, 2004). This role is located toward the alternative end of the traditional-alternative scale of IGO activities. Technically, what any IGO does is controlled by the wishes and votes of its members. In reality, many IGOs develop strong, relatively permanent administrative staffs.

These individuals often identify with the organization and try to increase its authority and role. Global expectations—such as "the UN should do something"— add to the sense that an IGO may be a force unto itself. Soon, to use an old phrase, the whole (of the IGO) becomes more than the sum of its (member-country) parts. Sometimes this independence is controversial, as we shall see in the discussions of the EU and UN that follow. In other cases, a degree of organizational independence is intended and established in the charters of various IGOs, such as the International Court of Justice (ICJ).

Supranational Organization

Some people believe that the world is moving and should continue to move toward a more established form of international government (Tabb, 2004). "The very complexity of the current international scene," one scholar writes, "makes a fair and effective system of world governance more necessary than ever" (Hoffmann, 2003:27). This model envisions a fourth role for IGOs, that of a **supranational organization,** one that has legal authority over its members. Such supranational government could be regional or global in scope.

In theory some IGOs already possess a degree of supranationalism in specialized areas, even if that supranationalism is extremely limited. While few states concede any significant part of their sovereignty to any IGO, in practice many accept limited IGO authority in the realm of "everyday global governance" (Slaughter, 2003:83). For example, countries now regularly give way when the World Trade Organization (WTO) rules that one of their laws or policies contravene the WTO's underlying treaty, the General Agreement on Tariffs and Trade (GATT).

Even more extensive supranational authority is exercised on a regional level by the European Union. As our later discussion will reveal, the EU not only has most of the structure of a full-scale government, but it makes policy, has courts, receives taxes, and in many other, if still limited, ways functions like a government of Europe.

The Potential Expansion of Supranational Authority

Those who favor expanding supranational authority take positions that range from proposals for relatively modest increases in the authority of the UN and other existing IGOs, through the establishment of reasonably powerful **regional governments,** to **world government.** Some advocates favor an evolutionary approach, with power shifting gradually from states to IGOs. Others believe that the problems the world is facing mean that major changes must be made quickly. Whatever the pace of change, the powers of any such global or regional government also range along a scale based on the degree of power-sharing between the central government and the subunits, as depicted in Figure 7.3 on page 200. *Unitary government* is at the end of the scale where the central government has all or most of the power and the subordinate units have little or none. In such a system, countries would be nonsovereign subunits that serve only administrative purposes.

Federal government would be a less dramatic alternative. A **federation,** or federal government, is one in which the central authority and the member units each have substantial authority. The United States and Canada are both federal structures, with Canada's 10 provinces having greater authority than the 50 U.S. states. Confederal government is the least centralized of the three arrangements. In a confederal government, members are highly interdependent and join together in a weak directorate organization while retaining all or most of their sovereign authority. The European Union provides a current example of what is, or at least approaches, a **confederation.**

Arguments for Expanding Supranational Authority   The arguments for greater global government begin with the criticism of the current state-based system detailed in chapter 6 (Volgy & Bailin, 2003;Wendt, 2004). The World Federalist Movement (WFM), for instance, takes the view that, "Ours is a planet in crisis, suffering grave problems unable to be managed by nations acting separately in an ungoverned world." Given this perspective, the WFM calls for "urgent progress in developing . . .

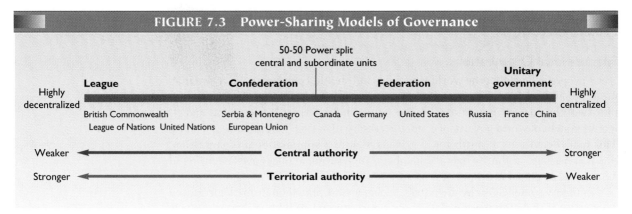

FIGURE 7.3   Power-Sharing Models of Governance

Whether at the national, regional, or global level, governments share power between the central government and territorial government in a variety of ways. In countries, territorial units are commonly termed states or provinces. In a global or regional government, countries would be the territorial unit. This figure shows the scale of possible power-sharing relationships. At one end of the scale, a league, the central government has little more than symbolic authority, and most power remains with the territorial units. At the other end of the scale, a unitary government, the central government monopolizes power and the territorial units perform only administrative functions. The most centralized international government organization today, the European Union, is a confederation.

world institutions . . . by which the world's people and nations can govern their relations." Moreover, the WFM argues, "These institutions must have actual and sufficient authority to make and enforce law in their given jurisdictions."[8]

It should be noted that the WFM and most others who favor greater global governance do not advocate the abolition of state sovereignty and the creation of an all-powerful world government. More common are calls for a federal structure, with countries retaining sovereignty over their internal affairs. It is unclear, however, where the line between international and domestic matters would be drawn in a globalizing world where more and more matters are "intermestic," with elements of both *inter*national and do*mestic* policy.

Arguments against Expanding Supranational Authority   There is also strong opposition to significantly expanded global governance. Among countries, the United States has in recent years been at the forefront of that opposition. It has refused to agree to numerous restrictions on its sovereignty, such as the Law of the Sea (LOS) Convention, the Kyoto Protocol to restrain the emission of global warming gases, and the treaty establishing the International Criminal Court. Some of this opposition is particular to the Bush administration, but it goes well beyond that. For example, President Bush endorsed the LOS Convention in 2004, yet it remains stalled in the Senate awaiting ratification (Coates, 2005).

Critics, whatever their nationality, raise numerous objections to greater global governance. First, they argue that there are practical barriers. Their assumption is that nationalism has too strong a hold and that neither political leaders nor masses would be willing to surrender substantial sovereignty to a universal body. Are we ready to "pledge allegiance to the United States of the World"? Second, critics of the world government movement pose political objections. They worry about the concentration of power that would be necessary to enforce international law and to address the world's monumental economic and social problems. A third doubt is whether any such government, even given unprecedented power, could succeed in solving world problems any better than states can. Fourth, some skeptics further argue that centralization would inevitably diminish desirable cultural diversity and political experimentation in the world. A fifth criticism of the world government worries about preserving democracy. With power concentrated in a central international government and little countervailing power left to countries, the seizure of the world government by authoritative forces might, in a stroke, roll back hundreds of years of democratic evolution.

The idea of regional government answers some of the objections to global government. Regions would still have to bring heterogeneous peoples together and overcome nationalism, but that would be an easier task than addressing even greater global heterogeneity. Moreover, regional governments would allow for greater cultural diversity and political experimentation than would a global government. Nevertheless, skeptics charge that even if regional government is slightly less objectionable than global government, regional government is at best the lesser of two evils. Opponents also contend that a world of regional governments would simply shift the axis of conflict from among states to among regions. Indeed, in the novel *Nineteen Eighty-Four,* George Orwell predicted in 1949 that the future would find world political control exercised by three regional governments (Oceania, Eurasia, and Eastasia) all perpetually at war with one another. Making matters worse, democracy was a memory. Oceania was ruled by the totalitarian iron hand of "Big Brother," and the other two megaregions were also presumably subject to authoritarian discipline. It is not hard to project the EU as the core of Eurasia, a U.S.-centered Oceania, and an Eastasia built around China. So while Orwell's vision did not come to pass by 1984, opponents of regional or global government might contend that perhaps he should have entitled the book *Twenty Eighty-Four.*

A third alternative for the future of global governance is the slow expansion of supranational authority in specialized IGOs. This is already occurring, as noted with regard to the WTO and is the most likely course in the foreseeable future. Even here, though, some critics rail against surrender of authority to an IGO.

Gradually through history our primary political loyalty has shifted from smaller units such as tribes and villages to larger units, especially countries. Some people believe that this trend should continue and that a world government should be established. The image of children starting out their day by saying "I pledge allegiance to the flag of the United States of the World" may seem strange, but a global government could evolve.

Web Link

For more on the view that U.S. sovereignty is at risk, visit the Web site of U.S. Representative Ron Paul (R-TX) at **http://www .house.gov/paul/** and browse the index of his weekly column, "Texas Straight Talk."

Regional IGOs: Focus on the European Union

The growth of regional IGOs has been striking. Prior to World War II there were no prominent regional IGOs. Now there are many. Most are specialized, with regional economic IGOs, such as the Arab Cooperation Council, the most numerous. Other regional IGOs are general purpose and deal with a range of issues. These include, for example, the African Union (AU, formerly the Organization of African Unity, OAU) and the Organization of American States (OAS).

Another noteworthy development regarding regional IGOs is that some of them are transitioning from specialized to general-purpose organizations. The Association of Southeast Asian Nations (ASEAN) was founded in 1967 to promote regional economic cooperation. More recently, though, ASEAN has begun to take on a greater political tinge, and, in particular, may serve as a political and defensive counterweight to China in the region. The Economic Community of West African States (ECOWAS) has also expanded its roles. It was created in 1975 to facilitate economic interchange, but it has since established a parliament and a human rights court. ECOWAS has also taken on regional security responsibilities and intervened in civil wars raging in the Ivory Coast, Liberia, and Sierra Leone. Beyond any of these examples of regional IGOs, the best example of regionalism is Europe. There, the European Union, with its 25 member-countries, has moved toward full economic integration. It has also achieved considerable political cooperation.

The Origins and Evolution of the European Union

The **European Union (EU)** has evolved through several stages and names. "What's in a name?" you might ask, echoing Shakespeare's heroine in *Romeo and Juliet*. As she discovered, the names Capulet and Montague proved important. So too, the name changes leading up to the current EU are important in the tale they tell.

Economic Integration

The EU's genesis began in 1952 when Belgium, France, (West) Germany, Italy, Luxembourg, and the Netherlands created a common market for coal, iron, and steel products, called the European Coal and Steel Community (ECSC). Its success prompted the six countries to agree to the Treaties of Rome (1958), which established the **European Economic Community (EEC)** to facilitate trade in many additional areas and the European Atomic Energy Community (EURATOM) to coordinate matters in that realm (Dinan, 2004).

Continued economic success led the six countries to found an overarching organization, the **European Communities (EC)**, in 1967. Each of the three preexisting organizations became subordinate parts of the EC. Then in 1993 a new name, the European Union, was adopted to denote both the existing advanced degree of integration and the EU's goal of becoming a single economic entity. Perhaps even more significant was the adoption in 2002 of a single currency, the euro, by most of the EU's members (Martin & Ross, 2004). Adding to the EU's momentum, 10 new members joined it in 2004, bringing the total to 25, as detailed in Figure 7.4. Four more countries have applied for EU membership, and the eventual, if not quite stated, goal of the EU is to encompass all the region's countries (Poole & Baun, 2004). In the words of one top EU official, "There will be no such things as 'in countries' and 'out countries'; rather there will be 'ins' and 'pre-ins.'"[9]

For about 30 years, European integration focused on economics. Members of the EC grew ever more interdependent as economic barriers were eliminated. Over the years, the EC members moved toward economic integration and empowering the EC by such steps as abolishing all tariffs on manufactured goods among themselves, establishing a common external tariff, bargaining collectively through the EC with other countries in trade negotiations, and creating a revenue source for the EC by giving it a share of each country's value-added tax (VAT, similar to a sales tax) and money raised by tariffs on imported goods. Making official what was already under way, the EC members agreed to the Single European Act (SEA) of 1987, which committed the EC to becoming a fully integrated economic unit.

Political Integration

There comes a point where economic integration cannot continue without also taking steps toward political integration. This occurs because it is impossible to reach

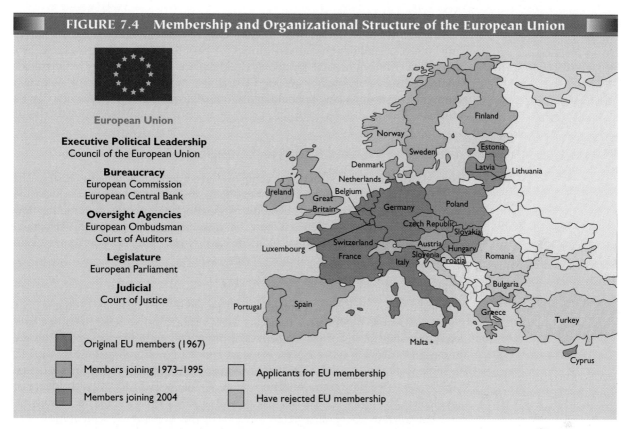

FIGURE 7.4   Membership and Organizational Structure of the European Union

European Union

Executive Political Leadership
Council of the European Union

Bureaucracy
European Commission
European Central Bank

Oversight Agencies
European Ombudsman
Court of Auditors

Legislature
European Parliament

Judicial
Court of Justice

Original EU members (1967)

Members joining 1973–1995

Members joining 2004

Applicants for EU membership

Have rejected EU membership

The world's most integrated regional organization is the European Union. It has expanded from the six original countries that established the European Economic Community in 1958 to 25 countries today. The EU's focus is primarily economic, but it has become increasingly integrated on matters of the environment, human rights, and other policy areas.

full economic integration among sovereign states whose domestic and foreign political policies are sometimes in conflict. Moreover, as the people unite economically, it is easier to think of becoming one politically.

Having reached this point, the EC's members moved forward by agreeing to the far-reaching Treaty on European Union (1993). Also known as the **Maastricht Treaty**, it laid the foundation for increased political integration. As one step in that direction, European citizenship was expanded. People can now travel on either an EU or a national passport, and citizens of any EU country can vote in local and European Parliament elections in another EU country in which they live. The Maastricht Treaty called for the EU to act increasingly as a political unit by eventually creating a common foreign and defense policy and a common internal policy relating to such issues as crime, terrorism, and immigration. Gradually, such ideas have moved toward reality. For example, the EU and the United States exchange ambassadors. Moving even further, the Treaty of Amsterdam (1999) strengthened EU political integration by such steps as enhancing the powers of the president of the EU Commission and the European Parliament (EP). Four years later, the Treaty of Nice (2003) set the stage for further expansion of the EU's membership by detailing political arrangements—such as the distribution of seats or votes in the EP—that would occur as new member-countries join the EU.

Even more recently, the EU has begun to take on the trappings of a state. It has a flag and has adopted the *European Anthem*. The anthem has no words in recognition

Web Link

You can hear the European Anthem at: http://europa.eu .int/abc/symbols/anthem/index _en.htm.

of the EU's linguistic diversity. However, its melody, the "Ode to Joy" movement of Ludwig van Beethoven's Ninth Symphony (1823), was chosen because it refers to Friedrich von Schiller's poem, "Ode to Joy" (1785). This verse expresses hope for a time when "All men become brothers" would replace "All that custom has divided." Adding substance to symbolism, the EU has also begun the process of creating a European constitution, an undertaking that we will explore in a later section (Cowles & Dinan, 2004).

The Government of the European Union

The EU's organizational structure is complex, but a brief look at it helps illustrate the extent to which a regional government exists. As with all governments, the structure and the authority of the various EU units play an important part in determining how policy is made (Meunier, 2000). Figure 7.4 gives a brief overview of this structure. The EU's government can be divided for analysis into its political leadership, bureaucracy, legislature, judiciary, and other review agencies.

Political Leadership

Political decision making is centered in the **Council of the European Union,** usually called the Council of Ministers. It meets twice a year as a gathering of the prime ministers and other heads of government, and on its own authority or along with the European Parliament it decides on the most important policy directions for the EU, including the direction of its Common Foreign and Security Policy. The Council meets more often with lesser ministers (such as finance ministers) in attendance to supplement the prime ministerial meetings. Assisting the Council is an administrative staff called the General Secretariat headed by the Secretary-General of the Council. This post has become increasingly important in recent years, with its incumbent (Spain's Javier Solana since 2004) speaking for the Council in international relations and exercising other visible and key roles.

Most Council sessions are held in Brussels, Belgium, the principal site of the EU administrative element. Decisions are made by a weighted-vote plan (termed "qualified majority voting"). Under this plan, there are 321 votes, with four countries (France, Germany, Great Britain, and Italy) each having 29 votes, and the votes of the other 21 members ranging from 27 (Spain and Poland) to 3 (Malta). Voting procedures are complex, but in some cases unanimity is required. In other cases, a measure is decided by the "qualified voting plan." Passage requires the votes of (a) a majority of countries, (b) 72.3% of all votes, and (c) the votes of countries that represent at least 62% of the EU's population. The precise details are not so important as seeing that the EU has adopted a voting plan that protects member-countries from being dominated by Germany, France, and the other larger members. This is something like the plan in the United States that gives states an equal vote in the Senate no matter what their population.

Bureaucracy

The EU's bureaucracy is organized under the **European Commission,** which administers policy adopted by the Council and the Parliament and can also propose legislation to those branches. There are 25 commissioners who serve five-year terms and act as a cabinet for the EU, with each commissioner overseeing an area of administrative activity. Although one commissioner is selected from each member-state, they are not supposed to represent their country's viewpoint. One of the commissioners is selected by the Council of the European Union to be **President of the Commission.**

This official serves as the EU's administrative head and is the overall director of the EU bureaucracy headquartered in Brussels.

The post has evolved into one of the most significant in the EU. A great deal of that evolution can also be attributed to Jacques Delors, a French national who served as president from 1985 through 1994 and who became known as "Mr. Europe" because of his strong advocacy of European integration. Delors and his staff created a core structure, informally referred to as "Eurocracy," which has a European point of view, rather than a national orientation. As of 2005, the Commission's president was José Manuel Barroso of Portugal.

One of many indications of the importance of the Commission, as well as the political integration of Europe, is the emergence of an ever larger, more active, and more powerful EU infrastructure. The EU's administrative staff has about quadrupled since 1970 to about 24,000 today. The annual number of EU regulations, decisions, and directives from one or the other EU body has risen from 345 in 1970 to over 600. The EU's 2005 budget was about $143 billion, raised primarily from payments by member-governments, tariff revenues, and the VAT.

> **Did You Know That:**
> The EU's 2005 budget ($147 billion) is larger than the budgets of all but 14 of the world's countries.

As occurs in the United States and every other country, the bureaucracy in the EU is a lightning rod for much of any dissatisfaction that exists with the government. To cite one example, the reputation of the Eurocrats was darkened by the chocolate imbroglio. What constitutes chocolate was the sticky issue facing EU regulators. The battle line was drawn between those EU countries that require chocolate to consist entirely of cocoa butter and the other EU members that allow up to 5% vegetable oil in chocolate. Representing the purists, the head of the Belgian chocolate company, Godiva, proclaimed that only "100% chocolate should be called . . . chocolate." Answering back for the freethinking chocolatiers, a representative of Great Britain's largest chocolate maker, Cadbury, urged, "Let's celebrate Europe's regional diversity and recognize that there are different ways of making chocolate." With regulators unable to resolve the issue, it reached the European Parliament. There the Godiva coalition won the first round when the legislators voted for purity. But the war was not over, for the Council of the European Union had to make the final gooey decision. "Whatever we do will be attacked from one side or the other," an EU spokesperson has complained. Compromise was the sweet solution. A ruling declared that chocolate with vegetable oil could be shipped throughout the EU. Moreover it could be labeled chocolate, but only in the nonpurist countries. In the purist countries, it would have to be labeled "family milk chocolate." Not that it has anything to do with families or milk. Ah well, as Forrest Gump mused, "Life is like a box of chocolates."

Oversight Agencies

The EU has two fairly unique regulatory oversight structures. One of these is the **European Ombudsman** who is appointed by the European Parliament. When EU residents, businesses, and institutions complain about an abuse of power or other alleged transgression by EU authorities, the office of the ombudsman investigates. If it feels that an injustice has been done, the office can recommend remedial action to EU agencies and can also make recommendations to the European Parliament for legislative action.

A second oversight institution is the **Court of Auditors.** Each member-country has one member on the Court, which directs a staff that oversees the EU budget to ensure that it is legally implemented, adheres to established policy, and is soundly managed. The Court has no independent corrective authority, but it can make recommendations to the Council and the Parliament.

Legislature

The **European Parliament (EP)** serves as the EU's legislative branch and meets in Strasbourg, France. It has 732 members who are elected to five-year terms, apportioned among the EU's 25 countries on a modified population basis. The most populous country (Germany) has 99 seats; the least populous country (Malta) has 5 seats. Delegates to the assemblies of most IGOs are appointed by their government, but members of the EP are elected by voters in their respective countries (Scully & Farrell, 2003). Furthermore, instead of organizing themselves within the EP by country, the representatives have tended to group themselves by political persuasion. The 2004 elections, for example, resulted in the center-right coalition, the European People's Party, winning the single biggest bloc of seats (37%), followed by the center-left Party of European Socialists (PSE) coalition with 28% of the seats. The remaining seats were divided among six other groups, ranging from a far left bloc to a far right bloc, each with approximately 5% of the seats. Reflecting Europe's propensity to elect more women to office than any other world region (see chapter 5), females made up 30% of the EP membership.

The EP's role began as a mostly advisory authority, but it has grown. It now has "co-decision" legislative authority with the Council of the European Union on the EU budget and a significant range of other policy matters. The EP also confirms the members of the European Commission and its president and can veto some regulations issued by it (Maurer, 2003). Demonstrating the EP's increasing assertiveness, it rejected the entire list of commissioners submitted in 2004 by the new President of the Commission, José Manuel Barroso. The issue was the nomination of Italy's Rocco Buttiglione as the EU's Commissioner for Justice, Freedom and Security. Numerous legislators objected to his comments that homosexuality is a "sin" and that the purpose of families is "to allow women to have children and to have the protection of a male who takes care of them."[10] Faced with solid opposition in the EP, Buttiglione finally stepped aside, Barroso nominated a new commissioner, and the legislators approved the slate.

Judiciary

The **Court of Justice** is the main element of the judicial branch of the EU. The 15-member court hears cases brought by member-states or other EU institutions and sometimes acts as a court of appeals for decisions of lower EU courts. The combined treaties of the EU are often con-

One indication the European Parliament (EP) is gaining authority within the EU is the upsurge of people and groups pressing the regional legislature to favor their cause. This photograph shows some of the hundreds of white laboratory rabbit models placed on the steps of the EP by supporters of animal rights. They were demonstrating for the allocation of more funding to develop ways to test drugs and other products without using animals.

sidered its collective "constitution" in lieu of a formal constitution. Like the EU's other institutions, the courts have gained authority over time. They can strike down both EU laws and regulations and those of member-countries that violate the basic EU treaties. In 2004, for example, the Court found for a woman, Man Levette Chen, in her suit against Great Britain. A Chinese national, Chen had given birth to a daughter in Northern Ireland. That did not give the daughter British citizenship, but it did make her a citizen of Ireland under Irish law, which gives citizenship to anyone born on the island. When Chen moved to Wales, British authorities refused her claim for residency in Great Britain. In its decision, the court found for Chen, ruling that the legal resident or citizen of any EU country may claim residency in any other EU country, and that the daughter would, in effect, be denied that right if her mother were forced out of Great Britain. Another bit of evidence of the mounting influence of the court is that its workload became so heavy that in 1989 the EU created a new, lower court, the Court of First Instance, which hears cases related to the EU brought by corporations and individuals.

The Future of the EU

The next major step toward an even more politically integrated EU was to have been a constitution. But the first substantial setback to the EU in its history came in May 2005 when French and then Dutch voters rejected the proposed EU constitution. These "no" votes probably ended any chance the constitution would ever take effect and left the future integrated development of the EU in considerable doubt.

Drafting the constitution began in 2002 when a convention chaired by former French President Valery Giscard d'Estaing met to write it. The resulting document was completed in 2004. Its details are complex, but it was designed to considerably strengthen the EU institutions, to give the EU greater authority in areas such as immigration, to extend the rights of EU citizens, to make passing of laws easier for the Council, and to create some new posts, such as a fixed-term (instead of rotating) president of the Council of the Europe Union and a foreign minister in order to strengthen the EU's executive branch. In sum, it would have moved the EU further toward the centralization of authority on the scale of the division of power in Figure 7.3 on page 200.

To take effect, however, the constitution required ratification by the member-states, with each able to decide its own ratification process (Gilbert, 2004; Calleo, 2003). Fifteen members opted to have their parliaments alone consider the issue. The other 10 states chose either a binding or nonbinding referendum as part of that process.

Initially, prospects for the adoption of the constitution seemed good. It enjoyed strong support among the most established leaders in Europe. Not only did the heads of every EU country sign it, but in January 2005 the EP endorsed it by a vote of 500 to 137, with 40 abstentions. Early polls also indicated solid public support. A poll in late 2004 in all EU countries found that of people who had decided, those favoring the constitution outnumbered those against it by a 3-to-1 margin. Moreover, there were more supporters than opponents in every country except Great Britain. The ratification process also began smoothly in November 2004 when Lithuania's parliament consented to the constitution by a lopsided 84 votes in favor and a mere 4 against. Parliaments in eight other countries added their ratifications by equally one-sided votes in the months that followed. And in the first referendum test, 77% of Spanish voters approved the document.

Did You Know That:

People generally dismissed the prediction of the great novelist Victor Hugo in 1849 that, "A day will come when you, France; you, Russia; you, Italy; you, England; you, Germany; you, all nations of the continent; without losing your distinctive qualities and glorious individuality, will be merged within a superior unit."

Nevertheless, there were growing doubts about ratification despite an overall rosy picture. Only 33% of the respondents to the November poll said they had a good idea of what was in the draft constitution, while 56% said they had little idea and 11% said they had no idea what was in it.[11] When the dates for referendums in a number of countries drew closer, opinion in some of them began to turn negative as the issues came into sharper focus. France was especially worrisome because of its size and importance to the EU and because French voters had approved the Maastricht Treaty by only a slim 2% margin in 1994.

President Jacques Chirac appeared on television a few days before the May 29, 2005, referendum in France and urged a yes vote. His appeal was unsuccessful, though, and 55% of French voters cast a no ballot. A few days later, the Dutch also defeated ratification, with 62% voting against it. No single factor caused the French or Dutch votes. Some of the negative sentiment had to do with domestic discontent with the French and Dutch governments that were supporting ratification. Still, the votes also signaled popular discontent with the simultaneous "wide and deep" pace of EU evolution. Voters were unsettled with the rapid pace of wider expansion in the number of EU member-countries at the same time the constitution called for even deeper EU political integration. For example, EU economic growth has lagged in recent years, unemployment is much higher than in the United States or Japan, and Western European workers worried that they would be competing for jobs with workers in the recently admitted East European countries and prospective member Turkey. Polls also showed discontent with what voters saw as the EU burgeoning bureaucracy and budget and concerns that they were losing control of their country to the EU. Among other points, voters were worried that EU rules would force them to accept increased numbers of immigrants from North Africa and elsewhere.

In the aftermath of the double body blow to the EU constitution, some supportive leaders put on a brave front and urged the process to go on with France, Holland, and any other country that said no being given a second chance to say yes. "Comments that one hears . . . that 'The Constitution is dead' are quite wrong, in my firm belief," Chancellor Gerhard Schröder declared.[12] Perhaps in the long run, the chancellor will be correct, but for the short-term the constitution went into limbo. Led by Great Britain, several countries canceled their pending referendums, and most leaders favor a time "of reflection" as one called it.

ANALYZE THE ISSUE
The European Union

Overall, the evolution of the EU has been one of the remarkable events of the past half-century (Gilbert, 2003). It does not take much imagination to foresee a day when the once-antagonistic states of Europe are forged into a United States of Europe. That is just one possibility, however. Each step toward integration encounters increasingly tougher barriers as political sovereignty and other traditional orientations are lessened. Making the change in people's minds from being German, French, or some other nationality to being European is crucial, yet it has only just begun and faces an uncertain future. (Hermann, Risse, & Brewer, 2004). This was amply demonstrated by the French and Dutch rejections of the EU constitution. What this means for the future is impossible to predict confidently. The most likely scenario is that Europe's leaders will draft a less far-reaching constitution and take other steps to ease the concerns of voters over such matters as loss of sovereignty, jobs, and immigration. However, it could be that Valéry Giscard d'Estaing will be proven correct in his prediction that rejection of the constitution might mean "the gradual falling apart of the European Union."[13] All that is certain, then, about the future of the EU is that the stakes of the constitutional debate are high, and progress of the EU toward true federation will be difficult.

The future of European integration faced a major test when French voters went to the polls in a May 2005 referendum to decide whether France should ratify the proposed EU constitution. A majority voted *non*, reflecting widespread sentiment that the EU was moving too fast to simultaneously widen its membership and deepen its integration. The French no vote, followed days later by the Dutch also rejecting ratification, doomed the constitution in its present form and cast doubts in some minds about the entire future of the EU.

Global IGOs: Focus on the United Nations

The growing level and importance of IGO activity and organization at the regional level is paralleled by IGOs at the global level. Of these, the United Nations is by far the best known and most influential (Ryan, 2000). Therefore, this section focuses on the UN, as a generalized study of the operation of IGOs and as a specific study of that key institution.

Structure, Rules, and Related Issues

How an institution is structured, its procedures, and other administrative details often play a crucial part in determining political outcomes. It is, for example, impossible to understand how the UN works without knowing that 5 of its members possess a veto in the Security Council and the other 186 do not. An outline of the UN's structure is depicted in Figure 7.5 on page 210.

Structure and process are also important because to be successful, an organization must reflect realities and goals and be flexible enough to change if it becomes outmoded. "Clearly we cannot meet the challenges of the new millennium with an instrument designed for the very different circumstances of the middle of the 20th century," the UN's secretary-general, Kofi Annan, points out.[14] To examine the structure and rules of the UN, we will take up matters of general membership, the structure of representative bodies, voting formulas, the authority of executive leadership, and the bureaucracy. Then we will turn to the matter of finance.

Membership Issues

There is a range of membership issues related to IGOs. Some concern membership in the overall organization and others concern membership in the various substructures within IGOs.

Web Link

If your college does not have one, you can help start a model UN program. Information is available on the Web site of the UN's Model UN Headquarters at **www.un.org/cyberschoolbus/modelun/links_6.asp**.

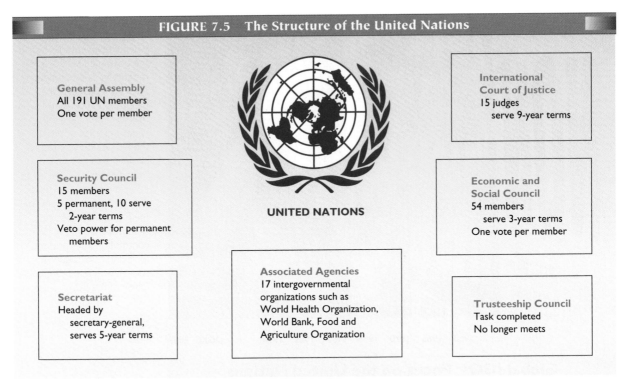

FIGURE 7.5   The Structure of the United Nations

General Assembly
All 191 UN members
One vote per member

Security Council
15 members
5 permanent, 10 serve
    2-year terms
Veto power for permanent
    members

Secretariat
Headed by
    secretary-general,
    serves 5-year terms

UNITED NATIONS

Associated Agencies
17 intergovernmental
organizations such as
World Health Organization,
World Bank, Food and
Agriculture Organization

**International
Court of Justice**
15 judges
    serve 9-year terms

**Economic and
Social Council**
54 members
    serve 3-year terms
One vote per member

Trusteeship Council
Task completed
No longer meets

The United Nations is a complex organization. It has six major organs and 17 associated agencies.

General Membership Issues   Theoretically, membership in the UN and most other IGOs is open to any state that is both within the geographic and functional scope of that organization and also subscribes to its principles and practices. In reality, politics is sometimes an additional standard. Today the UN has nearly universal membership, as Figure 7.6 shows, but that was not always the case.

Standards for admitting new members are one point of occasional controversy. One instance occurred in 1998 when the General Assembly voted overwhelmingly to give the Palestinians what amounts to an informal associate membership. They cannot vote, but they can take part in debates in the UN and perform other functions undertaken by states.

Successor state status can also sometimes be a political issue. When the UN recognized Russia as the successor state to the Soviet Union, it meant, among other things, that Russia inherited the USSR's permanent seat and veto on the Security Council. Taking the opposite approach, the UN in 1992 refused to recognize the Serbian-dominated government in Belgrade as the successor to Yugoslavia once that country broke apart. Instead, the General Assembly required Yugoslavia to (re)apply for admission. Once dictator Slobodan Milosevic was toppled, Yugoslavia (since renamed Serbia and Montenegro) (re)applied, and it was (re)admitted in 2000.

Withdrawal, suspension, or expulsion is another membership issue. Nationalist China (Taiwan) was, in effect, ejected from the UN when the "China seat" was transferred to the mainland. In a move close to expulsion, the General Assembly refused between 1974 and 1991 to seat South Africa's delegate because that country's apartheid policies violated the UN Charter. The refusal to recognize Yugoslavia in 1992 as a successor state was, in effect, an expulsion of that country based on its bloody repression of Bosnians, Croats, and others.

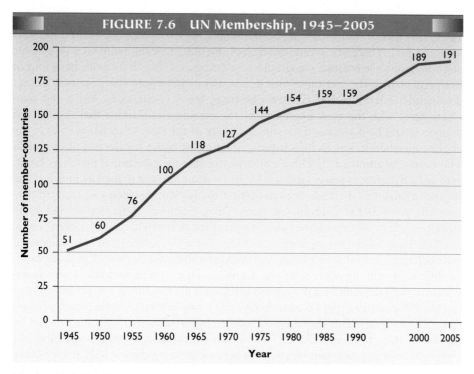

FIGURE 7.6   UN Membership, 1945–2005

Membership in the United Nations has risen rapidly. The 375% growth in UN membership is an indication of the increased number of states in existence and also of the UN's nearly universal membership.

Data source: UN Web site at http://www.un.org/overview/growth.htm.

Membership Issues within IGOs   Not every internal decision-making structure in an IGO necessarily has representatives from each member-country. At the core of the UN and other IGOs there is usually a **plenary representative body** that includes all members. The basis for plenary bodies is the mutual responsibility of all members for the organization and its policies and their equal role in deciding policy. The **UN General Assembly (UNGA)** is the UN's plenary organ. Such assemblies normally have broad authority within their organizations and are supposedly the most powerful elements of their organizations. In practice, however, the assembly may be secondary to the administrative structure or some other part of the organization.

A second type of representative body is a **limited membership council.** Based on the theory that smaller groups can operate more efficiently than large assemblies, there are many councils that have representatives only from some parent organization's membership. For example, the UN's Economic and Social Council (ECOSOC) has representatives from 54 members, elected by the General Assembly for three-year terms based on a plan of geographical representation. Membership is also sometimes limited on the theory that some members have a greater concern or capacity in a particular area. For example, the **UN Security Council (UNSC)** has five permanent members (the P5: China, France, Russia, the United Kingdom, and the United States). These five were the leading victorious powers at the end of World War II and were thought to have a special peacekeeping role to play.

Controversy over Membership on the Security Council   Like many IGO organs, the Security Council has a limited membership. Ten of its 15 members are chosen by the

UNGA for limited terms. The others are the P5 that have served continuously since 1945. This special status has long been a simmering issue in the UN, and it has now begun to boil. There are several sources of discontent. Some point to a *geographic and demographic imbalance.* Geographically, Europe and North America have four of five permanent seats, and those four permanent members are also countries of predominantly Eurowhite and Christian heritage. Many countries in Africa and elsewhere agree with the view expressed by the president of Zambia that the council "can no longer be maintained like the sanctuary of the Holy of Holies with only the original members acting as high priests, deciding on issues for the rest of the world who cannot be admitted."[15] Other critics charge that the permanent members are an *inaccurate reflection of power realities.* As the German mission to the UN puts it, "The Security Council as it stands does not reflect today's world which has changed dramatically since 1945."[16] From this perspective, Germany, India, Japan, and some other powerful countries have begun to press for permanent seats for themselves.

This issue heated up even more in 2005 after a UN review panel recommended and Secretary-General Kofi Annan endorsed expanding the Security Council's membership to 24. Among other reactions, Germany, Japan, India, and Brazil launched a joint campaign to claim four permanent seats, with the remaining two probably going to a Muslim country (Egypt is most likely) and a sub-Saharan African country (Nigeria or South Africa). This thrust was countered by a coalition of 40 countries (led by Argentina, Italy, Mexico, Pakistan, and South Korea) also favoring expansion but arguing against any new permanent seats because creating them would reduce other countries' chances of getting a rotating seat on the expanded 24-member council.

Neither the panel nor Annan recommended that the six new permanent members be given the same veto power as the P5 on the Security Council. Still, there was widespread speculation that adding permanent members would soon lead to a call for all permanent members, or none, to have a veto. Although this possibility understandably worries the P5, they have looked for ways to block it without seeming to be self-serving. For example, China proclaimed itself open to adding new members but opposed Japanese membership. A government spokesperson in Beijing complained that Japan has never apologized for its aggression and atrocities during World War II and argued that "only when a country respects history . . . only when a country is able to win trust from its neighboring countries, can it be able to play a greater role in international affairs." Similarly, a U.S. diplomat at the UN professed support for reform, but only if it could be done by "broad consensus" (which is unlikely) and only if the movement for reform avoided "artificial deadlines" (that is, deciding soon).[17]

Whatever might be fair, change will be hard to achieve. Any Charter revision must be recommended by a two-thirds vote of the UNSC, in which each of the P5 has a veto that they might well use to avoid surrendering or diluting their special status. If a reform plan did pass the Security Council, it would also have to be adopted by a two-thirds vote of the UNGA. There, agreement on any new voting formula would be difficult, given the sensitivities of the 191 countries. For example, the proposal that India have a permanent seat alarms Pakistan, whose UN representative has characterized the idea as "an undisguised grab for power and privilege."[18] Complicating matters even more is the dispute between countries wanting a permanent seat for themselves and the countries wanting more members but no new permanent ones. Therefore, the prospects for reform remain dim. Secretary-General Kofi Annan was undoubtedly right when he noted that despite "widespread agreement that the council should be enlarged," there remains "no consensus on the details."[19]

JOIN THE DEBATE
Changing Permanent
Membership and the
Almighty Veto Power in
the Security Council:
How Can Reform Strengthen
the UN Security Council?

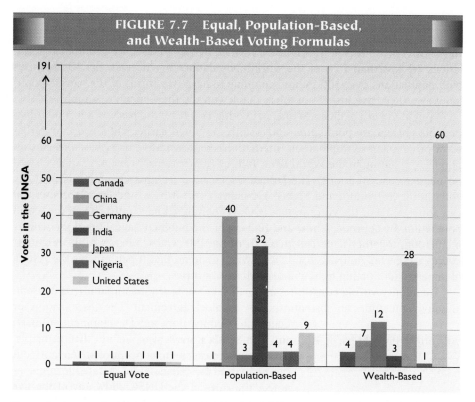

FIGURE 7.7   Equal, Population-Based, and Wealth-Based Voting Formulas

To see the impact of various voting formulas, imagine that the current 191 votes in the UNGA were allocated on the basis of equality, population, and wealth. Voting power would vary widely. Compare the United States and China, for example. Both, of course, would have the same vote in a one-country, one-vote system. In a population system, China would have far more votes than the United States. The reverse would be true in a wealth-based voting scheme, in which the United States would have almost nine times as many votes as China. Are any of these formulas fair? What would be a fair formula?

Data sources: World Bank (2004) and author's calculations.
Note: Voting weights were rounded to the nearest whole number, with all countries getting at least one vote.

Voting Issues

One of the difficult issues that any international organization faces is its formula for allocating votes. Three major alternatives as they exist today are majority voting, weighted voting, and unanimity voting. The implications of various voting formulas are evident in Figure 7.7.

Majority voting is the most common formula used in IGOs. This system has two main components: (1) each member casts one equal vote based on the concept of sovereign equality, and (2) the issue is carried by either a simple majority (50% plus one vote), reflecting the democratic notion that the will of the majority should prevail. The UNGA and most other UN bodies operate on this principle. A variation is **supermajority voting.** This requires more than a simple majority to pass measures. A two-thirds vote is most common, and some of the supermajority formulas, like the one used by the Council of Europe, can be quite complex.

The objection to equal voting power is that it does not reflect some standards of reality. Should Costa Rica, with no army, cast an equal vote with the powerful United

WEB POLL
The Place of Democratic Governance in International Organizations

States? Should San Marino, with a population of thousands, cast the same vote as China, with its more than 1 billion people? It might be noted, for example, that in the UNGA, two-thirds of the votes are wielded by 127 states whose combined populations are less than 15% of the world's population. By contrast, the 13 countries with populations over 100 million combine to have two-thirds of the world's population, yet they have just 7% of the available votes in the General Assembly.

Weighted voting allocates unequal voting power on the basis of a formula. Two possible criteria are population and wealth. As noted earlier, the European Parliament provides an example of an international representative body based in part on population. Voting in the World Bank and the International Monetary Fund is based on member contributions. The United States alone commands about 17% of the votes in the IMF, and it and France, Germany, Great Britain, and Japan together can cast almost 40% of the votes in that IGO, yet combined have only 10% of the world population. By contrast, China and India, which combined have 37% of the world's population, together have less than 5% of the IMF votes. This "wealth-weighted" voting is especially offensive to LDCs, which contend that it perpetuates the system of imperial domination by the industrialized countries.

Unanimity voting constitutes a fourth scheme. It requires unanimous consent, although sometimes an abstention does not block agreement. The Organization for Economic Cooperation and Development (OECD) and some other IGOs operate on that principle. Unanimity preserves the concept of sovereignty but can easily lead to stalemate. In a related formula, as noted, the rules of the UNSC allow any of the five permanent members to **veto** proposals. Taking exception to this arrangement, a Venezuelan diplomat described the veto as "an antidemocratic practice . . . not in accordance with the principle of the sovereign equality of states."[20]

Vetoes were cast frequently during the cold war, but have been infrequent since 1990. As Figure 7.8 shows, the USSR has cast many more vetoes than the other P5, but most of those came during the early years of the cold war. Since 1990, it is the United States that has most frequently used the veto, accounting for 72% of them, mostly on resolutions condemning Israel.

Although the use of the veto has declined dramatically, the power remains important. First, vetoes are still sometimes cast. In 2004, for example, the United States vetoed a resolution condemning Israel's assassination of the Hamas leader on the grounds that the resolution was "unbalanced" because it did not mention terror attacks on Israel. Second, the threat of a veto can persuade countries not to press an initiative. For example, the United States and Great Britain did not push for a Security Council authorization to take military action against Iraq in 2003 because it was clear that even if majority support could be gathered (which was doubtful), France and Russia would exercise their veto power. The veto can also be a dip-

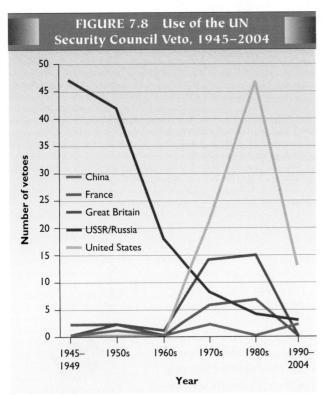

FIGURE 7.8 Use of the UN Security Council Veto, 1945–2004

Number of vetoes

China
France
Great Britain
USSR/Russia
United States

1945–1949   1950s   1960s   1970s   1980s   1990–2004

Year

The use of the veto in the UN Security Council has changed over the years. In the first two decades of the cold war, Russia cast the vast majority of vetoes, and it accounts for 48% of the 257 vetoes in UN history through 2004. In more recent years, it has been the United States that has cast the preponderant number of vetoes.

Source: Global Policy Forum at http://www.globalpolicy.org/security/membship/veto/vetosubj.htm. Calculations by author.

lomatic tool. The United States, for instance, has successfully pressured the UN to exempt U.S. troops serving as UN peacekeepers from the jurisdiction of the International Criminal Court by threatening to veto all UN peacekeeping operations.

Leadership

It is difficult for any organization to function without a single administrative leader, and virtually all IGOs have a chief executive officer (CEO). The UN's administrative structure is called the **Secretariat**, and the secretary-general is the CEO. The UN secretary-general and the heads of many other IGOs are more than mere administrators; they are important diplomatic figures in their own right.

The Selection of IGO Leaders

Critics sometimes dismiss IGOs as marginal players on the world stage. One indication that argument is not accurate is the intense struggle among member-countries over who will head various IGOs. Clearly, there must be much ado about something.

Selecting the UN Secretary-General   The process begins when the Security Council nominates a candidate for secretary-general. The General Assembly then elects that official for a five-year term. It is hardly the finest hour of democracy, though, because the Security Council controls the choice by always submitting only one name to the General Assembly. While the selection process may not be very democratic, it is highly political. For example, the story of the selection of the current secretary-general, Kofi Annan, begins in some ways with the selection of his predecessor in 1992. With no African having served in the UN's top office, that continent's countries claimed it was their turn and fielded several candidates. Most of these individuals had a history of criticizing the West, and the United States made it clear that it would veto them. The compromise choice was Egypt's Boutros Boutros-Ghali. He had a moderate reputation and had even been a Fulbright scholar at Columbia University. Concern that Boutros-Ghali was an Arab was eased by the fact that he is a Coptic Christian, not a Muslim, and his wife is Jewish. As it turned out, Washington guessed wrong, and Boutros-Ghali proved to be an assertive, sometimes acerbic secretary-general who often rankled the United States by, among other things, criticizing the Eurowhite-dominated Security Council for what he saw as a racially tinged tendency to pay more attention to matters in white regions (such as the Balkans crisis in Europe) than in nonwhite areas (such as the crises in Somalia and Rwanda in Africa). Whatever the validity of such charges, the result was that the United States blocked a second term for Boutros-Ghali.

Since most secretaries-general have served two terms, Africans argued it was still their turn, and sub-Saharan Africans were particularly intent on having one of their number recognized. After extensive maneuvering, the final choice was Annan, a career UN diplomat from Ghana. He had a reputation as a capable and moderate diplomat and administrator, and his personal history (a B.A. degree in economics from Macalaster College in St. Paul, Minnesota, an M.A. in management from MIT) helped assuage Washington's concern that a secretary-general from black Africa might prove too radical. Also helpful, according to some reports, was that Annan is married to Nane Lagergren, a Swedish lawyer, who is a niece of Raoul Wallenberg, the heroic Swedish diplomat noted for trying to save Jewish lives during World War II.

Selecting the CEOs of other IGOs   Sharp struggles over who will lead an IGO are not confined to the UN. For example, there have been spirited contests during changes in leadership at the WTO. In 1999 the focus was a determined effort by the LDCs to break the EDC's monopoly on the top jobs in the leading financial IGOs. The result was a compromise: an EDC national, Mike Moore of New Zealand, was selected with the understanding that in 2002 he would step down in favor of Thailand's Supachai Panitchpakdi, who would serve until 2005. The LDC challenge was also evident in 2004 when many non-Western countries backed Egyptian Mohamed El-Erian to head the IMF. Eventually the unbroken tradition of a European holding that position was preserved with the selection of Rodrigo de Rato y Figaredo of Spain, but it was just the latest in what promises to be the ongoing struggle of non-Western countries to play a greater role in the direction of IGOs and, indeed, the course of world politics. The basic point is that the jostling among countries, blocs, and regions to appoint one of their own or someone of their liking to the top jobs indicates how important these IGOs are. All that sound and fury must signify something.

The Role of IGO Leaders

An issue that swirls around IGO executives is their proper role. The role orientations of the UN secretary-general and other IGO leaders can range from activism to restraint (Kille & Scully, 2003). For the most part, the documents that established IGOs anticipated a restrained role. In the UN Charter, for example, the Secretariat is the last major organ discussed. That placement indicates the document's drafters intended a limited, largely administrative role for the secretary-general. That has not, however, been the history of the office.

Former UN Secretaries-General   Whatever was intended, the first two secretaries-general, Trygve Lie of Norway (1946–1953) and Dag Hammarskjöld of Sweden (1953–1961), were activists who steadily expanded the role of their office. Hammarskjöld argued that he had a "responsibility" to act to uphold the peace "irrespective of the views and wishes of the various member governments" (Archer, 1983:148). Hammarskjöld's approach was epitomized during the civil war that followed the independence of the Belgian Congo in 1960. The secretary-general aggressively used UN military forces to try to restore peace. It is somehow sadly fitting that he died in the area when his plane crashed after reportedly being shot down by one of the warring factions.

The Soviets were so upset at the activist and what they saw as a pro-Western stance of Hammarskjöld that they pressed for successors with more restrained conceptions of the role of secretary-general. Over time, however, secretaries-general have once again tended toward activism. The sixth secretary-general, Egypt's Boutros Boutros-Ghali (1992–1996), believed that "if one word above all is to characterize the role of the secretary-general, it is independence. The holder of this office must never be seen as acting out of fear or in an attempt to curry favor with one state or groups of states."[21] Just as Hammarskjöld's activism had led him into disfavor, so too did Boutros-Ghali's views, and he was forced from office after one term, as related above.

The Current UN Secretary-General   Kofi Annan of Ghana is the UN's seventh secretary-general, but he is the first to have spent almost his entire career as a UN diplomat rather than as a diplomat for his country. Annan joined UN service at age 24 and earned a solid reputation while serving in a variety of positions, including undersecretary-general for peacekeeping. After the contentious Boutros-Ghali, Annan's moderation and quiet demeanor helped his selection because Washington and some other capitals that wanted to rein in the secretary-general assumed he would be a cautious bureaucrat who would not act independently.

Predictions that Annan would be compliant were wrong. Although Annan is quite soft-spoken, he is also an activist who strongly supports the idea that the UN and its secretary-general are not beholden to any one country or bloc. He professes to admire collaboration and consensus, but adds that he is "comfortable . . . in the end not fearing to do things my way."[22] Despite his assertive approach and the disagreements with powerful countries that sometimes ensued, Annan's smoothly diplomatic approach avoided confrontations with Washington and other major capitals, and he was easily reappointed for a second term beginning in 2002. Adding to his accolades at that time, Annan received the Nobel Peace Prize for 2001 for his work toward making "a better organized and more peaceful world."

Annan's independence was clearly evident in 2003 when he differed with the United States about Iraq. He rejected as "not in conformity with the [UN] Charter" the U.S. argument that it had the legal authority to act militarily against Iraq without Security Council authorization.[23] Although the secretary-general has no vote, his position was undoubtedly influential in bolstering the countries on the Security Council that opposed action because many of them would echo the comment of Mexico's UN ambassador, "We always look for the guidance of the secretary-general and this is no exception."[24] After the war, the secretary-general characterized the preemptive action aspects of the Bush Doctrine as "a fundamental challenge to the principles on which, however imperfectly, world peace and stability have rested for the last 58 years."[25]

Scandal in the Secretariat   Midway through Annan's second term, scandal broke very close to him. Revelations of corruption in the oil-for-food program for Iraq that operated from 1996 to 2003 cast a deep shadow on Annan's tenure. Established by the Security Council, the program allowed Iraq to sell oil and use the receipts to buy food, medicine, and other humanitarian supplies under UN supervision. Persistent rumors about corruption in the $67 billion program led the Security Council in 2004 to launch an investigation headed by Paul Volcker, former head of the U.S. Federal Reserve Board. He found that Benon Sevan, Annan's appointee to run the program, was corrupt. According to the report, Sevan had persuaded the Iraqi government to sell oil through a Swiss firm that, in turn, gave kickbacks to the UN administrator. In payment for Iraq's cooperation, Sevan turned a blind eye to Saddam Hussein diverting billions of dollars away from food and medicine, toward banned uses. Making matters worse, the secretary-general's son, Kojo Annan, who worked for a company hired by the UN to monitor the oil-for-food program, had also been involved.

Volcker did not accuse Kofi Annan of being corrupt. As the report put it, "There is no evidence . . . [that the program] was subject to any affirmative or improper influence of the secretary-general."[26] Soon thereafter, Annan expressed "great relief" at being exonerated by the report, and when a journalist asked if he would resign, the secretary-general shot back, "Hell, no!"[27] Although it became clear as the investigation filed its reports that Annan would survive in office, his luster and his personal authority were undercut by the improprieties that came to light involving UN officials close to him and his son. Some governments began to imply that Annan might have at least indirect culpability. "It is probably an exaggeration to suggest that the Volcker report exonerated the secretary-general," a top U.S. State Department official commented.[28] In the end, even if Annan was not himself corrupt, the scandal eroded his personal stature to such a degree that his ability to lead effectively was compromised. It was a sad and ironic cloud over the stewardship of an exceptional secretary-general.

Even if Annan resigns, however, a new secretary-general will be elected, and the UN will continue its tasks, much as the United States was rocked by, not devastated by, the end of the disgraced Richard Nixon's presidency. Whether it is Annan or his successors, the debate over the proper role of top officials in other IGOs leaders will continue. The controversy is part of a struggle between the traditional approach versus the alternative approach to world politics. Traditionally, national states have sought to control IGOs and their leaders. As IGOs and their leaders have grown stronger, however, they have more often struck out independently down the alternative path. As Secretary-General Annan has commented, he and his predecessors have all carried out their traditional duties as chief administrative officer, but they have also assumed another, alternative role: "an instrument of the larger interest, beyond national rivalries and regional concerns."[29] Presidents and prime ministers are finding, comments one U.S. diplomat, that "you can't put the secretary-general back in the closet when it's inconvenient."[30]

Administration and Finance

No organization, no matter how well led, can be successful unless it is well organized and efficient and receives the resources it needs in terms of able staff and budget to accomplish its missions. So it is with the UN, and such matters as staff and finances are important to the function of the UN and other IGOs, even if they do not often capture the headlines.

Administration

The secretary-general appoints the other principal officials of the Secretariat. However, in doing so, he must be sensitive to the desires of the dominant powers in making these appointments and also must pay attention to the geographic and, increasingly, to the gender composition of the Secretariat staff. Controversies have occasionally arisen over these distributions, but in recent years the focus of criticism has been the size and effectiveness of the staffs of the UN headquarters in New York and its regional offices (Geneva, Nairobi, and Vienna). In this way, the UN is like many other IGOs and, indeed, national governments, with allegedly bloated, inefficient, and unresponsive bureaucracies that have made them a lightning rod for discontent with member-governments.

Administrative Reform   Over its existence, critics of the United Nations have regularly charged that it cost too much, employed too many people, and managed its affairs poorly. Many of these charges reflect animus toward the UN rather than a balanced evaluation, but even defenders of the UN have agreed that the operation of the organization needed to be improved. Soon after he became secretary-general, Annan reported to the General Assembly that, to a degree, "over the course of the past half century certain . . . [UN] organizational features have . . . become fragmented, duplicative, and rigid."[31] To address these issues, Annan undertook an extensive program to improve administration and restrain costs. Reflecting this effort, the UN's core budget has grown little in recent years. The secretariat has trimmed its core staff from 10,100 in 1997 to 9,100, and the total number of people working for the UN has remained static despite significantly increased peacekeeping operations. Many administrative changes were also instituted, with a U.S. government review in 2004 noting over 40 reforms that had fully or substantially been implemented.[32]

Gender diversification has been another notable reform. The UN has a relatively good record compared to most countries for increasing the percentage of management positions held by women. They now occupy more than 40% of the professional posts, up 11% since 1991. And among the most senior UN positions, women fill a third of the jobs.

Putting Charges of Maladministration in Perspective   As with almost any government bureaucracy, it is possible to find horror stories about the size and activities of IGO staffs. The oil-for-food program scandal and the evidence of sexual abuse of supposedly protected persons by UN peacekeeping troops and personnel that swept over the UN like a tsunami in 2004 are recent and particularly disturbing examples (Pilch, 2005). But the charges that the UN and its associated agencies are corrupt and a bureaucratic swamp need to be put in perspective.

One way to gain insight about the size of the UN staff is to compare it to U.S. city governments. While employment in the UN system has not increased since 1997 when Annan took office, the number of municipal employees in the United States has risen by more than 11%. The Secretariat's core staff (9,100 workers), which deals with a world population of 6.3 billion people, is smaller than the staff of the city of New Orleans (pop. 485,000; 9,900 employees). The total number of people (37,000) who work directly for the UN is smaller than the number of municipal employees of Chicago, and the entire UN system has fewer people (61,000) on the payroll than does New York City.

When evaluating UN administration it is important to acknowledge its flaws. There have been times of poor leadership and scandal at UN headquarters and in its various agencies. In the most recent of these, Secretary-General Annan was at least naive in not ensuring better oversight of the oil-for-food program and in not looking into why his son was so in demand as a consultant. Similarly, it is possible to find instances of ineptitude, wasted money, overstaffing, and other problems in the UN bureaucracy. However, it also important to recognize that all these problems occur in national governments, including the U.S. government. The basic point is that the standards one applies to the leaders of countries and those of IGOs should not differ. Nor should reactions to bureaucratic blundering. Within countries, problems may lead to the abolition of a particular agency, but the thrust is reform, not destruction of the entire government. From this perspective, it is more reasonable to address problems at the UN through reform rather than disbanding it.

In the same vein, it is important to see that reforming any large organization is difficult and usually a slow process. But the task is especially difficult in the UN where the secretary-general has 191 bosses, each with self-interested views of bureaucratic arrangements and all squabbling among themselves as to what is superfluous and what is vital. A 2004 review by the U.S. General Accounting Office highlighted the difficulty of implementing reforms requiring approval by membership. The report found that 70% of the 56 reforms that the secretary-general had initiated and could implement on his own authority had proceeded. By comparison, only 44% of 32 reforms needing member-country approval had made significant progress.[33] The implication of this data is that when members complain about the UN's operation, they might look to themselves as the barrier to needed changes.

Finance

All IGOs face the problem of obtaining sufficient funds to conduct their operations. National governments must also address this issue, but they have the power to impose and legally collect taxes. By contrast, IGOs have very little authority to compel member-countries to support them.

The United Nations is beset by severe and controversial financial problems. There are two main elements to the UN budget: the *core budget* for headquarters operations and the regular programs of the major UN organs and the *peacekeeping budget* to meet the expenses of operations being conducted by the Security Council. These two budgets for 2005 were, respectively, $1.5 billion and $3.9 billion. Additionally, there is a *voluntary contributions budget* of about $7 billion, which funds a wide range of UN-affiliated agencies such as the United Nations Children's Fund

(UNICEF) and the United Nations Environment Programme (UNEP). These three budgets and some special budget categories, such as funding international tribunals, brought the total UN budget for 2005 to about $13 billion.

The UN depends almost entirely on the assessment it levies on member-countries to pay its core and peacekeeping budgets. This assessment is fixed by the UNGA based on a complicated formula that reflects the ability to pay. According to the UN Charter, which is a valid treaty binding on all signatories, members are required to meet these assessments and may have their voting privilege in the General Assembly suspended if they are seriously in arrears. Ten countries each have assessments of 2% or more of the budget. They and their percentages of the core budget assessment are: the United States (22.0%), Japan (19.5%), Germany (8.7%), Great Britain (6.1%), France (6.0%), Italy (5.0%), Canada (2.8%), Spain (2.5%), Brazil (2.4%) and China (2.1%). At the other end of the financial scale, more than half the UN's members are assessed below .01%, with many paying the minimum assessment of 0.001%. The "target" voluntary budget payments are the same as the core budget. Because of their special responsibility (and their special privilege, the veto), permanent UNSC members pay a somewhat higher assessment for peacekeeping, with the U.S. share at 25%. The assessment scheme is criticized by some on the grounds that while the 10 countries with assessments of 2% or higher collectively pay almost 75% of the UN budget, they cast just 5% of the votes in the UNGA.

Such numbers are something of a fiction, however, because some countries do not pay their assessment. Member-states were in arrears on the core and peacekeeping budgets by $3.8 billion in early 2005. As a result, the UN's financial situation constantly teeters on the edge of crisis at the very time it is being asked to do more and more to provide protection and help meet other humanitarian and social needs. "It is," said a frustrated Boutros-Ghali just before he stepped down, "as though the town fire department were being dispatched to put out fires raging in several places at once while a collection was being taken to raise money for the fire-fighting equipment."[34] The analogy between the UN's budget and firefighting is hardly hyperbole. During 2005, the public safety (police and fire departments) budget of New York City was about 20% larger than the UN peacekeeping budget.

Just as it determines many things in this world, U.S. policy toward the UN's budget is a key to its financial stability. Some Americans think that their country overpays; others see the United States as a penurious piker. The decision box, "Santa or Scrooge? The United States and the UN Budget" asks you to sort out this controversy and decide the future of U.S. funding of the United Nation.

Activities of the UN and Other IGOs

Web Link

You can watch a wide range of UN activities, such as press conferences and Security Council meetings, at the UN Webcast site at http://www.un.org/webcast/index.asp.

The most important aspects of any international organization are what it does, how well this corresponds to the functions we wish it to perform, and how well it is performing its roles. The following pages will begin to explore these aspects by examining the scope of IGO activity, with an emphasis on the UN. Much of this discussion will only begin to touch on these activities, which receive more attention in other chapters.

Activities Promoting Peace and Security

The opening words of the UN Charter dedicate the organization to saving "succeeding generations from the scourge of war, which . . . has brought untold sorrow to mankind." The UN attempts to fulfill this goal in numerous ways.

Creating norms against violence is one. Countries that sign the charter pledge to accept the principle "that armed force shall not be used, save in the common inter-

WRITE THE POLICY SCRIPT

Santa or Scrooge? The United States and the UN Budget

From one perspective, Americans may feel like Santa Claus for their support of the United Nations. After all, the United States is just 1 of 191 UN members, yet it is assessed 22% of the UN's core budget and 25% of its peacekeeping budget. The United States also contributes to the budgets of the UN specialized agencies. For 2005 U.S. funding was about $530 million for the core budget, about $550 million for the peacekeeping budget, and about $900 million for the agencies, for a total just under $2 billion.

Two billion dollars sounds like a lot, but it is less extravagant from other perspectives. One is that total U.S. funding came to only about $10.26 per American. That is about 4% of what the average American spends each year going to movies. In another context, only $1 out of every $1,200 dollars in the U.S. budget ($2.4 trillion) for 2005 went to supporting the UN. Focusing on security, Washington spends more every 15 hours on its military forces than it did for the entire year on UN peacekeeping.

Ratcheting down the image of Santa Claus even more, and perhaps even casting Americans as Scrooge, is the fact that the United States is also the UN's biggest debtor. In early 2005, Washington owed $1.4 billion to the UN, accounting for 37% of all UN arrearages. This debt persists even after the United States in 2002 pressured the UN into reducing the U.S. assessments from 25% to 22% for the core budget and from 30% to 25% for the peacekeeping budget.

Most Americans think that their government should pay its debt. A 2002 poll that asked them whether they favored or opposed U.S. payment of its UN debt found 58% in favor, 32% opposed, and 10% unsure.[1] As for the annual payments, a 2003 survey found that 11% of Americans wanted to increase UN funding, 50% wanted to keep it the same, 37% wanted to decrease it, and 2% were uncertain.[2] How Americans would feel today about funding is unclear. On the one hand, the oil-for-food scandal and other frustrations have undercut American support of the UN. A 2005 poll showed considerable disenchantment among Americans with the UN. Yet the same survey recorded only 13% of its respondents as favoring a U.S. withdrawal from the UN, and almost 65% saying that the UN plays "a necessary role in the world today."[3]

What Do You Think?

How would you rewrite the script for the U.S. approach to the UN budget? Would you quickly pay off the U.S. debt or ignore it? How about the level of funding—should Santa Claus give less? Should Scrooge give more? Or is U.S. funding of the UN about right?

---

est" and further agree to "refrain in their international relations from the threat or the use of force except in self-defense." Reaffirming the charter's ideas, the UN (and other IGOs) condemned Iraq's invasion of Kuwait in 1990, Serbian aggression against its neighbors, and other such actions. These denunciations and the slowly developing norm against aggression have not halted violence, but they have created an increasing onus on countries that strike the first blow. When, for example, the United States acted unilaterally in 1989 to depose the regime of Panama's strongman General Manuel Noriega, the UN and the OAS condemned Washington's action. Five years later, when the United States toppled the regime in Haiti, Washington took care to win UN support for its action. Of course, norms do not always restrain countries, as the U.S.-led invasion of Iraq in 2003 demonstrates. Yet the efforts of U.S. and British diplomats to get a supportive UN resolution underlined the existence of the norm. Moreover, the angry reaction in many parts of the globe to the Anglo-American preemptive action and the postwar difficulties during the occupation may, in the long run, actually serve to reinforce the norm.

Providing a debate alternative is a second peace-enhancing role for the UN and some other IGOs. Research shows that membership in IGOs tends to lessen interstate military conflict (Chan, 2004). One reason is that IGOs serve as a forum in which members publicly air their points of view and privately negotiate their differences. The UN thus acts like a safety valve, or perhaps a soundstage where the world drama can be played out without the dire consequences that could occur if another

SIMULATION
The Work of
the United Nations

"shooting locale" were chosen. This grand-debate approach to peace involves denouncing your opponents, defending your actions, trying to influence world opinion, and winning symbolic victories.

Intervening diplomatically to assist and encourage countries to settle their disputes peacefully is another security role that IGOs play. IGOs engage in such steps as providing a neutral setting for opposing parties to negotiate, mediating to broker a settlement between opposing parties, and even deciding issues between disputants in such forums as the International Court of Justice.

Promoting arms control and disarmament is another international security function of IGOs. The International Atomic Energy Agency, an affiliate of the UN, helps promote and monitor the nonproliferation of nuclear weapons. The UN also sponsors numerous conferences on weapons and conflict and has also played an important role in the genesis of the Chemical Weapons Convention and other arms control agreements.

Imposing sanctions is a more forceful step to pressure countries that have attacked their neighbors or otherwise violated international law. As we will see in chapter 12, sanctions are controversial and often do not work. But there have been successes. In 2003, after 15 years of sanctions, Libya finally paid reparations to the families of the 280 people killed when a bomb planted by Libyan agents destroyed Pan Am Flight 103 over Lockerbie, Scotland, in 1988. The wheels of justice sometimes grind slowly, but grind they did. It also turns out that despite the mishandling of the sanctions on Iraq through 2003, they did constrict the funds flowing to Saddam Hussein enough to help forestall any thought he might have had of building weapons of mass destruction.

Peacekeeping is the best-known way that the UN and some other IGOs promote peace and security. This function is extensively covered in chapter 11, but a few preliminary facts are appropriate here. Through early 2005, the United Nations had mounted 60 peacekeeping operations, and they have utilized military and police personnel from most of the world's countries. These operations ranged from very lightly armed observer missions, through police forces, to full-fledged military forces. Never before have international forces been so active as they are now. The number of UN peacekeeping operations has risen markedly in the post–cold war era, as shown in Figure 7.9. As of February 2005, there were 17 UN peacekeeping forces of varying sizes in the field at locations throughout the world, with more than 67,000 troops and police from 103 countries deployed. Fortunately, UN peacekeeping forces have suffered relatively few casualties, but almost 2,000 have died in world service. For these sacrifices and contributions to world order, the UN peacekeeping forces were awarded the 1988 Nobel Peace Prize.

Social, Economic, Environmental, and Other Activities

In addition to maintaining and restoring the peace, IGOs engage in a wide variety of other activities. During its early years, the UN's emphasis was on security. This concern has not abated, but it has been joined by social, economic, environmental, and other nonmilitary security concerns. This shift has been a result of the ebb and eventual end of the cold war, the growing number of LDCs since the 1960s, realization that the environment is in danger, and changing global values that have brought an increased focus on human and political rights. "Peacekeeping operations claim the headlines," Secretary-General Annan has observed astutely, "but by far the lion's share of our budget and personnel are devoted to the lower-profile work of . . . helping countries to create jobs and raise standards of living; delivering relief aid to victims of famine, war, and natural disasters; protecting refugees; promoting literacy;

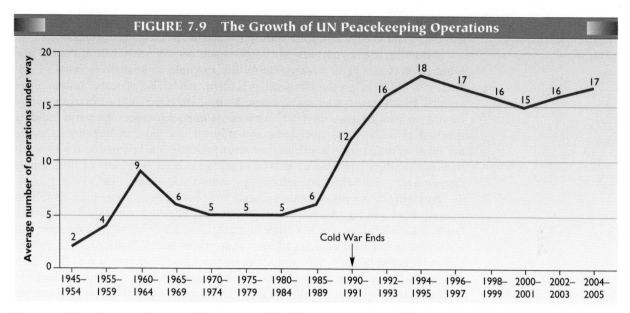

FIGURE 7.9 The Growth of UN Peacekeeping Operations

The end of the cold war and its standoff between the United States and the Soviet Union in the Security Council has allowed the UN to mount a significantly increased number of peacekeeping operations since the early 1990s.

Note: Number for each two years is the most missions during that period.
Data source: UN, Department of Peacekeeping Web site, http://www.un.org/depts./dpko/.

and fighting disease. To most people around the world, this is the face of the United Nations."[35] Recent examples of this effort include the UN program, headed by former President Bill Clinton, to bring aid to the victims of the tsunami that devastated Indonesia and other places in the Indian Ocean region in 2004, and the supply of emergency relief to people in the embattled region of Darfur in Sudan and the refugees from there who have fled to neighboring countries.

It would be impossible to list here, much less fully describe, the broad range of endeavors in which the UN and other IGOs are involved. Suffice it to say that they cover most of the issues that humans address at all levels of government. Many of these activities will be highlighted in subsequent chapters, so this discussion is limited to a few of the programs and successes of the UN and other IGOs.

Promoting *economic development* is an important role, with the United Nations Development Programme (UNDP), the World Bank, and a significant number of other global and regional IGOs working to improve the economic well-being of those who are deprived because of their location in an LDC, their gender, or some other cause. The UNDP alone supports more than 5,000 projects globally with a budget of $1.3 billion. The UN Development Fund for Women (UNIFEM) focuses on improving the lives of women in LDCs.

Advocating human rights is a closely related IGO function. Beginning with the Universal Declaration of Human Rights in 1948, the UN has actively promoted dozens of agreements on political, civil, economic, social, and cultural rights. The UN Commission on Human Rights has used its power of investigation and its ability to issue reports to expose abuses of human rights and to create pressure on the abusers through a process that one scholar has termed the "mobilization of shame" (Weisband, 2000). Currently, for example, the UN is at the heart of the global effort to free the estimated 250 million children who are forced to work instead of being sent to school, to end the sexual predation of children that is big business in some parts of the world, and to eliminate other abuses that debase the meaning of childhood.

Advancing international law and norms is another important role of the UN and other IGOs (Coate & Fomerand, 2004). For example, international courts associated with IGOs help establish legal precedent. IGOs also sponsor multinational treaties, which may establish the assumption of law. Over 300 such treaties have been negotiated through the UN's auspices. As one scholar sees the norm-building function of IGOs, "The procedures and rules of international institutions create information structures. They determine what principles are acceptable as a basis for reducing conflicts and whether governmental actions are legitimate or illegitimate. Consequently, they help shape actors' expectations" (Keohane, 1998:91).

Improving the quality of human existence has many aspects. More than 30 million refugees from war, famine, and other dangers have been fed, given shelter, and otherwise assisted through the UN High Commissioner for Refugees. A wide variety of IGOs also devote their energies to such concerns as health, nutrition, and literacy. For example, UNICEF, WHO, and other agencies have undertaken a $150 million program to develop a multi-immunization vaccine. This vaccine program is designed to double the estimated 2 million children who now annually survive because of such international medical assistance. The Food and Agriculture Organization (FAO) has launched a program to identify, preserve, and strengthen through new genetic techniques those domestic animals that might prove especially beneficial to LDCs. Western breeds of pigs, for example, usually produce only about 10 piglets per litter; the Taihu pig of China manages 15 to 20. The FAO hopes to use the latter and other appropriate animals to increase protein availability in the LDCs.

Guarding the environment is one of the newer roles of IGOs. Beginning with the UN Conference on Environment and Development (dubbed the Earth Summit) in 1992, the UN has sponsored several global meetings on the environment. These have resulted in the initiation of programs that will slow down, stop, or begin to reverse the degradation of the environment. IGOs are increasingly also requiring that envi-

Peacekeeping is the UN activity that is most often in the news, but the UN also addresses a broad range of the world's other needs. One UN function is disaster relief. This Sri Lankan man, who has received an aid pack provided by the UN High Commissioner for Refugees, is one of tens of millions that the UN has helped. His life was thrown into crisis by the 2004 tsunami that devastated many Indian Ocean countries.

ronmental impact statements accompany requests for economic development aid and in some cases are refusing to finance projects that have unacceptable negative impacts on the biosphere.

Encouraging independence through self-determination has long been a role of IGOs. The UN Trusteeship Council once monitored numerous colonial dependencies, but the wave of independence in recent decades steadily lessened its number of charges. When in October 1994 Palau gained its independence from the United States, the last trust territory was free. Therefore, the Trusteeship Council's mission was fulfilled and, while it continues to exist technically, it no longer meets.

Evaluating IGOs and Their Future

The United Nations has existed for more than fifty years. Most other IGOs are even younger. Have they succeeded? The answer depends on your standard of evaluation.

Ultimate goals are one standard. Article 1 of the UN Charter sets out lofty goals such as maintaining peace and security and solving economic, social, cultural, and humanitarian problems. Clearly, the world is still beset by violent conflicts and by ongoing economic and social misery. Thus, from the perspective of meeting ultimate goals, it is easy to be skeptical about what the UN and other IGOs have accomplished. One has to ask, however, whether the meeting of ultimate goals is a reasonable standard. There is, according to one diplomat, a sense that "failure was built into [the UN] by an extraordinary orgy of exaggerated expectations."[36]

Progress is a second standard by which to evaluate the UN and other IGOs. Is the world better off for their presence? That is the standard Kofi Annan appeals for when he implores, "Judge us rightly . . . by the relief and refuge that we provide to the poor, to the hungry, the sick and threatened: the peoples of the world whom the United Nations exists to serve."[37] Between its 40th and 50th anniversaries, the United Nations surpassed all previous marks in terms of numbers of simultaneous peacekeeping missions, peacekeeping troops deployed, and other international security efforts. During the 1990s alone, the UN also sponsored 12 conferences on a range of global concerns. This activity has continued apace, with conferences on racism (Durban, 2001), aging (Madrid, 2002), sustainable development (Johannesburg, 2002), financing for development (Monterrey, 2002), small islands (Mauritius, 2005), and the information society (Tunis, 2005) among those held in the first five years of the new century. These meetings have all focused attention on global problems and have made some contribution toward advancing our knowledge and enhancing our attempts to deal seriously with a wide range of economic, social, and environmental global challenges. Moreover, the people of the world tend to recognize these contributions, as Figure 7.10 shows. Thus, by the standard of progress, the UN and other IGOs have made a contribution.

What is possible is a third standard by which to evaluate the UN and other IGOs. Insofar as the UN

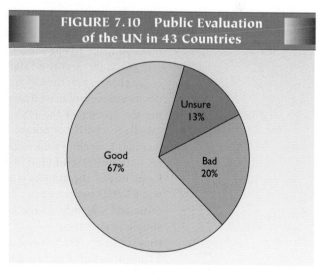

FIGURE 7.10 Public Evaluation of the UN in 43 Countries

The United Nations enjoys strong popularity around the world. When asked about the impact of the UN on their country, an average of 67% of the people in 43 countries characterized it as good. Kenyans were the most positive, with 93% saying good. There were only two countries (Argentina and Jordan) in which more people said bad than good. As for Americans, 72% responded good, 19% replied bad, and 9% were unsure.

Note: The question was, "Is the influence of the United Nations very good, somewhat good, somewhat bad, or very bad in your country?"
Data source: The Pew Research Center for People and the Press, "Views of a Changing World" (June 2003).

The UN and other IGOs have many limitations and problems. Yet they also make valuable contributions. Among other places, eastern Congo is one example of the UN in action in 2005. UN peacekeepers there do not have the numbers, arms, or authority to resolve the fighting among various factions in the region, yet the peacekeepers have increased the safety of the civilians. Some critics of the UN would diminish or even dismantle it. Another approach would be to reform and empower it. What do you think?

does not meet our expectations, we need to ask whether it is a flaw of the organization or the product of the unwillingness of member-states to live up to the standards that countries accept when they ratify the charter.

When the Security Council would not authorize action against Iraq, there were angry charges that the UN was not living up to its obligation to make Baghdad surrender its weapons of mass destruction (WMDs) and that it was weak and irrelevant. Raising the specter of the UN's defunct predecessor, President Bush told an audience, "We'll see whether or not the United Nations will be [like] the League of Nations when it comes to dealing with [Saddam Hussein] who for 11 years has thumbed his nose at resolution after resolution [to end Iraq's WMD program]."[38] Such derision is heard less frequently as the months after the war have dragged on with no evidence that there was a WMD program to be discovered. Thus the question must be asked whether the crisis and war showed the UN to be impotent or prudent. At a less dramatic level, simply paying their assessments regularly and on time is another thing more countries could do. The UN will also work better if countries try to make it effective. It is a truism, as Kofi Annan put it, that there is a "troubling asymmetry between what the member-states want of the [UN] and what they actually allow it to be."[39]

Whether alternatives exist is a fourth standard by which to evaluate the UN and other IGOs. John Bolton, whom President Bush nominated in 2005 as U.S. ambassador to the UN, once caustically commented that if 10 of the UN headquarters' 38 floors were eliminated "it wouldn't make a bit of difference."[40] Even if Bolton were correct and "there's no such thing" as a well-functioning UN, one must ask the question he never addressed: If not the UN and other international organizations, then what? Can the warring, uncaring world continue unchanged in the face of nuclear weapons, persistent poverty, an exploding population, periodic mass starvation, continued widespread human rights violations, resource depletion, and environmental degradation? Somehow the world has survived these plagues, but one of the realities that this book hopes to make clear is that we are hurtling toward our destiny at an ever-increasing, now exponential speed. In a rapidly changing system, doing things the old way may be inadequate and may even take us down a road that, although familiar, will lead the world to cataclysm. At the very least, as Secretary of State Madeleine Albright noted, "The United Nations gives the good guys—the peacemakers, the freedom fighters, the people who believe in human rights, those committed to human development—an organized vehicle for achieving gains."[41] This returns us to the question, If not the UN, then what? There may be considerable truth in the view of the British ambassador to the UN that "it's the UN, with all its warts, or it's the law of the jungle."[42] It is through this jungle that the road more familiar has passed, and following it into the future may bring what Shakespeare was perhaps imagining when he wrote in *Hamlet* of a tale that would "harrow up thy soul, [and] freeze thy young blood."

To repeat an important point, the UN and other IGOs are, in the end, only what we make them. They do possess some independence, but it is limited. Mostly their successes and failures reflect the willingness or disinclination of member-countries to cooperate and use them to further joint efforts. Kofi Annan urged support of the UN by quoting what Winston Churchill said to Franklin Roosevelt in 1941: "Give us the tools and we will do the job."[43] Whether or not that occurs is uncertain. What is clear is that critics of IGOs are too often narrowly negative. They disparage the organizations without noting their contributions or suggesting improvements. IGOs hold one hope for the future, and those who would denigrate them should make other, positive suggestions rather than implicitly advocating a maintenance of the status quo. Surely the UN has its flaws, but so does the status quo.

The ultimate question is what to do with IGOs in the years to come. Critics and supporters of the UN agree, as Kofi Annan commented in 2005, "The multilateral system is not delivering for its member-states the results that it should."[44] Some would blame the UN and other IGOs for this and abandon them. Others would try to make them vehicles of big-power diplomacy. Then there is the possibility that the main problem is the unwillingness of countries to increase the power and authority of the UN and other IGOs to address the increasingly globalized problems the world faces. Whatever the choice, there is a last bit of Shakespeare's wisdom, found in *Julius Caesar,* that is worth pondering. The playwright counsels us:

> There is a tide in the affairs of men
> Which, taken at the flood, leads on to fortune;
> Omitted, all the voyage of their life
> Is bound in shallows and in miseries.

Chapter Summary

An Overview of Intergovernmental Organizations

1. One sign of the changing international system is the rapid rise over the last century in the number of intergovernmental organizations (IGOs). There are many classifications of international organizations, including global, regional, and specialized IGOs.

2. Current international organization is the product of three lines of development: the idea that humans should live in peace and mutual support, the idea that the big powers have a special responsibility for maintaining order, and the growth of specialized international organizations to deal with narrow nonpolitical issues.

3. The rapid growth of all types of international organizations stems from increased international contact among states and people, increased economic interdependence, the growing importance of transnational issues and political movements, the inadequacy of the state-centered system for dealing with world problems, small states attempting to gain strength by joining together, and successful IGOs providing role models for new organizations.

4. There are significant differences among views on the best role for international organizations. Four existing and possible roles of IGOs are: providing an interactive arena, acting as a center for cooperation among states, evolving into an independent national actor, and becoming a supranational organization.

5. Some observers argue that international organizations are best suited to promoting cooperation among states rather than trying to replace the state-centered system. Still others contend that international organizations should concentrate on performing limited functional activities with the hope of building a habit of cooperation and trust that can later be built upon. Finally, many view international organizations as vehicles that should be manipulated to gain national political goals.

6. Some observers favor moving toward a system of supranational organization, in which some form of world government, or perhaps regional governments, would replace or substantially modify the present state-centered system.

Regional IGOs: Focus on the European Union

7. The EU provides an example of the development, structure, and roles of a regional IGO. The EU has evolved considerably along the path of economic integration and is by far the most integrated regional organization.

8. The movement toward political integration is more recent and is proving more difficult than economic integration. The French and Dutch re- jections of the proposed EU constitution were a significant setback in the process of EU expansion and integration. In is unclear, though, whether the negative votes would only cause a pause in EU progress toward becoming a United States of Europe or augured a stalling or even reversal of the trend of recent decades toward integration.

Global IGOs: Focus on the United Nations

9. The United Nations provides an example of the development, structure, and roles of a global IGO.

10. There are several important issues related to the structure of international organizations. One group of questions relates to membership and criteria for membership.

11. Voting schemes to be used in such bodies are another important issue. Current international organizations use a variety of voting schemes that include majority voting, weighted voting, and unanimity voting.

12. Another group of questions concerns the administration of international organizations, including the role of the political leaders and the size and efficiency of IGO bureaucracies. The source of IGO revenue and the size of IGO budgets are a related concern.

13. International organizations have many roles. Peacekeeping is one important role. Others include creating norms against violence, providing a debate alternative, intervening diplomatically, imposing sanctions, and promoting arms control and disarmament.

14. The UN and other international organizations perform other, varied functions: they promote international law, promote arms control, better the human condition, promote self-government, and further international cooperation.

15. However one defines the best purpose of international organization, it is important to have realistic standards of evaluation. The most fruitful standard is judging an organization by what is possible, rather than setting inevitably frustrating ideal goals.

For simulations, debates, and other interactive activities, a chapter quiz, Web links, PowerWeb articles, and much more, visit **www.mhhe.com/rourke11/** and go to chapter 7. Or, while accessing the site, click on Course-Related Headlines and view recent international relations articles in the *New York Times*.

Key Terms

confederation
Council of the European
  Union
Court of Auditors
Court of Justice
European Commission
European Communities
  (EC)
European Economic
  Community (EEC)
European Ombudsman

European Parliament
  (EP)
European Union (EU)
federation
functionalism
Hague system
Intergovernmental
  organizations (IGOs)
League of Nations
limited membership
  council

Maastricht Treaty
majority voting
neofunctionalism
plenary representative
  body
President of the
  Commission
regime
regional government
Secretariat
supermajority voting

supranational
  organization
UN General Assembly
  (UNGA)
UN Security Council
  (UNSC)
United Nations (UN)
unanimity voting
veto
weighted voting
world government

National Power and Diplomacy: The Traditional Approach

Then, everything includes itself in power,
Power into will, will into appetite.
—William Shakespeare, *Troilus and Cressida*

Bid me discourse, I will enchant thine ear.
—William Shakespeare, "Venus and Adonis"

This chapter begins with a fable by British Prime Minister Winston Churchill about the various forms of power among the zoo animals and how that affected their diplomacy. You will see in this chapter that human diplomacy, like that of the zoo residents, is substantially shaped by power.

O NCE UPON A TIME," began a fable told by British Prime Minister Winston S. Churchill, "all the animals in the zoo decided that they would disarm." To achieve that goal, the animals convened a diplomatic conference. There, Churchill's tale went:

> The Rhinoceros said when he opened the proceeding that the use of teeth was barbarous and horrible and ought to be strictly prohibited by general consent. Horns, which were mainly defensive weapons, would, of course, have to be allowed. The Buffalo, the Stag, the Porcupine, and even the little Hedgehog all said they would vote with the Rhino, but the Lion and the Tiger took a different view. They defended teeth and even claws, which they described as honourable weapons of immemorial antiquity. The Panther, the Leopard, the Puma, and the whole tribe of small cats all supported the Lion and the Tiger. Then the Bear spoke. He proposed that both teeth and horns should be banned and never used again for fighting by animals. It would be quite enough if animals were allowed to give each other a good hug when they quarreled. No one could object to that. It was so fraternal, and that would be a great step toward peace. However, all the other animals were very offended by the Bear, and the Turkey fell into a perfect panic. The discussion got so hot and angry, and all those animals began thinking so much about horns and teeth and hugging when they argued about the peaceful intentions that had brought them together, they began to look at one another in a very nasty way. Luckily the keepers were able to calm them down and persuade them to go back quietly to their cages, and they began to feel quite friendly with one another again.[1]

Sir Winston's allegory is instructive, as well as colorfully entertaining. It touches on the two related aspects of world politics that are our focus in this chapter.

Power is the first thing we will explore. It remains an essential element of diplomacy in a system based on self-interested sovereignty. In our world, like the zoo, the actors that possess the power to give rewards or inflict punishment are able to influence other actors. Power has many forms. Physical strength is one, and the rhino and the lion were both powerful in this way. Skill is another aspect of power. The turkey had little tangible strength, but perhaps it possessed guile and other intangible diplomatic skills to persuade some of the animals to adopt its views. Economic power is also important in diplomacy. The zookeepers controlled the food supply and may have used food as a positive incentive (more food) or negative sanction (less or no food) to persuade the animals to return to their cages.

Diplomacy is our second topic. It examines how countries apply power to achieve their goals in the international system. The zoo was the system in which the animals negotiated. Like the current international system, the zoo system was based on self-interest, with each group of animals selecting goals that were advantageous to itself, giving little thought to how they affected others. The zoo system also apparently allowed for some potential fighting because each of the animals tried to maximize its power potential and to minimize the power of the other animals. Thus, success in the zoo was based in part on the Darwinian law of the jungle. Notice, though, that the animals relied on negotiating skills, not threats or actual attacks, to initially advance their positions. They tried clever arguments, and they also formed coalitions, such as the "anti-teeth" alliance of Rhino, Buffalo, Stag, Porcupine, and Hedgehog working in opposition to the "pro-teeth" axis of the Lion, Tiger, and other similarly armed cats. As we shall see, diplomacy involves applying power through techniques ranging from raw military muscle to skillfully made arguments.

In the context of the traditional and alternative approaches to world politics, this chapter looks at the traditional way of establishing what policies will prevail in the world. This includes countries applying power in the diplomatic pursuit of their self-interest. Might may not make right, but traditionally in world politics it has usually made success. The alternative approach, discussed in chapter 9, involves the establishment of international law and norms of justice to regulate the conduct of international relations. Chapter 9 also examines the role of international courts in trying to ensure that the rule of law limits destructive behavior by states and individuals, much like the zookeepers helped establish rules to preserve order in their domain. That way who is right, rather than who is mightiest, has a better chance of prevailing.

National Power

"Until human nature changes, power and force will remain at the heart of international relations," according to a top U.S. official.[2] Not everyone would agree with such a gloomy realpolitik assessment, but it underlines the crucial role that power plays in diplomacy. When the goals and interests of states conflict, which side will prevail is often decided by who has the most power.

The Nature of Power

Power is an elusive concept. It is hard to define, measure, or describe exactly how it works. Harvard University dean and former top U.S. Defense Department official Joseph Nye (2000:55) writes that power "is like the weather. Everyone talks about it, but few understand it." Alluding to an even greater mystery, Nye confides that power is "like love . . . easier to experience than to define or measure." If the nature of power is so perplexing to a Harvard dean, then how can we begin to understand it? The first step is to see the dualistic nature of power as both an end (goal) and a means (asset, tool). Then we can turn to measuring power and examining its characteristics.

Power as a Goal

Because power is a key determinant of the course of events in the international system, countries try at minimum to preserve their power and hopefully to expand it. This is an almost inevitable consequence of the current international system that emphasizes self-reliance. Classic realists would go even further and see power accumulation as a rational response of humans pursuing their often-conflicting self-interests, whether as individuals or collectively, such as states. As discussed in chapters 1 and 5, liberals, postmodernists, constructivists, and feminists all think that it is possible to change the norms of power seeking and conflict. Even these theorists would concede, though, that countries continue frequently to conserve or augment their power.

This power seeking leads to an analysis of the concept of balance of power, which was introduced in chapters 2 and 3. Sometimes the term *balance of power* is used to describe the existing distribution of power, as in, "the current balance of power greatly favors the United States." More classically, though, the theory of **balance-of-power politics** put forth by realists holds that: (1) all states are power seeking; (2) ultimately, a state or bloc will attempt to become hegemonic, that is, dominate the system; and (3) other states will attempt to block that dominance by increasing their own power and/or cooperating with other states in an antihegemonic effort.

Whether or not seeking power is a constructive goal is highly controversial. Realists argue that it is, because building national strength and antihegemonic coalitions help preserve the independence of countries. They also argue that failure to balance or "underbalancing" leaves states vulnerable (Schweller, 2004). Liberals and others see balance-of-power politics as a never-ending formula for conflict and for wasting resources in a Quixotic quest to achieve the impossible dream, that is, true security.

Whether a balance of power is good or bad, however, and whether the term is used to describe an equilibrium or the existing distribution of power, the idea is much on the minds of national leaders. President Bush explicitly supported the idea when he wrote in his 2002 national security report, "The great strength of this nation must be used to promote a balance of power that favors freedom."[3] Freedom as he defined it included the full range of Bush's policy goals and the assumption that those would benefit the world. President Jacques Chirac was also concerned with the balance of power and the looming shadow of a hegemonic United States when in 2005 he urged French voters to ratify the EU constitution as a way of avoiding an "Anglo-Saxon, Atlanticist Europe. . . . dominated by America." Chirac envisions a powerful EU as a counterbalance to the United States (Hasseler, 2004). To achieve that, he warned the French, "We do not defend our interests alone. We can only defend them collectively, and if Europe is united. . . . Otherwise, we'll be swept away."[4]

Power as an Asset

Power is an asset as well as a goal. From this perspective, power is the sum of the various assets of a state that it can use to achieve its goals even when they clash with the goals of other international actors. One way to see this is to think about *power as money*, as a sort of political currency. Power and money are both assets that can be used to acquire things. Money buys things; power causes things to happen. Like money, power is sometimes used in a charitable way. But also like money, power is more often used for self-interest. Acquiring money and power both often require sacrifices, and those who use their financial or power assets imprudently may lose more than they gain. As with any analogy, however, you should be wary of overusing the comparison. There are differences between money and power. One is that political power is less liquid than money; it is harder to convert into things that you want. A second difference is that power, unlike money, has no standard measurement. Therefore it is much harder to be precise about how much power any country has.

One important issue about any asset is, how much is enough? If you think about money as a physical object, it is pretty useless. It is inedible, you cannot build anything useful out of money, and it will not even burn very well if you need to keep warm. Yet some people are obsessed with having money for its own sake. For them, acquiring money is an end in itself. Literature is full of such stories, ranging from Molière's *The Miser* to Dickens's classic *A Christmas Carol* and its tragic tale of Ebenezer Scrooge. The misers give up love, friendships, and other pleasures to get and keep money only to discover, in the end, that their money becomes a burden. Similarly, some people believe that countries can become fixated on acquiring power, especially military power, beyond what is prudently needed to meet possible exigencies. This, critics say, is unwise because power is expensive, it creates a temptation to use it, and it spawns insecurity in others.

THE NEW ATLANTIC WALL

This cartoon satirizes the reception French President Jacques Chirac (portrayed as a tank barrier) and German Chancellor Gerhard Schröder (pictured as a cannon emplacement) gave President Bush when he arrived in Europe in May 2005 for the 60th anniversary of Germany's surrender in World War II. The European "welcome" is characterized as similar to the greeting that German troops gave Allied forces on D-Day when they landed in France in 1944. Balance-of-power politics is arguably one reason for the recent strains in transatlantic relations, as the Europeans try to curb the hegemonic power of the United States on the world stage.

To such charges, realists would reply that the danger is not having too much power but not wisely using the power you have. Realists warn against wasting power on marginal goals, but they also caution against a country being too reluctant to use it as a tool to advance its national interests. Former Secretary of State Henry Kissinger, for one, argues that Americans are sometimes too-reluctant warriors and believes that "American leadership [needs] to articulate for their public a concept of the national interest and explain how that interest is served . . . by the maintenance of the balance of power" through a forceful U.S. presence on the world stage.[5]

Hard and Soft Power

The most common image of power involves the ability to make someone else do something or suffer the consequences. Often called **hard power,** this type of power rests on negative incentives (threats, "sticks") and on positive incentives (inducements, "carrots"). There is also **soft power,** the ability to persuade others to follow your lead by being an attractive example. As one scholar puts it, "A country may obtain the outcome it wants in world politics because other countries—admiring its values, emulating its example, aspiring to its level of prosperity and openness—want to follow it" (Nye, 2004:5).

The value and proper use of these two forms of power has been and remains an important debate in the United States and elsewhere. American neoconservatives and to a degree President Bush and like-minded leaders favor using hard power at least sometimes to advance American interests and even to spread freedom. The spread of democracy may be a positive outcome of the U.S. invasion of Iraq, and it was clearly in Bush's mind when he declared in his second inaugural address that "the policy of the United States [is] to seek and support the growth of democratic movements and institutions in every nation and culture, with the ultimate goal of ending tyranny in our world." The president assured his listeners that "this is not primarily the task of arms," but he also warned, "We will defend ourselves and our friends by force of arms when necessary."

Critics of this approach condemn it as counterproductive and argue that it is squandering the greatest U.S. asset, the attractiveness of America's personal liberty and economic prosperity. Citing poll results, such as those in Figure 8.1, showing that opinion about the United States has plummeted almost everywhere in the past several years, one analyst worries that "the United States' soft power—its ability to attract others by the legitimacy of U.S. policies and the values that underlie them—is in decline as a result" (Nye, 2004a:16). One reason this is a concern according to this view is that the United States needs the cooperation of other countries to combat terrorism and many other problems, but "When the United States becomes so unpopular that being pro-American is a kiss of death in other countries' domestic politics, foreign political leaders are unlikely to make helpful concessions, reducing U.S. leverage in international affairs."

To such commentary, an advocate of hard power would echo the words of President Bush, "We cannot defend America and our friends by hoping for the best. . . . The only path to peace and security is the path of action." As for world opinion, Bush has pledged to "respect the values, judgment, and interests of our friends and partners." Nevertheless, he asserted, "We will be prepared to act apart" if necessary and "will not allow . . . disagreements [with allies] to obscure our determination to secure . . . our fundamental interests and values."[6]

A final note on hard and soft power is not to construe their application as an "either-or" proposition. Soft power is certainly important, but even UN Secretary-

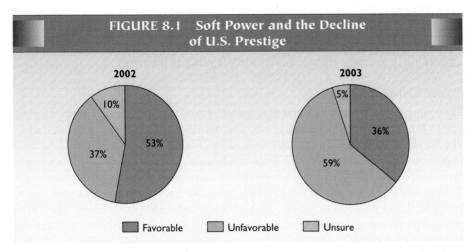

FIGURE 8.1 Soft Power and the Decline of U.S. Prestige

2002

2003

■ Favorable ■ Unfavorable ■ Unsure

A survey in 14 countries taken in 2002, then again in 2003 after the U.S. invasion of Iraq found that the percentage of respondents with a favorable opinion of the United States declined from a majority to a minority, while those with an unfavorable opinion grew from a minority to a majority of 59%. This decline in U.S. prestige arguably undercut U.S. "soft power" and the willingness of other governments to cooperate with Washington.

Note: The question was, "Please tell me if you have a very favorable, somewhat favorable, somewhat unfavorable or very unfavorable opinion of the United States."
Data Source: Pew Research Center for the People and the Press (2003).

General Kofi Annan has conceded, "You can do a lot with diplomacy, but of course you can do a lot more with diplomacy backed up by firmness and force."[7]

Measuring Power

At a general level, it is possible to measure or at least estimate power. There can be no doubt, for example, that China is more powerful than Mongolia. Beyond such broad judgments, there is no widely accepted formula for measuring power. It is easy enough to measure such tangible factors as per capita GNP or number of soldiers. But it is harder to assign weights to each to establish their relative importance to one another when constructing a power formula. Even harder is measuring and giving relative weights to intangible factors such as the diplomatic skill of a country's leaders or its soft-power ability to lead by example. These difficulties were illustrated by a study that reviewed four attempts by various scholars to devise formulas to measure national power during the cold war (Taber, 1989). The four often came to dramatically different conclusions because of different methods of measuring power. Two studies rated the Soviet Union the most powerful. One each rated the United States and China most powerful. One ranked China only seventh. Brazil ranked number three in one study, and India ranked number four in another study; yet two studies did not place either country in the top ten. The list need not go on to make the point that different formulas for measuring power yielded very different results.

These problems do not mean that we should abandon attempts to gauge national power. To repeat a point, states may legally be sovereign equals, but in power terms the reality is something akin to what George Orwell wrote in *Animal Farm* (1945), "All animals are equal, but some animals are more equal than others." Because ignoring this reality would be foolish, it is important to further increase our understanding of power by examining its complex characteristics.

Did You Know That:

King Frederick the Great of Prussia (1712–1786), once commented, "Diplomacy without arms is like music without instruments."

Web Link

View an online version of a recent attempt to measure national power at **www.rand .org/publications/MR/MR1110/**.

Characteristics of Power

Power is not a simple and stable phenomenon. Indeed, it is very much a political chameleon, constantly changing even while it remains the same.

Power Dynamics

Even simple measurements show that power is constantly in flux. Economies prosper or lag, arms are modernized or become outmoded, resources are discovered or are depleted, and populations rally behind or lose faith in their governments. No superpower from Rome, through imperial Britain, to the Soviet Union has maintained its status permanently. Each eventually declined and some even vanished, as did the USSR. To take their place, other countries have risen from humble beginnings to the rank of major power, as did the United States. Still others, like China today, may reemerge from a period of eclipse and strive to recapture their lost status (Tammen et al., 2002).

There are numerous reasons why power is so fluid. One system-level of analysis theory is that *power cycles* occur over a period of a few decades, or even as much as a century (Tessman & Chan, 2004; Colaresi, 2001). The cycles are demarcated by great-power or "systemic" wars, such as the two world wars, that reflect strains or power shifts within the system and act as political earthquakes, altering the system by destroying the major power status of declining powers and elevating rising powers to pole status. Then the process of power decay and formation begins anew. *Balance-of-power politics* is another system-level cause of change as countries form alliances and take other actions to avoid being dominated.

From a state-level-of-analysis perspective, several factors account for the rise or fall of a country's power. One involves the *sources of power*. The advent of nuclear weapons some 60 years ago instantly elevated the status of countries that have them. *Internal conditions* also affect an actor's power. The Soviet Union collapsed in part because it no longer commanded the loyalty of most of its citizens. Most Americans are patriotic, but the country cannot remain a superpower if its people are unwilling to bear the cost of being a leader in the international system. That does not mean the United States should lead, only that it cannot remain dominant unless it accepts the burdens, as well as the benefits of leadership.

ANALYZE THE ISSUE
Measuring a Country's Power

Absolute and Relative Power

By one standard, power that indisputably exists and can be potentially used is **absolute power**. One example is the approximately 5,000 nuclear warheads and bombs that are deployed on about 1,000 U.S. missiles and bombers. They indisputably exist, will have a specific impact if used, and in theory can be used by a president without any legal check on the ability to authorize their deployment.

SIMULATION
Creating Your Own
International Power Index

Whatever the theory may be, however, power does not usually exist in a vacuum. Since power is about the ability to persuade or make another actor do or not do something, calculating power is of limited use except to measure it against the power of the other side. When assessing capabilities, then, **relative power**, or the comparative power of national actors, must be considered. We cannot, for example, say that China is powerful unless we specify in comparison to whom. Whatever Beijing's power resources may be, China's relative power compared to another major power, such as Japan, is less than is China's relative power compared to a smaller neighbor, such as Vietnam.

A related issue is whether power is a **zero-sum game**. If a gain in power of one actor inevitably means a loss of power for other actors, the game is zero-sum. If an

The relative power of countries is dynamic and continually changing. One of the important trends on the world stage today is the growth of China's power, including its military capabilities. China's major campaign to increase its military power is captured in this photograph taken in Shanghai in 2005 of a martial display that includes the exhortation, "Strengthen National Power, Build a Solid National Defense."

actor can gain power without the power of other actors being diminished, then the game is non-zero-sum. Realists tend to see power as zero-sum; idealists usually portray it as non-zero-sum. Without delving too far into this controversy, we can say that the relative nature of power implies that sometimes, especially between antagonists, power approaches zero-sum. When China's Asian rival India tested nuclear weapons in 1998, it decreased China's relative power compared to India and arguably reduced China's influence in the countries to its southwest. Yet India's advance in power was non-zero-sum relative to another of its regional rivals, Pakistan, because that country tested its own nuclear weapons almost simultaneously with India. When the nuclear dust settled, India and Pakistan were in the same relative power position vis-à-vis each other as they had been before the blasts.

Power as Capacity and Will

Every country's power is determined substantially by its power assets: its military and economic strength, its leadership, the size and talents of its population, and numerous other factors. Together these make up a country's **power capacity**, its potential for exercising international power. By themselves, though, substantial power assets are not enough to create a powerful global presence. They give a country the capacity to exercise power, but to be effective they must be supplemented by a **will to power**. This is a country's willingness to use its capacity, to turn potential power into applied power. Japan offers a current example.

Economically Japan is the world's second most powerful country, with an annual GNP that is second only to that of the United States and larger than that of China, France, and Great Britain combined. Japan's 127 million well-trained people are also a significant asset. With little fanfare, Japan has also amassed a well-equipped military force supported by the world's second-largest annual military budget ($46 billion in 2004). Yet for all of this, Japan's global influence has been limited by its post–World War II reluctance to assert itself. Symbolically, the Japanese constitution forbids the "use of force as a means of settling international disputes." More importantly, the

Web Link

You can play a zero-sum game and a variety of other political strategy games such as "Free Rider" and "Prisoner's Dilemma" online at **www.egwald.com/ operationsresearch/ gameintroduction.php.**

Having the will to use the power you possess is an important power factor. Japan already has a significant military force and vast military potential. But the Japanese experience in World War II has made them very reluctant to use their military force. This photograph of Japanese personnel displaying the "rising sun" military flag symbolizes that in the past decade or so, quasi-pacifism has begun to change, and Japan has begun to take small steps to use its military abroad in support of its diplomacy.

Japanese have been unwilling to take an assertive stand, much less use their forces, to promote their views.

This attitude has begun to change. Polls show a growing sense of national pride in Japan, and recent prime ministers have found it politically wise to annually visit the Yasukuni Shrine, which honors Japan's troops killed in World War II. Japan has also very slowly begun to deploy military units abroad. They now participate in UN peacekeeping missions, and Tokyo deployed 600 noncombatant troops (engineering and medical units) to Iraq in 2003. Additionally, the Japanese navy is readying its first helicopter-carrier ship and intensifying commando training, both moves that will add to the country's ability to project its power further from its shores. This worries some of Japan's neighbors, especially when combined with recent renewed claims by Japan to islands and territorial waters lost to or in dispute with China, Russia, and South Korea since World War II. Yet another sign of growing Japanese assertiveness is the country's campaign for a permanent seat on the UN Security Council. "Japan is changing," the U.S. ambassador there recently commented. "I think Japan has decided, 'We're a great, big country, we're the second-largest economy in the world, and we probably have the second-largest navy in the Pacific. We want a seat on the Security Council. We want a role to play in the international arena.' I think all those changes are at work and will continue." Confirming that impression, Japan's foreign minister told reporters, "There are expectations that Japan play a greater role in dealing with international conflicts. And I believe that Japan must do so."[8] All this portends a Japan that will increasingly convert its power capacity into applied power and play a stronger role.

Objective and Subjective Power

Just as a country's power is influenced by its willingness to use its assets, so too it is influenced by what other countries perceive to be those assets and the intent to use them. **Objective power** consists of assets that you possess and that you are willing to use. As such, objective power is a major factor in determining whose interests prevail, as Iraq found out in 2003 in its war with the U.S.-led coalition forces.

A great deal of the power a country has is not applicable to every situation. During the classic military invasion of Iraq in 2003, U.S. tanks, warplanes, and other high-tech weaponry quickly defeated Iraq's poorly equipped military forces. In the "post-victory," occupation phase, however, modern weapons became much less useful. The type of urban combat this U.S. patrol faces in Mosul in northern Iraq puts American troops and the forces of the resistance on a more equal footing.

Subjective power is also important. It is common to hear politicians argue that their country cannot back down in a crisis or get out of an ill-conceived military action because the country's reputation will be damaged. Research shows that concern to be overdrawn (Mercer, 1996). Still, a country's power is to a degree based on others' perceptions of its current or potential power or its reputation for being willing (or not willing) to use it. Sometimes the perception that a country is not currently powerful can tempt another country. When asked for his evaluation of the U.S. military in 1917, a German admiral replied, "Zero, zero, zero." Based on this perception of U.S. power, Germany resumed submarine warfare against U.S. merchant shipping, a move that soon led to war with the United States. More recently, it appears that in both 1991 and 2003, Saddam Hussein's willingness to risk war with the United States was based in part on his perception that Americans would not be willing to sustain the cost and casualties necessary to invade Iraq and topple him.

Situational Power

A country's power varies according to the situation, or context, in which it is being applied. A country's **situational power** is often less than the total inventory of its capabilities. Military power provides a good example. During the last weeks of March and first weeks of April 2003, American and British forces faced those of Iraq in a classic conventional war situation. In that context, the conflict was one-sided with the U.S./U.K. forces quickly destroying and dispersing those of Iraq. During the postwar period, the conflict situation changed when forces opposed to the U.S./U.K. presence in the country began to use guerrilla warfare and terrorist tactics. Soon, more U.S. soldiers had died in the "postwar" period than during the war, and U.S. policy was in considerable disarray even though the American forces in Iraq were as numerous as the ones that had so easily toppled the regime of Saddam Hussein. The difference was that in the very different situation after "victory," a great deal of the U.S. high-tech weapons inventory, its heavy armored vehicles, and its air power were of no use in countering the resistance tactics in Iraq.

Before leaving this discussion of the characteristics of power, it is important to stress that power is multidimensional. In any given diplomatic situation, a country's

SIMULATION
Winning Wars Isn't Simple

hard and soft power may both come into play. Capacity and the will to power, the objective and subjective elements of power, and all the other characteristics of power may also be relevant. Therefore, it is important when analyzing power to consider *all* its dimensions *and* to place them in their proper relative and situational contexts. Only then can we begin to answer the question of who is powerful and who is not. To help with that process, our next step is to identify the various determinants of national power.

The Elements of Power

There are many ways to categorize the multitudinous elements of power. One common way is to group power assets into various functional categories. Two such categories, the national core and the national infrastructure, are central to the power of all countries because they serve as a foundation for the more utilitarian categories of national power, specifically military power and economic power. In the following sections, we will analyze these two central categories of national power; military and economic power will be discussed in chapters 10 and 12, respectively.

The National Core

The national state forms the basis of this element of power. The essence of a state can be roughly divided into three elements: national geography, people, and government.

National Geography

Shakespeare's King Henry VI proclaimed:

> Let us be backed with God and with the seas
> Which He hath given for fence impregnable, . . .
> In them and in ourselves our safety lies.

It is not clear what, if anything, God has ever done for England, but King Henry's soliloquy reminds us that the English Channel has helped save Great Britain from Napoleon, Hitler, and every other threat from Europe for nine centuries. Geographic factors that influence a country's power status include location, topography, size, and climate.

The *location* of a country, particularly in relation to other countries, is significant. The weight of China's army as a power factor is different in Beijing's relations with the United States and Russia. The huge Chinese army can do little to threaten the United States, far across the Pacific Ocean. By contrast, Russia and China share a border, and Chinese soldiers could march into Siberia. Location can be an advantage or a disadvantage. Spain was able to avoid involvement in either world war partly because of its relative isolation from the rest of Europe. Poland, sandwiched between Germany and Russia, and Korea, stuck between China and Japan, each has a distinctly unfortunate location. The Israelis would almost certainly be better off if their promised land were somewhere—almost anywhere—else. And the Kuwaitis probably would not mind moving either, provided they could take their oil fields with them.

A country's *topography*—its mountains, rivers, and plains—is also important. The Alps form a barrier that has helped protect Switzerland from its larger European neighbors and spared the Swiss the ravages of both world wars. The rugged mountains of Afghanistan bedeviled British and Soviet invaders in the past, and since 2001 they have frequently frustrated the efforts of U.S. and other coalition troops to corner and capture or kill remnants of the al Qaeda and Taliban forces. Topography can also work against a country. For example, the southern and eastern two-thirds of Iraq is a broad plain that provided a relatively easy invasion avenue for the mechanized U.S. and British forces in 2003. The Tigris and Euphrates river systems and the associated swampy areas provided some topographical defenses, but too few to make a difference.

A country's *size* is important. Bigger is often better. The immense expanse of Russia, for example, has repeatedly saved it from conquest. Although sometimes overwhelmed at first, the Russian armies have been able to retreat into the interior and buy time in exchange for geography while regrouping. By contrast, Israel's small size gives it no room to retreat.

A country's *climate* can also play a power role. The tropical climate of Vietnam, with its heavy monsoon rains and its dense vegetation, made it difficult for the Americans to use effectively much of the superior weaponry they possessed. At the other extreme, the bone-chilling Russian winter has allied itself with Russia's geographic size to form a formidable defensive barrier. Many of Napoleon's soldiers literally froze to death during the French army's retreat from Moscow, and 131 years later Germany's army, the Wehrmacht, was decimated by cold and ice during the sieges of Leningrad and Stalingrad. In fact the Russian winter has proved so formidable that Czar Nicholas I commented, "Russia has two generals we can trust, General January and General February."

People

A second element of the national core is a country's human characteristics. Tangible demographic subcategories include number of people, age distribution, and such quantitative factors as health and education. There are also intangible population factors such as morale.

Population   As is true for geographic size, the size of a country's population can be a positive or a negative factor. Because a large population supplies military personnel and industrial workers, sheer numbers of people are a positive power factor. It is unlikely, for instance, that Tonga (pop. 112,000) will ever achieve great-power status. A large population may be disadvantageous, however, if it is not in balance with resources. India, with 1.1 billion people, has the world's second-largest population, yet because of the country's poverty ($530 per capita GNP), it must spend much of its energy and resources merely feeding its people.

Age Distribution   It is an advantage for a country to have a large percentage of its population in the productive years (15–64 by international reporting standards). Some countries with booming populations have a heavy percentage of children who must be supported. In other countries with limited life expectancy, many people die before they complete their productive years. Finally, some countries are "aging," with a geriatric population segment that consumes more resources than it produces (Longman, 2004).

Worldwide, 28% of the Earth's population in 2005 was less than 15 years old; 7% was 65 or over; 65% was in the working-age years (15–64). Figure 8.2 on page 242 shows the age distributions of several countries, which you should compare. The figure also shows the dependency ratio of young and old people combined compared to the working-age population. Many analysts would contend that South Korea is relatively

MAP
Employment by
Economic Activity

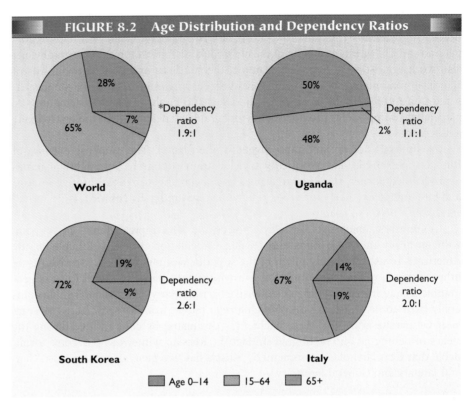

FIGURE 8.2 Age Distribution and Dependency Ratios

World
Uganda
South Korea
Italy

Age 0–14   15–64   65+

Most economically less developed countries (LDCs), like Uganda, are disadvantaged because their population has a high percentage of children. These youngsters add little to their country's economic vitality. While investing in them is wise policy, children consume resources for their education and general care that they will only begin to "repay" the system in terms of productivity and taxes when they become adults. A high percentage of senior citizens, as in Italy, is also economically suboptimal.

*Dependency ratio is a World Bank calculation of the ratio of the working-age population (ages 15–64) to the dependent population (age 14 and younger plus age 65 and older). Generally, the higher the ratio, the more economically advantaged a country is.
Data source: CIA (2005).

advantaged by its large working-age population, while Uganda, with numerous children, and Italy, with a high percentage of senior citizens, are relatively disadvantaged.

Countries like Italy that have such low birthrates that they are in a zero or even a negative population growth pattern are also disadvantaged as they experience progressive **demographic graying**. This occurs when a growing proportion of the population is of retirement age. Studies have found, for example, that a relatively large working-age population is positively correlated with per capita GDP growth and an increasing share of elderly citizens is negatively correlated with economic growth (UNDP, 2003:143). In addition to being a drag on the economy, a growing geriatric population also challenges a country's ability to pay the cost of providing pensions and other services to retired citizens. Demographic graying is already pronounced in the economically developed countries and is projected to increase. By 2025, for instance, an estimated 28% of Japan's population will be age 65 and older, and by 2050 fully a third of all Japanese will be of retirement age. In Europe, 30% of the population will be 65 or older in 2050, and the median age will be 51. The U.S. age distribution is still relatively good: 0–14 (21%), 15–64 (67%), and 65+ (12%). But

Americans are also graying, and the retirement-age population is projected to rise to 19% in 2025 and 21% in 2050. That is less worrisome than in most other economically developed countries (EDCs), but the U.S. Social Security and health care systems will still face a formidable challenge. Currently, for instance, there are 3.3 American workers contributing Social Security taxes to support each retiree. That number will decline to 2 workers per retiree by 2050.

Some analysts project that demographic graying "will become the transcendent political and economic issue of the 21st century" as declining birthrates and increasing longevity also begin to reshape the populations of many countries in East Asia, South America, and elsewhere beyond the developed countries. China provides a good example. Its one-child-per-couple policy instituted to restrain population growth coupled with increasing longevity means that a quarter of all Chinese will be senior citizens in 2050. That is a major challenge to a country in which only about one in four workers has a pension plan and that also has many fewer resources than EDCs to provide government support to its elderly.

In addition to pointing to the daunting costs of providing health care, housing, and other social service costs, one study asks, "As global aging progresses, who will be doing the work, paying the taxes, saving for the future, and raising the next generation?" (Peterson, 2001:3). How to address this problem is a major policy challenge for the United States and other EDCs, and one possible solution is presented for your consideration in the decision box, "Is Immigration a Solution to Demographic Graying?"

Education   An educated population is important to national power. Although there are education variations among all countries, LDCs are especially disadvantaged compared to EDCs. Namibia in southern Africa spends a greater percentage (7.9%) of its GNP on public support of education than does the United States (5.6%). Nevertheless, Namibia's relative poverty means that its efforts amount to only about $150 a year per student while the U.S. expenditure is nearly $10,700 per student. Given this financing gap, it will be hard, for example, for Namibia and other LDCs to create educational programs that will close the gap in research and development (R&D) scientists and technicians, who number 41 per every 10,000 people in the EDCs and only 4 per 10,000 people in the LDCs. To make matters worse for LDCs, many of them suffer a substantial "brain drain," an "outflow of highly educated individuals" to EDCs, where professional opportunities are better (Carrington & Detragiache, 1999:1).

The quality of a country's education system is not solely a function of funding, however. For example, almost all Americans are literate, yet there is growing concern that the U.S. educational system is not adequately preparing students to meet the requirements of the modern world. It may be that the basic 3 Rs—reading, 'riting, and 'rithmetic—that once served to train a workforce will no longer suffice in the 21st century. Instead, the requirements will be more like the 3 Cs—computers, calculus, and communications. Another problem may be that American students during their four years of high school spend an average of only about half as much time on core subjects as do students in Japan, France, and Germany. An additional difficulty may be discipline in American schools. Students in U.S. classrooms, for instance, are six times more likely to encounter discipline problems in the classroom than Japanese students.[9] Whatever the cause, a recent study in 26 mostly developed countries measuring the mathematic, scientific, and reading skills of 15-year-olds showed that American students finished 14th overall and below average in each of the three areas of study. Figure 8.3 on page 245 depicts some of the results.

Web Link

You can find the current and projected age distribution (population pyramid) of countries and territories around the world on the U.S. Census Bureau Web site at **www.census.gov/ipc/www/idbpyr.html.**

JOIN THE DEBATE
The Foreign Student Program in the United States: Does It Serve U.S. National Interests?

WRITE THE POLICY SCRIPT

Is Immigration a Solution to Demographic Graying?

Japan and Europe are facing a problem that could undermine their economic vitality and international power. They are graying demographically, with a growing percentage of their populations aged 65 or older. Increased longevity is one cause. Life expectancy in the EDCs is now 78 years, up 9% since 1975. Decreased fertility rates (the average number of children a woman will have) are the second cause of graying. In Western Europe and Japan, the rate is now 1.4, far below the replacement rate (about 2.1) needed to keep the population from declining and to produce younger adults to offset the older adults reaching retirement age.

A graying population is a double-barreled problem. One threat is that with relatively fewer children being born, the supply of future adults is waning. A relatively smaller workforce will cause labor shortages, a dropoff in consumer spending, and other problems that will harm economic growth. The second threat is that governments will struggle to pay for retirement, health care, and other programs that support senior citizens.

The United States is graying also, but less markedly than most EDCs. Whereas 30% of the population in Europe will be 65 or older in 2050, only 21% of Americans will be 65+ by mid-century. Immigration is the most important reason for the relative U.S. advantage. U.S. immigration has risen substantially and now averages about 1 million immigrants a year. The share of the U.S. population that is foreign-born grew from 6% in 1980 to 11% in 2000. Europe once provided most immigrants. Now most come from Latin America and Asia.

Immigrants help keep the percentage of the U.S. working-age population higher than in most other EDCs. Currently, 59% of all foreign-born Americans are between ages 25 and 54, whereas only 42% of native-born Americans are in that age group. Immigrants are also the reason that the U.S. fertility rate (2.1) is actually up since 1980 (1.8). Whites (2.0) and African Americans (2.1) are at about the replacement rate, but Asian Americans (2.3) and Hispanics (2.9) are above it. Thus it is these groups that are disproportionately producing the children of today and the adult workers of tomorrow.

Another thing many EDCs share is a heated debate about immigration policy. A 2005 survey of Americans found that 41% agreed with the statement, "Immigration adds to our character and strengthens the United States because it brings diversity, new workers, and new creative talent to this country." But 48% differed, saying, "Immigration detracts from our character and weakens the United States because it puts too many burdens on government services, causes language barriers, and creates housing problems." Another 10% said "both" or "it depends," and 1% were unsure.[1] Reflecting this division, another poll found that 33% of its respondents wanted to keep immigration at its current level, 14% wanted to increase it, 49% wanted to decrease it, and 4% were unsure.[2]

What Do You Think?

Should immigration continue at its current level, be increased, or be cut? If you favor an increase or decrease, by how much?

Yet another way to break down general educational statistics is to see how well a country trains various segments of its population. Most countries limit their power potential by underutilizing major elements of their population. For example, sexism limits the possible contribution of women in virtually all countries. In Bangladesh, for instance, 42% more male than female teenagers are enrolled in secondary school. Racial, ethnic, and other bases of discrimination add to this failure to maximize a population's potential. The fact that among adults over age 24 in the United States just 17% of African Americans and 11% of Latinos, compared to 27% of whites, have completed college means that the potential of a significant number of these disadvantaged people has been lost to the country.

Health　Health problems can also sap a country's power, with Russia providing a disturbing example. Among other health problems, Russia is experiencing a health crisis among its men due to widespread alcoholism and smoking. Drug addiction is also on the rise. Two-thirds of all adult Russian males smoke (2.5 times the U.S. rate), and the lung cancer death rate is twice that of the United States. To make matters worse, about 60% of all Russian men are alcohol abusers, with the average Russian

Web Link

Health-related data for countries can be found on the World Health Organization Web site at **www.who.int/countries/en/**.

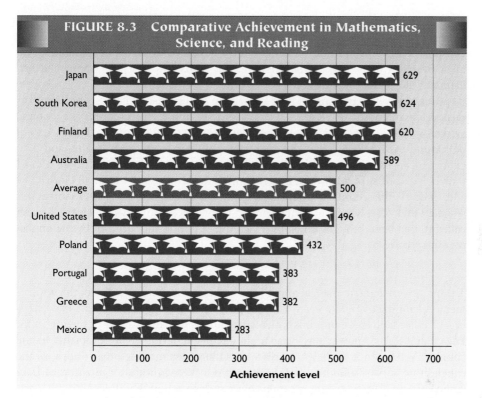

FIGURE 8.3 Comparative Achievement in Mathematics, Science, and Reading

Country	Achievement level
Japan	629
South Korea	624
Finland	620
Australia	589
Average	500
United States	496
Poland	432
Portugal	383
Greece	382
Mexico	283

National power rests in part on a well-educated populace. For Americans, this is something of a concern. The data in this figure is drawn from the overall scores amassed by 15-year-old students in 26 mostly developed countries for skills in reading, mathematics, and science. The results here are for the four countries with the highest and lowest scores, the United States, and the average of the 26 countries. As evident, American students finished below average, well below the leading countries, and not that far ahead of some relatively poor countries, such as Poland.

Note: The actual scores were reduced by 1000 to better highlight comparative data. That is, for example, the score for Japan was actually 1629.

Data source: Organization for Economic Development and Cooperation, *Education at a Glance, 2004.*

male drinking a quart of vodka every two days, supplemented by other alcohol. "Sobriety is no longer the moral norm in Russia," says one health official there.[10] The effect is lethal. Longevity for Russian males has declined to less than 59 years (compared to 73 years for Russian women). "Normally only during wartime do we see the kind of decreases in men's longevity that we've seen recently in Russia," a health official reports gloomily.[11] The threats to Russia's national strength are numerous. There are immense economic costs from lost productivity, added treatment, abandoned families, and other byproducts of alcoholism. Also, the country's population could drop by a third in the next two decades if current trends continue. A third issue relates to Russia's military strength. Officers there complain that most potential military recruits are so wasted from alcohol and drugs that they cannot withstand basic training. Overall, the internal health crisis has replaced any possible external enemy as "the clearest possible threat to national security," according to one Russian study.[12]

Morale World War II demonstrated yet another population-based element of national power, civilian morale. Early in the war, Great Britain and the Soviet Union reeled under tremendous assaults by the Nazi forces. Yet the Allies hung on. In October

Did You Know That:

Vodka has long undermined Russia's power. In 1373 the Russians lost a battle to the Tartars reportedly because the czar's forces were too inebriated to fight. The defeated Russians were thrown into a nearby river, which was then dubbed the Reka Pianaya, the Drunk River.

1940 during the darkest days of the war Winston Churchill told the British people, "Death and sorrow will be the companions of our journey; hardship our garment; constancy and valor our only shield. We must be united, we must be undaunted, we must be inflexible." The British answered Sir Winston's call. They remained undaunted; they held; they prevailed.

Conversely, low national morale can lead to civil unrest and even topple governments. The end of the USSR in 1991 provides an example. As the country's economic system went from bad to worse, the populace was increasingly disheartened. A 1990 poll found 90% believed that the country's economic situation was dire, and 57% expressed no confidence in the future. This profound pessimism led to an almost total collapse of support for the government of Soviet President Mikhail Gorbachev and, indeed, the country's political system. On December 25, 1991, Gorbachev resigned and dissolved the Soviet Union. The "evil empire," as President Reagan called it, had been brought down by a vacuum of public support, not by the opposing superpower.

Government

A third power element associated with the national core is the quality of the government. *Administrative effectiveness* is one aspect. It involves whether a state has a well-organized and effective administrative structure to utilize its power potential fully. For example, U.S. power has been undoubtedly undermined by problems in the country's intelligence agencies. Intelligence failures led, among other things, to the expenditure of vast amounts of U.S. power in a war with and occupation of Iraq, launched primarily to destroy weapons of mass destruction that in fact did not exist. Reflecting that, the 2005 report of a presidential commission bemoaned what it called "one of the most . . . damaging intelligence failures in recent American history." As for the cause of the catastrophe, the commission concluded:

> This failure was in large part the result of analytical shortcomings; intelligence analysts were too wedded to their assumptions about Saddam's intentions. But it was also a failure on the part of [the intelligence agencies]. . . . [They] collected precious little intelligence for the analysts to analyze, and much of what they did collect was either worthless or misleading. Finally, it was a failure to communicate effectively with policymakers. . . . The flaws we found . . . are still all too common. . . . The intelligence community is also fragmented, loosely managed, and poorly coordinated. . . . [Furthermore, it] is too slow to change the way it does business. It is reluctant to use new human and technical collection methods; it is behind the curve in applying cutting-edge technologies; and it has not adapted its personnel practices and incentives structures to fit the needs of a new job market.[13]

Leadership ability is a second aspect of government that adds or detracts from a country's power. For example, Prime Minister Winston Churchill's sturdy image and his inspiring rhetoric well served the British people during World War II. By contrast, the presidency of Russia's Boris Yeltsin, which had begun with heroics as he faced down tanks in the streets of Moscow in 1991, dissolved into incompetence as the ailing, often inebriated Yeltsin became an increasingly sad caricature of his former self.

The National Infrastructure

National power also rests on a country's infrastructure, which might be roughly equated with the skeleton of a human body or to a building's foundation and its framing or girders. To examine the infrastructure of the state as an element of national power, the following sections will discuss technological sophistication, transportation systems, and information and communications capabilities. Each of these factors is related to a country's power capacity.

Technology

"Everything that can be invented has been invented," intoned Charles H. Duell, commissioner of the U.S. Office of Patents, in 1899. He was obviously both in error and in the wrong job. Most of the technology that undergirds a great deal of contemporary national power has been invented since Duell's shortsighted assessment. Air conditioning modifies the impact of weather, computers revolutionize business and education, robotics speed industry, synthetic fertilizers expand agriculture, new drilling techniques allow for undersea oil exploration, microwaves speed information, and lasers bring the military to the edge of the Star Wars era. Thus, technology is an overarching factor and will be discussed as part of the tangible elements of power.

One source of U.S. strength is the considerable money that its government, corporations, and universities spend on research and development (R&D). During 2003 the United States spent $284 billion. That was almost three times as much as Japan ($106 billion) and more than the combined R&D spending of the 25 countries in the European Union ($201 billion). Another good measure of technological sophistication and capability is computing capacity. Needless to say, business, education, science, and other key elements of national power depend on computers, and, as Figure 8.4 shows, there is a vast disparity in national capabilities.

Transportation Systems

The ability to move people, raw materials, finished products, and sometimes the military throughout its territory is another part of a country's power equation. For

MAP
The Indebtedness of States

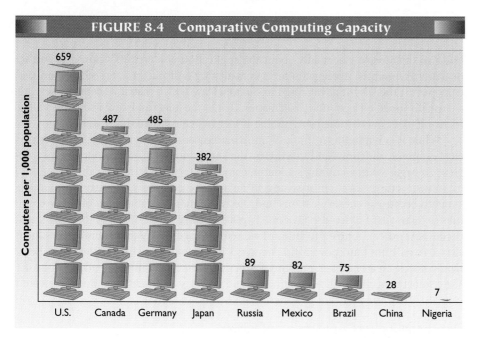

FIGURE 8.4   Comparative Computing Capacity

Computers per 1,000 population

U.S.	Canada	Germany	Japan	Russia	Mexico	Brazil	China	Nigeria
659	487	485	382	89	82	75	28	7

Computer capacity is a key element of a country's technological infrastructure. As this figure shows, there is a huge gap, called the "global digital divide," in global computing power.

Data source: World Bank (2005).

example, one of the major hurdles that Russia must overcome to invigorate its economy is its relatively limited and decrepit transportation systems. As one standard, for every 1,000 square miles of its land territory, the United States has 14 times as many miles of paved roads and four times as many miles of railroad track than does Russia. Inadequate transportation systems are also a problem for LDCs.

Information and Communications Systems

A country's information and communications capabilities are becoming increasingly important (Rothkopf, 1998). Satellites and computers have accelerated the revolution begun with radio and television. Photocopying machines, then fax machines, and now the Internet have dramatically changed communications. Enhanced communications technology increases the ability of a society to communicate within itself and remain cohesive. It also increases efficiency and effectiveness in industry, finance, and the military. Here again, the gap between LDCs and EDCs is wide. For example, U.S. annual per capita expenditures on information and communications ($3,309) are more than 50 times that of China ($58). There are, for example, approximately three times more television sets, six times more radios, three times more telephones, and 19 times more Internet users per capita in the United States than in China.

National Diplomacy

Now that we have explored power as the foundation of national diplomacy, we can turn to its conduct. First we will take up diplomacy as applied power, then we will examine the various settings in which diplomacy is conducted.

Diplomacy as Applied Power

National diplomacy is normally about the application of a country's power to further its national interests. Even goals such as mediating a dispute among other countries, empowering the UN, or advancing international law, which may not seem self-serving, are usually based on a country's calculation that in the long run it and its people will be better off in an international system that is less anarchical than the current one.

While it is common to think of applying power as using military forces or perhaps economic sanctions and incentives, the application of power is much more complex. To begin with, a country's economic and military might rest on the strength of its infrastructure. As such, a strong infrastructure adds to a country's diplomatic strength because a country's status and the willingness or reluctance of other countries to follow its lead are also aspects of applied power. Some of this is soft power that encourages other countries to support and emulate a country they admire. Prestige is also derived from hard power. As chapter 3 points out, the U.S. position as a hegemonic power creates an assumption of American leadership in many other countries. They sometimes chaff at U.S. dominance and even try to undercut it, but these countries also see it as important to system stability and prosperity.

Did You Know That:

Humorist Will Rogers once defined diplomacy as "Saying 'Nice doggie' until you can find a rock."

Direct and Indirect Application of Power

Diplomacy applies power directly and indirectly. The *direct diplomatic application of power* includes the use of economic sanctions or inducements and also threatening/offering them. Threatened or actual war is also a direct diplomatic use of power if, as chapter 10 explains, a country follows the advice given by the great Chinese strategist Sun Tzu some 2,500 years ago, "A government should not mobilize its army out of anger. . . . Act when it is beneficial; desist when it is not."[14] As diplomacy moves along the scale away from the overt use of economic and military muscle, it ranges from threats all the way to the argumentation of skilled diplomats who have little power other than their own abilities to support their country's goals.

The *indirect application of power* is subtler. It involves a communications process of a country skillfully advancing its policy preferences, skillfully crafting and arguing the merit of its position, and persuading others to join it in promoting those goals or at least to accede to them. Sometimes the power factor is clearly a looming factor. For example, a clear backdrop to the diplomacy over North Korea's nuclear weapons program is the U.S. ability to use its wealth to greatly benefit North Korea—or its military might in the extreme to obliterate it. Similarly, North Korea's ability to push a huge army over the border into South Korea or even possibly use missile-launched nuclear weapons to devastate South Korea or Japan are never far from the calculations of the diplomats. At other times, power is nearly invisible. When diplomats recently conducted negotiations to amend the U.S.-Barbados Tax Convention, American negotiators did not threaten war if Barbados did not cooperate in closing "offshore" tax havens. Still, faced with economic realities—the United States accounts for one-fifth of all exports from Barbados, and Barbados takes in less than one–one-thousandth of all U.S. exports—there was little doubt which country would be the loser if the issue ever led to mutual economic retaliation.

A Foundation for Analysis

Many diplomatic events of every type are used in the following pages to explore power-based diplomacy. More than any others, though, four recent or ongoing diplomatic events are used here to provide a foundation for our analysis. It is for this reason that you will encounter repeated references to the U.S.–North Korea confrontation over nuclear weapons, tensions between China and Taiwan, the U.S.-Afghanistan crisis, and the backdrop to the Iraq War in 2003.

The U.S.–North Korea confrontation centers on North Korea's nuclear weapons program (Cha & Kang, 2004; Howard, 2004). The confrontation began when the United States moved in 1993 to force North Korea (the Democratic People's Republic of Korea, DPRK) to halt its alleged nuclear weapons program after the DPRK announced it would withdraw from the Nuclear Non-Proliferation Treaty (NPT) and blocked the monitoring of its nuclear plant at Yongbyon by the International Atomic Energy Agency (IAEA). Threats and military moves escalated to the point in mid-1994 where war seemed possible. Then diplomacy lowered the flame of crisis. North Korea agreed to dismantle its nuclear energy program over 10 years and to allow IAEA inspections to resume. In return, the United States and other countries pledged to spend more than $5 billion to meet North Korea's energy needs by, for example, annually supplying it with about 138 million gallons of petroleum. Relations turned downward again after President Bush took office in 2001. His administration accused North Korea of cheating on the 1994 agreement. North Korea denied the charge, but said renewed U.S. threats were forcing it to once again make fissionable material and block IAEA inspections. The United States and others cut off the oil shipments to North Korea and demanded that it reverse its policy. Soon there was renewed talk of war.

China-Taiwan tensions and the U.S. involvement in them are rooted in Taiwan's curious status (Tucker, 2005; Tsang, 2004). An island located 100 miles east of south-central China, Taiwan became politically separated from China when the Nationalist government of Chiang Kai-shek fled there in 1949 after being ousted by the communist

The events surrounding North Korea's nuclear weapons program are one of the focal points of diplomacy presented and discussed in this chapter. In this 2005 photograph, North Korean leader Kim Jong Il is hung in effigy by South Koreans protesting in Seoul against North Korea's development of nuclear weapons.

forces of Mao Zedong. Since then, Taiwan has functioned as a de facto country, but China claims it as an integral part of China. Taiwan and other countries, including the United States, have found it diplomatically useful to continue the legal fiction that there is "one China." Recent tensions have centered on Taiwan's presidential elections in 1996, 2000, and 2004, when one or more candidates took stands that seemed to favor Taiwan declaring independence. Other trends in Taiwan also, Beijing fears, portend a declaration of independence by Taipei.

The crisis between Afghanistan and the United States in 2001 followed the 9/11 terrorist attacks. Washington concluded that the attacks had been directed by al Qaeda, which was then based in Afghanistan under the leadership of Osama bin Laden. President Bush demanded that bin Laden and the rest of the leadership of al Qaeda be turned over; the Taliban government in Kabul under the leadership of Mullah Mohammad Omar refused; war ensued (Tarzi, 2005).

The U.S.-Iraq crisis of 2002–2003 had been brewing since the end of the Persian Gulf War in 1991. The back-and-forth maneuvering over UN inspections, occasional U.S. bombing raids, and occasional mini-crises reached a full boil after President Bush assumed office in 2001. He was determined to take a firm stand against Iraq, and the 9/11 attack intensified his position. Tensions escalated in 2002 as the United States sought UN resolutions supporting armed intervention in Iraq and took other measures to bring pressure on the Security Council. Saddam Hussein followed a cat-and-mouse strategy of partially giving in to increased UN inspections for weapons of mass destruction (WMDs) and playing for time. The Iraqi maneuvers are even more curious in retrospect because, it seems, they did not have WMDs to hide. As is well known, the diplomats were unable to keep the peace, and the generals settled the matter on the battlefield.

The Context of Diplomacy

Although diplomats sometimes portray themselves as practicing an ancient and unchanging art form, diplomacy is in fact constantly evolving because of the context in which it is conducted. Certainly, diplomacy is in part ancient. Historical indications of negotiations and other diplomatic exchanges date back almost four millennia, and records from what appear to be embassies can be found from as far back as the time of the great Babylonian emperor, Hammurabi (1792–1750 B.C.). Diplomatic missions are described in Homer's *Iliad* (about 850 B.C.), and the Greeks, followed by the Romans, wrote treaties and used ambassadors to negotiate disputes. The Byzantine Empire, which flourished after Rome's collapse, began the practice of training negotiators and established the first department of foreign affairs.

Did You Know That:

The oldest surviving diplomatic document is a message on a tablet sent about 2,500 B.C. by Ibubu, chief minister to the king of Ebla (in modern Lebanon), to King Zizi of Hamazi (in modern Iran). In it Ibubu pledges goodwill, relates that he is sending Zizi a quantity of rare wood, and urges Zizi to "give me good mercenaries. Please send them" (Cohen, 1996:2).

In the 1600s, the rise of the state as the dominant political actor elevated diplomacy to an ongoing practice, rather than a usually ad hoc effort to settle specific issues, and also led to permanent bureaucracies to conduct diplomacy. Cardinal Richelieu, who served as chief minister (1624–1642) to King Louis XIII of France, consolidated all foreign affairs functions under one ministry. Then, during Louis XIV's reign (1643–1715), the minister of foreign affairs became a member of the king's cabinet, and permanent embassies were established in all the major capitals, with lesser-ranked missions in minor capitals. Soon thereafter, François de Callierres wrote the first diplomatic manual, *On the Manner of Negotiating with Sovereigns* (1716).

Also ancient and little changed is the basic role of the diplomat: Once it was to promote the interests of the sovereign, now it is to promote the national interest. English diplomat Sir Henry Wotton in 1604 defined an ambassador as "an honest man sent abroad to lie for his country." And some 350 years later and even less charitably, UN Secretary-General Trygve Lie (1946–1953) reputedly described a diplomat as someone "who can cut his neighbor's throat without having his neighbor notice it." Such characterizations are surely too cynical, but they do sharply make the point that far from being neutral go-betweens, diplomats focus on furthering their country's national interest. Or as Venetian ambassador Ermolao Barbaro put it in the 1400s, "the first duty of an ambassador is . . . to do, say, advise, and think whatever may best serve the preservation and aggrandizement of his own state" (Craig & George, 1995).

Despite many links to the past, diplomacy has also changed dramatically because of the evolving context of world politics. The early twentieth century serves as a benchmark in the transition to the modern-era diplomacy. In this evolving new context, the "old diplomacy" did not vanish, but it changed substantially. The eclipse of colonialism, advances in travel and communications, the spread of democracy, and other factors have all played a role in changing the context of diplomacy.

Expansion of Geographic Scope

For several hundred years through the end of the nineteenth century, diplomacy was dominated by the major European powers. Then the geographic scope began to expand. The two Hague Conferences (1899, 1907) on peace, particularly the second, with its 44 participants, included countries outside the European sphere. World War I (1914–1918) weakened European world dominance and World War II ended it. New powers—the United States, Japan, and China—began to assert themselves, and the last remnants of Europe's imperial dominion was doomed by the nationalistic self-determination that stirred in Asia and Africa. Today, the United Nations, with its nearly universal membership, reflects the truly global scope of diplomacy. This change is not a mere matter of numbers. For example, the context of diplomacy now includes greater cultural clashes over standards of justice and other matters than was true in the days of relatively homogeneous Eurocentric diplomacy.

Multilateral Diplomacy

Although there were a few multilateral conferences prior to 1900, such as the Congress of Vienna (1815), the normal form of negotiation was **bilateral diplomacy,** direct negotiations between two countries. The use of **multilateral diplomacy,** conferences involving a number of nations, has expanded greatly in the modern era. More than any event, the founding of the League of Nations in 1920 marked this change, and there are now about 250 permanent world and regional intergovernmental organizations (IGOs). Conferences to address specific issues and treaties are also more apt to be multilateral. Before 1900, for example, the United States attended an average of one multilateral conference per year. Now, the United States is a member

SIMULATION
An Adventure in Diplomacy

Web Link

Interactive historical maps representing world power in the early 20th century can be found at http://users.erols.com/ mwhite28/1907powr.htm.

of scores of international organizations and American diplomats participate daily in multilateral negotiations.

One reason that multilateral diplomacy has increased is that modern technology allows faster and more frequent contacts among countries. Second, many global concerns, such as the environment, cannot be solved by any one country or through traditional bilateral diplomacy alone. Instead, global cooperation and solutions are required. Third, diplomacy through multilateral organizations is attractive to smaller countries as a method of influencing world politics beyond their individual power.

A fourth factor promoting multilateral diplomacy is the growing expectation that important international actions, especially those using military force, will be taken within the framework of a multilateral organization. President Bush said in 2001 that he would act alone if necessary against Afghanistan, but he was also careful to engage in the multilateral diplomacy necessary to win both UN and NATO support for the U.S.-led campaign. In 2003, Washington and London invaded Iraq without UN or NATO support, but the importance of the expectation of multilateral approval was evident in both the Anglo-American effort to win such support and in the outpouring of criticism from abroad when they acted without it.

Leader-to-Leader Diplomacy

It was once rare for monarchs and other leaders to meet. Now modern transportation and communications have made it common. It was not until 1919 that an American president (Woodrow Wilson) traveled overseas while in office. Presidents now travel frequently. Bill Clinton holds the record as most traveled U.S. president. He made 54 trips to 133 countries and was out of the country for 229 days, or almost 8% of his presidency. One Republican derided Clinton as being "like the Energizer Bunny; he . . . continued to keep on going, and going, and going."[15] Such partisan criticism may be dangerous though, because Republican president George W. Bush departed on his first state visit only 27 days after his inauguration, and during his first term spent only six less days abroad (74) than did Clinton in his first four years. Even more common are trips of foreign leaders to Washington. Bush had 136 meetings with other leaders in his first 18 months as president. Indeed, the once-rare instances of leader-to-leader diplomacy have become nearly routine, with, for example, annual meetings of the leaders of the Group of Eight (G-8), the seven largest industrialized countries plus Russia, and Asia-Pacific Economic Cooperation (APEC), an IGO including the United States, China, and 19 other countries. Beyond such face-to-face meetings, it has become an almost everyday occurrence for leaders to talk with one another on the telephone. Presidents and other leaders tend to like personal diplomacy because they believe it pays off and can even lead to a dramatic breakthrough for which they can take credit. Foreign travel is also a way to escape domestic pressures. Clinton said he found foreign policy more "fun" because he could make policy "with less interference and static in Congress," whereas in domestic policy even the president was but "one of a zillion decision makers."[16]

Advantages of Leader-to-Leader Diplomacy   The wanderlust of many leaders certainly has advantages. For example, face-to-face **summit meetings** sometimes can have high symbolic value. One of the most significant moments in the more than 50 years since the outbreak of the Korean War (1950–1953) occurred in 2000, when the presidents of North and South Korea met for the first time. While a few agreements were reached, the real importance of the meeting in Pyongyang was the symbolic televised image of the two shaking hands, smiling, bantering, and drinking champagne. "Maybe nothing dramatic will happen right away," one South Korean noted, "but most people would agree that a surprising amount of progress and understanding has been achieved already."[17]

Another advantage is that leaders sometimes make dramatic breakthroughs. The 1978 Camp David Accords, which began the process of normalizing Egyptian-Israeli relations after decades of hostility and three wars, were produced after President Jimmy Carter, Egyptian President Anwar Sadat, and Israeli Prime Minister Menachem Begin isolated themselves at the presidential retreat in Maryland. A third advantage of leader-to-leader diplomacy is that it can facilitate communications and smooth relations. President George H. W. Bush believed that "The best diplomacy starts with getting to know each other."[18] If a personal meeting was not possible, he also liked the telephone. "If [another leader] knows the heartbeat a little bit from talking [with me], there's less apt to be misunderstanding."[19] Similarly, personal contact among leaders can promote mutual understanding, confidence, and even friendship. U.S.-Russia relations can be prickly, but they are probably eased somewhat by the fact that Presidents Bush and Putin get along personally. Said Bush of Putin after one meeting, "I like him. He's a good fellow to spend quality time with." Moreover, the president continued, "Because we've got a trustworthy relationship, we're able to move beyond any disagreement over a single issue."[20]

Disadvantages of Leader-to-Leader Diplomacy   Among its disadvantages, personal diplomacy between leaders may lead to misunderstandings. There are numerous instances when leaders have made and reached what each thought was a mutual agreement, only to find to their dismay that they had misunderstood each other. Furthermore, as tricky as personal contacts may be, the telephone may present even greater difficulties. Henry Kissinger argues that telephone contacts are especially problematic because "It is difficult to make a good record. You can't see the other side's expressions or body language."[21] A second problem is that while leaders can disavow mistakes made by lower-ranking officials, a leader's commitments, even if not wise, cannot be easily retracted. "When presidents become negotiators no escape routes are left," Kissinger warns (1979:12). "Concessions are irrevocable without dishonor."

Additionally, poor personal chemistry can damage relations between leaders. Kissinger (1979:142) comments that most world leaders are characterized by a "healthy dose of ego," and when two such egos collide, "negotiations can rapidly deteriorate from intractability to confrontation." For example, relations between President Bush and German Chancellor Gerhard Schröder turned sour in 2002 when the chancellor publicly castigated the president's policy toward Iraq. According to a U.S. diplomat, Bush felt "betrayed by Schröder," and even the chancellor had to admit, "This question about Iraq has gotten personal."[22] As for Bush, his feelings were so strong that he snubbed Schröder when the two attended a NATO summit in 2002. Among other insults, Bush scheduled one-on-one meetings with several leaders, but he could not find time for the chancellor of Germany. Even after the war, the break between the two leaders did not improve. "The personal relationship is not just damaged, it is broken, and I fear beyond repair," lamented a German official. "That is regrettable because personal trust in the negotiating parties is important for political cooperation."[23]

Less substantively, there is the sheer travail of travel, and leaders often complain about it. An arduous schedule and jet lag once caused Ronald Reagan to fall asleep while listening to a speech by the pope. And President George W. Bush, who normally goes to bed by 10:30 P.M. was so exhausted at the end of one foreign trip filled with what one reporter described as a "complete killer" schedule of late evening events, that he reportedly was nearly "sleep-walking through the final stages of the trip."[24]

Leader-to-leader diplomacy can be beneficial if leaders get along but can dampen diplomacy if they do not. The picture on the left of President George Bush and Russian President Vladimir Putin in Moscow in 2005 captures their warm relationship. The photo on the right of Bush and German Chancellor Gerhard Schröder with their backs to one another during a 2005 meeting in Mainz, Germany, symbolizes their strained relations. Bush was angered in 2002 because he believed that Schröder's vigorous opposition to proposed U.S. military action in Iraq was a partisan ploy to boost the prospects of the chancellor's party in Germany's parliamentary elections that year.

In addition to physical exhaustion, there are the culinary hazards of what has been waggishly labeled "mealpolitik." One peril is eating odd things to avoid injuring local sensitivities. President George H. W. Bush dined on boar's penis soup while visiting China in 1989, and Bill Clinton found moose lips—real ones, not the chocolate dessert—on his presidential plate during a 22-course state dinner in Russia. Unaccustomed food can also lead to gastric distress. Jimmy Carter was felled in Mexico City by diarrhea, which he undiplomatically called "Montezuma's revenge," and while in Tokyo, George H. W. Bush threw up on the Japanese prime minister during dinner. Meals can even become targets of criticism. When the younger President Bush visited Great Britain in 2003, he expressed the hope of stopping at a local pub. Prime Minister Blair arranged that, and the two had fish and chips and mushy peas at the Dun Cow Inn. But an uproar broke out in the press over the more than $1 million spent on security for the lunch, making it the most expensive fish-and-chips meal in history.

Democratized Diplomacy

Few countries were democracies before the 20th century, and in that context conducting diplomacy and agreeing to treaties and other international obligations was almost exclusively within the monarch's realm of authority. "*L'état, c'est moi*" (I am the state), Louis XIV supposedly proclaimed with some justification. Executive leaders still dominate the foreign policy–making process, but it is no longer their exclusive domain. Instead, **democratized diplomacy** is the norm, with legislatures, interest groups, and public opinion all playing a greater role.

Indeed, the importance of domestic politics in foreign policy making has given rise to **two-level game theory**. This holds that to be successful a country's diplomats must find a solution that is acceptable to both the other country at the international level and, at the domestic level, to the political actors (legislators, public opinion, interest groups) in the diplomat's own country. From this perspective, the diplomatic setting exists at the domestic as well as at the international level, and is influenced by the interplay of the two levels when leaders try to pursue policies that satisfy the actors at both levels. During the Taiwan crises, for instance, U.S. and Chinese leaders not only have had to find points of agreement between themselves, they also have had to fend off domestic forces pushing to escalate the crisis. Reflecting this, China's president told the U.S. ambassador at one point, "Any leader who lets this [Taiwan's independence] pass would be overthrown."[25] On the American front, one example of the pressure not to compromise was a 1996 resolution by House Republicans urging Clinton to commit the United States "to the defense of Taiwan."[26] To ensure that Clinton did not ignore their views, GOP legislators introduced the Taiwan Security Enhancement Act to substantially increase the U.S. commitment to Taiwan. "There is a lot of pent-up frustration about the administration's policy approach to China," a GOP aide noted.[27] The GOP did not push that bill to passage, but it served notice of the strong support of Taiwan in Congress.

Parliamentary Diplomacy

Within the context of spreading global democracy, another modern practice is **parliamentary diplomacy**. This includes debate and voting in IGOs as a supplement to negotiation and compromise. The maneuvering involved in parliamentary diplomacy was strongly evident in the UN during the U.S. campaign to win Security Council approval for an invasion of Iraq. That required the backing of 9 of the Council's 15 members and also required a "yes" vote or an abstention from each of the 5 permanent members with veto power. As the diplomacy heated up, the United States could count on four "yes" votes (its own, Great Britain, Spain, and Bulgaria). Germany and Syria were definitely "no" votes. Three permanent members—China, France, and Russia—also opposed war; a "no" vote by any of them was a veto. So U.S. diplomats concentrated on getting a majority vote, arguing that it would buttress a U.S-led invasion of Iraq by allowing Washington to claim that the will of the majority had been blocked by the veto power of a minority on the council. Thus the spotlight was on the remaining 6 members: Angola, Cameroon, Chile, Guinea, Mexico, and Pakistan.

Washington's strategy, according to one U.S. diplomat, was to "win backing like you would in Congress—going after votes one by one by one." And just like a campaign to influence votes in Congress, U.S. officials used a mixture of argumentation, threats, and promised rewards in the Security Council. Secretary of State Powell claimed, "We present our case. We don't threaten. We don't suggest that blackmail is in order."[28] But widespread reports indicated that, depending on how the six undecided countries voted, U.S. diplomats were offering them new or increased (or decreased) aid and trade opportunities and access to (or denial of) lucrative contracts to rebuild postwar Iraq and modernize its oil industry As one U.S. diplomat conceded, "We'll put it to them simply: Do you want to be part of reconstruction and all that means—or leave it to us?"[29] In the end, Washington probably did not have majority support, but it was certain that France and perhaps Russia would veto the U.S./U.K. resolution. To avoid that and the embarrassment of not even getting a symbolic majority, the British ambassador to the UN announced that Washington and London "have agreed that we will not pursue a vote."[30]

Open Diplomacy

Secrecy was once the norm in diplomacy. Negotiations were usually conducted in secret, and even treaties were often secret. Seeking change, Woodrow Wilson called for "open covenants, openly arrived at" in his Fourteen Points. He got his wish and in the context of expanded democracy since his time, the norm is **open diplomacy**, with negotiations and the contents of international agreements widely reported and documented. While this change is important to the principle of democratic government, it does have its disadvantages. Public negotiations are difficult. Disclosure of your bargaining strategy compromises your ability to win concessions. Public negotiations are also more likely to lead diplomats to posture for public consumption. Concessions may be difficult to make amid popular criticism. In sum, it is difficult to negotiate (or to play chess) with someone kibitzing over your shoulder. Indeed, domestic opposition to dealing with an adversary may be so intense that it may be impossible to negotiate at all.

Soon after the 9/11 terrorist attacks on the United States, the Bush administration made a series of demands on Pakistan that, in Washington's view, were crucial to the success of the U.S. response. Many of these, such as the right to use Pakistani military bases, were difficult for the government in Islamabad to accept because of the large number of militant Muslims in the country and the connection between Pakistani Pashtuns and their ethnic brethren who made up the bulk of the Taliban ranks in Afghanistan. Nevertheless, the requirements were presented strongly. "We're talking to Pakistanis in a way we've never talked to them before," one U.S. official commented.[31] The demands and the pressure were all applied in secret, however, because open diplomacy might have put Pakistan's government at risk of being overthrown if it accepted the U.S. requirements.

Public Diplomacy

ANALYZE THE ISSUE
Multi-track Diplomacy

Traditional diplomacy primarily involved trying to influence another country's leaders. That continues, but it has been supplemented by efforts to also influence a much wider array of subnational actors in other countries. One reason for this is that the communications revolution has placed leaders and other diplomats in public view more than ever before. Moreover, the spread of democracy means that how the media, public opinion, interest groups, and legislators react to other countries is much more important than it once was. As a result, international relations are also increasingly conducted through **public diplomacy**. This is the process of creating an image that enhances a country's ability to achieve diplomatic success by increasing its soft power. Commenting on this approach, UN Secretary-General Kofi Annan has said, "If I can't get the support of governments, then I'll get the support of the people. People move governments."[32]

In addition to traditional propaganda, public diplomacy includes shaping what leaders and other top diplomats say and do to play to public opinion abroad and otherwise conducting diplomacy in part as a public relations campaign. One scholar's concept of public diplomacy envisions a "theater of power" that is a "metaphor for the repertoire of visual and symbolic tools used by statesmen and diplomats." As players in the theater of power, leaders "must be sensitive to the impression they make on observers. . . . They surely [are] subject to the same sort of 'dramatic,' if not aesthetic, criticism of other kinds of public performances" (Cohen, 1987:i–ii).

Public diplomacy, which attempts to reach beyond leaders and influence public opinion, is illustrated by this billboard promoting the U.S. government agency USAID in the West Bank city of Ramallah. The billboard refers to U.S. aid to the Palestinians to improve their water supply and schools, and its Arabic text reads "More than 2000 classrooms built to teach children from one human to another."

Public diplomacy is practiced in all phases of a country's foreign policy effort. When President Bush traveled to Russia in May 2005 to join in ceremonies marking the sixtieth anniversary of VE Day (May 8, 1945), the end of World War II in Europe, he was careful to also schedule visits to two former Soviet republics, Latvia and Georgia, to demonstrate continued U.S. support of the countries against any outside interference, especially by their former overlord, Moscow. Among other things, Bush underlined that point by placing a wreath at a monument in Riga honoring those who died fighting for Latvian independence.

Governments also use a variety of agencies and other organizations to project their image. The United States, for one, operates or sponsors the Voice of America, Radio Free Europe/Radio Liberty, and Radio Martí. The U.S. Information Agency also produces Worldnet, a television service available globally, provides Web sites, and has other modern communications capabilities. Other efforts are contracted to private public relations firms. In one such effort in 2002 and 2003, the United States ran a $15 million television campaign in several Arab countries. Called "Shared Values," the media effort was meant to convince viewers that Americans were tolerant of Muslims and their beliefs and practices. In one spot, an Arab American female schoolteacher explained, "I wear a *hijab* (head covering) in the classroom where I teach. I have never had a child who thought it was weird or anything like that."[33]

WEB POLL
Public Diplomacy or Propaganda: The Media and National Power

The Conduct of Diplomacy

Diplomacy is a complex game of maneuvering in which the goal is to get other players to do what you want them to do. The players can number from two, in bilateral diplomacy, to many, in multilateral diplomacy. The rules of diplomacy are, at best, loose, and there is not just one mode of play. Instead, like all the most fascinating games, diplomacy is intricate and involves considerable strategy that can be employed in several ways. Thus, while diplomacy is often portrayed by an image of somber negotiations over highly polished wooden tables in ornate rooms, it is much more than that. Modern diplomacy is a far-ranging communications process (Starkey, Boyer, & Wilkenfeld, 2005; Steiner, 2004).

Diplomacy as a Communications Process

In essence, diplomacy is a communications process. It involves communicating to one or more countries or other actors what your goals, demands, requests, and other objectives are. Diplomacy also includes persuading other actors to support or comply with your objectives by communicating either the logic or morality of your point of view or by communicating your power to achieve your goal despite opposition. The diplomatic communication process is carried out through negotiation and signaling.

Negotiations occur when two or more parties communicate with one another, either directly or indirectly through an intermediary. It is very difficult to accomplish anything unless the different sides are talking. An important U.S. goal in the Middle East has been to encourage negotiations between the Israelis and Palestinians. As Secretary of State Colin Powell put it, "The world is in agreement that the solution will not be produced by terror or a response to terror—this is not going to get us there. What will get us there are political discussions and the sooner we can get them the better."[34] Most diplomatic communications are part of an exchange of views, but they can sometimes be one-sided. When, in 1972, South Vietnam resisted the U.S.-negotiated settlement, President Richard Nixon cabled President Nguyen Van Thieu that "all military and economic aid will be cut off . . . if an agreement is not reached" and that "I have . . . irrevocably decided to proceed . . . to sign [the agreement]. I will do so, if necessary, alone [and] explain that your government obstructs peace." "Brutality is nothing," Nixon told Kissinger. "You have never seen it if this son-of-a-bitch doesn't go along, believe me" (Kissinger, 1979:1420, 1469). Thieu went along.

Signaling entails saying or doing something with the intent of sending a message to another government. When leaders make bellicose or conciliatory speeches, when military forces are deployed or even used, when trade privileges are granted or sanctions invoked, or when diplomatic recognition is extended or relations are broken, these actions are, or at least should be, signals of attitude and intent to another country.

Signals can be quite direct and, indeed, sometimes leaders signal one another through the open airwaves rather than through diplomatic channels. One time this occurred was evident when the long-standing confrontation between Iraq and the United States finally led to a U.S. ultimatum. It was delivered publicly. "Saddam Hussein and his sons must leave Iraq within 48 hours. Their refusal to do so will result in military conflict, commenced at a time of our choosing," President George W. Bush declared on March 17, 2003. The following day, the Iraqi government retorted, "Iraq doesn't choose its path through foreigners and doesn't choose its leaders by decree from Washington."[35] That night war began.

Less direct signaling was evident in the U.S. invasion of Afghanistan after the 9/11 terror attacks. Certainly that was meant to attack al Qaeda and the Taliban government, but it was also a signal to others. "Let's hit them hard," Bush told the chairman of the Joint Chiefs of Staff when he directed the general to send ground troops as well as warplanes and missiles against Afghanistan. "We want to signal this is a change from the past," the president explained. "We want to cause other countries like Syria and Iran to change their views [about supporting terrorism]."[36]

The Rules of Effective Diplomacy

Delineating the methods of diplomatic communications is easy. Utilizing them effectively is hard. There is no set formula that will ensure success. There are, however, ways to improve your chances of diplomatic success whether you are an ambassador or an individual engaged in personal diplomacy. Some basic rules of effective diplomacy are:

Be realistic. It is important to have goals that match your ability to achieve them: "The test of a statesman is his ability to recognize the real relationship of forces" (Kissinger, 1970:47). North Korea's nuclear weapons program presents Washington with difficult policy choices. The ultimate U.S. goal might be to have the DPRK abandon the program and submit to international inspections without significant U.S. concessions but that is almost certainly an unrealistic goal. Also unrealistic is U.S. military action in any scenario short of an attack by the North on South Korea or Japan. Therefore, according to one analyst, the only "realistic" option for the United States is "to engage North Korea on a wide range of issues—especially its failed economy."[37] If that is true, then part of the solution is U.S. economic aid to North Korea in exchange for its abandoning its program. That was the approach of the Clinton administration, which reasoned pragmatically that making some concession was "better than war."[38] After early reluctance, the Bush administration came to the same conclusion. "The North Korean government can find the respect it desires and acquire the assistance it needs, if it is willing to make a strategic choice for peace," was the way Secretary of State Rice put it.[39]

Being realistic also means remembering that the other side, like yours, has domestic political problems that, again just like you, mean they have to engage in two-level diplomacy. It is impossible to be realistic about negotiations in the Middle East unless you understand that whatever concessions Palestinian and Israeli leaders might be willing to make, each is under tremendous pressure from hardliners. The efforts of Palestinian President Mahmoud Abbas to rein in militants has been met with attacks by extremists. Similarly, Israeli Prime Minister Ariel Sharon's announced 2005 withdrawal of its forces from Gaza created what he called an "atmosphere of a civil war" within Israel.[40]

Be careful about what you say. The experienced diplomat plans and weighs words carefully. Many observers feel that North Korea's antagonistic turn in 2002 may have been a defensive reaction to what it saw as threats and insults from President Bush. Associating North Korea with Nazi Germany by naming it a member of the axis of evil was inflammatory language. The following year on the eve of multilateral negotiations on North Korea's nuclear weapons program, U.S. diplomat John Bolton complicated diplomacy by calling the DPRK a "hellish nightmare" and its president, Kim Jong Il, a "tyrannical dictator" who makes "extortionist demands" and is "directly responsible for bringing economic ruin" to his country. Pyongyang responded by calling Bolton "scum."[41]

When in 2005 President Bush nominated Bolton as U.S. ambassador to the UN, such language came under attack, but it was no more strident than that of President Bush himself. At a news conference defending his nomination of Bolton, the president mentioned Kim Jong Il a dozen times, calling him, among other things, "a dangerous person . . . who starves his people" and who has set up "huge concentration camps." Even if true, such personal attacks on another leader usually detract from diplomacy. In this case, Bush's remarks led to a counterbarrage by the DPRK, which called the president a "hooligan bereft of any personality . . . and a Philistine whom we can never deal with."[42] A better approach, one Republican legislator suggested to

Secretary of State Condoleezza Rice during hearings, "is not to make inflammatory statements. We don't need to punch our chest and say how great we are and talk about the negative aspects of other societies."[43]

Seek common ground. Finding common ground is a key to ending disputes peacefully. A first step to seeking common ground is to avoid seeing yourself as totally virtuous and your opponent as the epitome of evil. As a study of how peace is made and maintained puts it, "Wars are seldom a struggle between total virtue and vice. . . . But when so conceived, they become crusades that remove the possibility of finding common ground after the battles are over" (Kegley & Raymond, 1999:249).

Be flexible. While adhering to core principles may be important, being flexible on everything other than the most vital points is often wise. While working with North Korea and other countries in the region to resolve the nuclear confrontation, Secretary of State Powell had it right when he observed, "There are different approaches about this: Should you talk? When should you talk? Would you negotiate? What do you put on the table? Those are all issues that are worth debating."[44]

Understand the other side. Try to understand what it is your opponent really wants and to appreciate an opponent's perspective even if you do not agree with it. For example, the U.S. response to North Korea's nuclear program arguably should be tailored to Pyongyang's real aims. North Korea has portrayed its move as a defensive response to U.S. "hostile policies" and asserted its right to possess "devices to save us from a nuclear attack."[45] This argument became even more prominent after the U.S. invasion of Iraq, with Pyongyang declaring the invasion "teaches all the sovereign states the lesson that there should be only a strong physical deterrent force to protect the sovereignty of the country and the nation."[46] Another possibility is that North Korea is playing a nuclear weapons card to try to get more aid, to force the United States to deal with it directly, and to force Washington to sign a nonaggression treaty. According to a former South Korean foreign minister, the North Korean strategy is, "They pile up all this leverage, or cards, and they figure each will cost something to undo to bring them back into the Non-Proliferation Treaty, to stop them from testing missiles, and to freeze their nuclear programs."[47] A third possibility is that North Korea is aggressively bent on becoming a nuclear weapons power. "It's still possible this is some sort of negotiating tactic," a former U.S. official commented, "but the weight of evidence is that they may have decided to start building up their nuclear weapons stockpile."[48]

Be patient. It is also important to bide your time. Being overly anxious can lead to concessions that are unwise and may convey weakness to an opponent. As a corollary, it is poor practice to set deadlines, for yourself or others, unless you are in a very strong position or you do not really want an agreement. Throughout the negotiations with North Korea, which were frustrating and included many setbacks, the Bush administration has avoided timelines. As a former U.S. ambassador to South Korea noted, "There seems to be a recognition in the administration that what is happening in North Korea is unpleasant, and possibly destabilizing, but it is not something that is taking place at 60 miles an hour. It is going to take six to twelve months before the North Koreans can produce additional plutonium."[49]

Leave avenues of retreat open. It is axiomatic that even a rat will fight if trapped in a corner. The same is often true for countries. Call it honor, saving face, or prestige; it is important to leave yourself and your opponent an "out." Ultimatums, especially public ones, often lead to war. Whatever its other merits, President Bush's demand that Saddam Hussein leave Iraq or face war left no room for him to maneuver, and war followed.

Options for Conducting Diplomacy

While the above rules are solid guidelines to effective diplomacy, the practice is still more art than science. Therefore, effective diplomacy must tailor its approach to the situation and the opponent. To do this, diplomats must make choices about the channel, level, visibility, type of inducement, degree of precision, method of communication, and extent of linkage that they will use.

Conducting Direct or Indirect Negotiations

One issue that diplomats face is whether to negotiate directly with each other or indirectly through an intermediary. *Direct negotiations* have the advantage of avoiding the misinterpretations that an intermediary third party might cause. As in the old game of "Gossip," messages can become garbled. Direct negotiations are also quicker. An additional plus is that they can act as a symbol.

Indirect negotiations may also be advisable. Direct contact symbolizes a level of legitimacy that a country may not wish to convey. For example, the Bush administration has resisted talking directly and bilaterally to North Korea because that would have handed a diplomatic victory to a country that the United States does not recognize. But Washington did reach out indirectly, with Secretary of State Colin Powell stressing to reporters, "We have a number of channels we're using" to communicate with Kim Jong Il's government.[50] For example, at one point North Korea dispatched two low-level diplomats to Santa Fe, New Mexico, to talk with Governor Bill Richardson, a former U.S. ambassador to the UN who had dealt with North Korea during the Clinton administration.

Conducting High-Level or Low-Level Diplomacy

The higher the level of contact or the higher the level of the official making a statement, the more seriously will a message be taken. It implies a greater commitment, and there will be a greater reaction. Therefore, a diplomat must decide whether to communicate on a high or a low level. North Korea was put on notice and U.S. allies in Asia were reassured in 2005 when Secretary of State Condoleezza Rice, commenting on the rumor of an impending nuclear weapons test by North Korea, noted pointedly, "I don't think anyone is confused about the ability of the United States to deter, both on behalf of itself and on behalf of its allies, North Korea's nuclear ambitions or gains on the (Korean) Peninsula." In case anyone doubted what "ability" meant, Rice added, "Of course, the United States maintains significant—and I want to underline significant—deterrent capability of all kinds [that is, including nuclear weapons] in the Asia-Pacific region."[51]

High-level diplomacy has its advantages. Verbal and written statements by heads of government are noted seriously in other capitals. It was major news in diplomatic circles when President Bush took the occasion of a trip to Asia for an international conference to reassure North Korea and to hold out the prospect of a written commitment not to attack it. "I've said as plainly as I can say that we have no intention of invading North Korea," Bush said, adding that while signing a nonaggression treaty with North Korea was still "off the table. . . . Perhaps there are other ways to say exactly what I said publicly on paper."[52] This move, in turn, caused a shift in North Korea's position from demanding a formal treaty to a more flexible willingness to meet with the United States and other countries to explore the president's intimated readiness to sign some document pledging nonaggression.

Low-level diplomacy is wiser at other times. Communications at a low level avoid overreaction and maintain flexibility. Dire threats can be issued as "trial balloons" by

Threats and counterthreats are one approach to diplomacy. This 2005 cartoon depicts China's threat that it will use military force to reincorporate Taiwan into "one China," especially if the Taiwanese declare independence, and the U.S. counterthreat, appearing from over the horizon to defend Taiwan against China if necessary.

cabinet officers or generals and then, if later thought unwise, disavowed by higher political officers. During the ongoing tensions over Taiwan, the principal leaders generally have avoided military threats, leaving that role to lesser officials. For example, an editorial in the Chinese military's newspaper, *Liberation Army Daily,* was far enough removed from official policy makers to warn provocatively that China would "spare no effort in a blood-soaked battle" if Taiwan declared independence.[53] From a position safely distant from the pinnacle of U.S. authority in the Oval Office, Undersecretary of Defense for Policy Walter Slocombe growled back that China would face "incalculable consequences" if it attacked Taiwan.[54]

Sometimes it is even prudent to use a representative who is not in the government at all. It is diplomatically impossible for top officials from China and Taiwan to meet face-to-face, so, at one juncture, Jeremy Stone, president of the American Federation of Scientists and a close friend of Taiwan's new president, was used as an intermediary. Stone, who also has a diplomatic background in arms control, visited President-elect Chen in Taiwan. He then flew to Beijing as an "unofficial representative of Taipei," according to one Chinese official. "What we're trying to do is find ways to communicate," explained a Taiwanese source.[55] A problem with such informal contacts is that they are sometimes suspect. Reports swirled in 2003 about last-minute peace feelers from Iraq through such intermediaries. They came to naught, however, in part because, one U.S. official who had been approached by a Lebanese businessman with a purported offer explained, "I had doubts about whether there was a real offer, because the Iraqis had a lot of [other] ways to get in touch with the U.S."[56]

Using Coercion or Rewards to Gain Agreement

Yet another diplomatic choice is whether to brandish coercive sticks or proffer tempting carrots. To induce an opponent to react as you wish, is it better to offer rewards or to threaten punishment? **Coercive diplomacy** can be effective when you have the power, will, and credibility to back it up (Lake, 2005). At one point when China became particularly alarmed about Taiwan's intentions, Beijing conducted military "training" operations near Taiwan. This demonstration of military might included, among other things, firing six nuclear warhead–capable missiles into the seas off Taiwan's coast. For its part, the United States responded to the implied Chinese threat by sending a major naval flotilla, centered around the carriers USS *Nimitz* and USS *Independence,* into the waters off Taiwan. The commanding admiral of the U.S. Seventh Fleet explained that "we do not want to see an escalation. China has said [it is] not going to attack Taiwan, and that's exactly what we want to see happen."[57]

There are also drawbacks to coercive diplomacy. If it does not work, then those who have threatened force face an unhappy choice. Not carrying out threats creates an image of weakness that may well embolden the opponent(s) and perhaps future opponents in crises to come. Yet putting one's military might and money where one's mouth is costs lives and dollars and is not necessarily successful either. Even if coercion does work, it may entail a long-term commitment that was not originally planned or desired. The Persian Gulf War with Iraq ended in February 1991, but U.S. forces have remained enmeshed in the region and fought and won another war with Iraq in 2003. Yet as of this writing more than two years later, the United States remains mired in the region, unable to either achieve stability or to withdraw, suffering mounting casualties on a near daily basis, and spending tens of billions of dollars on a policy that has become increasingly unpopular with the American public.

There are many times when *offers of rewards* may be a more powerful inducement than coercion. Threats may lead to war, with high costs and uncertain results. Instead, it may be possible to "buy" what you cannot "win." One song in the movie *Mary Poppins* includes the wisdom that "a spoonful of sugar helps the medicine go down," and an increase in aid, a trade concession, a state visit, or some other tangible or symbolic reward may induce agreement. Various forms of aid quelled the North Korean nuclear crisis in 1994, and rewards may again be the key to easing renewed tensions. At first the Bush administration refused to consider incentives, arguing that would be rewarding Pyongyang for reneging on the 1994 agreement. But the countries involved in the multilateral talks urged Washington to be more flexible because, a Chinese diplomat advised, progress "depends on if the United States can have . . . more specific proposals to induce North Korea back to the negotiating table."[58] The United States has continued to be reticent about using incentives but has hinted they might be possible, with President Bush saying that if Pyongyang halted its weapons program, then a "bold initiative" may be possible to halt "the suffering of the North Korean people."[59]

Often, the best diplomacy mixes carrots and sticks. As one U.S. State Department official commented recently, it is difficult to apply a "scientific cookie-cutter approach" that works consistently. "Sometimes it's the carrot, and sometimes it's the stick," he said, adding that the right mixture varies from situation to situation. "You can slice and dice this any way you want. Hopefully, you know, the sausage machine produces something that's halfway coherent at the end."[60]

Economic sanctions and other diplomatic sticks helped topple the regime of Slobodan Milosevic in October 2000. The new government refused, however, to turn him over for trial by the war crimes tribunal sitting in The Hague. What seemingly turned the trick was proffering an exceptionally attractive bunch of carrots to Belgrade. In an unspoken but obvious deal, the Yugoslav government extradited Milosevic in June 2001, and within hours the United States, the European Union, and other donor countries and organizations (such as the World Bank) that were meeting in Brussels pledged $1.28 billion in aid to the country.

Being Precise or Being Intentionally Vague

Most diplomatic experts stress the importance of being precise when communicating. There are times, however, when purposeful vagueness may be in order. *Precision* in both written and verbal communications is usually advantageous because it helps avoid misunderstandings. Being precise can also indicate true commitment, especially if it comes from the national leader.

Vagueness may sometimes be a better strategy. Being vague may paper over irreconcilable differences. "The Saudis have a nice way of doing things" when they do not wish to agree, says one U.S. official. "They say, 'We'll consider it.' It is not their style to say no."[61] Lack of precision can also allow a country to retreat if necessary. A degree of ambiguity was one hallmark of legislation passed by China's parliament in 2005 that authorized the use of force against Taiwan if "major events" move the island toward independence or if "possibilities for peaceful reunification are completely exhausted." Since China's leaders do not need permission from the rubber-stamp parliament, the act was meant as a strong signal to Taiwan. Still it left the leadership room to maneuver by not defining what a major event was or what would constitute the exhaustion of the possibilities for peaceful reunification. Adding to the statute's mixed message, Chinese Premier Wen Jiabao held a press conference soon after it was enacted and focused his remarks on other provisions of the law that call for more economic and cultural exchanges with Taiwan. "This is a law for advancing peaceful reunification. It is not targeted at the people of Taiwan, nor is it a war bill," Wen reassured his listeners with one breath, then, with another added a bit more ominously, "Only by checking and opposing Taiwan's independence forces will peace emerge in the Taiwan Strait."[62]

Communicating by Word or Deed

Diplomacy utilizes both words and actions to communicate. *Oral and written communications*, either direct or through public diplomacy, are appropriate for negotiations and also can be a good signaling strategy. The possibility that North Korea's nuclear weapons program might be a defensive reaction to fear of a U.S. attack led to numerous public and private American assurances that Pyongyang's concern was groundless. As Secretary of State Powell noted, "We have made it clear we have no aggressive intent."[63] Verbal threatening signals also have their place. Powell's successor, Secretary of State Rice, was clearly trying to put pressure on North Korea to resume talks when during a 2005 trip to South Korea she told reporters, "We need to resolve this issue. It cannot go on forever." Turning up the heat a few degrees, Rice added that if Pyongyang refused to end its nuclear weapons program through negotiations, "Then we will have to find other means to do it. . . . [There are] other options in the international system."[64] What that meant, ranging from economic sanctions to military force, she left unclear.

Signaling by action is often more dramatic than verbal signaling and it has its uses. When Secretary of State Rice visited South Korea in 2005, she signaled U.S. determination to defend that country by becoming the highest-ranking American official to ever visit Command Post Tango, a bunker built into a mountain that would serve as the command center during a war with North Korea. There are drawbacks to such physical signals, though, because it is harder to retreat from them than from words. When the Soviets threatened to blockade Berlin in 1961, President John F. Kennedy took the risky step of going there and publicly proclaiming himself a symbolic citizen of the threatened city. "*Ich bin ein Berliner,*" Kennedy's words rang out. By putting his personal honor on the line, Kennedy persuaded the Soviets to back down. He also gave Germans on both sides of the Berlin Wall a good chuckle by making a minor grammatical error. "*Ich bin Berliner*" (I am a Berliner) is what he meant to say. Inadvertently adding "*ein*" changed the meaning of *Berliner* to refer to a jelly doughnut locally called a *berliner.* This left the leader of the free world actually declaring, "I am a jelly doughnut."[65]

Various military actions, ranging from alerting forces, through deploying them, to limited demonstrations of force, can also be utilized. Although in the end the signal did not pressure Iraq into making concessions, the Pentagon was clearly broadcasting U.S. intent when in late 2002 it almost certainly leaked a classified report in which Secretary of Defense Donald Rumsfeld ordered U.S. forces deployed to the Persian Gulf area. Since the military usually prefers to mask its movements, many analysts concluded that the extraordinarily detailed report of aircraft carriers, Army divisions, bomber and fighter units, and other military elements being deployed was meant as a message to Iraq. An anonymous Defense Department official admitted as much, commenting, "We're going to continue to deploy forces in a steady and deliberate buildup to help the diplomatic process."[66]

By reverse logic, it is also possible to signal by not doing something. For all its frequently red-hot rhetoric, North Korea has not as of this writing tested a nuclear

---

Did You Know That:

Similar to President Kennedy's translation-related diplomatic faux pas about pastry, President Boris Yeltsin of Russia once inadvertently greeted his American counterpart with a hearty, "Welcome, Blin Clinton!" *Blin* means pancake in Russian.

weapon. Doing so, one analyst commented, would prove that it has the weapons it claims. But it would also dramatically increase tension and might even "cut off all their options for a diplomatic solution."[67] In a similar way, the United States has not boosted its forces in South Korea nor sent the Seventh Fleet with its nuclear weapons–capable warplanes and cruise missiles near the North Korean coast.

Linking Issues or Treating Them Separately

A persistent dispute is whether a country should deal with other countries on an issue-by-issue basis or link issues together as a basis for a general orientation toward the other country. Advocates of *linking issues* argue that it is inappropriate to have normal relations on some matters with regimes that are hostile and repressive. Those who favor *treating issues separately* claim that doing so allows progress on some issues and keeps channels of communications and influence open.

Critics of the Bush administration have charged that its professed commitment to promoting democracy is hypocritical. Among other things, they point to Bush's continued good relations with Russia despite the increased restrictions on democracy under the Putin government and the brutal campaign against the Chechen independence movement. From the administration's point of view, linking Russia's internal policies to U.S. relations with that country on a range of other matters would be foolhardy. Commenting on Bush's trip to Russia in 2005, a top administration official explained that while "the issue about the democracy and freedom agenda is at the center of the president's foreign policy, and he obviously wants Putin's support in that endeavor," it was also the case that "there's a lot more to our relationship with Russia than just this discussion [about democracy]." The official went on to explain, "here's an opportunity for [Bush and Putin] to talk about Iran and the Middle East and all these other things which we talked about, which reminds us all that the agenda with Russia is a broad one. We do have a lot of common interests, areas where we need to work together to achieve [them]."[68]

Cuba has been another matter, though, and delinkage of issues has not extended to that country. There have been a number of U.S. measures, including the Helms-Burton Act (1996), that instituted economic sanctions on Cuba and foreign companies doing business with Cuba in an attempt to weaken the government of President Fidel Castro. President Bush increased those in 2004, imposing additional sanctions as a "strategy that says, 'We're not waiting for the day of Cuban freedom, we are working for the day of freedom in Cuba.'"[69] What is unclear is why delinking is good policy toward Russia and not toward Cuba.

Maximizing or Minimizing a Dispute

Diplomats face a choice over whether to put a confrontation in a broad or narrow context. *Maximizing a dispute* by invoking national survival, world peace, or some other major principle may be advantageous because doing so increases credibility. At one point, China maximized the stakes of the Taiwan issue by having its premier publicly depict the matter as a "core principle" involving China's "territorial integrity."[70] The drawback of maximizing a dispute is that it makes it very hard to back away from confrontation if a settlement is not reached. President Bush maximized the stakes of the crisis with Iraq. Speaking before the UN General Assembly he declared that the world was being "challenged . . . by outlaw groups and regimes that accept no law of morality and have no limit to their violent ambitions," and he singled out Iraq's "weapons of mass murder" as the single greatest global threat.[71] By doing so, the president signaled U.S. resolve but he also painted himself into something of a corner. Given the dire picture he painted, he arguably would have appeared weak internationally and also been politically vulnerable domestically unless the Iraqis totally capitulated to U.S. demands or were defeated in a war to remove the threat (which, ironically, did not exist).

Minimizing a dispute may work positively to avoid overreactions. In contrast to its rhetoric about Iraq, the Bush administration sought to cool the atmosphere regarding North Korea by, among other things, refusing to call it a crisis. Describing it as the "C-word," one U.S. official said, "We are not thinking in those terms," and the administration labeled the North Korean decision to restart its nuclear facility as merely "regrettable," rather than using a more heated term. Some observes applauded the U.S. restraint, but others criticized it. "By feigning nonchalance, the Bush administration risks encouraging a dangerous regime to step even further forward," charged one critic, and he portrayed the use of the word "regrettable" as "the kind of word you use when the soup isn't very good before dinner."[72]

A final note is that despite the recitation of diplomatic rules and the analysis of the advantages and disadvantages of various diplomatic options in the preceding two sections, there is no substitute for skill and wisdom. Understanding how the game ought to be played does not always produce a win on the playing field of sports or a success at the negotiating table of diplomacy. Certainly you are advantaged if you know the fundamentals, but beyond that, individual capacity and field savvy provide the margin of victory.

Chapter Summary

National Power

1. National diplomacy is the process of trying to advance a country's national interest by applying power assets to persuade other countries to give way.

2. Power is the foundation of diplomacy in a conflictual world. National power is the sum of a country's assets that enhance its ability to get its way even when opposed by others with different interests and goals.

3. Measuring power is especially difficult. The efforts to do so have not been very successful, but they do help us see many of the complexities of analyzing the characteristics of power. These characteristics include the facts that power is dynamic, both objective and subjective, relative, situational, and multidimensional.

4. Two factors are significant when determining a country's power: tangible national assets or a country's power capacity, and more intangible, a country's will to power, the determination to apply power assets.

The Elements of Power

5. The major elements of a country's power can be roughly categorized as those that constitute (1) its national core, (2) its national infrastructure, (3) its national economy, and (4) its military. The core and infrastructure are discussed here and form the basis for economic and military power, which are analyzed in later chapters.

6. The national core consists of a country's geography, its people, and its government.

7. The national infrastructure consists of a country's technological sophistication, its transportation system, and its information and communications capabilities.

National Diplomacy

8. The functions of diplomacy include advancing the national interest through direct application of power, such as imposing sanctions against another country, or indirect power, such as skillfully advancing national interests and attempting to persuade other countries to follow the desired course.

9. Diplomacy is an ancient art, and some of the historical functions of diplomacy are still important. Diplomacy, however, has also changed dramatically during the past century. Seven characteristics describe the new approach to diplomacy: expanded geographic scope, multilateral diplomacy, parliamentary maneuvering, democratized diplomacy, open diplomacy, leader-to-leader communications through summit meetings, and public diplomacy.

10. These changes reflect the changes in the international system and in domestic political processes. Some of the changes have been beneficial, but others have had negative consequences. At the least, diplomacy has become more complex with the proliferation of actors and options. It has also become more vital, given the possible consequences should it fail.

The Conduct of Diplomacy

11. Diplomacy is a communication process that has three main elements. The first is negotiating through direct or indirect discussions between two or more countries. The second is signaling. The third is public diplomacy.

12. Good diplomacy is an art, but it is not totally freestyle, and there are general rules that increase the chances for diplomatic success. Among the cautions are to be realistic, to be careful about what you say, to seek common ground, to try to understand the other side, to be patient, and to leave open avenues of retreat.

13. There are also a wide variety of approaches or options in diplomacy. Whether contacts should be direct or indirect, what level of contact they should involve, what rewards or coercion should be offered, how precise or vague messages should be, whether to communicate by message or deed, whether issues should be linked or dealt with separately, and the wisdom of maximizing or minimizing a dispute are all questions that require careful consideration.

For simulations, debates, and other interactive activities, a chapter quiz, Web links, PowerWeb articles, and much more, visit **www.mhhe.com/rourke11/** and go to chapter 8. Or, while accessing the site, click on Course-Related Headlines and view recent international relations articles in the *New York Times*.

Online
*Learning*Center
with POWERWEB

Key Terms

absolute power
balance-of-power politics
bilateral diplomacy
coercive diplomacy
democratized diplomacy
demographic graying

hard power
multilateral diplomacy
objective power
open diplomacy
parliamentary diplomacy
power

power capacity
public diplomacy
relative power
situational power
soft power
subjective power

summit meetings
two-level game theory
will to power
zero-sum game

CHAPTER

9

International Law and Justice: An Alternative Approach

Which is the wiser here, Justice or Iniquity?
—William Shakespeare, *Measure for Measure*

The law hath not been dead, though it hath slept.
—William Shakespeare, *Hamlet*

Individuals are increasingly being tried in international tribunals such as the International
Criminal Court (ICC) for war crimes and other violations of international law. This
wall painting in Iraq depicts an Iraqi prisoner being tortured in Abu Ghraib prison by
American military and intelligence personnel. The United States refuses to join the
majority of countries that have ratified the ICC. As you read this chapter's discussion
of the ICC, ask yourself whether you agree with the U.S. stance.

THIS CHAPTER FOCUSES ON international law and justice in the conduct of world politics as an alternative to the power-based diplomatic pursuit of self-interest discussed in chapter 8. It would be naive to ignore the reality that most global actors emphasize their own interests. However, this is also true in domestic systems. What is different between global and domestic systems is not so much the motives of the actors as the fact that domestic systems place greater restraints on the pursuit of self-interest than the international system does (Joyner, 2005).

Legal systems are one thing that restrains the power-based pursuit of self-interest in a domestic system. Certainly, powerful individuals and groups have advantages in every domestic system. Rules are broken and the guilty, especially if they can afford a high-priced attorney, sometimes escape punishment. Still, laws in the United States cannot overtly discriminate under the "equal protection" clause of the Fourteenth Amendment to the Constitution; for example, an attorney is provided to indigent defendants in criminal cases. Thus, the law somewhat evens the playing field.

Justice is a second restraint on power in domestic systems. What is just and what is legal are not always the same. Justice involves what is "right" here, not just what is legal. Whether the word is *just, moral, ethical,* or *fair,* there is a greater sense in domestic systems than there is in the international system that justice should prevail, that the ends do not always justify the means, and that those who violate the norms should suffer penalties. Surely, there is no domestic system in which everyone acts justly (Amstutz, 2005). Yet the sense of justice that citizens in stable domestic systems have does influence their behavior.

This means that since it is possible to restrain power politics in the domestic system by the creation of legal systems and through a greater emphasis on what is moral and fair, then it is theoretically possible to use the same standards to curb the unbridled pursuit of interests in the international system. Accomplishing that will require major changes in attitudes and practices, but it can be done.

Fundamentals of International Law and Justice

What actors may and may not legitimately do is based in both international and domestic law systems on a combination of expectations, rules, and practices that help govern behavior. We will explore the fundamental nature of these legal systems and moral codes by looking first at the primitive nature, growth, and current status of international law; then by turning to issues of justice.

The Primitive Nature of International Law

All legal systems, domestic or international, evolve. Each advances from a primitive level to more sophisticated levels. As such, any legal system can be placed on an evolutionary scale ranging from primitive to modern. Note that modern does not mean finished; people in the future may consider our current legal systems to be rudimentary. This concept of a *primitive but evolving legal system* is important to understanding international law.

The current international legal system falls toward the primitive end of the evolutionary scale of legal systems. First, it does not have a formal rule-making (legislative) process as more sophisticated systems do. Instead, codes of behavior are derived from custom or from explicit agreements among actors. Second, there is little or no

Web Link

Some anthropologists study the development of law as part of the evolution of political systems. More on this focus can be found on the Web site of the Association for Political and Legal Anthropology at **www.aaanet** .org/apla/.

The injustices of war and other aspects of international relations led the Dutch jurist and statesman Hugo Grotius (1583–1645) to look for rules to govern conflict and other interactions among states. This effort earned him the title "father of international law."

Did You Know That:

The phrase *international law* was first used by England's Jeremy Bentham in "Principles of International Law" (1789). A utilitarian philosopher, Bentham argued that sovereigns should observe international law because it would be mutually beneficial to do so.

established authority to judge or punish violations of law. Primitive societies, domestic or international, have no police or courts. They rely on self-help techniques ranging from negotiation to violence and occasionally on mediation to resolve disputes. Viewing international law as a primitive legal system helps us to understand that international law does exist, even if it is not as developed as we might wish. Also, we can see that international society and its law may evolve to a higher order, as have domestic systems.

The Growth of International Law

International law has its beginnings in the origin of the states and their need to regulate their relations. Gradually, elements of ancient Jewish, Greek, and Roman custom and practice combined with newer Christian concepts to form the beginning of an international system of law. A number of theorists were also important to the genesis of international law. The most famous was Holland's Hugo Grotius (1583–1645), whose study *De Jure Belli et Pacis* (On the Law of War and Peace) earned him the title "father of international law." Grotius and others advanced ideas about the sources of international law, its role in regulating the relations of states, and its application to war and other specific circumstances. From this base, international law evolved slowly over the intervening centuries, as the interactions between the states grew and as the needs and expectations of the international community became more sophisticated.

During the last century or so, concern with international law has grown rapidly. Globalization has significantly expanded the need for rules to govern a host of functional areas such as trade, finance, travel, and communications. Similarly, our awareness of our ability to destroy ourselves and our environment, and of the suffering of victims of human rights abuses, has led to lawmaking treaties on such subjects as genocide, nuclear testing, use of the oceans, and human rights. Even the most political of all activities, war and other aspects of national security, have increasingly become the subject of international law. Aggressive war, for example, is outside the pale of the law. The UN's response of authorizing sanctions and then force against Iraq after that country invaded Kuwait in 1990 reflected that. So did the refusal of most countries to support what they saw as an unjustified U.S.-led invasion of Iraq in 2003.

The Practice of International Law

Those who discount international law contend that it exists only in theory, not in practice. As evidence, they cite war, human rights violations, and other largely unpunished examples of "lawlessness." What this argument misses is that international law is effective in many areas despite many holes in its coverage. There is substantial evidence in the behavior of states that they "do accept international law as law, and, even more significant, in the vast majority of instances they . . . obey it" (Joyner, 2000:243). Furthermore, the fact that the law is not *always* followed does not disprove its existence. There is, after all, a substantial crime rate in the United States and most other countries, but that does not mean they are lawless.

International law is *most effective* in governing the rapidly expanding range of transnational **functional relations**. These involve "low politics," a term that designates such things as trade, diplomatic rules, and communications. International law is *least effective* when applied to "high-politics" issues such as national security relations. When vital interests are involved, governments still regularly bend international law to justify their actions rather than alter their actions to conform to the law. Even in this realm, though, the law and standards of justice sometimes influence political decisions. Both international law and world values, for instance, are strongly opposed to states unilaterally resorting to war except in immediate self-defense. Violations such as Iraq's invasion of Kuwait still occur, but they are met with mounting global condemnation and even counterforce. Now even countries as powerful as the United States regularly seek UN authorization to act in cases such as Afghanistan in 2001 and Iraq in 2003, when not long ago they would have acted on their own initiative. It is true that the United States and Great Britain ultimately went ahead in 2003 without UN support, but that does not disprove the existence of the norm against unilateral war. Indeed, the widespread condemnation of the invasion shows the norm does exist, and the ability of the United States to ignore the norm demonstrates that power often continues to trump international law and justice.

Web Link

A good entry point for more information on international law and international courts is through the UN at http://www.un.org/law/.

The Fundamentals of International Justice

Concepts of just behavior stem from religious beliefs, from secular ideologies or philosophies, from the standard of equity (what is fair), or from common practice. We will see in our discussion of roots of international law that what a society considers just behavior sometimes becomes law. At other times, legal standards that are considered just are gradually adopted by a society. Insofar as just behavior remains an imperative of conscience rather than law, we can consider justice in a broad sense. Distinctions can be made between moral, ethical, equitable, and humanitarian standards and behavior, but the four individually and in sum equate to justice.

It would be wrong—given recurring war, gnawing human deprivation, persistent human rights violations, and debilitating environmental abuse—to imagine that justice is a predominant global force. Yet it would also be erroneous to use these ills to argue that law and justice do not play a role. Instead, as one scholar describes the balance between what is ideal and real, "Contrary to what the skeptics assert, norms do indeed matter. But norms do not necessarily matter in the ways or often to the extent that their proponents have argued" (Legro, 1997:31). This state of affairs is changing, though, through a growing body of ethical norms that help determine the nature of the international system. Progress is slow and inconsistent, but it exists. American and British forces did not drop nuclear weapons on Iraq in 2003, even though doing so arguably could have saved time, money, and the lives of American and British troops. Many countries give foreign aid to less developed countries. National leaders, not just philosophers and clergy, regularly discuss and sometimes even make decisions based on human rights. Consumers have rallied to the environmentalist cause to protect dolphins by purchasing only those brands of tuna whose cans feature the dolphin-safe logos. Thus the reality is that world politics operates to a degree within the context of international law and justice.

The International Legal System

International law, like any legal system, is based on four critical considerations: the philosophical roots of law, how laws are made, when and why the law is obeyed (adherence), and how legal disputes are decided (adjudication).

The Philosophical Roots of Law

Where does law originate? Ideas about what is right and what should be the law do not spring from thin air. Rather, they are derived from sources both external and internal to the society they regulate. *External roots,* those outside a society, provide one source of law. Those who look to external sources believe that some higher, metaphysical standard of conduct should govern the affairs of humankind. An important ramification of this position is that there is, or ought to be, one single system of law that governs all people.

Support for the theory of external sources can be subdivided into two schools. The **ideological/theological school of law** is one. This school holds that law is derived from an overarching ideology or theology. For instance, a substantial part of international legal theory extends back to early Western proponents of international law who relied on Christian doctrine for their standards. The writings of Saint Augustine and Saint Thomas Aquinas on the law of war are examples. There are also long-standing elements of law and scholarship in Islamic, Buddhist, and other religious traditions that serve as a foundation for just international conduct.

The **naturalist school of law** posits that humans, by nature, have certain rights and obligations. English philosopher John Locke argued in *Two Treatises of Government* (1690) that there is "a law of nature" that "teaches all mankind, who will but consult it, that all [people] being equal and independent [in the state of nature], no one ought to harm another in his life, health, liberty, or possessions." Since countries are collectives of individuals, and the world community is a collective of states and individuals, natural law's rights and obligations also apply to the global stage and form the basis for international law.

Critics of the theory of external sources of law contend that standards based on ideology or theology can lead to oppression. The problems with natural law, critics charge, are both that it is vague and that it contains such an emphasis on individualism that it almost precludes any sense of communitarian welfare. If a person's property is protected by natural law, then, for instance, it is hard to justify taking any individual's property through taxes levied by the government without the individual's explicit agreement.

Internal roots, those from within the society, are a second basis of law. Some legal scholars reject the idea of divine or naturalist roots and, instead, focus on the customs and practices of society. This is the **positivist school of law**, which advocates that law reflects society and the way people want that society to operate. Therefore, according to positivist principles, law is and ought to be the product of the codification or formalization of a society's standards.

Critics condemn the positivist approach as amoral and sometimes immoral, in that it may legitimize immoral, albeit common, beliefs and behavior of a society as a whole or of its dominant class. These critics would say, for instance, that slavery was once widespread and widely accepted, but it was never moral or lawful, by the standards of either divine principle or natural law.

How International Law Is Made

Countries usually make domestic law through a constitution (constitutional law) or by a legislative body (statutory law). In practice, law is also established through judicial decisions (interpretation), which set guidelines (precedent) for later decisions by the courts. Less influential sources of law are custom (common law) and what is fair (equity). Compared to its domestic equivalent, modern international lawmaking is much more decentralized. There are, according to the Statute of the International Court of Justice, four sources of law: international treaties, international custom, the general principles of law, and judicial decisions and scholarly legal writing. Some students of international law would tentatively add a fifth source: resolutions and other pronouncements of the UN General Assembly. These five rely primarily on the positivist approach but, like domestic law, include elements of both external and internal sources of law.

International treaties are the primary source of international law. A primary advantage of treaties is that they **codify**, or write down, the law. Agreements between states are binding according to the doctrine of *pacta sunt servanda* (treaties are to be served/carried out). All treaties are binding on those countries that are party to them (have signed and ratified or otherwise given their legal consent). Moreover, it is possible to argue that some treaties are also applicable to nonsignatories. When a large number of states agree to a principle, it begins to take on systemwide legitimacy. The 1948 Convention on the Prevention and Punishment of the Crime of Genocide, for

ANALYZE THE ISSUE
Law and Justice:
Finding Its Place in the
Current International System

Multilateral treaties are a prime source of international law. The four treaties (1949) and two supplementary protocols (1977) that collectively are called the Geneva Conventions form an important part of the law of war. Too often those rules have been ignored, as they allegedly were by President Charles Taylor of Liberia. But the principle expressed by the sign seen here on a wall in Liberia's capital, Monrovia, is increasingly being enforced. A month after this picture was taken in July 2003, Taylor was forced to flee to Nigeria, where he is in exile. That country's president announced that Taylor may be extradited to Sierra Leone for trial by the international tribunal that has indicted him.

example, has been ratified by most states. Therefore, genocide has arguably become a crime under international law, and that standard is binding on all states whether or not they are party to the treaty. Now people are being tried, convicted, and sentenced for genocide, whether or not their country ratified the antigenocide treaty.

International custom is the second most important source of international law. The old, and now supplanted, rule that territorial waters extend three miles from the shore grew from the distance a cannon could fire. If you were outside the range of land-based artillery, then you were in international waters. Maritime rules of the road and diplomatic practice are two other important areas of law that grew out of custom. Sometimes, long-standing custom is eventually codified in treaties. An example is the Vienna Convention on Diplomatic Relations of 1961, which codified many existing rules of diplomatic standing and practice.

General principles of law are a third source of international law. The ancient Roman concept of *jus gentium* (the law of peoples) is the foundation of the general principles of law. By this standard, the International Court of Justice (ICJ) applies "the general principles of law recognized by civilized nations." Although such language is vague, it has its benefits. It encompasses "external" sources of law, such as the idea that freedom of religion and freedom from attack are among the inherent rights of people. More than any other standard, it is for violating these general principles that Slobodan Milosevic, the former president of Yugoslavia, was brought to trial in 2002 at the international tribunal in the Netherlands. The charges against Milosevic included nine counts of violating specific treaty law, the 1949 Geneva Conventions. But the indictment was also based on *jus gentium*, including 13 counts of "violations of the laws or customs of war," such as "murder; torture; cruel treatment; [and] wanton destruction of villages . . . not justified by military necessity"; and 10 counts of "crimes against humanity," such as "persecutions on political, racial or religious grounds; extermination; murder; imprisonment; torture; [and] inhumane acts (forcible transfers)."[1]

Judicial decisions and scholarly writing also add to the law. In many domestic systems, legal interpretations by courts set precedent according to the doctrine of *stare decisis* (let the decision stand). This doctrine is specifically rejected in Article 59 of the Statute of the International Court of Justice, but in practice judges on both domestic and international courts cite other legal decisions in justifying their own rulings. One scholar argues that this has created a "global community of courts," whose judges "are in many ways creating their own version of [an international legal] system—a bottom-up version . . . shaped by a deep respect for each other's competences and the ultimate need, in a world of law, to rely on reason rather than force" (Slaughter, 2003: 219). Judicial review, deciding whether a government law or action is constitutional, is another possible role of international judicial bodies. Many domestic courts have this authority but the European Court of Justice is the only international court to have conducted judicial review.

International representative assemblies are arguably a fifth source of international law. Compared to the generally recognized preceding four sources of international law, the idea that laws can come from the UN General Assembly or any other international representative assembly is much more controversial. Clearly, to date, international law is not statutory. The General Assembly cannot legislate international law the way that a national legislature does. Yet, UN members are bound by treaty to abide by some of the decisions of the General Assembly and the Security Council, which makes these bodies quasi-legislative. Some scholars contend that resolutions approved by overwhelming majorities of the General Assembly constitute international law because such votes reflect international custom and/or the general princi-

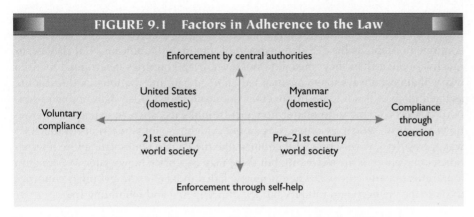

FIGURE 9.1   Factors in Adherence to the Law

Two crucial factors in international law are how the law is enforced and what encourages compliance. These factors differ over time and for different societies.

ples of law. We may, then, be seeing the beginnings of legislated international law, but, at best, it is in its genesis. Certainly, UN resolutions and mandates often are not followed, but some would argue that this means that the law is being violated rather than that the law does not exist.

Adherence to the Law

Adherence to the law is a third essential element of any legal system. As Figure 9.1 represents, people obey the law because of a mixture of voluntary and coerced compliance, and they enforce the law through a mixture of enforcement by central authorities and enforcement through self-help.

Compliance with the Law

Obedience to the law in any legal system—whether it is international or domestic, primitive or sophisticated—is based on a mix of voluntary compliance and coercion. *Voluntary compliance* occurs when the subjects obey the law because they accept its legitimacy, that is, people abide by rules because they accept the authority of the institution that made the rules (a legislature or a court) and/or agree that the rules are necessary for the reasonable conduct of society. *Coercion* is the process of gaining compliance through threats of violence, imprisonment, economic sanction, or other punishment.

Any society's legal system can be placed somewhere along the compliance scale between complete reliance on voluntary compliance and complete reliance on coercion. Voluntary compliance is usually more important, but there are wide variations among societies. Americans tend to obey the law voluntarily; in Myanmar (Burma) obedience to the laws of the country's military junta is primarily a function of force.

Compliance with international law is mostly voluntary rather than based on coercion. Pragmatic legitimacy is the key to international voluntary compliance. Countries recognize the need for a system that is made predictable by adherence to laws. Therefore they follow the law because it is in their interest that other countries follow it (Goldsmith & Posner, 2005). For this reason, functional international law governing day-to-day relations between states has expanded. Legitimacy based on norms is less well established, but it has also grown. Aggression, violation of human rights, and other unacceptable practices still occur, but they increasingly meet with widespread condemnation. Unilateral military action is, for example, becoming ever more difficult for a country to launch without meeting severe criticism. Such events continue to occur, as the U.S.-led invasion of Iraq in 2003 indicates. But they occur much less often than they once did. Moreover, even countries determined to go to war will almost always make a concerted effort to gain international authorization, as the diplomacy leading up to the 2003 war again shows. Also, failure to win support subjects a country, no matter how just it thinks its cause, to extensive international criticism, which, as noted, was amply evident in global reactions to the 2003 war against Iraq. A very powerful country like the United States can ignore international opposition in the short run, but there may be a price to pay later. Washington found this out after the war when it mostly failed in its effort to get other countries to share the financial and military burden of occupying and rebuilding Iraq.

Enforcement of the Law

In all legal systems, enforcement relies on a combination of *enforcement through self-help* and *enforcement by central authorities*. Primitive societies rely primarily on self-help and on mediation to enforce laws and norms. As a primitive society evolves, it begins to develop enforcement authorities. Domestic systems have done this, and they rely mostly on a central authority to provide law enforcement organizations (usually the police) and sanctions (fines, prison) to compel compliance with the law. Still, even advanced legal systems recognize the legitimacy of such self-help doctrines as self-defense.

As a primitive society, the global community system continues to focus on self-help for enforcement, and neither law enforcement organizations nor sanctions are well developed at the international level. Yet there is observable movement along the evolutionary path toward a more centralized system. For example, war criminals were punished after World War II. More recently, indictments have been handed down for war crimes in Bosnia and elsewhere, and some of the accused have been tried, convicted, and imprisoned. Economic and diplomatic sanctions are becoming more frequent and are sometimes successful. Armed enforcement by central authorities is even less common and rudimentary. Because of their ad hoc nature, the UN-authorized military action against Iraq in 1991 and the NATO intervention in Kosovo in 1999 were more akin to an Old West sheriff authorizing posses to chase the outlaws than true police actions, but they did represent a step toward enforcement of international law by central authorities.

Adjudication of the Law

How a political system resolves disputes between its actors is a fourth key element in its standing along the primitive-to-modern evolutionary scale. As primitive legal systems become more sophisticated, the method of settling disputes evolves from (1) primary reliance on bargaining between adversaries, through (2) mediation/conciliation by neutral parties, to (3) **adjudication** (and the closely related process of arbitration) by neutral parties. The international system of law is in the early stages of this developmental process and is just now developing the institutions and attitudes necessary for adjudication.

International Courts

There are a number of international courts in the world today. Their genesis extends back less than a century to the Permanent Court of International Arbitration established by the Hague Conference at the turn of the century. In 1922 the Permanent

Court of International Justice (PCIJ) was created as part of the League of Nations, and in 1946 the current **International Court of Justice (ICJ)**, which is associated with the UN, evolved from the PCIJ. The ICJ, or so-called World Court, sits in The Hague, the Netherlands, and consists of 15 judges, who are elected to nine-year terms through a complex voting system in the UN. By tradition, each of the five permanent members of the UN Security Council has one judge on the ICJ, and the others are elected to provide regional representation, as is evident in the map on page 278.

In addition to the ICJ, there are a few regional courts of varying authority and levels of activity. These include the European Court of Justice (ECJ), the European Court of Human Rights, the Inter-American Court of Human Rights, the Central American Court of Justice, and the Community Tribunal of the Economic Community of West African States. None of these has the authority of domestic courts, but like the ICJ, the regional courts are gaining more credibility.

The ECJ is particularly notable for the number of cases it hears (665 in 2004) and its authority to make decisions and to have those rulings followed in areas that were once clearly within the sovereign realm of states. In 2000, for example, the court ruled that a German law barring women from holding combat positions in the military was discriminatory and that "national authorities could not . . . adopt the general position that the composition of all armed units . . . had to remain exclusively male."[2] Soon thereafter, the German army began to train women for combat. An important pending decision relates to Microsoft Corporation's appeal of a decision by the EU Commission fining the software giant $613 million for monopolistic practices such as bundling Explorer and other programs with its Windows operating system. After the EU's Court of First Instance ruled against the U.S. firm in 2005, it filed a further appeal with the ECJ. That ruling will have a major financial impact on Microsoft and, by extension on both the U.S. stock market and possibly the way that software is sold all over the world.

Additionally, people or governments sometimes change their behavior rather than face an adverse ruling by the ECJ or some other international court. One example involved a British law setting the age of consent at 16 for heterosexuals and 18 for homosexuals. When a 17-year-old British homosexual sued in the ECJ, arguing that the two-year differentiation was discriminatory, the House of Commons lowered the age of consent for homosexuals to 16 rather than pursue an almost certain losing case. The House of Lords blocked the measure, however, with one opponent, the Earl of Longford, reasoning, "A girl is not ruined for life by being seduced. A young fellow is." This logic escaped many. "Lord Longford is 92," wrote a columnist in the *Observer* of London, "but he acts like a man twice his age."[3] The deadlock ended when, for only the fourth time since World War I, Commons overruled the Lords by once again approving the change, thereby making it law.

Jurisdiction of International Courts

Although the creation of international tribunals during this century indicates progress, the concept of sovereignty remains a potent barrier to adjudication. The authority of the ICJ extends in theory to all international legal disputes. Cases come before the ICJ in two ways. One is when states submit legal disputes between them. The second is when one of the organs or agencies of the UN asks the ICJ for an advisory opinion.

From 1946 through 2005, the court has averaged only about two new cases annually. Although this number has increased slightly in recent years, it remains relatively low, given the ICJ's broad jurisdiction and the number of issues facing the world and its countries. More than any other factor, the gap between the court's

SIMULATION
The World Court: Creating a Trial for the Classroom

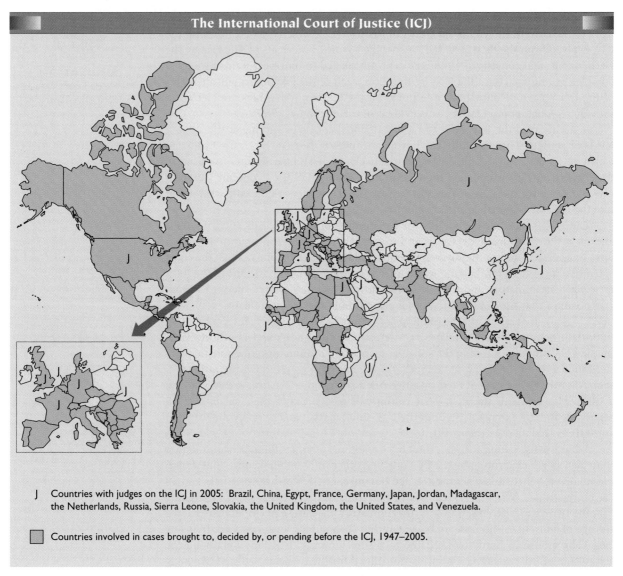

The International Court of Justice (ICJ)

J   Countries with judges on the ICJ in 2005: Brazil, China, Egypt, France, Germany, Japan, Jordan, Madagascar, the Netherlands, Russia, Sierra Leone, Slovakia, the United Kingdom, the United States, and Venezuela.

☐   Countries involved in cases brought to, decided by, or pending before the ICJ, 1947–2005.

The International Court of Justice (ICJ), which sits in The Hague, the Netherlands, draws both its judges and its caseload from around the world. This map shows the home countries of the ICJ's 15 judges in 2005, and the 81 countries that have been a party in cases before the ICJ between 1947 and 2005.

MAP
The International Court
of Justice (ICJ)

jurisdiction and its actual role is a matter of the willingness of states to submit to decisions of the ICJ, to litigate cases before it, and to abide by its decisions. Although all UN member-countries are technically parties to the ICJ statute, they must also sign the so-called *optional clause* agreeing to be subject to the compulsory jurisdiction of the ICJ. About two-thirds of all countries have not done so, and others that once were adherents to the optional clause have withdrawn their consent. For example, when Nicaragua filed a case in 1984 with the ICJ charging that U.S. support of the Contra rebels and its mining of Nicaraguan harbors violated international law, the United States argued that the charges were political and, therefore, that the court had no jurisdiction. When the ICJ ruled that it did have jurisdiction in the case, the United States withdrew U.S. consent to the optional clause.

It should be noted that nonadherence to the optional clause does not entirely exempt a country from ICJ jurisdiction. It is common for treaties to have a clause that commits the signatories to submit disputes arising under the treaty to the ICJ. One such treaty that has brought two suits against the United States in the ICJ in recent years is the Vienna Convention on Consular Relations (1963). In it the signatories, including the United States, agree to settle disputes arising from the treaty in the ICJ. The treaty permits countries to assist their citizens who have been accused of serious crimes in another country. Mexico in 2003 brought a case to the ICJ contending that various U.S. states were violating the treaty in several death penalty cases by not allowing German and Mexican consular officials access to 51 accused or condemned individuals.

Effectiveness of International Courts

There are some important limits on the impact of the ICJ and other international courts. The *jurisdictional limits* just discussed are one restraint. *Lack of enforcement* is a second impediment to the effectiveness of international courts. All courts rely heavily on the willingness of those within their jurisdiction to comply voluntarily or, when that fails, on a powerful executive branch to enforce court decrees. Effective domestic courts have these supports. By contrast, countries are often reluctant to follow the decisions of international courts, and the UN Secretariat, which is the ICJ executive branch, does not have the authority or power to enforce ICJ rulings. This allows countries to sometimes ignore ICJ rulings.

In *United States of America v. Mexico,* for example, the ICJ found for Mexico and directed the United States to ensure that its subdivisions (the states) provided relief to the prisoners. However, the federal U.S. Circuit Court of Appeals held that the ICJ's decision was not binding. The case reached the U.S. Supreme Court in 2005 and took an odd turn when the Bush administration seemed to come down on both sides of the issue. On the one hand, the administration's brief asked the U.S. high court to uphold the Court of Appeals. On the other hand, the brief said that the president would use his "constitutionally based foreign affairs power" to direct the state courts to give new hearings to the Mexican nationals as required in the ICJ decision. Many legal experts were doubtful that such presidential authority existed, and that uncertainty plus the White House's seeming ambiguity toward the ICJ ruling "will launch a million law review articles" one attorney commented.[4] The status of the issue became even murkier when the Supreme Court reversed its decision to hear the case and dismissed it on the grounds that it was moot in light of Bush's declared intention to make the states abide by the treaty requiring home-country notification. The justices chose not to address whether the president had the authority to take that action, meaning that the case would probably once again wind up before the high court.

Given the limitations on the effectiveness of international courts, it is tempting to write them off as having little more than symbolic value. Such a judgment would be in error. The ICJ, for instance, does play a valuable role. Its rulings help define and advance international law. Furthermore, the court can contribute by giving countries a way, short of war, to settle a dispute once diplomacy has failed. The current ICJ case filed in 2004 by Bulgaria against Ukraine over their maritime border in the Black Sea provides a good example. More important than the details of the dispute is the fact that unlike many disagreements throughout history over land and

International courts have no independent power to force compliance with their decisions. The International Court of Justice ruled in 2004 that the security wall that Israel is building between it and the West Bank, and in some places in the West Bank, violates international law. The Palestinians and other demonstrators seen here during a rally before the wall in the West Bank town of Qalqilya are predicting the wall will fall, but that is unlikely in the near future. Israel rejects the ICJ's decision, and there is no practical way to enforce it. Does this mean that there is something wrong with the ICJ or is the problem the willingness of countries to uphold its rulings?

maritime borders that have resulted in war, the existence of the ICJ provides Bulgaria and Ukraine a way to come to a peaceful resolution.

ICJ advisory opinions also help resolve issues between IGOs and may even help establish general international law. In separate actions, the UN General Assembly and the World Health Organization each asked the ICJ to rule on the legality of using nuclear weapons. The court ruled in 1996 that "the threat or use of nuclear weapons would generally be contrary to the rules of international law applicable in armed conflict," but went on to say that it was unable to "conclude definitively whether the threat or use of nuclear weapons would be lawful or unlawful in an extreme circumstance of self-defense, in which the very survival of a state would be at stake."[5] While the ICJ's ruling was not as all-encompassing as some antinuclear advocates hoped, the decision does put any leader considering the use of nuclear weapons except in extremis on notice that he or she could wind up the defendant in some future war crimes trial.

In what may be an even higher profile instance of an advisory ruling, the General Assembly in December 2003 requested that the ICJ take up the legality of the 435-mile-long barrier wall that Israel is constructing along the Israel–West Bank border and through parts of the West Bank. The Palestinians claimed that Israel intends to use the barrier to annex part of the West Bank and the city of Jerusalem in violation of various agreements and UN resolutions. Israel argued that the structure is meant to make it harder for suicide bombers and other terrorists to infiltrate the country. The ICJ ruled against Israel in 2004, saying it was "not convinced that the specific course Israel has chosen for the wall was necessary to attain its security objectives" and that the "wall, along the route chosen . . . gravely infringes a number of rights of Palestinians residing in the territory occupied by Israel." Therefore, the ICJ concluded, "The construction of such a wall accordingly constitutes breaches by Israel of various of its obligations under the applicable international humanitarian law and human rights instruments."[6] As an advisory opinion, the court's ruling had no immediate impact, and Israel and its supporters denounced it. An Israeli spokesperson predicted that the decision "will find its place in the garbage can of history," and a White House official said of the ICJ, "We do not believe that that's the appropriate forum to resolve what is a political issue."[7] It is not surprising, then, that Israel has continued to build the wall, but how the ICJ decision will influence the long history of the Middle East conflict remains to be seen.

Whatever the outcome of a specific case, there is evidence that countries are gradually becoming more willing to utilize the ICJ, the ECJ, and other international courts and to accept their decisions. The map of the ICJ's justices and cases on page 278 shows that countries around the world have justices on the court and almost half are or have been a party to its cases. Now more than 60 countries, including Canada, India, and the United Kingdom, adhere to the optional clause giving the ICJ compulsory jurisdiction over their international legal disputes. In sum, it is true that the international judicial system is still primitive, but each of the some 160 opinions issued by the PCIJ and the ICJ since 1922 is one more than the zero instances of international adjudication in previous centuries.

Applying International Law and Justice

Law and justice are easy to support in the abstract, but it is much more difficult to agree on how to apply them. To examine this, we will look at issues of cultural perspective, issues of applying international law and standards of justice equally to states and individuals, and issues of pragmatism.

Law and Justice in a Multicultural World

As the international legal system evolves and expands to incorporate diverse peoples, one problem it faces is the "fit" between differing culturally based concepts of law and justice. Most of international law and many of the international standards of justice that currently exist and influence world politics are based on the concepts and practices of the West. This is a result of U.S. and European dominance, though, and does not mean that Western concepts are superior to those held in other parts of the world. Now, in a changing international system, Africans, Asians, Latin Americans, and other non-Westerners are questioning and sometimes rejecting law based on Western culture.

Law and Cultural Perspectives

Western and non-Western precepts of law and justice differ on numerous points. The *Western view* of law is based on principles designed to protect the long-dominant power of this bloc of states. Order is a primary point, as is sovereignty. Closely related is the theory of property, which holds that individuals (and states) have a "right" to accumulate and maintain property (wealth). This is a major philosophical underpinning of capitalism. Western law also relies heavily on the process and substance of law rather than on equity. Thus, there is an emphasis on courts and what the law is rather than on what is fair. One current controversy that touches on both property rights and "law versus fairness" involves HIV/AIDS and patents held by Western pharmaceutical firms. Patent drugs, which can be as much as 50 times more expensive than generic equivalents, are beyond the financial means of most less developed

Web Link

Those interested in a career in international law or other applied aspects would do well to check out the Web site of the American Society of International Law at **www.asil.org/**.

countries (LDCs). Even though the pharmaceutical companies have slashed prices by as much as 90% on some drugs sold in LDCs, these countries argue the drugs are still financially out of reach. They claim that their right to try to respond to the epidemic by producing the drugs themselves is more important than the Western emphasis on property rights. LDCs add that it is unfair, whatever the law may be, for the poor to suffer untreated because they cannot afford drugs that, in essence, are only available to wealthy individuals and countries.

The *non-Western view* of international law is influenced by the different cultural heritage of non-Western states, by the recent independence of those states, and by the history of exploitation their people have often suffered at the hands of the West. These states claim that since they had little or no role in determining the rules that govern the international system, they are not necessarily bound by preexisting agreements, principles, or practices. Instead, they support sovereignty and reject aspects of international law that they claim are imperialistic abridgments of that principle. They insist on noninterference, which, for example, was one reason that many LDCs opposed the American and British intervention in Iraq in 2003. Whatever their sympathies with the plight of the Iraqis under Saddam Hussein, and whatever the LDCs' views of whether or not he posed an international danger, they are concerned that they could be the target of a future intervention. The LDCs also are keenly aware that such interventions are only launched against weaker countries and that the more powerful economically developed countries are, in effect, exempt from intervention no matter what the issue (Farer, 2003; Lang, 2003).

The LDCs also reject weighted voting schemes that favor the rich and powerful, such as those in the UN Security Council, the World Bank, and the International Monetary Fund. The LDCs often emphasize equity over the substance and process of law. For them, the important standard is justice, especially in terms of what they consider to be the unjust maldistribution of wealth in the world that leaves a few countries wealthy and most countries poor. A final note about multiculturalism and its interface with international law and justice is that there are differing cultural perspectives on human rights. This topic is covered in detail in chapter 14.

Standards of Law for States and Individuals

Yet another issue to consider about the application of international law is whether states and individuals should be judged by the same standards (Erskine, 2003). Traditionally countries have generally not been held accountable, and they have acted and continue to often act in ways that would be reprehensible for individuals. Imagine if as a private person you were arguing with your neighbors, and you laid siege to their house and managed to significantly reduce their ability to feed their children and buy them medicine. As a result, some of your neighbors' children died. Would any dispute justify such actions? Most people would think not and would consider you a heinous criminal.

In a somewhat analogous situation, the United States and other countries continued UN-authorized economic sanctions against Iraq between its invasion of Kuwait in 1990 and the fall of Saddam Hussein in 2003. Whatever the cause of the sanctions, one impact was that the lack of food, medicine, and other basics contributed to the deaths of several hundred thousand more Iraqi children than would have died in normal circumstances. Surely those sanctions were at least partly the result of Iraq's obdurate refusal during most of the time to grant unimpeded access to UN arms inspectors. But does that settle the question? It is hard to conceive of a circumstance where we as individuals could legally or morally take action against a person that would injure that person's children. Is it moral, should it be legal, that we—the collective of states in the UN—assailed the Iraqi children to punish Iraq's regime?

Of course, we recognize differences between justifiable and inexcusable actions, but where do you draw the line? Some have argued that the state cannot be held to individual moral standards. Realist philosopher and statesman Niccolò Machiavelli wrote in *The Prince* (1513) that a ruler "cannot observe all those things which are considered good in men, being often obliged, in order to maintain the state, to act against faith and charity, against humanity, and against religion." Taking the same view, American diplomat George Kennan (1986:204) argued that the "functions, commitments and moral obligations of governments are not the same as those of the individual. . . . [A government's] primary obligation is to the interests of the national society it represents, not to the moral impulses that individual elements of that society may experience."

Those who believe that the standards of justice and morality guiding individuals should also govern countries argue that neither national interest nor sovereignty legitimizes unjust actions. A philosopher and statesman who took this view was Thomas Jefferson. While secretary of state (1789–1793), Jefferson argued that since a society is but a collection of individuals, "the moral duties which exist between individual and individual" also form "the duties of that society toward any other; so that between society and society the same moral duties exist as between the individuals composing them" (Graebner, 1964:55).

Questions about what principles should guide the foreign policy of countries are not abstract because countries are increasingly being held accountable for their actions in the court of international opinion and sometimes even in courts of law. While it is true that the cornerstone of the state system continues to be sovereignty, it is no longer a legal absolute. Instead, it is being eroded by a growing number of law-making treaties that limit states' actions. Sovereignty is also being slowly restricted by the international community's growing norms condemning aggression, unrestrained attacks on civilians, human rights abuses, and other unacceptable acts of governments. As UN Secretary-General Kofi Annan puts it, sovereignty "was never meant as a license for governments to trample on human rights and human dignity. Sovereignty implies responsibility, not just power."[8] Views such as this led, for instance, to international action that ended apartheid in South Africa (1993) and forced the military junta in Haiti to flee (1994), and to the NATO bombardment of Yugoslavia until it ceased its ethnic cleansing policy in Kosovo (1999). Also, as we will discuss further below, international tribunals are increasingly holding individual leaders responsible for their actions and for those of their subordinates.

There are numerous policy areas where international law is applicable to the actions of states. Many of these are covered in other chapters. Chapter 14, for example, examines the international law of human rights, and Chapter 15 takes up international law regarding the biosphere. Of all the policy areas, though, the oldest and arguably still the most critical is the law of war.

States, War, and International Law

Most of the early writing in international law focused on the law of war. This issue continues to be a primary concern of legal scholarship, but what has changed is that in addition to issues of traditional state-versus-state warfare, international law now also attempts to regulate revolutionary and internal warfare and terrorism.

Illustrating these diverse concerns is the long debate on when and how war can be justifiably fought. "Just war" theory has two parts: the cause of war and the conduct of war. Western tradition has believed that *jus ad bellum* (just cause of war) exists in cases where the war is (1) a last resort, (2) declared by legitimate authority, (3) waged in self-defense or to establish/restore justice, and (4) fought to bring about peace. The same line of thought maintains that *jus in bello* (just conduct of war) includes the standards of proportionality and discrimination. Proportionality means that the amount of force used must be proportionate to the threat. Discrimination means that force must not make noncombatants intentional targets (Rengger, 2002).

As laudable as limitations on legitimate warfare may seem, they present problems. One difficulty is that the standards of when to go to war and how to fight it are rooted in Western-Christian tradition. The parameters of *jus in bello* and *jus ad bellum* extend back to Aristotle's *Politics* (ca. 340 B.C.) and are especially associated with the writings of Christian theological philosophers Saint Augustine (Aurelius Augustinus, A.D. 354–430) and Saint Thomas Aquinas (1225–1274). As a doctrine based on Western culture and religion, not all the restrictions on war are the same as those derived from some of the other great cultural-religious traditions, including Buddhism and Islam (Silverman, 2002). Another difficulty with the standards of just war, even if you try to abide by them, is that they are vague and controversial (Butler, 2003).

Just Cause of War

The concept of *jus ad bellum*, the just cause of war, no longer exists only in theory. After World War II, the Nuremberg and Tokyo war crimes tribunals held German and Japanese leaders accountable for, among other things, waging aggressive war. More recently, UN tribunals have punished those found guilty of war crimes in the Balkans and in Rwanda. Adding to the case that aggressive war is a criminal offense under international law, the treaty that established the International Criminal Court (ICC) gives it jurisdiction "with respect to . . . the crime of aggression." Although the ICC charter does not define aggression, it does state that judging acts of war "shall be consistent with the relevant provisions of the [UN] Charter." Among these is the mandate that members "refrain in their international relations from the threat or use of force against the territorial integrity or political independence of any state." The Charter recognizes "the inherent right of individual or collective self-defense if an armed attack occurs," but apart from that contingency, the document directs that it is the Security Council that "shall determine the existence of any threat to the peace . . . or act of aggression and . . . decide what measures shall be taken." The Charter also stresses that every effort at a peaceful settlement should be made before resorting to force. These clauses closely parallel the traditional standards—that to be just, war must be the last resort, declared by legitimate authority, waged in self-defense or to establish/restore justice, and fought to bring about peace.

WEB POLL
Just War?

Despite all the precedent and new initiatives related to *jus ad bellum*, it remains, like many points of law, less than fully precise, especially in the abstract. Therefore, it is worthwhile to examine a specific case, the U.S.- and British-led invasion of Iraq in 2003, to explore the intricacies of *jus ad bellum* (Rodin, 2005). To find that Washington and London conducted a just war, the answer must be "yes" to all of the following questions:

Was the war the last resort? President George W. Bush argued it was. He told Americans, "For more than a decade, the United States and other nations have pursued patient and honorable efforts to disarm the Iraqi regime without war. . . . Every measure has been taken to avoid war."[9] President Jacques Chirac of France disagreed. He told reporters that he believed the "disarmament" of Iraq could "be done in a peaceful way," and that "War is always the worst of solutions. It's always a failure. . . . Everything should be done to avoid it."[10]

Was the U.S./U.K. action taken under legitimate authority? The United States made a legal argument that the authority to act did exist from the UN under earlier

Security Council resolutions. As President Bush put it, "the Security Council did act in the early 1990s. Under Resolutions 678 and 687—both still in effect—the United States and our allies are authorized to use force in ridding Iraq of weapons of mass destruction." Taking an opposing view, Secretary-General Annan declared just before the war that if "action is taken without the authority of the Security Council, the legitimacy and support for any such action will be seriously impaired."[11]

Was the war waged in self-defense or to promote justice? Bush argued that the Untied States was threatened by the possibility that Iraq might give weapons of mass destruction (WMDs) to terrorists or someday use them itself. "The danger is clear," the president proclaimed, that the "United States has the sovereign authority to use force in assuring its own national security," and that "before it is too late to act, this danger will be removed." A statement issued by the heads of 60 Christian organizations disagreed. Explaining the group's position, Episcopal Bishop John B. Shane argued that just war theory differentiates between "anticipatory self-defense, which is morally justified, and preventive war, which is morally prohibited." In the case of Iraq, he continued, "I don't see the threat from Iraq to the United States as an imminent threat, so . . . military action against Iraq is inappropriate."[12]

Was the war fought to bring about peace? Here again, President Bush argued "yes." He told Americans, "The cause of peace requires all free nations . . . to work to advance liberty and peace" in the Persian Gulf region. Taking a very different view of U.S. motives, one Middle East analyst contended that the U.S. invasion of Iraq "has to do with oil and to do with empire—getting control of Iraq's enormous oil resources." The analyst then explained her belief that the motive was "not just about importing oil to the United States." Instead, "The issue is control, undermining OPEC [Organization of Petroleum-Exporting States], and controlling access to oil for Germany, Japan, and the rest of Europe. This would give the United States tremendous political and economic clout in the rest of the world."[13]

When thinking about *jus ad bellum* and Iraq, fairness requires that you not apply 20-20 hindsight. If, in domestic law, a police office shoots someone, the issue is whether the officer had reasonable cause to think that the individual presented a clear and present danger of injury or death to the officer. Whether that was ultimately true is not the standard. In the same way, the fact that WMDs were never found is not applicable to determining whether President Bush and Prime Minister Tony Blair reasonably believed that a significant and imminent threat existed. In the same way, it is their intentions at the onset of the war, not the success or failure of the postwar occupation of Iraq in bringing about justice and peace that is the standard to apply.

This woman demonstrating in New York City's Times Square in 2003 clearly feels that war with Iraq is justified. Do you agree after reading the section of this chapter on *jus ad bellum,* the just cause of war?

Web Link

The U.S. legal case for the Iraq war is in a State Department paper, "Decade of Defiance" (6/12/02), at **www.state.gov/ p/nea/rls/13456.htm**. An Australian government agency takes the opposite view, in "'Disarming' Iraq under International Law" (2/26,03) at **www.aph .gov.au/library/pubs/cib/ 2002-03/03cib16.htm**.

Just Conduct of War

In the realm of *jus in bello,* there are some clear guidelines about what is unacceptable. The Hague Conferences (1899, 1907) and the Geneva Conventions of 1949 set down some rules regarding impermissible weapons, the treatment of prisoners, and other matters. Other treaties have banned the possession and use of biological and chemical weapons, and the ICJ has ruled that in most circumstances the use of nuclear weapons would be illegal. Most recently, the treaty establishing the International Criminal Court includes an extensive list of actions that constitute war crimes.

Still, many uncertainties exist about *jus in bello*. The treatment of prisoners provides one example. There is no dispute that U.S. military personnel and perhaps CIA operatives as well violated those standards in their egregious abuse of Iraqi prisoners of war at Abu Ghraib Prison and elsewhere in Iraq. But there is less clarity about whether the provision of the Geneva Conventions relating to the treatment of prisoners of war is applicable to the status of irregular Iraqi "fedayeen" forces that fought in the war and a small number of non-Iraqi mujahedin combatants. Similar questions relate to Taliban and al Qaeda fighters captured by the United States in Afghanistan and held at the U.S. naval base at Guantánamo Bay, Cuba. The U.S. administration eventually took the position that Taliban prisoners were subject to the Geneva Conventions' provisions, but that al Qaeda members were "enemy combatants," not prisoners of war, on the grounds that they were not members of a national military organization. As such, al Qaeda prisoners can be tried by military courts, and they do not have the protection of the Geneva Conventions or many of the rights accorded U.S. citizens and foreigners tried in U.S. civilian courts.

Another uncertainty about *jus in bello* involves how to gauge proportionality. Almost everyone would agree, for instance, that France, Great Britain, and the United States would not have been justified in using their nuclear weapons against Yugoslavia in 1999 to force it to withdraw from Kosovo or against Afghanistan in 2001 for refusing to surrender the al Qaeda terrorists. But what if Iraq had used chemical weapons against the forces of those three countries during the Persian Gulf War in 1991 or against U.S. and British forces in 2003? Would they have been justified if they had retaliated with nuclear weapons? Some people even argue that using nuclear weapons under any conditions would violate the rule of discrimination and would thus be unjust.

The *jus in bello* standard of discrimination also involves matters of degree rather than clear lines. There was heavy bombing, some of it in urban areas, during the invasion of Iraq. American officials went to great lengths to give assurances that all efforts were being made to avoid unnecessary civilian casualties. For example, Secretary of Defense Donald H. Rumsfeld told reporters, "The targeting capabilities and the care that goes into targeting, to see that the precise targets are struck and other targets are not struck is as impressive as anything anyone could see—the care that goes into it, the humanity that goes into it."[14] Others disagreed. One survey of people in 20 countries found that an average of 60% did not believe the United States tried hard enough to avoid civilian casualties, compared to 35% who believed that it did, and 5% who were unsure. As detailed in Figure 9.2, 82% of Americans thought that their country had tried very hard to avoid killing and wounding civilians, and a majority of people in 7 other countries agreed. But in the other 12 countries, a plurality or majority of respondents disagreed. As this discussion illustrates, the law and justice of war remain highly controversial. Most observers would support neither of the two polar views: (1) that the United States could not be held responsible no matter what the level of civilian casualties; (2) that knowingly taking actions that would kill any civilians violates the standards of *jus in bello*. It is, however, easier to question two extreme views than to clearly demarcate the dividing line between what is just and unjust.

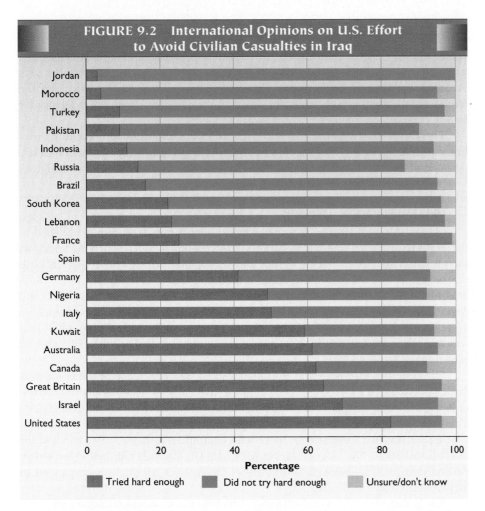

FIGURE 9.2   International Opinions on U.S. Effort to Avoid Civilian Casualties in Iraq

Legend: Tried hard enough | Did not try hard enough | Unsure/don't know

The Bush administration said, and most Americans agreed, that U.S. forces were trying very hard to avoid civilian casualties during the aerial and ground campaigns against Iraq in 2003. More often than not, respondents in Israel, Great Britain, Canada, Australia, Kuwait, Italy, and Nigeria agreed with that assessment, but a plurality or majority of the other 12 countries where the survey was taken did not think the U.S. campaign had taken sufficient care to avoid killing and wounding civilians.

Data source: The Pew Research Center for People and the Press, "Views of a Changing World," June 2003.

Applying International Law and Justice to Individuals

International law has begun recently to deal with the actions of individuals. A series of precedents in the 20th century marked this change. It is possible to divide these developments into three topics: post–World War II tribunals, current international tribunals, and the International Criminal Court.

Post–World War II Tribunals

The first modern instances of individuals being charged with crimes under international law came in the aftermath of the horrors of World War II. In the Nuremberg and Tokyo war crimes trials, German and Japanese military and civilian leaders were tried for waging aggressive war, for war crimes, and for crimes against humanity.

ANALYZE THE ISSUE
Nuremberg Trials

Nineteen Germans were convicted at Nuremberg; 12 were sentenced to death. Similar fates awaited convicted Japanese war criminals. Seven were hanged. Many Germans and Japanese also went to prison. Some important precedents were established. One was that those who ordered criminal acts or under whose command the acts occurred were just as liable to punishment as those who actually carried out the crimes. Another important precedent was that obeying orders was not a defense for having committed atrocities.

There were efforts in the UN as early as 1948 to establish a permanent international tribunal to deal with genocide and other criminal affronts to humankind. Little came of the effort, however, and there were no subsequent war crimes tribunals for almost the next half-century.

Current International Tribunals

After languishing for nearly 50 years, international tribunals were reestablished in the 1990s to deal with criminal violations of international law. The driving force was the atrocities that occurred in Bosnia and in Rwanda during the 1990s. In both places, people on all sides were abused, injured, and killed; in Bosnia it was the Muslims who were the principal victims and the Serbs who inflicted the most death and degradation between 1990 and 1995. In Rwanda the Hutus were the murderous aggressors in 1994 and the Tutsis the victims of genocide in a ghastly slaughter that was recently revisited in the 2004 film *Hotel Rwanda* and the 2005 HBO special *Sometimes in April*.

The atrocities in Bosnia and Rwanda shocked the conscience of the world and made it obvious, as a former UN official put it, that "a person stands a better chance of being tried and judged for killing one human being than for killing 100,000."[15] This jarring reality led to the establishment in 1994 of a tribunal for Bosnia and another for Rwanda to prosecute those who committed atrocities. The tribunal for the Balkans sits in The Hague, the Netherlands. The Rwanda tribunal is located in Arusha, Tanzania. In 1999, the authority of the Balkans tribunal was expanded to include war crimes in Kosovo.

The Hague tribunal has indicted over 150 individuals as war criminals, and 95% of them have been arrested. Charges have been dropped for about 10% of the accused. Of those whose trials were completed by mid-2005, 90% have been convicted of committing crimes such as genocide, murder, rape, and torture. Sentences have ranged up to 40 years in prison, and the convicted war criminals have been transferred from their cells in the Netherlands to other countries in Europe to serve their time (Kerr, 2004).

The most important of the trials in The Hague began in 2001 against Slobodan Milosevic, the former president of Yugoslavia, who was extradited to The Hague to stand trial for crimes against Bosnian Muslims and Croats in the early 1990s and against Muslim Kosovars in the late1990s. Milosevic declared both the court and the indictment illegal, telling the court, "The whole world knows this is a political trial."[16] Unfazed, the court entered not guilty pleas to all charges, and the prosecutors began presenting their case in February 2002 in a trial that is still continuing in 2005.

The Rwanda tribunal has made headway more slowly than its counterpart in The Hague, but it became the first international tribunal since the Tokyo War Crimes trials after World War II to punish a head of government when former Rwandan Prime Minister Jean Kambanda pleaded guilty to genocide and was sentenced to life in prison. Through mid-2005, the tribunal has completed the trials of 25 individuals, almost all of whom were convicted, and was trying another 25 people. Hutu civilian and military leaders have made up most, but not all, of the convicted and accused.

Web Link

Links to documents of the Nuremburg trials and to such related sites as the U.S. Holocaust Memorial Museum are available on Yale University's Web site at **www.yale.edu/ lawweb/avalon/imt/imt.htm.**

For instance, a Belgian-born Italian citizen, Georges Henry Joseph Ruggiu, who was a radio journalist in Rwanda, was sentenced to 12 years in prison for inciting genocide. Among the many other chilling calls to mayhem he broadcast in 1994: "You [Tutsi] cockroaches must know you are made of flesh. . . . We will kill you."[17]

Following a somewhat different pattern, a joint UN-Sierra Leone tribunal was established in 2002 to deal with war crimes that occurred in the civil war in Sierra Leone beginning in 1996. In that afflicted country, rebels killed and mutilated many thousands of noncombatants in an attempt to terrorize the population. The rebels' favorite gruesome tactic was to hack off part of one or more of their victims' limbs so that the maimed individuals would serve as living reminders not to oppose the Revolutionary United Front (RUF). By mid-2005, 13 individuals from the RUF and other militia forces had been indicted and 11 of them were in custody. The tribunal has also indicted former Liberian President Charles Taylor on charges of aiding the RUF. He is in exile in Nigeria; its government may surrender him to the tribunal or send him back to Liberia to face trial in that country's courts (Romano, Nollkaemper, & Kleffner, 2005).

Yet another joint tribunal, this time linking the UN and Cambodia, began to finally get under way in 2005 after countries pledged sufficient funds for its operation. It is intended to prosecute members of Cambodia's former Khmer Rouge regime for the deaths of approximately 1.7 million people (about 25% of the population) during its reign of terror (1975–1979). Whether the tribunal will achieve any success amid the complexities of Cambodian politics is uncertain.

The increasing application of international law to individuals, as well as countries, is captured in this picture of Jean-Paul Akayesu, handcuffed and surrounded by UN security personnel, as he arrives for his trial at the International Criminal Tribunal for Rwanda. A former mayor, Akayesu was charged with leading a massacre of 2,000 people and other crimes in 1994 during the violence in which Hutus slaughtered hundreds of thousands of Tutsis. The court convicted Akayesu of nine counts of genocide, inciting mass rape, and other crimes against humanity and sentenced him to life in prison, which he is serving in Mali.

The International Criminal Court

The advent of ad hoc international tribunals has put war criminals at peril. But the world has also begun to recognize, as President Clinton said, that "the signal will come across even more loudly and clearly if nations all around the world . . . establish a permanent international court to prosecute . . . serious violations of humanitarian law."[18] To that end, the UN convened a global conference in 1998 to create a permanent International Criminal Court (ICC). During the conference, most countries favored establishing a court with broad and independent jurisdiction. Secretary-General Annan agreed, calling on the delegates in Rome to "not flinch from creating a court strong and independent enough to carry out its tasks. It must be an instrument of justice, not expediency."[19]

Some countries, including the United States, wanted a much weaker ICC. The crux of U.S. opposition to a strong ICC was the fear that U.S. leaders and military personnel might become targets of politically motivated prosecutions. "The reality is that the United States is a global military power and presence. . . . We have to be careful that it does not open up opportunities for endless frivolous complaints to be lodged against the United States as a global military power," explained the U.S. delegate to the talks.[20] The U.S. stand drew strong criticism. For one, an Italian diplomat expressed disbelief "that a major democracy . . . would want to have an image of insisting that its soldiers be given license never to be investigated."[21]

Web Link

The Cambodian Master Performers Program supports the revival of the traditional art forms of Cambodia that were largely destroyed by the Khmer Rouge. You can view its Web site at **www.cambodianmasters.org.**

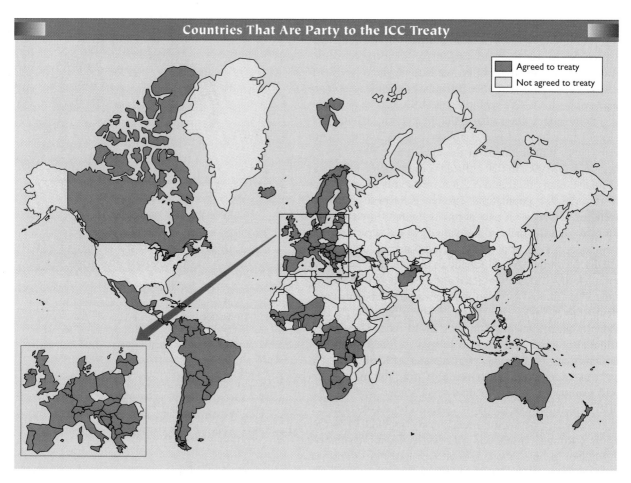

Countries That Are Party to the ICC Treaty

Agreed to treaty
Not agreed to treaty

When Mexico's Senate unanimously ratified the ICC Treaty in May 2005, their country became the 100th party to agree to the treaty.

MAP
Countries That are Party to the ICC Treaty

In the end, some of the reservations of the United States and some other countries were met, but over 80% of the 148 countries attending voted to create a relatively strong court. The treaty gives the ICC jurisdiction over wars of aggression, genocide, and numerous "widespread and systematic" crimes committed as part of "state, organization, or group policy" during international and internal wars. National courts remain the first point of justice, and the ICC is authorized to try cases only when countries fail to do so. The UN Security Council can delay a prosecution for a year, but the vote to delay or proceed is not subject to veto (Broomhall, 2004).

The ICC treaty became operational in 2002 after 60 countries had adhered to it, and by mid-2005 the number of ratifications stood at 100. The creation of the court means, French President Jacques Chirac commented, that "starting now, all those who might be inclined to engage in the madness of genocide or crimes against humanity will know that nothing will be able to prevent justice."[22] The countries that had adhered to the ICC treaty met in 2003 and elected the court's 18 judges, including Canada's Philippe Kirsch as the president of the court, and the ICC's chief prosecutor, Luis Moreno-Ocampo of Argentina. The court began to operate the following year. Several African countries filed complaints with the ICC in 2004 and 2005 alleging atrocities by various forces in the long and gruesome fighting in the central

The newly formed International Criminal Court has begun its first investigations. One of these, on a complaint by Uganda, is against rebels operating in that country and allegedly committing numerous atrocities, including wounding this young boy with a machete during an attack on his village.

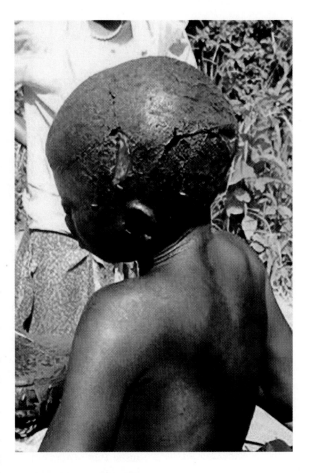

African area that encompasses parts of the Democratic Republic of Congo, Uganda, Sudan, and the Central African Republic, and the ICC prosecutor has launched an investigation. ICC prosecutors began a second investigation in 2005 after the Security Council asked the ICC to address alleged criminal acts committed in the civil war afflicting the Darfur region of Sudan.

There is little doubt that the creation of the ICC represents an important step in the advance of international law. Still, it is not clear how effective it will be. Germany, France, Great Britain, South Korea, Brazil, and a number of other notable countries have ratified the ICC treaty, but the United States, China, Russia, India, Japan, and some other important states have not. The United States remains staunchly opposed. President Clinton signed the treaty for technical reasons, but declined to submit it to the Senate for ratification unless revisions were made. His successor, President Bush, has even stronger reservations, and in 2002 he directed the State Department to inform the UN that the United States "does not intend to become a party to the [ICC treaty]" and "has no legal obligations arising from its signature (to the treaty)."[23] In another action, the president threatened to veto all UN peacekeeping operations unless the Security Council exempted U.S. troops from possible prosecution by the ICC. This issue has been resolved for now by a series of one-year exemptions from prosecution by the ICC that the Security Council has given to U.S. peacekeepers. The Bush administration has also negotiated bilateral agreements with dozens of countries, including some of those who have ratified the ICC treaty, agreeing that neither country will surrender the other's citizens to the ICC for prosecution.

Given its hegemonic role in the international system, the U.S. position on the court is sure to be important—perhaps critical to its success (Ralph, 2005). Little change is likely while President Bush is in office. Most Americans also oppose having U.S. troops subject to trial by the ICC. This is evident in Figure 9.3 comparing American attitudes on this question with those of people in several other countries. But some observers are optimistic about the U.S. stance in the long run. For one, the ICC's chief judge, Philippe Kirsch, predicts, "In the end, this court is going to become universal. It will not happen overnight. I think it may take a few decades to reach universality, but I believe it is only a question of time."[24] Perhaps Judge Kirsch is correct and American attitudes will eventually change. Most movie viewers probably supported the idea of sending the odious dictator of the fictional country Matoba to the ICC for prosecution in the 2005 film *The Interpreter,* starring Nicole Kidman and Sean Penn, and perhaps in time the ICC will seem less threatening. Even the Bush administration relented just a bit when in 2005 it abstained rather than vetoed the Security Council resolution that referred the situation in Darfur to the ICC for investigation and possible prosecution.

JOIN THE DEBATE
The International Criminal Court: To Ratify or Not to Ratify—That is the Question

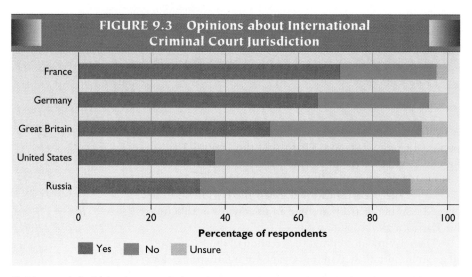

FIGURE 9.3 Opinions about International Criminal Court Jurisdiction

Opinions varied widely when people in various countries were asked whether they would agree to their soldiers being subject to the jurisdiction of the International Criminal Court. French citizens were the most willing to see that happen; Russians were the least favorable.

Note: The question asked was: In your opinion, should the International Criminal Court be allowed to try [your country's] soldiers accused of war crimes if [your country's] government refuses to try them, or not?
Data source: The Pew Research Center for People and the Press, "Views of a Changing World," June 2003.

The Pragmatic Application of Law and Justice

In a perfect world, everyone would promote justice, act morally, obey the law, and insist that others conduct themselves in the same way. Moreover, what is legal, just, and moral and what is not would be clear. Finally, our choices would always be between good and evil, not, as usually occurs, between relative degrees of good or of evil. In our imperfect world, standards and choices are often much murkier, which leads to several questions regarding the prudence of applying standards of law, justice, and morality.

Can ends justify means? One conundrum is whether an act that by itself is evil can be justified if it is done for a good cause. Some believe that ends never justify means. The philosopher Immanuel Kant took a position of **moral absolutism** in his *Groundwork on the Metaphysics of Morals* (1785) and argued that ends never justify means. He therefore urged us to "do what is right though the world should perish."

Others disagree and argue that faced with complex choices, lofty goals do sometimes justify acts that most people consider morally abhorrent in the abstract. Terrorism is a case in point. For example, the Middle East terrorist group Hamas justifies suicide bombings against Israeli civilians on the grounds that the "heroic martyrdom operations . . . represent the sole weapon" available to the Palestinian people. The statement goes on to argue that "denying the Palestinian people the right of self-defense and describing this as terrorism, which should have been linked with the occupation [of Palestinian lands by Israel], violates all laws and norms which granted the people the right of self-defense" and that "considering the Palestinian resistance as a terrorist act and an outlaw legitimizes occupation because it delegitimizes its resistance."[25]

On the other side are potential victims of terrorism who debate whether torturing terrorists to learn about and abort planned attacks is justified. The 1998 film *The Siege* took the moral position that FBI agent "Hub" Hubbard (Denzel Washington) was the hero when he arrested General William Deveraux (Bruce Willis) for torturing a suspected terrorist to death in an effort to gain information about other terrorist cells in a besieged New York City. But Americans are not so sure who was right, as a 2005 poll revealed. It found that only 27% of them responded that torture was "never justified." By contrast, a strong majority thought torture was justified: "often" (15%), "sometimes" (30%), or at least "rarely" (24%).[26]

In practice, the primitive international political system can make the strict application of strong moral principles, adherence to international law, and other such altruistic acts unwise and even dangerous. Clearly, most of us do not take such an absolute position. Nor do we practice **amorality**. Instead, most people adhere to **moral relativism**. They believe that actions must be placed in context. For example, most Americans explicitly or implicitly accept capital punishment and the atomic bombings of Hiroshima and Nagasaki as somehow justified as retaliation or even as an unfortunate necessity to a better end. The problem, again, is where to draw the line. That problem is presented to you in the box, "Would You Kill This Baby?" on page 294.

Should we judge others by our own standards? The issue about whether to judge others rests on two controversies. The first, which we have already addressed, is whether one should apply standards of international law and justice given the divergent values of a multicultural world. Some claim that doing so is cultural imperialism; others believe that at least some universal standards exist.

A second objection to any country or even the UN imposing sanctions or taking other action against a country for committing supposedly illegal, unjust, or immoral acts is that it violates the sovereignty of the target country. Americans overwhelmingly supported sanctions and even war against Iraq for its invasion of Kuwait in 1990. Most Americans would have been outraged over the violation of U.S. sovereignty, however, had the UN imposed sanctions on the United States for what many, perhaps most people around the world considered the illegal U.S. invasion of Iraq in 2003. A third concern stems from what one might call "selective interventions." The United States has intervened in Haiti and Iraq at least partly in the name of democracy, yet in 1990 it sent its forces to defend Saudi Arabia and liberate Kuwait, both of which are ruled by distinctly undemocratic monarchies. Strong U.S. sanctions exist against communist Cuba, but U.S. trade with communist China is booming. Such selective interventions lead to a fourth concern: the suspicion that the invocation of international law and justice is often a smokescreen to cover old-fashioned imperialist intentions (Welsh, 2004; Orford, 2003).

Is it pragmatic to apply standards of legality and justice? Another objection to trying to apply moral principles is based on self-interest. Realists maintain that national interest sometimes precludes the application of otherwise laudable moral principles. They further contend that trying to uphold abstract standards of justice casts a leader as a perpetual Don Quixote, a pseudo knight-errant whose wish "To dream the impossible dream; to fight the unbeatable foe; . . . [and] to right the unrightable wrong," while appealing romantically, is delusional and perhaps dangerous. One danger is that you waste your reputation, your wealth, and the lives of your soldiers trying to do the impossible. A second peril springs from the reality that since not all states act morally, those who do are at a disadvantage: "Nice guys finish last."

Those who disagree with this line of reasoning contend that it fails the test of courageously standing up for what is right. They might even recall the remonstration of President John F. Kennedy, who, evoking Dante Alighieri's *The Divine Comedy* (1321), commented, "Dante once said that the hottest places in hell are reserved for those who in a period of moral crisis maintain their neutrality."[27] More pragmatically, advocates of applying principles of law and justice contend that greater justice is necessary for world survival. This argument deals, for example, with resource

Did You Know That:

A 2002 U.S. Justice Department memo relating to the treatment of terrorist suspects argued, "For an act to constitute torture as defined [in U.S. law] it must inflict pain . . . equivalent in intensity to the pain accompanying serious physical injury, such as organ failure, impairment of bodily function, or even death."

WRITE THE POLICY SCRIPT

Would You Kill This Baby?

Here is a chance for you to rewrite the script and change the future. The setting is Braunau, Austria. The address is 219 Salzberger Vorstadt in a building known as the Gasthof zum Pommer. There, on Easter Sunday, April 20, 1889, a child was born. It is a year later, and you have been transported back to that time and are standing in the room with the baby boy. You are contemplating whether to kill him. If you do, you will be immediately transported back to the 21st century and will be beyond the reach of the Austrian police.

The infant is Adolf Hitler, the fourth child of Alois Schickelgruber and Klara Hitler. He is a normal, cute baby, as you can see in the accompanying picture. His parents love him, and their neighbors think he is adorable. Unlike anyone in Braunau or indeed the world in 1890, however, you know what the future holds. Baby Adolf will grow up to be the führer of Nazi Germany. His Third Reich will be responsible for the horrors of World War II and the genocidal acts against Europe's Jews, Gypsies, and others. You know that he will die by his own hand on April 29, 1945, in a bunker in Berlin. But by then it will be too late. Tens of millions of people will have died in the war in Europe, and 6 million Jews and other people deemed undesirable will have perished in death camps. Should you kill the baby now?

All this may seem macabre, but the point is to struggle with whether the laudable ends sometimes justify distressing means. A moral absolutist would not kill young Hitler. Someone who is amoral would have no qualms about doing it. However, most people, probably including you, are moral relativists who make moral decisions in a context. Complicating the decision even further, the world drama is partly an improvisational play. So in a caution much like *Star Trek*'s "prime directive," interfering with the future is risky because you cannot be absolutely sure of what will occur in the 1930s and the first half of the 1940s if there is a simple marker reading "Adolf Hitler, 1889–1890" at the resting place in Braunau. Perhaps the Holocaust and World War II will never occur. Or perhaps a different German führer will come to power, one who is smart enough to defeat Great Britain before attacking Russia, to not declare war on the

United States in 1941, to focus on developing an atomic bomb, and to ultimately win World War II.

What Do You Think?
Should you rewrite the script of history by taking a pillow and smothering baby Adolf?

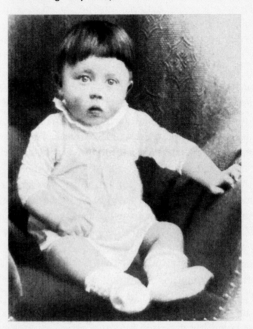

Would you kill this baby? Imagine you have been transported back to early 1890 and you are standing just out of this picture. No one but you and the child are present. The baby in this picture is Adolf Hitler, about a year after his birth on April 20, 1889, in Braunau, Austria. Given your knowledge of the horrors of World War II and the Holocaust, would you kill baby Adolf? Would the end justify the means? This and other issues are raised if one attempts to apply moral standards to the formation and conduct of foreign policy.

distribution. It contends that it is unjust to support a system in which a large part of the world remains both impoverished and without self-development possibilities. The inevitable result, according to this view, will be a world crisis that will destroy order as countries fight for every declining resource.

One way out of the dilemma about when and to what degree law, justice, and other principles should apply to foreign policy may be to begin with the observation that it is not necessary to choose between moral absolutism and amorality. Instead, there is a middle ground of moral relativism that relies on **moral pragmatism** as a guiding principle. There is a secular prayer that asks for the courage to change the wrongs one can, the patience to accept the wrongs that one cannot change, and the wisdom to know the difference. From this perspective, a decision maker must ask, first, whether any tangible good is likely to result from a course of action and, second, whether the good will outweigh negative collateral consequences. By the first standard, taking high-flown principled stands when it is impossible or unlikely that you will affect the situation is quixotic. By the second standard, applying standards of justice when the overall consequences will be vastly more negative also fails the test of prudence. But not taking action when change is possible and when the good will outweigh the bad fails the test of just behavior.

The Future of International Law and Justice

The often anarchic and inequitable world makes it easy to dismiss idealistic talk of conducting international relations according to standards of international law and justice. This view, however, was probably never valid and certainly is not true now. An irreversible trend in world affairs is the rapid growth of transnational interaction among states and people. As these interactions have grown, so has the need for regularized behavior and for rules to prescribe that behavior. For very pragmatic reasons, then, many people have come to believe, as one analyst notes, that "most issues of transnational concern are best addressed through legal frameworks that render the behavior of global actors more predictable and induce compliance from potential or actual violators" (Ratner, 1998:78). The growth of these rules in functional international interactions has been on the leading edge of the development of international law. Advances in political and military areas have been slower, but here too there has been progress. Thus, as with the United Nations, the pessimist may decry the glass as less than half full, whereas, in reality, it is encouraging that there is more and more water in the previously almost empty glass.

All the signs point to increasing respect for international law and a greater emphasis on adhering to at least rudimentary standards of justice. Violations of international standards are now more likely to draw criticism from the world community. It is probable, therefore, that international law will continue to develop and to expand its areas of application. So too will moral discourse have an increasing impact on the actions of the international actors. There will certainly be areas where growth is painfully slow. A particular barrier is the change in the U.S. attitude from being a champion of international law and legal institutions after World War II to being a skeptic today (Murphy, 2004). There will also be those who violate the principles of law and justice and who sometimes get away with their unlawful and unjust acts. But, just as surely, there will be progress.

Chapter Summary

Fundamentals of International Law and Justice

1. International law can be best understood as a primitive system of law in comparison with more developed domestic law. There are only the most rudimentary procedures and institutions for making, adjudicating, and enforcing international law. This does not mean, however, that international law is impotent, only that it is in an earlier stage of development than domestic law.

2. As a developing phenomenon, international law is dynamic and has been growing since the earliest periods of civilization. This growth accelerated in the 20th century because increasing levels of international interaction and interdependence required many new rules to govern and regularize contacts in trade, finance, travel, communication, and other areas. The possible consequences of war have also spurred the development of international law.

3. Thus far, international law is most effective when it governs functional international relations. International law works least well in areas of "high politics," where the vital interests of the sovereign states are at stake. Even in those areas, though, international law is gradually becoming more effective.

4. Justice is another factor in establishing the rules of the international system. It acts as a guide to action and as the basis for some international law.

The International Legal System

5. The international legal system has four essential elements: its philosophical roots, lawmaking, adherence, and adjudication.

6. The roots of law for any legal system may come from external sources, such as natural law, or from within the society, such as custom.

7. Regarding lawmaking, international law springs from a number of sources, including international treaties, international custom, general principles of law, and international representative assemblies. Some scholars argue that resolutions and other pronouncements of the UN General Assembly should be included as a significant influence.

8. Regarding adherence, international law, again like primitive law, relies mainly on voluntary compliance and self-help. Here again, though, there are early and still uncertain examples of enforcement by third parties, a feature that characterizes more advanced systems.

9. The fourth essential element of a legal system, adjudication, is also in the primitive stage in international law. Although there are a number of international courts in the world today, their jurisdiction and their use and effectiveness are limited. The International Court of Justice and other such international judicial bodies represent an increasing sophistication of international law.

Applying International Law and Justice

10. In a culturally diverse world, standards of international law and justice have encountered problems of fit with different cultures. Most current international law and many concepts of justice, such as the stress on individualism, are based on Western ideas and practices, and many non-Western states object to certain aspects of international law as it exists.

11. The changes in the world system in this century have created a number of important issues related to international law. Among these are the status of sovereignty, the legality of war and the conduct of war, rules for governing the biosphere, and observing and protecting human rights.

12. International law has been interpreted as applying to states. Now it is also concerned with individuals. Primarily, it applies to the treatment of individuals by states, but it also has some application to the actions of individuals. Thus people, as well as countries, are coming to have obligations, as well as rights, under international law.

13. It is not always possible to insist on strict adherence to international law and to high moral standards, yet they cannot be ignored. One middle way is to apply principles pragmatically.

The Future of International Law and Justice

14. With the growth of international interaction in the last century, international law has developed, and rudimentary standards of justice are being established. Although this growth has sometimes been slow, there will definitely be continued progress in the future.

For simulations, debates, and other interactive activities, a chapter quiz, Web links, PowerWeb articles, and much more, visit **www.mhhe.com/rourke11/** and go to chapter 9. Or, while accessing the site, click on Course-Related Headlines and view recent international relations articles in the *New York Times*.

Online *Learning*Center with POWERWEB

Key Terms

adjudication
amorality
codify
functional relations

ideological/theological
    school of law
International Court of
    Justice (ICJ)

jus ad bellum
jus in bello
moral absolutism
moral pragmatism

moral relativism
naturalist school of law
pacta sunt servanda
positivist school of law

National Security: The Traditional Road

Be wary then; best safety lies in fear.
—William Shakespeare, *Hamlet*

Cry "Havoc," and let slip the dogs of war.
—William Shakespeare, *Julius Caesar*

Few would dispute the truth of U.S. Civil War General William Tecumseh Sherman's exclamation, "War is hell!" Yet violence continues to be a regular part of world politics. This chapter explores such topics as why war continues and how political violence is used.

WAR IS AN ENIGMA. On the one hand, we have condemned it throughout history, and that refrain has become particularly persistent in recent centuries (Mueller, 2004). "O war, thou son of hell," Shakespeare has a character cry out in *King Henry VI, Part 2.* "War is hell," General William Tecumseh Sherman lamented, remembering the U.S. Civil War and "the shrieks and groans of the wounded." And General of the Army Dwight D. Eisenhower confessed, "I hate war . . . its brutality, its futility, its stupidity." War may be hell, but it is also a regular part of our political world. Perhaps that is because insecurity has also always been part of the human condition. "We make war that we may live in peace," Aristotle suggested in his *Nicomachean Ethics* (325 B.C.).

In this and the following chapter we will explore the human search for safety and how that relates to accumulating military power as an asset, organizing to use it, and applying it as a political tool. National security, the traditional approach, is the focus of this chapter. It takes up the history and causes of warfare between states and also examines how they amass military power as an asset and use it as a diplomatic tool. Then chapter 11 contemplates international security, an alternative path to safety. As you will see, some people believe that security can be best achieved by disarming, not arming, and that creating collective security forces is a better approach than traditional self-reliance.

WEB POLL
Your Knowledge of History

War and World Politics

Whatever the ultimate cost or morality of war, it is difficult to disagree with the classic observation of scholar Max Weber (1864–1920) that, "The decisive means for politics is violence. Anyone who fails to see this is . . . a political infant" (Porter, 1994:303). Reality compels us, then, to examine military power and to grasp the role that force plays in the conduct of international politics.

War: The Human Record

War is as ancient as humanity (Cioffi-Revilla, 2000). One reasonable number, as shown in Figure 10.1, is that there were almost 1,000 wars during the millennium that just ended. Looking even farther back, it is possible to see that the world has been totally free of significant interstate, colonial, or civil war in only about 1 out of every 12 years in all of recorded human history. The data also shows that war is not a tragic anachronism waged by our less civilized ancestors. To the contrary, political violence continues. Two ways to gauge this are by frequency and severity.

Frequency provides bad news. Over the last ten centuries, as Figure 10.1 shows, wars between countries have become more frequent, with some 30% occurring since 1800. Although the frequency of war in the 1900s declined somewhat from the horrific rate in the 1800s, and that ebbing has continued into the early 21st century, the number of civil wars increased (Eriksson & Wallensteen, 2004). This means that the overall incidence of interstate and intrastate warfare remains relatively steady.

Severity is worse news. Again as evident in Figure 10.1 on page 300, about 150 million people have died during wars since the year 1000. Of the dead, an astounding 75% perished in the 20th century and 89% since 1800. Not only do we kill more soldiers, we also now kill larger numbers of civilians. During World War I, six soldiers died for every civilian killed (8.4 million soldiers and 1.4 million civilians). World War II killed two civilians for every soldier (16.9 million troops and 34.3 million

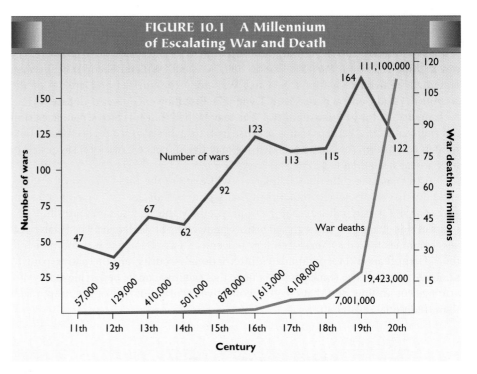

FIGURE 10.1 A Millennium of Escalating War and Death

This figure shows the long-term trend in the rise of both the frequency and severity of war. Beginning in the year 1000, the number of wars in each century has usually increased. The soaring death toll of the 20th century's wars, which accounted for 75 percent of the millennium's total, is a truly alarming figure.

Data sources: Eckhardt (1991); author. Eckhardt defines a war as a conflict that (1) involves a government on at least one side and (2) accounts for at least 1,000 deaths per year of the conflict.

civilians). The worst news may lie ahead. A nuclear war could literally fulfill President John F. Kennedy's warning in 1961 that "mankind must put an end to war, or war will put an end to mankind."

The Causes of War: Three Levels of Analysis

Why war? This question has challenged investigators over the centuries (Caplow & Hicks, 2002). Philosophers, world leaders, and social scientists have advanced many different theories about the single root cause of war, but it is more likely that there is no one reason why people fight. Given this, it is reasonable to discuss the causes of war by classifying them according to system-level analysis, state-level analysis, and individual-level analysis, as detailed in chapter 3.

System-Level Causes of War

Wars may be caused by a number of factors related to the general nature of the world's political system (Cashman, 1999). To illustrate that here, we can touch on four system-level variables.

The distribution of power. As noted in chapters 3 and 8, some analysts believe that the stability of the international system is influenced by factors such as the system's number of poles (big powers), their relative power, and whether the poles and their power are stable or in flux. Conflict is likely to occur, for example, when a system is experiencing a significant power transition because some powers are rising and others are declining. "Great powers are like divas. They enter and exit the stage with great tumult," one analyst observes (Zakaria, 1996:37). Postwar alliances that concentrate power by bringing victorious major countries together have also been found to be "war prone" (Gibler & Vasquez, 1998:805).

The anarchical nature of the system. Some systems analysts argue that wars occur because there is no central authority to try to prevent conflict and to protect countries. Unlike domestic societies, the international society has no effective system of law creation, enforcement, or adjudication. When the gap between U.S. demands on Iraq and what Iraq was willing to do proved unbridgeable, there was no court that could either subpoena Iraqi records or enjoin an American attack. War ensued. This self-help system causes insecurity. Therefore, countries acquire arms in part because other countries do, creating a tension-filled cycle of escalating arms → tensions → arms → tensions.

System-level economic factors. The global pattern of production and use of natural resources is one of the system-level economic factors that can cause conflict. This was evident in 1990 when Iraq endangered the main sources of petroleum production by attacking Kuwait and threatening Saudi Arabia. A U.S-led coalition of countries dependent on petroleum rushed to defend the Saudis and to liberate the Kuwaitis (and their oil). The global gap between wealthy and poor countries is another system-level factor. Some analysts believe that the highly uneven distribution of wealth between countries and regions is one reason that a great deal of terrorism is rooted in the South.

System-level biosphere stress. Overconsumption of biosphere resources is yet another possible system-level cause of conflict. Water provides one example. This basic resource is becoming so precious in many areas that, as you will see in chapter 15, there are growing concerns that countries might soon go to war with one another over disputes about water supplies. "When the empire of man over nature can no longer be easily extended," one scholar writes, "then the only way for one people to increase its standard of living is by redistributing the sources or fruits of industry from others to themselves. The surest way to do this is by extending man's empire over man" (Orme, 1998:165).

State-Level Causes of War

War may result from the very nature of states. There are also several theories of war that have to do with the internal processes and conditions of countries (Finnenmore, 2004).

Militarism. States inherently tend toward militarism, according to some scholars. One writes, "It is impossible to understand the nature of modern politics without considering its military roots" (Porter, 1994:xix). The argument is that as warfare required more soldiers and more increasingly expensive weapons, it created a need for political units with larger populations and economies. This gave rise to the state.

Externalization of internal conflict. A theme found in movies such as *Wag the Dog* (1997, with Robert De Niro and Dustin Hoffman) and *Canadian Bacon* (1995, with Alan Alda and John Candy) is that of a faltering government trying to stay in power by fomenting a foreign crisis in order to rally the populace and divert its attention. Scholars call this ploy diversionary war or the externalization of internal conflict (Meernik & Ault, 2005; Pickering & Kisangani, 2005). Evidence indicates, for instance, that revolutionary regimes will attempt to consolidate their power by

One possible state-level cause of war occurs when a leader who is in political trouble at home tries to divert the country's attention by creating a foreign crisis. In 1998, President Bill Clinton was mired in a scandal involving sexual intimacy with White House intern Monica Lewinsky. After terrorist bombings of U.S. embassies in Kenya and Tanzania by al Qaeda, he ordered a cruise missile attack on a factory in Khartoum, Sudan. Clinton asserted the factory was producing chemical weapons for terrorists and for Iraq. Sudanese officials insisted it made only medicine. The Sudanese women demonstrating in this picture reflect the view that Clinton created an international crisis to divert Americans' attention from his infidelity.

Data source: CNN.com, August 25, 1998.

fomenting tension with other countries (Mitchell & Prins, 2004; Andrade, 2003). It is also the case that countries are more likely to go to war while they are experiencing times of economic distress.

Type of country. There are analysts who believe that some types of countries, because of their political structure (democratic, authoritarian) or their economic resources and wealth, are more aggressive than others. Of particular note, chapter 6 discusses democratic peace theory—the idea that democratic countries are not prone to fighting with one another.

Political culture. Some scholars believe that a nation's political culture is correlated to warlike behavior. No nation has a genetic political character. Nations, however, that have had repeated experiences with violence may develop a political culture that views the world as a hostile environment. It is not necessary for the list to go on to make the point that how states are organized and how they make policy can sometimes lead to conflict and war among them.

Individual-Level Causes of War

It may be that the causes of war are linked to the character of individual leaders or to the nature of the human species. "In the final analysis," one scholar writes, "any contemplation of war must return to . . . the nature of humanity, which yet stands as the root cause of war and the wellspring of history's inestimable tragedy" (Porter, 1994:304).

Human characteristics. Those who have this perspective believe that although it is clear that human behavior is predominantly learned, there are also behavioral links to the primal origins of humans (Rosen, 2004). Territoriality, which we examined in chapter 3, is one such possible instinct, and the fact that territorial disputes are so frequently the cause of war may point to some instinctual territoriality in humans. Another possibility, some social psychologists argue, is that human aggression, individually or collectively, can stem from stress, anxiety, or frustration. The reaction of the German society to its defeat and humiliation after World War I is an example.

Individual leaders' characteristics. The personal traits of leaders may also play a role in war (Bennett & Stam, 2004). One study concludes, "The personalities of the leaders . . . have often been decisive. . . . [Usually] a fatal flaw or character weakness in a leader's personality was of critical importance. . . . [and] spelled the difference between the outbreak of war and the maintenance of peace" (Stoessinger, 1998:210). A leader may have a personality that favors taking risks, when caution might be the better choice, or might have a psychological need for power. While discounting some of the more strident characterizations of Saddam Hussein as a madman, most personality analyses characterize him as driven to seek power and to dominate, traits that made it hard for him to cooperate completely with UN arms inspectors. Individual experiences and emotions also play a role, and it is not fatuous to ask what the impact of Iraq's attempt to assassinate former President George H. W. Bush in 1993 was on his son's view of that country once he became president.

Military Power as an Asset

For good or ill, military power is an asset that often determines whether a country will prevail or not in a heated international dispute. Therefore, it is appropriate to first consider the nature of military power that provides the sword for policy makers to wield.

Amassing and Measuring Military Power

Countries in an anarchical political system that emphasizes self-help have traditionally followed the advice of the early-fifth-century Roman military thinker Flavius Vegetius Renatus, "If you want peace, prepare for war." That preparation has involved amassing military power. It is an asset based on an array of tangible factors, such as numbers of weapons and troops, and intangible factors, such as military morale, leadership, and a country's political reputation.

Military Spending

Defense spending is one of the largest categories in most countries' budgets. Global military spending soared during the cold war, peaking at nearly $1 trillion in 1987. After the end of the cold war, defense spending dropped significantly, bottoming out in 1998 at about $730 billion a year in current dollars (value that year) or under $700 billion in constant dollars (value controlled for inflation, real dollars). Then spending began to rise again and stood in 2003 at $879 billion in constant year 2000 dollars or $949 billion in current dollars. Post-9/11 increases in U.S. defense spending were the largest component of the growth. These changes are depicted in Figure 10.2 on page 304. By another measure, military spending by the world governments equals about 10% of their collective budgets and some 2.5% of the world gross domestic product (GDP). For more details on national budgets see Table 1.1 on page 12.

Within Figure 10.2 it is also worth noting that military spending of the world's economically less developed countries (LDCs) increased steadily during the period. The LDCs spent over $314 billion (current dollars) on their militaries in 2003. The amount was equivalent to almost 5% of their collective GNPs, a percentage that the LDCs especially can ill afford because of their crying needs for spending on economic development, education, and health. A final point worth noting about military spending is that it has increased in some countries and regions much faster than average. During the decade 1994–2003, it grew by over 25% in constant dollars, with China's spiraling arms spending (+143%) being the driving force, followed by India (+51%).

Weapons

Comparison of two countries' or alliances' military might are often focused on number of weapons. Quantity is certainly an important consideration. Knowing that the United States had 16,000 tanks and Iraq had 1,900 tanks prior to their war in 2003 is one indication of the relative power of the two countries' armored forces. Had the

SIMULATION
What Would You Spend
for Security?

MAP
Sizes of Armed Forces

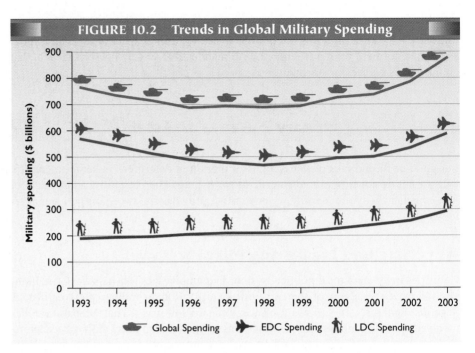

FIGURE 10.2 Trends in Global Military Spending

Global military spending peaked in the late 1980s, declined into the late 1990s, then increased again, reaching $879 billion in constant dollars shown here (or $949 billion in current dollars). Notice that while LDC spending is much lower than that of the EDCs, it grew steadily. Moreover, military spending consumes nearly twice as much of the GDP of the LDCs as it does of the EDCs.

Notes: Expenditures calculated in 2000 dollars. For this chart, EDCs includes the countries of Eastern Europe, including Russia, as well as those of Western Europe, Oceania, the United States, and Canada.
Data source: Stockholm International Peace Research Institute (SIPRI), 2004.

Web Link

The Federation of American Scientists maintains an excellent site with details about American military weaponry at **www.fas .org/man/index.html**. Other countries' systems can be explored by keying "rest of world" in the Search function.

potential combatants been the United States and Russia or China, Moscow's 21,000 tanks or Beijing's 11,000 tanks would have made for a much different military situation.

Numbers are only part of the military weapons equation, however, with quality at least equally important. The quality factor was evident during the U.S. wars against Iraq in 1991 and 2003. Both were showcases for high-tech warfare. For one, Iraq's aging tank force was no match for U.S. main battle tanks capable of maneuvering at nearly highway speeds, using thermal sights and computerized targeting, firing shells coated with depleted uranium that can destroy almost any armored opponent, and clad in depleted uranium armor capable of repelling the shells fired by Iraqi tanks. Even had the number of tanks been substantially in Iraq's favor, it is probable that its vintage Soviet-export tanks would have been overwhelmed by U.S. armor.

For all the advantages of sophisticated weapons, there are drawbacks. An F-22, one of the newest U.S. fighters, is a technological marvel that can defeat any other fighter. Each costs $150 million, though, compared to a less excellent, but still good Russian-built SU-30 fighter, which is available for export at $37 million each. Second, high-tech weapons are often also more difficult to operate and repair. Third, the effectiveness of military hardware is very situational. Therefore, a country's military systems need to be appropriate to the challenges they will face. American technology twice easily overwhelmed the Iraqis in the relatively open terrain near the Persian Gulf but was not able to prevail during the war in densely forested Vietnam against an even less sophisticated opponent than Iraq.

The quality and quantity of a country's weapons are one way of measuring national military power. This photograph shows a convoy of MIAI Abrams tanks of the U.S. 3rd Infantry Division crossing the Euphrates River during the American push into Baghdad in early April 2003. The outcome of the Iraq war was determined in significant part by the wide edge in the number and quality of weapons that U.S. forces enjoyed over Iraqi forces.

Personnel

As with weapons, a number of quantitative and qualitative factors determine the capabilities of a country's military personnel. These include the quantitative size of the force and its training, morale, and leadership.

Number of Troops   There are nearly 20 million men and women in the world's military forces. Generally, size matters. With over a third of the world total, China (2.5 million troops), Russia (1.5 million), the United States (1.4 million) and India (1.3 million) have the military personnel to play a major regional and even global role. By contrast, Belize, with about 1,000 troops, has very little military muscle to use as a diplomatic asset. Sheer size is not, however, the only quantitative factor. The number of troops that a country has must be measured against the scope of their deployments and reasonable estimates of their potential use. For example, the large U.S. force become less dominant when its global commitments are considered. Indeed, U.S. forces have been stretched thin by their deployment in Iraq, requiring an extensive, long-term call-up of reserve units. By comparison, Brazil (288,000 troops) has a force that is concentrated in the home country and is large enough both to defend it against any likely aggressor and to give it important regional sway.

Training   Good training significantly improves the quality of a country's military force. This is especially true given the complicated nature of many of today's high-tech weapons. Pilot training provides one example. Considerable flight time is critical for fighter pilots because of the complex weapons systems they use, but providing practice is costly. Therefore, significant differences in training exist. The countries of the North Atlantic Treaty Organization (NATO) generally meet the alliance's standard of providing fighter pilots with 180 to 200 hours of inflight training annually. Russia's standard is about half of that, but the strains on the country's economy leave its pilots reportedly receiving only about 20 hours a year in the air to hone their skills. In a clash between NATO and Russian air forces, this difference would probably bode ill for Russia's combat aviation forces.

Did You Know That:

The world's smallest army is the Vatican's 110-man Swiss Guard. The original force was formed from Swiss mercenaries who had defended Pope Clement VII during the sacking of Rome in 1527 by, oddly, Charles V, the Holy Roman Emperor.

Morale An army that does not fight with spirit cannot win. Historian Stephen Ambrose, who served as a consultant for Steven Spielberg's 1998 film *Saving Private Ryan,* believed that "in the end success or failure on D-Day [came] down to a relatively small number of junior officers, noncoms, and privates." According to Ambrose, "If the men coming in over the beaches [had] flopped down behind the seawall and refused to advance, if the noncoms and junior officers [had] failed to lead their men up and over the seawall . . . in the face of enemy fire—why, then, the Germans would [have won] the battle and thus the war."[1]

Morale, of course, is not inherent. Russian soldiers fought with amazing valor during World War II despite conditions that, in many cases, were far worse than those that American troops faced. Yet in more recent times, the morale of Russia's soldiers has been sapped by their substandard living and working conditions; they have been poorly paid, housed, equipped, and trained. In the aftermath of the collapse of Iraq's army in 2003, some Russian military experts were worried that a similar fate might await Russia's army in a war. "Go on the street and ask who is ready to defend the motherland, and you will immediately see unpleasant parallels," fretted retired General Andrei Nikolayev, who chairs the defense affairs committee in the lower house of parliament, the State Duma. "The outcome of a war depends on the army's morale."[2]

Leadership Military leadership also plays a significant role for good or ill. There is little doubt that U.S. and British forces would have defeated the Iraqi military in 2003, but Saddam Hussein's practice of placing those most loyal to him, rather than the best officers, in command of his country's armed forces and creating many specialized units instead of a central command helped speed the rapid collapse of Iraq's army. According to one Iraqi colonel, the multiple units, some commanded by Saddam Hussein's sons, were created because "he was afraid the regular army might rise up against him." Added an Iraqi general, "There was no coordination between these armies—they hate[d] each other."[3]

Military Power and Political Reputation

Whatever tangible power a country may possess, its ability to influence others will depend partly on how those others perceive its capacity and will. National leaders commonly believe that weakness tempts their opponents, while a reputation for strength deters them. This has been an issue for the United States in recent decades because some observers believe, as one French general put it, that Americans want "zero-dead wars."[4] The image was formed amid the reluctance of the United States to commit ground forces in the aftermath of the frustrating Vietnam War and was heightened by the U.S. withdrawal in the face of casualties in Lebanon in 1983. The thinking goes that this reputation emboldened U.S. opponents, including perhaps Saddam Hussein, who argued before he invaded Kuwait, "The nature of American society makes it impossible for the United States to bear tens of thousands of casualties."[5]

Subsequent U.S. military responses did little to dispel the image that American public opinion would not tolerate significant U.S. casualties. These events included the month-long air assault on Iraq before U.S. ground forces moved forward in 2001, the U.S. withdrawal from Somalia in 1993 after the loss of troops (depicted in part in the 2001 movie *Blackhawk Down*), and the exclusive use of air power to pound Yugoslavia into submission during the Kosovo crisis in 1999. Because President Bush believed U.S. power was being undermined by the widely held image that Americans were "flaccid" and "wouldn't fight back," he was adamant in 2001 about "putting boots on the ground" (committing ground forces) in Afghanistan.[6] Still, the actual use of U.S. troops was generally limited in favor of using anti-Taliban Afghani forces. Bush again committed ground forces in 2003, but this time the military began its ground operations after a much shorter aerial assault against Iraq than had occurred in 1991. Moreover, while the American public has clearly been distressed by the number of U.S. troops killed and wounded during the war and occupation of Iraq, it has not demanded a U.S. withdrawal. One indication of that was a late-2004 poll that recorded 58% of Americans in favor of keeping U.S. force in Iraq "until civil order is restored there, even if that means continued U.S. military casualties," compared to 39% that supported withdrawal, and 3% who were unsure.[7] Whether this will change foreign doubts about Americans' will to persist in the face of casualties is unclear.

Military Power: The Dangers of Overemphasis

Given the importance of military power as a tool of national defense and diplomacy, it is not uncommon for people to assume that the phrase "too much military power" must be an oxymoron. Exactly how much is enough is a complex question, but it is certain that there are clear dangers associated with overemphasizing military power. Three such perils deserve special mention. They are insecurity, temptation, and expense.

Military power creates insecurity. One result of amassing power is the "spiral of insecurity." Efforts by one country to increase its power to achieve security are frequently perceived by other states as a threat. They then seek to balance power, which the first country sees as threatening, causing it to acquire even more power, and so on ad infinitum, in an escalating spiral. As chapter 11's discussion of disarmament details, the arms races are not automatic. Still, the interaction of one country's power and other countries' insecurity is an important factor in world politics.

Military power creates temptation. A second peril of amassing excess military power is the temptation to use it in a situation that is peripheral to the national interest (Fordham, 2004). The United States went to war in Vietnam despite the fact that President Lyndon Johnson derided it as a "raggedy-ass fourth-rate country." One reason Americans intervened in Vietnam was because of a so-called arrogance of power. Had U.S. military power been more modest, the United States might have emphasized diplomacy or maybe even acquiesced to the reunification of North and South Vietnam. One can never be sure, but it is certain that it is hard to shoot someone if you do not own a gun.

Military power is expensive. A third problem with amassing military power is that it is very expensive. At $2.1 billion, each U.S. B-2 bomber costs more than the entire military budget of two-thirds of the world's countries. In addition to short-term budget

This American demonstrating in Reno, Nevada, in 2005 wants the United States to withdraw its troops from Iraq. Some people argue that Americans have been too quick to withdraw their support from U.S. military operations once casualties begin to mount and that this tendency weakens U.S. power by emboldening its enemies. From this perspective, withdrawing from Iraq before the new Iraqi government is stabilized would further damage U.S. prestige. Do you agree?

The drawing of Uncle Sam reaching beyond his grasp illustrates the view that U.S. power is declining because of "imperial overstretch," whereby the country spends too much on military power in an effort to become and remain a superpower. Other observers argue that any decline that has occurred is the result of overspending on what they see as economically unproductive programs such as care for the elderly. This might be called "social overstretch."

pressure, there is a longer-range concern related to high military spending. A scholar who studied the decline of great powers between 1500 and the 1980s concluded that "imperial overstretch" was the cause of their degeneration (Kennedy, 1988). His **imperial overstretch thesis** is that former superpowers spent so much on military power that, ironically, they weakened their strength by siphoning off resources that should have been devoted to maintaining and improving the country's infrastructure. Kennedy's study did not include the Soviet Union, but it is arguable that the collapse of the USSR followed the pattern of overspending on the military while starving the country's economic core. Declinists warn that the United States is also guilty of imperial overstretch and could go the way of other great powers that rose, dominated, then declined. Indeed, declinists see the Bush Doctrine as hastening a U.S. downturn. "America is marching in the well-trod footsteps of virtually all of the imperial powers of the modern age," one analyst writes. "The Bush rhetoric of preventive war is a disconcerting reflection of the disastrous strategic ideas of those earlier keepers of the imperial order" (Snyder, 2002:2).

The imperial overstretch thesis has many critics (Levey & Brown, 2005). Some argue that far more danger is posed by a "lax Americana" than by any effort to create a "pax Americana." The reasoning, as detailed in chapter 3, is that a U.S. failure to exercise leadership as the hegemon puts the international system in danger of falling into disorder.[8] Similarly, critics of the declinist thesis warn that a rush to peace is only slightly less foolish than a rush to war. One study that reviewed the sharp cuts in U.S. military spending after World War II, the Korean War, and the Vietnam War concluded, "In each case the savings proved only temporary, as declining defense budgets eroded military readiness and necessitated a rush to rearm in the face of new dangers abroad" (Thies, 1998:176).

Critics of Kennedy's thesis also disagree with his analysis of the economic cause of decline. They agree that *overconsumption* (spending that depletes assets faster than the economy can replace them) at the expense of reinvestment (spending that creates infrastructure assets) causes decline. But whereas Kennedy argues that excessive military spending causes overconsumption, his critics say that excessive social spending is the problem. This might be termed the **social overstretch thesis**. "Whether in the form of bread and circuses in the ancient world or medical care for the lower classes and social security for the aged in the modern world," the argument goes, it is social spending on the least economically productive segments of a society that financially drains it (Gilpin, 1981:164). This is especially apt to be true in the United States and other "graying" countries that have increasing segments of their populations reaching retirement age and beginning to consume the equivalents of U.S. Social Security, Medicare, and other programs supporting senior citizens. Consider, for example, Figure 10.3. It shows that since 1960, U.S. military spending has declined while spending on social programs has increased significantly as a percentage of the U.S. budget. It is also the case, however, that U.S. military spending accounts for more than 40% of world military spending. Which, if either, category would you cut to increase spending on education, transportation, communications, and other infrastructure programs?

Applying Military Assets to Diplomacy

War is sometimes a spasm of violence begun by an irrational leader or set off by an emotional reaction. Normally, however, a country's military assets are part of its overall power that can be used directly or indirectly to help the country achieve its diplomatic goals. As German strategist Carl von Clausewitz argued in *On War* (1833): "War is not merely a political act, but also a political instrument, a continuation of political relations, a carrying out of the same by other means." Or as Chinese premier Zhou En Lai reportedly commented in 1954, "War is a continuation of diplomacy by other means."

Applications from Intimidation to Attack

Military power may be applied in several escalating ways. These range from serving as a diplomatic backdrop, through threats, to using military forces to defeat an opponent (Cimballa, 2002; Nathan, 2002). It also should be noted that the options provided by the five levels of violence form a multiple menu. That is, they are often exercised concurrently.

The very existence of significant military power establishes a *diplomatic backdrop* that influences other countries. This is what one U.S. diplomat meant by "Diplomacy without force is like baseball without a bat."[9] Military strength not only deters opponents, it also influences friends and neutrals. One reason the United States has been, and remains, a leader of the West is because massive U.S. conventional and nuclear military power creates a psychological assumption in others that Washington will play a strong role. This reality is what led one U.S. ambassador to China to put a photograph of a U.S. aircraft carrier on his office wall with the caption, "90,000 tons of diplomacy."[10]

Overt threats are the next step up the escalation ladder. That is what President Bush did in his address on March 17, 2003, when he declared, "Saddam Hussein and his sons must leave Iraq within 48 hours. Their refusal to do so will result in military conflict, commenced at a time of our choosing" and that the only way for "Iraqi military units to avoid being attacked and destroyed" was to follow the "clear instructions they would be given by U.S. forces." *Indirect intervention* is a further escalation and includes the use of any of a number of techniques to apply military power while avoiding a commitment of your armed forces to direct combat. One example is supplying arms or providing training and advisers to another government or to a rebel force. Another is conducting covert operations using special military forces, intelligence agents, or mercenaries in another country to conduct clandestine operations.

Limited demonstrations are well up the escalatory ladder. These involve overtly wielding restrained conventional force to intimidate or harass rather than defeat an opponent. On two occasions (1993 and 1996), for example, the United States attacked Iraqi military installations with cruise missiles in retaliation for Baghdad's attempt to assassinate former President Bush, then to pressure Iraq to end military operations against the Kurds in the northern part of Iraq.

Direct action is the most violent application of a country's military assets. It involves using full-scale force to attempt to defeat an opponent. Within this context,

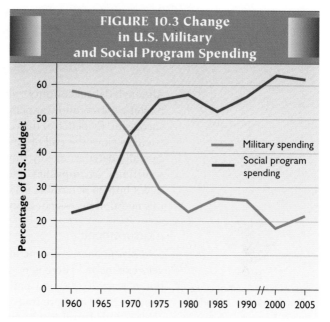

FIGURE 10.3 Change in U.S. Military and Social Program Spending

Many analysts agree that a country's power declines if it does not invest in its infrastructure, but they disagree about what diverts funds from that investment. Imperial overstretch theory argues that defense spending is the drain; social overstretch theory contends that appropriations for welfare, elderly care, and other such programs are sapping the economy. This figure shows the relative changes in U.S. military and social spending, but it does not answer the question of whether either or both are too high, too low, or about right.

Note: The 2005 budget is the president's budget request. Military spending includes spending of the Department of Veterans Affairs.
Data source: U.S. Office of Management and Budget: http://w3.access.gpo.gov/usbudget/fy2004/pdf/spec.pdf.

the level of violence can range from highly constrained conventional conflict, as occurred in Iraq in 2003, to unrestricted nuclear war.

The Effectiveness of Force

Although debate continues about the root cause(s) of war, there is no doubt that one reason weapons and war persist in the international system is that they are sometimes successful. Evidence of the continuing use of force is clear in the map of international conflicts since the end of WW II on pages 312–313. The threat of violence may successfully deter an enemy from attacking you or an ally. The actual use of force also sometimes accomplishes intended goals. Given these realities, we should ask ourselves how to determine if force will be effective by utilitarian standards. Answering this question necessitates looking at measurements and conditions for success.

Measurement

MAP
International Conflicts in the
Post–World War II World

Web Link

An up-to-date calculation of the ongoing cost of the Iraq war and occupation for the United States is available at **http://costofwar** **.com/**.

Cost/benefit analysis is one of two ways of measuring the effectiveness of war. War is very expensive. There is no accurate count of the deaths in the 2003 war with Iraq but at least 20,000 and perhaps as many as 45,000 Iraqi soldiers were killed and another 2,200 or more Iraqi civilians perished. The invading U.S.-led forces had 378 soldiers killed, and that number had risen during the occupation to over 2,800 (90% of whom were Americans) by late 2005. As far as the financial costs, U.S. spending on the war and the subsequent occupation was approaching the $200 billion mark in 2005. Have the results been worth the loss of life, human anguish, and economic destruction? Although such trade-offs are made in reality, it is impossible to arrive at any objective standards that can equate the worth of a human life or political freedom with dollars spent or territory lost.

Goal attainment is the second way to judge the effectiveness of force. Generally, the decision for war is not irrational because leaders usually calculate, accurately or not, their probability of successfully achieving their goals. This calculation is called the "expected utility" of war. In the words of one study, "Initiators [of war] act as predators and are likely to attack [only] target states they know they can defeat" (Gartner & Siverson, 1996:4). By this standard, war does sometimes work. Indeed, the expected utility of force is especially apt to be positive when a major power starts the war. One study found that from 1495 to 1991, great powers that initiated wars won 60% of them (Wang & Ray, 1994). What is more, the initiators' success rate is going up. During the first three centuries (1495–1799), the initiators won 59% of the wars they fought. But during the last two centuries (1800–1991), the success rate increased, with the initiators winning 75% of the wars. Of course, as Miguel de Cervantes noted in *Don Quixote* (ca. 1615), "There is nothing so subject to inconsistency of fortune as war." Leaders often miscalculate and, as Saddam Hussein did in 1990, start a war they ultimately lose. Also, it is sometimes hard to evaluate whether goals were attained. If the U.S. goal in 2003 was to defeat Iraq and topple Saddam Hussein, it certainly succeeded. However, to the extent the goal was to destroy Iraq's weapons of mass destruction (WMDs), the invasion was a failure since they did not exist. Finally, to the degree that the goal was to bring democracy to Iraq, the verdict is still out about whether Iraq's future will be one of democracy or an internal bloodbath as various religious factions fight for power.

Conditions for Success

The next question, then, is: When does force succeed and when does it fail to accomplish its goals? There is no precise answer, but it is possible to synthesize the findings

of a variety of studies and the views of military practition-
ers to arrive at some rudimentary rules for the successful
use of military force, especially in cases of intervention
when a country has not been directly attacked.[11] Note that
these criteria do not guarantee success. They only improve the chances. With that caveat in mind, a country
improves its chances of success during an intervention
when military force is:

1. Used in areas where it has a clearly defined,
   preferably long-standing, and previously demonstrated commitment.
2. Supported firmly and publicly by most of the
   country's leaders.
3. Supported strongly by public opinion.
4. Utilized to defeat other military forces, not to
   control political events.
5. Applied early and decisively, not after extended
   threatening and slow escalation.
6. Meant to achieve clear goals and does not change
   or try to exceed them.

The Changing Nature of War

Warfare has changed greatly over the centuries because of three factors.

Technology has rapidly escalated the ability to kill. Successive "advances" in the
ability to deliver weapons at increasing distances and in the ability to kill ever more
people with a single weapon have resulted in mounting casualties, both absolutely
and as a percentage of soldiers and civilians of the countries at war.

Nationalism has also changed the nature of war. Before the 19th century, wars
were generally fought between the houses of nobles with limited armies. The French
Revolution (1789) changed that. War began to be fought between nations, with
increases in intensity and in numbers involved. France proclaimed that military service was a patriotic duty and instituted the first comprehensive military draft in
1793. The idea of patriotic military service coupled with the draft allowed France's
army to be the first to number more than a million men (Avant, 2000).

As a result of technology and nationalism, the scope of war has expanded. Entire
nations have become increasingly involved in wars. Before 1800, no more than 3 of
1,000 people of a country participated in a war. By World War I, the European powers called 1 of 7 people to arms. Technology increased the need to mobilize the population for industrial production and also increased the capacity for, and the
rationality of, striking at civilians. Nationalism made war a movement of the masses,
increasing their stake and also providing justification for attacking the enemy
nation. Thus, the lines between military and civilian targets have blurred. Modern
technology has, at other times, also reversed the connection between war effort and
the nation (Coker, 2002). The high-tech forces deployed by the United States and its
allies against Iraq (1991, 2003) and Yugoslavia (1995, 1999) and the quick victories
that ensued largely separated the war effort from the day-to-day lives of Americans.

Strategy has also changed. Two concepts, the power to defeat and the power to
hurt, are key here. The **power to defeat** is the ability to seize territory or overcome

One reason that war
continues is because it
sometimes achieves its goals.
The United States wanted to
topple Saddam Hussein, it
chose war to accomplish that
in 2003, and it achieved its
goal, as this photograph
of a U.S. soldier draping
an American flag over the
head of a statue of Saddam
Hussein in Baghdad attests.

International Conflicts in the Post–World War II World

War is a continuing reality in the international system. The conflicts since World War II have been less cataclysmic than that global conflagration, but the ongoing use of force means that the world cannot be sure that World War III does not lie in the future. The possibility of conflict also means that the military instrument is used in many ways, ranging from an intimidating diplomatic backdrop to a full-scale assault on an opponent.

	Conflict[1]	Start Date	Major Belligerent Countries[2] (in alphabetical order)	
1	Palestine	1948	Egypt Iraq Israel	Jordan Lebanon Syria
2	Korean	1950	China North Korea South Korea United Nations: United States and 11 other countries	
3	Soviet-Hungarian	1956	Hungary	Soviet Union
4	Sinai	1956	Egypt France	Israel United Kingdom
5	Sino-Indian	1962	China	India
6	Kashmir	1965	India	Pakistan
7	Vietnam	1965	Australia North Vietnam South Korea	South Vietnam United States
8	Six-Day	1967	Egypt Israel	Jordan Syria
9	Soviet-Czech	1968	Czechoslovakia	Soviet Union
10	Football	1969	El Salvador	Honduras
11	Indo-Pakistani	1971	India	Pakistan
12	Yom Kippur	1973	Egypt Israel	Syria
13	Cyprus	1974	Cyprus	Turkey
14	Ogaden	1977	Ethiopia	Somalia
15	Cambodian-Vietnamese	1978	Cambodia China	Vietnam
16	Ugandan-Tanzanian	1978	Tanzania	Uganda
17	Afghanistan	1979	Afghanistan	Soviet Union
18	Persian Gulf	1980	Iran	Iraq
19	Angola	1981	Angola Cuba	South Africa
20	Falklands	1982	Argentina	United Kingdom
21	Saharan	1983	Chad	Libya
22	Lebanon	1987	France Israel Lebanon	Syria United States
23	Panama	1989	Panama	United States
24	Persian Gulf	1990	Iraq United Nations: United States and 7 other countries	
25	Yugoslavia	1990	Bosnia-Herzegovina	Croatia Serbia
26	Peruvian-Ecuadorian	1995	Ecuador	Peru
27	Albania	1995	Albania	Yugoslavia (Serbia-Montenegro)
28	Rwanda	1995	Burundi	Rwanda
29	East Timor	1995	Indonesia	New Guinea insurgency
30	Cameroon	1996	Cameroon	Nigeria
31	Northern Iraq	1996	Iraq	Kurdish insurgency
32	Eritrea	1997	Eritrea	Yemen
33	Iraq	1998	Great Britain Iraq	United States
34	Democratic Republic of the Congo	1998	Angola Chad Congo	Namibia Sudan Zimbabwe
35	Kosovo	1999	Albania NATO	Yugoslavia
36	Chechnya	1999	Chechnya	Russia
37	"War on Terrorism"	2001	Afghanistan (Taliban) al-Qaeda organization Great Britain	United States Others
38	Iraq	2003	Great Britain Iraq	United States

[1] "Conflict" implies at least 1,000 battle deaths.
[2] "Belligerent" implies country supplied at least 5% of the combat troops in the conflict.

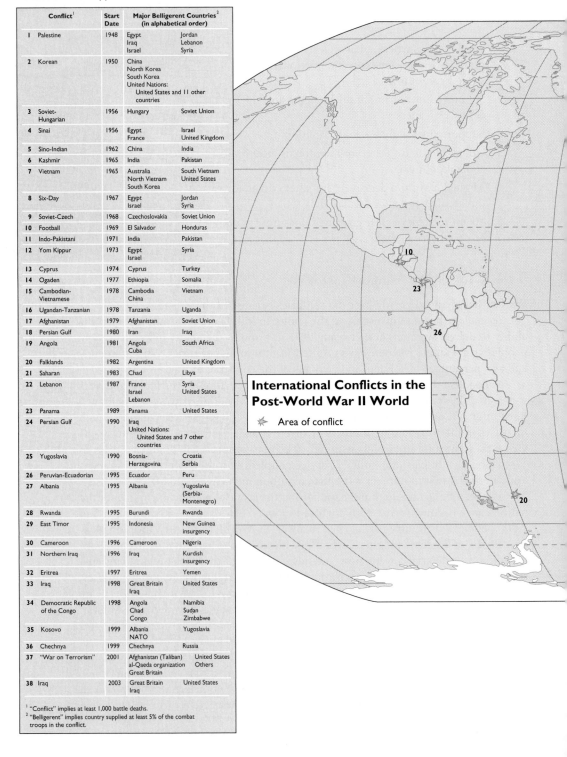

International Conflicts in the Post-World War II World

✳ Area of conflict

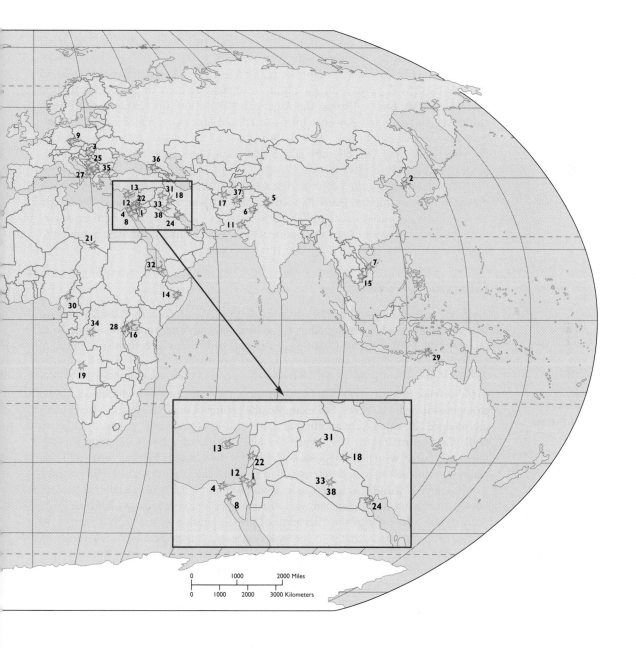

enemy military forces and is the classic goal of war. The **power to hurt,** or coercive violence, is the ability to inflict pain outside the immediate military sphere (Slantchev, 2003). It means hurting some so that the resistance of others will crumble. The power to hurt has become increasingly important to all aspects of warfare because the success of the war effort depends on a country's economic effort and, often, the morale of its citizens. Perhaps the first military leader to understand the importance of the power to hurt in modern warfare was General William Tecumseh Sherman during the U.S. Civil War. "My aim was to whip the rebels, to humble their pride, to follow them to their inmost recesses, and [to] make them fear and dread us," the general wrote in his memoirs.[12]

Traditionally wars were fought with little reference to hurting. Even when hurting was used, it depended on the ability to attack civilians by first defeating the enemy's military forces. During the American Revolution, for example, the British could have utilized their power to hurt—to kill civilians in the major cities they controlled—and they might have won the war. Instead they concentrated on defeating the American army (which they could not catch, then grew too strong to overpower), and they lost.

In the modern era, the power to defeat has declined in importance relative to the power to hurt. Terrorism, guerrilla warfare, and nuclear warfare all rely extensively on the power to hurt to accomplish their ends. Even conventional warfare sometimes uses terror tactics to sap an opponent's morale. The use of strategic bombing to blast German cities during World War II is an example.

Classifying Warfare

There are numerous ways to classify warfare. One has to do with causality and intent, and distinguishes among offensive, defensive, and other types of conflict. *Wars of aggression* are those that do not meet the standards of *jus ad bellum* (just cause of war) analyzed in chapter 9. *Defensive warfare* can include immediate self-defense, such as Kuwait's futile and short-lived resistance to Iraq's invasion in 1990, or coming to the defense of a country suffering aggression. Defense can also include responding to aggression against others. For example, the countries in NATO and other alliances are pledged to protect one another, and a coalition of countries waged the Persian Gulf War against Iraq in 1991 when the UN authorized action to liberate Kuwait. Often, of course, who is the aggressor and who is the victim is unclear, with each side claiming to be acting in self-defense or to be justifiably righting some other wrong.

Preemptive warfare is one such scenario that defies the simple dichotomy between offensive and defensive war. Whether preventive war is justified has been hotly debated recently in the aftermath of the declaration of the Bush Doctrine, as discussed in chapter 2, that, "To forestall or prevent hostile acts by our adversaries, the United States will, if necessary, act preemptively." Putting theory into practice, U.S. forces moved against Iraq in March 2003. Countries have long struck first to forestall what they believed to be an impending attack, and the line between preemption as aggression (which violates international law) and preemption as self-defense (which does not) is not precise. Even in much more constrained domestic situations, a potential victim confronted by someone with a loaded gun does not have to wait to be shot at before exercising his or her right of self-defense. What the law generally says is that you must be reasonably afraid that you or someone with you faces immediate death or injury and your response must be proportionate to the threat. Thus the justifiability of a preemptive war must be evaluated within its context. The general public also holds this view, as evident in Figure 10.4.

SIMULATION
Classifying Wars

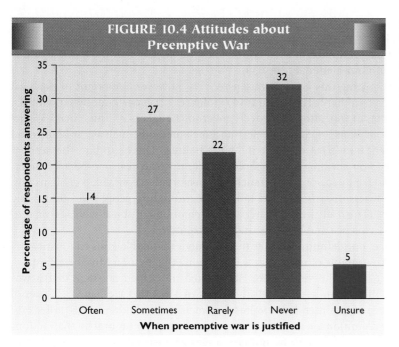

FIGURE 10.4 Attitudes about Preemptive War

For most people, the use of preemptive war is not a matter of absolute right or wrong. From one perspective, this data indicates that a majority (54%) of the respondents in 20 countries think that preemptive war is rarely if ever justified. Another way to look at the data, though, is to see that only 32% find no circumstances that would justify preemptive warfare. Among Americans, the responses were often 22%, sometimes 44%, rarely 17%, never 13%, and unsure 4%.

Note: The question was: Do you think that using military force against countries that may seriously threaten our country, but have not attacked us, can often be justified, sometimes be justified, rarely be justified, or never be justified?

Data source: The Pew Research Center for People and the Press, "Views of a Changing World," June 2003.

Another approach to classifying war focuses on the weapons and tactics employed. Adopting this strategy, the remainder of this chapter discusses four categories of tactics and weapons: terrorism, unconventional military force, conventional force, and weapons of mass destruction.

Terrorism

When a quadrennial survey taken in 1999 asked Americans to name two or three top foreign policy concerns, only 12% mentioned terrorism. Four years later, with 9/11 on their minds, 75% of Americans identified terrorism as a critical threat, more than chose any other foreign policy issue.[13] Like the unknown in a horror movie, the shadow of terrorism may be greater than its actual presence, yet it has become an important component of international violence. For instance, there were more than 3,000 terrorist attacks during the period 1994 through 2003, and they wounded almost 25,000 people worldwide and killed approximately 6,000. Almost half of these deaths occurred during the 9/11 attacks.

The Nature and Limits of Terrorism

One of the challenges of examining terrorism is that there is no widely accepted definition. This is not just a problem of semantics. It has affected initiatives to establish treaties and other international efforts to combat terrorism. Most specifically, the UN has struggled intermittently for years to draft a comprehensive treaty on terrorism. Several treaties have been concluded, including one in 2005 to thwart nuclear terrorism. But a general agreement has failed in part because of definitional disagreements. For instance, many LDCs want wording to indicate that armed struggles for national liberation, against occupation, or against a racist regime should not be considered terrorism. "The simple fact is that terrorism means different things to different people," one diplomat explained after one frustrating negotiation. "We couldn't find common political ground on several issues—despite the fact that the entire world is preoccupied with international terrorism."[14]

While recognizing this lack of consensus, it is, however, important to establish how the word is used here. **Terrorism** is (1) violence; (2) carried out by individuals, nongovernmental organizations, or covert government agents or units; that (3) specifically targets civilians; (4) uses clandestine attack methods, such as car bombs and hijacked airliners; and (5) attempts to influence politics. This definition stresses that terrorism focuses on harming some people in order to create fear in others by targeting civilians and facilities or systems (such as transportation) on which civilians rely. The objective of terrorists is not just killing and wounding people and destroying physical material. Instead the true target is the emotions of those who see or read about the act of violence and become afraid or dispirited.

By inference, our definition rejects the argument that noble ends can justify terrorist means. An example of this claim was made in 2005 by Abu Musab al-Zarqawi, al Qaeda's chief of operations in Iraq. He asserted in a taped message that it was acceptable to kill "all infidels with all the kinds of arms that we have. . . . even if armed infidels and unintended victims—women and children—are killed together."[15] The definition of terrorism here also rejects the argument that actions taken by military forces against military targets that also result in civilian casualties should be classified as terrorism. Some would question why a civilian dissident who detonates a car bomb in a market, killing numerous noncombatants, is a terrorist, but a military pilot who drops a bomb that kills numerous noncombatants near the target is not a terrorist. There are two replies to this objection. The first is that intent is important. Terrorists intend to kill noncombatants. With rare exception, uniformed personnel attack military or hostile targets. Noncombatants may be inadvertently killed or wounded, but they are not the object of the attack.

This perspective does not mean all military actions are acceptable. When they are not, however, they are properly classified as war crimes under the principles of *jus in bello* (just conduct of war) discussed in chapter 9, and the perpetrators should be brought to justice in national or international courts. An additional note is that not all attacks categorized as terrorism by the United States fall within the definition of terrorism used here. For example, Washington condemned as terrorism the October 2000, attack on the destroyer USS *Cole* while it was refueling in Aden. Yet despite the fact that it was suicide

Terrorism can be distinguished from military actions in that terrorism specifically targets noncombatants. This little girl being held by her uncle was wounded by a car bomb detonated by insurgents in Iraq. The blast was one of a series of car bombings that day that killed 19 civilians and wounded 194 more in an effort to undermine the U.S. occupation of Iraq by destabilizing its society.

bombers operating a small boat laden with explosives that mangled the ship and killed 17 crew members, the fact that the target was a military vessel puts the act beyond the definition of terrorism used here. A final point is that like all definitions of terrorism, there are gray areas. For example, the attacks on American and other forces in Iraq during the postwar occupation fulfill the definition of guerrilla warfare rather than terrorism because they target military forces. Yet the use of car bombs that may kill dozens of civilians in order to also kill one or a few soldiers are at least war crimes and probably terrorism because they violate the standards of discrimination in *jus ad bellum* (just conduct of war). This is especially the case when the perpetrators are outside fighters, such as al Zarqawi (a Jordanian), rather than Iraqis.

Sources of Terrorism

Two sources of political terrorism concern us here. One is state terrorism; the second is transnational terrorism. As we shall see, they are closely linked.

State Terrorism

To argue that most acts, even if horrific, committed by uniformed military personnel are not properly regarded as terrorism does not mean that countries cannot engage in terrorism. They can, through **state terrorism.** This is terrorism carried out directly by an established government's clandestine operatives or by others who have been specifically encouraged and funded by a country.

From the U.S. perspective, the State Department repeatedly listed Cuba, Iran, Iraq, Libya, North Korea, Sudan, and Syria as countries guilty of state terrorism. Iraq has been deleted from the list, and reforms in Libya could also lead to its deletion. Each of these countries vehemently denies being involved in terrorism, and some of the U.S. allegations would fall outside the definition of terrorism used here. Not all would, though. For example, state terrorism would include Syria's almost certain involvement in the 2005 assassination of former Lebanese Prime Minister Rafiq Hariri, a strong opponent of Syria's long-time occupation of much of Lebanon. There have also been accusations of state terrorism against the United States. "We consider the United States and its current administration as a first-class sponsor of international terrorism, and it along with Israel form an axis of terrorism and evil in the world," a group of 126 Saudi scholars wrote in a joint statement issued in 2002.[16]

Here again, most, but not all, such charges fall outside the definition of terrorism used here. An example involves Washington's alleged complicity in assassinations and other forms of state terrorism practiced internally by some countries in Latin America and elsewhere during the anticommunist fervor of the cold war. A secret document declassified in 1999 records the anguished views of an American diplomat in Guatemala regarding U.S. support of the Guatemalan army against Marxist guerrillas and their civilian supporters. After detailing a long list of atrocities committed by the army, the American diplomat told his superiors in Washington, "We have condoned counter-terror . . . even . . . encouraged and blessed it. . . . Murder, torture, and mutilation are all right if our side is doing it and the victims are Communists."[17]

Transnational Terrorism

The changes in the world that have given rise to a rapid increase in the number of international nongovernmental organizations have also expanded the number of terrorist groups that are organized and operate internationally and that commit **transnational terrorism.** One source, the U.S. State Department's 2004 edition of its "Report on Foreign Terrorist Organizations," lists 40 such groups, including al Qaeda, and there are dozens of other such organizations that one source or another label as terrorist.

Al Qaeda is surely the most famous of these, and its origins and operations provide a glimpse into transnational terrorism. According to U.S. sources, al Qaeda (the Base) was founded by Osama bin Laden, the son of a wealthy Saudi family, in the late 1980s to support Arabs fighting in Afghanistan against the Soviet Union. Once the Soviets were driven from Afghanistan in 1989, bin Laden's focus shifted to the United States. He was outraged by the presence of U.S. forces in Saudi Arabia near Mecca and Medina, the two holiest cities of Islam, and by American support of what he saw as Israel's oppression of Palestinian Muslims. Reflecting this view, he issued a *fatwa,* a religious call, in 1998 entitled "Jihad Against Jews and Crusaders," which proclaimed that "to kill the Americans and their allies—civilians and military—is an individual duty for every Muslim who can do it in any country in which it is possible to do it."[18] Subsequently according to U.S. officials, bin Laden and his followers masterminded a number of other terrorist attacks. These included the 1998 bombings of the U.S. embassies in Nairobi, Kenya, and Dar es Salaam, Tanzania, which killed more than 300 people and injured thousands of others. Of course, al Qaeda's most devastating attack was the 9/11 assault, and the group has been linked to other terrorist activities ranging from the attack on the USS *Cole* to the al Zarqawi-led campaign against Iraq's new government and the outside military forces there.

Bin Laden was based in Sudan from 1991 to 1996 when he moved the headquarters of al Qaeda to Afghanistan after international pressure forced the government of Sudan to expel him. Additionally, investigators have discovered links to al Qaeda operatives, bank accounts, and activities in more than 50 countries. There is no accurate count of how many individuals are part of al Qaeda, but it and other closely associated extremist groups had and probably still have several thousand members. In addition to al Qaeda's own members, it trained many thousands of terrorists for other groups in its camps in Afghanistan and elsewhere. They derived their funding in part from bin Laden's vast personal wealth, in part from contributions from sympathizers around the world, and perhaps in part from donations from sympathetic governments. Al Qaeda also established a sophisticated global network of bank accounts and other financial vehicles that allowed them to move money easily around the world.

The Record of Terrorism

International terrorism has become a regular occurrence. U.S. State Department data issued in 2004 indicates that the number of attacks rose from 165 in 1968 to peak at 665 in 1987. Since then, despite annual ups and downs, the number of attacks steadily decreased, as evident in Figure 10.5. Then the number shot up in 2004. The State Department counted 651 attacks taking 1,907 lives in 2004, but downplayed the increase, claiming that it was an anomaly caused by the high number of attacks by insurgents in Iraq. These were taken into count because they caused civilian casualties even if aimed at U.S. personnel and Iraqi government forces. Others charged that the statistics showed that U.S. policy was promoting rather than reducing terrorist activity.

Geographically, international terrorism has been widespread, with all regions other than North America suffering frequent terrorist attacks. For the period 1998–2003, Latin America suffered the most terrorist attacks (692). By contrast, North America was the target of the fewest attacks (6), although one of those was the

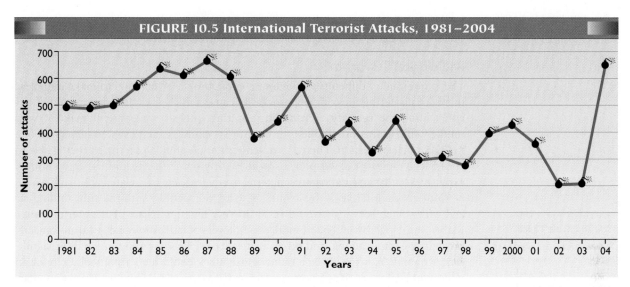

FIGURE 10.5 International Terrorist Attacks, 1981–2004

Terrorism is a constant in the world. It spiked upward in the mid-1980s, but then generally declined. The sharp increase in 2004 is a result of the attacks inside Iraq and what the State Department calls a more extensive review than done in previous years. Administration defenders said that the 2004 data was not comparable to previous years; critics charged that it showed that the U.S. war on terrorism was failing.

Data source: U.S. Department of State, *Patterns of Global Terrorism 2003,* issued April 2004, and *Country Reports on Terrorism 2004,* issued April 2005; and various news reports in April 2005.

9/11 attack series that killed almost 3,000 people. In 2003, 35 Americans were killed and 29 were wounded in 60 attacks around the world targeting Americans.

Terrorist Weapons and Tactics

The explosions that tore apart the World Trade Center and Pentagon and buried their victims under tons of rubble, the mangled remains of Israeli civilians in a bomb-shattered bus, the hollow stares of hostages held as pawns in the macabre game that terrorists play—these are the images of terrorism that have too often gripped us. For all the ghastly history of terrorism using conventional weapons, future possibilities are even more disturbing. Now there is a new, more terrible threat—radiological, nuclear, biological, and chemical terrorism (Enders & Sandler, 2005; Gurr & Cole, 2000; Tucker, 2000). As a recent U.S. National Intelligence Estimate described the situation, for the first time "U.S. territory is more likely to be attacked" with radio-logical, biological, or chemical weapons using "ships, trucks, airplanes or other means" than by weapons of mass destruction from another country using its military missiles or bombers.[19]

Conventional Weapons Terrorism

With relatively few exceptions, most terrorist attacks have used bombs, guns, and other conventional weapons. Data compiled by the U.S. State Department for 2003 indicates, for example, that of the attacks that year on American targets, 75% involved some type of ground-delivered bomb, and 12% utilized firearms. Kidnap-ping, arson, and a skyjacking accounted for the remaining attacks. Even the attacks on the World Trade Center and Pentagon in 2001, as horrific as they were, would fall under the category of conventional weapons terrorist attacks.

Radiological Terrorism

The extraordinary difficulty of obtaining enough nuclear material to make a nuclear bomb, of mastering the complex process to cause a nuclear chain reaction, and of circumventing the security surrounding existing nuclear weapons all make it very unlikely that in the foreseeable future terrorists could get and use a mini version of a military nuclear weapon. There is a much greater possibility of terrorists being able to construct a radiological weapon, a so-called dirty bomb that would use conventional explosives to disperse radioactive material over a large area. A related approach would be to destroy a nuclear power plant, spewing radioactivity into the surrounding air and water. Such scenarios would result in very few immediate or near-term deaths. Rather, the danger would be from increased levels of radiation causing future cancers, pregnancy complications, and other medical risks. There is also potential for significant economic damage, since a radiological attack could render parts of a city or an important facility (such as a port) unsafe, perhaps for years. Thus, as one expert characterized the impact of a dirty bomb to Congress, "The effects are not instantaneous. You have long-term potential health hazards, and you also have longer-term psychological, social, and political impacts that can go on weeks, months, maybe years."[20]

The concern over the possibility of terrorists acquiring the material to fashion a radiological weapon has grown in recent years. According to the International Atomic Energy Agency (IAEA), there are hundreds of thousands of known industrial, medical, and other sites and thousands more "orphaned" (unregulated) sites that possess highly radioactive material, such as cobalt-60, caesium-137, strontium-90, and iridium-192l. IAEA data also indicates that there have been over 600 confirmed cases of trafficking in stolen radiological material since 1993, and that thefts continue at an accelerating pace, as shown in Figure 10.6. Most of the known incidents have involved radiological material. However, about a third have involved nuclear material, and 18 of these cases included highly enriched (weapons-grade) uranium or plutonium.

Of all possible sources, however, Russia is the most likely. That country is dismantling many of its nuclear weapons, and it needs to store tons of plutonium and uranium. Russia's desperate economic condition adds to the problem. There is concern that impoverished Russian military and scientific officials might be willing to sell radioactive material to terrorist groups or states. Additionally, the partial breakdown of governmental functions throughout the former Soviet republics (FSRs) creates the possibility that the material to make a radiological bomb could be stolen.

Chemical and Biological Terrorism

Public awareness of the possibility of chemical or biological attack grew after the 9/11 attacks. There was alarm when it was learned that one of the suicide hijackers had made repeated trips to rural airports to learn about crop dusters. Anxiety was further heightened by the spread of anthrax through the U.S. mail to postal facilities, news organizations, and congressional offices. The resulting atmosphere spawned a spate of doomsday images of chemical and biological attacks that would leave millions dead. Most experts consider such scenarios overdrawn, and it is important to have a balanced understanding of the possibilities of chemical or biological attack and the impact of such attacks.

Causes for concern. There surely are worrisome realities. The tons of chemical weapons and agents seized from Iraq in 1991 after the Persian Gulf War bear testi-

---

Did You Know That:

It takes about 17.5 pounds of plutonium to make a bomb with the explosive yield (about 15 kilotons of TNT) of the atomic bomb dropped on Hiroshima.

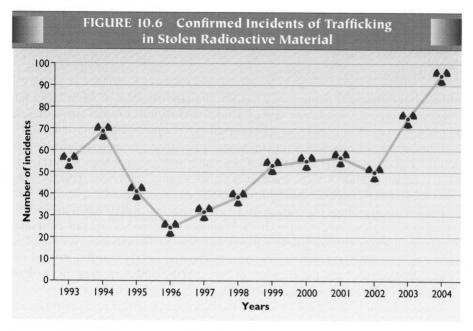

FIGURE 10.6   Confirmed Incidents of Trafficking in Stolen Radioactive Material

Between 1993 and 2003 there were 650 confirmed incidents of criminal trafficking in stolen radioactive material and almost certainly many more undetected illegal cases. About one-third of the confirmed cases involved nuclear material. It is unclear whether the sharp increase in 2003 and 2004 reflects more trafficking or better crime detection.

Data source: International Atomic Energy Agency Illegal Trafficking Database.

mony to the amount of such weapons in the world and the proliferation of the ability to produce them. Biological weapons are also a threat. For example, the U.S. Office of Technology Assessment estimates that a light plane flying over Washington, D.C., and its surrounding area and releasing just 220 pounds of anthrax spores using a common crop sprayer could deliver a fatal dose to 3 million people.[21] It would be comforting to think that no one would use such weapons, but that is not the case. Iraq used chemical weapons against Iran and rebellious Kurds in the 1980s, and in 1995 a Japanese terrorist group, Aum Shinrikyo (Supreme Truth), used nerve gas in an attack that killed 12 people and injured 5,000 on a Tokyo subway station. What is worse, a panel of UN experts has warned that the risk of terrorists groups "acquiring and using weapons of mass destruction . . . continues to grow."[22]

Calls for calm. While it is impossible to rule out a biological or chemical attack that takes tens of thousands of lives, it is probably more realistic to see the likelihood of such an attack as remote because of the significant difficulties of amassing and delivering enough of a chemical or biological agent to cause widespread death and injury. According to one scientist, "When one retreats from the hyperbole and examines the intricacies involved in executing a mass casualty attack with [biological or chemical] agents, one is confronted with technical obstacles so high that even terrorists that have had a wealth of time, money, and technical skill, as well as a determination to acquire and use these weapons [would have difficulty doing so]."[23] This implies that the impact of a chemical or biological terrorist attack is most likely to be similar to that of a radiological attack. The psychological impact will far outweigh the actual casualties. This is what occurred during the anthrax incidents in the United States in late 2001. They caused only five deaths and about a dozen

Did You Know That:

Routine smallpox vaccinations in the United States ended in 1972. Prior to the 9/11 attacks, the existing U.S. stock of smallpox vaccine could have protected only 3% of Americans in the event of a smallpox attack.

other infections, but that was enough to virtually close down Congress for a time and to frighten millions.

The Causes of Terrorism

Although the attacks of September 11, 2001, brought terrorism to the front of the international agenda, it has long existed. Understanding the causes of terrorism and its recent record are important parts of combating it (Laqueur, 2004; Sinclair, 2004).

Untangling the causes of terrorism is much like trying to understand why war occurs. At the *system level of analysis,* it is possible to argue that such political violence is in part a product of the global unequal distribution of wealth. This has long existed, but globalization has brought the wealth gap into sharper focus and has also created a sense of cultural dislocation with its Westernizing impact. When the world's leaders met in Monterrey, Mexico, in 2002 to discuss globalization and economic development, many speakers made a connection between poverty and violence. The president of the UN General Assembly depicted poverty as "the breeding ground for violence and despair," and the president of Peru told the conference that "to speak of development is to speak also of a strong and determined fight against terrorism."[24]

State-level analysis of the 9/11 attacks might argue that terrorism is partly caused by the continuing bloodshed between Israelis and Palestinians and the overwhelming view among Muslims that the United States favors Israel. Other possible state-level factors are the presence of U.S. forces in the Middle East, especially those in Saudi Arabia near the holiest sites of Islam in Mecca and Medina, and the U.S. support of authoritarian regimes in Saudi Arabia and elsewhere. On the *individual level of analysis,* one looks into the psychological drives of terrorists ranging from Osama bin Laden to the numerous suicide bombers who have blown themselves to pieces attacking Israelis in cafés, shops, and meeting rooms (Post, 2004). Like general war, there is little agreement among analysts about the causes of terrorism along these dimensions.

On a more pragmatic level, terrorism occurs because, like war, it is effective. As one leading expert puts it, "Terrorism has proved a low-cost, low-risk, cost-effective and potentially high-yield means of winning useful tactical objectives for its perpetrators, such as massive publicity, securing the release of large numbers of terrorist prisoners from jail, and the extortion of considerable sums to finance the purchase of more weapons and explosives and the launching of a wider campaign."[25] From this perspective, terrorism usually is not the irrational acts of crazed fanatics. Instead, it is usually carried out by those who consider it a necessary, legitimate, and effective tool to rid themselves of what they consider oppression. It is necessary, its proponents say, because it may be the only way for an oppressed group to prevail against a heavily armed government.

Moreover, modern conditions are ripe for terrorist operations. First, technology has increased the power of the weapons available to terrorists. Explosives have become more deadly, huge airliners can be made into piloted missiles, and there is an increasing danger of terrorists obtaining the material and means to launch a biological, chemical, or radiological attack. Second, increased urbanization has brought people together so that they are more easily attacked, especially when they are gathered in such high-profile places as skyscrapers and sports stadiums. With eerie premonition, a U.S. senator warned in 1999, that Americans were vulnerable to attack on targets that might be "selected for their symbolic value, like the World Trade Center in the heart of Manhattan."[26] Third, modern communications have also made terrorism more efficacious because the goal of the terrorist is not to kill or injure, as such. Instead, the aim of terrorism is to gain attention for a cause or to create widespread anxiety that will, in turn, create pressure on governments to negotiate with terrorists and accede to their every demand. Without the media to transmit the news of their acts, terrorist attacks would affect only their immediate victims, which would not accomplish the terrorists' goals.

Combating Terrorism

The most immediate concern about terrorism is how to combat it. That is made difficult by the clandestine methods used by terrorists and also by the fact that, like other forms of political violence, there is no agreement on what causes terrorism. The U.S.-led "war on terrorism" in recent years has emphasized military and economic strategies to disrupt and destroy terrorist organizations and their ability to operate. Epitomizing this approach, a U.S. State Department report argues, "The world is fighting terrorism on five fronts: diplomatic, intelligence, law enforcement, financial, and military."[27] The report then explains how diplomacy had created cooperation to fight terrorism, how intelligence agencies had worked to identify terrorists and uncover their plans, how law enforcement agencies around the world have detained thousands of suspected terrorists since 9/11, and frozen hundreds of millions of dollars in assets of suspected terrorist groups and sympathizers, and how military operations have dealt heavy blows to terrorists in Afghanistan and elsewhere.

What the report does not mention are any efforts to address many of the causes of terrorism discussed earlier. Critics say it is a major error not to realize that the current wave of terrorism is prompted in significant part by turmoil in the Middle East, especially between Israelis and Palestinians, and the pattern of economic and cultural threat that globalization poses to many in less developed countries. As one such critic put it, "We need to understand the root causes behind terrorism" because "military action will not prevent future terrorism, but only delay it."[28] In a debate that in some ways resembles the one on the war on drugs, some people say that too much is being spent on countering the problem and not enough on trying to cure it.

ANALYZE THE ISSUE
NATO

JOIN THE DEBATE
Understanding the
National Security Threats
of the 21st Century:
Are Military Means the Best
Way to Combat Terrorism?

Unconventional Force

As used here, **unconventional force** means outside intervention in local conflict through unconventional means including supplying arms and conducting special operations. This approach allows countries to use their military assets to support their policies while, at the same time, limiting their involvement.

Arms Transfers

The global flow of arms can be properly considered as a form of intervention because it usually strengthens either a government or antigovernment rebels favored by the supplying country. Thus to a substantial degree, the international flow of weapons is an indirect way to intervene abroad.

Arms Transfers: Where and Why

The export and import of arms has long been important economically and politically. It reached new heights during the cold war, as the two hostile superpowers struggled

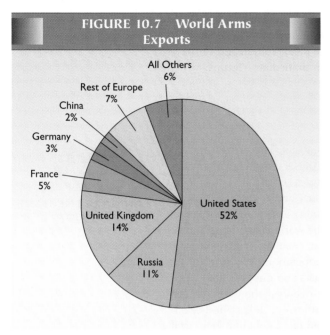

FIGURE 10.7 World Arms Exports

World arms exports for 2000–2003 came to about $148 billion, with the United States being the major arms supplier. About two-thirds of all arms exports went to LDCs.

Data Source: Richard F. Grimmett, "Conventional Arms Transfers to Developing Nations, 1996–2003," Congressional Research Service report, August 26, 2004.

for influence. About two-thirds of the arms that flowed in the world during the cold war were exported by the United States and the Soviet Union, while LDCs were the destination of about two-thirds of the flow of weaponry. Annual global arms transfers peaked late in the cold war, then declined considerably into the late 1990s measured in constant dollars and have generally been steady since then. Between 2000 and 2003, arms transfers totaled about $148 billion. U.S. weaponry contributed almost half the supply, as Figure 10.7 indicates. Russia ranked second and a number of Western European countries were also major exporters. About two-thirds of all weapons still flow to LDCs. Countries in Asia, especially the Middle East, and North Africa were the largest importers, with Saudi Arabia alone accounting for 16% of the world arms imports. Latin America and sub-Saharan Africa received only 4% each of the arms flow.

Several motives prompt countries to sell and give weapons to other countries or to insurgent groups. One of these, as noted, is political support of the recipient government or rebel group. A second and related factor is supplying arms as a way of furthering desired cooperation with another government. Critics chastised the decision of the Bush government to sell F-16 fighters and other advanced weapons systems to Pakistan in 2005, contending that it fueled an arms race with India, and that Pakistan had a record of exporting nuclear weapons and missile technology in violation of the Nuclear Non-Proliferation Treaty. From a different perspective, the White House believed that it needed Pakistan's continued cooperation for the U.S. antiterrorist effort, its operations in Afghanistan, and other efforts. As Secretary of State Rice explained that view, "If you look at it, there is an entire arc there that is very important to American interests in the future, and we're going to pursue all of those relationships on their own terms, and in this context the F-16 issue with Pakistan makes sense."[29]

National economic benefit is yet another, and now perhaps the predominant, motive behind arms exports. This is especially true for the world's leading arms merchant, the United States. For example, the sale of F-16 fighters is crucial to the economic well-being of Lockheed Martin Company and the approximately 12,000 workers at its Fort Worth, Texas, plant. A majority of the more than 4,200 F-16s produced or ordered since the fighter first flew in 1976 have gone to other countries, and in recent years virtually the entire production of F-16s is for export. Thus, the economic welfare of Texas is not just linked to U.S. military needs; it also depends in part on the thousands of F-16s that have been sold to over 20 countries around the world. To ensure that economic health, the administration also provides incentives. Most U.S. military aid requires recipient countries to buy specific U.S. military weapons and supplies, which Washington then pays for. In 2003 and 2004, the Bush administration extended to Pakistan a $4.3 billion, multiyear military aid package. Much of it will be spent buying about two dozen F-16s, which, with their support packages, sell for up to $100 million each.

Arms Transfers: Drawbacks

There can be little doubt that arms transfers may help recipient countries meet legitimate defense needs, may be a valuable diplomatic tool, and may help the economy of the supplying country. It is also true, however, that the global flow of arms entails drawbacks to both the importing and the exporting countries. *Cost* is one concern, especially for LDCs. At least some of the billions of dollars that LDCs spend annually on arms might be better spent on funding economic development or social programs. *Increased violence* is a second problem because, at least sometimes, the arms flow increases the level and perhaps the frequency and intensity of violence between countries and within countries. One study concludes that the consequences of the flow of weapons, especially to the LDCs, are "likely to be severe" because they "now possess the capacity to conduct wars of greater intensity, duration, and reach" and because "there is a high correlation between the growing diffusion of war-making material and the increased tempo of global violence" (Klare & Lumpe, 2000:173).

Countries sometimes sell weapons to entice other countries to cooperate, or to reward them for doing so. In 2005, to reward Pakistan for its cooperation in the war against terrorism, President George Bush ended the embargo on the sale of F-16 fighters and other U.S. warplanes to Pakistan. His father had instituted the embargo when he was president in 1990 in response to Pakistan's nuclear weapons program.

Facing one's own weapons is a third problem that may occur. Countries that you supply today can wind up an opponent tomorrow. Also, weapons may later be sold by recipients to yet other governments or dissident groups, be stolen, or otherwise wind up in the vast arms black market. *Hypocrisy* is a fourth problem. It is hard to persuade others not to do what you are doing. Indications that the European Union (EU) in 2005 was about to end its ban on weapons sales to China prompted a major U.S. diplomatic effort to keep the ban in place. As one top U.S. official explained, "We see China continuing a military buildup, which is viewed as threatening by its democratic neighbors. We believe that the EU's lifting of the embargo would negatively affect regional stability as well as American security interests."[30] However, Washington struggled to make its case, given its status as the world's leading arms supplier, with many nondemocracies among the recipients. French President Jacques Chirac and others were prone to see the U.S. position as stemming from its desire to maintain its hegemonic position, a level of influence many European leaders seek to diminish. Diplomacy barred openly calling the American position hypocritical, but even after meeting with President Bush, Chirac told reporters that the U.S. position was "not justified" and that, "With regard to China, Europe intends to remove the last obstacles to its relations with this important country."[31]

Special Operations

Not all military action involves the use of large numbers of uniformed troops against other organized military forces in classic battle scenarios. Some approaches to violence fall under the heading of special operations.

Special operations include overtly or covertly sending one's own special operations forces (SOFs), intelligence operatives, or paramilitary agents into another country to conduct such small-unit activities as commando operations and intelligence gathering. When these actions are aimed at an opponent's armed forces or other military targets, then the activity falls under the general heading of special operations warfare. The use of SOFs as a form of military intervention has increased in recent decades for several reasons. First, there has been an increase in civil strife within countries. Second, attempts to topple governments or to create separatist states are now usually waged using guerrilla tactics, rather than the conventional tactics normally used in the past. More than any single reason, this change in tactics has occurred because the preponderance of high-tech weapons available to government forces makes it nearly suicidal for opposition forces to fight conventionally. Third, covert intervention avoids the avalanche of international and, often, domestic criticism that overt interventions set off. Fourth, clandestine operations allow the initiating country to disengage more easily, if it wishes, than would be possible if it overtly committed regular military forces.

Covert operations also have drawbacks. Escalating involvement can be a major problem. Interventions can begin with supplying weapons. If the arms flow does not bring victory, then the next step may be to send in advisers and special operations forces. Even if the supplier country has its doubts about wanting to commit its own armed forces, the process of intervention often causes that country's prestige to become associated with the fate of the recipient country or rebel group that is being supported. Therefore, if things continue to go badly for the recipient, then the supplier may be tempted to engage in limited combat support, and, finally, to commit to a full-scale military intervention with its own troops. This is how the United States waded ever deeper into the quagmire in Vietnam and how the Soviet Union fell into the abyss in Afghanistan.

Since the events of 9/11, SOFs have received renewed attention in the United States. President George W. Bush has dramatically increased the size of and funding for U.S. SOFs. In addition to their use in Afghanistan and Iraq, the president has deployed SOF units to Colombia to assist in the war against leftist guerrilla armies there and to the Philippines to help that country's army in the war against Abu Sayyaf, a Muslim rebel group. Whatever the justification of any specific use of SOFs, they can also lead to intervention where prudence might otherwise recommend restraint, as discussed in the earlier section on overstretch.

Web Link

For contrasting analyses of U.S. national security policy, visit the sites of the conservative Center for Security Policy at **www .centerforsecuritypolicy.org** and the liberal Center for Defense Information at **www.cdi.org/.**

Conventional Force

The most overt form of coercive intervention is for a country to dispatch its own forces to another country. That intervention can range from such limited demonstrations of power as the numerous U.S. aerial and cruise missile attacks on Iraq between 1991 and 2003 to the global warfare seen during World War I and World War II. With the exceptions of the U.S. atomic attacks on Hiroshima and Nagasaki in 1945 and some use of chemical weapons, wars have been waged using conventional weapons.

The **conventional warfare** that has been the norm throughout most of history is distinguished from other types of warfare by the tactics and weapons used. The overt use of uniformed military personnel, usually in large numbers, is what separates conventional tactics from special operations and terrorism. As for weapons, it is easier to indicate what conventional weapons are not than what they are. Generally, conventional weapons are those that rely on explosives for impact but are not nuclear/radiological, biological, or chemical weapons.

Goals and Conduct

Carl von Clausewitz's earlier cited dictum that war is a form of diplomacy implies three principles that civilian and military decision makers should keep in mind.

(1) *War is a part of diplomacy, not a substitute for it.* Therefore, channels of communication to the opponent should be kept open in an attempt to limit the conflict and to reestablish peace. (2) *Wars should be governed by political, not military, considerations.* Often commanders chafe under restrictions, as General Douglas MacArthur did during the Korean War (1950–1953) over his lack of authority to attack China. When generals become insubordinate, as MacArthur did, they ought to be removed from command, as he was. (3) *War should be fought with clear political goals.* When goals are not established or are later ignored, disaster looms. After the Persian Gulf War, some criticized President George H. W. Bush for not driving on to Baghdad and unseating Saddam Hussein. Others strongly defended him for halting hostilities once U.S.-led forces had achieved the stated UN goal in 1991 of liberating Kuwait. By doing so, he ended the killing and stayed within the legal confines of the UN resolution that authorized the action. Moreover, in retrospect, invading Iraq in 1991 and unseating Saddam might have led to the same morass for U.S. forces that bogged them down after the 2003 war.

The fact that most wars are fought within limits does not mean that those boundaries are never violated. **Escalation** occurs when the rules are changed and the level of combat increases. Increasing the scope and intensity of a war, however, has always been dangerous, and it is particularly so in an era of nuclear, biological, and chemical (NBC) weapons. Not long after their entry into the war in Vietnam in the mid-1960s, Americans began to realize that continuing the war within the limits it was being fought offered little chance of victory and carried a heavy cost in lives and economics. Escalating the war by invading North Vietnam might have brought China into the war and increased the cost monumentally. Also, many Americans were sickened by the human cost to both sides; if the war had continued or escalated, there surely would have been an increase of deep divisions within the United States. Ultimately, the United States could have achieved a military victory by "nuking" North Vietnam and killing everyone there. Americans finally accepted, though, that victory was not the only thing. American troops began to withdraw from Vietnam in 1969; all U.S. troops were gone by 1973; Vietnam was reunited under Hanoi's control in 1975.

Avoiding Unchecked Escalation

The dangers of escalation and the prudence of keeping limited wars limited make it important to understand how to avoid unchecked escalation. As with most things political, there is no set formula. There are, however, a few useful standards.

Keep lines of communication open. The basic principle is that escalation (or de-escalation) should be a deliberate strategy used to signal a political message to the enemy. Accordingly, it is also important to send signals through diplomatic or public channels so that the opponent will not mistake the escalation as an angry spasm of violence or misconstrue the de-escalation as a weakening of resolve.

Limit goals. Unlimited goals by one side may evoke unlimited resistance by the other, so limiting goals is another way to avoid unchecked escalation. It is usually appropriate, for instance, that a goal should fall short of eliminating the opponent as a sovereign state! Even where unconditional victory is the aim, obliteration of the enemy population is not an appropriate goal.

Restrict geographical scope. It is often wise to limit conflict to as narrow a geographical area as possible. American forces refrained from invading China during the Korean War. Similarly, the Soviets passed up the temptation to blockade Berlin in 1962 in response to the U.S. blockade of Cuba.

Observe target restrictions. Wars can be controlled by limiting targets. Despite their close proximity, the Arabs and Israelis have never tried to bomb each other's capitals. Iraq's launch of Scud missiles against Tel Aviv and other Israeli cities in 1991 was, by contrast, a serious escalation, but it was not repeated in 2003.

Limit weapons. Yet another way to keep war limited is to adhere to the principle that the level of force used should be no greater than the minimum necessary to accomplish war aims. The stricture on weapons has become even more important in an era when there is such a great potential for the use of limited, on-the-battlefield NBC weapons. In addition to moral issues, even the limited use of NBC weapons might well set off a serious escalation that could lead to strategic nuclear war or massive biological and chemical attacks. This stricture has been followed in all international wars in recent decades, with the exception of the Iran-Iraq war in the 1980s during which Iran used mustard gas (which causes chemical burns to the lungs) and Iraq used mustard gas and tabun (a nerve agent).

Weapons of Mass Destruction

The world's history of waging war primarily with conventional weapons does not guarantee that this restraint will continue. Science and technology have rapidly increased the ability of countries to build, deploy, and potentially employ devastating **weapons of mass destruction (WMDs).** The term was first used by the British press in 1937 to describe German bombers deployed to Spain in support of the eventually successful effort of fascist forces to overthrow the government during that country's civil war (1936–1939). Now, however, the term weapons of mass destruction is used to denote nuclear, biological, and chemical weapons in the amounts and potencies that are available to national militaries and can cause horrific levels of death and injury to enemy forces or civilian targets. In the pages that follow, we will deal briefly with biological and chemical weapons, then turn to a more extensive examination of nuclear weapons and strategy.

Web Link

The horror of German bombing in Spain is presented in Pablo Picasso's iconic painting, *Guernica,* depicting people in that city under air attack. View it at **www .pbs.org/treasuresoftheworld/ guernica/gmain.html.**

Biological Weapons

Biological warfare is not new. As early as the 6th century B.C., the Assyrians poisoned enemy wells with a parasitic fungus called rye ergot that caused gangrene and convulsions. More catastrophically, the Tartar army besieging Kaffa, a Genoese trading outpost in the Crimea in 1346, catapulted plague-infected corpses and heads over the walls to spread the disease among the defenders. Many of those who fled back to Italy carried the disease with them and, according to some historians, set off the Black Death that killed millions of Europeans. North America first experienced biological warfare in 1763 when, during an Indian uprising, the British commander in North America, Sir Jeffrey Amherst, wrote to subordinates at Fort Pitt, "Could it not be contrived to send the smallpox among those disaffected tribes of Indians?"[32] As it turns out, Sir Jeffrey's prompting was unnecessary. Soldiers at the fort had already given disease-infected blankets to members of the Shawnee and Delaware tribes.

The specter of biological warfare still looms large. Although the 1972 Biological Weapons Convention (BWC) bans the production, possession, and use of germ-based *biological weapons,* there are persistent rumors that some countries maintain bioweapons stocks or are seeking them. North Korea, Iran, Russia, and Syria are

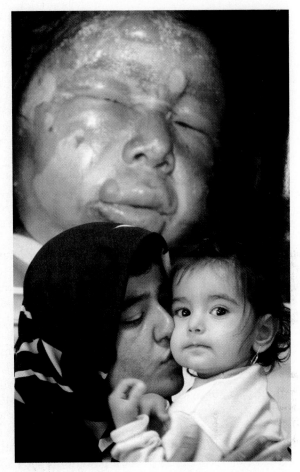

Chemical weapons remain a threat because humans have them and have shown they will use them against other humans. This 2004 photograph shows one of the luckier victims of a chemical weapons attack. An Iranian woman, Asmar Saeedpour, kisses her daughter Elaheh, while posing in front of an image of what the woman looked like in the aftermath of an Iraqi chemical attack on her town in 1987, during the 1980–1988 Iran-Iraq war. Iran claims that about 100,000 Iranians were killed or injured by chemical attacks during the war.

most often mentioned. Such possibilities are given credence by relatively recent evidence of bioweapons activity. For example, a top Russian official admitted in 1992 that the Soviet Union had been violating the BWC by conducting biological weapons research and, among other things, had amassed 20 tons of smallpox. The UN-led inspections of Iraq after the 1991 Persian Gulf War indicated that the country also had a germ warfare program that had, at minimum, produced 132,000 gallons of anthrax and botulism toxins.

Chemical Weapons

Of the three components of NBC warfare, chemical weapons are the most prevalent because they are relatively easy and inexpensive to produce. Indeed, they have earned the sobriquet of "the poor man's atomic bomb." As CIA director John M. Deutch told Congress, "Chemicals used to make nerve agents are also used to make plastics and [to] process foodstuff. Any modern pharmaceutical facility can produce biological warfare agents as easily as vaccines or antibiotics."[33]

Most ominously of all, chemical weapons have been used recently. Both Iran and Iraq used them during their grueling war (1980–1988), and Iraq used them internally to attack rebellious Kurds. UN inspections in Iraq after the Persian Gulf War also discovered huge stores of chemical weapons, including over 105,000 gallons of mustard gas; 21,936 gallons of tabun, sarin, and other nerve gases; and over 453,000 gallons of other chemicals associated with weapons. Some of this supply was contained in munitions, such as 12,786 artillery shells filled with mustard gas and 18 warheads or bombs filled with nerve agents. There is no evidence that any chemical weapons were used during the war, but traces of mustard gas and sarin were detected on the battlefield. These may have been released inadvertently when the allied attacks destroyed Iraqi weapons depots, and some analysts suspect that exposure to these chemicals may be the cause of Gulf War syndrome, which has afflicted many veterans of the war.

Nuclear Weapons

The Bible's Book of Revelation speaks of much of humankind suffering a fiery death during an apocalyptic end to the world: A "hail of fire mixed with blood fell upon the

Web Link

For a look at the impact of a nuclear attack, go to the PRB site http://www.pbs.org/wgbh/amex/ bomb/sfeature/index.html.

earth; and . . . the earth was burnt up. . . . The sea became blood . . . and from the shaft rose smoke like the smoke of a great furnace and the sun and the air were darkened." Whatever your religious beliefs, such a prophecy is sobering because we now have the capability to sound "the blast of the trumpets" as Revelations put it, by loosing the awesome array of nuclear weapons that we possess.

Nuclear Weapons States and Their Arsenals

The world joined in a collective sigh of relief when the cold war ended. Almost overnight, worry about the threat of nuclear war virtually disappeared from the media and from general political discussion. Unfortunately, the perception of significantly greater safety is illusory. It is true that the number of strategic nuclear weapons has declined. Nevertheless, there continues to be a huge number of extremely powerful nuclear weapons in the arsenals of several states, and yet other countries aim to acquire such WMDs.

The United States and Russia   The United States and Russia remain the nuclear Goliaths. In 2005, the U.S. deployed strategic-range (5,550 kilometers/3,416.8 miles) arsenal included 4,226 nuclear warheads and bombs and 951 **strategic-range delivery vehicles** (missiles and bombers). Russia's deployed strategic inventory was 3,814 weapons and 885 delivery vehicles. Additionally, the United States has 780 deployed tactical (shorter-range, battlefield) nuclear weapons, and Russia has some 3,400.

Washington and Moscow have both long relied on a triad of strategic weapons systems that include (1) submarine-launched ballistic missiles (SLBMs) carried aboard ballistic missile nuclear submarines (SSBNs), (2) land-based intercontinental ballistic missiles (ICBMs), and (3) bombers. Most ICBMs are located in silos, although Russia has some that are railroad-mobile. ICBMs and SLBMs carry up to ten warheads, with multiple warhead missiles having multiple independent reentry vehicle (MIRV) capability, allowing each warhead to attack a different target. The most powerful of these explosive devices is currently deployed on some of Russia's ICBMs, each of which carries between 6 and 10 MIRV 750-kiloton warheads. The largest American weapons are those SLBMs that carry eight 475-kiloton warheads.

Nuclear weapons designed for tactical use also come in a relatively miniaturized form. Among currently deployed tactical nuclear weapons, the explosive power of U.S. B-61 bombs can be as low as 0.3 kilotons (30 tons of TNT), a yield that is approximately nine times as powerful as the ammonium nitrate bomb that destroyed the Federal Building in Oklahoma City on April 19, 1995.

Did You Know That:

The array of 750-kiloton warheads on Soviet ICBMs each has an explosive yield 50 times larger than that of the atomic bomb dropped on Hiroshima in 1945.

Other Nuclear Weapons States   China, France, Great Britain, India, and Pakistan all openly have nuclear weapons, and Israel and (perhaps) North Korea have undeclared nuclear weapons, adding another 1,300 or so nuclear devices to the volatile mix of over 13,000 deployed tactical and strategic nuclear devices. There are another 14,000 or so such weapons in U.S. and Russian reserve inventories or waiting for disassembly. Additionally, several countries, most notably Iran, have or are suspected of having nuclear weapons development programs, and another 30 countries have the technology base needed to build nuclear weapons.

The Role of Nuclear Weapons

Given the reality of the huge number of nuclear weapons that still exist and the increase in the number of countries that have them, it would be unwise to discount the continuing impact of nuclear weapons on world politics. One role that nuclear weapons play is to be a part of the "backdrop" of power and influence. There can be little doubt that the continuing importance of Russia, despite its tremendous travails, rests in part on its still-immense nuclear arsenal. Deterrence is a second role played by nuclear weapons. Whether or not nuclear weapons will always deter conventional or nuclear attack is uncertain, but at least sometimes they have been and remain a restraining factor that deters an opponent from attacking in the first place or that limits an opponent's weapons or tactics. It is not unreasonable to conjecture, for instance, that the nuclear option that the United States, France, and Great Britain all had in the Persian Gulf War may have helped deter Saddam Hussein from using his chemical weapons in 1991. The United States again used its nuclear weapons in 2003 to threaten Iraq. Among a number of allusions by various officials to the possible use of nuclear weapons if U.S. forces faced WMDs, Secretary of Defense Donald Rumsfeld publicly declared that the administration would "not foreclose the possible use of nuclear weapons if [so] attacked."[34] Similarly, Secretary of State Condoleezza Rice's pointed remark in 2005 that, "the U.S. maintains significant—I want to underline significant—deterrent capability of all kinds in the Asia-Pacific region," served as a barely disguised warning to North Korea that any use of its WMDs might evoke a U.S. nuclear response.[35]

Actual use is a third role for nuclear weapons. Strategic analysts envision several scenarios that could lead to nuclear war. An *irrational leader,* one who is fanatical, deranged, drunk, or otherwise out of control is one possible cause of nuclear war. For instance, Russian generals were reportedly worried about what hard-drinking President Boris Yeltsin (1990–1999) might do during a crisis. A second scenario, a *calculated attack,* could also occur if one country felt that it could deliver a first strike that would disable all or most of its opponent's strategic forces and force it into submission. An unprovoked nuclear attack could also come as a result of a nuclear country attacking a nonnuclear country, especially if that country used chemical or biological weapons against the nuclear country.

Last gasp nuclear war could come as a final attempt to fend off conventional defeat. This scenario is called the Samson option after the biblical character who pulled a building down on himself in order to slay his captors. Some analysts believe that a key reason behind Israel's nuclear arsenal is to have the Samson option if its vaunted conventional forces are ever overwhelmed by numerically superior Arab invaders (Beres, 2004; Moaz, 2004). *Inadvertent nuclear war* based on bad information or misperceptions might also occur and is one of the most likely scenarios. False intelligence that a nuclear attack is imminent or even under way, for example, might cause a leader to inadvertently strike first. Such an event nearly occurred in 1995 when Russian radar detected what appeared to be an incoming missile fired over the Norwegian Sea, and Moscow prepared to launch a retaliatory strike on the United States. Only at the last moment was it determined that the radar blip was an outgoing Norwegian scientific rocket, not an incoming U.S. missile. "For a while," said a Russian defense official, "the world was on the brink of nuclear war."[36] This was neither the first nor last such close call. The time for American and Russian leaders to make decisions in a nuclear crisis is short—at most 30 minutes—given the flight time of a nuclear missile between the two countries. Leaders of countries close to one another, like Pakistan and India, would have much, much less time to respond. This will decrease the time to confirm reports that a nuclear attack has been launched or is about to be launched. It will also vastly increase the chances of erroneously launching what a leader sees as a counterstrike, but what, in fact, is a first strike.

Escalation in a deadly spiral is a final, not unlikely, path to nuclear war. History has demonstrated that leaders are willing to risk nuclear war even when there is no immediate and critical threat to national security. Perhaps the closest the world has

Did You Know That:

Eighteen Japanese survived the atomic attack on Hiroshima and also (three days later) the atomic blast in Nagasaki, where they and others had fled seeking safety after the first mushroom cloud.

ever come to nuclear war was during the 1962 Cuban missile crisis, when the Soviets risked nuclear war by placing missiles with nuclear warheads in Cuba, and the United States risked nuclear war by threatening to invade Cuba and attack the Russian forces guarding the missiles unless Moscow withdrew them.

Nuclear Deterrence and Strategy

There are issues about a country's nuclear arsenal and doctrines that seldom enter the public debate, but that are crucial to an effective and stable arsenal. The two main issues are (1) how to minimize the chance of nuclear war and (2) how to maximize the chance of survival if a nuclear exchange does occur. It is not possible here to review all the factors that impinge on these issues, but we can illustrate the various concerns by examining deterrence and then several specific issues about strategy.

Deterrence

The concept of deterrence remains at the center of the strategy of all the nuclear powers. **Deterrence** is persuading an enemy that attacking you will not be worth the cost. Deterrence relies on two factors. *Capability* is the first. Effective deterrence requires that even if you are attacked you must be able to preserve enough strength to retaliate powerfully. Of all current strategic weapons systems, SLBMs are least vulnerable to attack and therefore the most important element of deterrence. Fixed-silo ICBMs are the most vulnerable to being destroyed in an attack. *Credibility* is the second foundation of deterrence. It is also necessary for an opponent to believe that you can and will use your weapons if attacked. Perception is a key factor. The operational reality will be determined by what the other side believes rather than by what you intend. You might be thinking at this point, Why would a country not respond to an attack? In the sometimes perverse logic of nuclear war, as we shall see, there are times when doing so might not be an option. This leads some analysts to believe that relying exclusively on retaliation is not a credible deterrent stance and that, therefore, countries should be able and willing to initiate a nuclear war in an extreme circumstance.

Mutual assured destruction (MAD) advocates would base deterrence exclusively on having the ability and will to deliver a devastating counterstrike. They believe that deterrence is best achieved if each nuclear power's capabilities include (1) a sufficient number of weapons that are (2) capable of surviving a nuclear attack by an opponent and then (3) delivering a second-strike retaliatory attack that will destroy that opponent. In essence, this approach is *deterrence through punishment*. If each nuclear power has these three capabilities, then a mutual checkmate is achieved. The result, MAD theory holds, is that no power will start a nuclear war because doing so will lead to its own destruction (even if it destroys its enemy).

An alternative approach to deterrence is **nuclear utilization theory (NUT)**. Its advocates contend that the MAD strategy is a crazy gamble because it relies on rationality and clear-sightedness when, in reality, there are other scenarios (discussed earlier) that could lead to nuclear war. Therefore, NUT supporters prefer to base deterrence partly on *deterrence through damage denial* (or limitation). This requires the ability and willingness to destroy enemy weapons before the weapons explode on one's own territory and forces. The ways to do this are to prevent weapons from being launched by either destroying an enemy's command and communications structure or the weapons themselves before the weapons are launched and/or destroying the weapons during flight.

Nuclear Strategy

The rapid reconfiguration of the political world and nuclear weapons inventories has muted the MAD-NUT debate, which was born during the Soviet-American nuclear confrontation. Still, the two approaches remain relevant to a number of current weapons and strategy issues. To illustrate these issues, we can examine two, the first-use option and missile-defense systems.

The First-Use Option   One long-standing debate is when, if ever to employ the **first-use option**, the possibility of being the first country to use its nuclear weapons in a conflict between nuclear powers or against a nonnuclear country. The NATO alliance long held that it might launch a nuclear strike to destroy oncoming, overwhelming Soviet ground forces. More recently, Presidents Bush, the father and the son, each indirectly warned Saddam Hussein that if Iraq used biological or chemical weapons in the impending wars (1991 and 2003), Iraq faced U.S. nuclear retaliation. Similarly, President Clinton issued Presidential Decision Direction 60 (PDD-60) indicating he might respond with nuclear weapons to a biological or chemical attack on the United States.

MAD advocates are very leery of first-use. They warn that using nuclear weapons against another nuclear power could lead to uncontrolled escalation. As for using nuclear weapons against a nonnuclear country, MAD supporters worry that doing so could undermine the norm against nuclear warfare and make it easier in the future for other nuclear powers to use their weapons against nonnuclear foes. NUT advocates argue that there are scenarios when first-use would be good policy. One is when faced with a major attack by biological or chemical weapons. NUT advocates reason that these are WMDs and therefore deterring their use or responding to them with another type of WMD, nuclear weapons, is valid. A second scenario in which NUT supporters would use nuclear weapons first is one in which their country faced a nuclear attack and decided to used nuclear weapons to kill off enemy's leadership, destroy its communications and control system, and disarm it before it could attack by obliterating as many of its nuclear weapons as possible. This approach is roughly akin to the Bush Doctrine's advocacy of preemptive war in the realm of conventional warfare. MAD supporters believe the preemptive nuclear first-strikes could be launched in error, much as the Iraq War was in 2003, and that the result might well be an apocalyptic nuclear counterstrike.

Currently, the first-strike debate centers on two issues. One is the aforementioned controversy over whether to use nuclear weapons to deter against and retaliate for biological and chemical attacks. Whether to develop a new generation of very low-yield (less than 5 kilotons) tactical nuclear weapons ("mini-nukes") is the second issue. In 2005, the Bush administration asked Congress to fund development of a "robust nuclear earth penetrator" weapon, informally dubbed a "bunker buster." Secretary of Defense Donald Rumsfeld argued that there are 10,000 hardened targets in 70 countries that are potential adversaries and that, "At the present time, we don't have a capability of dealing with that. We can't go in there and get at things in solid rock underground."[37] Critics oppose the proposal as promoting first-use and also contend that even low-yield weapons would kill a huge number of civilians. "It is beyond me as to why you're proceeding with this program when the laws of physics won't allow a missile to be driven deeply enough to retain the fallout, which will spew in hundreds of millions of cubic feet if it's at 100 kilotons," one senator responded to Rumsfeld.[38] Legislators eventually rejected funding for mini-nukes after a congressional study estimated that one might kill as many as a million people if used in an urban area, but it is likely that the White House will persist in its effort to add bunker busters to the U.S. arsenal.

Missile Defense Systems   Another long-standing controversy in the area of nuclear planning is whether or not to build a national missile defense system (NMDS), also called a ballistic missile defense (BMD) system or an anti-ballistic missile (ABM) system. After early attempts to build such weapons failed, constructing a NMDS was barred by the U.S.-USSR Anti-Ballistic Missile (ABM) Treaty (1972). A decade later, President Ronald Reagan renewed the controversy by proposing the Strategic Defense Initiative (SDI, labeled "Star Wars" by its critics) to develop BMD capability. Reagan's vision of a comprehensive shield from missile attack was abandoned as too expensive and technically infeasible.

Advances in technology and concern about future possible nuclear attacks by "rogue states" such as North Korea once again raised the issue of building a BMD system in the late 1990s. Some basic research occurred late in the Clinton administration, but that effort has been greatly speeded up by President Bush. Soon after entering office he gave Moscow the required one-year notice that the United States would withdraw from the ABM Treaty in 2002. He also directed the Pentagon to build a NMDS. It is a challenging task that needs to overcome the immense technical difficulties of reliably attacking missiles early in their flight or shooting down warheads traveling through space at 18,000 miles per hour among numerous decoy warheads. The NMDS will also be expensive. Annual funding during the Bush administration has averaged about $9 billion. Supporters of a NMDS contend it can be ready by about 2015 at a cost of about $150 billion. Opponents doubt it will ever work acceptably, and put the eventual cost as high as $1 trillion. The Pentagon had pledged to deploy the first 20 interceptors in Alaska and California by the end of 2005, but that goal was problematic given that tests in relatively controlled situations had only achieved a 50% success rate by early that year.

Whatever the merits of the technical and financial arguments, they are not as important as the question of whether a NMDS should be built even if it is technically and financially feasible (Cimballa, 2003). NUT supporters favor the project because it follows the damage-denial strategy by, hopefully, allowing you to destroy all or some of your opponent's weapons in flight. They also argue that if an enemy believes that its weapons may not get through, it will be less likely to attack and risk retaliation. NMDS advocates also point out that even if it never got to the point where it could provide safety from a large nuclear attack from Russia, the system would provide a degree of protection from North Korea, Iran, and other "rogue states."

MAD proponents claim that a NMDS would make the world more dangerous, not less, by reigniting the nuclear arms race and destabilizing deterrence. They contend the arms race would resume as other nuclear powers deployed a massive number of delivery devices capable of overwhelming any defensive system even after they had suffered a first-strike. Destabilization would arguably occur for two reasons. First, a NMDS might tempt its possessor to strike first in a crisis, since the NMDS would be most effective against a reduced retaliatory strike rather than a full-scale first-strike by an opponent. Second, other countries would worry about that possibility, and would be tempted to launch their own first-strike if they believed that a U.S. first-strike was coming. The other country would reason that since many of its weapons would be destroyed by a U.S. first-strike and that the U.S. NMDS would deflect the remaining weapons in the retaliatory strike, the only chance for survival might be to go first. In such a scenario, the chance of inadvertent nuclear war would soar.

Web Link

The Claremont Institute maintains a pro-NMDS site at **www.missilethreat.com,** and an anti-NMDS link is on the main page of the organization Nuclearfiles at **www.nuclearfiles.org/.**

WRITE THE POLICY SCRIPT

Da or *Nyet* to a First Strike on the United States?

The year is 2010. You are president of Russia. The post–cold war hopes for American-Russian friendship have been replaced by intense hostility, and war with the United States looms. A crisis began four months ago when the ethnic Russians who make up 30% of Latvia's population revolted amid charges of ethnic abuse. The ferocious retaliation by the Latvian authorities against your ethnic brethren outraged you and all Russians, and you ordered your army to occupy Latvia to stop the slaughter. Unfortunately for you, Latvia had joined NATO in 2004, and fleeing Latvian leaders called on the alliance to respond. NATO units are now massed near your border and off your coast, with American military units a major part of these threatening forces.

Your military staff is urging you to strike now rather than wait for what they say is an inevitable attack by the U.S.-led alliance. Your advisers point out that the United States is building a defense against ballistic missiles, and they estimate that it is now capable of destroying 90% of up to 1,000 incoming warheads. Beyond that number, though, the United States is still defenseless because of the limited number of missile interceptors it has deployed so far. Your commanders press you to use 2,100 (70%) of your 3,000 warheads to attack U.S. strategic delivery systems. Your experts estimate that 1,200 of your warheads will get through to their targets, destroying 80% of them. Your strike on the U.S. strategic force leaves you 300 warheads (10%) to use to devastate the NATO forces along your borders, and 600 (20%) to be kept in reserve to deter a retaliatory strike.

You protest that the Americans will surely strike back, perhaps even before your warheads hit their targets. But your generals make two powerful counterarguments. One, they contend that you can deter the U.S. president from immediately retaliating by, at the moment you launch your attack, sending the White House a message on the hotline saying that you are only targeting U.S. strategic weapons sites and warning that a retaliatory U.S. strike will force you to wipe out the American population by firing your remaining 600 warheads at U.S. cities. Second, the officers point to alarming intelligence reports that the Americans, who are also doing their math, might launch a first-strike on you. The U.S. calculation is that if they use 70% of their 3,000 warheads they can destroy 80%, or 2,400 of your warheads in a preemptive strike. You will then have to capitulate because you know that the U.S. missile defense system could destroy 540 (90%) of the remaining 600 warheads in your feeble counterstrike, and the Americans can use their remaining 900 nuclear weapons to obliterate Russian civilization. Your advisers know they are asking you to make a cosmic roll of the dice, but they argue that while you may be damned if

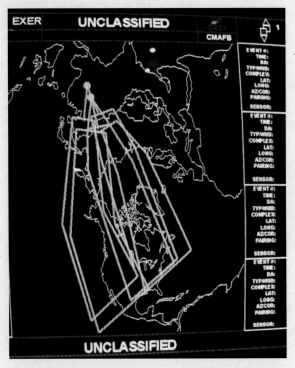

Nuclear war has been called unthinkable, but you are asked here to place yourself in the position of a Russian president and think about the supposedly unthinkable. If you say *da* and launch a nuclear strike on the United States, this photo is something like what American generals would be looking at while advising your counterpart, the U.S. president, about the U.S. response to your attack. The computer screen image at the North American Aerospace Defense Command Center deep inside Cheyenne Mountain in Colorado shows a simulated missile attack by China on the United States.

you act now, you surely will be damned if you wait. Thus you must think about the unthinkable, a preemptive nuclear strike. The skies are heavy over Moscow this morning, and your aching brain screams for relief from the pressure. But there is none. You are the president.

What Do You Think?

As Russia's president in this situation would you strike first or wait? What does the scenario and your decision tell you about the debate over whether developing an NMDS will destabilize nuclear deterrence?

Thus, the issue about whether to proceed with developing a NMDS is a huge gamble. We are betting not only many billions of dollars but also our very lives on a policy choice without knowing whether such a system will add or detract from the chances of nuclear war. How would you write the script about the development of such a system? To help answer that, ponder the dilemma you are presented in the decision box, "*Da* or *Nyet* to a First Strike on the United States?"

Chapter Summary

War and World Politics

1. War is organized killing of other human beings. Virtually everyone is against that. Yet war continues to be a part of the human condition, and its incidence has not significantly abated. Modern warfare affects more civilians than it traditionally did; the number of civilians killed during war now far exceeds that of soldiers.

2. The study of force involves several major questions: When and why does war occur? When it does happen, how effective is it? What conditions govern success or failure? What options exist in structuring the use of force?

3. Although much valuable research has been done about the causes of war, about the best we can do is to say that war is a complex phenomenon that seems to have many causes. Some of these stem from the nature of our species, some from the existence of nation-states, and some from the nature and dynamics of the world political system.

Military Power as an Asset

4. Military power is both tangible and intangible. Tangible elements of power, such as tanks, are relatively easy to visualize and measure. Intangible elements of military power, such as morale and reputation, are much more difficult to operationalize.

5. Acquiring military power also has drawbacks. It creates the temptation to use it, it makes others insecure, and it is costly. Some people argue, and others disagree, that spending too many resources on military power is a major factor in the decline of once-mighty countries. Another argument debates whether quantity or quality provides the best defense.

Applying Military Assets to Diplomacy

6. Force can be used, threatened, or merely exist as an unspoken possibility. When it is used, its suc-

cess requires much planning and skill. Studies have determined the ideal conditions for successful use of military force. If force is to be used, it should be employed as a means, or tool, rather than, as sometimes happens, as an end in itself.

7. Force does not have to be used to have an impact. The possession of military power creates a backdrop to diplomacy, and the overt threat of force increases the psychological pressure even more. The tools of force can be applied through arms sales and other methods of intervention. When it is used, force can range from a very limited demonstration to a full-scale nuclear attack.

8. The nature of war is changing. Technology has enhanced killing power; nationalism has made war a patriotic cause. As a result, the scope of war has expanded, which has also changed the strategy of war. The power to defeat is a traditional strategy of war, while the power to hurt has increased in significance and incidence.

Terrorism

9. The definition of terrorism—what acts are terrorist—has been an ongoing controversial issue. The sources of terrorism can be state-sponsored or transnational, and terrorist acts have taken place in all regions of the world, with some fluctuations in their numbers over the years.

10. Terrorist weapons and tactics have become important issues that states and policy makers must combat, as modern conditions have facilitated the growth of terrorist activities. Apart from using conventional weapons, terrorist threats include the potential use of radiological, chemical, and biological weapons.

11. Governments around the globe have devoted increasing resources and cooperative efforts to find new strategies to combat terrorism as well as to address its root causes.

Unconventional Force

12. Warfare can be classified into three categories: unconventional warfare (including arms transfers, special operations), conventional warfare, and weapons of mass destruction warfare (including nuclear, biological, and chemical weapons).

13. Arms transfers and special operations are unconventional methods of warfare. These have assumed more importance in recent times.

Conventional Force

14. Conventional warfare has been the norm throughout most of history. The goals and conduct of war include avoiding unchecked escalation.

Weapons of Mass Destruction

15. Biological, chemical, and nuclear weapons are now developed to the point where they can cause horrific levels of death and destruction. The debate (MAD versus NUT) involving how to structure nuclear weapons systems and doctrines is an example of the issues that arise as the ability to conduct war continues to change and new technology develops new weapons.

For simulations, debates, and other interactive activities, a chapter quiz, Web links, PowerWeb articles, and much more, visit **www.mhhe.com/rourke11/** and go to chapter 10. Or, while accessing the site, click on Course-Wide Content and view recent international relations articles in the *New York Times*.

Key Terms

conventional warfare	mutual assured destruction (MAD)	social overstretch thesis	transnational terrorism
deterrence	nuclear utilization theory (NUT)	special operations	unconventional force
escalation		state terrorism	weapons of mass destruction (WMDs)
first-use option	power to defeat	strategic-range delivery vehicles	
imperial overstretch thesis	power to hurt	terrorism	

CHAPTER 11

International Security: The Alternative Road

Weapons! arms! What's the matter here?
    —William Shakespeare, *King Lear*

Out of this nettle, danger, we pluck this flower, safety.
    —William Shakespeare, *King Henry IV, Part 1*

This chapter presents alternatives to seeking security through national defense. Alternative approaches include international security forces, arms control and disarmament, and, as these Japanese pacifists marching in Tokyo in 2005 suggest, total rejection of violence as a form of human interaction.

ECURITY IS THE ENDURING YET elusive quest. "I would give all my fame for a pot of ale, and safety," a frightened boy cries out before a battle in Shakespeare's *King Henry V.* Alas, Melpomene, the muse of tragedy, did not favor the boy's plea. The English and French armies met on the battlefield at Agincourt. Peace—and perhaps the boy—perished. Today most of us similarly seek security. Yet our quest is tempered by the reality that while humans have sought safety throughout history, they have usually failed to achieve that goal for long.

Thinking about Security

Perhaps one reason that security from armed attack has been elusive is that we humans have sought it in the wrong way. The traditional path has emphasized national self-defense by amassing arms to deter aggression. Alternative paths have been given little attention and fewer resources. From 1948 through 2005, for example, the world states spent about $41 trillion on their national military budgets, and the UN spent approximately $40 billion on peacekeeping operations. That is about $1,000 spent on national security for each $1 spent on peacekeeping. It just may be, then, that the first secretary-general of the United Nations, Trygve Lie, was onto something when he suggested that "wars occur because people prepare for conflict, rather than for peace."[1]

The aim of this chapter is to think anew about security from armed aggression in light of humankind's failed effort to find it. Because the traditional path has not brought us to a consistently secure place, it is only prudent to consider alternative, less-traveled-by, paths to security. These possible approaches include limiting or abandoning our weapons altogether, creating international security forces, and even adopting the standards of pacifism.

A Tale of Insecurity

One way to think about how to increase security is to ponder the origins of insecurity. To do that, let us go back in time to the hypothetical origins of insecurity. Our vehicle is a parable. Insecurity may not have started exactly like this, but it might have.

A Drama about Insecurity

It was a sunny, yet somehow foreboding autumn day many millennia ago. Og, a caveman of the South Tribe, was searching for food. It had been a poor season for hunting and gathering, and Og fretted about the coming winter and his family. The urge to provide security from hunger for his family carried Og northward out of the South Tribe's usual territory and into the next valley.

It was the valley of Ug of the North Tribe. The same motivations that drove Og also urged Ug on, but he had been luckier. He had just killed a large antelope and Ug was feeling prosperous as he used his long knife to clean his kill. At that moment, Og, with hunting spear in hand, happened out of the forest and came upon Ug. Both the hunters were startled, and they exchanged cautious greetings. Ug was troubled by the lean and hungry look of the spear-carrying stranger, and he unconsciously grasped his knife more tightly. The tensing of his ample muscles alarmed Og, who instinctively dropped his spear point to a defensive position. Fear was the common denominator. Neither Og nor Ug wanted a confrontation, but they were trapped. Their disengagement negotiation went something like this (translated):

Web Link

The Bulletin of the Atomic Scientists has calculated a "Doomsday Clock" since 1947 to estimate how close humankind is to midnight (nuclear annihilation). The clock's history and "current time" are at **www.thebulletin .org/doomsday_clock/**.

Ug: You are eyeing my antelope and pointing your spear at me.

Og: And your knife glints menacingly in the sunlight. But this is crazy. I mean you no harm; your antelope is yours. Still, my family is needy and it would be good if you shared your kill.

Ug: Of course I am sympathetic, and I want to be friends. But this is an antelope from the North Tribe's valley. If there is any meat left over, I'll even give you a little. But first, why don't you put down your spear so we can talk more easily?

Og: A fine idea, Ug, and I'll be glad to put down my spear, but why don't you lay down that fearful knife first? Then we can be friends.

Ug: Spears can fly through the air farther. . . . You should be first.

Og: Knives can strike more accurately. . . . You should be first.

And so the confrontation continued, with Og and Ug equally unsure of the other's intentions, with each sincerely proclaiming his peaceful purpose, but with each unable to convince the other to lay his weapon aside first.

Critiquing the Drama

Think about the web of insecurity that entangled Og and Ug. Each was insecure about providing for himself and his family in the harsh winter that was approaching. Security extends farther than just being safe from armed attacks. Ug was a "have" and Og was a "have-not." Ug had a legitimate claim to his antelope; Og had a legitimate need to find sustenance. Territoriality and tribal differences added to the building tension. Ug was in "his" valley; Og could not understand why unequal resource distribution meant that some should prosper while others were deprived. The gutting knife and the spear also played a role. But did the weapons cause tension or, perhaps, did Ug's knife protect him from a raid by Og?

We should also ask what could have provided the security to get Og and Ug out of their confrontation. If Og's valley had been full of game, he would not have been driven to the next valley. Or if the region's food had been shared by all, Og would not have needed Ug's antelope. Knowing this, Ug might have been less defensive. Assuming, for a moment, that Og was dangerous—as hunger sometimes drives people to be—then Ug might have been more secure if somehow he could have signaled the equivalent of today's 911 distress call and summoned the region's peacekeeping force, dispatched by the area's intertribal council. The council might even have been able to aid Og with some food and skins to ease his distress and to quell the anger he felt when he compared his ill fortune with the prosperity of Ug.

The analysis of our parable could go on and be made more complex. Og and Ug might have spoken different languages, worshipped different deities, or had differently colored faces. That, however, would not change the fundamental questions regarding security. Why were Og and Ug insecure? More important, once insecurity existed, what could have been done to restore harmony?

Seeking Security: Approaches and Standards of Evaluation

Now bring your minds from the past to the present, from primordial cave dwellers to yourself. Think about contemporary international security. The easiest matter is determining what our goal should be. How to achieve it is, of course, a much more challenging question.

| | | | | Primary | |
Security Approach	Sources of Insecurity	World Political System	Armaments Strategy	Peacekeeping Mechanism	Strategy
Unlimited self-defense	Many; probably inherent in humans	State-based national interests and rivalries; fear	Have many and all types to guard against threats	Armed states, deterrence, alliances, balance of power	Peace through strength
Limited self-defense	Many; perhaps inherent, but weapons intensify	State-based; limited cooperation based on mutual interests	Limit amount and types to reduce capabilities, damage, tension	Armed states; defensive capabilities, lack of offensive capabilities	Peace through limited offensive ability
International security	Anarchical world system; lack of law or common security mechanisms	International political integration; regional or world government	Transfer weapons and authority to international force	International peacekeeping/peace enforcement	Peace through law and universal collective defense
Abolition of war	Weapons; personal and national greed and insecurity	Options from pacifistic states to global village model	Eliminate weapons	Lack of ability; lack of fear; individual and collective pacifism	Peace through being peaceful

TABLE 11.1   Four Approaches to Security

Concept source: Rapoport (1992).

The path to peace has long been debated. The four approaches outlined here provide some basic alternatives that help structure this chapter on security.

Approaches to Security

There are, in essence, four possible approaches to securing peace. The basic parameters of each are shown in Table 11.1. As with many, even most matters in this book, which approach is best is part of the realist-liberal debate.

Unlimited self-defense, the first of the four approaches, is the traditional approach of each country being responsible for its own defense and amassing weapons it wishes for that defense. The thinking behind this approach rests on the classic realist assumption that humans have an inherent element of greed and aggressiveness that promotes individual and collective violence. This makes the international system, from the realists' perspective, a place of danger where each state must fend for itself or face the perils of domination or destruction by other states.

Beyond the traditional approach to security, there are three alternative approaches: *limited self-defense* (arms limitations), *international security* (regional and world security forces), and *abolition of war* (complete disarmament and pacifism). Each of these will be examined in the pages that follow. Realists do not oppose arms control or even international peacekeeping under the right circumstances. Realists, for instance, recognize that the huge arsenals of weapons that countries possess are dangerous and, therefore, there can be merit in carefully negotiated, truly verifiable arms accords. But because the three alternative approaches all involve some level of trust and depend on the triumph of the spirit of human cooperation over human avarice and power-seeking, they are all more attractive to liberals than to realists.

Standards of Evaluation

Now that we have identified the approaches to seeking security, the question is which one of them offers the greatest chance of safety. There is no clear answer, so it

ANALYZE THE ISSUE
Choosing an Alternative Path

Security is relative and a state of mind. Like this 19-year-old college student in Thailand who was taken hostage by a man so high on methamphetamines that he had cut himself, individuals can suddenly fall victim to violent crime. Yet most people do not carry guns because they feel safe in their domestic system. The police responded to this woman's peril and eventually subdued her assailant and freed her. By contrast, there is no one who will necessarily aid international victims of aggression. Therefore, countries in the anarchical international system rely on self-protection and create armies to defend themselves.

is important to consider how to evaluate the various possibilities. To do this, begin by considering the college community in which you live. The next time you are in class, look around you. Is anyone carrying a gun? Are you? Probably not. Think about why you are not doing so. The answer is that you feel relatively secure.

The word "relatively" is important here. You are not absolutely safe because dangerous people who might steal your property, attack you, and even kill you are lurking in your community. There were 14,408 homicides, 93,433 reported rapes, and 1,273,418 other violent crimes in the United States during 2003. Criminals committed another 10,535,527 burglaries, car thefts, and other property crimes, which cost the victims about $17 billion. Thus, it is clear that you are not absolutely secure. Yet most of us feel secure enough to forgo carrying firearms.

The important thing to consider is why you feel secure enough not to carry a gun despite the fact that you could be murdered, raped, beaten up, or have your property stolen. There are many reasons. *Domestic norms* against violence and stealing are one reason. Most people around you are peaceful and honest and are unlikely, even if angry or covetous, to attack you or steal your property. Established *domestic collective security forces* are a second part of feeling secure. The police are on patrol to deter criminals; you can call 911 if you are attacked or robbed; courts and prisons exist to deal with perpetrators. *Domestic disarmament* is a third contributor to your sense of security. Most domestic societies have disarmed substantially, shun the routine of carrying weapons, and have turned the legitimate use of domestic force beyond immediate self-defense over to their police. *Domestic conflict-resolution mechanisms* are a fourth contributor to security. There are ways to settle disputes without violence. Lawsuits are filed, and judges make decisions. Indeed, some crimes against persons and property are avoided because most domestic political systems provide some level of social services to meet human needs.

To return to our stress on relative security, it is important to see that for all the protections and dispute-resolution procedures provided by your domestic system, and for all the sense of security that you usually feel, you are not fully secure. Nor are countries and their citizens secure in the global system. For that matter, it is unlikely that anything near absolute global security can be achieved through any of the methods offered in this chapter or anywhere else. Therefore, the most reasonable standard by which to evaluate approaches to security is to compare them and to ask which makes you more secure.

Limited Self-Defense through Arms Control

The first alternative approach to achieving security involves limiting the numbers and types of weapons that countries possess. This approach, called **arms control**, aims at lessening military (especially offensive) capabilities and lessening the damage even if war begins. Additionally, arms control advocates believe that the decline in the number and power of weapons systems will ease political tensions, thereby making further arms agreements possible.

Web Link

A site that provides a valuable overview of disarmament is that of the UN Department for Disarmament Affairs at http://disarmament.un.org/.

Methods of Achieving Arms Control

There are many methods to control arms in order to limit or even reduce their number and to prevent their spread. These methods include numerical restrictions; research, development, and deployment restrictions; categorical restrictions; and transfer restrictions. Several of the arms control agreements that will be used to illustrate the restrictions are detailed in the following section on the history of arms control, but to familiarize yourself with them quickly, peruse the agreements listed in Table 11.2 on page 344.

Numerical restrictions. Placing numerical limits above, at, or below the current level of existing weapons is the most common approach to arms control. This approach specifies the number or capacity of weapons and/or troops that each side may possess. In some cases the numerical limits may be at or higher than current levels. For example, the first and second Strategic Arms Limitations Talks treaties, the two Strategic Arms Reduction Treaties (START I and II), and the Treaty of Moscow (2002) were structured to significantly reduce the number of American and Russian nuclear weapons. Although START II never went into effect because Russia's Duma refused to ratify it, both countries later agreed to cuts in their nuclear arsenals that in many cases will exceed the reductions outlined in the treaty.

Categorical restrictions. A second approach to arms control involves limiting or eliminating certain types of weapons. The Intermediate-Range Nuclear Forces Treaty (INF) eliminated an entire class of weapons—intermediate-range nuclear missiles. The new Anti-Personnel Mine Treaty will make it safer to walk the Earth.

Development, testing, and deployment restrictions. A third method of limiting arms involves a sort of military birth control that ensures that weapons systems never begin their gestation period of development and testing or, if they do, they are never deployed. The advantage of this approach is that it stops a specific area of arms building before it starts. For instance, the countries that have ratified the Nuclear Non-Proliferation Treaty (NPT) and that do not have such weapons agree not to develop them. The U.S. Congress has barred the development of new types of low-yield tactical nuclear weapons (mini-nukes), and refuses to lift that ban despite repeated requests by the Bush administration to do so.

TABLE 11.2 Selected Arms Control Treaties			
Treaty	Provisions	Date Signed	Number of Parties
Treaties in Force			
Geneva Protocol	Bans using gas or bacteriological weapons	1925	133
Limited Test Ban	Bans nuclear tests in the atmosphere, space, or underwater	1963	124
Non-Proliferation Treaty (NPT)	Prohibits selling, giving, or receiving nuclear weapons, materials, or technology for weapons. Made permanent in 1995	1968	189
Biological Weapons	Bans the production and possession of biological weapons	1972	162
Strategic Arms Limitation Talks Treaty (SALT I)	Limits U.S. and USSR strategic weapons	1972	2
Threshold Test Ban	Limits U.S. and USSR underground tests to 150 kt	1974	2
SALT II	Limits U.S. and USSR strategic weapons	1979	2
Intermediate-Range Nuclear Forces (INF)	Eliminates U.S. and USSR missiles with ranges between 500 km and 5,500 km	1987	2
Missile Technology Control Regime (MTCR)	Limits transfer of missiles and missile technology	1987	33
Conventional Forces in Europe Treaty (CFE)	Reduces conventional forces in Europe	1990	30
Strategic Arms Reduction Treaty (START I)	Reduces U.S. and USSR/Russian strategic nuclear forces	1991	2
Chemical Weapons Convention (CWC)	Bans the possession of chemical weapons after 2005	1993	169
Anti-Personnel Mine Treaty (APM)	Bans the production, use, possession, and transfer of land mines	1997	144
Treaty of Moscow	Reduces U.S. and Russian strategic nuclear forces	2002	2
Treaties Not in Force			
Anti-Ballistic Missile (ABM) Treaty	U.S.-USSR pact limits anti-ballistic missile testing and deployment. U.S. withdrew in 2002	1972	n/a
START II	Reduces U.S. and Russian strategic nuclear forces. Not ratified by Russia	1993	1
Comprehensive Test Ban Treaty (CTBT)	Bans all nuclear weapons tests. Not ratified by U.S., China, Russia, India, and Pakistan	1996	121

Notes: The date signed indicates the first date when countries whose leadership approves of a treaty can sign it. Being a *signatory* is not legally binding; becoming a *party* to a treaty then requires fulfilling a country's ratification procedure or other legal process to legally adhere to the treaty. Treaties to which the Soviet Union was a party bind its successor state, Russia.

Data sources: Numerous news and Web sources, including the United Nations Treaty Collection at http://untreaty.un.org/.

Progress toward controlling arms has been slow and often unsteady, but each agreement listed here represents at least an attempted step down the path of restraining the world's weapons.

Geographic restriction. A fourth approach is to prohibit the deployment of any weapons of war in certain geographic areas. The deployment of military weapons in Antarctica, the seabed, space, and elsewhere is, for example, banned. There can be geographic restrictions on specific types of weapons, such as the Treaty for the Prohibition of Nuclear Weapons in Latin America (1989).

Transfer restrictions. A fifth method of arms control is to prohibit or limit the flow of weapons and weapons technology across international borders. Under the

NPT, for example, countries that have nuclear weapons or nuclear weapons technology pledge not to supply nonnuclear states with weapons or the technology to build them.

This review of the strategies and methods of arms control leads naturally to the question of whether they have been successful. And if they have not been successful, why not? To address these questions, in the next two sections we will look at the history of arms control, then at the continuing debate over arms control.

The History of Arms Control

Attempts to control arms and other military systems extend almost to the beginning of written history. The earliest recorded example occurred in 431 B.C. when Sparta and Athens negotiated over the length of the latter's defensive walls. Prior to the beginning of the 20th century, however, arms control hardly existed. Since then there has been a buildup of arms control activity. Technology, more than any single factor, spurred rising interest in arms control. Beginning about 1900, the escalating lethality of weapons left many increasingly appalled by the carnage they were causing on the battlefield and among noncombatants. Then in midcentury, the development of nuclear, biological, and chemical weapons of mass destruction (WMDs) sparked a growing sense that an apocalyptic end of human life had literally become possible.

Arms Control through the 1980s

The multilateral Hague Conferences (1899, 1907) were the first modern attempts at arms control. Although limited in scope, they did place some restrictions on poison gas and the use of other weapons. The horror of World War I further increased world interest in arms control. The Washington Naval Conference (1921–1922) established a battleship tonnage ratio among the world's leading naval powers and, for a time, headed off a naval arms buildup. There were several other bilateral and multilateral arms negotiations and agreements in the 1920s and 1930s, but they all had little impact on the increasing avalanche of aggression that culminated in World War II. Arms control efforts were spurred even more by the unparalleled destruction wrought by conventional arms during World War II and by the atomic flashes that leveled Hiroshima and Nagasaki in 1945. One early reaction was the creation in 1946 of what is now called the International Atomic Energy Agency (IAEA) to limit the use of nuclear technology to peaceful purposes.

The intensity of the cold war blocked arms control during the 1950s, but by the early 1960s worries about nuclear weapons began to overcome even that impediment. The first major step occurred in 1963 with the Treaty Banning Nuclear Weapon Tests in the Atmosphere, in Outer Space and Under Water (the Limited/Partial Test Ban Treaty). Between 1945 and 1963, there were on average 25 above-ground nuclear tests each year. After the treaty was signed, such tests (all by nonsignatories) declined to about three a year, then ended in the 1980s. Thus, the alarming threat of radioactive fallout that had increasingly contaminated the atmosphere was largely eliminated.

Later in the decade, the multilateral nuclear **Non-Proliferation Treaty** (**NPT**) of 1968 pledged its parties (adherents, countries that have completed their legal process to adhere to a treaty) not to transfer nuclear weapons or in any way to "assist, encourage, or induce any nonnuclear state to manufacture or otherwise acquire nuclear weapons." Nonnuclear adherents also agree not to build or accept nuclear weapons and to allow the IAEA to establish safeguards to ensure that nuclear facilities are used exclusively for peaceful purposes. Overall, the NPT has been successful in that many countries with the potential to build weapons have not. Yet the

NPT is not an unreserved success, as discussed below in the section on its renewal in 1995 and subsequent five-year reviews.

During the 1970s, with cold war tensions beginning to relax, and with the U.S. and Soviet nuclear weapon inventories each passing the 20,000 mark, the pace of arms control negotiations picked up. The **Anti-Ballistic Missile Treaty (ABM)** of 1972 put stringent limits on U.S. and Soviet efforts to deploy national missile defense systems (NMDS), which many analysts believed could destabilize nuclear deterrence by undermining its cornerstone, mutual assured destruction (MAD). As discussed in chapter 10, President Bush withdrew the United States from the ABM Treaty in 2002 to pursue the development of a NMDS.

The 1970s also included important negotiations to limit the number, deployment, or other aspects of WMDs. The most significant of these with regard to nuclear weapons were the **Strategic Arms Limitation Talks Treaty I (SALT I)** of 1972 and the **Strategic Arms Limitation Talks Treaty II (SALT II)** of 1979. Each put important caps on the number of Soviet and American nuclear weapons and delivery vehicles. Moscow and Washington, already confined to underground nuclear tests by the 1963 treaty, moved to limit the size of even those tests to 150 kilotons in the Threshold Test Ban Treaty (1974). In another realm of WMDs, the **Biological Weapons Convention** of 1972, which virtually all countries subsequently signed and ratified, pledged those countries with biological weapons to destroy them, and obligated all parties not to manufacture new ones.

Arms control momentum picked up even more speed during the 1980s as the cold war began to wind down. The **Missile Technology Control Regime (MTCR)** was established in 1987 to restrain the proliferation of missiles. The odd designation "regime" is used for the agreement because, according to the U.S. State Department, the MTCR is an "informal political arrangement" through which signatory countries pledge not to transfer missile technology or missiles with a range greater than 300 kilometers.[2] The MTCR has slowed, although not stopped, the spread of missiles. The countries with the most sophisticated missile technology all adhere to the MTCR, and they have brought considerable pressure to bear on China and other noncompliant missile-capable countries.

A second important agreement was the U.S-Soviet **Intermediate-Range Nuclear Forces Treaty (INF)** of 1987. By eliminating an entire class of nuclear delivery vehicles (missiles with ranges between 500 and 5,500 kilometers), it became the first treaty to actually reduce the global nuclear arsenal. The deployment of such U.S. missiles to Europe and counter-targeting by the Soviet Union had put Europe at particular risk of nuclear war.

Arms Control since 1990: WMDs

The years since 1990 have been by far the most important in the history of the control of WMDs. The most significant arms control during the 1990s involved efforts to control nuclear arms, although progress was also made on chemical weapons.

Strategic Arms Reduction Treaty I   After a decade of negotiations, Presidents George H. W. Bush and Mikhail Gorbachev signed the first **Strategic Arms Reduction Treaty I (START I)** in 1991. The treaty mandated significant cuts in U.S. and Soviet strategic-range (over 5,500 kilometers) nuclear forces. Each country was limited to 1,600 delivery vehicles (missiles and bombers) and 6,000 strategic explosive nuclear devices (warheads and bombs). Thus, START I began the process of reducing the U.S. and Soviet strategic arsenals, each of which contained more than 10,000 warheads and bombs.

The world remains menaced by deadly arsenals of nuclear weapons, but arms control efforts in the last several decades have substantially reduced the number of these weapons that are deployed. Here, an explosion is destroying a U.S. Minuteman III missile silo near Petersburg, North Dakota, in August 2001. This silo was 149th and last to be destroyed under U.S.-Soviet Strategic Arms Reduction Treaty I of 1991.

Strategic Arms Reduction Treaty II   Presidents Boris Yeltsin and George Bush took a further step toward reducing the mountain of nuclear weapons when they signed the **Strategic Arms Reduction Treaty II (START II)** in 1993. Under START II, Russia and the United States agreed that by 2007 they would reduce their nuclear warheads and bombs to 3,500 for the United States and 2,997 for Russia. The treaty also has a number of clauses relating to specific weapons, the most important of which was the elimination of all ICBMs with multiple warheads (multiple independent reentry vehicles, MIRVs). The U.S. Senate ratified START II in 1996, but Russia's Duma delayed taking up the treaty until 2000. Then it voted for a conditional ratification, making final agreement contingent on a U.S. pledge to abide by the ABM Treaty. When President Bush did the opposite and withdrew from the ABM Treaty, Moscow announced its final rejection of START II. As a result, the reduction of U.S. and Russian strategic nuclear weapons slowed, but it continued as both countries sought to economize. Cuts have continued under the Treaty of Moscow discussed below, but the provision requiring elimination of all MIRV-capable ICBMs died, and both countries maintain a significant number of these missiles (U.S.–360; Russia–245).

The Treaty of Moscow   Even while START II was in limbo pending Russia's ratification, Presidents Bill Clinton and Boris Yeltsin agreed in 1997 on the broad principles for a third round of START aimed at further cutting the number of nuclear devices mounted on strategic-range delivery systems to between 2,000 and 2,500. That goal took on greater substance in May 2002 when President George W. Bush met with President Vladimir Putin in Moscow and the two leaders signed the Treaty Between the United States of America and the Russian Federation on Strategic Offensive Reductions, more generally called the **Treaty of Moscow.** Under its provisions, the two countries agree to cut their arsenals of nuclear warheads and bombs to no more than 2,200 by 2012. However, the Treaty of Moscow contains no provisions relating to MIRVs.

Web Link

The lead U.S. office for arms control is the State Department's Bureau of Arms Control at **http://www.state.gov/t/ac/**.

Did You Know That:

START I is about 700 pages long. The Treaty of Moscow is 3 pages long.

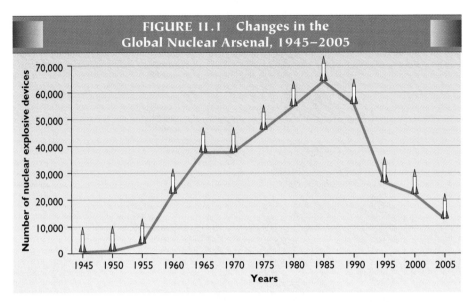

FIGURE 11.1 Changes in the Global Nuclear Arsenal, 1945–2005

The mountain of strategic and tactical nuclear warheads and bombs grew rapidly from 1945 to 1986 when it peaked at 65,057. Then it began a steep decline and in 2005 stood at an estimated 12,741.

Notes: Data includes all acknowledged nuclear weapons countries only and would be between 100 to 200 more for 2005 if unacknowledged nuclear weapons countries were included.

Data source: Bulletin of the Atomic Scientists Web site at http://www.thebulletin.org. Calculations for 2005 by author.

Most observers hailed the new agreement, and it was soon ratified by both countries' legislatures. There were critics, however, who charged that it was vague to the point of being "for all practical purposes meaningless." Four of the treaty's clauses sparked the allegation that it lacked teeth. For one, there is no schedule of reductions from existing levels as long as they are completed by 2012. Second, the treaty expires that year if the two sides do not renew it. Thus the two parties could do nothing, let the treaty lapse in 2012, and never have violated it. Third, either country can withdraw with just 90 days notice. And fourth, both countries will be able to place dismantled weapons in reserve, which would allow them to be rapidly reinstalled on missiles and deployed.

Such concerns, although important, are somewhat offset by the fact that between 2002 and 2005, the U.S. stockpile of deployed nuclear warheads and bombs declined 36% and Russia's arsenal dropped 22%. Moreover these reductions are part of an overall trend that has lowered the mountain of global nuclear weapons by 80% between 1986 and 2002, as Figure 11.1 illustrates. If the reductions outlined in the Moscow treaty are put into place, and if the nuclear arsenals of China and the other smaller nuclear powers remain relatively stable, the world total of nuclear weapons in 2012 will be further reduced by about 25%. Even now the silos at several former U.S. ICBM sites are completely empty, some of the bases have even been sold, and part of the land has reverted to farming, bringing to fruition the words from the Book of Isaiah (2:4), "They shall beat their swords into plowshares, and their spears into pruning hooks."

The Comprehensive Test Ban Treaty   Banning all tests of nuclear weapons has been another important arms control effort. Following the first atomic test on July 16,

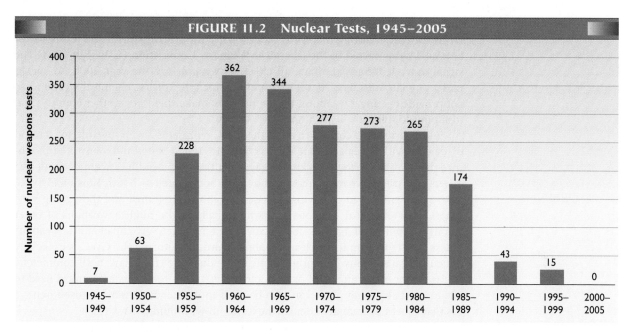

FIGURE 11.2   Nuclear Tests, 1945–2005

There were 2,051 known nuclear weapons tests between August 1945 and May 1998. As of this writing, no further tests have been held, raising the hope in many that the 2,051st test, conducted by Pakistan, will be the last. The goal of the Comprehensive Nuclear Test Ban Treaty is to turn that hope into a universal international commitment, but the unwillingness of several of the existing nuclear-weapons countries to ratify the treaty leaves further tests possible.

Data source: Bulletin of the Atomic Scientists, 45/6 (November/December 1998); author's calculations.

1945, the number of tests mushroomed to 171 blasts in 1962. Then testing began to ebb in response to a number of treaties (see Table 11.2), a declining need to test, and increasing international condemnation of those tests that did occur. For example, Australia's prime minister in one of the milder comments labeled France's series of underground tests in 1995 on uninhabited atolls in the South Pacific "an act of stupidity."[3] Those tests, China's two in 1996, and the series that India and Pakistan each conducted in 1998 brought the total number of tests since 1945 to 2,051. As shown in Figure 11.2, no further tests have been conducted through mid-2005, although there is concern that North Korea may break the de facto moratorium.

Those who share the goal of having the number of nuclear tests frozen forever at 2,051 have pinned their hopes on the **Comprehensive Test Ban Treaty** (**CTBT**). The treaty was concluded in 1996 and 120 countries have become parties to it. Nevertheless, it has not gone into force. The reason is that it does not become operational until all 44 countries that had nuclear reactors in 1996 ratify it, and 11 of them, including the United States, have not. In the U.S. case, President Bill Clinton signed the treaty, but the Republican-controlled Senate rejected it in 1999. His successor, President Bush, is unwilling to try to resurrect the treaty, in part because his administration favors developing and possibly testing mini-nukes, as discussed earlier. Thus testing remains a possibility, and any new tests could set off a chain of other tests. As the Russian newspaper *Pravda* editorialized, "The Moscow hawks are waiting impatiently for the USA to violate its nuclear test moratorium. . . . If the USA carries out tests . . . , the Kremlin will not keep its defense industries from following the bad U.S. example. They have been waiting too long since the end of the cold war."[4]

Chemical Weapons Convention Nuclear weapons were not the only WMDs to receive attention during the 1990s. Additionally, the growing threat and recent use of chemical weapons led to the **Chemical Weapons Convention (CWC)** in 1993. The signatories pledge to eliminate all chemical weapons by the year 2005; to "never under any circumstance" develop, produce, stockpile, or use chemical weapons; to not provide chemical weapons, or the means to make them, to another country; and to submit to rigorous inspection.

As with all arms control treaties, the CWC represents a step toward, not the end of, dealing with a menace. One issue is that the United States and many other countries that are a party to the treaty have not met the 2005 deadline. Second, about two dozen countries have not agreed to the treaty. Some, such as North Korea and Syria, have or are suspected of having chemical weapons programs, and they, along with others, view chemical weapons as a way to balance the nuclear weapons of other countries. Some Arab nations, for instance, are reluctant to give up chemical weapons unless Israel gives up its nuclear weapons. Third, monitoring the CWC is especially difficult because many common chemicals are dual-use (they have both commercial and weapons applications). For example, polytetrafluoroethene, a chemical used to make nonstick frying pans, can also be used to manufacture perfluoroisobutene, a gas that causes pulmonary edema (the lungs fill with fluid).

Arms Control since 1990: Nuclear Non-Proliferation

Stemming the spread of nuclear weapons to additional countries has arguably been the greatest arms control challenge since the end of the cold war. A recent poll of Americans found that 74% of them believed that "preventing the spread of nuclear weapons" should be "a very important" U.S. foreign policy goal, a support level 2% higher than even combating international terrorism.[5] The centerpiece of the nuclear containment campaign, as noted earlier, is the Non-Proliferation Treaty (NPT) of 1968.

The Record of the NPT Clearly the record of the NPT is not one of complete success. In contrast to the decline in the number of nuclear weapons that has occurred since the end of the U.S.-Soviet confrontation in the early 1990s, the number of countries with nuclear weapons has increased. India, Israel, and Pakistan never agreed to the NPT, and North Korea withdrew its ratification in 2003. All have developed nuclear weapons or believably claim to have done so. This doubles the number of countries with nuclear weapons from the time the NPT was first signed. As the accompanying map indicates, there are now seven countries that openly possess nuclear weapons, one (Israel) whose nuclear arsenal is an open secret, and one (North Korea) that probably has nuclear weapons. Several other countries such as Iran have or had active programs to develop nuclear weapons, and unless the diplomats from the European Union can persuade Iran to change course, it too will arm itself with nuclear weapons. Yet further proliferation is not hard to imagine. For example, nuclear weapons test by North Korea would put heavy pressure on neighboring South Korea and Japan to develop a nuclear deterrent. The list could go on.

Yet despite the proliferation that has occurred, it would be an error to depict the NPT as a failure. Now all but four countries are party to the NPT. Furthermore, somewhat offsetting the march of India, Pakistan, North Korea, and perhaps Iran to become nuclear weapons countries, other pretenders to that title have given up their nuclear ambitions. Libya ratified the NPT in 2004 and agreed to dismantle its nuclear weapons and missile programs and allow IAEA inspections. Why Libya abandoned its 30-year effort to develop nuclear weapons and the missiles to deliver

MAP
The Spread of
Nuclear Weapons

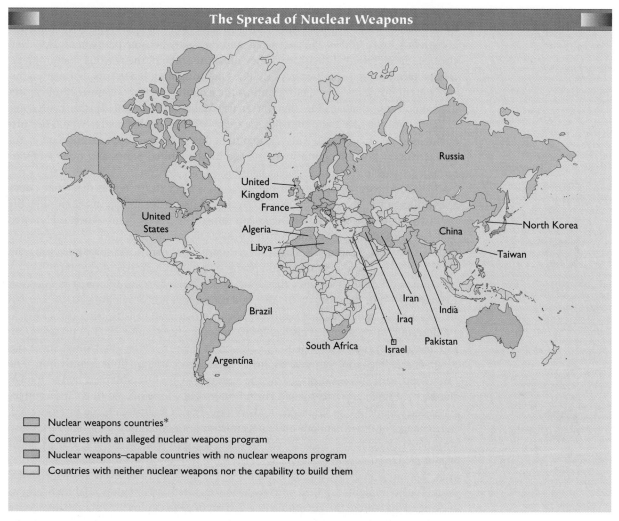

The Spread of Nuclear Weapons

Russia

United Kingdom

France

United States

Algeria

Libya

China

North Korea

Taiwan

Brazil

Iran

India

Iraq

South Africa

Israel

Pakistan

Argentina

☐ Nuclear weapons countries*

☐ Countries with an alleged nuclear weapons program

☐ Nuclear weapons–capable countries with no nuclear weapons program

☐ Countries with neither nuclear weapons nor the capability to build them

Efforts such as the Nuclear Non-Proliferation Treaty have slowed, but not stopped, the proliferation of nuclear weapons. There are now nine declared and undeclared nuclear weapons countries. Numerous other countries have the ability and, in some cases, the desire to acquire nuclear weapons.

*Israel has never acknowledged that it has nuclear weapons. North Korea claims to have nuclear weapons and most experts believe this to be true.

them is uncertain, but among the reasons cited by various analysts were the negative impact of the long-term sanctions on the Libyan economy, the cost of continuing the faltering program, and fear that it would become a target of U.S. military action, as Iraq had. Similarly, Argentina and Brazil halted their nuclear programs in the early 1990s and adhered to the NPT in 1995 and 1997 respectively. Algeria and South Africa both also had nuclear weapons programs, and South Africa may have even tested a weapon, before they both changed course and also became party to the NPT (1995 and 1991 respectively). Beyond these countries that once pursued nuclear weapons, there are many countries such as Canada, Germany, and Japan that long ago could have developed nuclear weapons and have not.

Challenges to Halting Proliferation Under the NPT's provisions, the treaty was temporary and its parties were to gather in 1995 to decide whether to make it permanent (Braun & Chyba, 2004). This occurred, and the treaty became permanent. However, the negotiations were difficult, and they illustrate some of the reasons that proliferation is hard to stop (Singh & Way, 2004). One stumbling block was that many nonnuclear countries resisted renewal unless the existing nuclear-weapons countries set a timetable for dismantling their arsenals. Malaysia's delegate to the conference charged, for instance, that renewing the treaty without such a pledge would be "justifying nuclear states for eternity" to maintain their monopoly.[6] One important factor in overcoming this objection was a pledge by the United States and other nuclear-weapons states to conclude a treaty banning all nuclear tests.

Did You Know That:

Pakistan's biggest missile, the Ghauri, is named after Mohammad Ghauri, the 12th-century leader who began the Muslim conquest of Hindu India. India's Agni missile bears the name of the Hindu god of fire.

A second reason that nuclear proliferation is difficult to stem is that some countries still want such weapons. Israel developed its nuclear weapons soon after the NPT was first signed, India and Pakistan joined the nuclear club when each tested nuclear weapons in 1998, and North Korea declared in 2005, "We . . . have manufactured nuclear weapons."[7] The reverberations of North Korea's weapons program and the diplomacy to persuade Pyongyang to end it are covered in chapter 8.

Iran is yet another country that appears determined to acquire nuclear weapons. Even though Iran is a party to the NPT and claims that it is developing only a peaceful nuclear energy program, most outsiders believe that Tehran is nearing the ability to produce nuclear weapons. This has led to ongoing efforts since 2003 to pressure Iran to comply with the NPT. Whether by design or happenstance, the United States has acted as the "bad cop" by pressing for at least economic sanctions against Iran. The "good cop" role has been played by the European Union represented by the foreign ministers of France, Germany, and Great Britain. They have offered Iran various diplomatic carrots, including admission to the World Trade Organization and economic aid, in exchange for it permanently ending its nuclear enrichment program. They have also threatened to refer the issue to the UN Security Council, where the United States would be free to demand that sticks in the form of economic sanctions be applied to Iran. Looming large in the background is the possibility of even stronger sticks. Numerous comments by U.S. officials have suggested Washington might aid groups seeking to overthrow the government in Tehran or even deploy U.S. aircraft and cruise missiles to attack Iran's nuclear facilities. A similar possibility is a military strike by Israel, much like the one that destroyed Iraq's Osiraq nuclear reactor in 1981.

The continuing challenges to the NPT were also highlighted in the stalemated quinquennial (every five years) review meeting in 2005. Washington pressed to focus attention on the nuclear programs of North Korea and Iran, but Iran and its supporters rejected such an agenda. Many nonnuclear countries complained that the United States continued to try to maintain a nuclear weapons advantage by reneging on its pledge in Article 6 of the NPT "to pursue good-faith negotiations on effective measures relating to . . . nuclear disarmament." Critics say this means complete nuclear disarmament. American and other diplomats argue that the sizeable reductions in the U.S. and Russian arsenals constitute nuclear disarmament and satisfy the treaty. A similar charge by nonnuclear countries is that by rejecting the CTBT, Washington has ignored its 1995 agreement to join a treaty barring all nuclear weapons testing in return for nonnuclear countries' support for making the NPT permanent. American representatives opposed the tabling of either of these charges at the review session. In another agenda stalemate, Muslim countries wanted to spotlight Israel's nuclear weapons; U.S. diplomats opposed doing so. A further agenda standoff featured American diplomats wanting to condemn Iran's alleged nuclear weapons program, and some other delegations taking exception to doing so. When the conference opened, UN Secretary-General Kofi Annan cautioned the delegates that, "If we are truly committed to a nuclear weapon–free world, we must move beyond rhetorical flourish and political posturing, and start to think seriously how to get there."[8] During a month of wrangling, the delegates largely ignored that advice. When the meeting adjourned with no progress, a frustrated Mohamed ElBaradei, head of the IAEA, lamented, "The conference after a full month ended up where we started, which is a system full of loopholes, ailing, and not a road map to fix it."[9]

Arms Control since 1990: Conventional Weapons

Arms control efforts since the advent of nuclear weapons in 1945 have emphasized restraining these awesome weapons and, to a lesser degree, the other WMDs and their delivery systems. In the 1990s, the world also began to pay more attention to conventional weapons inventories and to the transfer of conventional weapons.

Conventional Weapons Inventories   The virtual omnipresence of conventional weapons and their multitudinous forms makes them more difficult to limit than nuclear weapons. Still, progress has been made. One major step is the **Conventional Forces in Europe Treaty (CFE)**. After 17 years of negotiation, the countries of the North Atlantic Treaty Organization (NATO) and the Soviet-led Warsaw Treaty Organization (WTO) concluded the CFE Treaty in 1990 to cut conventional military forces in Europe from the Atlantic to the Urals (the ATTU region). In the aftermath of the cold war, adjustments have been made to reflect the independence of various European former Soviet republics (FSRs) and the fact that some of them have even joined NATO. Such details aside, the key point is that the CFE Treaty as amended reduced the units (such as tanks and warplanes) in the ATTU region by about 63,000 and also decreased the number of troops in the area.

An additional step in conventional weapons arms control came in 1997 with the **Anti-Personnel Mine Treaty (APM)**, which prohibits making, using, possessing, or transferring land mines. Details of the creation of the APM Treaty and directions for what you can do to support or oppose it can be found in the Play a Part in Your World box "Adopt a Minefield." By mid-2005, 144 countries had ratified the APM Treaty, and it has an important impact. When the treaty was signed, 131 countries possessed a total of 260 million mines. That number has dropped 24% as these countries have destroyed their stockpiles. Additionally, the associated effort to clear land mines has removed some 5 million of the deadly devices and millions of other pieces of unexploded ordinance from former battle zones. The APM Treaty has not been universally supported, however. Three key countries (China, Russia, and the United States) were among those that have not adhered to it, arguing that they still need to use mines. For example, U.S. military planners consider land mines to be a key defense element against a possible North Korean invasion of South Korea.

Conventional Weapons Transfers   Another thrust of conventional arms control in the 1990s and beyond has been and will be the effort to limit the transfer of conventional weapons. To that end, 31 countries in 1995 agreed to the Wassenaar Arrangement on Export Controls for Conventional Arms and Dual-Use Goods and Technologies. Named after the Dutch town where it was negotiated, the "pact" directs its signatories to limit the export of some types of weapons technology and to create an organization to monitor the spread of conventional weapons and **dual-use technology**, which has both peaceful and nonpeaceful applications.

A more recent attempt to control conventional weapons is the work of the UN Conference on the Illicit Trade in Small Arms and Light Weapons (2001). It is a huge

PLAY A PART IN YOUR WORLD

Adopt a Minefield

A common sight throughout the United States are roadside adopt-a-highway signs naming one or another group that has pledged to keep a section of the road clear of litter. Fortunately for Americans, a discarded beer can or fast-food wrapper is about the worse thing they might step on while working along the country's roadways or in its fields and forests.

People in many other countries are not so lucky. In the fields of Cambodia, along the paths of Angola, and dotting the countryside in dozens of other countries, land mines wait with menacing silence and near invisibility to claim a victim. Mines are patient, often waiting many years to claim a victim, and they are also nondiscriminatory. They care not whether their deadly yield of shrapnel shreds the body of a soldier or a child. Cambodian farmer Sam Soa was trying to find his cow in a field near his village when he stepped on a mine. "I didn't realize what had happened, and I tried to run away," he remembers.[1] Sam Soa could not run away, though; the bottom of his left leg was gone. Millions of land mines from past conflicts remain in the ground in several dozen countries, and each year these explosive devices kill or maim about 10,000 civilians each year, one-third of them children.

The effort over the past three decades to ban land mines and clear existing ones has been a testament to the power of individuals at the grass roots. For example, Jody Williams of Vermont, a former "temp agency" worker in Washington, converted her horror at the toll land mines were taking into action. In 1991, she and two others used the Internet to launch an effort that became the International Campaign to Ban Landmines (ICBL). "When we began, we were just three people sitting in a room. It was utopia. None of us thought we would ever ban land mines," she later told a reporter.[2] Williams had underestimated herself. Seventy-five percent of the world countries have now ratified the Anti-Personnel Mine Treaty, and Williams's work in fostering the 1997 pact won her that year's Nobel Peace Prize.

Be Active!

If you share Williams's view, much remains to be done to get the United States and other countries that have not agreed to the APM Treaty to do so and to clear existing minefields. Certainly the efforts of individual countries and the UN and other IGOs will be important. But individuals can also get involved through such organizations as the ICBL, a network of 1,400 NGOs in 90 countries (http://www.icbl.org), or Adopt-a-Minefield (www.landmines.org/). No pro-land mine NGOs exist, but you can find President Clinton's rationale for not signing the treaty at the Department of Defense site, www.defenselink.mil/ speeches/1997/s19970917-clinton.html. The Bush administration has followed Clinton's lead. Whatever your opinion, let your members of Congress and even the president know what you think.

Reflecting the tragedy of many children, as well as adults, who are killed or maimed by old land mines each year, this sign, erected with the help of UNICEF, warns of a minefield in Sri Lanka. One of the many ways you can get involved in world politics is by supporting an NGO or IGO involved in the international effort to rid the world of land mines.

task considering the estimated 639 million small arms and light weapons (revolvers and rifles, machine guns and mortars, hand grenades, antitank guns and portable missile launchers) that exist in the world, mostly (60%) in civilian hands. To address this menacing mass of weaponry, the conference called on states to curb the illicit trafficking in light weapons through such steps as ensuring that manufacturers mark weapons so that they can be traced, and tightening measures to monitor the flow of arms across borders. Most of these arms were initially supplied by the United States, Russia, and the European countries to rebel groups and to governments in less developed countries, then eventually found their way into the multibillion-dollar global arms black market. The UN program is nonbinding, but it does represent a first step toward regulating and stemming the huge volume of weapons moving through the international system. Speaking at a UN conference to review progress in curbing the illicit arms trade, Chairperson Kuniko Inoguchi of Japan commented, "I would not claim we have achieved some heroic and ambitious outcome," but she did point to heightened awareness of the problem and to the greater willingness of countries to cooperate on the issue as evidence that the world's countries had "started to implement actions against small arms and explore what the United Nations can do."[10]

The Barriers to Arms Control

Limiting or reducing arms is an idea that most people favor. Yet arms control has proceeded slowly and sometimes not at all. The devil is in the details, as the old maxim goes, and it is important to review the continuing debate over arms control to understand its history and current status. None of the factors that we are about to discuss is the main culprit impeding arms control. Nor is any one of them insurmountable. Indeed, important advances are being made on a number of fronts. But together, these factors form a tenacious resistance to arms control.

International Barriers

Security concerns constitute perhaps the most formidable barrier to arms control. Members of the realist school of thought have strong doubts about whether countries can maintain adequate security if they disarm totally or substantially. Realists are cautious about the current political scene and about the claimed contributions of arms control.

Worries about the possibility of future conflict are probably the greatest barrier to arms control. For example, the anxiety during the cold war that spawned a huge arms buildup had no sooner begun to fade than fears about the threat of terrorists and "rogue" states with WMDs escalated in the aftermath of 9/11. In the United States that spurred the Bush administration to move toward building mini-nukes, as discussed in chapter 10.

At least to some degree, nuclear proliferation is also a product of insecurity. India's drive to acquire nuclear weapons was in part a reaction to the nuclear arms of China to the north, which the Indian defense minister described as his country's "potential number one enemy."[11] India's program to defend itself against China raised anxieties in Pakistan, which had fought several wars with India. So the Pakistanis began their program. "Today we have evened the score with India," Pakistan's prime minister exulted after his country's first test.[12] Similarly, North Korea has repeatedly maintained that its interest in having nuclear weapons is to protect itself against the United States. Many Americans discount that rationale, but it is not all that far-fetched given the U.S. invasion of Iraq and other uses of force.

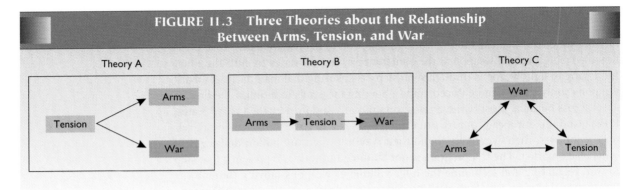

FIGURE 11.3 Three Theories about the Relationship Between Arms, Tension, and War

Theory A approximates the realist view, and Theory B fits the idealist view of the causal relationship between arms, tension, and use. Theory C suggests that there is a complex causal interrelationship between arms, tension, and war in which each of the three factors affects the other two.

Much the same argument about a dangerous world helps drive other military spending and works against reductions. The United States is the world's most powerful country and spends more on its military each year than the next five or six countries combined. Yet security worries drive it to spend even more. Presenting Congress in 2005 with an approximately half-trillion-dollar annual and supplementary (for Iraq and Afghanistan) budget request, Secretary of Defense Donald Rumsfeld argued the immense funding was needed because:

> To the seeming surprise of some, our enemies have brains. They're constantly adapting and adjusting to what we're doing. They combine medieval sensibilities with modern technology and media savvy to find new ways to exploit perceived weaknesses and to weaken the civilized world. We must employ the lessons of the past three-and-a-half years of war to be able to anticipate, adjust, act and react with greater agility.[13]

Doubts about the value of arms control create a second international barrier. Realists, for one, have doubts about arms control and its supposed benefits. Realists begin with the belief that humans arm themselves and fight because the world is dangerous, as represented by Theory A in Figure 11.3. Given this view, realists believe that political settlements should be achieved before arms reductions are negotiated. The skeptics therefore reject the idea that arms control agreements necessarily represent progress (Kydd, 2000). In fact, it is even possible from this perspective to argue that more, not less weapons, will sometimes increase security.

Liberals, by contrast, agree with Homer's observation in the *Odyssey* (ca. 700 B.C.) that "the blade itself incites to violence." This is represented by Theory B in Figure 11.3, and it represents the belief that insecurity leads countries to have arms races, which leads to more insecurity and conflict in a hard-to-break cycle (Gibler, Rider, & Hutchison, 2005). From this perspective the way to increase security is by reducing arms, not increasing them.

While the logic of arms races seems obvious, empirical research has not confirmed that arms races always occur (McGinnis & Williams, 2001). Similarly, it is not clear whether decreases in arms cause or are caused by periods of improved international relations. Instead, a host of domestic and international factors influence a country's level of armaments. What this means is that the most probable answer to the chicken-and-egg debate about which should come first, political agreements or arms control, lies in a combination of these theories. That is, arms, tension, and wars all promote one another, as represented in Theory C of Figure 11.3.

Concerns about verification and cheating constitute a third international barrier to arms control. The problem is simple: Countries suspect that others will cheat. This worry was a significant factor in the rejection of the CTBT by the U.S. Senate. A chief opponent characterized the treaty as "not effectively verifiable" and therefore "ineffectual because it would not stop other nations from testing or developing nuclear weapons. . . . The CTBT simply has no teeth."[14]

There have been great advances in verification procedures and technologies. Many arms control treaties provide for **on-site inspections (OSI)** by an agency such as the IAEA or even the other side, but in some cases weapons and facilities can be hidden from OSI. **National technical means (NTM)** of verification using satellites, seismic measuring devices, and other equipment have also advanced rapidly. These have been substantially offset, however, by other technologies that make NTM verification more difficult. Nuclear warheads, for example, have been miniaturized to the point where one could literally be hidden in a good-sized closet. Dual-use chemicals make it difficult to monitor the CWC, and the minute amounts of biological warfare agents needed to inflict massive casualties make the BWC daunting to monitor. Therefore, in the last analysis, virtually no amount of OSI and NTM can ensure absolute verification.

Because absolute verification is impossible, the real issue is which course is more dangerous: (1) coming to an agreement when there is at least some chance that the other side might be able to cheat, or (2) failing to agree and living in a world of unrestrained and increasing nuclear weapons growth? Sometimes, the answer may be number 2. Taking this view while testifying before the U.S. Senate about the Chemical Weapons Convention, former secretary of state James A. Baker III counseled, "The [George H. W.] Bush administration never expected the treaty to be completely verifiable and had always expected there would be rogue states that would not participate." Nevertheless, Baker supported the treaty on the grounds that "the more countries we can get behind responsible behavior around the world . . . , the better it is for us."[15]

Ultimately, the decision with the most momentous international security implications would be to opt for a world with zero nuclear weapons. Whether you favor overcoming the many barriers to that goal or would consider such an effort a fool's errand is asked in the decision box, "Is 'Zero-Nukes' a Good Goal?"

Domestic Barriers

All countries are complex decision-making organizations, as chapter 3 discusses. Not all leaders favor arms control, and even those who do often face strong opposition from powerful domestic political actors. This opposition may be rooted in ideological differences and policy doubts noted above. In addition to these international barriers, opposition to arms control often stems from such domestic barriers as national pride and the interrelationship among military spending, the economy, and politics.

National pride is one domestic barrier to arms control. The adage in the Book of Proverbs that "pride goeth before destruction" is applicable to modern arms acquisitions. Whether we are dealing with conventional or nuclear arms, national pride is a primary drive behind their acquisition. For many countries, arms represent a tangible symbol of strength and sovereign equality. EXPLOSION OF SELF-ESTEEM read one newspaper headline in India after that country's nuclear tests in 1998.[16] LONG LIVE NUCLEAR PAKISTAN read a Pakistani newspaper headline soon thereafter.

WRITE THE POLICY SCRIPT

Is "Zero-Nukes" a Good Goal?

Most of the commentary on nuclear weapons takes the view that they are dangerous and that reducing their number will create a safer world. By extension, a "zero-nuke" world, one with no nuclear weapons, would be even safer yet and, therefore, is a goal to work toward. The logic is straightforward. Nuclear weapons have horrific destructive power. Even a relative handful could cause devastating casualties and damage to large countries and virtually wipe out many smaller ones. Because weapons that do not exist cannot hurt you, it would seem that if nuclear arms cuts are considered progress, then having no such weapons would be the ultimate success.

Alternatively, it may be that nuclear weapons may actually provide safety by making war between nuclear-armed countries too terrible to fight. Taking this view, British Prime Minister Winston Churchill observed early in the atomic age, "It may be that we shall by a process of sublime irony" come to a point "where safety will be the sturdy child of terror and survival the twin brother of annihilation" (Nogee & Spanier, 1988:5). Arguably Sir Winston's point was well taken; during the cold war, despite its intense hostility, the United States and the Soviet Union avoided war and its risk of nuclear counterstrikes and mutual destruction. That was the view of British Prime Minister Margaret Thatcher, who told Soviet President Mikhail Gorbachev in 1987 that, "A world without nuclear weapons would be less stable and more dangerous for all of us."[1]

Some analysts make much the same point in the post–cold war world. For example, one top U.S. government nuclear weapons expert argues that "the world, in fact, would become more dangerous, not less dangerous, were U.S. nuclear weapons to be absent. The most important role for our nuclear weapons is to serve as a 'sobering force,' one that can cap the level of destruction of military conflicts and thus force all sides to come to their senses."[2]

Not all top U.S. officials agree with this view. For instance, a number of former high-ranking U.S. military officers were among the 57 retired generals and admirals from countries with nuclear weapons who published a 1996 manifesto declaring that nuclear weapons are "of sharply reduced utility" in the post–cold war world, calling for "substantially reducing their numbers," and proclaiming that "the ultimate objective . . . should be the complete elimination of nuclear weapons from all nations" (Schultz & Isenberg, 1997:87).

What Do You Think?

Do you favor a zero-nuke world? Assume this could be achieved by a treaty in which all the countries with nuclear weapons agreed to turn them over to the International Atomic Energy Agency for immediate destruction, in which all non-nuclear countries agreed not to develop nuclear weapons, and in which all countries agreed to unlimited and unscheduled IAEA inspections to verify treaty compliance. Do not debate the possibility of cheating. For our scenario here, the treaty is foolproof, and the issue is whether the world would be safer with zero nuclear weapons or if Churchill was right when he warned, "Be careful above all things not to let go of the atomic weapon until you are sure, and more sure than sure, that other means of preserving the peace are in your hands."[3]

"Five nuclear blasts have instantly transformed an extremely demoralized nation into a self-respecting proud nation . . . having full faith in their destiny," the accompanying article explained.[17] Such emotions have also seemingly played a role in Iran's alleged nuclear weapons program. "I hope we get our atomic weapons," Shirzad Bozorgmehr, editor of *Iran News*, has commented in 2003 on the international pressure on Tehran to comply with the Non-Proliferation Treaty. "If Israel has it, we should have it. If India and Pakistan do, we should, too," he explained.[18]

Military spending, the economy, and politics interact to form a second domestic barrier to arms control. Supplying the military is big business, and economic interest groups pressure their governments to build and to sell weapons and associated technology. Furthermore, cities that are near major military installations benefit from jobs provided on the bases and from the consumer spending of military personnel stationed on the bases. For this reason, defense-related corporations, defense plant workers, civilian employees of the military, and the cities and towns in which they reside and shop are supporters of military spending and foreign sales. Additionally, there are often bureaucratic elements, such as ministries of defense, in alliance with

Weapons building is an important part of the economies of the United States and many other countries. As a result, defense industries, their workers, their communities, and the legislators who represent them join to resist cuts in defense spending or restraints on the international sales of arms.

ARES. caglecartoons.com/espanol

the defense industry and its workers. Finally, both interest groups and bureaucratic actors receive support from legislators who represent the districts and states that benefit from military spending. This alliance between interest groups, bureaucracies, and legislators forms a military-industrial-congressional complex that has been termed the **iron triangle**.

Web Link

A PBS interactive site for the Global Security Simulator at which you try to reduce the danger from WMDs is at **www .pbs.org/avoidingarmageddon/ getInvolved/involved_01.html.**

International Security Forces

The idea of forming international security forces to supplement or replace national military forces is a second approach to seeking security on the road less traveled by. This approach would enhance, not compete with, the first approach, arms control. Organizing for international security would emphasize international organizations and de-emphasize national defense forces. Thus, the creation of international security forces and the first approach, arms control, are mutually supportive.

International Security Forces: Theory and Practice

The idea of seeking security through an international organization is not new. Immanuel Kant foresaw the possibility over two centuries ago in *Idea for a Universal History from a Cosmopolitan Point of View* (1784). "Through war, through the taxing and never-ending accumulation of armament . . . after devastations, revolutions, and even complete exhaustion," Kant predicted, human nature would bring people "to that which reason could have told them in the beginning": that humankind must "step from the lawless condition of savages into a league of nations" to secure the peace. These ideas have evolved into attempts to secure the peace through such international structures as the Concert of Europe, the League of Nations, and the United Nations (Price & Zacher, 2004). An increased UN peacekeeping role has been especially evident, and other international governmental organizations (IGOs) also have occasionally been involved in international security missions.

An important point is that while our discussion here will focus on the UN as a global organization, much of what is said is also applicable to regional IGOs and their security forces. The **North Atlantic Treaty Organization (NATO)** is providing international security forces in Afghanistan, Bosnia-Herzegovina, and Kosovo province. Also in Europe, the European Union took on its first peacekeeping mission in 2003 when it assumed that role in Macedonia from NATO, and a second EU initiative sent its peacekeepers to the Congo later that year. Additionally on the continent, the **Organization for Security and Cooperation in Europe (OSCE)** has taken on some functions of a regional security structure. Established in 1973, the OSCE now has 55 members, including almost all the countries of Europe, Kazakhstan and several other states in Central Asia, and Canada and the United States. Operationally, it has begun limited field activities to prevent or settle conflicts. These efforts primarily involve sending monitors and other personnel to try to resolve differences, and in 2005, OSCE missions were operating along the border between Georgia and Russia, in Kosovo, and in more than a dozen other countries or hot spots. The largest OSCE peacekeeping effort involved the dispatch of 6,000 troops from eight countries to Albania in 1997 when that country's political system collapsed into anarchy amid factional fighting.

Beyond Europe, the **Economic Community of West African States (ECOWAS)** has dispatched troops over the past decade or so to Guinea-Bissau, Ivory Coast, Liberia, and Sierra Leone. In July 2003, for example, ECOWAS troops from Nigeria, Ghana, Mali, and Senegal entered Liberia on a UN-authorized mission to try to bring an end to the civil war there. At the end of that year, ECOWAS peacekeepers not only remained in that country, but also in Ivory Coast and Sierra Leone. On the other side of the South Atlantic Ocean, the Organization of American States (OAS) has advanced peace on a number of fronts, including helping to settle the long and seemingly intractable border dispute between Ecuador and Peru. The potential cause of war was eliminated in 1998 when the presidents of the two countries met in Brazil to sign the Acta de Brasilia demarcating their border and establishing Argentina, Brazil, Chile, Spain, and the United States as the guarantors of the pact.

Collective Security

One theory behind the use of international security forces through the UN and other IGOs is the concept of **collective security**. This idea was first embodied in the Covenant of the League of Nations and is also reflected in the Charter of the United Nations.

The Theory of Collective Security   Collective security is based on three basic tenets. First, all countries forswear the use of force except in self-defense. Second, all agree that the peace is indivisible. An attack on one is an attack on all. Third, all pledge to unite to halt aggression and restore the peace by supplying to the UN or other IGOs whatever material or personnel resources are necessary to deter or defeat aggressors and restore the peace.

This three-part theory is something like the idea that governs domestic law enforcement. First, self-defense and the defense of someone in the case of an attack or dire threat that could lead to death or serious injury are the only times an individual can use force legally. Second, acts of violence are considered transgressions against the collective. If one person assaults another, the case is not titled the victim versus the aggressor (such as *Jones v. Smith*); it is titled the society versus the aggressor (*Ohio v. Smith*); the prosecutor takes legal action and presents the case on behalf of the people. Third, domestic societies provide a collective security force, the police, and jointly support this force through taxes.

Collective security, then, is not only an appealing idea but one that works—domestically, that is. It has not, however, been a general success on the international scene. In part, applying collective security is limited by problems such as how, in some cases, to tell the aggressor from the victim. But these uncertainties also exist domestically and are resolved. The more important reason that collective security fails is the unwillingness of countries to subordinate their sovereign interests to collective action. Thus far, governments have generally maintained their right to view conflict in terms of their national interests and to support or oppose UN action based on their nationalistic points of view. Collective security, therefore, exists mostly as a goal, not as a general practice. Only the UN-authorized interventions in Korea (1950–1953) and in the Persian Gulf (1990–1991) came close to fulfilling the idea of collective security. The United States and Great Britain tried to convince the Security Council in 2003 that the situation in Iraq warranted a third such collective security action, but that effort failed.

Collective Security, Preemption, and Iraq The refusal of the Security Council to authorize action against Iraq and the subsequent American- and British-led invasion raised a storm of controversy over whether that action had violated the UN Charter. President George Bush and Prime Minister Tony Blair argued that they were justified in ordering action as a matter of self-defense. Secretary-General Annan disagreed, as detailed in the chapter 2 box, "Is Preemptive War Good Policy?" At the center of the dispute is the meaning and interface between Article 51 of the Charter, recognizing that every country retains "the inherent right of individual or collective self-defense if an armed attack occurs," and Article 39, which states that except in cases of self-defense, the UN Security Council has the sole authority to "determine the existence of any threat to the peace, breach of the peace, or act of aggression and . . . decide what measures shall be taken."

Not unexpectedly, an international panel subsequently appointed by Annan supported his view. In its late-2004 report, the High-Level Panel on Threats, Challenges, and Change said that while nations could act in self-defense if under attack or facing an incontrovertible and imminent attack, preemption was another matter. The report concluded that on the question of the legality of a preemptive attack,

> The short answer is that if there are good arguments for preventive military action, with good evidence to support them, they should be put to the Security Council, which can authorize such action if it chooses to. If it does not so choose, there will be, by definition, time to pursue other strategies, including persuasion, negotiation, deterrence and containment—and to visit again the military option. For those impatient with such a response, the answer must be that, in a world full of perceived potential threats, the risk to the global order and the norm of nonintervention on which it continues to be based is simply too great for the legality of unilateral preventive action, as distinct from collectively endorsed action, to be accepted. Allowing one to so act is to allow all.[19]

This reasoning cheered those critical of Washington and London, but it did not address some of the political realities that are often involved in securing Security Council authorization. France, for example, may well have truly believed that more time to conduct inspections for WMDs was needed. It is also the case, though, that Paris saw the issue as a chance to frustrate American power and to reduce its hegemonic sway at least marginally. Thus the views of the secretary-general and the panel he appointed may have been technically correct but they were also politically naïve. What the views did not adequately address is the possibility of members blocking action by the Security Council for reasons not connected to the crisis even if action is warranted.

MAP
Current Peacekeeping
Operations

Peacekeeping

What the United Nations has been able to do more often is to implement a process commonly called **peacekeeping**. Apart from using military force, peacekeeping is quite different from collective security. The latter identifies an aggressor and employs military force to defeat the attacker. Peacekeeping takes another approach and deploys an international military force under the aegis of an international organization such as the UN to prevent fighting, usually by acting as a buffer between combatants. The international force is neutral between the combatants and must have been invited to be present by at least one of the combatants.

Some of the data regarding the use of UN peacekeeping forces and observer groups to help restore and maintain the peace is given in chapter 7, but it bears repeating briefly here. Between 1945 and 2005, the United Nations sent over 9 million soldiers, police officers, and unarmed observers drawn from two-thirds of the world's countries to conduct 60 peacekeeping or truce observation missions. Almost 2,000 of these individuals have died in UN service. The frequency of such UN missions has risen sharply, as can be seen in Figure 7.9 on page 223. In mid-2005, there were 18 UN peacekeeping forces of varying size, totaling nearly 67,000 troops, police, and military observers drawn from 103 countries in the field in Africa, Asia, Europe, and the Middle East, as shown in the accompanying map. The cost of these operations was about $4.5 billion in FY2005 (fiscal year, July 1, 2004 to June 30, 2005).

Several characteristics of UN peacekeeping actions can be noted. First, most have taken place in LDC locations, as evident on the map. Second, UN forces have generally utilized military contingents from democracies and from smaller or nonaligned powers (Lebovic, 2004). Canada and Fiji have contributed personnel to virtually all peacekeeping efforts, and the Scandinavian countries and Ireland have also been especially frequent participants. The end of the cold war has made it possible for the troops of larger powers to take a greater part in international security missions, and in 2005, American, British, Chinese, French, German, and Russian troops and police personnel were in the field as UN peacekeepers.

Did You Know That:

In mid-2005, the five countries with the most UN peacekeepers were Pakistan (9,914), Bangladesh (8,208), India (6,176), Nepal (3,565) and Ethiopia (3,416).

Peacekeeping Issues

There are a number of important issues related to UN peacekeeping. Some of those are discussed elsewhere. For example, chapter 7 outlines the budget restraints and the unwillingness of numerous countries to pay their dues for peacekeeping to the United Nations. Yet another issue covered in chapter 7 is the use of the veto power held by the five permanent members of the UN Security Council and the growing number of countries that are voicing their discontent with a system they claim is neither fair nor any longer resembles world power realities. A third issue, addressed in chapter 9 on international law, is the demand made by the United States that its troops serving with UN peacekeeping forces be exempted by the Security Council from the jurisdiction of the International Criminal Court, and the threat of Washington to withhold its dues or veto new and continuing missions if the American stipulations are not met. As the U.S. ambassador to the UN put it while threatening to veto the renewal of the UN mission in Bosnia, "We will not ask them [American peacekeepers] to accept the additional risk of politicized prosecutions before a court whose jurisdiction over our people the government of the United States does not accept."[20] Two other issues involved with peacekeeping are whether UN forces should play a relatively passive peacemaking role or a more assertive peace enforcement function and how to ensure that humanitarian interventions by UN and other IGO military police forces are not neocolonialism by another name.

Web Link

The site of the UN's Department of Peacekeeping Operations is at http://www.un.org/Depts/dpko/.

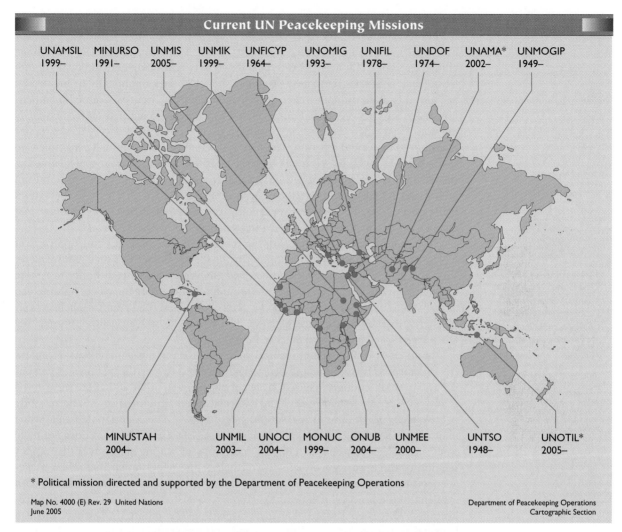

Current UN Peacekeeping Missions

| UNAMSIL 1999– | MINURSO 1991– | UNMIS 2005– | UNMIK 1999– | UNFICYP 1964– | UNOMIG 1993– | UNIFIL 1978– | UNDOF 1974– | UNAMA* 2002– | UNMOGIP 1949– |

| MINUSTAH 2004– | UNMIL 2003– | UNOCI 2004– | MONUC 1999– | ONUB 2004– | UNMEE 2000– | UNTSO 1948– | UNOTIL* 2005– |

* Political mission directed and supported by the Department of Peacekeeping Operations

Map No. 4000 (E) Rev. 29 United Nations
June 2005

Department of Peacekeeping Operations
Cartographic Section

The United Nations has played a valuable peacekeeping role. This map shows the 18 peacekeeping operations active in mid-2005. It is a testament to the ever-growing record of UN peacekeeping that the map would have become too confusing if it had included the other 43 peacekeeping missions that the UN had undertaken and concluded in its history. The Nobel Peace Prize for 1988 was awarded to the soldiers who have served in peacekeeping missions, thousands of whom have been killed or wounded in UN service.

Notes: UNTSO—UN Truce Supervision Organization
UNMOGIP—UN Military Observer Group in India and Pakistan
UNFICYP—UN Peacekeeping Force in Cyprus
UNDOF—UN Disengagement Observer Force
UNIFIL—UN Interim Force in Lebanon
MINURSO—UN Mission for the Referendum in Western Sahara
UNOMIG—UN Observer Mission in Georgia
UNMIK—UN Interim Administration Mission in Kosovo
UNAMSIL—UN Mission in Sierra Leone
MONUC—UN Mission in the Democratic Republic of the Congo
UNMEE—UN Mission in Ethiopia and Eritrea
UNOTIL—UN Mission of Support in East Timor
UNMIL—UN Mission in Liberia
UNOCI—UN Operation in Côte d'Ivoire
MINUSTAH—UN Stabilization Mission in Haiti
ONUB—UN Operation in Burundi
UNMIS—UN Mission in the Sudan
UNAMA—United Nations Assistance Mission in Afghanistan
Source: http://www.un.org/Depts/dpko/dpko/home.shtml.

Peacekeeping and Peace Enforcement   For all the contributions that UN peacekeeping efforts have made, they have sometimes been unable to halt fighting quickly (or even at all) or to keep the peace permanently. The numerous reasons for the limited effectiveness of UN forces can be boiled down to two fundamental and related problems: First, countries frequently do not support UN forces politically or financially. Second, it is often difficult to get the self-interested UN Security Council members, especially the five veto-wielding permanent members, to agree to authorize a UN mission. Even when the mission is authorized, it is often given a very narrow scope of authority to act and few troops. When, for example, the UN initially sent forces to the Balkans in 1992, the secretary-general asked for 35,000 peacekeepers. However, the Security Council authorized only 7,000 troops restricted to light arms and not authorized to take strong action. These limits prevented the peacekeepers from being effective and even led, at one point, to UN troops being taken hostage and chained to potential targets to deter threatened action by NATO forces.

The mounting frustrations with the reactive, passive peacekeeping approach of UN forces led to an upsurge of support for the idea of proactive **peace enforcement**. This new role would involve heavily armed UN forces with the authority to restore and maintain the peace. Such UN units would not only intervene where fighting had already broken out. They could also be deployed to imperiled countries before trouble starts, thereby putting an aggressor in the uncomfortable position of attacking UN forces as well as national defense forces.

In an effort to implement change, successive secretaries-general have called on UN members to better fund and equip UN forces and to give them sufficient personnel and a broad enough mandate (rules of engagement) that will allow them to be effective. A report issued in 2000 by a special panel appointed by Annan to study peacekeeping operations made several key points.[21] The report noted that when major forces are needed to respond to aggression, "the United Nations does not wage war." Instead, to respond, it relies on "coalitions of willing states, with the authorization of the Security Council." Nevertheless, the panel urged that when peacekeepers are deployed, "The United Nations must be prepared to deal effectively with spoilers [of the peace] if it expects to achieve a consistent record of success in peacekeeping." One step toward that goal, according the report, is closing "the gap between verbal postures and financial and political support for prevention" by the UN's member-states. The panel also recommended a change in posture for UN troops. For example, instead of maintaining impartiality toward all combatants, the report said that when one side was clearly at fault, the UN should take a more assertive stand. To implement this, it recommended bigger and better equipped forces with enough freedom of action to be "a credible deterrent," to "mount an effective defense against violent challengers," and when faced with flagrant violence "to stop it." Additionally, the panel called for the UN to have a "rapid and

JOIN THE DEBATE
The United Nations and the Establishment of International Peace: Debating the Scope of UN Peacekeeping Mandates

This Nigerian soldier serving as a UN peacekeeper in Sierra Leone is representative of most peacekeeping forces. They are lightly armed and do not have sufficient personnel, equipment, and authority to launch proactive operations. Criticism of such forces as ineffective misses the point that political decisions establish these limits. Different decisions by the countries of the UN Security Council could create more potent and effective peacekeeping forces.

effective deployment capacity" so that it could deploy peacekeepers more rapidly. This could involve options ranging from national troops predesignated and trained for UN missions to a standing UN military force.

Reflective of the gap between the member-states' rhetoric and reality, such calls for a more effective UN peace-enforcing ability have often drawn accolades from national leaders and sometimes even pledges of support. However, change has been slow and limited. As one analyst explains the resistance of countries to further empowering the UN, "Robust peace enforcement is beyond the capacity of the United Nations. The Security Council does not have the stomach for it, contributing countries don't want to put their troops under other commanders and then have to answer questions at home when their troops get killed."[22]

Peace Enforcement: Humanitarian Intervention or Neocolonialism?   Doubts about a more aggressive UN military role are not just based on nationalism and other such factors. There is also a concern that creating a more powerful, proactive UN will undermine the sovereignty of the smaller LDCs and that the UN will become a neo-colonial tool of the big powers. In the words of one UN report, "there is the understandable and legitimate concern of member-states, especially the small and weak among them, about sovereignty."[23] The chaos and abuses that engulf weak countries sometimes render them mere legal fictions that have no coherent government, and they are considered so-called failed states. In such a situation, other states may have powerful emotional and political incentives to intervene, either to alleviate the suffering or to take political advantage of the turmoil. One observer notes, for example, that "the new rule whereby human rights outrank sovereignty must still prevail, because the old rule is simply dead." The problem, the analyst continues, is the "places where this new rule could be applied all too easily: weak states" (Luttwak, 2000: 61). That, arguably, allows powerful states like China to continue to abuse human rights while small countries may be "invaded" by international security forces and have their sovereignty abridged.

Other commentators worry that once the barrier of sovereignty is breached, the powerful countries will have license through the UN to impose their will on weaker countries. That suspicion is not voiced only from within LDCs; it also receives some scholarly support. An analysis of the record from 1945 to 1990 led one study to conclude that the political consideration the countries applied to supporting peacekeeping led to a record during the cold war "bordering on imperialism" by the Western countries and that a post–cold war "expansion of UN peacekeeping activities . . . [might] signal an era in which sovereignty is eroded, but only for non-Western states" (Neack, 1995:194).

WEB POLL
The United Nations and
International Security

International Security and the Future

What does the future hold for international security? While there are certainly many impediments on the path to international security, it would be foolish to dismiss the idea as impossible. First, it is in almost everyone's interest to prevent or contain crises, and there is a growing recognition that cooperation through the use of an international security force may often be a more effective way to maintain or restore peace than is continued reliance on unlimited national self-defense in a world capable of producing and using nuclear, biological, and chemical weapons. As such, the existence of peacekeeping has been largely a functional response to an international problem, and the increased number of missions, whether by the UN or one of the regional organizations, is evidence that the international security efforts are necessary, have achieved notable successes, and almost certainly have become a permanent part of world politics (Fortna, 2004).

Second, it is important to see that many of the shortcomings of previous international security missions have not been due to an inherent failure of the UN. Certainly the UN has problems, as any large political and bureaucratized organization does (Jett, 2000). But the central problem, at least in Kofi Annan's view, is that the UN has "been asked to do too much with too little."[24]

Efforts to create the nucleus of a UN ready force continue but remain controversial. Events in the first years of the new millennium somewhat revived interest in strengthening UN forces and giving them more proactive authority. As has occurred too often, UN forces, this time in Sierra Leone in 2000, were outnumbered and outgunned by hostile forces and suffered other problems inherent in trying to deploy an army made up of various national contingents with little ability to work as a unified force. The worst moment came when rebels took several dozen UN peacekeepers hostage. In the aftermath of this humiliation, the Security Council more than tripled UN forces in the country to 17,500 and gave them broader authority to initiate action against the rebels. The improved UN position played an important role in creating enough stability to allow for elections in 2002. As a report more than a year later described the situation, "No one forgets . . . rebels and disenchanted government soldiers . . . hacking and burning anything that stood in their way. . . . The United Nations then arrived in force, and give or take a few hiccups, the peace has held." Now, instead of murderous troops, the capital, Freetown, has to deal with having "become one vast traffic jam," and residents have the security to complain that "a large contributor to the jam is the UN peacekeeping mission. . . . The UN's white jeeps and armored cars are everywhere."[25] Stability has continued to take hold in Sierra Leone, and it is expected that the Security Council will feel confident in the country's ability to order its own affairs to end the UN peacekeeping mission there at the end of 2005.

Another approach for the immediate future may be to distinguish types of international security efforts, including peacekeeping and peace enforcement missions, and to handle them differently. The UN's undersecretary-general for peacekeeping has contended, "Peace enforcement and serious peace restoration campaigns will . . . be the responsibility of a coalition of interested countries using their own forces but with a green light from the Council."[26] This model is much like the NATO-led interventions in Bosnia in 1995 and in Kosovo in 1999 and the International Force in East Timor in 1999. This Australian-led multinational force restored stability in East Timor before handing over responsibility for the territory to the UN in 2000. According to this model, peace enforcement would be up to heavily armed regional forces, with peacekeeping assigned to more lightly armed UN contingents. As one U.S. diplomat explains it, "There has to be a peace to keep before the blue helmets are put on the ground."[27] In the case of East Timor, at least, the model worked well. Peace was restored and protected, and the UN established a transitional administration that prepared East Timor for full independence in May 2002.

This model also resembles the intervention in Afghanistan beginning in 2001. The initial action was taken under UN authority by a U.S.-led coalition of forces that routed al Qaeda and toppled the Taliban government. Then in 2002 the UN Security Council turned over authority to the NATO-led International Security Assistance Force to provide security in Kabul in support of the efforts of the interim government to begin the reconstruction of the country's physical and political structures.

While the exact configuration of international security forces in the future is not clear, there can be little doubt that they have become an integral part of world poli-

Does peacekeeping work? Sometimes it does. Liberia is one of the recent success stories. After years of excruciatingly violent civil war, more than 16,000 UN peacekeepers were deployed to the West African country beginning in 2003, and they helped restore a degree of stability and peace. In this picture, a UN peacekeeper takes possession of the weapon of a teenage soldier who was a member of the rebel group. The teenager was one of about 100,000 combatants who were disarmed.

tics in the little more than half a century since they were first deployed. Certainly, they experience problems given their political and financial restraints. The Security Council process of authorizing action is also frequently criticized by countries that oppose a particular operation or favor commencing one when there is not enough support in the council to do so. This was the case in 2003 when the UN came under a barrage of disparagement because it did not authorize an invasion of Iraq. But a majority of people in most countries continued to support the UN and thought that the problem was with the United States, not with the United Nations. Even a majority of Americans continued to express support. When asked in June 2003 about their basic opinion of the UN, 66% of American respondents replied "favorable," 32% replied "unfavorable," and 2% were unsure.[28] And even though most Americans were disappointed that the UN had not supported action, more of them (50%) than not (42%) were willing to concede (with 8% unsure) that the UN can still "function effectively as an international peacekeeping force."[29] Thus, in one form or another, international security forces are here to stay, and their use is likely to increase.

Abolition of War

The last of the four approaches to security that we will examine in this chapter looks toward the abolition of war. For our purposes, we will divide the discussion into two parts: complete disarmament and pacifism.

Complete Disarmament

The most sweeping approach to arms control is simply to disarm. The principal argument in favor of disarmament is, as noted, the idea that without weapons people will not fight. This rests in part on sheer inability. **General and complete disarmament (GCD)** might be accomplished either through unilateral disarmament or through multilateral negotiated disarmament.

In the case of *unilateral disarmament,* a country would dismantle its arms. Its safety, in theory, would be secured by its nonthreatening posture, which would prevent aggression, and its example would lead other countries to also disarm. Unilateral disarmament draws heavily on the idea of pacifism, or a moral and resolute refusal to fight. The unilateral approach also relies on the belief that it is arms that cause tension rather than vice versa. *Negotiated disarmament* between two or more countries is a more limited approach. Advocates of this path share the unilateralists' conviction about the danger of war. They are less likely to be true pacifists, however, and they believe one-sided disarmament would expose the peace pioneer to unacceptable risk.

The GCD approach has few strong advocates among today's political leaders. Even those who do subscribe to the ideal also search for intermediate arms limitation steps. Still, the quest goes on. The UN Disarmament Committee has called for GCD, and the ideal is a valuable standard by which to judge progress as "real."

Pacifism

SIMULATION
Make Love Not War

The second war-avoidance approach, pacifism, relies on individuals. As such, it very much fits in with the idea that people count and that you can affect world politics if you try. Unlike other approaches to security, **pacifism** is a bottom-up approach that focuses on what people do rather than a top-down approach that stresses government action.

Pacifism begins with the belief that it is wrong to kill. Leo Tolstoy, the Russian novelist and pacifist, told the Swedish Peace Conference in 1909, "The truth is so simple, so clear, so evident . . . that it is only necessary to speak it out completely for its full significance to be irresistible." That truth, Tolstoy went on, "lies in what was said thousands of years ago in four words: *Thou Shalt Not Kill.*"

Beyond this starting point, pacifists have varying approaches. There are *universal pacifists,* who oppose all violence; *private pacifists,* who oppose personal violence but who would support as a last resort the use of police or military force to counter criminals or aggressors; and *antiwar pacifists,* who oppose political violence but would use violence as a last resort for personal self-defense.

The obvious argument against pacifism is that it is likely to get one killed or conquered. Those who support pacifism make several counter-contentions. One is that there is a history of pacifism being effective. As one scholar points out, "Non-violence is as old as the history of religious leaders and movements." The analyst goes on to explain that "traditions embodied by Buddha and Christ have inspired successful modern political movements and leaders [such as] . . . the Indian struggle for independence under the leadership of [Mohandas K.] Gandhi and the struggle of the American blacks for greater equality under the leadership of Martin Luther King, Jr." (Beer, 1990:16).

Gandhi was the great Indian spiritual leader. He began his career as a London-trained attorney earning what was then an immense sum of £5,000 annually practicing in Bombay. Soon, however, he went to South Africa, where, earning £50 a year, he defended Indian expatriates against legal white oppression. Gandhi returned to India in 1915 to work for its independence. He gave up Western ways for a life of abstinence and spirituality. Gandhi believed that the force of the soul focused on (to use the Hindi) *satyagraha* (truth seeking) and *ahimsa* (nonviolence) could accomplish what resorting to arms could not. He developed techniques such as unarmed marches, sit-downs by masses of people, work stoppages, boycotts, and what might today be called "pray-ins," whereby *satyagrahi* (truth seekers) could confront the British nonviolently. "The sword of the *satyagrahi* is love," he counseled the Indian people (Lackey, 1989:14). Gandhi became known as Mahatma (great soul) and was the single most powerful force behind Great Britain's granting of independence to India in 1947. The Mahatma then turned his soul toward ending the hatred and violence between Hindus and Muslims in independent India. For this, a Hindu fanatic, who objected to Gandhi's tolerance, assassinated him in 1948. Earlier, after the United States had dropped atomic bombs on Japan, Gandhi was moved to write that "mankind has to get out of violence only through nonviolence. Hatred can be overcome only by love. Counter-hatred only increases the surface as well as the depth of hatred." One has to suspect that had he been able to, Gandhi would have repeated this to the man who shot him.

Pacifists, especially antiwar pacifists, would also make a moral case against the massive, collective violence that is war. They would say that no gain is worth the loss. This view, they would argue, has become infinitely more compelling in the nuclear age. Consider the description of Nagasaki filed by the first reporter who flew over the city after a U.S. bomber dropped an atomic bomb, killing at least 60,000 people. "Burned, blasted, and scarred," he wrote, "Nagasaki looked like a city of death." It was a scene, he continued, of "destruction of a sort never before imagined by a man and therefore is almost indescribable. The area where the bomb hit is absolutely flat and only the markings of the building foundations provide a clue as to what may have been in the area before the energy of the universe was turned loose" (Lackey, 1989:112). Pacifists contend that even by the standards of just war conduct (*jus in bello*) adopted by nonpacifists, any nuclear attack would be unconscionable.

A final point about pacifism is that it is not an irrelevant exercise in idealist philosophy. There are some countries, such as Japan, where at least limited pacifism represents a reasonably strong political force. Moreover, in a changing world, public

Web Link

"Shakespeare's Pacifism," an article by Steven Marx in *Renaissance Quarterly* (1992) arguing that the Bard's plays shifted from being militaristic to favoring pacifism is available at **http://cla.calpoly.edu/~smarx/Publications/pacifism.html**.

These peace activists are displaying a banner with an aphorism of the great Indian pacifist leader (Mohandas K.) Mahatma Gandhi. Pacifists believe that retaliation is never justified and that the only way to peace is to stop killing altogether.

opinion, economic measures, and other nonviolent instruments may create what is sometimes called a "civilian-based defense." Indeed, there are efforts, such as the Program on Nonviolent Sanctions in Conflict and Defense at Harvard University's Center for International Affairs, that are working to show that those who favor non-violence should not be considered "token pacifists" who are "tolerated as necessary to fill out the full spectrum of alternatives, with nonviolent means given serious considerations only for use in noncritical situations" (Bond, 1992:2). Instead, advocates of this approach believe that the successes of Gandhi, King, and others demonstrate that proactive techniques, including nonviolent protest and persuasion, noncooperation, and nonviolent intervention (such as sit-ins), can be successful (Schell, 2003).

It is true that pacifists are unlikely to be able to reverse world conflict by themselves. They are a tiny minority everywhere. Instead, pacifism may be part of a series of so-called peace creation actions. It is an idea worth contemplating.

Chapter Summary

Thinking about Security

1. The goal of the chapter is to discuss alternative paths to security. Security is not necessarily synonymous with either massive armaments or with disarmament. There are four approaches to security: unlimited self-defense, limited self-defense, international security, and abolition of war. The first was the subject of the last chapter. This chapter investigates the other three.

2. There are four possible approaches to ensuring security. They involve restrictions on the number of arms; their development, testing, and deployment; restrictions on certain types of weapons; and the transfer of weapons. Additionally, the standards of evaluation are determined by domestic norms, domestic collective security forces, domestic disarmament, and the established domestic conflict-resolution mechanism. Despite all of the protections and dispute-resolution procedures provided by a domestic system, security is a relative term, thus making full security impossible.

Limited Self-Defense through Arms Control

3. Some people believe that, because of the nature of humans and the nature of the international system, unlimited self-defense is the prudent policy. Advocates of this approach are suspicious of arms control.

4. Limited self-defense is one means of alternative security. People who favor limited self-defense would accomplish their goals through various methods of arms control.

5. From the standpoint of pure rationality, arms control, or the lack of it, is one of the hardest aspects of international politics to understand. Virtually everyone is against arms; virtually everyone is for arms control; yet there are virtually no restraints on the explosive arms escalation in which we are all trapped. It is a story that dates back far into our history, but unless progress is made, we may not have a limitless future to look forward to.

6. There are many powerful arguments against continuation of the arms race. Arms are very costly, in direct dollars and in indirect impact on the economy. Arms are also very dangerous and add to the tensions that sometimes erupt in violence.

7. During the 1990s, efforts increased to regulate arms. Several START treaties, renewal of the Nuclear Nonproliferation Treaty (NPT), the Comprehensive Test Ban Treaty (CTBT), conventional weapons inventories, conventional weapons transfer regulation, and biological and chemical arms control are among the efforts made. There are heavy domestic pressures from the military-industrial-congressional complex and sometimes from the public against arms control.

8. There are a number of ways to implement approaches to arms control, including arms reductions, limits on the expansion of arms inventories, and prohibitions against conventional arms transfers and nuclear proliferation.

International Security Forces

9. Some people favor trying to achieve security through various international security schemes. Collective

security, peacekeeping, and peace enforcement are among the most significant attempts of an international security effort. The most likely focus of this approach would be the United Nations with a greatly strengthened security mandate and with security forces sufficient to engage in peace enforcement, rather than just peacekeeping.

plete disarmament. This makes violence difficult and may also ease tensions that lead to violence. Individual and collective pacifism is another way to avoid violence. Pacifists believe that the way to start the world toward peace is to practice nonviolence individually and in ever-larger groups.

Abolition of War

10. Abolition of war is a fourth approach to security. One way to avoid war is through general and com-

For simulations, debates, and other interactive activities, a chapter quiz, Web links, PowerWeb articles, and much more, visit **www.mhhe.com/rourke11/** and go to chapter 11. Or, while accessing the site, click on Course-Wide Content and view recent international relations articles in the *New York Times*.

Key Terms

Anti-Ballistic Missile Treaty (ABM)

Anti-Personnel Mine Treaty (APM)

arms control

Biological Weapons Convention

Chemical Weapons Convention (CWC)

collective security

Comprehensive Test Ban Treaty (CTBT)

Conventional Forces in Europe Treaty (CFE)

dual-use technology

Economic Community of West African States (ECOWAS)

general and complete disarmament (GCD)

Intermediate-Range Nuclear Forces Treaty (INF)

iron triangle

Missile Technology Control Regime (MTCR)

national technical means (NTM)

Non-Proliferation Treaty (NPT)

North Atlantic Treaty Organization (NATO)

on-site inspections (OSI)

Organization for Security and Cooperation in Europe (OSCE)

pacifism

peace enforcement

peacekeeping

Strategic Arms Limitation Talks Treaty I (SALT I)

Strategic Arms Limitation Talks Treaty II (SALT II)

Strategic Arms Reduction Treaty I (START I)

Strategic Arms Reduction Treaty II (START II)

Treaty of Moscow

National Economic Competition: The Traditional Road

Our wealth increased
By prosperous voyages I often made.
—William Shakespeare, *The Comedy of Errors*

I greatly fear my money is not safe.
—William Shakespeare, *The Comedy of Errors*

In this chapter and the next one, you will be asked to evaluate different approaches to the global economy. One, economic nationalism, argues that tariffs and other protectionist measures are valid ways to protect a country's industries and workers. Representing this view, this billboard in South Carolina, sponsored by the American Manufacturing Trade Action Coalition, urges voters to use their electoral muscle to persuade elected officials to favor protectionism.

GIVEN THE DEGREE TO WHICH this text has already discussed the interplay of politics and economics, you have probably concluded correctly that, to a significant extent, economics is politics and vice versa. This chapter and the next will continue to explore the **international political economy (IPE)**, that is, how economics and politics intertwine. The subject of this chapter is economic competition among countries, the traditional IPE approach (Goddard, Cronin, & Dash, 2003). We begin by explaining IPE theories and also the general state of the world economy before turning to national economic competition. Then chapter 13 discusses international economic cooperation, the alternative IPE path.

It is important before delving into the subject to familiarize yourself with the distinctions between some economics terms that you will encounter frequently in this and the next chapter. **Gross national product (GNP)**, also called gross national income (GNI), is the value of all domestic and international economic activity by a country's citizens and business. **Gross domestic product (GDP)** is the value of all economic activity within a country by its own and foreign individuals and companies. Some sources use raw numbers to report GNP and GDP, while other adjust these two measures for **purchasing power parity (PPP**, as in GNP/PPP, GDP/PPP). This process adjusts the GNP and GDP to a relative value against the U.S. dollar based on differentiations in the cost of food, housing, and the cost of other "local" purchases. For example, the unadjusted 2003 per capita GNPs of the United States and Mexico are $37,870 and $6,230 respectively. Because it is the standard against which other currencies are measured, the U.S. GNP/PPP remains the same ($37,870), while Mexico's GNP/PPP ($8,950) is 44% more than its unadjusted GNP because of the lower cost of living in Mexico. By contrast, Japan's per capita GNP/PPP ($28,620) is 17% lower than its unadjusted GNP ($34,510) because of its relatively high cost of living compared to the United States.

Both measures have advantages and disadvantages. GNP does not take prices of locally produced and consumed items into account. But GNP-PPP misses the fact that many items we all consume come through international trade, and the prices of a barrel of imported petroleum or an imported computer are pretty much the same, whether you are paying for them in U.S. dollars, Mexican pesos, or Japanese yen. Finally, it is important to understand the difference between **current dollars** and **real dollars**. Current (inflated) dollars report values in terms of the worth of the currency in the year being reported. Real (constant, uninflated) dollars express value in terms of a base year adjusted for inflation. For example, if your current dollar earnings are $50,000 a year in 2005 and $70,000 in 2006, but there is 10% inflation annually, then using 2005 as the base year, your real dollar earnings in 2006 would be just $63,000.

A final technical note is about sources and statistics. You may find that the data used here for any given indicator may vary somewhat from another source. The reason is that for most of the data the methodology used to calculate it varies among reporting organizations, such as the World Bank, IMF, WTO, UN, and U.S. government. Second, the data itself is imperfect. For example, if you have ever been paid for an odd job such as cutting grass or babysitting and not reported the income, then you have detracted from the precise calculation of your country's GNP. Economic data for poorer countries is especially imperfect, given the limited resources those countries' governments have to collect statistics. None of this means that you can ignore the data. Instead, it means that it is best to concentrate on trends, such as the rapid growth of international trade, and on major differences, such as the per capita income gap between the wealthy and poor countries. For instance, whatever the precise amount, trade has risen vastly during the last half-century. Also, whether the per

MAP
Gross National Income
Per Capita

capita GNP gap between Americans and Mexicans is $31,640, as presented above, or is $30,000 or $33,000, the key point is that it is huge.

Theories of International Political Economy

As chapter 1 discusses, many political scientists believe that economic forces and conditions are the key determinants of the course of world politics. The various theories that these scholars have advanced to explain the interaction between politics and economics can be roughly divided into economic nationalist, economic internationalist, and economic structuralist approaches. Each of these three approaches purports to describe how and why conditions occur and also offers prescriptions about how policy should be conducted. These descriptions and prescriptions are summarized in Table 12.1. You should further note that economic nationalism is a realpolitik school of IPE, while economic internationalism and, especially, economic structuralism are liberal schools.

Economic Nationalism

The core of **economic nationalism** is the realpolitik belief that the state should use its economic strength to further national interests. By extension, economic nationalists also advocate using a state's power to build its economic strength. Epitomizing this view, the first U.S. secretary of the treasury, Alexander Hamilton, argued that "the interference and aid of [the U.S.] government are indispensable" to protect American industry and to build U.S. economic strength (Balaam & Veseth, 1996:23). Given their realist roots, economic nationalists believe that conflict characterizes international economic relations and that the international economy is a zero-sum game in which one side can gain only if another loses. From the economic nationalist perspective, political goals should govern economic policy because the aim is to maximize state power in order to secure state interests.

To accomplish their ends, economic nationalists rely on a number of political-economic strategies such as exploiting weaker countries. *Colonialism* (imperialism) seeks national economic gain by directly controlling another land and its people. It was this motive that propelled Europeans outward to conquer and build the great colonial empires. Classic colonialism has largely died out, but many observers charge that **neocolonialism** (neoimperialism, indirect control) continues to exist, with the powerful **economically developed countries (EDCs)** of the North dominating and exploiting the **less developed countries (LDCs)** of the South. Economic nationalists also advocate furthering their country's policy goals by using *economic incentives,* such as foreign aid and favorable trade terms, and *economic disincentives,* such as sanctions. For example, a U.S. State Department official justified putting "pressure on the Cuban government through the embargo and [other sanctions]" on the grounds that they "can be and are a valuable tool for . . . protecting our national interests."[1] *Protectionism,* such as tariffs, and *domestic economic support,* such as tax breaks for companies that manufacture exports, are a third set of tools that economic nationalists favor. Because they favor using economic measures as a policy tool, economic nationalists are suspicious of free trade and many other aspects of economic globalization on the grounds that it takes away important economic levers and thus reduces their state's sovereignty and its power.

TABLE 12.1	Approaches to International Political Economy		
	Economic Nationalism	Economic Internationalism	Economic Structuralism
Associated terms	Mercantilism, economic statecraft	Liberalism, free trade, free economic interchange, capitalism, laissez-faire	Marxism, dependency, neo-Marxism, neoimperialism, neocolonialism
Primary economic actors	States, alliances	Individuals, multinational corporations, IGOs	Economic classes (domestic and state)
Current economic relations	Competition and conflict based on narrow national interest; zero-sum game	National competition but cooperation increasing; non-zero-sum game	Conflict based on classes of countries; wealthy states exploit poor ones; zero-sum game
Goal for future	Preserve/expand state power; secure national interests	Increase global prosperity	Eliminate internal and international classes
Prescription for future	Follow economic policies that build national power; use power to build national economy	Eliminate/minimize role of politics in economics; use politics	Radically reform system to end divisions in wealth and power between classes of countries
Desired relationship of politics and economics	Politics controls economic policy	Politics used only to promote domestic free markets and international free economic interchange	Politics should be eliminated by destruction of class system
View of states	Favorable; augment state power	Mixed; eliminate states as primary economic policy makers	Negative; radically reform states; perhaps eliminate states
Estimation of possibility of cooperation	Impossible; humans and states inherently seek advantage and dominance	Possible through reforms within a modified state-based system	Only possible through radical reform; revolution may be necessary
Views on development of LDCs	No responsibility to help. Also could lose national advantages by creating more competition, higher resource prices	Can be achieved through aid, loans, investment, trade, and other assistance within current system. Will ultimately benefit all countries	Exploitation of countries must be ended by fundamentally restructuring the distribution of political and economic power

Conceptual sources: Isaak (2000). Balaam & Veseth (1996), Gilpin (1996), author.

Analysts take very different approaches in describing how the international political economy works and in prescribing how it should work.

Economic Internationalism

A second theoretical and policy approach to IPE, **economic internationalism**, is often also associated with such terms as capitalism, laissez-faire, economic liberalism, and free trade. Economic internationalists are liberals. They believe that international economic relations should and can be conducted cooperatively because, in their view, the international economy is a non-zero-sum game in which prosperity is available to all. To spread prosperity, economic internationalists favor freeing trade and other forms of economic interchange from political restrictions. Therefore, economic internationalists (in contrast to economic nationalists) oppose tariff barriers, domestic subsidies, sanctions, and any other economic tools that distort the free flow of trade, investments, and currencies.

The origins of economic liberalism lie in the roots of **capitalism**. One early proponent of capitalist theory, Adam Smith, wrote in *The Wealth of Nations* (1776) that people seek prosperity "from their regard to their own interest" and that this self-interest constituted an "invisible hand" of competition that created the most efficient economies. Therefore, he opposed any political interference in trade. Smith argued that "if a foreign country can supply us with a commodity cheaper than we ourselves can make it, better buy it of them with some part of the produce of our own industry, employed in a way in which we have some advantage."

The pure capitalism advocated by Smith has few adherents today. Instead, most modern economic liberals favor a "mixed economy" using the state to modify the worst abuses of capitalism by preventing the formation of monopolies and by taking other steps to ease the brutal competition and unequal distribution of wealth inherent in capitalism. At the international level, the liberal approach of modified capitalism makes its adherents moderate reformers who would alter, but not radically change either capitalism or the state-based international system. Instead they would use intergovernmental organizations (IGOs), such as the International Monetary Fund (IMF), to promote and, when necessary, to regulate international economic interchange. Modern liberals also favor such government interference as foreign aid and a degree of concessionary trade agreements or loan terms to assist LDCs to develop.

In sum, modern economic liberals generally believe in the capitalist approach of eliminating political interference in the international economy. They are modified capitalists, though, because they also favor using IGO and national government programs for two ends: (1) to ensure that countries adopt capitalism and free trade and (2) to ease the worst inequities in the system so that future competition can be fairer, and current LDCs can have a chance to achieve prosperity. Thus economic liberals do not want to overturn the current political and economic international system.

Economic Structuralism

Advocates of the third major approach to IPE, **economic structuralism**, believe that economic structure determines politics; they argue that the way the world is organized economically determines how world politics is conducted. Economic structuralists contend that the world is divided between have and have-not countries and that the "haves" (the EDCs) work to keep the "have nots" (the LDCs) weak and poor in order to exploit them. To change this, economic structuralists favor a radical restructuring of the economic system to end the uneven distribution of wealth and power. There are several subsets of economic structuralist thought.

Marxist theory is the first of these subsets. It is based on the ideas of Karl Marx, who with Friedrich Engels in *The Communist Manifesto* (1848) depicted the struggle between the propertied and powerful *bourgeoisie* and the poor and oppressed *proletariat* over the distribution of wealth as the essence of politics. The first Soviet Communist Party chief, V. I. Lenin, applied Marxism to international politics. He argued in *Imperialism: The Highest Stage of Capitalism* (1916) that capitalist, bourgeois leaders had duped their proletariat workers into supporting the exploitation of other proletariat peoples through imperialism. Thus, the class struggle also included an international class struggle between bourgeois and proletariat countries and peoples.

Dependency theory, like Marxism, holds that underdevelopment and poverty in the LDCs is the result of exploitation by the EDCs. However, dependency theorists focus on nationalist effort and, unlike Marxists, do not believe that the workers of the world would unite if freed of their respective bourgeoisie masters. Dependency theorists contend that the EDCs' exploitation of the LDCs is driven by the EDCs'

Web Link

For a site lauding the virtues of capitalism, go to **www.capitalism .org/**. For an opposing view, visit the Web site of the World Socialist Movement at **www .worldsocialism.org/**.

need for cheap **primary products** (such as oil), large external markets for the EDCs' expensive **manufactured goods**, profitable investment opportunities, and low-wage labor. Because this economic structure enriches the EDCs and impoverishes the LDCs, dependency theories argue that the EDCs follow policies designed to keep LDCs dependent. For this reason, economic structuralists call the system that has been created *neocolonialism* because it operates without colonies but is nevertheless imperialistic. The dependency of LDCs is maintained in a number of ways. Some are subtle, such as giving rich countries much greater voting power in the IMF and some other IGOs, thereby allowing the EDCs to manipulate the world economy to their advantage. Other techniques are less subtle. These include corrupting and co-opting the local elite in LDCs by allowing them personal wealth in return for governing their countries to benefit the North or, if the local elite is defiant, using military force to overthrow it and replace it with a friendlier regime.

World systems theory traces the current global economic inequality to the rise of the Western political and economic domination, especially following the Western-centered industrial revolution in the mid-1700s. Theorists who take this perspective contend that the evolution of the Western-dominated capitalist system has distorted development, leaving vast economic, social, and political disparities between the core of the international system (the EDCs) and the periphery (the LDCs). As for countries such as South Korea, which have achieved considerable prosperity, world system theorists are apt to argue that these semiperiphery states have achieved success only by dutifully serving the interests of the EDCs. Like all economic structuralists, world systems theorists favor dramatic changes to the prevailing economic model of Western-dominated capitalism. Sharing the view of dependency theorists, and unlike their Marxist counterparts, world system theorists do not believe that capitalism and the state system should be wiped away. Yet even those not totally opposed to capitalism are skeptical of it. They contend that it can be supported only if it is radically reformed from exploitive capitalism to cooperative capitalism, which recognizes the moral and practical advantages of ensuring at least minimally acceptable economic and social conditions for all.

Whatever their exact theoretical perspective, economic radicals would argue, for example, that the U.S. role in the Persian Gulf region dating back to World War II epitomizes neoimperialism. The devil's bargain, in the view of structuralists, is this: The United States protects or tries to protect the power of obscenely rich, profoundly undemocratic rulers of oil-rich states, such as Saudi Arabia and Kuwait, as it did in 1991. In return, the king and emir keep the price of oil down, which benefits the economies of the United States and the other oil-importing EDCs. Crude oil sold for an average of about $20 a barrel (equal to 42 gallons) in 1990. After the Persian Gulf War through 1999, oil prices dropped to an average of about $17 a barrel, a significant economic advantage to the United States and other imported-oil-dependent countries. Then, beginning in 2000, oil prices began to rise, and when the U.S. invaded Iraq in 2003, economic radical theorists were suspicious that Washington was motivated, at least in part, by the prospects of driving down prices by dominating and increasing Iraqi oil production. From this perspective, it is possible to argue that, in light of the continued oil price increases, the postwar pressure on the Arab oil states

GOMAA
AL AHRAM WEEKLY
Cairo
EGYPT

Poverty Line

This Egyptian editorial drawing captures the view of economic structuralists, who believe that the world's wealthier countries want the world's less developed countries to remain poor in order to dominate and exploit them.

to democratize is not the result of a sincere U.S. concern with democracy but a threat to undermine the autocratic "oil sheiks" if they do not reduce petroleum prices.

Before turning to the main theme of this chapter, national economic competition, it is important to set the stage by surveying the state of the world economy. This analysis contains two parts. First, we will see that the world economy is globalizing and becoming increasingly interdependent. Second, we will take up the often-dramatic differences in economic circumstances that exist among the world's countries.

The World Economy: Globalization and Interdependence

Economic interchange across political borders predates written history. Trading records extend back to almost 3000 B.C., and archaeologists have uncovered evidence of trade in the New Stone Age, or Neolithic period (9000–8000 B.C.). Since then, economics has become an ever more important aspect of international relations. This is evident in expanding world trade and the resulting increased interrelationship between international economic activity and domestic economic circumstances. It has reached the point that we can speak of true economic **globalization** and its accompanying **interdependence** among countries. We can see this by examining trade, investment, and monetary exchanges and by looking at both the general expansion of these factors and the uneven pattern of each.

Trade

In the quest for prosperity, the international flow of goods and services is a vital concern to all world states. **Merchandise trade** is most frequently associated with imports and exports. These goods are tangible items and are subdivided into two main categories: primary goods (raw materials) and manufactured goods. **Services trade** is less well known but also important. Services include things that you do for others. When U.S. insurance companies earn premiums for insuring foreign assets or people, when American movies earn royalties abroad, when U.S. trucks carry goods in Mexico or Canada, the revenue they generate constitutes the export of services. Note that exported services do not have to be performed overseas. American colleges and universities, for example, are one of the country's largest exporters of services. More than 586,000 foreign students studying at U.S. colleges spent over $12 billion for tuition, room, board, and the other aspects of college life ranging from textbooks to pizzas. Whatever their nature, services are a major source of income for countries, amounting to more than 20% of the entire flow of goods and services across international borders.

Expanding Trade

Whether merchandise or services, trade is booming. In 1913 it totaled only $20 billion. In 2004 world trade stood at $11.1 trillion. Even considering inflation, this represents a tremendous jump in world commerce, as indicated in Figure 12.1. Trade growth has been especially rapid during the post–World War II era of significant tariff reductions. During the 1913–1948 period of world wars, depression, and trade protectionism, trade increased at an average annual rate of only 0.8%. The postwar period has seen average annual increases at a rate of approximately 9% overall, with

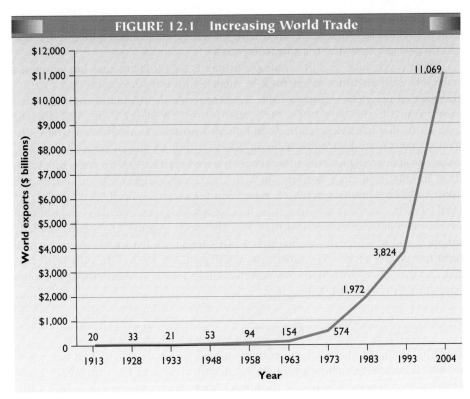

FIGURE 12.1   Increasing World Trade

Trade, measured here in current dollar exports, has grown meteorically during recent decades. This growth is one sign of the vastly increased importance of international economic relations to individual countries and their citizens.

Data source: IMF (various years).

a somewhat slower rate (5%) since 1990. The rapid growth of trade has been caused by a number of supply and demand factors and the implementation of a free trade philosophy.

Factors Promoting Expanded Trade

A number of supply and demand factors have spurred increased trade. First, *improved production technology* has increased the supply of goods. The industrial revolution, which began in 18th-century Europe, led to mass manufacturing. As production rates sped up, manufacturers increasingly had to seek markets for their burgeoning supply of goods farther away and even across national borders. This, in turn, created an *increased demand for resources* to supply the factories. Trade in raw materials imported by the industrialized European countries peaked during the 19th century and through World War II, as increased demand outstripped domestic resource availability. This demand has decreased for several reasons, such as the use of synthetic materials in the manufacturing process. Today, primary products account for only about one-fifth of all goods in international trade. *Materialism* is a third factor that accounts for increased trade. The rise in the world's standard of living, especially in the industrialized countries, has also contributed to "demand" pressure on international trade as people have sought more material goods and improved services. A fourth factor, *improved transportation,* has increased our ability to carry the growing supply of materials and manufactured goods and to meet the demand for them. Modern developments in transportation technology have also greatly decreased per-unit transportation costs.

Wide acceptance of a *free trade philosophy* is a fifth factor that has promoted trade. The early advocacy of free trade by Adam Smith and others came into vogue in the wake of the global trauma of the great economic depression of the 1930s and World War II in the early 1940s. One cause for these miseries, it was said, was the high tariffs that had restricted trade and divided nations. To avoid a recurrence, the United States took the lead in reducing barriers to international trade. As a result, countries accounting for 80% of world commerce began in 1947 to cooperate to reduce international trade barriers through the General Agreement on Tariffs and Trade (GATT). This and a series of related efforts have dramatically decreased world tariff barriers. American import duties, for example, dropped from an average of 60% in 1934 to a current level of less than 4%. The tariffs of other EDCs have similarly dropped, and while the duties charged by LDCs tend to be higher, the average global tariff rate is only about 15%. Tariffs, as we will soon see, are not the only trade barrier, but their sharp reductions have greatly reduced the cost of imported goods and have strongly stimulated trade.

SIMULATION
Free Trade or
Domestic Industry?
You Make the Decision

International Investment

Trade has not been the only form of international economic activity that has grown rapidly. A parallel globalization of international investment has created increased financial interdependence among countries. For example, Americans had $7.2 trillion in investments, bank deposits, property, stocks, and other assets abroad in 2004, making not only individual investors but also the health of the entire U.S. economy dependent to a degree on the state of the world economy. Conversely, foreigners had a $9.6 trillion stake in the United States, and the ebb and flow of those funds into the country are also a central factor in Americans' prosperity, or lack of it. Of the variety of assets that countries have in one another, the two most important types are foreign direct investments and foreign portfolio investments.

Foreign Direct and Portfolio Investment

When Americans invest in British or Nigerian companies, or when Canadians invest in U.S. corporations, a web of financial interdependency is begun. There are two types of foreign investments, **foreign direct investment (FDI)**, which involves buying a major stake in foreign companies or real estate, and **foreign portfolio investment (FPI)** in stocks and bonds on a smaller scale that does not involve controlling companies or owning real estate. Such investments have long existed, but they have accelerated greatly in recent decades as Figure 12.2 shows for FDI. American individuals and corporations are the leading investors, with $2.7 trillion in FDI and another $2.4 trillion in FPI abroad in 2004. Investors in other EDCs and a few from LDCs have added many billions of dollars to the international flow of investment capital.

The flow of investment capital into and out of countries is an important factor in their economic well-being. FDI and, to a degree, FPI help support and expand local

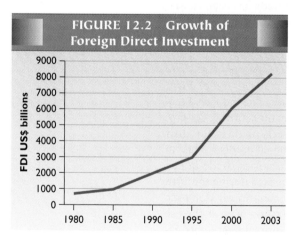

FIGURE 12.2 Growth of Foreign Direct Investment

One indication of economic globalization is the rapid increase in recent decades of the total foreign direct investment (FDI) capital that people and corporations have invested in other countries. The rise from $693 billion in 1980 to over $8.2 trillion in 2003 is a 1090% increase.

Data source: United Nations Conference on Trade and Development businesses, thus supplying jobs. Foreign investors can also help finance a country's budget deficit. The U.S. Treasury would be in dire straits if it were not for the $1.5 trillion in bonds (40% of the total deficit) it has sold to foreigners to fund the chronic U.S. federal budget deficits. Foreign investments also create earnings for investors. American investors earned $294 billion in 2003 alone from their overseas investments.

International Investment and Multinational Corporations

The world's **multinational corporations (MNCs)**, also called transnational corporations (TNCs), account for the lion's share of the global FDI. MNCs are businesses that operate in more than one country. These operations can involve sales outlets, mines and other natural resource–extraction processes, farms and ranches, manufacturing plants, or offices that supply banking and other services. MNCs date back at least to the Dutch East India Company in 1602, but it was not until after World War II that they began to expand in number and size at a rapid pace. Now over 60,000 MNCs exist, and they pack enormous economic muscle. Their annual revenues (gross corporate product, GCP) provide one good measure. The top 500 MNCs alone had a collective GCP of $14.9 trillion in 2003. That is equal to an astounding 43% of the world's collective GNP ($34.5 trillion) that year. Figure 12.3 presents a second perspective on GCP by comparing the revenues of the largest MNC with the GNPs of a number of countries.

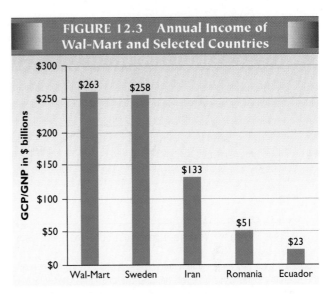

FIGURE 12.3 Annual Income of Wal-Mart and Selected Countries

By comparing the gross corporate product (revenues) of the world's largest MNC, Wal-Mart, with the gross national product (GNP) of countries, you can get an idea of the enormous economic power of multinational corporations. As this figure shows, Wal-Mart's 2003 GCP ($263 billion) is about equal to the 2003 GNP of Sweden, twice as big as that of Iran, five times that of Romania, and ten times the GNP of Ecuador. At the furthest extreme, Wal-Mart's GCP dwarfs the $50 million GNP of São Tomé and Príncipe, the world's smallest national economy, by an astronomical ratio of 5,260:1.

Data sources: World Bank, 2005; *Fortune,* July 24, 2004.

The immense wealth of the largest MNCs gives them considerable influence (Navaretti & Venables, 2004). For example, Wal-Mart is the world largest MNC, with 2003 revenues of $263 billion and 1.5 million employees. These numbers give Wal-Mart an "economy" the size of Sweden's, and there are about 50 countries with populations smaller than Wal-Mart's workforce. The United States is one country that has been dramatically affected by Wal-Mart's decisions. Over the past few decades the company has shifted from buying mostly from U.S. suppliers to using overseas sources. This policy has cost many American jobs, but it also has improved the standard of living for its U.S. shoppers by keeping prices down. Wal-Mart also influences the countries from which it buys. Its biggest supplier is China, and Wal-Mart has pressured manufacturers there to cut costs while maintaining quality. Supporters claim this has caused needed improvements in China's manufacturing efficiency. Critics say that the pressure from Wal-Mart has caused Chinese companies to lower workers' already low wages and cut their skimpy benefits even further.

Did You Know That:

If Wal-Mart were a country, it would be the world's sixth-largest importer of goods from China, slightly ahead of Germany.

Monetary Relations

The globalization of trade and investments means that **monetary relations** have become an increasingly significant factor in both international and domestic economic

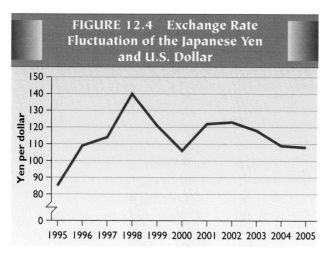

Currencies vary in their value against one another. As you can see, the exchange rate of Japan's yen (¥) and the U.S. dollar between 1995 and 2005 varied from a low of $1 = ¥85 in 1995 to a high of $1 = ¥140 in 1998 before settling into a narrower exchange range and being at $1 = ¥108 in mid-2005. Changes in exchange rates have an important impact on the flow of trade, investment, and other international financial transactions.

Note: Yen value was for June 1 of each year.
Data source: U.S. Federal Reserve Board

Web Link

The historical exchange rate between the U.S. dollar and a range of other currencies can be found at **www.eh.net/hmit/ exchangerates/.**

ANALYZE THE ISSUE
The IMF and the International
Political Economy

health. *The globalization of money* is one aspect. There is a torrent of money amounting to about $700 trillion a year circulating around the world. Much of this flow involves exchanging one country's currency for another's, markedly increasing the importance of **exchange rates**. These are the values of currencies in relation to each other—for example, how many U.S. dollars per Japanese yen and vice versa. Exchange rates are important because they strongly influence the flow of trade and investment. Consider, for example, the changes in the exchange rate of the U.S. dollar and the Japanese yen in Figure 12.4. It shows that the U.S. dollar in 1998 was 61% stronger versus the yen than it was in 1995, and in 2005 was 27% weaker than it was in 1998. Weak and strong should not be equated with good and bad, though, because exchange rates are a two-edged sword. During the late 1990s the strengthening yen was good if you were an American consumer buying a car made in Japan because it would require fewer of your dollars to buy it. But if you were a U.S. autoworker, the strengthening dollar was bad because you might get laid off due to competition from low-cost foreign cars. The flip side, of course, is that a weakening dollar is good for U.S. exporters and bad for U.S. consumers of foreign imports.

To accommodate the globalization of money, there has been a parallel *globalization of financial services,* such as banking. In recent decades, banks have grown from hometown to national to multinational enterprises. Another indicator of increased international financial ties is the level of international lending by private banks. Just the top 25 multinational banks controlled assets of over $20 trillion in 2004, giving them immense financial power in the global economy because of the influence they have over the flow of loans, investment capital, and other financial transactions across borders. For example, American banks have about $500 billion in foreign assets (such as overseas loans) and $800 billion in foreign liabilities (such as foreign deposits in the banks). Moreover, many are involved in international financial services beyond traditional banking. For example, the world's largest bank, Japan's Mizuho Financial Group (assets: $1.29 trillion), has such nonbanking subsidiaries as a brokerage firm, a credit card company, and a venture capital firm. The second largest bank, Citigroup (assets: $1.26 trillion), owns, among other companies, Travelers Insurance, Diners Club International, and the Smith Barney brokerage house.

A third aspect of monetary relations is the *international regulation of money.* As trade, transnational investing, and other forms of international economic interchange increased during the 20th century, it became clear that some mechanisms needed to be created to help regulate the rapidly expanding flow of currencies across borders. The most pressing problem was, and still is, how to stabilize the values of currencies against one another. To that end, there have been a number of regional and global efforts to keep exchange rates stable and to otherwise ensure that currency issues do not impede economic activity. Globally, the International Monetary Fund (IMF), which is detailed in chapter 13, has the primary responsibility for attempting to maintain monetary stability. Regionally, the most advanced efforts have been in the European Union, which has the European Central Bank and now a common currency, the euro.

The World Economy: Diverse Circumstances

Every country, whatever its domestic economic system, has citizens whose circumstances range from wealthy to poor. Similarly, the countries of the world range from rich to destitute.

Traditionally, analysts have divided the world's countries into two spheres. One, the **North**, consists of the generally prosperous EDCs. The other sphere, the **South**, is composed of the relatively, and in some cases absolutely, poor LDCs. The poorest of these LDCs are low-income countries also referred to as **least developed countries (LLDCs)**. Table 12.2 compares the North and South using four income categories (high, upper middle, lower middle, and low) established by the World Bank. The North-South designations result from the fact that most EDCs lie to the north in North America and Europe and most LDCs are farther to the south in Africa, Asia, and Central and South America.

It is important to note that the North and South categories are somewhat fluid. For one, some oil-producing countries, such as Kuwait, which are usually classified as part of the South, fall into the high-income group. Second, there is a handful of **newly industrializing countries (NICs)** in the South that have made strong progress in modernizing their economies. Four of these (Israel, Malta, Singapore, and South Korea) have achieved high-income status. Also worth noting is the status of Russia, other former Soviet republics (FSRs), and the former post-communist countries of Eastern Europe. Some of these have a reasonable industrial base, but only one, Slovenia falls in the high-income group. Russia and most of the other European FSRs are middle-income countries, and Tajikistan and most of the other Asian FSRs are low-income countries.

> **Did You Know That:**
> The world had 691 billionaires with collective assets of $2.2 trillion in 2005. The richest was Bill Gates with a net worth of $46.5 billion, an amount about equal to the 2005 GNP of Vietnam and its 81 million people.

TABLE 12.2   Country Economic Classifications

Category	Income Range Per Capita GNP	Number of Countries	% of World Population	Average Per Capita GNP	Average Per Capita GNP/PPP
North: High Income	≥$9,657	39	16%	$28,550	$29,450
South:	≤$9,656	151	84%	$1,280	$4,320
Upper-Middle Income	$9,656–$3,126	35	05%	$5,340	$9,900
Lower-Middle Income	$3,125–$786	55	42%	$1,480	$5,510
Low Income	<$785	61	37%	$450	$2,190

Data source: World Bank (2005).

Whether you measure economic circumstance in per capita GNP or per capita GNP/PPP, the world is generally divided into two spheres, a prosperous North and a substantially to desperately poor South. The North, which includes a small minority of the world's countries and even a smaller minority of its population, generates an average per capita income that is 22 (GNP) or 7 (GNP/PPP) times the average for the rest of the world.

North-South Patterns

Despite not being a precise division, the North-South dichotomy is used in this analysis because it captures the reality that there is a great divide in the world pattern of economic and social circumstances. In addition to their economic circumstances, most of the countries of the South share a history of having been colonially or neo-colonially dominated by one or another EDC, often within living memory. According to economic structuralists, this dependency relationship continues to a great degree today.

North-South Economic Patterns

The economies of LDCs are not quite different from, rather than just poor mirrors of, those of the EDCs. *Trade differences* are one distinction. Overall, the 20% of the countries that are EDCs with their 16% of the world population exported 75% of all the goods and services in 2004. That left a scant quarter of all exports for the vast majority of countries and people that make up the South. Moreover, China accounted for 33% of all LDC exports, while many other LDCs had few. For example, sub-Saharan Africa, with 11% of the world population, managed to ship only 1.5% of world exports. Trade differences are depicted in Figure 12.5. It also makes a difference what countries export. A diverse range of manufactured goods and services exports account for more than 90% of what EDCs sell abroad. By contrast, manufactured goods and services make up only 69% of middle-income country exports and only 50% of low-income country exports. These LDCs rely more than do EDCs on the export of primary products, such as food, fibers, fuels, and minerals. This disadvantages the LDCs because the price of primary products is often unstable and also has generally has not risen as fast as the price of manufactured goods.

Similarly, *investment differences* also favor the North. First, the North has the flow of most investment capital. Of the 50 largest MNCs, 60% are U.S. companies, 32% are European firms, and 5% are Japanese companies, leaving only 3% of the largest MNCs located elsewhere. Therefore the flow of profits mostly benefits the North. Second, about 70% of all FDI, and an even greater percentage of FPI, flows from one EDC to another, rather than to the South where the need is greatest. Furthermore, the NICs and a few other countries such as China receive most of the investment capital, and most LDCs receive little or none.

North-South Societal Patterns

Economic data can seem dry until you realize the social implications of differences in per capita GNP and similar statistics. Consider what it means for their comparative quality of life that on a per capita basis, the people who live in the EDCs produce $63 for every $1 produced by those living in the LLDCs. In these countries, about 1.1 billion people live in **extreme poverty**, which the World Bank defines as less than $1 a day. Another 1.7 billion people struggle to sustain themselves on between $1 and $2 a day, with the two impoverished groups combining to make up about 46% of the world's population. In societal terms, these numbers translate into poor health care, limited education, lack of safe water, in-

FIGURE 12.5 Share of Exports of the North and South

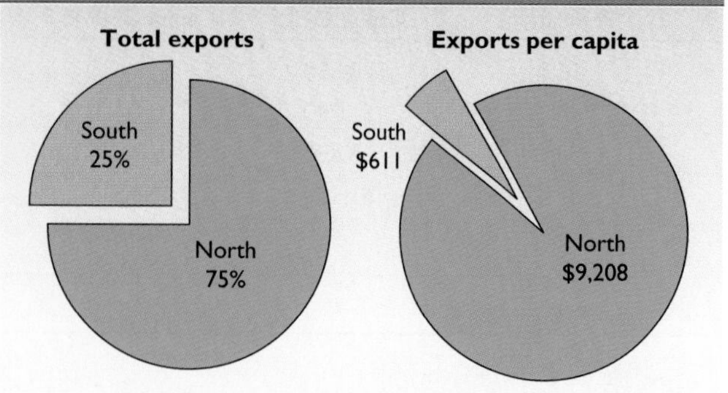

The pattern of world trade is very uneven. The North exports more than 3 times as much in goods and services as does the South in overall dollars and 15 times as much on a per capita basis.

Data source: World Bank (2005).

adequate nutrition, and other grim realities. For example, 39% of all adults in LLDCs are illiterate; less than 1% of EDC adults are. Medical facilities in the South are overwhelmed. Each physician in an LLDC is responsible for about 2,500 people, 10 times as many people as a physician in the North. Moreover, hundreds of millions of people in the South have no access to any kind of health care. These conditions lead to disease and death on a wide scale. A child born in an LLDC is 18 times more likely to die before age 5 than a child in an EDC. Having children is also risky, with the maternal mortality rate in LLDCs 31 times higher than in EDCs. Overall, just 58% of the people in LLDCs (compared to 91% in EDCs) live to age 65, and the average person in a low-income country dies 20 years earlier than a resident in a high-income country.

Evaluating the North-South Gap

Although annual data about economic and societal factors are important in evaluating the indisputable gap between North and South, they do not tell the whole story. Trends are of at least equal importance. Are things getting better or worse? On this question, the data is mixed and somewhat subject to interpretation. There is also a highly uneven pattern of development.

Mixed Data on Development

Statistics about development in the South present a classic good news–bad news scenario. On the economic dimension, trade provides one example. Yes, LDCs are disadvantaged in trade because goods and services are only 68% of their exports, but that figure has improved from 55% in 1990. As a result trade has increased from being 34% to 49% of the average LDC's GNP. Similarly, while FDI still mostly flows between EDCs and what goes to LDCs is concentrated in a few of them, the overall dollars of FDI going into the LDCs increased 8 times between 1990 and 2001. There are also many signs of progress for the LDCs on the societal front. Compared to 1990, 7% less of the world's population is living in extreme poverty. Education has improved during that time, with adult literacy up 8%. Health in the LDCs is also better. For example, a child in an LDC is now 33% more likely to survive to age 5 than was true in 1990, and for adults their life expectancy is up by two years. In light of this data, how you evaluate the condition of LDCs depends in part on your standard of comparison. Relative to 1990, LDCs are doing better than they were. Relative to the EDCs, a huge and in some cases growing gap still exists.

It is also important to see that statistics sometimes seem to tell almost contradictory stories. Per capita GNP provides an example. From a positive perspective, the per capita GNP growth of the LDCs (4.9%) measured in real dollars since 1990 has far exceeded the growth of the EDCs (2.1%). Yet at the same time, as evident in Figure 12.6, the relative economic gap between North and South is much greater than it once was. Even worse, the dollar gap

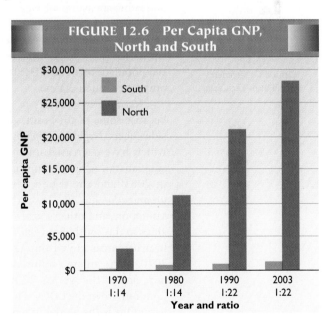

FIGURE 12.6   Per Capita GNP, North and South

The economic ratio of the per capita GNPs of North and South expanded 65% between 1970 and 2003. The dollar gap grew by nine times, going from about $3,000 in 1970 to approximately $27,000 in 2003.

Data source: World Bank (2005).

has increased considerably. The reason for this outcome is the much lower base of per capita wealth in the LDCs. For example, compare an LDC with a per capita GNP of $2,000 and an EDC with a per capita GNP of $10,000. The gap is $8,000. If the LDC's GNP grew at 4.9% (compounded) for 5 years, it would be $2,540. The EDC growing at 2.1% would have a per capita GNP of $11,095 after 5 years. Thus, even though in this example the LDC's economy grew much faster than the EDC's, the dollar gap in their respective per capita GNPs widened from $8,000 to $8,550.

Uneven Patterns of Development

The good news about the growth in the economies of the LDCs and the improvements in their societal conditions is also tempered by uneven patterns of development. *Disparity between countries* is one warp in the overall picture of economic growth in the South. Some regions such as East Asia have made major economic and societal strides. At the other end of the regional spectrum, sub-Saharan Africa has struggled and in some cases lost ground. Its average GNP growth rate has been only about half of the other LDCs. The region's exports are only 35% manufactured goods and services, compared to 68% for all LDCs. Less than 2% of all global FDI goes to the region, and more than half of that goes to just one country, South Africa. Life expectancy in the region has actually declined from 50 years in 1990 to 46 years now, and two-thirds of the population will not live to age 65. About a third of sub-Saharan Africans were malnourished in 1990, and no improvement has been made. The child mortality rate has fallen from a horrific 19% in 1990, but is still a disturbing 17%. The litany of woes need not continue to make the point that the overall data for the LDCs does not always reflect the wide array of circumstances among them.

Disparity within countries is a second characteristic of LDC economic development that can make the overall data deceiving. All countries have disparities in income and other measures of wealth within their population, but unequal distribution is particularly strong within most LDCs. More than in EDCs, the LDCs tend to have a very small, very wealthy upper class and a vast, very poor lower class. Figure 12.7 shows the percentage of income earned by the wealthiest and poorest 20% each of the populations of an LDC (Brazil), an EDC (Japan), and the world's largest economy (the United States).

Negative by-products of development are a third aspect of the uneven pattern because some of the South's advances have been partially offset by several negative side effects. *Explosive population growth* has occurred as a result of medical advances, which have decreased infant mortality and increased longevity. The population of sub-Saharan Africa, for instance, rose 236% from 210 million in 1960 to 705 million in 2003, and the region is expected to reach 866 million people by 2015. *Rapid urbanization* has also beset the South, as the hope of finding jobs and better health, sanitation, and other social services has set off a mass migration from rural areas to cities in the South. Between 1965 and 2003 the share of the South's population living in urban areas grew from 22% to 43%, and it is projected to reach 53% in the year 2020. There are now approximately 175 cities in LDCs with populations over 1 million, and of the world's 20 most populous cities, all but 3 (Tokyo, New York, and London) are in the LDCs. This rapid urbanization process has created a host of problems. One is the weakening of social order. Older tribal, village, and extended-family loyalties are being destroyed, with few new offsetting values and other social support systems to take their place. Second, the hope of employment is often unfulfilled, and unemployment and poverty in many cities is staggering. Third, struggling LDC governments are often unable to meet the sanitary, housing, and other needs of the flood of people moving to or being born in the cities. About a quarter of the South's urban

MAP
Central Government
Expenditures Per Capita

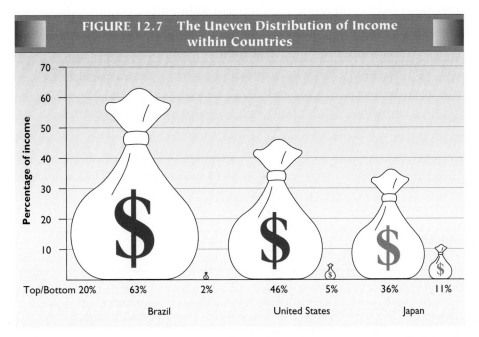

FIGURE 12.7   The Uneven Distribution of Income within Countries

The unequal distribution of income within countries is shown for each of three countries by a pair of moneybags. One represents the percentage of the country's income that goes to the wealthiest 20% of its citizens and the other, the percentage of the country's income that goes to the poorest 20% of its citizens. All countries have unequal distributions, but LDCs generally have the greatest inequality. Notice that in Japan, the wealthiest 20% make only about 3 times as much as the country's poorest citizens. In Brazil the top 20% make about 31 times what the poorest 20% receive. The "wealth gap" in the United States is greater than in most EDCs.

Data source: World Bank (2005).

population is living in conditions below the minimum standard for health. For example, in Dhaka, the capital of Bangladesh, only 22% of the households are connected to a sewer, and in Indonesia's capital, Jakarta, only half the households have access to safe drinking water.

Industrial and environmental dangers have also been undesirable by-products of development. The impact of development on the environment is detailed in chapter 15, but a brief note of the dangers is appropriate here. One problem is rapid deforestation due to demands for wood, expanding farm and ranch acreage, and general urban growth. Loss of these forests increases soil erosion and has numerous other deleterious effects. LDC industrial development also adds to air, water, and soil pollution, and most major cities in the LDCs are now far more polluted than are major metropolitan areas in the EDCs.

Web Link

The Population Reference Bureau has good commentary, maps, and data on urbanization in the South and the rest of the world at **www.prb.org/** Content/NavigationMenu/PRB/ Educators/Human_Population/ Urbanization2/Patterns_of _World_Urbanization1.htm.

National Economic Power

Having set the stage by reviewing the state of the world economy, we can now turn to economic nationalism, the traditional state-centric approach to international political economy. While it is true that there has been considerable movement toward liberalizing international economic relations in recent decades, economic nationalism

TABLE 12.3 Measures of U.S. Financial Power			
Financial Measure	Evaluation	United States	Comparison
GNP	Excellent	$11 trillion	32% of world GNP
Per capita GNP	Excellent	$37,870	5th highest in world
Per capita GNP/PPP	Excellent	$37,870	4th highest in world
Real GNP growth	Very good	4.4%	2.5%: other EDCs
Inflation	Good	1.9%	1.7%: other EDCs
Unemployment	Fair	5.5%	7.2%: other EDCs
Budget balance as % of GNP	Poor	3.4% deficit	1.5%: deficit other EDCs
Interest payments as % of budget	Poor	11.2%	6.2%: other EDCs
Balance of payments as % of GNP	Very poor	5.7% deficit	2.1%: surplus other EDCs

Data source: IMF, *World Economic Outlook,* April 2005.
Note: All data are for either 2003 or 2004.

The strengths of the U.S. economy are its sheer size, wealth, healthy growth, and low inflation. There are several worrisome aspects, though, including a growing budget deficit, high interest payments to finance the national debt, and a huge deficit in the U.S. balance of payments, the measure of all money coming into and leaving the country.

remains the dominant practice in global economic affairs for two reasons. First, states remain the principal actors. Second, these states most often acquire economic power, formulate economic policy, and use their economic assets to benefit themselves, not the global community.

It is axiomatic that to pursue economic statecraft effectively, a country needs to possess considerable economic power. Chapter 8 explains the national infrastructure (technological sophistication, transportation systems, information and communications capabilities) that provides part of the basis for building a powerful economy. In addition to these factors, the determinants of national power include financial position, natural resources, industrial output, and agricultural output.

Financial Position

The center of any country's economic power is its basic financial position. To think about that, consider Table 12.3 and the criteria of financial strength detailed there for the United States. Certainly, the U.S. economy is by far the world's largest, it is prosperous, and it is immensely powerful. But also, like the biblical Goliath, it has worrisome vulnerabilities. Most of the U.S. weaknesses are associated with lack of financial discipline. For example, the U.S. government had a budget deficit for 48 of the 56 years during the period FY1950–FY2006. One result of chronic deficit spending is that Americans are paying huge sums in interest ($260 billion in FY2006), a third of it to foreigners, on the $5 trillion in federal bonds sold to finance the debt. Poor financial restraint is also evident in the huge U.S. deficit in its **balance of payments**, a measure that represents the entire flow of money into and out of a country's economy. Since its last surplus in 1989, the United States has amassed ever-larger balance-of-payments deficits, both in dollars and as a percentage of the country's GNP. The $666 billion deficit in 2004 equaled a very worrisome 5.7% of the U.S. GNP.

The greatest single factor in the balance-of-payments deficit is the U.S. trade deficit. Americans have rung up a **net trade** (exports minus imports) deficit during all but two years since 1971. The $617 billion trade deficit for 2004 was the largest ever and accounted for 93% of the overall balance-of-payments deficit. The primary source of the trade deficit is the seemingly insatiable American appetite for imported goods. U.S. exports increased by 4.5% annually between 1997 and 2005, but imports grew at an even faster pace, 7.7%. Thus far, the immense U.S. economy has been able to absorb these negative trends in U.S. budget and balance-of-payments deficits, but no country is invulnerable forever to economic realities. Even for the financially mightiest of countries, deficit spending, accumulating significant foreign debts, and other such practices can weaken a country's financial position over time and even lead to collapse.

Natural Resources

The possession, or lack, of energy, mineral, and other natural resources has become an increasingly important power factor as industrialization and technology have advanced. Natural resources affect power in three related ways: (1) The greater a country's self-sufficiency in vital natural resources, the greater its power. (2) Conversely, the greater a country's dependency on foreign sources for vital natural resources, the less its power. (3) The greater a country's surplus (over domestic needs) of vital resources needed by other countries, the greater its power.

The key here is not just production; it is production compared to consumption. Oil is the most obvious example. The United States produces about 5.5 million barrels of crude oil a day, a rate second only to world leader Saudi Arabia (1 barrel = 42 gallons). Yet Americans consume about 16 million barrels a day, about three times what they produce. As a result, the United States has to import more than 10.5 million barrels of petroleum each day. One concern is that U.S. petroleum dependency makes the country vulnerable to disruptions of the flow of oil that it needs to maintain prosperity. Second, sharp energy price increases due to political manipulation or, as occurred in 2004 and 2005, a supply-demand crunch can hamper economic growth. Third, the dependency causes a huge outflow of financial resources. With imported petroleum costing Americans about $60 per barrel in mid-2005, they were spending about $578 million a day (or $211 billion a year) importing oil.

Did You Know That:
Americans, who make up about 5% of the world population, consume about 25% of its petroleum.

By contrast, possessing a surplus of oil or any other vital resources is a power asset. As is evident in Figure 12.8 on page 390, oil reserves are highly concentrated in the world. For many countries with oil, the so-called black gold has been a major source of revenue. Saudi Arabia, for example, exported about $200 billion in oil during 2005. Oil has also increased the global political focus on the petroleum-producing countries and on their diplomatic power, especially the countries in the Middle East, which account for about two-thirds of world petroleum reserves.

Industrial Output

Even if a country is bountifully supplied with natural resources, its power is limited unless it can convert those assets into industrial goods. On a global basis, industrial production is highly concentrated. For instance, just five countries (China, Japan, Russia, the United States, and South Korea) produce 57% of the world's steel. Vehicle production is another indication of industrial concentration, as indicated in Figure 12.9 on page 391. It shows that in 2004 the three biggest vehicle manufacturers (Germany, Japan, and the United States) made 44% of the global total. Those 3 plus

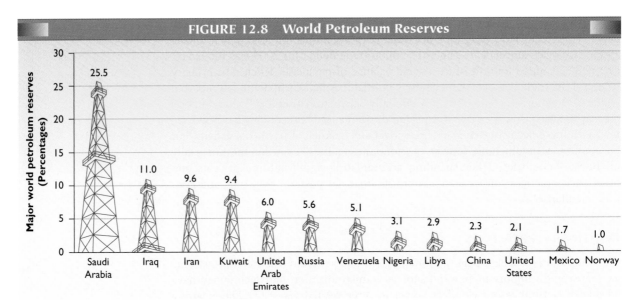

FIGURE 12.8 World Petroleum Reserves

The 13 countries with 1% or more of the world's oil reserves control more than 85% of the resources. The concentration of about two-thirds of the reserves in the Middle East has given that region great geopolitical importance.

Data source: U.S. Energy Information Administration.

the other 7 countries that make up the top 10 vehicle producers accounted for 78% of world production. About 85% of the world's countries (including all those in Africa) produce no, or only a negligible number of, vehicles.

Agricultural Output

It is not common to equate food production with power. Yet a country's agricultural capacity is an important factor. Self-sufficiency varies widely in the world. The United States is basically able not only to supply its own needs but also to earn money from agricultural exports. With less than 5% of the world's population, it produces 16% of the world's cereal grains and 18% of its meat. Other countries are less fortunate. Some have to use their economic resources to import food. Sub-Saharan Africa is in particularly desperate shape. Senegal, for one, needs to import machinery, fuel, and other products necessary to diversify and industrialize its economy, yet it must spend 30% of its import funds to buy food. By contrast, food accounts for just 5% of American imports. Others have insufficient funds to buy enough food and face widespread hunger. About a third of all sub-Saharan Africans are undernourished. In their region, per capita food production has declined by 29% since 1970. By comparison, U.S. per capita production rose 25% over the same period.

Another significant agricultural factor is the percentage of economic effort that a country must expend to feed its people. Countries are relatively disadvantaged if they have larger percentages of their workforce engaged in agriculture, and thus not available for the manufacturing and service sectors. For example, over half of China's workforce is in agriculture compared to only 2% of all U.S. workers. A country is also at a disadvantage if it has to spend a significant part of its economic effort (measured as a percentage of GDP) to feed its people. Here again, China is relatively disadvantaged by having to devote 15% of its GDP to farming, compared to just 2% for

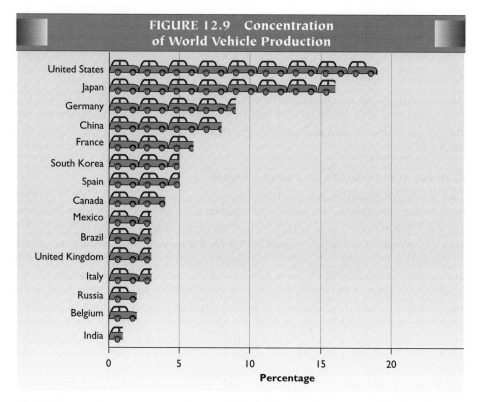

FIGURE 12.9   Concentration of World Vehicle Production

Global industry is highly concentrated. The 10 countries with the largest vehicle production accounted for more than three-fourths of the world total of about 64 million vehicles in 2004.

Data source: International Organization of Motor Vehicle Manufacturers.

the United States. A major problem for China and similarly disadvantaged countries is that they are inefficient because they have so little farm machinery. As one measure, Americans have almost three times more tractors per square mile of farmland than do the Chinese.

National Economic Competition

One of the most important economic changes within countries since the end of the 1800s has been the expansion of governments' regulation of their national economies. Even countries like the United States that see themselves as bastions of capitalism have myriad laws that significantly restrain economic competition by barring monopolistic practices and other unwanted manifestations of capitalism. Furthermore, most countries have accepted the notion that the self-interest of individual citizens must be balanced to some degree with the collective welfare of the national society. In contrast to domestic systems, the international system is still a largely unregulated arena in which countries pursue their economic self-interests in competition with other countries and in which there is little sense of shared responsibility for the welfare of the global society. As chapter 13 discusses, this dog-eat-dog image of the international political economy is not quite as stark as it once was. Nevertheless, competition and self-reliance, not cooperation and mutual assistance, are the prevailing IPE realities. This struggle for advantage and prosperity exists between and within the North and South.

North-North Economic Competition

Although the North is extraordinarily advantaged compared to the South, the EDCs face many economic challenges. In addition to the normal competitive tensions of the system, economic and political changes are creating strong competitive pressures on the EDCs.

Changes in the North's Economic Climate

One factor increasing economic tensions within the North is that its economic growth rate has slowed. The average annual real GDP growth rate of the EDCs during the 1980s was 3.4%; during the 1990s that declined to 2.3%; and between 2000 and 2005 it rebounded only marginally to 2.4%. Europe and Japan were particularly in the doldrums during 2000–2005, with Japan's economy at a nearly stagnant 0.9% annual growth rate, and the EU's at 1.7%. The EDCs slowing economies have sharpened the competition among them to export their products to one another and to the LDCs and to protect their domestic economies against imports. Adding to this pressure, there is increasing competition from China and a few other LDCs in the manufacturing and service sectors. Making matters worse, companies in the North have tried to deal with the competition in some cases by reducing their workforces and using robotics and other high-tech manufacturing processes to replace workers. In other cases, companies have eliminated entire plants, laid off their employees, and moved operations overseas to take advantage of cheaper labor. Many of the displaced workers are either unemployed or find jobs in the usually lower-paying service sector. Now even service sector jobs are increasingly subject to foreign competition. In what is called "outsourcing," companies in the United States and other EDCs are hiring workers abroad to do data entry work, to respond to service telephone calls and e-mail inquiries, to write software, and do many other service jobs. Such economic impacts have created mounting domestic pressures on the governments of the EDCs to protect jobs. For example, a recent survey of Americans that asked them to name their high priority foreign policy goals found that more Americans listed protecting jobs from foreign competition as a high priority (78%) than those who chose stopping the spread of nuclear weapons (73%) or combating international terrorism (71%).[2]

Changes in the North's Political Climate

Declining political accord is also increasing the sense of rivalry among the EDCs. The end of the cold war and the looming threat of the Soviet Union lessened the need for strategic cooperation among the industrialized Western allies. As a result, the long-standing economic disputes among the so-called trilateral countries (Japan, the United States/Canada, Western Europe) that had once been suppressed in the name of allied unity have become more acrimonious. The strains between the United States, on one hand, and France, Germany, and other European countries, on the other, over the U.S. determination to topple the Iraqi regime of Saddam Hussein in 2003 is but one of the latest examples of the discord.

The United States and most of Europe have also parted ways on a range of political issues. There is broad resentment of President George W. Bush's unilateralist approach to foreign policy and many of his specific policies. Europeans were distressed by his refusal to support the Kyoto Protocol on the environment, by his rejection of the International Criminal Court, by his abrogation of the Anti-Ballistic

Web Link

The best source for data on the economic position of the North is the Web site of the Organization for Economic Cooperation and Development at **www .oecd.org.** The most recent data overview can be found by entering "Economic Outlook" and the current year in the search window of the OECD's home page to find the latest issues of its monthly publication of that name.

Unions are one of the interest groups that favor many economic nationalist measures. These members of the Teamsters union in New Hampshire oppose the possible creation of the Free Trade Area of the Americas (FTAA) as an extension of the bad policy making that they think led to the North American Free Trade Agreement (NAFTA) among the United States, Canada, and Mexico.

Missile Treaty, and, perhaps most of all, by his military action against Iraq. These political strains have enhanced the U.S.-European rivalry and entwined it with the European concern about U.S. hegemony. As one example, President Jacques Chirac used fear of the United States as a key point in his appeal to French citizens to ratify the EU constitution, as discussed in chapter 7. Chirac told one group of voters in the nation that "genuine European power" was needed to counter "the United States, and other emerging economic blocs, like China, India, Brazil and South America, [and] Russia." And he warned, "Only our political power at the heart of the European Union today allows us to defend our interests: should we vote 'no,' we will no longer have any power."[3]

North-South Economic Competition

Three factors are particularly responsible for increased economic competition and tension between North and South. One is that the LDCs are now asserting with mounting intensity their claim that they have a right to a much greater share in the world's economic wealth. A second factor is the North's general rejection of the LDCs' demands for economic concessions. Third, a number of LDCs have become major exporters of manufactured goods and, to a lesser degree, services that directly compete with the EDCs' products and services, thus undermining EDC dominance in those economic areas.

The South's Reform Agenda

A basic point to understand the perspective of the South is that many people there share parts of the structuralist argument that by design or happenstance the international system works to the advantage of the EDCs and serves to keep the LDCs relatively poor and dependent. As a result, the LDCs have joined together to insist on a more equitable distribution of global financial resources. To promote that, a coalition of them cooperated to convene the first United Nations Conference on Trade and

Development (UNCTAD) and to create an LDC organization, the Group of 77, both in 1964. Now the Group of 77 has grown to 132 members, and there is an ongoing UNCTAD organization that includes all countries with UN membership and serves as a vehicle for the LDCs to discuss their needs and to press demands on the North.

The new LDC organization soon led to an assertive South pressing the North to reform its policies and the international economic system. Proposals were first put forward in the Declaration on the Establishment of a **New International Economic Order (NIEO)**, which was drafted by UNCTAD and approved by the UN General Assembly in 1974. These largely unmet demands have regularly been reiterated, refined, and expanded by UNCTAD and the Group of 77. A recent reassertion occurred at 2005 summit meeting of the South's leaders in Doha, Qatar (the first was in Havana, Cuba, in 2000). The leaders adopted the "Doha Program of Action" that reiterated a number of earlier declarations and pledged its signatories to "continue strengthening the unity and solidarity among countries of the South, as an indispensable element in the defense of our right to development and for the creation of a more just and equitable international order."[4] The document asserted the need for policy change in these areas:

1. *Trade reforms,* such as lowering EDC barriers to agricultural imports, which will expand and stabilize markets for LDC exports.
2. *Monetary reforms* that will create greater stability in the exchange rates of LDC currencies and will also moderate the sometimes sudden and significant ebb and flow of FDI and FPI into and out of the LDCs.
3. *Institutional reforms* that will increase the influence of the South over the policy decisions of the International Monetary Fund, the World Bank, and other such international financial agencies. Currently, as chapter 13 details, wealthy countries have a much larger vote in these institutions than do poorer countries.
4. *Economic modernization* of the LDCs with significant assistance by the EDCs through such methods as relaxing patent rights to permit easier technology transfers to the LDCs.
5. *Greater labor migration* for LDC workers seeking employment in the more prosperous EDCs.
6. *Elimination of economic coercion,* including the use of sanctions, which the South tends to see as a tool by which the EDCs punish and control LDCs.
7. *Economic aid* to the South by the North that steadily increases to meet the UN's target of 0.7% of each EDC's GNP, to be spent on promoting the development of the LDCs. The current aid level is a bit over 0.2%.
8. *Debt relief* granted by the EDCs, the World Bank, and the IMF, based on reducing the money owed to them by many LDCs and eliminating the debt for the poorest LLDCs. Currently, the LDCs owe about $2.4 trillion and have annual debt service payments over $400 billion.

The North's Response to the South's Reform Agenda

To say that the North has ignored the South's plight would be inaccurate. But it would also be misleading to say that the North has gone very far to meet the South's demands. One reason for the North's limited response is the view of many that the main barriers to the South's development are internal issues, including political instability, inefficient market controls, and corruption. Taking that view, President Bush

Web Link

A good source for the South's view on the international political economy is the Web site of the Group of 77 at **www.g77.org**.

told one international development conference that LDCs had not done enough to reform themselves and that, "The lesson of our time is clear: When nations close their markets and opportunity is hoarded by a privileged few, no amount—no amount—of development aid is ever enough." Instead of more aid, the president continued, the LDCs needed to accept "a higher, more difficult, more promising call . . . to encourage sources that produce wealth: economic freedom, political liberty, the rule of law and human rights."[5]

Domestic resistance within the EDCs is a second factor that has limited their response to the LDCs. Many of the changes that the LDCs want are very unpopular in the EDCs. Greater labor migration is an example. One survey of the United States, Canada, Japan, and four Western European EDCs found that an average of 71% of their people opposed increased immigration.[6] Foreign aid also faces stiff opposition in most EDCs. A 2004 poll of Americans found 64% saying that U.S. foreign aid was too high and only 9% thinking it was too low. Another 24% thought the aid level was about right, and 2% were unsure.[7] As a result of this attitude in the United States and elsewhere, the $69 billion foreign aid in 2004 was actually less in real dollars than in 1995. Moreover, as Figure 12.10 shows, foreign aid as a percentage of the EDC's GNP has gone down, instead of up toward 0.7% as the LDCs and the UN advocate. Yet other steps that would help LDCs are opposed by one or another powerful interest group in the EDCs. For instance, numerous LDCs have important sugar crops, yet their exports to the United States are limited by an array of strict quotas and high tariffs that the U.S. sugar lobby has persuaded the U.S. government to impose. These are a sweet deal for American sugar producers, leaving the 2004 price of U.S. sugar more than three times the world market price. However, the protection is a bitter pill for American consumers, annually costing them an extra $2 billion for sugar, soda, and other products containing sugar, and for poor LDCs that cannot export their crop freely to the United States.

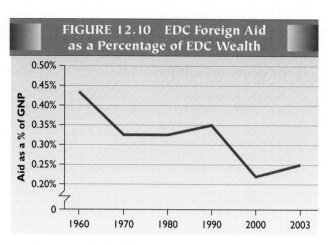

FIGURE 12.10   EDC Foreign Aid as a Percentage of EDC Wealth

The EDCs now give a smaller percentage of their wealth as economic aid to the LDCs than in earlier years.

Data source: Organization of Economic Cooperation and Development.

New Developments in North-South Competition

A relatively recent and growing development in North-South relations is that a few LDCs are beginning to compete with the EDCs for markets, resources, and other economic assets, creating global repercussions. China is the prime example. With a per capita GNP of only $1,100, China is distinctly an LDC. Yet its overall annual GNP of $1.6 trillion is the world's fifth largest, just behind Great Britain and just ahead of France. Among other things, China's large economy has increased its needs for energy imports, which the EDCs also need. Between 2000 and 2004, China's petroleum consumption increased 38%, and its oil imports increased 40%. It now consumes 8% of the world's annual oil supply, second only to the United States. Soaring oil prices are one outcome of the sharply increased demand for petroleum. Another outcome of China's hunger for oil, and one that would have seemed inconceivable not long ago, occurred in 2005 when the government-controlled China National Offshore Oil Corporation (CNOOC) outbid Chevron to purchase control of a major U.S. oil company, Unocal (originally Union Oil Company of California,

WRITE THE POLICY SCRIPT

Sanctions on China?

Confrontation and an eventual showdown form the plotline of such classic western films as *High Noon* (1952) starring Gary Cooper and even of such light-hearted westerns as *Shanghai Noon* (2000) starring Jackie Chan and Owen Wilson. Now another showdown is brewing, this time between China and the United States over the exchange rate of the yuan. If it were made into a movie, *Shanghai Noon 2*, Jackie Chan's character Chon Wang and Owen Wilson's Roy O'Bannon would no longer be partners. Instead, they would be facing one another at high noon, just as Gary Cooper's Marshal Will Kane had to confront Frank Miller and his murderous gang.

The path to conflict in *Shanghai Noon 2* begins with the U.S. trade deficit with China. It has been steadily mounting and reached $162 billion in 2004. That year, China exported $5.67 worth of goods to the United States for every $1 in American goods it bought.

U.S. officials put part of the blame for the deficit on China's policy of maintaining an artificially high exchange value of 8.3 yuan to the dollar at a time when the dollar weakened against most other currencies. Some experts say China should revalue the yuan by as much as 40% to reach a fair exchange rate. In 2005, U.S. Secretary of the Treasury John Snow called on Beijing to act "without delay," and Congress threatened to enact a 27.5% increase in the U.S. tariff on Chinese goods unless Beijing gave way.

Beijing initially called the U.S. position and threats "unacceptable."[1] Then in response to increasingly urgent U.S. demand, China relented, but just a bit. In July 2005, it agreed to devalue the yuan by 2%, far short of the 40% artificial difference with the U.S. dollar that some analysts claimed existed. China also agreed to let the yuan fluctuate further in the future, but again placed strict limits on how much. Most analysts agreed that the marginal devaluation would do little to change the U.S.-China trade pattern, and one of the legislators sponsoring the retaliatory tariff characterized the devaluation as a "baby step."[2]

The key argument for confronting China is that trade deficits cost Americans workers their jobs. "Until [the Chinese] start playing by the rules, our manufacturing industry will continue to bleed jobs," charged Senator Lindsey Graham (R-SC).[3] Another argument for retaliating against China might be termed the "enough's enough" argument. It does not focus on one thing, but on the pattern of China allegedly not playing fairly by keeping the value of the yuan high, by continuing to allow the massive pirating of U.S. movies and software, and by a range of other practices that distort trade and investment.

Those who opposed sanctions on China make several counterarguments. One is that a major revaluing of the yuan or imposing sanctions on China will not save jobs. Former Federal Reserve Board Chairman Alan Greenspan told Congress that "few if any American jobs would be protected" because if the price of Chinese goods increased, the affected items would be imported from other low-cost countries rather than supplied by U.S. manufacturers. Opponents of retaliation against China also warn that substantially revaluing the yuan or increasing the tariff would

founded 1890) for $18.5 billion. China had earlier bought such U.S. businesses as the personal computer division of IBM, but the strategic importance of oil led to such an outburst of opposition to the Unocal deal within the United States that CNOOC withdrew its offer. However, China's quest for oil assets continues. Among other places, China is a major investor in several oilfield ventures in Canada. This also potentially affects Americans because Canada is the largest supplier of U.S. petroleum imports, accounting for about 20% of the total in 2005. China has also agreed to invest heavily in the oil sector of Venezuela, the third leading supplier (15%) of U.S. petroleum imports (Mexico, at 18% is second).

Trade is another source of tension between China and the North. A major factor in the 2004 record U.S. trade deficit was the $162 billion imbalance in trade with China (U.S. exports to China: $197 billion, U.S. imports from China: $359 billion). The European Union also had a major trade deficit of about $80 billion with China in 2004. At least one cause, according to U.S. officials, is that China has manipulated the exchange rate of its currency, the yuan, to keep it artificially low relative to the dollar. In May 2005, U.S. Secretary of the Treasury called on China to relax its controls on the yuan "without delay," and legislation was introduced in Congress threat-

In this photograph, a Bank of China teller is displaying 100 yuan currency notes with the face of Mao Zedong. The value of the yuan relative to the U.S. dollar is among the many economic issues causing tension between Washington and Beijing. If you were a U.S. policy maker, would you practice patient diplomacy to resolve the issues or would you favor sanctions to retaliate against China?

harm most Americans. For instance, China produces about 90% of the world's toys, and the price of the nearly $18 billion in toys that the U.S. imports annually from China would increase, making birthdays, and other gift-giving occasions more expensive. It is also the case that China has used part of the inflow of U.S. currency to amass $230 billion in U.S. Treasury bonds (second only to Japan), thereby helping the U.S. government finance its budget deficit. A falling yuan would reduce bond purchases, the reduced demand would push up the interest rate the U.S. Treasury has to pay to sell its supply of bonds, and an increase in the Treasury rate would push up U.S. consumer interest rates on credit cards, mortgages, student loans, and other debt.

What Do You Think?

Imagine you are the U.S. senator from your state and that China has made only small adjustments in its international economic policy. Write the U.S. foreign economic policy script. Would you vote for or against a major tariff increase on Chinese goods?

ening a substantial increase in the U.S. tariff on Chinese goods unless Beijing met the U.S. demands. The European Union has experienced similar trade tensions with China, particularly over the flood of textiles from China that has displaced EU workers in that industry. In July, China relented a bit, but it revalued the yuan by only 2% (or about one-fourth of a cent), and to quell rumors that further changes could be expected, the Bank of China advised, "The notion that the 2% revaluation is only an initial adjustment and that the central bank will further adjust the rate in the foreseeable future is wrong."[8] You can decide on possible U.S. actions to improve its trade balance with China by reviewing the issue in the box "Sanctions on China?"

South-South Economic Competition and Tension

Although the South generally shows a united front in calling on the North for economic reform, the LDCs are also in competition with one another. One example is oil. Increased prices benefit those few LDCs that export oil, but they are very harmful to the economies of oil-importing LDCs, which are much less able to afford to pay the higher prices than are the EDCs.

Additionally, LDCs compete among themselves for investment capital from the North and for its markets. Again, China provides a good example. Chinese goods are flooding the United States, the EU, and the other countries of the North, but only 10% of the factories exporting goods are owned by the Chinese. The rest are owned by the EDCs' multinational corporations. At one time these factories may have been in the United States and other countries of the North and employed those countries' workers. But in most cases, the plants had long ago left the North and had gone to such LDCs as Mexico. In the past few years, however, Mexico's role as a provider of low-cost exports to the United States has been substantially undercut by China, where an average factory worker's wages are less than half those of the average Mexican worker. As a result, production dropped 30% between 2000 and 2002 in Mexico's *maquiladora* manufacturing zone near the U.S. border, some 850 maquiladora factories shut down, and employment in the zone declined by 20%. Since then the economic fortunes of the maquiladoras and their Mexican workers have improved somewhat, but that has come in part at the cost of wage restraints for low-paid workers and tax breaks to lure MNCs back to the border.

Applied Economic Nationalism

Economic nationalism is more than a theory. It also has been and remains a powerful force in determining the economic and political policies of the world's sovereign states. Economic nationalists believe that a state's political, military, and economic powers are inextricably linked, leading them to advocate interfering in the international political economy in three ways. One is manipulating a country's international economic policy to preserve or, even better, to enhance the national economy. The second is using a country's economic power to accomplish its political goals. The third is using a country's military and other noneconomic power resources to achieve its economic goals.

Using Economic Means to Achieve Economic Ends

Globalization is increasingly linking the economies of all countries, and chapter 13 takes up the argument that in the long run the chances of prosperity of every country are improved if all other countries have sound economies. Be that as it may, all countries still follow the traditional approach of shaping their economic policy primarily to promote their own prosperity; the welfare of the world is a secondary issue. To accomplish their self-interested goals, all states practice **protectionism** to some degree by using a variety of tools to manipulate the flow of trade, investments, and other forms of economic interchange into and out of the country. Each of these protectionist measures has benefits and drawbacks, a cost-benefit analysis that is taken up in the chapter 13 section on debating the future of globalization, cooperation, and interdependence.

Trade and Investment Barriers

Countries can erect a range of barriers to limit import or foreign investment. These include tariffs, nontariff barriers, monetary manipulation, and investment restrictions.

Tariff Barriers   Restrictions on trade and investments are the most familiar form of protectionism. Of the tools available, **tariffs** are the most widespread. Tariff rates are quite low relative to what they once were, but two qualifications are important. One is that tariff rates for EDCs are generally much lower than those for LDCs, which believe they need higher rates to protect their smaller industries from being over-powered by foreign competition. For example, the average U.S. tariff is 4% compared to 10% for China, 31% for Brazil, and 46% for India. Second, globally and for almost every country individually, the average tariff on agricultural products is much higher than it is on manufactured products. U.S. tariffs on agriculture average 9.8% in contrast to 3% on manufactured goods.

Beyond the normal tariff levels, countries sometimes impose economic sanctions by increasing import duties in response to an alleged abuse of international trade rules by other countries. In 2002, for example, President Bush ignited a global trade dispute when he imposed a 30% tariff on steel imports, in response to the faltering U.S. steel industry's complaint that foreign competitors were violating trade rules by selling their product below cost to U.S. customers. Some countries imposed immediate retaliatory tariffs on U.S. exports. Russia, which stood to lose $750 million a year in steel sales, barred $800 million in U.S. poultry imports, setting off what the press, with tongue in beak, quickly dubbed the "cold chicken war." Other steel-exporters threatened countersanctions. For instance, the EU announced plans to impose retaliatory 100% tariffs on about $2 billion in U.S. goods, an amount equal to its losses to the U.S. steel tariff. Finally, the face-off was defused when President Bush rescinded the tariff hike amid a range of pressures including the threatened counter-tariffs and a negative ruling by the World Trade Organization.

Nontariff Barriers   A less-known but more common way that countries restrict trade is by using **nontariff barriers (NTBs)**. *Health and safety standards* are one form of NTB. These are sometimes reasonable regulations to protect the well-being of the importing country's citizens. At other times, they are simply an excuse for protectionism, and trade disputes are common over whether the restriction is reasonable or protectionist. One current example is the EU's ban on the importation of genetically modified (GM) crops, a barrier that hurts farmers in the United States and many other countries that grow and seek to export GM crops. These countries reject the EU's position that GM crops pose a health threat and claim it is an ill-disguised effort to protect Europe's inefficient farms. According to one U.S. trade official, "the EU's legal structure for regulating biotechnical products is badly broken and driven much more by politics than by science."[9]

Quotas that limit the number of units that can be shipped are another form of NTB. The European Union, as noted earlier, places quotas on textile imports from China that will limit the annual growth rate on imports to 10% through 2008. Quotas are sometimes tied into tariffs. The United States sets quotas on imported raw and refined sugar by estimating U.S. sugar production, subtracting that from estimated U.S. needs, and permitting an amount of sugar imports equal to the difference at a low tariff rate of $33 a ton. Any imports beyond that quota face a tariff of $353 a ton. This added to the world price of sugar ($179 a ton) drive the price of nonquota sugar to over $532 a ton. This effectively protects the U.S. sugar industry, which sells its product domestically for $520 a ton.

Administrative requirements are a third type of NTB. These are particularly important in limiting service imports. For example, many countries license architects, engineers, insurance agents, stock and bond traders, and other professionals, and these licensing requirements can be used to make it difficult for foreign professionals and companies to provide services in another country. One study that compared licensing and similar restrictions that 34 countries place on domestic (citizens, companies)

ANALYZE THE ISSUE
E-Commerce and the WTO

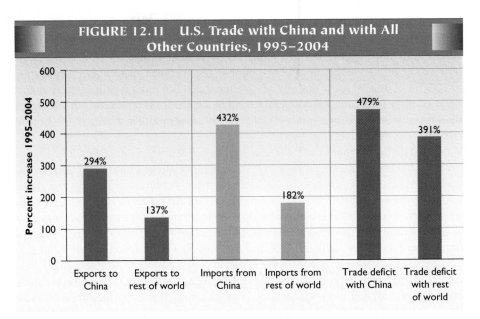

FIGURE 12.11 U.S. Trade with China and with All Other Countries, 1995–2004

China's monetary policy kept the yuan fixed to the value of the U.S. dollar between 1994 and 2004 at the same time the dollar declined against most other major currencies. As a result, U.S. imports from China and the U.S. deficit with China rose faster than U.S. trade with all other countries during 1995–2004. But the soaring imports and trade deficit with the rest of the world despite a much weaker dollar indicate that American consumer demand may be a more important factor in the dismal and steadily worsening U.S. trade picture. For this reason, Beijing's 2% revaluation of the yuan in 2005 will do little or nothing to change U.S.-China trade patterns.

Data source: U.S. Bureau of the Census.

and foreign service providers found that countries almost uniformly put more difficult requirements on foreign providers of accounting, banking, engineering, legal, telecommunications, transportation, and other services.[10]

Monetary Barriers Another way that a country protects its domestic producers by limiting imports and promoting exports is by manipulating the exchange rate so that its currency is weaker against other currencies than it would be if it were allowed to float, that is, trade freely. As discussed earlier, Washington alleges (and Beijing denies) that China is keeping the value of the yuan artificially low versus the U.S. dollar. Between 1994 and mid-2005, as noted above, China managed to keep the value of its currency at a steady 8.3 yuan = $1 even though during the same period the dollar weakened by 46% against a "market basket" of currencies monitored by the IMF. This monetary manipulation is one reason that U.S. exports from China and the trade deficit with it have risen faster when compared with the rest of the world, as shown in Figure 12.11. The minor 2% devaluation of the yuan in July 2005 is unlikely to have a dramatic effect on the flow of trade between China and the United States or the other EDCs.

Investment Barriers Most countries want to attract international investment because it brings outside capital into their national economy. Yet countries are also wary of outside control of their companies and real estate. The most common form of investment restriction limits foreign ownership of companies. All countries have some limits. For example, foreigners are barred from controlling airlines in the European Union, Canada, and the United States. Japan does not allow foreign ownership of its telecommunications companies. Only citizens may own fishing and energy enterprises in Iceland. Some countries directly control companies, such as Mexico's state-owned oil monopoly Petróleos Mexicanos.

Trade and Investment Supports

In addition to erecting protectionist barriers to foreign trade and investment, countries also try to increase the economic prospects of their domestic products and producers through a variety of support techniques. Subsidies, dumping, and cartels are three of note.

Subsidies Countries give tax breaks, provide low-cost services (such as energy and transportation), and offer various other forms of financial support to subsidize domestic producers, who can then lower the price they charge for their product. Less direct supports include such techniques as funding research for product development and undertaking government trade promotion campaigns (advertising). Agriculture is the most heavily subsidized economic sector. The EDCs provide an estimated $280 billion annually in support of agricultural business ("agribusiness") in those countries. On average 30% of all agricultural income in the EDCs comes from subsidies. The United States is on the low end of the subsidization scale, providing 18% of all agricultural receipts. The EU at 33% of receipts is about average, and Japan at 56% on the high end. Many LDCs also give subsidies, with Mexico (17%) an example. Like other forms of economic intervention, agricultural subsidies benefit one segment of a country's economy at the expense in taxes and prices of the country's citizenry and also at the expense of foreign competitors.

> **Did You Know That:**
> Cotton growers in poor countries are harmed by a U.S. cotton subsidy program that in 2003 gave American farmers $3.2 billion in cotton acreage subsidies and $1.6 billion in export credits. The total ($4.8 billion) in subsidies was greater than the market value ($3.9 billion) of the U.S. crop that year.

Subsidies can also play an important part in the competitive position of manufactured goods. For example, a major trade dispute broke out in 2005 between the United States and the European Union, with each charging the other was violating international trade rules by subsidizing competing new commercial airliners. At the center of the dispute are Boeing's 787 jetliner, which is scheduled to enter service in 2008, and the Airbus 380, which is being developed by Airbus, a subsidiary of the European Aeronautic Defense and Space Company (EADS) and is scheduled for deliveries beginning in 2010. At stake are tens of billions of dollars in orders plus the prestige of being the leading commercial aircraft producer, a title long-time champion Boeing lost to Airbus in 2004. The most important U.S. charge is that the EU will not only loan Airbus $1.7 billion at very low rates to develop the 380, but will not require Airbus to repay the loan unless the plane proves profitable. In reply, the EU points to a $3.2 billion tax break given by the state of Washington to Boeing to persuade it to build the 787 in the company's plant near Seattle. As part of the dogfight over who will prevail, the United States filed a complaint with the World Trade Organization (WTO) claiming that Airbus has benefited over the years from $15 billion in illegal subsidies, and the EU counterfiled, accusing the United States of channeling $23 billion in subsidies to Boeing.

The United States and the European Union are engaged in a dogfight over the rivalry between commercial airliner producers Boeing and Airbus. The stakes run into billions of dollars. Each combatant accuses the other of illegally subsidizing their aircraft industry, and each has filed charges against the other in the World Trade Organization.

Dumping Yet another trade tactic is dumping. This occurs when a company, often with the support of its national government, violates trade laws by selling its products

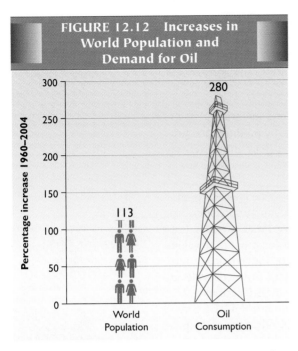

FIGURE 12.12 Increases in World Population and Demand for Oil

Oil price increases have had less to do with the efforts of the cartel OPEC than with increased per capita consumption. Between 1960 and 2004, world petroleum consumption rose more than twice as fast as the population grew.

Data sources: UN Population Fund; U.S. Department of Energy.

abroad at a price lower than what it sells them for at home. When in 2005, for instance, Vietnamese Prime Minister Phan Van Khai became the first of his united country's leaders ever to visit the United States, one item on his and President Bush's agenda was the 27% tariff on shrimp imports from Vietnam imposed by U.S. International Trade Commission after it found that Vietnam was dumping the seafood on the U.S. market. Similar punitive tariffs were also put on other countries' shrimp, ranging up to 112% on Chinese shrimp. Such matters may seem small, but they are not for the U.S Southern Shrimp Alliance, which faces competition from imported shrimp worth $5 billion annually.

Cartels Countries, especially EDCs, also have occasionally tried to control trade by establishing cartels. A **cartel** is an international trading agreement among producers who hope to control the supply and price of a primary product. The first cartel was established in 1933 to regulate tea, but the decade of the 1960s, when 18 came into existence, was the apex of cartel formation. They ranged in importance from the Organization of Petroleum Exporting Countries (OPEC) to the Asian and Pacific Coconut Community. Cartels, however, have not always proven to be successful. Even OPEC has had to struggle to maintain prices in the face of internal economic and political disputes (such as the Iraq-Iran war in the 1980s), the production of about 60% of the world's petroleum by non-OPEC countries, and other factors. Over the years, price increases, including sharp rises in 2004–2005, have had less to do with the efforts of OPEC to increase prices by manipulating supply than with the increasing demand for oil by an energy-addicted world, as evident in Figure 12.12.

Using Economic Means to Achieve Noneconomic Political Ends

Tariffs, quotas, and the other tools of economic nationalist policy are primarily used to achieve economic ends, such as the protection of domestic producers. However, it is not uncommon for countries to also use a range of economic techniques to support noneconomic political goals.

National Security Restrictions

All of the countries that produce major military weaponry require government approval of foreign sales. In many cases there are blanket prohibitions of sales to other countries that are considered current or potential enemies. As circumstances change, such bans can prove controversial. For example, the EU is considering dropping the West's long-time embargo on selling high-tech weapons to China. The United States, among others, strongly opposes this move for various reasons, including the possibility that U.S. forces could face European-supplied weaponry if China were to invade Taiwan. Another often-controversial area involves "dual-use" goods, anything from supercomputers to nuclear plant machinery to chemicals that can be used for both civilian and military purposes. As one example, the United States restricts the sale of the most advanced semiconductors, computers, avionics equipment, and other high-tech items to China. One official explained the U.S. position, "We continue to have significant differences with China on security and foreign policy issues that dictate a cautious way forward in our overall political, economic, and strategic relationship."[11]

Economic Incentives

States regularly offer economic incentives to induce other states to act in a desired way. Incentives include providing foreign aid, giving direct loans or credits, guaranteeing loans by commercial sources, reducing tariffs and other trade barriers, selling or licensing the sale of sensitive technology, and a variety of other techniques. Sometimes incentives are meant to achieve an economic goal, but more often specific offers (as distinct from, say, general foreign aid) is aimed at achieving a political goal. For example, the efforts by the EU to persuade Iran to give up its alleged nuclear weapons development program and the similar effort by the United States and other countries to convince North Korea to give up its program both involve the offer of energy aid and significant other economic incentives.

Economic Sanctions

Countries can also use their economic power in a negative way by applying sanctions. As noted above, sanctions sometimes are applied during economic disputes, but the most significant sanctions usually have a political goal. They are most commonly applied in a generally hostile atmosphere when "there are expectations of frequent conflict with the target" (Drezner, 1998:728). Methods include raising trade barriers, cutting off aid, trying to undermine another country's currency, and even instituting blockades.

The History of Sanctions   The use of **economic sanctions** dates back to at least 432 B.C. when the city-state of Athens embargoed all trade with another city-state, Megara, an ally of Athens' bitter rival Sparta. Despite being ancient, though, sanctions were uncommon until fairly recently (Elliot & Oegg, 2002). Increased use has occurred, in part, because countries are more willing to ignore sovereignty and impose penalties on oppressive governments, because economic interdependence makes target countries more vulnerable to sanctions, and because they are an alternative to war. For example, the United States imposed sanctions on Syria in 2004 because of its alleged support for terrorism, its occupation of Lebanon, and its chemical weapons program. Overall, the U.S. government in 2005 had economic embargoes (no trade) in place against Burma (Myanmar), Cuba, Iran, and Sudan; and limited sanctions on Iraq, Liberia, Libya, North Korea, and Zimbabwe. It should be noted that sanctions can be imposed by international organizations as well as by individual countries. During its history, the UN has used sanctions against 17 countries. About half of those, almost all of them arms embargoes, were in place in 2005 (Cortright & Lopez 2000).

The Effectiveness of Sanctions   Economic sanctions are a blunt instrument that attempts to economically bludgeon a target country into changing some specific behavior. As such, their effectiveness is mixed. Sometimes they can be effective. In one recent case, the sanctions first imposed on Libya in the early 1990s almost certainly played a role in its 2003 agreement to end its program of building weapons of mass destruction and to allow inspections by the International Atomic Energy Agency and other international agencies.

Did You Know That:

The longest-standing sanctions were put into place against Cuba by the United States in 1963 under its Trading with the Enemy Act.

It is also the case, though, that, more often than not, sanctions fail to accomplish their goal. Some analysts place their success rate as low as 5%, but even more optimistic assessments indicate that sanctions change the behavior of a target country about one-third of the time (Elliott & Oegg, 2002). Thus while scholars disagree on the exact success rate, "something of a conventional wisdom has emerged," one writes, "suggesting that, while sanctions may serve domestic political or symbolic purposes, they are not particularly effective at inducing target states to change their behavior" (Morgan, 2005:1). Moreover, even when sanctions are successful, their impact is most often only part of what caused a change in behavior by the target state. In the case of Libya, "What forced [its leader Muammar] Gaddafi to act was a combination of things—U.N. sanctions . . . his international isolation after the Soviet Union's collapse . . . and internal economic problems [caused in part by the sanctions] that led to domestic unrest," one analyst commented. An additional factor, according to a U.S. official, was that "the invasion of Iraq sent a strong message to governments around the world that if the United States feels threatened by weapons of mass destruction, we are prepared to act against regimes not prepared to change their behavior."[12]

Studies also indicate that sanctions are most likely to be effective in certain circumstances (Lacy & Niou, 2004; Drezner, 2000; Shambaugh, 2000). These include instances when (1) there is strong multilateral cooperation; (2) the target is politically unstable and/or economically weak; (3) those imposing the sanctions are strong economically; the targeted country has substantial trade with the targeting countries; (4) sanctions are put into effect quickly and decisively to maximize psychological impact; and (5) the targeting countries are not themselves harmed significantly by the cost of maintaining the sanctions (Drezner, 2000; Shambaugh, 2000).

One reason sanctions are used despite their limited impact is because they nevertheless do work sometimes. A second reason is that judging whether sanctions will work or even have worked or not is sometimes difficult. It could be argued, for example, that the UN sanctions on Iraq after its defeat failed because they never did force the regime of Saddam Hussein to fully comply with the conditions imposed by the Security Council. However, a case could also be made that the sanctions did prevent Iraq from having the funds to rearm and, perhaps, to develop WMDs that could threaten the region. A third reason that sanctions are used is that they also have a symbolic value even if they do not cause another country to change its behavior. Simply put, just as you might choose not to deal with an immoral person, so too countries can express their moral indignation by reducing or severing their interactions with an abhorrent regime (Baldwin, 2000).

The Drawbacks of Sanctions   Countries that apply sanctions must be wary of their potential negative impact on unintended victims. One such difficulty is that sanctions may harm economic interests other than those of the intended target. The UN sanctions imposed on Iraqi oil exports between 1991 and 2003 cost Jordan and Turkey many millions of dollars annually by way of lost revenues. Both countries would have earned revenues for the use of pipelines that run from Iraq through them and on to ports from which the oil is shipped. Economic interests in the targeting country can also be harmed. For instance, U.S. sanctions barring trade with other countries reduced American exports by about $15 billion a year. That is a tiny part of the U.S. economy, but, as one study notes, "the costs of sanctions are never spread evenly" across the economy. For example, the analysis continues, "the long-standing U.S. embargo on Cuba arguably has a much larger impact on Florida than on other states" (Hufbauer & Oegg, 2003:8).

A third criticism of sanctions is that they are often the tool used by EDCs to continue their dominance of LDCs. Of the 71 incidents of sanctions applied during the 1970s and 1980s, 49 of the cases (69%) involved EDCs placing sanctions on LDCs (Rothgeb, 1993). A fourth charge against sanctions is that they may constitute a rogue action in the view of many countries that do not support them. For the 13th consecutive year and by a vote of 179 to 4, the UN General Assembly in 2004 condemned the unilateral U.S. sanctions against Cuba that have been in place since the early 1960s. A fifth criticism is that sanctions often harm the innocent. Taking this view, President Fidel Castro of Cuba has called them "noiseless atomic bombs" that "cause the death of men, women, and children."[13] Iraq provides a good example of Castro's point. There, the UN sanctions in place between 1991 and 2003 and the defiant stance of the government in Baghdad had a brutal impact. Scant supplies of food and medicine for the civilian population were among the hardships. The effects were especially devastating for children. Various studies by the UN, Harvard University's School of Public Health, and others all found that the sanctions caused (beyond normal expectations) over 1 million Iraqi children to be malnourished and upward of 500,000 to have died. This deleterious effect is evident in Figure 12.13, which compares the child mortality rate in Iraq to that of its neighbors.

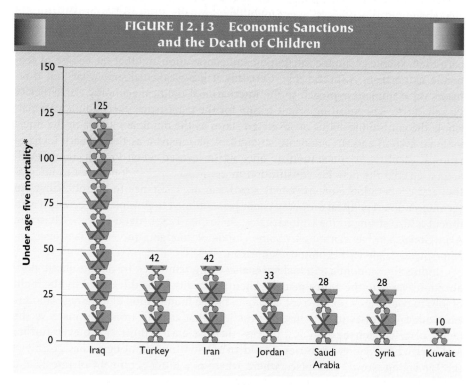

FIGURE 12.13   Economic Sanctions and the Death of Children

The year before sanctions were imposed on Iraq, its child mortality rate and those of its neighbors were about the same. By 2002, the last full year of the sanctions, the child mortality rate in Iraq had risen 51% and was four times higher than the average for its neighbors, whose child mortality rate had declined 59%. It is debatable whether the sanctions were the cause or whether the fault lies with the unwillingness of the Iraqi regime to redistribute funds away from its military to child nutrition and health care. But there is little doubt that without the sanctions, 15,000 or more Iraqi children would probably have lived past age five than did.

*The number of children who die before age five per 1,000 children born.
Data source: World Bank (2004).

The Future of Economic Nationalist Policy

There can be no doubt that global economics during the last half-century has been marked by three main stories. The first has been the almost complete triumph of capitalism over competing economic models, especially Marxism and socialism. Even two (China and Vietnam) of the four remaining officially communist countries have largely adopted capitalism, with Cuba and North Korea the last holdouts still following the Marxist model.

The second important development has been a steady movement toward ever greater economic interdependence based on an increasingly free exchange of trade, investment, and other financial activity. An array of statistics presented in this and the following chapter show conclusively that the movement of goods, services, investment capital, and currencies across borders has expanded exponentially. Furthermore, as chapter 13 discusses, the international system has created the EU, IMF, World Bank, WTO, and numerous global and regional organizations and arrangements to facilitate and promote free international economic interchange. A third important change, also a topic in chapter 13, has been the growth of a sense of global responsibility to the plight of the poorer countries. One indication is that foreign economic aid comes to over $69 billion annually. Prior to World War II it did not exist.

For all this evidence, it would be erroneous to conclude that the world is on a path to inevitable economic integration and cooperation and that the eclipse of economic nationalism is inescapable. Certainly it has weakened somewhat, but it remains the dominant approach to the international political economy (Helleiner & Pickel, 2005). The most important reason for the persistence of economic nationalism is the continuing status of sovereign states as the dominant actors in the international system and the enduring strength of nationalism as the primary focus of political identity. As integrationists once again learned when French, then Dutch voters rejected the new EU constitution in 2005, nationalist opposition to integration and cooperation remains potent. Furthermore, resistance to liberal changes in the international political economy is not just confined to Europe. Protectionist sentiment is also strong in the United States. As former U.S. Federal Reserve Chairman Alan Greenspan has cautioned, "Some clouds of emerging protectionism have become increasingly visible on today's horizon."[14]

Indirectly, economic nationalism is also being reinforced by doubts about globalization. Many in the North perceive their prosperity to be threatened by the flight of jobs to countries with low-cost labor and by the immigration of low-wage laborers from other countries to take many of the jobs that are left. Ironically, many in the South perceive globalization as a process that has enriched the North even further and harmed the poorer countries. President Hosni Mubarak of Egypt has portrayed the "emerging world" as a place where "there is a bitter sentiment of injustice, a sense that there must be something wrong with a system that wipes out years of hard-won development because of changes in market sentiment."[15] Such views have prompted UN Secretary-General Kofi Annan to characterize globalization as "fragile" and to warn, "The unequal distribution of benefits and the imbalances in global rule-making, which characterize globalization today, inevitably will produce backlash and protectionism."[16] All this lends credence to one analyst's observation that, "We have gotten used to the idea that globalization will inevitably succeed, but I am not so sure anymore."[17]

WEB POLL
National and Global
Economic Demands:
Where Do Your Loyalties Lie?

Chapter Summary

Theories of International Political Economy

1. Economics and politics are closely intertwined aspects of international relations. This interrelationship has become even more important in recent history. Economics has become more important internationally because of dramatically increased trade levels, ever-tightening economic interdependence between countries, and the growing impact of international economics on domestic economics. The study of international political economy (IPE) examines the interaction between politics and economics.

2. There are many technical aspects to explaining and understanding the international political economy, and it is important to understand such concepts as gross domestic product, gross national product (and purchasing power parity for those), and current and real dollars.

3. The approaches to IPE can be roughly divided into three groups: economic nationalism (mercantilism), economic internationalism (liberalism), and economic structuralism.

4. The core of the economic nationalist doctrine is the realist idea that the state should harness and use national economic strength to further national interest. Therefore, the state should shape the country's economy and its foreign economic policy to enhance state power.

5. Economic internationalists are liberals who believe that international economic relations should and can be harmonious because prosperity is available to all and is most likely to be achieved and preserved through cooperation. The main thrust of economic internationalism is to separate politics from economics, to create prosperity by freeing economic interchange from political restrictions.

6. Economic structuralists hold that world politics is based on the division of the world into have and have-not countries, with the EDCs keeping the LDCs weak and poor in order to exploit them. There are two types of economic structuralists. Marxists believe that the entire capitalist-based system must be replaced with domestic and international socialist systems before economic equity can be achieved. Less radical economic structuralist theories include dependency and world systems theory, which stress reform of the current market system by ending the system of dependency.

The World Economy: Globalization and Interdependence

7. Globalization and interdependence have increased at an exponential rate since the beginning of the second half of the 20th century, with a rapid rise in the level of economic interchange (trade, investments and other capital flows, and monetary exchange) in the international political economy.

The World Economy: Diverse Circumstances

8. The world is generally divided into two economic spheres: a wealthy North and a much less wealthy South. There are some overlaps between the two spheres, but in general the vast majority of the people and countries of the South are much less wealthy and industrially developed than the countries of the North and their people. The South also has a history of direct and indirect colonial control by countries of the North.

9. While a wealth gap persists between North and South, and in some ways has grown, the data must be carefully analyzed. By many measures, economic and social conditions in the South have improved greatly during recent decades. Also, data about overall improvements in the South is skewed downward by the worsening conditions in sub-Saharan Africa.

National Economic Power

10. Economic nationalism still remains the dominant approach in global economic affairs even though the trend toward international economic liberalization has grown in importance.

11. The stronger role being played by international economics means that political relations between countries have been increasingly influenced by economic relations. Domestically also, politics significantly affect economic policy. Domestic political pressures are important determinants of tariff policies and other trade regulations. Trade can also be used as a diplomatic tool.

12. Economic strength is a key element of every country's overall power. Economic power is based on financial position, natural resources, industrial output, and agricultural output.

National Economic Competition

13. There is economic competition across the analytical categories of countries, including North-North competition, North-South competition, and South-South competition.

Applied Economic Nationalism

14. Countries attempt to advance their economic policy and prosperity by using their economic power through a mixture of protectionist barriers and incentives in the areas of trade and investment. While each approach is sometimes successful, both incentives and, particularly, sanctions are difficult to apply successfully and have numerous drawbacks.

15. Countries also use their economic power to try to advance their political goals. Sanctions are a particularly controversial tool because they have a low rate of success and because they often harm unintended victims.

The Future of Economic Nationalist Policy

16. Although globalization and interdependence are undermining economic nationalism, it remains the driving force behind states' international economic policy. Moreover, persistent state sovereignty, nationalism, and problems with globalization are all helping to maintain the central role of economic nationalism in world politics.

For simulations, debates, and other interactive activities, a chapter quiz, Web links, PowerWeb articles, and much more, visit **www.mhhe.com/rourke11/** and go to chapter 12. Or, while accessing the site, click on Course-Wide Content and view recent international relations articles in the *New York Times*.

Key Terms

balance of payments
capitalism
cartel
current dollars
dependency theory
economic internationalism
economic nationalism
economic sanctions
economic structuralism
economically developed countries (EDCs)
exchange rates
extreme poverty

foreign direct investment (FDI)
foreign portfolio investment (FPI)
globalization
gross domestic product (GDP)
gross national product (GNP)
interdependence
international political economy (IPE)
least developed countries (LLDCs)

less developed countries (LDCs)
manufactured goods
Marxist theory
merchandise trade
monetary relations
multinational corporations (MNCs)
neocolonialism
net trade
New International Economic Order (NIEO)

newly industrializing countries (NICs)
nontariff barriers (NTBs)
North
primary products
protectionism
purchasing power parity (PPP)
real dollars
services trade
South
tariffs
world systems theory

International Economic Cooperation: The Alternative Road

Join we together, for the public good.
—William Shakespeare, *King Henry VI, Part II*

*For my part, I had rather bear with you than bear you;
yet I should bear no cross if I did bear you,
for I think you have no money in your purse.*
                    —William Shakespeare, *As You Like It*

An indication of how far economic interdependence, as part of the larger phenomenon of globalization, has evolved is represented in this image. Balloons decorate the Temple of Heaven in Beijing, the capital of officially communist China, in preparation for the 2005 meeting of the Fortune Global Forum. Sponsored by the decidedly capitalist magazine, *Fortune*, the forum annually gathers global business leaders, heads of state, and other notables to discuss world business issues. At the end of the chapter, you are asked if you support the economic internationalism that this meeting represents.

THIS CHAPTER IS THE SECOND of two that examine the international political economy (IPE). Chapter 12, the first of the pair, takes up economic nationalism, the traditional approach to the international political economy. That path is characterized by self-interested economic competition among countries. Economic nationalism persists as the dominant set of values behind the international economic policy of states. But it is not unchallenged. Instead, economic internationalists and structuralists believe that the global economic future will be better if countries cooperate economically, or even integrate their economies. This chapter assesses the alternative route of greater international cooperation. This assessment will first examine global cooperation, then turn its attention to regional efforts. As you will see, one aspect of cooperation among the economically developed countries (EDCs) of the North is an effort to ensure that their relative prosperity continues. An even more important goal of economic cooperation, arguably, is to improve the circumstances of the less developed countries (LDCs) of the South. Therefore we will pay particular attention to what is needed for economic development and the programs that are addressing that need.

Economic Cooperation and Development: Background and Requirements

The thought of moving toward a very different way of dealing with the international economy is more than theory. It is a process that has made substantial progress and one that many think can and should become the dominant paradigm in the future. At the global level, it is appropriate to first look at basic IPE theory and the origins of economic cooperation. Then we will turn to detailing the development needs of the South, the most important focus of international economic cooperation today.

IPE Theory and Cooperation

Chapter 12 details the three main IPE theories, economic nationalism, economic internationalism, and economic structuralism. Still, it is appropriate to also briefly consider them here, with an emphasis on what each says about cooperation and development.

Economic nationalists operate from a realpolitik orientation and believe that each country, be it North or South, should look out for itself first and foremost by promoting its own national interest when formulating policy related to trade, investment, and aid. They also view the political economy as a zero-sum game in which gains made by some players inevitably mean losses for other players. As for development, economic nationalists are apt to be wary of giving extensive aid or other forms of economic assistance to the LDCs. One reason is that today's LDC could become tomorrow's competitor, just as China has become. Economic nationalists are particularly averse to taking steps such as ending agricultural subsidies, which would help LDCs that export such products but would hurt farmers in the EDCs. Furthermore, economic nationalists suspect that the South's calls for greater equity are, in essence, attempts to change the rules so that the LDCs can acquire political power for themselves.

Economic internationalists believe that international economic policy should emphasize cooperation. In their view, the global economy is a non-zero-sum game in which prosperity is available to all because the economic advancement of countries does not have to come at the expense of other countries. From this perspective, economic internationalists favor generally unfettered economic interchange. They therefore oppose tariff and nontariff barriers (NTBs) and incentives, the very tools that economic nationalists heartily endorse. As for LDC development, economic internationalists contend that the major impediments are the South's weakness in acquiring capital, its shortage of skilled labor, and some of its domestic economic policies, such as centralized planning and protectionism. These difficulties can be overcome, according to economic internationalists, through free trade, foreign investment supplemented by loans, foreign aid, and reduced government interference in the economy. Such policies will allow unimpeded international economic exchange among states, benefiting all of them. This view that the global economy is not a zero-sum game leads economic internationalists to believe that it is possible to integrate LDCs into the world economic system by eliminating system imperfections while maintaining the basic structure and stability.

Economic structuralists argue that how the world economy is structured determines the conduct of world politics. They portray a world split between rich countries (the EDCs, the North) and poor countries (the LDCs, the South), and they contend that the EDCs consciously strive to keep the LDCs poor and dependent so that the EDCs can exploit them. From this perspective, economic structuralists maintain that the political-economic organization of the world's patterns of production and trade must be radically altered for the LDCs to develop. To accomplish this, economic structuralists believe that not only should the LDCs be given substantial economic assistance and concessions, but that they should also be politically empowered and given a greater say over the operation of IGOs such as the IMF and World Bank.

The Origins of Economic Cooperation

The World Economic Forum (WEF) in Davos, Switzerland, the leading NGO proponent of globalization, represents more than 1,000 of the globe's largest multinational corporations. Although little known among the public, the WEF's annual meeting draws many of the world's political, economic, and social elite. Among those attending in 2005 were such business leaders as Microsoft's Bill Gates, such political leaders at British Prime Minister Tony Blair and Deputy U.S. Secretary of State Robert Zoellick, such activist celebrities as singer Bono and actor Angelina Jolie, and such other noted individuals as former U.S. President Bill Clinton. The WEF's mission is opposed by, among others, the World Social Forum, which annually brings together thousands of anti-globalization advocates in Porto Alegre, Brazil, at the same time as the Davos meeting.

The liberal idea of creating global **interdependence** based on free economic interchange and cooperation for the economic good of all dates back several hundred years. It was slow to take hold, though, and did not begin to shape international economic relations to any great extent until the 1930s and 1940s. The violence of two world wars and the economic dislocation during the Great Depression in the 1930s led an increasing number of leaders to rethink current policies, and they agreed with the view that unrestrained economic nationalism had played a role in causing these disasters. To avoid such catastrophes in the future, the United States led the EDCs of the anti-Axis alliance and then the anticommunist West to create the foundation of a new international economic order. During the years 1943–1948, the EDCs created a number of global and regional intergovernmental organizations (IGOs) to promote economic stability and the free flow of trade and capital across national boundaries. Most notable among these IGOs are the World Bank, the International Monetary Fund (IMF), and the General Agreement on Tariffs and Trade (GATT, both a treaty and an organization; the organization was

Did You Know That:

Within two years after Congress enacted the highly protectionist Smoot-Hawley Tariff in 1930 and the European countries retaliated with their own protectionist tariffs, U.S. imports from Europe declined 71% and U.S. exports to Europe dropped 67%.

renamed the World Trade Organization, WTO). The United Nations also came into existence, and it has grown to have numerous economic agencies and responsibilities.

The immediate post–World War II era also saw the first major foreign aid program. The United States launched the European Recovery Program (the Marshall Plan), which gave over $13 billion (or about $100 billion in current dollars) to the countries of Western Europe between 1948 and 1951. Certainly there was some degree of humanitarian concern with Europe's plight, but the main U.S. motives were political self-interest (to strengthen Western Europe against communism) and an economic self-interest (to revive major trading partners so that they could buy U.S. exports).

Development in the South: Requirements

The economic cooperation that began after World War II with a focus on the EDCs gradually shifted its emphasis to the economic development of the South (Seligson & Passé-Smith, 2003). This occurred for several reasons, such as the general return to prosperity of the North, the independence movements that changed dozens of colonies into countries, and a growing awareness of the economic plight of the South. Overall, considerable progress has been made, and, as detailed in chapter 12, the socioeconomic conditions in most of the countries in the South have improved substantially during the past few decades. As that chapter also pointed out, however, the pattern of positive change in the South is not even. First, there are many areas of the South, including sub-Saharan Africa, where conditions remain dismal and have even deteriorated. Second, development has been a mixed blessing for the LDCs. Partially offsetting the benefits, development has also brought with it increased pollution and a range of other ills.

Despite the negative by-products, LDCs are justifiably determined to promote their development. To do that their greatest need is capital to build roads, modernize communications, expand power supplies, build industry, and do all the other things necessary to create a stable and prosperous economy. The problem is that because the LDCs are poor, they find it difficult to raise capital internally. Therefore, the LDCs need massive inflows of **development capital** from the EDCs to expand and diversify their economies. "Uganda needs just two things," according to its president. "We need infrastructure and we need foreign investment. That is what we need. The rest we shall do ourselves."[1] Obtaining capital from the EDCs is also important because only **hard currency**, such as American dollars, Japanese yen, and European Union euros, are widely accepted in international transactions. Most LDC currencies are not. So if Guatemala wants to bring in the foreign expertise, equipment, and material to improve its port facilities at San José, it will need dollars or some other hard currency because the suppliers are unlikely to accept quetzals.

Four main sources of convertible currencies are available: loans, investment, trade, and aid. Unfortunately, there are limitations and drawbacks to each. Unless significant changes are made to increase the flow of development capital to the LDCs and to distribute it more broadly among all LDCs, the majority of them are destined to remain relatively poor for the foreseeable future. It is also the case that the LDCs need to institute some internal reforms so that they can better utilize their own capital resources and those that flow in from the EDCs.

Loans

One source of hard currency is loans extended by private or government sources. Based on a number of economic factors, the LDCs moved in the 1970s to finance their development needs by borrowing heavily from external sources. By 1982 LDC international debt had skyrocketed to $849 billion, and while the rate of increase has eased, the total debt owed by the LDCs has continued to grow and stood at $2.9 trillion in 2004. Banks and other private institutional and individual bondholders are the largest creditors, followed by IGOs (such as the IMF and World Bank) and governments.

Borrowing abroad to meet current domestic needs is common. The United States, for example, owes foreigners $1.5 trillion on the bonds the U.S. Treasury has sold them to finance the U.S. national debt. Both borrowers and lenders must manage money carefully, however. Many LDCs have struggled to meet their **debt service** (principal plus interest) on their loans. A standard measurement of any country's ability to meet its debt payments is the amount of its annual debt service compared to its annual export earnings. As Figure 13.1 shows, in 1980, the LDCs needed to devote only a manageable 8% of their trade earnings to payments on their debt. Within a few years, that percentage had skyrocketed. That set off a broad crisis that pushed Argentina, Brazil, Mexico, Nigeria, and several other LDCs to the edge of bankruptcy and also threatened the financial well-being of the lenders, who stood to lose billions of dollars. The debt crisis was finally solved through a massive intervention by the EDCs and the IMF to refinance most of the debt and to forgive some of it. The affected LDCs had to meet fiscal reform requirements negotiated with the IMF and other lenders.

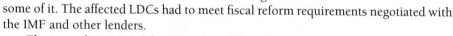

FIGURE 13.1   LDC Debt Service as a Percentage of Exports

LDCs began to take on increasing debt in the early 1980s as a result of a desire to modernize and pressure to pay sharply rising oil prices. The share of the LDCs' export earnings that they had to pay to meet their debt service (principal plus interest) rose from 8% in 1980 to 26% in 1987, fell somewhat, then hit 27% in 1998 before beginning to fall to a 20-year low of 14% in 2004. However, the sharp oil price hikes in 2005 could once again cause an upward trend in the LDCs debt service line for 2005 and beyond.

Data source: IMF (2005).

The immediate LDC debt crisis abated, but the issue of LDC debt remains troubling for several reasons. One concern is that the LDCs still have a towering debt of nearly $3 trillion. Second, as also evident in Figure 13.1, the debt burden remained high, falling below 20% only in 2003 and 2004. Even at the relatively modest 14% level in 2004, the LDCs had to pay out $437 billion in much-needed capital. Third, the LDCs remain vulnerable. Most are energy importers, and the steep rise in the price of petroleum that began in 2004 could again force them to borrow heavily to keep their economies going. Fourth, the overall data about the declining debt burden disguises the crushing debt of a group of countries designated Heavily Indebted Poor Countries (HIPCs) by the World Bank and IMF. There are 38 HIPCs, 32 of them in Africa, that are in such desperate economic condition that almost any debt payment is nearly impossible without taking money away from already poorly funded education, health, and other social programs.

There are also several countries with huge debts that threaten their stability. Argentina (debt: $166 billion), Brazil ($236 billion), and Mexico ($140 billion) are among the most indebted. Such countries, even though they are not low income, face a constant threat from their debt. In 2001 and into 2002, for example, a combination of Argentina's monetary policies, its faltering economy, and its immense debt set off a political and financial crisis that weakened the value of the peso by 71%, sent inflation up to 65%, caused the economy to shrink, tripled unemployment, and caused several governments to fall. Internal reforms and IMF assistance eased the

Did You Know That:

Argentina's University of Buenos Aires has opened a museum commemorating foreign debt. Its first major exhibit is entitled "Foreign Debt: Never Again." Among other things, it features a mock kitchen symbolizing the disastrous "economic recipes" Argentina adopted.

The ability of many less developed countries to develop economically is being hindered by their heavy foreign debt. These countries use such a high percentage of what they take in from exports and other external sources of capital to pay the principal and interest on their debt that they have insufficient funds remaining to invest in the development of their economies. The debt crisis has eased somewhat in the past few years, but the debt burden remains a major problem for many LDCs.

MAP
Global Flows of
Investment Capital

MAP
Exports of Primary Products

crisis, and Argentina has begun to recover, but it will take years to repair all the economic damage.

What is clear from this discussion of the experience of LDCs with loans in the last decades is that borrowing is not a sound way to finance development. Certainly loans can play a positive role in moderation and to meet short-term needs, but they present a perilous path to long-term development.

Private Investment

A second source of capital for LDCs is private investment through foreign direct investment (FDI) and foreign portfolio investment (FPI), as discussed in chapter 12. The flows of investment capital are growing in importance for LDCs. For example, the annual net inflow of FDI into the LDCs grew eightfold between 1990 and 2004 from $20 billion to $167 billion. FPI is also important, and stood at a net $53 billion in 2004. However, FPI is volatile. The funds tend to be short-term investments, and the flow can turn sharply negative when investors lose confidence. During the eight years 1997–2004, the first three years saw a total net inflow of $90 billion into the LDCs, but the following three years had a net outflow of $97 billion, before returning to a net inflow of $63 billion the final two years. Sudden outflow can disrupt a country's economy, and helped cause financial crises in Mexico in 1995, much of Asia in the late 1990s, and Argentina in 2001.

As with other overall data, the seemingly huge flow of investment capital into the LDCs is only part of the story. One less positive aspect of the details is that most investment capital goes to only a handful of LDCs. This is evident in Figure 13.2, which shows that 72% of the money went to just seven countries. The neediest region, sub-Saharan Africa, got just 6%, an amount about one-seventh of what was invested in China in 2003. Thus for most LDCs, investment funds are not a major source of development capital.

Trade

Export earnings are a third source of development capital. In theory, the vast size of the world market makes trade the optimal source of hard currency for LDCs. Yet, in reality, the LDCs are disadvantaged by the pattern and terms of international trade.

There are several sources of LDC trade weakness. First, as detailed in chapter 12 and Figure 12.5, the LDCs have 84% of the world's people yet command only 25% of world trade. With exports equal to only $611 per person, they provide nowhere near the economic stimulus generated by the North's exports, which are over $9,208 per capita. Second, just a few LDCs account for a lion's share of all the goods exported by the South. China alone exports 33% of all the South's goods, another four LDCs export 23% of the goods, and the handful of petroleum and natural gas exporters share another 14% of the exports. This means that about one-sixth of the LDCs account for about 70% of the South's exports.

Third, most LDCs need to import more than they can export. Therefore most of their export earnings go toward payment for imports rather than toward investment in development. Fourth, many LDCs' exports are too dependent on primary products, including fibers, foodstuffs, fuels, and other minerals and raw materials. With the exception of energy-exporting countries, a rule of thumb is that the more depen-

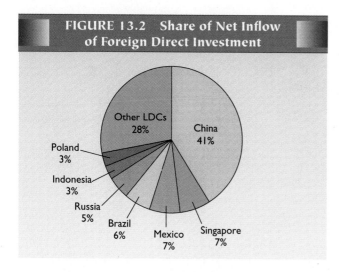

FIGURE 13.2   Share of Net Inflow of Foreign Direct Investment

China 41%
Other LDCs 28%
Poland 3%
Indonesia 3%
Russia 5%
Brazil 6%
Mexico 7%
Singapore 7%

There was a net inflow of over $165 billion in foreign direct investment into the LDCs in 2003. However, the impact of this capital on development of the South was mitigated by the fact that seven countries received almost 75% of the FDI, with China alone taking in 41%.

Note: China includes investments in Hong Kong.
Data source: World Bank (2005).

dent a country is on the export of primary products, the poorer that country is likely to be. Between 1990 and 2002, the LDCs' manufactured goods as a share of all exported goods rose from 50% to 60%, but this still compares unfavorably with the North's 80%. Moreover, more primary products, in some cases a single commodity, make up at least 75% of the exports of more than 50 LDCs. The map on page 416 shows the percentage of primary products that make up each country's exports.

Dependence on one or a few primary products for export earnings leaves LDCs disadvantaged because of several factors. *Product instability* is one factor. When, for example, the disease pod rot attacks the cocoa crop in Ghana, it loses a substantial portion of one of its leading exports. *Price weakness* also afflicts most primary products. During the past decades, world demand for products such as cotton and other natural fibers has declined due to the development of synthetics, and sugar sales have been undercut by artificial substitutes and by dietary changes. Lower demand has led to level or even reduced prices in keeping with the classic economic relationship of greater supply and less demand. Between 1970 and 2004, the price of cotton fell 42% and the price of sugar dropped 48% in real dollars. Making matters worse, the price of manufactured goods has risen steeply, which means that most of the primary products the LDCs export have lost value against the manufactured goods the LDCs need to import. This "double trouble" relationship is shown in Figure 13.3.

The use of trade, then, to acquire capital and to improve economic conditions has not been highly effective for most LDCs. Their pattern of merchandise trade deficits, overreliance on primary product exports, and price weaknesses are all disadvantages for LDCs in their trade relations with the EDCs.

Foreign Aid

A fourth possible external source of capital for LDCs is foreign aid. In some ways the flow of official development assistance (ODA) to LDCs has been impressive, amounting to about $4 trillion (measured in 2005 real dollars) since World War II. For 2004, ODA was $69 billion. Currently, 95% of all foreign aid that is given comes from the 22 EDCs that are members of the **Development Assistance Committee (DAC)** of the Organization for Economic Cooperation and Development (OECD). Most assistance is extended through **bilateral aid** (country to country), with a smaller amount being channeled through **multilateral aid** (via the United Nations, the World Bank, and other IGOs). Without disparaging the value or intent of foreign aid, the primary issue with foreign aid is that there is not enough of it to serve as a major source of

Did You Know That:

For the first time since the Mexican-American War of 1848, Mexican military forces entered the United States in 2005. This time Mexican troops were delivering foreign aid in the form of disaster relief supplies to American victims of Hurricane Katrina along the Gulf Coast.

Exports of Primary Products

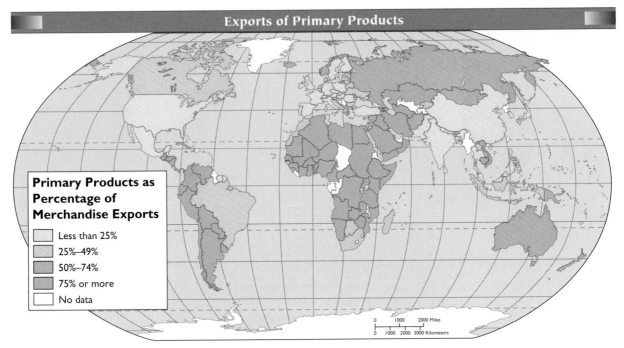

Primary Products as Percentage of Merchandise Exports

- Less than 25%
- 25%–49%
- 50%–74%
- 75% or more
- No data

The less developed countries of the South are disadvantaged compared to the economically developed countries of the North. One reason is that the LDCs are much more reliant on primary products for export earnings. The dependency is a disadvantage because the demand for and price of primary products is unstable. Also, over the long term the value of primary products rises more slowly than manufactured products. Therefore most LDCs have increasing difficulty earning the foreign capital needed for economic development. This map shows the distribution of countries according to the percentage of their exports accounted for by primary products.

development capital (Travis & Zahariadis, 2002). On the face of it, $69 billion in aid seems to be an enormous amount, but it appears less monumental when seen as only about $30 for each of the 2.3 billion people living in low-income countries.

Internal Reforms

Although not a capital need as such, internal reforms are a closely associated and controversial topic. One criticism of the LDCs is that development funds and other assistance programs have had effects ranging from suboptimal to failure because of protectionism, corruption, and problems within the LDCs. President Bush, Prime Minister Tony Blair of Great Britain, some other EDC leaders, and the IMF and World Bank have all pressed countries to open their economies further to trade and investment, to privatize state-run enterprises, and to assure greater "transparency," something of a code word for reducing corruption. Symbolic of this thrust, the World Bank's *World Development Report 2005* is subtitled *A Better Investment Climate for Everyone*. The volume argues (p. xii) that "improving the climate for investment in developing countries is essential to provide jobs and opportunities." The report says that some countries have taken steps to improve their investment climate. Nevertheless, it continues, "Progress remains slow" because many "governments still saddle firms and entrepreneurs with unnecessary costs, create substantial uncertainty and risks, and even erect unjustified barriers to competition." In its table rating countries by their investment climate, the report takes up such standards as the unpredictability of how officials interpret regulations, bribes, confidence in the court system, crime, tax rates, and the amount of bureaucratic red tape.

Did You Know That:

A World Bank survey of businesspeople found that 98% of those doing business in Bangladesh reported having to pay bribes to officials, the highest in the 53 LDCs examined. Armenia, at 36%, was least corrupt.

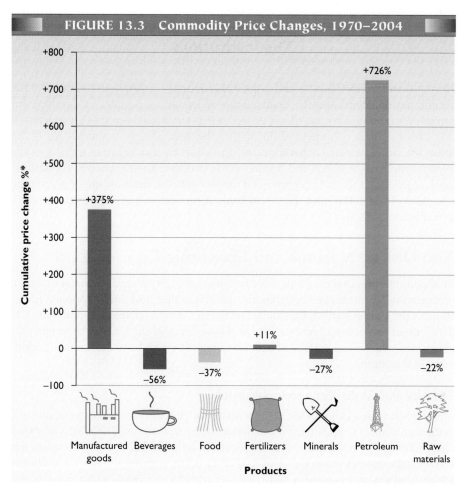

FIGURE 13.3 Commodity Price Changes, 1970–2004

Measured in real dollars, the price of manufactured goods increased substantially between 1970 and 2004, while the price of all primary products except oil either declined or grew at a slower rate than manufactured goods. As a result, LDCs that rely on primary products other than oil for export earnings have had an increasingly difficult time earning enough foreign capital through their exports to modernize their economies. Compounding the problem, most LDCs have to import petroleum, against which their primary product exports have lost even more value than against manufactured goods.

*Measured in real dollars
Data source: World Bank (2005).

Certainly, some of these factors, such as being safe from crime, would elicit no dispute. Others are more controversial. For example, leaders in LDCs wonder how the United States would do on the regulatory predictability scale, given that Washington is populated by hordes of lobbyists trying to influence government, as well as armies of attorneys trying to interpret, and to a degree manipulate, government regulations. Another criticism is that the demand for reductions in taxes and regulations serves to improve the profits of capitalist corporations, not the welfare of the people. There are yet other objections, but as you will see in several subsequent discussions of North-South relations, there is suspicion among many in the LDCs that the calls for "reform" are in truth an effort to advance the interests of the EDCs and their corporations and to continue their neocolonial domination of the South.

JOIN THE DEBATE
Is Debt Relief Good for
the Global Economy?

Economic Cooperation and Development: The Institutions

Having examined the theories and origins of economic cooperation, the status of the South's development, and the inadequacies of its various sources of development capital, we now turn to the efforts to facilitate international economic cooperation and advance the development of the South. The most obvious manifestation of the move toward economic cooperation and globalization that began in earnest in the 1940s is the array of global and regional IGOs that have been created to try to regulate and enhance the world economy. Of the global IGOs, the most important are the UN, the WTO, the IMF, and the World Bank. A number of EDC institutions and regional institutions also play a role.

The United Nations and Economic Cooperation

In addition to peacekeeping and other activities, the UN serves as a global umbrella organization for numerous agencies and programs that deal with economic issues through the United Nations Economic and Social Council (UNESCO), and other UN divisions and associated agencies. The economic focus of the UN can be roughly divided into two categories: global economic regulation and the economic development of the South.

The UN and Global Economic Regulation

The UN is involved in a number of areas related to global economic cooperation such as the regulation of transnational (or multinational) corporations (TNCs/MNCs). Many observers argue the MNCs need to be regulated by IGOs because globalization has allowed businesses to escape a great deal of domestic regulation. "Are we really going to let the world become a global market without any laws except those of the jungle?" France's president asked at a UN-sponsored economic conference.[2] In response to such concerns, the UN's Center for Transnational Corporations was established as part of the effort to create global standards and regulations to limit the inherently self-serving practices of capitalist corporations.

The UN and Development

The second focus of UN economic activity has been development of the LDCs. One role that the UN has played since 1981 is to sponsor North-South economic summit conferences that have helped increase international awareness among the policy makers of the North about the need for development, have elicited expressions of concern, and have even brought some financial support. For example, the Millennium Summit held at the UN in 2000 brought together 150 national leaders who established eight goals to be reached by 2015 in such areas as reducing extreme poverty, increasing education, and improving health. It is unlikely that most, perhaps any of the goals will be met completely, but setting a standard by which progress can be measured is an important step.

The Millennium Summit also agreed that in 2002 the leaders of North and South should meet again at the UN-sponsored **International Conference on Financing for Development (ICFD)** held in Monterrey, Mexico. The conference was attended by 50 national leaders, including President George Bush, the heads of the top financial IGOs, and other world leaders. UN Secretary-General Kofi Annan called on the

Web Link

You can get the details of the goals set by the Millennium Summit at **www.un.org/millenniumgoals/**.

EDCs to increase annual economic aid from the current .025% of their GNPs to .07% (an increase in 2004 aid from $69 billion to $193 billion). Some leaders, such as France's President Jacques Chirac, supported that goal, but President Bush and most other EDC officials were much more cautious. Still, the pressure to respond to the South's needs had an effect, with Bush, for example, announcing he would ask Congress to increase U.S. economic aid by 50% within three years. Congressional appropriations fell short of that mark, but U.S. international assistance did increase by about 30%.

The UN also has numerous programs to promote development. For example, the **UN Development Programme (UNDP)** was established in 1965 to provide both technical assistance (such as planning) and development funds to LDCs. The UNDP spends about $3 billion annually, has offices in 134 LDCs, and focuses on grassroots economic development, such as promoting entrepreneurship, supporting the Development Fund for Women, and transferring technology and management skills from EDCs to LDCs.

Another important UN organization, the **UN Conference on Trade and Development (UNCTAD)**, was founded in 1964 to promote the positive integration of the LDCs into the world economy. Virtually all countries are members of UNCTAD. UNCTAD primarily gives voice to the South, especially at the summit conferences it holds every four years. The most recent of these, held in São Paulo, Brazil, in 2004, emphasized "ways to make trade work for development," and called on the North to increase its support for achieving the goals set by the Millennium Summit.

A related organization is the **Group of 77 (G-77)**, a name derived from the Joint Declaration of the Seventy-Seven Countries that the LDCs issued at the end of the first UNCTAD conference. Since then the G-77 has expanded to include 132 members. It has recently tried to increase its profile by holding its first summit meeting since it was founded in the mid-1960s. That meeting, in Havana, Cuba, in 2000, as well as the second summit in Doha, Qatar, in 2005, have played an important role in having the leaders of the LDCs gather, establish their development agenda, and press the EDCs to support it, as discussed in chapter 12.

SIMULATION
IGOs and Economic
Cooperation

Trade Cooperation and Development: The WTO

While the UN addresses the broad range of global economic issues, there are a number of IGOs that focus on one or another specific area of economic interchange. One of the most prominent of these is the **World Trade Organization (WTO)**. It was founded in 1947, and until 1995 the organization had the same name as its underlying treaty, the **General Agreement on Tariffs and Trade (GATT)**. Whatever its name, the organization's initial membership of 23 countries has expanded to 148 members, and most of the nonmembers are seeking to join. In keeping with the GATT's original mission, the reduction of trade barriers, the WTO has sponsored a series of trade negotiations called "rounds" that have greatly enhanced the free flow of trade and capital. Although the WTO was established and remains a general trade organization, its latest series of negotiations, the Doha Round, heavily focuses on North and South perspectives on the intersection of economic globalization and development. Before turning to that, however, it is important to take a look at the WTO itself.

The Structure and Role of the WTO

The function of the WTO is to deal with the complexities of the GATT and to handle the disputes that will inevitably arise under the GATT. WTO headquarters are in Geneva, Switzerland, and currently headed by Director-General Pascal Lamy of France,

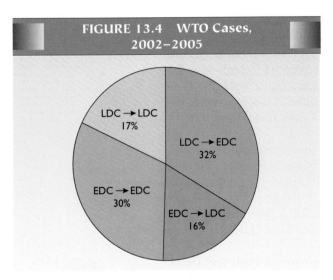

FIGURE 13.4   WTO Cases, 2002–2005

The pattern of the 75 WTO cases filed between mid-2002 and mid-2005 indicates that all economic types of countries are both complainants and respondents. Most commonly, EDCs are respondents, but that is not surprising given their high level of trade and the resulting sensitivity of other EDCs and of LDCs to perceived violations of GATT rules.

Note: The country type (EDC or LDC) to the left of the symbol → is the complainant; the country type to the right of the arrow is the respondent: complainant → respondent.
Data source: WTO at www.wto.org. Calculations by author.

a former trade commissioner of the European Union (EU), who took office in 2005. Countries can file complaints against one another for alleged violations of the GATT. The WTO uses three-judge panels to hear the complaints, and if a panel finds a violation, the WTO may impose sanctions on the offending country. Each country has one vote in the WTO, and sanctions require a two-thirds vote. While any country can withdraw from the WTO by giving six months' notice, that country would suffer significant economic perils because its products would no longer be subject to the reciprocal low tariffs and other advantages WTO members accord one another.

Despite grumbling by critics about countries losing their sovereignty, the WTO judicial process has been busy, with 20 to 30 cases being filed annually in recent years. The 2002–2005 case pattern, illustrated in Figure 13.4, shows that all types of countries are both complainants and respondents. The United States was involved in 43% of those cases, 10 times as a complainant and 23 times as a respondent. It is reasonable to conclude that the frequency of the U.S. status of respondent is almost surely a function of the size of the U.S. economy, rather than any tendency to target the United States, given the fact that the European Union was involved in 36% of all cases, filing 11 complaints and responding to 19 others.

The significance of the WTO hearing process was evident in the dispute that flared up in 2005 between the United States and the EU, each charging that the other was violating GATT rules by subsidizing their commercial airliner manufacturing industry. As detailed in chapter 12, both took their cases to the WTO, but they also began negotiations with one another to seek the equivalent of an out-of-court settlement. Such resolutions are not uncommon. The most difficult times arise when a WTO ruling runs counter to the desires of a powerful interest group in a respondent country and requires a change in domestic law. When in 2005 the WTO decided in favor of Brazil's complaint that U.S. subsidies to its cotton farmers violated GATT rules, powerful members of Congress from cotton-growing states decried the WTO's intervention in supposedly domestic American matters. But the U.S. Secretary of Agriculture called on Congress to work with the administration to find a way "to comply with the ruling."[3] Typical of many cases, an effort will be made to ease the impact on the U.S. cotton industry. But simply rejecting the WTO finding would expose the United States to sanctions that would hurt other areas of American commerce, would encourage other countries to reject WTO rulings that favored the United States, and, indeed, would imperil the WTO and the entire structure of economic globalization that Washington has so steadily promoted for over a half-century.

Revising the GATT: The Doha Round

As noted earlier, the GATT has been revised in a series of negotiations. The eighth and most recently completed of these, the **Uruguay Round**, was convened in Punta del Este, Uruguay, in 1986 and was not concluded until 1994. The resulting GATT revisions further reducing economic barriers are complex beyond our telling here, addressing about 10,000 products and myriad businesses and other commercial interchanges. There were for example, four paragraphs on the importation of "soft-ripened cow's milk cheese" and how to distinguish that kind of cheese from other kinds of cheese.

What is important, though, is that, overall, the countries that signed the Uruguay Round document agreed to reduce their tariffs $744 billion over a 10-year period by cutting them one-third on average. Agricultural tariffs were included in the GATT for the first time, and the agreement also further reduced or barred many NTBs. The signatories also agreed to institute within five years effective protection of intellectual property, such as patents, copyrights, trade secrets, and trademarks. These changes did not end the process of economic globalization, however. Instead, they set the stage for the next round of negotiations to further enhance the free flow of global trade and finance.

This newest round of negotiations began when the WTO decided during one of its periodic ministerial meetings, which had gathered in Doha, Qatar, in 2001, to reach agreements in just three years, less than half the time it took to complete the Uruguay Round. The **Doha Round** failed to meet that deadline, and the story of the stalled negotiations is in considerable part about conflict between North and South priorities on further development and globalization.

North-South disagreements came to a head in 2003 during Doha Round negotiations being held in Cancún, Mexico. The EDCs wanted to focus on the so-called Singapore issues, named for the location of the 1996 ministerial meeting at which they were introduced. The issues include matters that mostly require reform in the South such as competition (the EDCs want to restrict cartels and price fixing), transparency (ensuring corruption does not hinder trade), intellectual property rights (protecting the patents of EDC companies), government procurement (ensuring foreign companies can compete), and investment restrictions (such as limits of foreign ownership of business and real estate). By contrast, LDCs wanted to focus on reducing EDCs' barriers to agricultural imports. A particular target is the approximately $300 billion in annual subsidies that the EDCs give to their farmers and agribusinesses. These subsidies allow EDC agricultural products to be sold at artificially low prices, thereby often pricing LDC exports of those products out of the global market (Cline, 2004).

Unable to reach a compromise, the talks in Cancún collapsed. LDC delegates blamed the EDCs. "They were not generous enough; there was just not enough on the table for developing countries," argued the delegate from Jamaica.[4] Reflecting the EDC view, the EU commissioner of agriculture rejoined, "If I look at the recent extreme proposal co-sponsored by Brazil, China, India and others [in Cancún], I cannot help [having] the impression that they are circling in a different orbit. If they want to do business, they should come back to Mother Earth. If they choose to continue their space odyssey they will not get the stars, they will not get the moon, they will end up with empty hands."[5]

As of this writing little progress has been made, and a meeting set to convene in Hong Kong in July 2005 seems to offer little prospects of a breakthrough. As the head of the WTO put it, "I am afraid we have to face the facts. These negotiations are in trouble. . . . Everyone has a generalized commitment to progress, but when it comes to the specifics, the familiar defensive positions take over."[6]

Monetary Cooperation in Support of Development: The IMF

As trade and the level of other international financial transactions have increased, the need to cooperate internationally to facilitate and stabilize the flow of dollars, marks, yen, pounds, and other currencies has become vital. To meet this need, a

Did You Know That:
Indicative of the complexity of modern trade negotiations, the 1994 GATT revision is some 26,000 pages long and weighs about 385 pounds.

number of organizations, of which the **International Monetary Fund (IMF)** is the most important, have been established. As with many other aspects of international economic cooperation, the focus of the IMF has shifted substantially toward concerns with LDC development.

The genesis of the IMF in the early 1940s was rooted in the importance the United States placed on monetary stability and the easy convertibility from one currency to another, as discussed in chapter 12. To this end, Washington organized a conference of World War II Allies in 1944 at Bretton Woods, New Hampshire. There the delegates established the IMF. Thus, like the WTO, it was created by the West, with the United States in the lead, as part of the liberalization of international economic interchange. At first the IMF followed a system under which currencies were exchanged against the U.S. dollar on a "fixed-rate" tied to the price of gold. This worked for a time, but by the early 1970s a new system was put in place that relied on "free-floating" currency relations. Under this system, supply and demand determined the exchange rate of currencies.

The Role of the IMF

The IMF began operations in 1947 with 44 member-countries, a number that had grown to 184 in 2005. Its headquarters are in Washington, D.C. The managing director of the IMF since 2004 is Rodrigo de Rato y Figaredo, formerly Spain's economic minister. The IMF's primary function is to help maintain exchange-rate stability by making short-term loans to countries with international balance-of-payments problems because of trade deficits, heavy loan payments, or other factors. In such times, countries can use the IMF's loan to help meet debt payments, to buy back its own currency (thus maintaining exchange-rate stability by balancing supply and demand), or take other financial steps.

The IMF receives its usable funds from hard currency reserves ($327 billion in 2005) principally placed at its disposal by EDCs and from interest on loans it has made to countries that draw on those reserves. IMF resources are expressed in terms of **special drawing rights (SDRs)**, a virtual currency whose value is based on an average, or market basket, value of several currencies. In mid-2005, the exchange rate was 1 SDR = $1.45, and the IMF had over $90 billion in loans and available credit out to 82 countries, all of them LDCs. This fact reflects the IMF's increasing concern with the finances and development of the LDCs. In addition to its normal operations, the IMF has the Poverty Reduction and Growth Facility (PRGF) program that provides loans at "concessional" (very low) interest rates to low-income countries, and another program to provide loans at concessional rates to very poor countries under the Heavily Indebted Poor Countries (HIPC) Initiative. What the IMF attempts to do in its loans to LDCs is stabilize their currencies so that the countries can avoid high inflation and other economically destructive consequences of monetary destabilization. Figure 13.5 indicates that this funding has risen steadily.

Controversy about the IMF

Although the IMF has played a valuable role and has many supporters, it is also often criticized. The controversies regarding the IMF may be divided into two categories: voting and conditionality.

Voting   One criticism centers on the formula that determines voting on the IMF board of directors. Voting is based on how much each member-country contributes to the IMF's resources. On this basis, the United States has over 17% of the votes, 242 times the voting strength of Palau's 0.07%. By another calculation, the United States

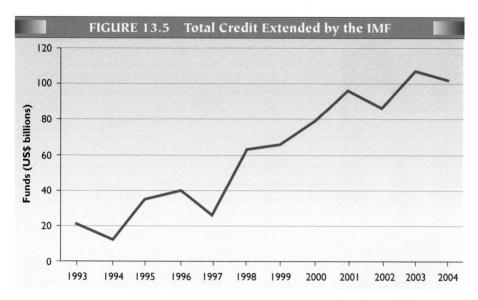

FIGURE 13.5 Total Credit Extended by the IMF

The IMF now extends all of its loans to LDCs in an effort to increase their financial stability and advance their development. As evident here, the funding available for this effort has risen considerably from the early 1990s.

Note: Sources express data in SDRs; conversion to dollars by author using average SDR rate for each year.
Data source: IMF Web site at http://www.imf.org/external/index.htm.

and just seven other large EDCs control a majority of the IMF vote under the wealth-weighted system. The weight of the EDC vote is a key reason why the director-general of the IMF has always been a Western European. This record and the voting apportionment leads critics of the IMF to charge that it is undemocratically controlled by the North and is being used as a tool to dominate the LDCs.

Conditionality　Critics also accuse the IMF of imposing unfair and unwise conditions on countries that borrow from it. Most IMF loans are subject to **conditionality.** This refers to requirements that the borrowing country take steps to remedy the situations that, according to the IMF, have caused the recipient's financial problems. These conditions generally press the LDCs to move toward capitalism and free international economic exchange by such steps as privatizing state-run enterprises, reducing barriers to trade and investment, and devaluing currencies to increase exports and decrease imports. The IMF also often requires borrowing governments to reduce their budget deficits by cutting domestic programs and/or raising taxes.

While such requirements may seem reasonable, one objection is that *IMF conditions violate sovereignty* by interfering in the recipients' policy-making processes. When the IMF and Argentina were negotiating the provisions of an IMF loan to that country in 2002 amid its financial crisis, many Argentine political leaders denounced the IMF's demand that they slash their budget deficit. One official growled that the IMF "should go to hell." "The only thing lacking is for us to pull down the Argentine flag and replace it with the IMF's," he continued.[7] Second, some critics have contended that *conditionality maintains the dependency relationship,* whether that is intended or not. For example, Argentina's president characterized IMF conditions as reflecting the "domination" of the LDCs by the EDCs.[8]

Third, critics charge that *IMF conditions often harm economies in LDCs* by requiring fiscal austerity and other stringent conditions that are counterproductive. During

Web Link

The Heritage Foundation and the *Wall Street Journal* compile an annual Index of Economic Freedom rating countries for how closely they adhere to unfettered capitalism. The index is available at **www.heritage .org/research/features/index/ index.cfm.**

Critics of the International Monetary Fund argue that the conditions it imposes on a country before it can receive IMF help are often harmful. Argentina had to agree to cut government spending to get IMF assistance, and in this photograph, teachers in Buenos Aires are protesting cuts to the education budget with mock skeleton signs reading "The future of our children." Defenders of the IMF argue that the conditions are necessary to correct the problems that led to the need for assistance.

the IMF-Argentina negotiations, Harvard economist Jeffrey Sachs compared the IMF's approach to "the 18th-century medical practice in which doctors 'treated' feverish patients by drawing blood from them, weakening the patients further and frequently hastening their deaths."[9] A related fourth charge is that *IMF conditions often destabilize governments* by forcing them to institute policies that cause a domestic backlash. Reflecting on riots that occurred in Argentina, one observer commented, "The IMF has the wrong idea if they think . . . any president can immediately make the kinds of reforms they are demanding and still be left standing in the morning."[10] A fifth line of criticism contends that *the IMF conditions undermine social welfare* by pushing countries to cut their budget, thereby reducing social services, laying off government workers, and taking other steps that harm the quality of life of their citizens. Taking that view, Argentina's president portrayed the IMF's conditions as "delaying education and the good health of Argentina's children."[11]

Defense of the IMF Those who defend the IMF rejected these charges. With respect to the voting formula, defenders argue that since it is the EDCs that provide the funds, they should have a proportionate share of the say in how they are invested. As for conditionality, the IMF acknowledges that its demands often cause hardship. But it argues that the required reforms are necessary to correct the problems that led the borrower-country into financial difficulty in the first place in order to avoid a continuing cycle of crisis and loans.

Taking this view during Argentina's economic meltdown, the head of the IMF, argued that, "without pain, [Argentina] won't get out of this crisis, and the crisis—at its root—is homemade."[12]

Perhaps both the critics and defenders of the IMF have a point; the agreement between Argentina and the IMF to refinance the country's debt reflected a compromise in which Argentina agreed to some conditions and the IMF considerably reduced its requirements. Like other compromises, it left many on both sides dissatisfied. Some talked of an IMF "cave in," while others protested that "if the national government . . . with the IMF . . . [causes] utility rate increases, there will be more hunger and there will be more unemployment."[13]

Development Cooperation: The World Bank Group

A third type of multilateral economic cooperation involves granting loans and aid for the economic development of LDCs. The most significant development agency today is the **World Bank Group**, commonly referred to as just the World Bank. The designator "group" stems from the fact that the World Bank consists of several distinct agencies.

World Bank Operations

Like the IMF, the World Bank was established in the World War II era to promote the postwar economic prosperity of the United States and its allies. However, like the IMF, the World Bank's priorities have shifted to assisting the development of the South. Reflecting this, the World Bank's 2004 report declares that its mission is "to fight poverty and improve living standards for people in the developing world."

Almost every country is a member of each agency of the World Bank Group. One agency, the *International Bank for Reconstruction and Development* (IBRD, established 1946) has lending policies that resemble those of a commercial bank in that the IBRD analyzes the financial worth of projects it funds and charges some interest. In 2004, the IBRD made $11 billion in loans to fund 87 projects in 33 countries. A second agency, the *International Development Association* (IDA, created 1960) focuses on making loans at no interest to the very poorest countries to help them provide better basic human services (such as education, health care, safe water, and sanitation), to improve economic productivity, and to create employment. During 2004, the IDA extended $9 billion in loans to fund 158 projects in 62 countries, most of them in sub-Saharan Africa.

The third agency, the *International Finance Corporation* (IFC, founded 1956) makes loans to companies in LDCs and guarantees private investment for projects supporting development. This contrasts with the IBRD and the IDA, which mostly make loans to governments for public projects. The IFC's loans for 2004 came to $4.8 billion to 217 private enterprises in 65 countries. Because of the unstable business climates in many countries, many of the IFC's loans are risky. The fourth of the World Bank Group agencies, the *Multilateral Investment Guarantee Agency* (MIGA, created 1988) promotes the flow of private development capital to LDCs by providing guarantees to investors for about 20% of any losses they might suffer due to noncommercial risks (such as political instability). In 2004, MIGA issued $1.1 billion in guarantees.

Controversy about the World Bank Group

Like the IMF, the World Bank has done a great deal of good, but it has also come under criticism. Many object to the fact that, like the IMF, the World Bank is dominated by the EDCs. It also uses a wealth-based voting formula. This gives the United States 16% of the votes and, along with Western Europe, majority control of the organization. One result is that the president of the World Bank is and always has been an American. The tenth and current (since 2005) head of the World Bank, Paul Wolfowitz, was deputy secretary of defense and a major architect of the Bush administration's invasion of Iraq. Moreover, Wolfowitz had little or no experience with banking, development, or the LDCs. Even some relatively conservative sources in the West were concerned by President Bush's nomination of Wolfowitz, with the *Financial Times* of Great Britain editorially warning, "The world would view a bank directed by Mr. Wolfowitz as no more than an instrument of U.S. power and U.S. priorities."[14] Whatever the concerns may have been, Wolfowitz's selection by the World Bank's Board of Directors was virtually assured because of the size of the U.S. vote and because he would get European support based on the informal arrangement of a Western European head for the IMF and an American head for the World Bank.

From the perspective of the South, the North's domination of the World Bank limits its ability to understand the views and problems of the LDCs. A harsher interpretation in line with economic structuralism is that the EDCs use the World Bank and other IGOs to maintain neoimperialist control of the South. For example, Malaysian economist and activist Martin Kohr charges, "Economically speaking, we are more dependent on the ex-colonial powers than we ever were. The World Bank and the IMF are playing the role that our ex-colonial masters used to play."[15]

Critics also grumble that the World Bank provides too little funding. Figures such as the nearly $600 billion the World Bank has distributed in its history and the $26 billion it loaned LDCs in 2004 sound less impressive in light of the fact that in real dollars, World Bank funding is no greater than it was in 1995 despite the North's rhetoric about being committed to increasing development funds for the South. A third criticism charges that the World Bank is too conservative in the distribution of its loans. Almost a quarter of World Bank loans in 2004 went to just seven countries (Argentina, Brazil, China, Mexico, Russia, South Korea, and Turkey), none of which was in dire economic straits. Critics also charge that the World Bank's conservatism causes it, like the IMF, to use its financial power to impose the capitalist economic model on recipient countries.

Web Link

For a critique of the IMF and World Bank, go to the Bretton Woods Project site at **www.brettonwoodsproject.org/**. The institutions defend themselves at **www.worldbank.org** and **www.imf.org**.

Economic Cooperation and Development: EDC Institutions

As globalization progressed in the latter half of the 20th century, the countries of the North created several organizations made up of EDCs to help ensure their post–World War II economic health. While these organizations still do that to some degree, they, like the IMF and other economic IGOs, have expanded their focus to include development.

Organization for Economic Cooperation and Development

Of the two major EDC organizations, the first to be created was the **Organization for Economic Cooperation and Development (OECD)**. It was established in 1961 by the United States, Canada, 15 Western European countries, and Turkey. It has subsequently admitted several LDCs that have close economic ties to an EDC, such as Mexico, or that are relatively prosperous, such as South Korea. Still, the bulk of the OECD's 30 member-states are EDCs, making the organization something of a "rich man's club." The OECD serves as a forum for member-countries to discuss economic issues, it generates copious statistics and numerous studies, and it offers economic advice and technical assistance. It has also become increasingly involved with the LDCs and such issues as globalization and sustainable development, and it has established links with some 70 LDCs, ranging from Brazil, China, and Russia to the low-income, or least developed countries (LLDCs), in sub-Saharan Africa and elsewhere.

The Group of 8 (G-8)

If the OECD is a reasonably exclusive club of prosperous member-countries, the **Group of Eight (G-8)** is equivalent to the executive board. The G-8 does not have a formal connection to the OECD, but it does represent the pinnacle of economic power. The G-8 began in 1975 as the Group of Seven (G-7) to coordinate economic policy among the seven most economically powerful noncommunist countries (Canada, France, Germany, Great Britain, Italy, Japan, and the United States). In 1997 the G-7 became the G-8 when it added Russia in recognition of its economic potential and geostrategic importance. The president of the Commission of the EU also regularly attends.

The apex of G-8 activity comes at its annual summit meeting. These have increasingly concentrated on development and other matters related to the LDCs. One indication of this focus on the LDCs is that a number of them have been invited as participating nonmembers to each G-8 summit since 2000. At the 2005 summit in Scotland, these countries included Algeria, Brazil, China, Ethiopia, Ghana, India, Mexico, Nigeria, Senegal, South Africa, and Tanzania. Also indicative of the G-8's orientation was its agenda in 2005. During a meeting that was overshadowed by four coordinated terrorist suicide bombings in the London transportation system, the G-8 leaders announced that they would double aid for Africa to $50 billion by 2010. They also agreed to end agricultural subsidies that distort trade, thereby addressing the complaint of many LDCs that their potential agricultural exports were being unfairly disadvantaged. Also, the G-8 leaders agreed to begin a series of meetings designed to end the standoff between the United States and much of the rest of the world on setting mandatory limits to the emission of "greenhouse gases" that promote global warming (see chapter 15). A key U.S. objection is that limits in the Kyoto Protocol apply only to EDCs and do not require the LDCs, including such major polluters as China, to also reduce their emissions.

Opinions on the importance of the G-8 vary widely. One factor is that the high-profile summits become an important part of the public diplomacy regarding development. Prior to the 2005 meeting, for example, music promoter Bob Geldof organized Live 8 popular music concerts in ten cities. They were broadcast around the world and starred such groups and performers as U2, Coldplay, Sting, Elton John, the Who, Pink Floyd, and Green Day. Adding to the public pressure, HBO aired a movie, *The Girl in the Café*, about a young woman who travels to the G-8 summit with a British financial expert and confronts the gathered leaders, charging them with not doing enough to meet the UN millennium goals to alleviate poverty and its social ills. Like most major meetings of the leading economic institutions, the summit also drew thousands of antiglobalization protesters.

As for the importance of the G-8 and its resolutions, one analyst depicts it as emerging as a "shadow world government."[16] A less expansive view, according to another scholar, is that G-8 members "do comply modestly with the decisions and consensus generated [at their summit meetings]."[17] There are also opinion differences over whether

Web Link

The University of Toronto includes the G8 Information Centre at **www.g7.utoronto.ca/**.

The Group of Eight (G-8), which consists of the seven leading economic powers plus Russia, has increasingly turned its attention to assisting the most impoverished countries of the South. To encourage the G-8 to do even more, especially for Africa, music entertainers from many countries organized free Live 8 concerts around the world in 2005 to increase public awareness and pressure on the decision makers gathered in Scotland for the annual G-8 meeting. Here, American rapper Snoop Dogg performs at the Live 8 concert in Hyde Park, London.

the G-8 is a positive or negative force. Representing the range of opinions, some observers applauded the decisions of the 2005 summit. U2 lead singer Bono, a cofounder of DATA (Debt AIDS Trade Africa), exulted, "We've pulled this off. The world spoke, and the politicians listened." More cautiously, Bob Geldof advised, "It is only time that will decide whether this summit is historic or not. The check has been written and signed, now we need to cash it."[18] Yet other views were neutral or negative. Sue Mbaya, director of the Southern Africa Regional Poverty Network, was even more hesitant. "As optimistic as we would like to be," she said, "we should be wary based on [the G-8] track record, which has often been far short compared to the pledges." Mbaya expressed suspicion of the G-8's sincerity in light of the fact that its pledge of added aid had been made on the condition that African countries reduce corruption and institute other reforms. She called demand for reform "the latest trick on the conditionalities front," and warned that it could be used "as a loophole" by the G-8 to renege on its pledge.[19]

Regional Economic Cooperation and Development

In addition to the activity promoting economic cooperation and development from a global perspective, there is also an important effort under way at the regional level. This regional activity does not exclusively involve the LDCs. Still, similar to global cooperation, regional ties have become extensively intermeshed with and important to the development of the South.

One area of cooperation is finance through nine regional development banks. In terms of loan commitments, the largest of these (and their loans in 2004) were the Inter-American Development Bank ($6.1 billion), the Asian Development Bank ($4.1 billion), the African Development Bank ($2.4 billion), and the European Bank for Reconstruction and Development ($3.5 billion), which focuses on projects in the LDCs in Eastern Europe and in Russia and the former Soviet republics. There are other regional banks, but they are much less well funded, as exemplified by the Caribbean Development Bank which, despite its region's pressing needs, only had the assets to make $223 million in loans in 2004. In addition to the development banks, there are numerous IGOs that are dedicated to promoting economic cooperation and development among groups of countries based on their geographical region (such as the 12-member Black Sea Economic Cooperation Zone), culture, or some other link (for example, the 21-member Arab Monetary Fund).

Multilateral **regional trade organizations (RTOs)** provide an even more numerous and rapidly expanding example of the growth of regional economic cooperation. There are about 30 RTOs, ranging from the tiny Melanesian Spearhead Group (Fiji, Papua New Guinea, Solomon Islands, and Vanuatu) to the huge European Union. Indeed, there are very few countries that are not members of an RTO, and numerous countries are in two or more. Some are little more than shell organizations that keep their goals barely alive, yet each represents the conviction of its members that, compared to standing alone, they can achieve greater economic prosperity by working together through economic cooperation or even economic integration. RTOs are particularly important to the development plans of the South. One indication is that about 75% of all the RTOs have memberships that are exclusively made up of or include LDCs, and several other RTOs mix EDC and LDCs. This pattern is evident if we look at the RTOs in the various global areas. We will discuss the leading RTOs in the following sections, and Table 13.1 provides a selective list of some of the others.

TABLE 13.1 Select Regional Trade Organizations

Regional Trade Organization	Members
Caribbean Community and Common Market	Antigua & Barbuda, Bahamas, Barbados, Belize, Dominica, Grenada, Guyana, Haiti, Jamaica, St. Kitts & Nevis, St. Lucia, St. Vincent & the Grenadines, Suriname, Trinidad & Tobago
Central American Common Market	Costa Rica, El Salvador, Guatemala, Honduras, Nicaragua
Commonwealth of Independent States	Azerbaijan, Armenia, Belarus, Georgia, Kazakhstan, Kyrgyz Republic, Moldova, Russia, Tajikistan, Turkmenistan, Ukraine, Uzbekistan
Common Market for Eastern and Southern Africa	Angola, Burundi, Comoros, Democratic Republic of Congo, Djibouti, Egypt, Eritrea, Ethiopia, Kenya, Madagascar, Malawi, Mauritius, Namibia, Rwanda, Seychelles, Sudan, Swaziland, Uganda, Zambia, Zimbabwe
Economic and Monetary Community of Central Africa	Cameroon, Central African Republic, Chad, Republic of Congo, Equatorial Guinea, Gabon
Economic Community of West African States	Benin, Burkina Faso, Cape Verde, Côte d'Ivoire, Gambia, Ghana, Guinea, Guinea-Bissau, Liberia, Mali, Niger, Nigeria, Senegal, Sierra Leone, Togo
Economic Cooperation Organization	Afghanistan, Azerbaijan, Iran, Kazakhstan, Kyrgyz Republic, Pakistan, Tajikistan, Turkey, Turkmenistan, Uzbekistan
Eurasian Economic Community	Belarus, Kazakhstan, Kyrgyz Republic, Russia, Tajikistan
European Free Trade Association	Iceland, Liechtenstein, Norway, Switzerland
Gulf Cooperation Council	Bahrain, Kuwait, Oman, Qatar, Saudi Arabia, United Arab Emirates
Latin American Integration Association	Argentina, Bolivia, Brazil, Chile, Colombia, Cuba, Ecuador, Mexico, Paraguay, Peru, Uruguay, Venezuela
Southern African Development Community	Angola, Botswana, Democratic Republic of Congo, Lesotho, Malawi, Mauritius, Mozambique, Namibia, South Africa, Swaziland, Tanzania, Zambia, Zimbabwe
South Asian Preferential Trade Arrangement	Bangladesh, Bhutan, India, Maldives, Nepal, Pakistan, Sri Lanka
South Pacific Regional Trade and Economic Cooperation Agreement	Australia, Fiji, Kiribati, Marshall Islands, Micronesia, Nauru, New Zealand, Papua New Guinea, Solomon Islands, Tonga, Tuvalu, Vanuatu, Western Samoa
West African Economic and Monetary Union	Benin, Burkina Faso, Côte d'Ivoire, Guinea Bissau, Mali, Niger, Senegal, Togo

There are about 30 regional trade organizations, and they are present in all the world's major geopolitical regions. The main commentary examines many of these RTOs, and this table provides a selective list of other RTOs that are not noted.

The Western Hemisphere

Proposals for regional economic cooperation date back to a U.S. effort in 1889 to create a hemispherical customs union that would reduce trade barriers among the hemisphere's countries and adopt common external tariff and nontariff barriers. The notion of RTOs in the Western Hemisphere then lay dormant for almost a century until globalization began to convert the idea into reality. Beginning in the 1960s, as Table 13.1 indicates, groups of nations began to establish RTOs.

The North American Free Trade Agreement

The largest RTO in the Western Hemisphere, measured in trade volume, is the **North American Free Trade Agreement (NAFTA)** among Canada, Mexico, and the United

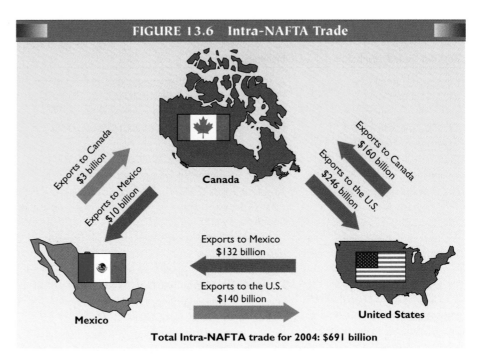

FIGURE 13.6 Intra-NAFTA Trade

Canada

Exports to Canada
$3 billion

Exports to Mexico
$10 billion

Exports to Canada
$160 billion

Exports to the U.S.
$246 billion

Exports to Mexico
$132 billion

Exports to the U.S.
$140 billion

Mexico

United States

Total Intra-NAFTA trade for 2004: $691 billion

The North American Free Trade Agreement has accounted for a rapid rise in trade among Canada, Mexico, and the United States since the treaty went into effect in 1994. There are now plans for a Western Hemisphere free trade zone, the Free Trade Area of the Americas.

Data source: IMF (2005).

ANALYZE THE ISSUE
Is NAFTA a Success
or Failure?

States. The 2,000-page agreement, which took effect in 1994, established schedules for reducing tariff and nontariff barriers to trade by 2004 in all but a few hundred of some 20,000 product categories and by 2009 for all products. NAFTA also reduced or eliminated many restrictions on foreign investments and other financial transactions and facilitated transportation by allowing trucking largely unimpeded access across borders. There is a standing commission with representatives from all three countries to deal with disputes that arise under the NAFTA agreement.

NAFTA has had an important impact on the three trading partners. For example, intra-NAFTA trade is a key component of the exports of all three partners, as can be seen in the data on merchandise trade in Figure 13.6. Mexico and Canada are especially dependent on intra-NAFTA trade, with 89% and 87% of their exports respectively going to the United States and to one another. The United States is least dependent, albeit still heavily so, with NAFTA trade accounting for 37% of U.S. exports.

A vigorous debate continues in each of the three countries about the pros and cons of NAFTA. Canada is the least affected because it has relatively little interchange with Mexico and because preexisting U.S.-Canada trade was already quite high. For Americans, there certainly have been losses. Many American businesses have relocated their facilities to Mexico, establishing *maquiladoras,* manufacturing plants just south of the border. These produce goods for export to the United States. According to a U.S. Department of Labor study, U.S. job losses from this shift of production and from Mexican imports totaled 507,000 between late 1993 and late 2002. Yet economists point out that those jobs would have probably gone to other LDCs if they had not been shifted to Mexico. Furthermore, American consumers benefited from lower prices for goods imported from Mexico. Such gains often are less noticed, however, than are losses. As one economist explains, "The gains are so thinly spread across the country that people don't thank NAFTA when they buy a mango or inexpensive auto parts."[20]

NAFTA has had the greatest effect on Mexico, in large part because both the size and the strength of its economy are so much less than those of the United States and Canada. Some aspects have been clearly positive. For example, NAFTA has diversified Mexico's economic base by increasing the percentage of its exports that are manufactured goods. The country's maquiladora program, dating back long before NAFTA, was set up to promote industrialization by giving special tax and other advantages to industries in a zone near the U.S. border. But after NAFTA went into effect, the maquiladora zone boomed, doubling its production and tripling its workers by 2000. Then fortunes turned down in the zone, in part because of competition from China for the U.S. market. Data for 2003 and 2004, however, shows a new upswing. Moreover, Mexico's GDP growth rate nearly tripled in the decade after NAFTA, compared to the decade before it. And the country's 2003 per capita GNP of $6,230 (2003) was 50% higher than that of Argentina and Brazil, the next wealthiest countries in Central and South America. Reflecting on such data, Mexican President Vincente Fox contends, "NAFTA gave us a big push. It gave us jobs. It gave us knowledge, experience, technological transfer."[21]

It is also true that for Mexicans, as well as for Americans and Canadians, NAFTA has had some very negative effects on some, such as displaced workers. Some segments of Mexico's economy have been particularly hard hit. For example, corn farmers in central and southern Mexico have suffered greatly from the incoming tidal wave of subsidized U.S. corn, which increased about 1,400% between 1993 and 2004. Many Mexicans worry about the loss of their culture amid the influx of Pizza Huts, KFC outlets, and other elements of American culture and recall the reputed lament of President Porfirio Diaz (1876–1880; 1884–1911), "Poor Mexico, so far from God, so close to the United States."

The Free Trade Area of the Americas

At the same time that NAFTA went into effect in 1994, efforts were under way to create a much broader hemispheric RTO tentatively named the **Free Trade Area of the Americas (FTAA)** that would include all or most of the countries in North, Central, and South America, and in the Caribbean. To that end, the heads of every country in the Western Hemisphere except Cuba, which was barred at U.S. insistence, met in 1994 at the Summit of the Americas in Miami, Florida, and agreed to create a free trade zone in the hemisphere by 2005. Soon, the optimistic predictions of the summit meeting gave way to difficult and slow negotiations. Subsequent summits in Santiago, Chile (1999), Quebec City, Canada (2001), Monterrey, Mexico (2004) and Mardel Plata, Argentina (2005) failed to reach any breakthroughs, and 2005, the original target date for an FTAA agreement, passed into history without one.

The disagreements that have ensnared the FTAA negotiations are very similar to the North-South issues that have beset the WTO's Doha Round, as discussed earlier. As much as the hemisphere's LDCs are anxious to improve their access to the U.S. markets, they are equally nervous about dropping their protections and being drowned in a tidal wave of American imports and services, and about having American investors snap up local businesses and other property. There is also resistance to the FTAA in the United States, especially among some interest groups. Unions fear that American jobs will wind up in the hands of underpaid Central and South Americans; agricultural organizations are determined to protect their subsidies. Other

Did You Know That:

Maquiladora is derived from the Spanish word *maquila,* the charge levied by millers to process grain, and was used since most of the maquiladora plants processed parts produced in the United States into finished products. The verb *maquilar* means to assemble.

WEB POLL
How Far Should Western Hemispheric Free Trade Go? You Be the Judge

Web Link

For an anti-FTAA group, go to **www.stoptheftaa.org/default .html**. A pro-FTAA site is at **www.floridaftaa.org/web/home .aspx** and is associated with the bid of Miami, Florida, to become the headquarters city of the FTAA.

groups fear that an FTAA will eventually increase labor migration, as the EU has done among its member-countries, leading to a greater inflow of Latin Americans into the United States than already exists.

There is also disagreement between the United States and some Latin American countries over the U.S. pressure on them to adopt a U.S.-style capitalist economy. Expressing the U.S. position, President George Bush told the 2004 summit meeting, "We must also chart a clear course toward a vibrant free market."[22] To many of his listeners, though, such language means accepting what they see as the unregulated, one-sided globalization that in their view makes the rich richer and, at best, leaves the poor somewhere between poorer and no better off. Taking this view of globalization, Brazil's President Luiz Inácio Lula da Silva depicted the 1990s as "a decade of despair" caused by "a perverse [globalization] model that wrongly separated the economic from the social, put stability against growth and separated responsibility from justice."[23] And Venezuelan President Hugo Chávez predicted that if it worked like other aspects of globalization, the FTAA would be "an infernal machinery that, minute by minute, produces an impressive number of poor."[24]

For now, the fate of the FTAA remains unclear. Official pronouncements hold out hope for an agreement in the near future, but such optimism has existed for over a decade without real results. In the interim, the United States has signed many bilateral economic agreements with countries in the hemisphere and also served as the driving force behind the impending establishment of the Central American Free Trade Association (CAFTA). That eventuality came closer in mid-2005 after the Congress approved the agreement. If the other member-countries all also support the agreement, which seems likely, CAFTA will within a few years eliminate tariffs on about 80% of the products that flow in trade among the association's members (Costa Rica, Dominican Republic, El Salvador, Guatemala, Honduras, Nicaragua, and United States). Whether the coming of CAFTA will advance or impede the FTAA negotiations remains to be seen.

Mercosur

Whatever the future of the FTAA, and in addition to CAFTA, a number of countries have undertaken or continued efforts to establish or expand their own trade treaties. The **Southern Common Market (Mercosur)** is of particular note. Mercosur was established in 1995 by Argentina, Brazil, Paraguay, and Uruguay. Since then, Bolivia, Chile, Peru, and Venezuela have become associate members. Including just its four full and four associate members, Mercosur is a market of 301 million people with a combined GDP of $864 billion, as shown in Figure 13.7.

A number of issues, including Argentina's economic crisis, have slowed the negotiations to expand Mercosur, but that effort has recently been reinvigorated by Brazil. President Lula da Silva is trying to strengthen the organization as a counter-weight to the United States in the hemisphere. "We have to unite," he told an audience. "We need to create a South American nation. The more policies we have in common, the better we will be able to succeed in big negotiations, above all in trying to break down WTO's protectionist barriers and prevent the FTAA becoming an instrument that suffocates our chances of growth."[25] Taking a step in that direction, the South American leaders, meeting in Cuzco, Peru, in 2004 agreed to create a new RTO by merging Mercosur and the Andean Community (Bolivia, Colombia, Ecuador, Peru, Venezuela), which already includes several Mercosur associate members, by 2007, and by eliminating all tariffs over the following 12 years. The new RTO, which would also include Guyana and Suriname, was named the South American

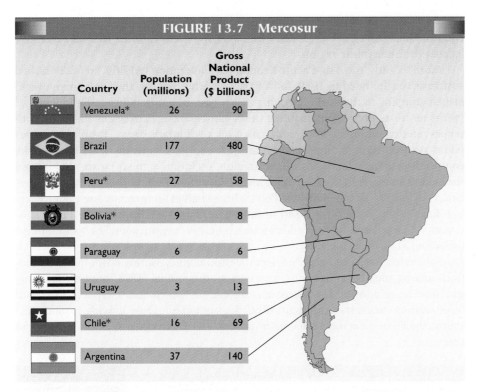

FIGURE 13.7   Mercosur

Country	Population (millions)	Gross National Product ($ billions)
Venezuela*	26	90
Brazil	177	480
Peru*	27	58
Bolivia*	9	8
Paraguay	6	6
Uruguay	3	13
Chile*	16	69
Argentina	37	140

Mercosur is an important RTO. A key issue for the Western Hemisphere is whether Mercosur and the hemisphere's other RTOs will unite into a single free trade organization, the Free Trade Area of the Americas, or become two rival trade blocs, one made up of Mercosur and the other countries of their continent in the South American Community of Nations and the other a yet nonexistent RTO composed of the countries of the North American Free Trade Agreement and Central American Free Trade Organization.

*associate members
Data source: World Bank (2005).

Community of Nations (CSN, after Comunidad Sudamericana de Naciones) and, according to the plans announced in 2004, would eventually emulate the EU with its own currency, a continental parliament, and a common passport. Whether the two-page Cuzco Declaration forming the CSN will ever be transformed into a functioning CSN is an open question that will take years to resolve.

Asia and the Pacific

In Asia, the first RTO was the **Association of Southeast Asian Nations (ASEAN)** established in 1967. It now includes Brunei, Cambodia, Indonesia, Laos, Malaysia, Myanmar (Burma), the Philippines, Singapore, Thailand, and Vietnam. The ASEAN countries have a combined population of over 525 million, a GNP of approximately $686 billion, and total exports of about $466 billion. Like the EU and some other RTOs, ASEAN is also expanding its responsibilities to include development, health, and other matters. For example, the disaster management program it developed in 2002 facilitated a coordinated response when in 2004 a tsunami devastated coastal areas in Indonesia and other member-countries. ASEAN is working to forge greater political cooperation among its members and to bargain as a group with external countries and other trade organizations. Some observers view the RTO as a counterbalance to China in the region.

SIMULATION
APEC

More recently, the **Asia-Pacific Economic Cooperation (APEC)**, an oddly named structure, was founded in 1989. Its Web site declares that it is the "only intergovernmental grouping in the world operating on the basis of non-binding commitments . . . [with] no treaty obligations required of its participants . . . decisions made by consensus, and commitments . . . undertaken on a voluntary basis." Despite its amorphous nature, APEC is important because among its 21 members are most of the countries of the greater Pacific Ocean region, including China, Japan, Russia, and the United States. Additionally, APEC members account for 42% of the world population, about 60% of the global GDP, and almost half of all merchandise trade. There is a small APEC secretariat based in Singapore, but it is symbolic of APEC's still-tentative status that it has not added a word such as "organization" or "community" to the end of its name.

Somewhat like the G-8, APEC facilitates numerous routine economic consultations among members. Its focus, however, is the annual APEC summit meeting, which serves as a forum for discussions among the United States, Japan, China, and other leading members. Although APEC does not claim to be moving toward RTO status, there have been agreements in principle, for example, to achieve "free and

Although it is a very loose grouping that shuns even calling itself an organization, the Asia-Pacific Economic Cooperation forum annually brings together the leaders of 21 countries that border the Pacific Ocean and its seas to discuss mutual concerns. This photograph taken at the 2004 meeting in Santiago, Chile, shows some of the assembled leaders including (top row, left to right) President of Taiwan Chen Shui-bian, Australian Prime Minister John Winston Howard, and U.S. President George W. Bush; and (bottom row, left to right) Prime Minister of Thailand Thaksin Shinawatra and Prime Minister of Brunei Sultan Haji Hassanal Bolkiah, as they pose for a photograph wearing traditional Chilean ponchos.

open trade and investment" in the Asia-Pacific region. Japan and the United States are to remove all their barriers by the year 2010, with the rest of the APEC members achieving a zero-barrier level by 2020. It remains unclear whether this will occur, given such factors as China's huge trade surplus with the United States and Japan's uncertain economy. Beyond this, few specific agreements have resulted from these summits, but they are part of a process of dialogue that helps keep lines of communication open.

Other Global Areas

The impulse for regional ties has not been confined to the Americas and the Asia-Pacific region. In Europe, the 25-member European Union is by far the most extensive regional effort. Given the expanded coverage of the EU in chapter 7, further commentary here is unnecessary other than to point out that with a population about 50% larger than the U.S. population and with a collective GNP that rivals that of the United States, the EU is a powerful economic force. The setback to EU political integration when French and Dutch voters rejected its constitution in 2005 does not detract from its importance as an RTO. To some degree, competing with it is one factor that has driven the creation of other RTOs. Also worth noting is that the EU's role in development is mixed. On the positive side, it has institutions like the European Development Fund that channel funds to LDCs, especially former European colonies. The EU has also taken a number of steps to reduce trade barriers to LDC products. On the negative side, the EU still maintains high agricultural subsidies that harm LDCs, and it follows many of the other policies that the LDCs consider unfair.

Still other RTOs exist in Africa, the Middle East, and elsewhere, as indicated in Table 13.1 on page 429. Most bring LDCs together and represent an effort to advance their mutual development. Yet because these RTOs are made up of countries with weak economies, their goal of increasing the members' economic strength is something akin to trying to build a solid structure on quicksand. Indeed, as a last note about RTOs, it may be that they detract from development. The WTO argues that their proliferation has created a patchwork of agreements that undermine global trade liberalization (Haftel, 2004). According to the WTO's director-general, RTOs are an unsatisfactory substitute for global trade liberalization because "they are by their very nature discriminatory. None has really succeeded in opening markets in sensitive areas like agriculture. They add to the complexities of doing business by creating a multiplicity of rules. And the poorest countries tend to get left out in the cold."[26]

Cooperation and Development: Debating the Future

There is no doubt that the expansion of world trade, investment, and currency exchange has profoundly affected countries and their citizens. Economic interdependence has inexorably intertwined personal, national, and international prosperity. Domestic economics, employment, inflation, and overall growth are heavily dependent on foreign markets, imports of resources, currency exchange rates, capital flows, and other international economic factors. Globalization is a reality.

The process of globalization has also brought the issue of development much more to center stage than it was in the past. Globalization has had advantages and disadvantages for all countries, but there is widespread agreement that both within countries and among countries those with the greatest wealth have benefited the most and those with the least wealth have gained the least and, in some cases, have been harmed. That has brought increasing resistance to globalization in the South and from those sympathetic to its stand (Drainville, 2004).

Globalization and the cooperation it entails are also beginning to have a significant impact on the way we organize our world politically. Globalization and sovereignty are not mutually exclusive, but cooperation requires that countries surrender some of their sovereign rights to make unilateral policy and accept international rules. The authority of the WTO to find a country's trade practices legal or illegal serves as an example. Some see this diminution of sovereignty as acceptable, even a positive development. Others are appalled by it.

There are yet other arguments for and against globalization and its accompanying commitment to cooperate and support development, and it is to this debate that we can now turn. Consider the arguments below, and then decide where you stand. Even better, take action to support globalization, modify its course, or reverse it. This much is sure: the script for the future remains unwritten. Because there is little likelihood that the major upheavals favored by economic structuralists will take place, we will shape the argument as a choice between economic internationalism and economic nationalism.

The Case for Economic Internationalism

Economic internationalists make a number of arguments in favor of furthering free economic interchange and increasing support for development. They advance both economic and noneconomic reasons to support their case (Bhagwati, 2004).

Economic Advantages

According to economic internationalists, there are several economic advantages to globalization and to assisting the LDCs as part of that process. These positive results include general prosperity, the benefits of specialization, the cost of protectionism, the advantages of competition, and the advancement of the LDCs through the provision of development capital.

General Prosperity   Economic internationalists argue that unhindered trade and other forms of free economic exchange promote prosperity. Especially since the mid-20th century, trade has accounted for a rapidly growing share of the world's economic activity. Trade in 1960 equaled 12% of the collective GDPs of the world's countries. That share grew to 24% in 2003. This means that more and more of what countries and their workers produce goes abroad. Without trade, then, or with a marked decline in trade, national economies would slow, perhaps stall, or might even decline. Figure 13.8 demonstrates that trade growth helps drive economic expansion by comparing the annual growth of two inflation-adjusted measures: world trade and the world's collective GDP.

A corollary of this argument, according to economic internationalists, is that EDC prosperity will be increased by the development of the South. Although assisting the LDCs will require a substantial short-term cost to the North in aid, debt reductions, and other assistance, many analysts argue that in the long run this investment would create a world in which many more of the 1.3 billion Chinese, 1.1 billion Indians, and the other 2.9 billion people living in the LDCs could buy products labeled "Made in America," visit the United States as tourists, and otherwise benefit the U.S. economy.

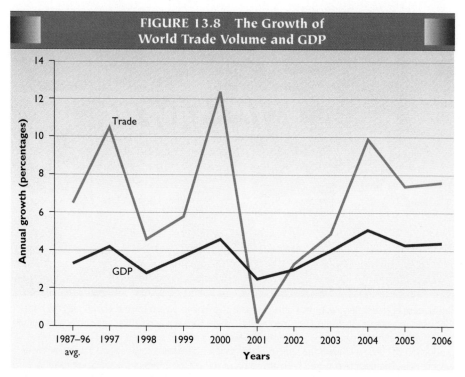

FIGURE 13.8   The Growth of World Trade Volume and GDP

World trade grows faster than the world's collective GDP almost every year. This means that trade expansion is responsible for most of the global economic expansion and the prosperity that brings to countries, their businesses, and their workers. Each year an increasing amount of the goods and services that the average country produces are exported rather than consumed domestically.

Note: Both trade and GDP growth are calculated in real dollars adjusted for inflation. Data for 2005 and 2006 are IMF estimates.

Data source: IMF (2005).

Benefits of Specialization   One long-standing economic theory holds that all countries will benefit if each sells what it can produce most efficiently. Among those who have propounded this idea are English economists David Ricardo in *On the Principles of Political Economy and Taxation* (1817) and John Stuart Mill in *Principles of Political Economy* (1848). Ricardo developed the theory of "competitive advantage," which held that everyone would benefit if each country produced and exported its most cost-efficient products. Based on this view, Mill argued that trade's "advantage consists in a more efficient employment of the productive forces of the world."

The Cost of Protectionism   Protecting jobs from foreign imports has a tremendous emotional appeal, but most economists argue that trade barriers result in higher prices because tariff costs are passed on to consumers or because consumers are forced to buy more expensive domestically produced goods. The U.S. Federal Reserve Bank argues that "protectionism is pure poison for an economy" and estimates that each American job that is saved by protectionism costs an average of $231,289, with an overall cost of nearly $100 billion annually to U.S. consumers.[27] How does a protected job cost over $200,000? The cost includes not just the higher price of the protected items but downstream products as well. For example, protecting sugar not only raises its price to consumers, it also raises prices of candy, soft drinks, and many

Tariffs, quotas and other trade restraints can be a two-edged sword for the economies they are supposed to protect. Such measures protect U.S. sugar growers and refiners, but they also put all the Americans in this picture out of work. The high cost of U.S. sugar led Kraft Foods to shift production of LifeSavers from the United States to Canada, where sugar sells at the much lower world price. The people pictured here are some of the 600 workers at the LifeSaver plant in Holland, Michigan, who were laid off when, after 60 years, the plant closed in 2003. Wrigley, Brach, Fannie Farmer, and other well-known U.S. candy and gum makers have also closed some or all their U.S. plants and moved production abroad.

other products. The higher price of candy also exposes that industry and its jobs to foreign competition. LifeSavers, Jaw Breakers, and Red Hots used to be made in the Chicago area. Now they are produced in Canada using cheaper sugar, and Chicago has lost half its candy manufacturing jobs since 1970. These wages are lost, unemployment compensation is paid, and the rippling costs add up higher and higher.

Promotion of Competition   A third contention by economic internationalists is that free economic interchange promotes beneficial competition. Without foreign competition, the argument goes, domestic manufacturers have a captive market, which can have a variety of ill effects, such as price fixing and lack of innovation. For example, American automakers did not begin to offer U.S. consumers well-built, inexpensive, fuel-efficient small cars until pressure from foreign competition forced them to reshape their product and modernize their production techniques.

Providing Development Capital   Fourth, economic internationalists maintain that free economic interchange increases the flow of investment capital to the LDCs. The IMF calculates that between 1997 and 2005 alone, a net $1.3 trillion (investments minus withdrawals) foreign direct investment (FDI) flowed into the LDCs to bolster their economic development. FDI also benefits EDCs. It is also the case that MNC-directed investments provide EDCs with a wide variety of economic benefits. Jobs are one example. Foreign-owned MNCs employ 6.3 million people in the United States, pay them $350 billion a year, and contribute tens of billions of dollars in U.S. federal, state, and local taxes.

Noneconomic Advantages

Arguably, there are also several noneconomic advantages to economic internationalism. These include advancing world cooperation, inhibiting conflict, and promoting democracy.

World Cooperation   A fifth, and this time political, argument made by economic internationalists is that free economic interchange promotes world cooperation. The logic is that if countries can trade together in peace, their interactions will bring greater contact and understanding. Cooperation will then become the rule rather than the exception, and this, it is thought, will lead to political cooperation and interaction. The move toward the political integration of Europe, which began with economic cooperation, is the most frequently cited example.

Decreased Violence   A sixth, and again political, argument for free economic interchange is that it restrains conflict by promoting interdependence, which makes fighting more difficult and more unlikely (McDonald, 2004; Pevehouse, 2004). In the words of one study, "Higher levels of economically important trade . . . are associated with lower incidences of militarized interstate disputes and war" (Oneal & Russett, 1997:288). One link between peace and trade is the contention that a high degree of interdependence among countries may dissuade or even prevent them from fighting. If oil and iron are necessary to fight, and if Country A supplies Country B's oil, and B supplies A's iron, then they are too enmeshed to go to war.

ANALYZE THE ISSUE
International Economic
Cooperation

A related argument is that the North will be more secure as the South achieves prosperity. This view contends that the poor are becoming increasingly hostile toward the wealthy. Modern communications have heightened the South's sense of relative deprivation—the awareness of a deprived person (group, country) of the gap between his or her circumstances and the relatively better position of others. Research shows that seeing another's prosperity and knowing that there are alternatives to your own impoverished condition causes frustration and a sense of being cheated, often leading to resentment and sometimes to violence. Perhaps it was the 9/11 attacks that provided the wake-up call, but when world leaders met in Monterrey, Mexico, in 2002 to discuss LDC development, a constant theme was the connection between poverty and violence (Li & Schaub, 2004). "Poverty in all its forms is the greatest single threat to peace [and] security," the head of the WTO told delegates.[28] Similarly, UN Secretary-General Kofi Annan has warned, "Left alone in their poverty, [very poor] countries are all too likely to collapse or relapse into conflict and anarchy, a menace to their neighbors and potentially, as the events of the 11th of September so brutally reminded us, a threat to global security."[29]

Promoting Democracy   A seventh, and once more political, argument advanced by some economic internationalists is that the openness required for free economic exchange promotes democracy. The idea is that it is difficult to simultaneously have a free enterprise system and an authoritarian political system. Gradually the habits of independent decision making inherent in a capitalist system, the flow of ideas within the country and between it and the outside world, and the growth of powerful financial interests all work to undercut the authoritarian political regimes. For example, during the past few years, such newly industrializing countries as Mexico, South Korea, and Taiwan have had their first truly democratic elections either ever, or in many decades. Particularly appealing is the thought that globalization will eventually moderate China's authoritarian government. According to one analyst, "Global markets and information technology are multiplying the channels through which outside actors can influence Chinese society and, simultaneously, undermining the regime's strict control" (Moore, 2001:63; Li & Reuveny, 2003).

The Case for Economic Nationalism

There are also several political and economic arguments for economic nationalism. Some of these involve trade or some other single aspect of international economic exchange; other arguments are more general.

Economic Advantages

Economic nationalists advance a number of economic arguments to support their position. These include the benefits of protecting the domestic economy, diversification, and compensating for existing distortions.

Protecting the Domestic Economy The need for economic barriers to protect threatened domestic industries and workers from foreign competition is a favorite theme of economic nationalists. "I'm not a free trader," a U.S. secretary of commerce once confessed. "The goal," he said, "is to nurture American workers and industry. It is not to adhere to some kind of strict ideology."[30] An associated argument seeks protection for new or still small, so-called infant industries. This is an especially common contention in LDCs trying to industrialize, but it is also heard worldwide. Many economists give the idea of such protection some credibility, at least in the short term.

Economic nationalists also argue that the positive impact of creation or preservation of jobs by the inflow of investment is offset by the loss of jobs when MNCs move operations to another country or when MNCs create new jobs in another country rather than in their own home country. American MNCs, for example, employ about 1.9 million more workers in other countries than foreign MNCs employ American workers in the United States. Furthermore, these opponents say, forcing well-paid workers in the United States and elsewhere to compete with poorly paid workers in LDCs depresses the wages and living conditions in EDCs in what they call "a race to the bottom." The U.S. clothing industries, for example, have been devastated, with their combined workforce dropping 57% from 2.1 million in 1980 to 900,000 in 2003.

Lost jobs and wages must also be measured in terms of the ripple effect that multiplies each dollar several times. A worker without a job cannot buy from the local merchant, who in turn cannot buy from the building contractor, who in turn cannot buy from the department store, and so on, rippling out through the economy. Displaced workers also collect unemployment benefits and may even wind up on public assistance programs. These costs are substantial and diminish the gains derived from free trade. Finally, there is the psychological damage from being laid off and from other forms of economic dislocation that cannot be measured in dollars and cents.

Diversification Another economic nationalist argument holds that economic diversification should be encouraged. Specialization, it is said, will make a country too dependent on a few resources or products; if demand for those products falls, then economic catastrophe will result. In reality, no modern, complex economy will become that specialized, but the argument does have simplistic appeal.

Compensating for Existing Distortions Yet another economic nationalist argument is that protectionism and other trade distortions continue, and that nice-guy free-

Economic nationalists argue that tariffs, quotas, and other trade tools can be used to rectify the abuses of other countries. China is a leading target for many U.S. economic nationalists, who argue that sanctions should be imposed on Chinese exports to the United States. This picture shows Chinese vendors with pirated Microsoft Windows software for sale in Beijing for as little as 10 yuan (83 cents). American economic nationalists criticize China for saying it cannot control software piracy at the same time it successfully suppresses political dissent.

traders will finish last when faced with such realities as cartels that set petroleum prices and governments that use tariffs, subsidies, currency manipulation, and other techniques to benefit themselves at our expense. As an example, take the issue raised in chapter 12 of China's refusal to substantially revalue its artificially low currency, the yuan, against the dollar. The economic nationalist argument is that the United States should retaliate against China by raising tariffs and setting quotas or even embargos on Chinese goods (Shambaugh, 2004).

Putting Domestic Needs First   According to economic nationalists, citizens forge a government and support it to look after their welfare and safety, not to lead idealistic quests to solve other people's problems. From this perspective, the amounts of funding recommended by the UN and other development advocates are prohibitive. It would cost the EDCs nearly $200 billion extra a year to increase foreign aid to the recommended level of 0.7% of their GNPs. Debt forgiveness, trade concessions, and other financial measures would add to the annual expenses. With most EDCs already running annual budget deficits, the added funds would mean higher taxes for their people, fewer social programs for them, or larger deficits.

Noneconomic Advantages

Economic nationalists also argue that their perspective protects national sovereignty, enhances national security, and permits the beneficial use of their country's economic power as a policy tool. There is an additional argument that globalization is harming the welfare of many individuals and also increasing damage to the environment.

National Sovereignty   One of the fastest-growing sources of sentiment against globalization is the belief of many people that the process is eroding their country's national sovereignty. Many people are shocked to find that sometimes their country's laws and regulations must give way when they clash with rules of the WTO or some other international organization or agreement.

A closely related phenomenon involves the fear that foreign investors will gain control of your country's economy and will be able to influence your political processes and your culture. In the late 1980s the value of the dollar plunged and set off a feeding frenzy of acquisition as foreign investors snapped up such quintessential American brand names as Capitol Records (Great Britain), Roy Rogers (Canada), Alka-Seltzer (Germany), and 7–Eleven (Japan). Cries rang out that the British, among others, were coming. One member of Congress fretted that "for the first time since the Revolution, Americans are being subjected to decisions and dictates from abroad."[31] In time, the flow of FDI reversed itself, and American acquisitions abroad once again outpaced foreign buying of U.S. companies and other assets. But American sensitivities are now rising anew, this time in response to the recent bids by Chinese investors to take control of such brand names as Maytag, RCA, and IBM's personal computer line.

National Security   A related economic nationalist argument involves national defense. The contention is somewhat the reverse of the "conflict inhibition," pro–free trade argument made earlier. Protectionists stress that the country must not become so dependent on foreign sources that it will be unable to defend itself. In recent years, the U.S. government has acted to protect industries ranging from specialty steels to basic textiles, partly in response to warnings that the country was losing its ability to produce weapons systems and uniforms. Economic nationalists also warn of the dangers of unchecked FDI acquisitions by foreign investors. A Chinese company's bid to take control of the major U.S. oil company Unocal sparked the warning from one analyst that, "Clearly, in today's China, we are up against a country that has a strategy to acquire U.S. critical technology companies. If we continue to ignore it—let alone enable it by acquiescing to the sale of companies like Unocal—we will do so at our peril."[32] Many Americans agreed, and the ensuing uproar in the United States ultimately persuaded the Chinese company to withdraw its bid to acquire Unocal.

Also under the rubric of national security, there is the issue of what can be called strategic trade. The question is how far a country should go in restricting trade and other economic interchanges with countries that are or may become hostile. Currently, the primary focus of the strategic trade debate is on dual-use technology that has peaceful uses but also has military applications. Here too, China is the cause of the greatest current concern. The export of U.S. computers and other high-tech items to China has led one staff member in Congress to worry that there has been a serious undermining of U.S. national security due to relaxed restrictions on export of "dual-use technologies," and that "The Chinese threat of a 'high-tech Pearl Harbor' is well within their reach."[33]

Policy Tool   Yet another economic nationalist argument maintains that trade "follows the flag" (Keshk, Pollins, & Reuveny, 2004). This means that politics determines economic relations, more than the other way around, and that trade is a powerful political tool that can be used to further a country's interests. The extension or withdrawal of trade and other economic benefits also has an important—albeit hard-to-measure—symbolic value. Clearly, economic tools can be used to promote a country's political goals, and free economic interchange necessarily limits the availability of economic tools to pursue policy. A current example is the U.S. embargo on most trade with and travel to Cuba, which has existed since 1960. It is justified, President Bush has argued, because "Well-intentioned ideas about trade will merely prop up this dictator, enrich his cronies, and enhance the totalitarian regime"[34]

Social and Environmental Protection   The chairman of Dow Chemical Company once confessed, "I have long dreamed of buying an island owned by no nation and establishing the world headquarters of the Dow company on . . . such an island, beholden to no nation or society" (Gruenberg, 1996:339). Critics of MNCs claim that such statements confirm their suspicions that these global enterprises use their ability to move operations around the globe to undercut protections relating to child labor, minimum wages, and many other socioeconomic standards and also to escape environmental regulations. In the estimate of one analyst, "National governments have lost much of their power to direct their own economies because of the power of capital to pick up and leave." The result of the "quantum leap in the ability of transnational corporations to relocate their facilities around the world," he continues, is to make "all workers, communities and countries competitors for these corporations' favor." This competition, he worries, has set off "a 'race to the bottom' in which wages and social and environment conditions tend to fall to the level of the most desperate" (Brecher, 1993:685).

Critics of globalization also charge that, among other evils, the race to the bottom will mean gutting desirable social programs. Europe has built an extensive social welfare support system through government programs and mandates on industries (such as health insurance for workers, paid vacations, and other benefits). Such programs and benefits are costly, however, and European economies struggle to meet them while also keeping the price of their products low enough to be competitive in world markets or even at home compared to imported goods and services. Similarly, critics worry that countries that attempt to maintain high standards of environmental protection or institute new safeguards will be penalized by companies moving their production facilities and jobs elsewhere.

The Globalization Debate in Perspective

To return to the point with which we began this section, the clash between the forces of economic internationalism and those of economic nationalism will be one of the most pivotal struggles in the years ahead (Helleiner & Pickel, 2005). The rapid globalization process that began after World War II has brought the world much closer to a truly global economy than seemed possible not long ago. The EDCs have generally prospered, and even most of the LDCs have improved their health, education, and many other social conditions. Moreover, globalization enjoys substantial public support worldwide, as Figure 13.9 shows.

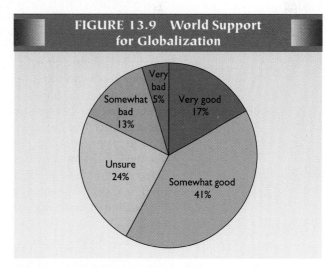

FIGURE 13.9   World Support for Globalization

Support for globalization is broad but somewhat tentative, according to a survey of people in 44 countries around the world. When asked, "Do you think globalization is a very good thing, somewhat good, somewhat bad, or a very bad thing?" 58% of the respondents chose one of the good replies and only 18% chose one of the bad options. From another perspective, though, only 17% of those surveyed gave globalization their unqualified blessing, while 65% thought it was only somewhat good or were unsure.

Data source: Pew Research Center for People and the Press, *Global Attitudes Project* (2002). Calculations by author.

WRITE THE POLICY SCRIPT

Economic Nationalism or Economic Internationalism?

Economic internationalists favor few restrictions on free trade and investment. They believe that a mostly unfettered flow of goods, services, and capital will, in the long term, advance the prosperity of all countries. Economic nationalists disagree. They see the international economy as a generally zero-sum game in which prosperity of some often comes at the expense of others. Therefore, economic nationalists believe that restrictions are often warranted to protect their country's economy and to advance its political interests.

You can test where you stand by deciding on three U.S. economic policy issues discussed in this chapter. One involves the continuation of the long-standing economic embargo on Cuba. The second is the U.S. membership in the Central American Free Trade Association (CAFTA), which the Senate supported by a vote of 54 to 45 and the House consented to by a razor-thin vote of 217 to 215. The third

involves various resolutions introduced in Congress that helped block the acquisition of the U.S. energy company, Unocal, by Chinese investors.

What Do You Think?

Assume that you are a member of Congress facing votes today on three issues. For each issue, a yea vote casts you as an economic internationalist; a nay vote aligns you with the economic nationalists. Cast your vote!

	Yea	Nay
Repeal the embargo on Cuba	____	____
Approve U.S. membership in CAFTA	____	____
Permit Chinese acquisition of Unocal	____	____

The advances that globalization has made and general support for it does not mean, however, that it is an unmitigated success. The changes associated with globalization have occurred in a largely unregulated international system, and, as a result, the benefits and costs that accompany most change have been unequally distributed. Other countries, their citizens, and even many people in prosperous countries have either not benefited or have been harmed. This has left the global public somewhat cautious about globalization, as Figure 13.9 can also be interpreted (Kaltenthaler, Gelleny & Ceccoli, 2004).

For here the key question is not the world's opinion, but yours. Should globalization proceed or be halted? You can also take the position that globalization is good in theory, but the practice so far has been unsatisfactory and needs to be reformed. If that is your view, what would you do to make globalization a positive process? Of course, answering such questions in the abstract and responding to them in a specific situation are not quite the same, so the decision box, "Economic Nationalism or Economic Internationalism?" asks you to make some policy choices.

Chapter Summary

Economic Cooperation and Development: Background and Requirements

1. This chapter assesses the alternative route of economic nationalism and focuses on the approach advocated by economic internationalists and struc-

turalists, which stresses global economic cooperation with a particular emphasis on the economic development of the South.

2. The idea of creating global interdependence based on free economic interchange and cooperation for

the economic good of all dates back several hundred years, but it did not begin to significantly shape international economic relations until about 60 years ago.

3. There has been considerable improvement in the socioeconomic development of the South, but those positive indications should not obscure other, more distressing realities in many LDCs.

4. To modernize their economies, the LDCs need to get more development capital, the four main sources of which are loans, investment, trade, and aid. Unfortunately, there are limitations and drawbacks to each. The South also needs to undertake internal reforms.

Economic Cooperation and Development: The Institutions

5. Numerous IGOs and international programs focus on economic cooperation, and most give the development of the South top priority. The largest general IGO, the UN, maintains a number of efforts aimed at general economic development, with an emphasis on the less developed countries (LDCs).

6. The IMF is the primary IGO dedicated to stabilizing the world's monetary system. The IMF's primary role in recent years has been to assist LDCs by stabilizing their currencies and reducing their foreign debt. There is, however, considerable controversy over how the IMF is run and the conditions it attaches to its loans.

7. The World Bank Group is the best known of the IGOs that provide developmental loans and grants to LDC. Like the IMF, there is controversy about the governance of the World Bank and its policies.

8. The are two main economic organizations associated with the North, the OECD and the G-8, but they also devote considerable attention to LDC development.

Regional Economic Cooperation and Development

9. In addition to the activity promoting economic cooperation and development at the global level, there are also important efforts under way at the regional level. The most important of these is the expansion in the number and size of regional trade organizations.

10. Receiving particular attention here are NAFTA, the FTAA, and Mercosur in the Western Hemisphere; ASEAN and APEC in the Asia-Pacific Region. The EU in Europe is detailed in chapter 7, and other RTOs are of less significance.

11. There is disagreement whether the growth in the number and membership of regional trade organizations and the establishment of other forms of preferential trade agreements is a positive or negative development for global economic cooperation, and, by extension, cooperation in other areas.

Cooperation and Development: Debating the Future

12. There are significant arguments on both sides of the question of whether or not to continue to expand economic globalization, including advancing both free international economic interchange and LDC development. Economic internationalists advance a series of economic and noneconomic arguments in support of their view. Economic nationalists counter with their own set of economic and noneconomic contentions.

For simulations, debates, and other interactive activities, a chapter quiz, Web Links, PowerWeb articles, and much more, visit **www.mhhe.com/rourke11/** and go to chapter 13. Or, while accessing the site, click on Course-Wide Content and view recent international relations articles in the *New York Times*.

Key Terms

Asia-Pacific Economic
 Cooperation
 (APEC)
Association of Southeast
 Asian Nations
 (ASEAN)
bilateral aid
conditionality
debt service
Development Assistance
 Committee (DAC)
development capital
Doha Round

Free Trade Area of the
 Americas (FTAA)
General Agreement on
 Tariffs and Trade
 (GATT)
Group of 77 (G-77)
Group of 8 (G-8)
hard currency
interdependence
International Conference
 on Financing for
 Development
 (ICFD)

International Monetary
 Fund (IMF)
multilateral aid
North American Free
 Trade Agreement
 (NAFTA)
Organization for
 Economic Cooperation
 and Development
 (OECD)
regional trade
 organizations
 (RTOs)

Southern Common
 Market (Mercosur)
special drawing rights
 (SDRs)
UN Conference on Trade
 and Development
 (UNCTAD)
UN Development
 Programme (UNDP)
Uruguay Round
World Bank Group
World Trade
 Organization (WTO)

Preserving and Enhancing Human Rights and Dignity

The sun with one eye vieweth all the world.
—William Shakespeare, *Henry VI, Part I*

And your true rights be term'd a poet's rage.
—William Shakespeare, "Sonnet XVII"

This woman in India and many others argue that human rights are universal: the same for everyone, everywhere. Others contend that human rights are based in culture and can vary across the world. Ask yourself which view you support as you begin this chapter, and then see if your stance changes after you have finished reading the chapter.

NDIVIDUALS AND GROUPS suffering human rights abuses or whole segments of humanity living in conditions so deplorable that they violate what is arguably the human right to live in dignity are travesties that have existed throughout history and continue today. What is new is a rising global consciousness of such travesties, a condemnation of them, and a resolve to ease the suffering of the oppressed. That is what this chapter is about. We will begin by looking at the nature of human rights, then turn to areas of concern and what is being done at the international level to improve conditions.

Unlike chapters 4 through 13, which contrast the traditional and alternative approaches in successive chapters, this chapter includes both the traditional approach and the alternative approach to human rights. On the international level, the traditional approach to human rights abuses in other countries has usually been to ignore them or at best to denounce them but do nothing to alleviate the situation. There are two main reasons for this traditional approach. One is the legal concept of sovereignty that is so ingrained in the traditional international system. Sovereignty gives countries absolute control over what happens within their borders. Since most human rights violations occur within state borders they have been traditionally seen as a domestic affair and no one else's business. Second, nationalism has created a we–they complex, as discussed in chapter 4. To a significant degree, our sense of responsibility and even of human caring is much greater for members of our we-group, our nation, than for people of other nations, the they-groups. Thus, traditionally, if members of a they-group were suffering, well, that was a shame, but really not something we should be obligated to address.

While this traditional approach to human rights continues as the dominant modality of international politics, things are beginning to change slowly to provide an alternative approach. Technology is one factor. There is a much more extensive and graphic detailing of human rights through television and the Internet. Hearing and reading about human rights abuses do not have anywhere near the emotional impact of seeing images of torture, rape, and other abuses in vivid color on the television screens and computer monitors in the intimate surroundings of our family rooms and bedrooms. Such images are harder to ignore than the reporting in other media, and have added to slowly changing attitudes about abuses. The World War II era was an important turning point. Shocked by the Holocaust, the horrendous treatment of the Chinese, Koreans, and others by the Japanese, and other horrific abuses of human rights, the victorious nations of the world proclaimed in the Preamble to the United Nations Charter that they were establishing the new IGO in part, "To reaffirm faith in fundamental human rights, in the dignity and worth of the human person, [and] in equal rights of men and women." It is easy to dismiss such words as mere lofty rhetoric, and, in truth, the "talk" has been far greater than the "action."

Yet it is also the case, as we shall see, that real changes have begun to take hold. Human rights are now "on the table" in diplomatic discussions within international governmental organizations (IGOs) and among countries, and there are hundreds, perhaps thousands, of international nongovernmental organizations (NGOs) whose focus is promoting human rights. More importantly, the international community is sometimes taking action. To preview the many instances of action that are discussed below, the former president of Yugoslavia is on trial before an international tribunal for abusing human rights and other crimes, and UN peacekeepers are in the Darfur region of Sudan trying to protect the population from marauding militia backed by the government in Khartoum. Such prescriptive steps remain a minor theme relative to the still dominant traditional approach of remaining on the sidelines, but a start down an alternative path has been made.

MAP
Human Rights: Political Rights and Civil Liberties

Web Link

For links to a wide variety of human rights–oriented organizations and material go to the "Human Rights, Globalization and Disaster Relief" page of the Human Rights Interactive Network at **www.webcom .com/hrin/**.

The Nature of Human Rights

Before moving to a detailed discussion of human rights, it is important to explain the broad concept of human rights used here and also some of the controversies in defining human rights. This will entail discussions of proscriptive and prescriptive rights, universal and culture-based rights, and individual and community rights.

Proscriptive and Prescriptive Human Rights

We are generally used to thinking about human rights in terms of freedom from specific abuses or restrictions that are proscribed (forbidden). Most commonly, certain actions by governments are proscribed. The U.S. Bill of Rights, for example, prohibits (except in extreme cases) the government from abridging individual Americans' rights to exercise their religion or free speech and from committing a variety of other abuses. **Proscriptive rights** also include those things that the government cannot do to groups, such as discriminate based on race, ethnicity, gender, or other inherent demographic characteristics. The obligation to respect many of these proscriptive rights also extends to private individuals and organizations. For instance, employers in the United States may not decide to hire only white males. Such rights are also called negative rights, because they negate the legitimacy of actions by governments and others.

Many people believe that beyond proscriptive rights, humans are entitled to enjoy a range of **prescriptive rights**. They include the basic necessities that a government is arguably prescribed (obligated) to try to provide in order to assure certain qualitative standards of life for everyone in the community. By the standard of prescriptive rights, every person has the right to exist in at least tolerable conditions. Among these are receiving adequate education, nutrition, housing, sanitation, health care, and the other basics necessary to live with dignity and security and to be a productive individual. Whether society is defined in narrow national terms or broader global terms is a matter of controversy. Such rights are also called positive rights because they place a positive obligation on societies and their governments to ensure they are met.

Whatever the focus, though, one scholar suggests that the most fruitful way to think about human rights is to begin with the idea that "ultimately they are supposed to serve basic human needs." These basic human needs, which generate corresponding rights, include, among others (Galtung, 1994:3, 72):

- "Survival needs—to avoid violence": The requisite to avoid and the right to be free from individual and collective violence.
- "Well-being needs—to avoid misery": The right to adequate nutrition and water; to movement, sleep, sex, and other biological wants; to protection from diseases and from adverse climatological and environmental impacts.
- "Identity needs—to avoid alienation": The right to self-expression; to realize your potential, to establish and maintain emotional bonds with others; to preserve cultural heritage and association; to contribute through work and other activity; and to receive information about and maintain contact with nature, global humanity, and other aspects of the biosphere.
- "Freedom needs—to avoid repression": The right to receive and express opinions, to assemble with others, to have a say in common policy; and to choose in such wide-ranging matters as jobs, spouses, where to live, and lifestyle.

The degree to which proscriptive and prescriptive rights should be used as a standard to judge countries is increasingly being debated internationally. For example, the United States, which emphasizes proscriptive rights, regularly criticizes China for a wide range of rights abuses. Typically, a U.S. State Department annual review of global human rights characterized China as an "authoritarian state" whose "human rights record throughout the year remained poor" on such matters as freedom of speech and religion.[1] China countered by accusing the United States of violating prescriptive human rights. "Human rights protection provided by the U.S. Constitution is very limited," a Chinese government report asserted. It noted, for instance, that in the United States there is no right to "food, clothing, shelter, education, work, rest, and reasonable payment."[2]

One source of differing views about prescriptive and proscriptive rights can be traced to how much a society believes that individual success or failure is based on each person's effort or outside forces such as that person's place in society. Americans and Canadians have a much stronger sense that individuals are responsible for their own personal success and other conditions than do people elsewhere in the world. One survey found, for example, that 65% of Americans disagreed with the statement, "Success in life is pretty much determined by forces outside our control," with only 32% agreeing and 3% unsure. The percentages for Canadians were almost identical. By contrast, in 44 other countries worldwide the combined percentages came close to being reversed. On average, only 35% of the respondents in those countries disagreed, with 58% agreeing and 7% unsure. The percentages broken down for different geographical groups are presented in Figure 14.1. Given the differences, it is hardly surprising that there are different views of prescriptive and proscriptive liberty. This became apparent in a survey that asked people in the United States, four Western European countries, and five Eastern European countries which they thought more important for a government to do: (1) follow the proscriptive liberty standard of not interfering in people's freedom to pursue their goals, or (2) adhere to the prescriptive liberty standard of acting to ensure that no one in the society is in need. Among Americans, 58% favored the proscriptive liberty approach. Only 33% of Western Europeans and 29% of Eastern Europeans took this view. Instead, 59% of Western Europeans and 60% of Eastern Europeans (compared to 33% of Americans) favored the prescriptive liberty approach (with the remainder of each group unsure).[3]

As you read the balance of this chapter, think about how you feel about proscriptive rights and prescriptive rights. What proscriptive rights, "freedoms from" specific abuses do you possess? Also ponder prescriptive rights. Doing so is more challenging because they are probably less familiar to you and whether they even exist is debatable. The ultimate question, which is posed in a decision box at the end of the chapter, is what rights you would include and exclude in a global bill of rights.

Universal and Culture-Based Rights

Scholars generally agree that a right is a justified claim to something. To say, for instance, that you have a right to freedom of religion means you have a legitimate claim to believe whatever you wish. However, a key question is what justifies claiming a right. Where does it come from? As noted in chapter 9, there are two schools of thought about where rights originate.

The Source of Rights

Universalists believe that all humans possess the same rights and that they are immutable. This perspective begins with the idea that rights originate from outside a

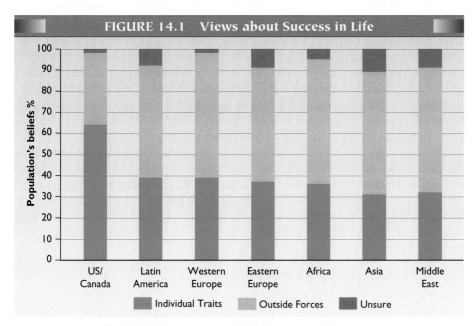

FIGURE 14.1   Views about Success in Life

Population's beliefs % (y-axis, 0 to 100)

Categories (x-axis): US/Canada, Latin America, Western Europe, Eastern Europe, Africa, Asia, Middle East

Legend: Individual Traits | Outside Forces | Unsure

One determinant of how a society perceives prescriptive and proscriptive rights is based on how it feels about success. People in some countries emphasize the importance of individual talent and effort in achieving success rather than the influence of outside forces, such as what country a person is born in, or whether a person is a member of a privileged or disadvantaged demographic group in their country. Americans and Canadians are much more likely than people elsewhere to attribute success to individual characteristics. Indeed, it is interesting to note in this chart that the percentage of people believing that outside forces pretty much control success is fairly consistent across geographic areas, except for the United States and Canada, which on average have percentages almost exactly opposite of everyone else.

Note: The question was whether or not people agreed that "Success in life is pretty much determined by forces outside our control." For clarity, the "agree" answer is labeled "outside forces," and the "disagree" answer is labeled "individual traits."
Data source: The Pew Research Center for People and the Press, "Views of a Changing World, 2003," June 2003.

society. Among the possible external sources, theology leads many universalists to believe that rights are granted by a deity and therefore may not be transgressed by humans. A second external source is the very nature of human existence. Universalists who believe in natural rights contend that people inherently possess such rights as the right to life, which may not be legitimately abridged. Whatever the specific source, those who contend that rights originate outside a society and transcend it are called universalists.

Relativists contend that rights are relative to culture. That is, rights are the product of a society's contemporary values. Relativists therefore assert that in a world of diverse cultures, no single standard of human rights exists or is likely to exist short of the world becoming completely homogenized culturally. The cultural relativist point of view also means that rights are not timeless; they can change with changing social norms.

To see the difference between the two views of rights, consider capital punishment. Whether they cite the theological commandment, "Thou shalt not kill," the natural right to life, or some other external source, many universalists believe that the death penalty is an abomination that violates the human rights of the executed individual. Universalists would note that about two-thirds of all countries have either abolished the death penalty or have not used it in so long that it has been de

WEB POLL
The Sources of Human Rights:
Are You a Universalist or
a Cultural Relativist?

MAP
Capital Punishment

facto abolished. Moreover, in 2004, only 25 countries executed anyone, and four of these countries accounted for 97% of the estimated 3,797 executions. China, with about 3,400 executions, accounted for by far the most. It was followed by Iran (159), Vietnam (64), and the United States (59). Relativists would reply that the legitimacy of executing criminals after judicial due process is based on the cultural beliefs of their people reflected in the policy of their government. To support their case, relativists might point, for instance, to a 2005 survey in which 70% of American respondents expressed the belief that capital punishment is "morally acceptable," compared to 25% who held it be "morally unacceptable," and 5% who were uncertain.[4] Such disagreements over whether a right is universal or culturally relative are not simply abstract arguments. One political repercussion is that numerous countries refuse to extradite accused individuals to a country if they might be sentenced to death. Such stands includes a number of statements from countries, such as Belgium, that they will not extradite terrorist suspects to the United States unless given assurance that they will not be executed.

Applying Universalism and Relativism

Given the differences in perspective between cultures, the question arises as to whether it is reasonable to try to apply human rights standards to international relations. Relativists contend that trying to impose human rights standards on the world stage constitutes **cultural imperialism**. Advocates of this view are apt to note that the prevailing definitions of human rights substantially reflect the values of the dominant Western powers and are much less attuned to some of the beliefs of Asian, African, and other societies. One American scholar writes, for instance, "We must understand and learn from other traditions while seeing them as historically conditioned—and this includes our own tradition. What we must not do . . . is elevate our own tradition to the status of 'universalism.' This is just rehashed cultural imperialism and has its roots in the dogmatic religious outlooks of the past and present." In sum, he argues, "We should realize that we create our own values, reacting to the times and climes, and rational people can disagree on what these values are."[5]

Others reject such claims of cultural imperialism as poor attempts to justify the unjustifiable. They argue that the nature of humankind is not based on culture, and, therefore, human rights are universal (Donnelly, 2003). President Chandrika Kumaratunga of Sri Lanka, for one, has expressed the opinion that "of course, every country has its own national ethos, but . . . when people talk about a conflict of values, I think it is an excuse that can be used to cover a multitude of sins" (Franck, 1997:627). Seconding this view, Secretary-General Kofi Annan told an audience in Iran, there is "talk of human rights being a Western concept, . . . [but] don't we all suffer from the lack of the rule of law and from arbitrariness? What is foreign about that? What is Western about that? And when we talk of the right [of people] . . . to live their lives to the fullest and to be able to live their dreams, it is universal."[6]

Individual and Community Rights

An issue closely related to the debate over cultural relativism is the controversy over the respective rights of individuals and society. Imagine a scale that ranges, on one end, from **individualism**, a value system in which the rights of an individual are more important than those of the society to, at the other end, **communitarianism**, a value system in which the good of the community takes precedence over the good of the individual. Western states would generally fall toward the individualistic end of the scale; non-Western states would generally fall farther toward the communitarian end of the scale. Singapore, for example, does not extend all the "Miranda rights" and other legal protections given to suspects in the United States. Singapore also imposes punishment that Americans might think is "cruel and unusual," including the extremely painful caning of a convict's bared buttocks with a rattan cane for about 30 crimes ranging from attempted murder through vandalism. To defend their position, Singapore officials point to the fact that people there are threatened by a vastly lower crime rate than found in most major U.S. cities. "We believe that the legal system must give maximum protection to the majority of our people. We make no apology for clearly tilting our laws and policy in favor of the majority."[7]

Proscriptive Human Rights

Most rights that societies and their states extend (the relativist view) or recognize as inherent (the universalist view) are proscriptive rights that prohibit the government and often others (such as organizations and companies) from doing certain things. Although they overlap, these rights can be subdivided into individual rights, such as freedom of speech and assembly, and group rights, which involve prohibitions against discriminating against categories of people based on ethnicity, gender, race, and other such "in-born" factors. These are often thought of as civil rights.

Rights are abused for many reasons. For example, oppression of individual rights often comes at the hands of dictators, who violate them by arbitrarily arresting and punishing people; by depriving them of their property without the due process of law; and by abridging their freedom to freely speak, organize, travel, and associate with other individuals and groups.

As for group rights, whether the focus is race, ethnicity, gender, sexual orientation, religious choice, or some other trait, there are few human characteristics or beliefs that have not been the target of discrimination and abuse somewhere in the world. One important cause, as discussed in chapter 4, is the "we–they" sense of group identification often associated with nationalism. This leads people to value the group they identify with and to see those in other ("they") groups as different. Too frequently, different does not mean "I'm OK, you're OK," but instead means that you are inferior and someone to be feared or oppressed. Evidence of such attitudes extends as far back into history as we can see. Genocide is a modern term, but the practice is ancient. The Roman philosopher and statesman Seneca (ca. 8 B.C.–A.D. 65) wrote in *Epistles* that Romans were "mad, not only individually, but nationally" because punished "manslaughter and isolated murders" while accepting "the much vaunted crime of slaughtering whole peoples."

Other sources of discrimination and abuse of groups within a society or across borders come from any one or a combination of feelings of superiority, lack of tolerance, or lack of concern. For example, the status of women has always been determined in significant part by the traditional assumption of most men and even many women that male dominance is natural. The reasoning, Plato explained in *The Republic*, is that men are the "watchdogs of the flock" and should bear the burden of conducting war and "the other duties of guardianship," whereas "in these duties the light part must fall to the women because of the weakness of their sex." The work of Charles Darwin also lent a patina of scientific theory to the practice of male dominance, based on his argument in *The Descent of Man* (1871) that "man is more courageous, pugnacious and energetic than woman, and has a more inventive genius." Darwin went on to assert that "the chief distinction in the intellectual powers of the two sexes is [shown] by man's attaining to a higher eminence, in whatever he takes up, than can woman—whether requiring deep thought, reason, or imagination, or merely the use of the senses and hands." Such attitudes are less pervasive than they once were, but they continue to exist widely, overtly or covertly, and are especially strong in some societies. This was documented in a survey's finding that approval of gender equality ranged from a high of 82% in Western countries, through 60%–65% in Asia and sub-Saharan Africa, to 55% in Muslim countries (Inglehart & Norris, 2002, 2003).

Human Rights: Problems and Progress

With some exceptions, the abuses of individual and group rights occur within countries. As such, they have traditionally been treated as domestic matters and beyond the scope of world politics. This attitude is beginning to change, and that in turn has brought international pressure on governments to respect the basic rights of their citizens.

Human Rights Problems

It is likely that you, like most of the people who read this book, live in the United States, Canada, or some other country where individual and group rights, while far from ideal, have progressed over time. Indeed, it is hard for those of us fortunate enough to live in such countries to imagine how widespread and how harsh oppression can be. Whether or not you agreed with the U.S.-led invasion of Iraq in 2003, there can be no doubt that President George Bush was correct in his 2004 State of the Union message when he asserted, "Had we failed to act . . . Iraq's torture chambers would still be filled with victims—terrified and innocent. The killing fields of Iraq—where hundreds of thousands of men and women and children vanished into the sands—would still be known only to the killers." The victims were not just individuals who opposed Saddam Hussein's regime. Whole groups were attacked with near genocidal intensity. The Sunni-dominated regime ruthlessly oppressed Shiite Muslim political activity and dealt even more harshly with the Kurds, many of whose villages were attacked with chemical weapons during the 1980s and then razed after survivors had been herded into trenches and executed by bullets to the brain. Detailing lurid tales of repression would be easy, for there are many, but perhaps it is best to turn to the data about the continuing widespread abuse of individual rights. Among other sources of evidence is one survey that ranked countries' respect for civil liberties such as freedom of religion and expression on a scale of 1 (free) to 7 (oppressive). Figure 14.2 illustrates that individual rights are still moderately to severely restricted in most of the

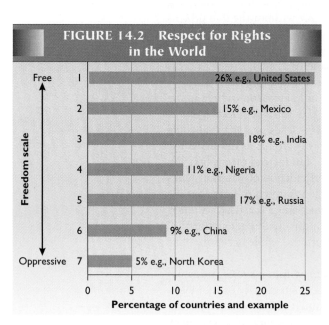

FIGURE 14.2   Respect for Rights in the World

Oppression of individual and group rights remains common. Although 41% of all countries fall into the laudable 1 and 2 categories, 31% fall into categories 5–7, which includes those countries where rights are tenuous at best and brutally abused at worst.

Notes: Percentages do not equal 100 because of rounding. Scores are based on a rating system of 1 to 7 used by Freedom House to evaluate civil liberties. An example of a country in each category is included.
Data source: Freedom House, *Freedom House Survey 2005* at http://www.freedomhouse.org/research/survey2005.htm. Calculations by author.

world's countries. Indeed, 55 countries fall at or below the seriously oppressive score of 5. It is a sad note on the travails of the Iraqi people that their country had managed to progress only from a 7 before the war to a 5 in 2004.

Human Rights Progress

It would be naive to argue that the world has even begun to come close to resolving its numerous human rights issues; it would be equally wrong to deny that a start has been made and that one aspect of globalization is the increased concern for and application of human rights principles (Cardenas, 2004; Tomuschat, 2004; Moravcsik, 2000). The way to evaluate the worth of the efforts that we are about to discuss is to judge their goals and to see them as the beginnings of a process that only a few decades ago did not exist at all. Whatever country you live in, the protection of human rights has evolved over an extended period and is still far from complete. The global community has now embarked on an effort similar to your country's effort (Hawkins, 2004). It will take time, however, and it will be controversial (Monshipouri, et al., 2003; Brysk, 2002). The UN is at the center of the international human rights effort. It has sponsored numerous human rights treaties that, along with human rights in general, are monitored by the Office of the United Nations High Commissioner on Human Rights (OHCHR). The UN Commission on Human Rights (UNCHR) is a second important UN organization. It consists of 53 member-countries elected for three-year terms by the United Nations Economic and Social Council (ECOSOC), and during its annual meetings it is often the site of clashes over human rights. For example, during the 2005 meeting, Cuba introduced a resolution criticizing the U.S. treatment of suspected terrorist prisoners at the U.S. naval base at Guantánamo Bay, and the United States sponsored resolutions condemning Cuba and a number of other countries for human rights abuses. The commission has also come under criticism for having members that are not committed to human rights. In 2001, the United States was denied the seat it had held since the commission was formed in 1947 by countries that objected to the U.S. refusal to support the International Criminal Court. The United States regained its seat in 2003, but refused to attend for a time in 2004 after Sudan was elected a member despite the well-documented atrocities occurring in its Darfur region, to which the government lent at least passive support.

Of the various UN-sponsored human rights treaties, the most far-reaching is the **Universal Declaration of Human Rights**, which was overwhelmingly adopted by the UN General Assembly in 1948. The Universal Declaration clearly supports the universalist approach, rather than the relativist approach to human rights by declaring in Article 1, "All human beings are born free and equal in dignity and rights," and by further proclaiming in Article 2, "Everyone is entitled to all the rights and freedoms set forth in this Declaration, without distinction of any kind."

Because it is not a treaty, the declaration does not directly bind countries, but its overwhelming passage makes it arguably part of the global norms. Many of the rights enunciated in the Universal Declaration are also included in two multilateral treaties: the International Covenant on Civil and Political Rights (ICCPR, 1966) and the International Covenant on Economic, Social and Cultural Rights (ICESCR, 1966). About 75% of all countries have agreed to these pacts, but there are some major exceptions. For example, China has not become a party of the ICCPR, and the United States has not ratified the ICESCR. In addition to these two basic treaties and the Universal Declaration, there are numerous other UN-sponsored covenants that address the rights of specific groups, as will be detailed below.

There are also several multilateral treaties that address specific types of abuse. Of these, the Convention against Torture and Other Cruel, Inhuman or Degrading

ANALYZE THE ISSUE
Human Rights

Web Link

The Web site of the UN High Commissioner for Human Rights is **www.ohchr.org/english/**.

The UN's Universal Declaration of Human Rights was drafted in 1948. It is the most fundamental statement of global human rights, and most countries have agreed to it. The decision box at the end of this chapter asks your view of the various clauses of the declaration and whether you would call for any changes in these clauses or make additions.

Web Link

Among the most well-known NGOs promoting human rights are Amnesty International at **www.amnesty.org/** and Human Rights Watch at **www.hrw.org/**.

ANALYZE THE ISSUE
The Rights of Our Enemies

Treatment or Punishment (1984) has drawn considerable recent attention because of confirmed and alleged abuses of prisoners by U.S. personnel in Iraq, Afghanistan, and elsewhere. The treaty, which the United States became a party to in 1994, defines torture as "any act by which severe pain or suffering, whether physical or mental, is intentionally inflicted on a person for such purposes as obtaining . . . information [or a confession]. Additionally, the treaty specifies, "No exceptional circumstances whatsoever, whether a state of war or a threat of war, internal political instability or any other public emergency, may be invoked as a justification of torture." A number of low-ranking military personnel associated with the proven abuses have been punished, but the larger issue is the tactics authorized by the Bush administration for use during questioning of suspected terrorists (see chapter 9) and whether those interrogation techniques violate the UN treaty. There are also a number of regional conventions and IGOs that supplement the principles and efforts of the UN. The best developed of these are in the European Union (EU) and include two human rights covenants and the European Court of Human Rights. Domestic courts also increasingly apply human rights law (Jayawickrama, 2003). Additionally, there are a substantial number of NGOs, such as Amnesty International and Human Rights Watch, that are concerned with a broad range of human rights. These groups work independently and in cooperation with the UN and regional organizations to further human rights. They add to the swell of information about, and criticisms of, abuses and help promote the adoption of international norms that support human rights.

Barriers to Progress on Human Rights

It would be foolish to imagine that being a party to one, some, or even all of these treaties by itself prevents a country from abusing human rights. Iraq ratified both the

ICCPR and the ICESCR in 1971, yet throughout its 33 years, Saddam Hussein's regime egregiously abused many, even most, of the rights set forth in both covenants. Indeed, the impact of such treaties, the efforts of IGOs and NGOs, and the general progress of human rights have, as noted, been mixed. One problem is sovereignty. Countries jealously guard it and reject outside criticism of their internal practices. After the United States criticized China's human rights record in 2005, Premier Wen Jiabao shot back, "No country should . . . view itself as the incarnation of human rights that can reign over other countries and give orders to the others."[8] Another barrier is political selectivity, which disposes all countries to be shocked when opponents transgress against human rights and to ignore abuses by themselves, by their allies, and by countries that they hope to influence. The United States regularly proclaims its commitment to the global spread of democracy, yet continues to support the governments of Saudi Arabia and several other unabashedly authoritarian regimes. Making matters worse, the self-proclaimed U.S. role of championing democracy and human rights was badly undercut by the disclosures of abuses inflicted on prisoners in Iraq at Abu Ghraib prison and elsewhere and on Muslim detainees at Guantánamo Bay. When the U.S. State Department issued its 2005 report on human rights and criticized numerous other countries, many of them retorted that, in essence, Americans should address their own abuses before pointing a finger at anyone else. The Russian Foreign Ministry charged that the report once again showed a "double standard" and that, "Characteristically off-screen is the ambiguous record of the United States itself." Venezuela's vice president portrayed United States as "not qualified from any point of view" to lecture others on human rights, and a Mexican official said that Washington criticizing other countries' human rights records was like "the donkey talking about long ears"—the Spanish-language equivalent of "the pot calling the kettle black."[9]

Another impediment is the claim that cultural standards are different, and, therefore, what is a human rights violation in one country is culturally acceptable in another (De Bary, 2004). A third issue is the standard of sovereignty, which continues to be used by some countries to reject outside interference in domestic abuses, and by other countries as a reason for ignoring those abuses. There are repeated signs, however, that the sovereignty defense is wearing thin. For example, when Americans were asked in late 2002 whether the record of Saddam Hussein's "human rights violations are enough to require the United Nations to support U.S. military action against Iraq," 50% replied yes, only 34% said no, and 16% were unsure.[10]

While it would be wrong to overestimate the advance of human rights, it would equally be an error not to recognize that progress has been achieved in the advancement of human rights by declarations of principle, by numerous treaties, and by the work of the UN, Amnesty International, and other IGOs and NGOs. The frequency and horror of the abuses that they highlight increasingly are penetrating the international consciousness, disconcerting the global conscience, and having a positive effect on the world stage. To see that more clearly and to also see how much remains to be done, it is appropriate to turn to the status of human rights for women, children, and several other groups.

Women's Rights

In our discussion of the status of the rights of a diversity of demographic groups, it is appropriate that we begin with the largest of all minority groups, women. The status of women has improved in recent decades, but only somewhat and slowly.

Women's Rights Problems

Economic and educational deprivations seem to pale when compared to the violence inflicted on women. They are subject to abuse during international and internal armed conflicts and to domestic abuse in their homes.

JOIN THE DEBATE
Democracy, Islam, and Iraq: Can Iraq Be Considered Truly Democratic If Women There Are Not Given the Same Rights As Men?

Political, Economic, and Social Discrimination Females constitute about half the world's population, but they are a distinct political-economic-social minority because of the wide gap in societal power and resources between women and men. Chapter 6 detailed the gap between the percentage of women in the population and in positions of political power, and this disadvantage need not be reiterated here beyond the basic statistics that only about 5% of countries are headed by women; they make up only about 8% of all national cabinet ministers, 16% of the membership of national legislatures, and about 9% of the world's judges. In a few countries women are still not allowed to vote, much less hold national office. One intriguing question is the future of Iraq. For all the horrors that occurred under Saddam Hussein, it can at least be said that in Iraq women enjoyed more equality with men than in most other Arab states. That is threatened, however, by pressure within Iraq to revert to more traditional social and legal approaches under Islamic law. Many Iraqi women are rightfully worried by such pronouncements as the statement by Iraq's Prime Minister Ibrahim al-Jaafari that, "Islam makes a woman the responsibility of her husband." He also noted that "a man is worth two women" according to the Koran, but then retreated a bit by cautioning, "We have to be careful about taking verses in isolation."[11] Would a freely elected Iraqi government that revoked the civil and political rights of Iraqi women be a democracy?

Women are also disadvantaged economically. Compared to men, women are much less likely to have a salaried job, are much less likely to hold a professional position, more likely to be illiterate, and more likely to be living below the poverty line. There is no country in the world where women wage earners make as much as men. Norway, where women average 74 cents to every dollar earned by men, is the best; in more than half of all countries the ratio is less than 50 cents to the dollar. Of all such statistics, none is more telling than the fact that women constitute approximately 70% of all those living below the poverty line in their respective countries. Women also suffer from a range of types of social discrimination. In many countries they are less likely to be literate, and even when they go to school much less likely to go on to secondary school, let alone college or technical training.

The degree of gender discrimination differs significantly among countries, with the gap between men and women generally narrower in economically developed countries (EDCs) than in less developed countries (LDCs). Nevertheless, female disadvantages are universal, as the Gender Gap map in chapter 5, page 159 shows.

Women, Armed Conflict, and Abuse The image of men fighting and dying in wars while women wait safely at home is substantially a myth. In many armed conflicts, women noncombatants suffer as much or more than male soldiers and civilians. A recent UN Development Fund for Women (UNIFEM) report, *War, Women, and Peace* (2002), begins with the observation of the study panel members that while they had read the distressing statistics about the extensive violence suffered by women noncombatants in conflict, nevertheless,

> We were completely unprepared for the searing magnitude of what we saw and heard in the conflict and post-conflict areas we visited . . . [and] for the horrors women described. Wombs punctured with guns. Women raped and tortured in front of their

husbands and children. Rifles forced into vaginas. Pregnant women beaten to induce miscarriages. Fetuses ripped from wombs. Women kidnapped, blindfolded, and beaten on their way to work or school. We heard accounts of gang rapes, rape camps, and mutilation. Of murder and sexual slavery. We saw scars of brutality so extreme that survival seemed for some a worse fate than death. (p. 9)

Often such attacks on women are not individual acts of sexual aggression. Instead, according to the report, women's "bodies become a battleground over which opposing forces struggle" (p. 10). Rape, and forced impregnation and birth, and sexual slavery are not uncommon, and women are also kidnapped and used as servants to soldiers. To escape such fates, many women flee and become refugees. In fact, up to 80% of all refugees from violence are women and their children. Such women find themselves in dire conditions. Many die of disease; others "are forced . . . to become sex workers . . . their bodies . . . a form of exchange that buys the necessities of life" (p. 11). Desperation often continues after women return home—if that is what razed dwellings, dead husbands and other family members, and no means of economic support can be termed. Much of this goes unnoticed. As the UNIFEM report puts it, "Violence against women in conflict is one of history's great silences" (p. 9).

Women, Society, and Abuse   All the abuses noncombatant women suffer are but a small proportion of physical abuse that women endure globally. According to the UN, at least one-third of all women have been beaten, coerced into sex, or otherwise abused at least once in their life, and, depending on the country, 40% to 70% of all female murder victims are killed during domestic violence.

Another form of assault on women comes through sex-selective abortions or the neglect of infant girls. Globally, there are about 60 million fewer girls (age 0 to 15) than normal population figures would expect. The reason is that female fetuses are aborted more often than male fetuses after ultrasound technology is used to determine sex or, more grimly, girl infants are allowed to die through neglect more often than boys. "Society needs to recognize this discrimination," a recent UN Population Fund (UNFPA) study counsels. "Girls have a right to live just as boys do. Moreover, a missing number of either sex, and the resulting imbalance can destroy the social and human fabric as we know it."[12]

Other girls are subjected to female genital mutilation (FGM), sometimes euphemistically called female circumcision. This procedure ranges in severity from, at minimum, a clitoridectomy (the excision of the clitoris), which deprives a female of all sexual sensation, to infibulation, the cutting away of all of a female's external genitalia and labial tissue. It is widely performed on adolescent and preadolescent girls in central and North Africa, and the UN estimates that as many as 130 million women and girls alive currently have undergone the procedure and that each year another 2 million are subjected to it. Beyond the psychological trauma, FGM, which is usually performed by individuals without medical training operating in unsanitary settings, is extraordinarily painful and dangerous, carrying a significant rate of infection.

Another unhappy fate awaits over 2 million impoverished women in many countries who annually are sold or forced to go into de facto slavery in their own countries or abroad. Some become domestic servants, who are often mistreated. The sale of young women and even girls (and young men and boys) into heterosexual or homosexual slavery is also relatively common in some places. Most of the women in sexual servitude are located in the LDCs, but many are also in the EDCs (Hughes, 2000). All countries have laws against sexual slavery and child prostitution, but male-dominated governments do little to enforce them. Economic incentives are one

> **Did You Know That:**
>
> Less than half the world's countries have laws against domestic abuse.

reason that governments ignore the problem. Prostitution is a huge business in Southeast Asia, as elsewhere, and the UN has estimated that the revenue generated by sex tourism and other aspects of the illicit sexual trade ranges between 2% and 14% of the GNPs of Indonesia, Malaysia, Thailand, and the Philippines.[13] According to the UN report, the "revenues [the sex trade] generates are crucial to the livelihoods and earning potential of millions of workers beyond the prostitutes themselves."

Women's Rights Progress

Some of the most vigorous international human rights efforts in recent years have focused on women. The most significant progress has been made in the realm of identifying the maltreatment of women as a global problem, identifying some of the causes and worst abuses, and defining women's rights. This has placed the issue of women solidly on the international agenda (Antrobus, 2004; Kerr, Spenger, & Symington, 2004). For example, the UN General Assembly's Third Committee, which specializes in social, cultural, and humanitarian issues, spent less than 2% of its time discussing women's rights from 1955 to 1965. That percentage had risen almost sevenfold by the mid-1980s, and, indeed, has become the second most extensively discussed issue (after racial discrimination) in the Third Committee.

A major symbolic step occurred when the UN declared 1975 as International Women's Year and the kickoff of a Decade for Women. Numerous conferences brought women together to document their status. Funding for projects to benefit women was begun through the establishment of such structures as the UN Fund for Women (UNIFEM). The adoption of the **Convention on the Elimination of All Forms of Discrimination Against Women (CEDAW, the treaty)** in 1979 led the way in defining women's rights on an international level. As of March 2005, 180 countries had agreed to the treaty, with the United States one of the few that had not.

This rise in the level of consciousness also led to a number of other institutional changes at the UN. It created the Division for the Advancement of Women, which is responsible for addressing women's issues and promoting their rights. In this role, the division administratively supports both the Commission on the Status of Women (CSW), which is the main UN policy-making body for women, and the Committee on the Elimination of Discrimination Against Women (CEDAW, the committee), which monitors the implementation of the 1979 convention on women's rights. The division has also organized four UN world conferences on women.

Of these, the most important was the fourth **World Conference on Women (WCW)**, which convened in Beijing in 1995 and was attended by some 3,000 delegates from 180 countries, including the U.S. delegation headed by Hillary Rodham Clinton and Secretary of State Madeleine Albright. Additionally, about 30,000 delegates representing some 2,000 NGOs gathered at the parallel NGO convention in nearby Huairou. The meetings constituted the largest conclave of women in history. Not only did women meet and strengthen their already formidable network of women's groups, but their message was carried outward by the 2,500 reporters who covered the conferences. The final report of the WCW demanded an end to discrimination against and the abuse of women, called for their economic empowerment, and urged public and private organizations to lend their moral and economic support to the cause of advancing the status of women worldwide. While the Beijing conference's platform was not binding on states, it set a standard that has had an impact. The following year, for example, the Hague tribunal for war crimes in the Balkans for the first time held that sexual abuse was a war crime and indicted eight Bosnian Serb soldiers for the rape of Bosnian Muslim women.

Web Link

One of the many NGOs promoting the rights of women is the International Women's Rights Action Watch at http://iwraw.igc.org/.

Five years later a special UN General Assembly session and a parallel NGO conference, collectively called the Beijing + 5 Conference, brought 10,000 delegates together in New York City to review the progress of the goals adopted by the WCW. In addition to continuing the important networking of women and the pressure on governments to address women's issues, Beijing + 5 adopted goals such as increasing the availability and affordability of treatment for women and girls with HIV and AIDS.

Finally, there have been advances in other contexts to further the rights of women. One notable stride, which is discussed in chapter 9, was the recent founding of the **International Criminal Court (ICC)**. Its underlying treaty defined war crimes to include violence "committed as part of a widespread or systematic attack directed against any civilian population," including such offenses as "rape, sexual slavery, enforced prostitution, forced pregnancy, enforced sterilization, or any other form of sexual violence of comparable gravity." Currently accused war criminals are being prosecuted in several existing international tribunals for such depravities, and the world has now served notice that rape and related abuses are war crimes. The ICC, now investigating alleged war crimes, including sexual abuse, in Sudan and other countries, is described by MADRE, a U.S.-based women's rights NGO, as "a critical new tool in the defense of human rights for women and their families around the world."[14]

Although women remain disadvantaged politically, economically, and socially everywhere, their status and rights have advanced considerably in recent decades. One recent victory came in Kuwait in 2005, where these women are celebrating after their country's parliament passed a law granting women the right to vote and stand for election for the first time.

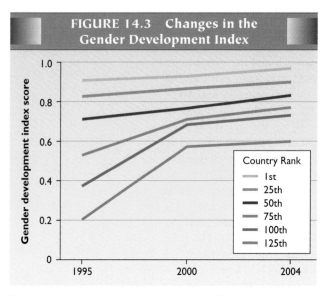

FIGURE 14.3 Changes in the Gender Development Index

The UN Development Programme's Gender Development Index evaluates the status of women compared to men within countries by using a number of health, education, and economic criteria. A score of 1, at the top of the scale, would mean statistical equality. In general terms, a 0.9 would mean women measure 90% compared to men's 100%, a 0.6 would be 60%, and so on. This figure presents the scores for the top ranked country (1st) and the countries ranked 25, 50, 75, 100, and 125 on the GDI in the UNDP's 1995, 2000, and 2004 reports. Notice two things. One is the upward trend of all six lines, a direction that shows that the score for each rank improved each year. This indicates that women's equality advanced and did so broadly. Second, note that the score for the lower ranks increased dramatically, while the scores of the upper ranks, with less disparity to begin with, rose more slowly.

Data source: UNDP, *Human Development Report* (1995, 2000, 2004). Calculations by author.

There is also evidence that the rising international condemnation of the abuse of women is having some impact on norms and practices within countries. Data for a number of societal opportunity measures indicates that the gap between men and women is narrowing. For example, the difference in the literacy rate of men and women worldwide narrowed from 11% in 1990 to 7% in 2002. There has been a 6% increase in percentage of national legislative seats held by women. Women's share of paying jobs in the manufacturing and service sectors has increased 3.5% to 35%. The percentage of countries with laws against domestic violence has nearly doubled to 47%. Regarding a more specific concern, several countries where FGM has been practiced have passed laws against it, and there are indications that the procedure is on the decline. Women in Kuwait won the right to vote and hold office in 2005. Yemen, a country that annually finishes near the bottom of both the United Nations Development Programme's (UNDP) gender development index (GDI), has ratified CEDAW, created a Ministry of Human Rights, and appointed a woman as its first head. All these advances and many more are also evident in the upward trend shown in Figure 14.3 of the GDI, a measure of women's conditions relative to men using a variety of health, education, and economic measures. Surely, reforms have come slowly and there continues to be significant global disparity in the conditions of men and women across the political-social-economic spectrum. Yet there has been progress.

Children's Rights

Children are not commonly considered a political group, but they are perhaps the most vulnerable of all humans. Also, children have rights like all humans, and those rights are all too often violated (Ensalaco & Majka, 2005).

Children's Rights Problems

If anything, the abuses that children suffer globally have received even less notice than those of women. In addition to the lack of adequate nutrition, medical care, and education that prevent a vast number of children in many countries from achieving a fulfilling life or even surviving at all, they endure a variety of abuses. Being forced to work is one of them. According to the International Programme for the Elimination of Child Labour (IPEC), a division of the International Labor Organization (ILO), there are 246 million children aged 5 to 14 that are performing more than light or casual economic work. About 75% of these children are engaged in what the ILO classifies as hazardous work. Among children ages 5 to 9, 12% work, and that rises to nearly 25% between ages 10 and 14. Adding further to the problem, about half the working children age 10 and under do so full-time and do not go to school. Child labor ranges from about 2% of all children in the EDCs to as high as 29% in sub-Saharan Africa.

The most disturbing statistics of all relate to the 8.4 million children involved in what IPEC terms "unconditional worst forms of child labor." This includes children in five categories (and the number of children in each): internationally trafficked children (1.2 million), forced and bonded labor (5.7 million), armed conflict (so-called boy soldiers, 0.3 million), prostitution and pornography (1.8 million), and illicit activities (such as drug sales, 0.6 million). Child prostitution is especially prevalent in southern Asia and Latin America. There are many reasons—ranging from abuse at home to economic desperation—why children turn to prostitution; it is also the case that many children are sold by their families. A recent UN report related the example of Lam, a 15-year-old Vietnamese girl who was sold by her grandmother to purveyors for a brothel in Cambodia. According to the report, the price for girls like Lam ranges between $50 and $200. Other individuals are kidnapped by sex-slavers to supply the multibillion-dollar sex trade. An astronomical rate of AIDS and other sexually transmitted diseases are among the myriad dangers these children face.

The treatment of children is certainly the proper concern of national governments, but it is also an international issue. It is estimated that each year 10 to 12 million men travel internationally as "sex tourists" to exploit children. An unknown but substantial number of children are transported across international borders for sexual purposes, and technology has brought child pornography to the Internet. Clothes, shoes, and other products manufactured by children are sold in international trade; you may be wearing one of these products even as you read these words. The wars and civil strife that ruin the lives of boy soldiers and other children are often rooted in world affairs.

Children's Rights Progress

Serious international efforts to protect children's rights have only recently begun, symbolically kicked off in 1979, which was designated by the UN as the International Year of the Child. The United Nations Children's Fund (UNICEF) is the most important single agency promoting the rights of children, but it is supported by numerous other IGOs and NGOs. Their common goal, in the words of UNICEF's executive director, is to "ensure that exploitive and hazardous child labor becomes as unacceptable in the next century as slavery has become in this. Children should be students in school, not slaves in factories, fields, or brothels."[15]

One noteworthy advance is the **Convention on the Rights of the Child,** which was adopted unanimously by the UN General Assembly in 1989 and made available for signature and ratification by the world's countries. The treaty defines a wide range of collective and individual rights in such areas as the sexual exploitation of children, the use of boy soldiers, and the diversion of children from their education to work. It is a mark of hope that the convention garnered enough ratifications to go into force in less than a year and also quickly became the most widely ratified human

The UN and associated agencies are slowly moving to institute economic regulations to end corruption, labor abuses, and other problems. Child labor is one such concern, with the International Labor Organization a leader in the effort to create a world where scenes such as the one pictured here cease to exist. This young girl is at work carrying bricks at a construction site in Myanmar rather than going to school and playing as she should be. Bricks such as the eight she is carrying weigh between 3 and 4 kilos each, meaning that the total weight pressing down on her neck and spine is somewhere between 53 and 71 pounds.

rights treaty in history. Indeed, as of early 2005, every country in the world save the United States and the failed state of Somalia was a party to the treaty. Among other concerns in the United States was whether the convention would abridge the possibility in some U.S. states that minors convicted of capital crimes can be executed once they reach age 18. However, the U.S. Supreme Court declared such executions unconstitutional in the 2005 case *Roper v. Simmons,* and that could open the way for U.S. ratification of the treaty. It is worth noting that the Supreme Court recognized the U.S. isolation on child rights in its decision. In the majority opinion, Justice Anthony M. Kennedy declared that the court's stand "finds confirmation in the stark reality that the United States is the only country in the world that continues to give official sanction to the juvenile death penalty."[16]

A second important effort on behalf of children has come through a series of global conferences on the rights and welfare of children. In 1990, 71 heads of state and senior officials from 88 other countries met at the World Summit for Children at UN headquarters, adopted the Declaration on the Survival, Protection and Development of Children, and put forth a 10-point Plan of Action. The world countries also joined together during the first and second World Congresses Against Commercial Sexual Exploitation of Children. Both were widely attended, with the second congress drawing 3,050 persons from 136 governments, 283 NGOs, and 23 IGOs. The authority of such international meetings is severely limited, but they do serve a valuable function by focusing attention on issues. As one official of the first congress noted, "There can be no more delusions—no one can deny that the problem of children being sold for sex exists, here and now, in almost every country in the world."[17]

The increasing awareness of child labor and determination to end it is also evident in many other ways. For example, an ILO-sponsored international conference led to an agreement known as the Worst Forms of Child Labour Convention (1999). The convention bars countries from inflicting on children any form of compulsory labor similar to slavery (including being forced to become a child soldier), using children for illicit activities (prostitution, pornography, drug trafficking), and having children do work that is inherently dangerous. As of mid-2004, the treaty had been ratified by 151 countries and become part of international law. Another indication of growing support is that only 6 countries contributed to the ILO's International Programme on the Elimination of Child Labour (IPEC) when it was founded in 1992, now 80 do. A 2005 report by the head of the ILO also cites evidence of progress in such factors as the number of countries passing new or tougher child labor laws and the adoption of codes of conduct by multinational corporations barring the use of child laborers. "The global challenge remains daunting," the ILO director-general concedes in the report, but he also advised, "We can take heart that already there has been a great deal of progress achieved in knowledge and experience, as well as an impressive worldwide movement to combat child labor."[18]

Web Link

One way to learn more about child labor is to see the documentary *Stolen Childhoods* released in 2005. More on the film and about how to get involved in halting child labor can be found at **www.stolenchildhoods .org/mt/index.php.**

Ethnic, Racial, and Religious Group Rights

Among humans, the "we–they" complex is most destructive when it engenders hostility toward "others" and often violent oppression of "others" based on their ethnicity, race, and religion. There is hope, though. Tolerance can be taught to many, and it can be enforced for those who do not want to learn.

Group Rights Problems

Strife and oppression based on ethnicity, race, and religion are still unsettlingly common. There are racial and religious overtones in the gruesome violence in Sudan between the government dominated by Arab-heritage Muslims and the black Christians and animists of the southern part of the country, and similarly between the government and the black Muslims in the western region or Darfur. Fighting between the mostly Buddhist Sinhalese who control the government and the mostly Hindu Tamil minority has beset Sri Lanka for many years. People in Northern Ireland divide themselves between warring Protestant and Catholic factions, and in Cyprus fences and troops have to separate Greek-heritage citizens from Turkish-heritage citizens. Religious fundamentalism has strengthened in recent decades and has sparked numerous efforts in India, Israel, several Muslim countries, and elsewhere to align the legal codes and religious laws of their respective countries and to force everyone, regardless of their personal beliefs, to follow those theocratic laws. It hangs in the balance whether Iraq will become a tolerant democracy, an oppressive quasi-theocracy, or will dissolve into civil war among Shiite Muslims, Sunni Muslims, and Kurdish Muslims. Even in countries where there is no move to supplant civil with theocratic law, religious intimidation is not uncommon.

Most of the worst instances of oppression are in the LDCs, but the EDCs do not escape the stain. The persecution of Jews and Gypsies, properly called Roma, did not perish with Adolf Hitler's Nazi Third Reich. Instead, they persist in Europe and elsewhere. In July 2005, the European Court of Human Rights found racist motivations in an incident in Romania in which an altercation between Romas and ethnic Romanians ended when Romanians, encouraged by police, surrounded a house in which several Roma men were hiding and set it on fire. One man burned to death; those who fled the flames were beaten to death. Charges brought against the town police were dismissed by a Romanian court, which commented, "The Roma community has marginalized itself, shown aggressive behavior and deliberately denied and violated the legal norms acknowledged by society. Most of the Roma have no occupation and earn their living by doing odd jobs, stealing and engaging in all kinds of illicit activities."[19]

Web Link

Learn more about the Roma and their human rights concerns at http://www.romani.org/index.html.

Anti-Semitism also troubles Europe and other EDCs. Between 1989 and 2004, Tel Aviv University's annual review on global anti-Semitism recorded a sixfold increase in major anti-Semitic incidents to 482. Russia is one country with a worrisome record. There a poll found 59% of Russians agreeing with the statement, "Jews have too much power in the world of business." Such attitudes are evident even in the government. In a 2005 incident, 20 members of the Duma, Russia's parliament, sent a letter to the equivalent of the country's attorney-general calling for a ban of all Jewish groups. The legislators, all members of the Rodina (Motherland) Party, argued that the move was necessary because, "The whole democratic world today is under the financial and political control of the Jews. We would not want our Russia, which is subject to a permanent illegal war seeking to prevent its rebirth, to find itself among unfree countries."[20] President Vladimir Putin said the letter had shamed Russia, and the Duma voted overwhelmingly to condemn it, but no sanctions on the offending legislators were forthcoming.

The list of ethnic, racial, and religious divisions, oppression, and violence could go on at length, but that is not necessary here. Chapter 4 details the world's ethnonational divisions and chapter 5 does the same for religion. The question is what is being done to address the problem.

Group Rights Progress

The international effort to increase ethnic, racial, and religious tolerance and to eliminate their worst forms quickly is only a few decades old. It has made progress, but negative attitudes are so widespread and deep-seeded that change has been limited.

One early notable advance came in South Africa. Years of international pressure through economic sanctions and other penalties finally compelled South African whites to surrender political power in 1994, ending official racism through the apartheid system that permitted 6.5 million whites to dominate the other 29 million black, Asian, and "colored" (mixed-race) people.

The global effort to combat intolerance has also been furthered by a series of international conferences to highlight the problem and seek solutions. The first two met in Geneva, Switzerland, in 1978 and 1983. The third, the World Conference against Racism, Racial Discrimination, Xenophobia and Related Intolerance (WCAR) convened in Durban, South Africa, in 2001. The meeting brought together official delegations from 160 countries. Like most UN conferences, there was also an unofficial parallel conference that included representatives of hundreds of NGOs ranging alphabetically from ABC Ulwazi (South Africa) to the Zoroastrian Women's Organization (Iran).

Unfortunately the Durban conference fell into acrimonious debate over what the South saw as blunt candor and what the North regarded as undiplomatic truculence. The South's mood was captured in the comments of the host, South Africa's President Thabo Mbeki, who told the delegates that it was important to acknowledge that:

> There are many in our common world who suffer indignity and humiliation because they are not white. Their cultures and traditions are despised as savage and primitive and their identities denied. . . . To those who have to bear the pain of this real world, it seems the blues singers were right when they decried the world in which it was said, "If you're white you're all right; if you are brown, stick around; if you are black, oh brother! Get back, get back, get back!"[21]

Wrangling focused on two issues. One was the demand by African countries that the countries of Western Europe and the United States that had once been involved in the slave trade apologize and perhaps pay reparations. The other sore point was the effort by Muslim countries to label Israel a "racist apartheid state" and to demand an end to the "ongoing Israeli systematic perpetration of racist crimes, including war crimes, genocide, and ethnic cleansing."[22] When some countries insisted on bringing a resolution including this language to a vote, Canada and several European countries downgraded their delegations, and the U.S. delegation withdrew altogether from the conference. "I have taken this decision with regret," Secretary of State Colin Powell said. "[But] I know that you do not combat racism by conferences that produce declarations containing hateful language," he concluded.[23] Who was to blame is debatable, but it is certain that in the end the conference accomplished little because, as an Australian representative lamented, "Far too much of the time at the conference was consumed by bitter divisive exchanges on issues which have done nothing to advance the cause of combating racism."[24]

More positively, efforts to define the rights of ethnic, racial, and religious groups have been part of the major human rights documents such as the International Covenant on Economic, Social, and Cultural Rights and the Convention on the Prevention and Punishment of the Crime of Genocide. There have also been some specific agreements, such as the **International Convention on the Elimination of All Forms of Racial Discrimination** (1969). It is a step forward that 170 countries, including the United States, have been willing to agree to this document, which, among other things, proclaims that its signatories are "convinced that . . . there is no justification for racial discrimination, in theory or in practice, anywhere."

There are also regional efforts. At a 2005 conference in Sofia, Bulgaria, eight countries (Bulgaria, Croatia, the Czech Republic, Hungary, Macedonia, Romania, Serbia and Montenegro, and Slovakia) pledged to begin a 10-year program to improve the social and economic status of Eastern Europe's Roma people. One observer optimistically noted, "There has been a huge lack of political will on behalf of the countries that are now participating in this effort," and called it "a huge leap forward in this respect." More cautiously, a Roma activist commented, "It is now at the level of good will and speeches. How it will work we will have to wait and see."[25] Both were right.

Such international and regional efforts have been supplemented by some levels of enforcement. The earlier international pressure on South Africa to end legal racism was an important step. The international tribunals investigating and trying war crimes committed in the Balkans and in Rwanda are further evidence that persecution based on ethnicity, race, or religion are increasingly considered an affront to the global conscience, as are the investigations that the ICC has begun into atrocities in Sudan and elsewhere.

The Rights of Indigenous Peoples

The history of the world is a story of mass migrations and conquests that have often left the indigenous people of a region as a minority in national political systems imposed on their traditional tribal or other political structures. All together, there are approximately 5,000 indigenous groups with a total of 300 million people residing in more than 70 countries on five continents.

Indigenous Peoples' Rights Problems

Almost everywhere, the world's 370 million indigenous peoples live in socioeconomic circumstances that are below those of the non-native population of their country. For example, the socioeconomic status of Mexico's indigenous peoples, such as the Mayas, is 21% below that of the country's general population according to the UNDP. There is also a long history in many countries of trying to force indigenous groups to adopt mainstream culture by giving up their language, customs, and other aspects of their culture.

One of the particular efforts of indigenous peoples in recent years has been their attempt to protect their traditional home areas politically and environmentally from the incursion of the surrounding cultures. The spread of people and commercial activities such as logging and mining into the vast interior areas of the Amazon River system has increasingly degraded the health, environment, and other aspects of the life of the indigenous peoples of that region. The Yanomami people of Brazil and Venezuela provide an example. The Yanomami (the word means "human being") had little contact with outsiders before the mid-1980s when the lure of gold brought prospectors and miners far up Brazil's rivers and into the Yanomami's forest retreats. The invasion has left the Yanomami devastated by the diseases, mercury, and other toxins brought by the miners, and, on occasion, by violence aimed at forcing the tribe off its lands. Their numbers have shrunk since the mid-1980s by about 10%, to 19,000.

Beyond the Amazon basin, similar stories are common. Representatives of the Khwe people of Botswana traveled to the annual UN Commission on Human Rights convention in Geneva, Switzerland, to seek help in fending off their threatened expulsion from the Kalahari Desert to make way for tourism facilities. "We came without any promise of getting anything done," said John Hardbattle, leader of the First People of the Kalahari organization. "We felt that if we can't get help at the UN, then we won't get it anywhere else."[26] As Hardbattle recognized, the ability of aboriginal groups to resist the hunger of powerful outside forces for resources and land is limited. They depend in part on gaining world attention and help. That has just begun, as we will see later.

Indigenous Peoples' Rights Progress

The UN General Assembly proclaimed 1993 to be the International Year of the Indigenous Peoples. The following year, representatives of some of the more than 5,000 indigenous peoples agreed to an International Covenant on the Rights of Indigenous Nations that prescribed relations among the groups and between each of them and the country in which it is located. The increased focus on the plight of many groups led the General Assembly to further designate 1995 to 2004 as the International Decade of the Indigenous Peoples and to subsequently extend that to a second decade (2005–2014). Additionally, in 2000 the UN Economic and Social Council established the UN Permanent Forum on Indigenous Issues (UNPFII) as an advisory body. Its purpose, declared Mary Robinson, UN High Commissioner for Human Rights, is "to give indigenous peoples a unique voice within the United Nations system."[27] The UNPFII has a permanent staff, meets annually, and serves to study problems faced by indigenous populations and to bring those issues to the attention of the UN and other IGOS. The efforts of indigenous people have also been furthered by numerous NGOs, including the International Indian Treaty Council, the World Council of Indigenous Peoples, the Inuit Circumpolar Conference, and the Unrepresented Nations and Peoples' Organization. The causes of indigenous peoples were also furthered when the Nobel Peace Prize Committee made its 1992 award to Rigoberta Menchú of Guatemala in recognition of her efforts to advance the rights of her Mayan people in her country and to further the welfare of indigenous people globally.

Refugee and Migrant Workers' Rights

Driven by war, economic desperation, and other factors, the movement of humans ranging from individuals to entire nations has occurred throughout history. "Migration is the visible face of social change," a report by UNFPA explains.[28] This face is evident in the early 21st century. According to the Office of the High Commissioner for Human Rights (OHCHR) there were 19.2 million refugees in 2005. While still distressingly high, this number was well below its peak during recent decades, as indicated in Figure 14.4. About 45% are internally displaced. These refugees have been forced to flee to another part of their country by violence, famine, or some other disaster. Another 9.2 million, whom the OHCHR calls its "core constituency," were members of groups that had fled their country to a neighboring country. An additional nearly 1 million people had fled as individuals or in small groups to another country and were seeking political or humanitarian asylum. Beyond those classes of people and beyond the UNHCR data, many millions of others have legally or illegally entered other countries to find work.

Refugee and Migrant Workers' Rights Problems

Human history is a story of populations either migrating in their entirety or expanding to new territories. When those on the move or expanding have come to dominate their new homes, they have often reduced the indigenous population to second-class citizenship, as discussed in the section above. Where the newcomers have not dominated, it is they who have often been relegated to second-class status or even worse through discrimination and nativist violence against them. This latter pattern is a tale of current times, and the tide of refugees and immigrants, legal and illegal, has been met with increasing resistance. When asked whether immigrants have a good or bad effect on their country, a plurality of people in 28 countries replied bad, with a plurality in 13 countries answering good, and 3 countries evenly divided on the issue.

When queried about increasing restrictions on people coming to their country, citizens' reactions to immigrants, refugees, foreign workers, and other outsiders were even starker. On average, a resounding 72% of the respondents favored stricter controls. Only 22% opposed stricter controls, with 6% unsure. Opposition was very high in the EDCs, especially the United States, Canada, and Western Europe, where, on average, 76% wanted tougher restrictions. But opposition was even slightly higher in Latin America (77%) and sub-Saharan Africa (79%). East Europeans (67%), Asians (61%), and Middle Easterners (66%) were also solidly for raising barriers to entry.[29]

To a degree, the feelings against immigrants, refugees, and others entering a country may result from racial, ethnic, religious, and other biases. But there are other causes. As discussed in chapter 5, people in most countries see their national cultures being diluted by the cross-acculturation associated with globalization. Coping with refugees and economically driven illegal immigrants is costly. Countries donate billions of dollars to assist refugees overseas, and many countries also spend vast sums on their border patrols and on other domestic programs to stem the influx of refugees and undocumented immigrants, to assist those who are admitted or who slip in, and to return some of those who do arrive to their country of origin. Such costs can be a severe strain for LDCs that suffer a large influx of refugees, and the funds available through the UN and other IGOs and private NGOs are almost never adequate to fully house, feed, and otherwise care for the refugees. There are also other potential problems. For one, when refugees have fled from fighting, the conflict may sometimes spread to the new area to which they have gone.

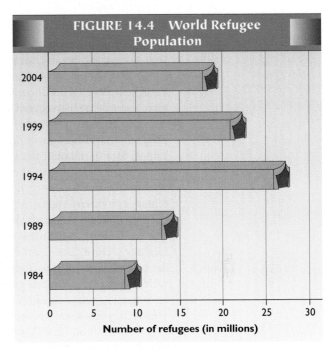

FIGURE 14.4 World Refugee Population

Number of refugees (in millions)

The decline in internal ethnonational wars since the early 1990s (see chapter 4) has been accompanied by a decline in the number of refugees. Each year's total is represented here by a tent, the most common type of shelter for refugees. Whatever any year's total, there is always a huge number of displaced people in the world who have been forced from their homes by violence, hunger, and other causes. The UN High Commissioner for Human Rights is the lead international agency involved in feeding, sheltering, and otherwise easing the suffering of refugees and hopefully one day helping them return to their homes and rebuild their lives.

Data source: UNHCR, Helping Refugees 2004.

Whatever attitudes may be about the inflow of refugees and immigrants, it is certain that the tide will be unending as long as people in some countries are subject to endemic violence and poverty. The Kevin Costner movie *Field of Dreams* revolved around the line, "If you build it, they will come." To those who daily face death, disease, and hunger, any safe haven, especially the EDCs' societies of relative peace and material wealth, represents a field of dreams. And people in danger and destitution will come. Barriers can lower the stream, but arguably a better way that would address the cause and also avoid the perpetual spending of vast sums on aid, immigration control, and other programs is to help the South develop quickly and achieve political stability so that it can build a field that at least meets minimum needs of sustenance and safety. It is conceivable that if Mexico's standard of living were to increase substantially, for example, many of its citizens would no longer undergo the dislocation and risk the physical danger that leaving home and slipping into the United States entails. "We have a good argument now, a very concrete one," for helping the LDCs, the prime minister of Denmark told a UN conference, "which is, if you don't help the Third World . . . , then you will have these poor people in your society."

Refugee and Migrant Workers' Rights Progress

International efforts on behalf of refugees have provided very mixed results. There have been a number of efforts to define the status and the rights of both international and internal refugees. An early effort was the Convention Relating to the Status of Refugees (1951). This document charged the UN with providing assistance to people who were being persecuted in their countries or who feared persecution if they returned to their home countries. The convention also defined the basic rights of refugees and minimum standards for their treatment and has served, among other things, as a foundation for subsequent efforts on behalf of refugees. It is also true, though, that it is one of the least widely ratified of the UN's major human rights treaties. Because of concerns that they might be required to open their borders to refugees or extend rights to those who managed to arrive unbidden, only 142 countries have signed and ratified it, with the United States among the missing countries.

Aid to refugees, while scant compared to their actual need, presents a somewhat brighter picture. The effort on behalf of displaced persons in the early 1950s led to the creation of the UN High Commissioner for Refugees (UNHCR) in 1951 with wide responsibility for refugee rights and needs. Among other things, it oversees the feeding and sheltering of refugees and works toward restoring them to their homes. The agency has a staff of about 5,000, who are located in 120 countries, and a budget of $1.4 billion (2004), or about $70 per refugee that year. Also formed in 1951 was the International Organization for Migration (IOM), a body specifically concerned with the movement of refugees either to new homes or back to their former homes, as appropriate. Additionally, there are a number of IGOs, such as the International Red Cross (and its Muslim counterpart, the International Red Crescent), Oxfam, and others, that are involved in providing food, clothes, shelter, and other necessities. Individual countries also help in various ways, such as making donations to the UNHCR and with individual efforts to provide aid to refugee camps. The United States is the largest donor, accounting for about one-third of the UNHCR's

The Office of the United Nations High Commissioner for Refugees (UNHCR) assists those who have been internally displaced by political violence and natural disasters as well as those who have fled across international borders. Here a mother and her baby wait for food in a UNHCR refugee camp in Sri Lanka that was established after a tsunami devastated the coastal areas of many countries in the Indian Ocean in late 2004.

2004 budget. A few countries also permit a certain number of refugees to immigrate. In 2004, 95% of the total went to just three countries, the United States (53,000), Australia (16,000), and Canada (11,000).

Countries have been much less willing to recognize any international role in protecting the rights of migrant workers and their families, who are seen as much more of a domestic matter than refugees. Indicative of that attitude is the history of the Convention on the Protection of the Rights of All Migrant Workers and Members of Their Families. It extends the rights noted in several other UN human rights to all migrants, both legal and illegal, and obligates states to protect their rights equally with citizens. The treaty was submitted by the UN General Assembly to states for ratification, but few have responded positively. As of 2005, only 27 countries were party to the treaties, and none of these included the United States or any other EDC.

Prescriptive Human Rights

Compared to the proscriptive rights that we have been discussing, prescriptive human rights are much less often recognized or enumerated by countries or in international law. Yet they exist. South Africa's post-apartheid constitution (1996), for one, obligates the government to ensure that everyone has access to adequate food at all times. The U.S. Constitution mostly includes proscriptive rights, but it does prescriptively specify in Article IV, "The United States shall guarantee to every state in the union a republican form of government, and shall protect each of them against invasion and . . . domestic violence." In other words, the U.S. federal government is obligated to ensure that all states maintain a democratic form of government, to repel invaders, and to preserve domestic order. Many U.S. state constitutions are more expansive in codifying prescriptive rights. For instance, the Connecticut constitution declares in Article VIII, "There shall always be free public elementary and secondary schools in the state. The general assembly shall implement this principle." Note that the article does not say children cannot be barred from school (a proscriptive right); it obligates the state to provide free elementary and secondary schooling. Moreover, the article mandates the General Assembly to act ("shall"). Less clearly, there has been an effort at both the U.S. federal and state levels to establish the notion that providing many basic services (such as housing, food, and health care for the needy) are obligations on the government, not merely options. This move is evident in the vast array of federal programs, such as food stamps and Medicare, which provide funding according to a formula (rather than by specific legislative appropriation) and which are commonly referred to as "entitlement programs." This phrase is meant to imply a prescriptive obligation. Such programs have not been held to be a right by the federal courts. Nevertheless, some Americans believe that entitlement programs do address rights and therefore are prescriptive obligations, not a choice, and it is not unthinkable that in time the courts could agree.

Although the Universal Declaration of Human Rights that the United States, among others, voted for and, indeed, helped draft, mostly contains proscriptive rights, it does also enumerate prescriptive rights. Article 22 specifies that:

> Everyone, as a member of society, has the right to social security and is entitled to realization, through national effort and international co-operation and in accordance with the organization and resources of each State, of the economic, social and cultural rights indispensable for his dignity and the free development of his personality.

Being more specific about some of these prescriptive rights, Article 25 states in part:

> Everyone has the right to a standard of living adequate for the health and well-being of himself and of his family, including food, clothing, housing and medical care and necessary social services, and the right to security in the event of unemployment, sickness, disability, widowhood, old age or other lack of livelihood in circumstances beyond his control.

Certainly one set of pressing problems involves preserving and enhancing human dignity by protecting and improving the physical condition of humans. These issues are partly economic in nature and are being addressed by the international economic cooperation efforts discussed in chapter 13. It is also the case, in the view of many, that food, health, and the other quality of life matters that we will take up in this section fall under the rubric of human rights. For example, the UN-sponsored World Food Summit that met in 1996 reasserted the principle found in the Universal Declaration by declaring that there is a "right to adequate food and the fundamental right of everyone to be free from hunger."[30] If, indeed, there is such a right, then an obligation exists. As one scholar explains it, "Since adequate food is a human right, the obligations apply internationally. The rights and the corresponding obligations do not end at national borders. Under human rights law, the international community is obligated to create conditions that will end hunger in the world" (Kent, 2002). A right to adequate nutrition, to a reasonable standard of health, and to a basic education are not the only ones that some people lay claim to as prescriptive rights, but they will serve to illustrate the need and the response.

A final important point about prescriptive rights is that those who are without adequate health, education, and the other necessities that support survival and a decent level of dignity are not spread evenly across the globe. This is evident in the accompanying map showing the pattern of the Human Development Index. This is a measure established by the UNDP that includes various measures of health, education, and per capita income. As you can see, the 54 countries the UNDP rates as having "high human development" (levels 8 and 9) are mostly in Europe and North America. The 33 low human development countries (levels 4 and below) are in Africa and southern Asia, with the remaining 85 medium human development countries (levels 5 through 7) concentrated in South America, northern Asia and the Middle East.

Adequate Nutrition

Just over two centuries ago, Thomas Malthus predicted in his *Essay on the Principle of Population* (1798) that the world's population would eventually outpace the world's agricultural carrying capacity. To date, human ingenuity has defied his predictions. The question is whether it can continue to do so, given the rapidly increasing global population.

There are two basic food problems. One is the *short-term food supply*. The UN's Food and Agriculture Organization (FAO) estimates that 815 million people, about 20% of the world population, are undernourished. Sub-Saharan Africa, where 33% of the people are undernourished, is the most severely affected region. In addition to the death of 15 million people annually from starvation or diseases stemming from malnutrition, food shortages rob individuals and their societies of part of their future. Poor nutrition among pregnant women leads to 20 million "low birthweight" (less than 5.5 pounds) babies being born each year in the LDCs. In some countries, including India, more than 30 percent of all children are born underweight. Infant

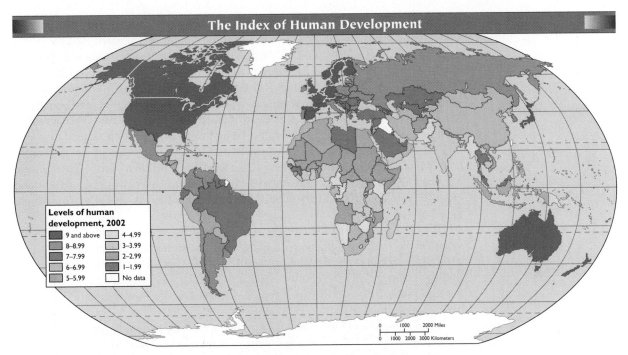

The Index of Human Development

Levels of human development, 2002
- 9 and above
- 8–8.99
- 7–7.99
- 6–6.99
- 5–5.99
- 4–4.99
- 3–3.99
- 2–2.99
- 1–1.99
- No data

The level of human rights and dignity around the world is measured in part by the Index of Human Development. The index, which was developed by the United Nations Development Programme, Includes such gauges as health, literacy, income, and education. As you can see, the level of development that people enjoy or endure, as the case may be, varies greatly.

mortality for such infants is four times the normal rate. Moreover the malnourishment that they have already suffered and continue to experience, not just in calories but also in protein, vitamins, minerals, and other nutritional necessities, stunts their growth both physically and cognitively in ways that often limit them for the rest of their lives and deprive their societies of talents and vigor that might have developed.

The *long-term adequacy* of the food supply is also a significant issue. There have been important strides in the LDCs over the past few decades toward agricultural self-sufficiency. The food supply and crop yields (amount produced per acre) have grown over 50% since 1970 due to the "green revolution" (the development and widespread introduction of high-yielding rice, wheat, and other grains), the increased use of fertilizers and pesticides, better irrigation, more mechanization, and other agricultural advances. For all LDCs, food production grew by 35% during 1994 and 2004, far outpacing their population growth (16%). But among the poorest countries (the LLDCs, low-income countries) where the problem has been most acute, the food production index during the decade increased only at the same rate as the population, 30% each. One result is that undernourishment in middle-income LDCs stood at 10% in 2004 and at 25% in the low-income LDCs.

Causes of the Food Problem

Population growth is one cause. The annual growth rate of the world population has slowed measurably during the past two decades. However, the LLDCs still have a growth rate that is about 50% higher than the rest of the world. Growth rates are expected to continue to decline among all categories of countries, but the relative gap between the LLDCs and other countries is not expected to narrow. As a result,

Web Link

The World Food Programme has an interactive world hunger map at **www.wfp.org/country _brief/hunger_map/map/ hungermap_popup/map _popup.html**.

agriculture will be hard pressed to keep up in some parts of the world. Additionally, slower population growth does not mean no growth; it is estimated that the world population may reach 9 billion by about 2050. The ability to increase yields per unit of farmland is not infinite, which means that new acreage will have to be devoted to agriculture. This clearing of land is causing deforestation, aggravating a range of problems such as greenhouse warming, wildlife habitat destruction, and water pollution from pesticide and fertilizer runoff. Accelerating the problem is the fact that a great deal of current agricultural land is being lost to urbanization, degradation due to ill-use, and other causes. The FAO calculates that 38% of the world's original cropland (some 2.1 million square miles, almost two-thirds the area of the United States) has been lost to agriculture, and that a combination of increasing population and loss of arable land has cut the world's cultivated land to six-tenths of an acre per mouth to feed.

It is also important to note that some countries are already not keeping up. Whether the problem is inability to afford modern methods and technology, lack of adequate water and arable land, or political strife, many countries are in serious trouble. There are 38 LDC countries whose per capita food production declined during the 1990s. Cuba had the worst record, with an average annual drop of 6.5% in its per capita production.

Maldistribution of food is a second problem. In 2000 the world produced enough food to allow for 2,757 calories per person in the world. Thus, for now at least, the world has the agricultural capacity to feed everyone adequately. Resources and consumption, however, are concentrated in relatively few countries. In the EDCs, daily food consumption averages a waist-expanding 3,240 calories a day. In significant segments of the South calorie intakes were at belt-tightening low levels. The sub-Saharan countries of Africa, for example, averaged only 2,183 calories per capita daily. Some countries in that region are in especially desperate shape. The people of Burundi average only 1,640 calories a day, 68% of them are undernourished, one of every six babies has a low birthweight, and 57% of the children are stunted.

Nutritional content represents a third, and even greater gap between the ability of the North and South to meet dietary needs. Protein deficiency is particularly common in the LLDCs. Most people in Africa, for instance, consume less than 60 grams of protein per day per capita and in some countries they average as little as 30 grams. The recommended daily intake is about 55 grams for sedentary individuals, which means that in the LLDCs, where manual labor is the norm, protein deficiency is also the norm. The lack of protein is especially detrimental to children because of the role it plays in developing both healthy bodies and brain tissue, and there are over 300 million children in LDCs who suffer from stunted growth, poor cognitive development, and other ills due to protein malnutrition. Vitamin A deficiency, also common in LLDCs, is the cause of visual impairment in over 100 million children a year. Adding to the nutritional woes of the South, over 800 million people suffer from iodine deficiency, which inhibits motor skill development and also, according to the FAO, causes losses of 10 to 15 points on IQ tests. It is a sad testimony to how little is done to ease some of these problems, that iodine deficiency could be largely eliminated through the distribution of iodized salt at an annual cost of about 4 cents per recipient.

Political strife is a fourth problem. In many countries with severe food shortages, farms have been destroyed, farmers displaced, and food transportation disrupted by internal warfare. Sierra Leone, one of the recent tragic examples, now produces 19% less food than the already meager supply it managed to provide in 1991 before it was overtaken by strife.

The International Response to the Food Problem

A number of international efforts are under way. Some deal with food aid to meet immediate needs, while others are dedicated to increasing future agricultural productivity.

Emergency Food Aid   Supplying food aid to areas with food shortages is a short-term necessity to alleviate malnutrition and even starvation. Grains constitute about 95% of food aid. The United States is by far the largest food aid donor. In 2004, it contributed $1.3 billion in food, which constituted 51% of all food aid. The next nearest countries, Japan and Great Britain, donated about 5% each. Some of the aid is given bilaterally, but a good deal of the assistance goes through a number of multilateral food aid efforts. The UN's World Food Programme (WFP) is the largest. It distributes food in crisis situations, delivering over 5 million tons of food in 2004 to feed 113 million people in 80 countries. About 80% of WFP aid goes to countries that have experienced food emergencies because of natural causes or political strife; the other 20% goes to development projects. In 2004, the WFP received $2.9 billion in grains and other foodstuffs. While these contributions are laudable, they meet only about two-thirds of the emergency food needs identified by the WFP and amounted in 2001 to only about $26 per WFP individual recipient. There are also a variety of NGOs, such as Food for the Hungry International, that are active in food aid.

Specific Nutritional Needs   Numerous programs also exist to address the lack of adequate dietary vitamins and minerals and other nutritional problems. Iodine deficiency provides an example. The 1990 World Summit for Children set the goal of eliminating iodine deficiencies by 2000. That did not occur, but substantial progress has been made. With WHO and UNICEF in the lead among IGOs and such NGOs as Kiwanis International also playing a leading role, the proportion of LDC households using iodized salt has risen from less than 20% in 1990 to over 70% today. As a result, 50 million more children who are born each year are now protected against learning impairment and other problems related to iodine deficiency than would have been the case without the international programs.

Agricultural Development   The development of agricultural techniques and capabilities is crucial to remediate conditions in countries that already cannot adequately feed their people and to meet the needs of the 9 billion people that will constitute the world's population less than five decades from now. On a bilateral basis, many countries' programs include agricultural development aid. There is also a multilateral effort. The oldest agricultural IGO is the FAO. Founded in 1945, it has 188 members and an annual budget of approximately $750 million. The FAO supplies food aid and technical assistance to LDCs through field offices in 78 countries. The agency has been criticized for a variety of its policies, including putting too much emphasis on short-term food aid and not enough effort into long-range agricultural growth. This, in addition to the growing recognition of the food problem, has led to the establishment of several other global food efforts.

One of these is the International Fund for Agricultural Development (IFAD), a specialized UN agency. IFAD began operations in 1977 and is specifically dedicated to environmentally sustainable agricultural development projects in rural areas of the poorest LDCs. The agency raises its funds through the voluntary contributions of its 164 member-countries, and disburses about $400 million annually in loans and grants to support projects in agriculturally struggling countries. These efforts are supplemented by several UN-associated organizations involved in various donor, investment, and research efforts in agriculture. Finally, there are a variety of regional and specialized organizations that address agricultural issues.

World Food Conferences   A key event in both the effort to increase both short- and long-term food was the 1974 World Food Conference held in Rome. Among its other actions, the conference sponsored the creation of IFAD and various structures associated with the UN Economic and Social Council to monitor the global food supply and its delivery to needy countries and people.

A second global conference, the 1996 **World Food Summit**, met in Rome and was attended by the heads of more than 80 governments and representatives from more than 100 other governments. Reflecting the declining commitment of the EDCs to foreign aid, though, the leaders of most of the EDCs were not present. The United States, for example, sent its secretary of agriculture. Without the strong support of the EDCs, though, there was little of immediate substance that the summit could accomplish. It did, however, establish the goal of reducing the number of undernourished people from 800 million to 400 million by 2015. It also reaffirmed the UN's traditional standard that the EDCs should devote 0.7% of their respective GDPs to development aid, including food and agricultural assistance. Third, in a move that rankled Washington and some other capitals, the conference resolved that "food should not be used as an instrument for political and economic pressure."[31] This swipe at economic sanctions came just days after the UN General Assembly voted overwhelmingly to urge the United States to end its embargo against Cuba. The delegates also declared their belief in "the right of everyone to have access to safe and nutritious food [and] . . . the fundamental right of everyone to be free from hunger." The recognition of a prescriptive right to adequate nutrition had little immediate meaning, but such rhetorical flourishes are often one of the building blocks that change attitudes and eventually lead to action.

The continuing problems with supplying adequate calories and nutrition to a large number of LDCs occasioned a review of the efforts since the 1996 conference. The World Food Summit—Five Years Later conference, organized by the FAO, was held in Rome during June 2002. The fifth year review was necessary, in the estimation of Jacques Diouf, the FAO's director-general, because little progress was being made toward achieving the goal to cut the number of malnourished people in half, set by the 1996 conference. "There is very little evidence," according to Diouf, "of the large-scale purposive action needed to get to grips with the underlying causes of hunger."[32]

Adequate Health Standards

Those who believe that humans have prescriptive rights would put living in reasonably healthy conditions and having access to adequate health care on the list of those rights. Reality is far from this ideal.

Health Needs

The state of medical care, sanitation, and other conditions related to health in some areas of the world is below a level imaginable by most readers of this book. While health care is well below EDC standards in most LDCs, it is in the LLDCs that the greatest need exists. As one measure, the EDCs annually spend $105 per capita on health care for every $1 spent by the LLDCs (Ghobara, Huth, & Russett, 2004). By another measure, there are 10 times as many physicians per person and 5 times as

Child Mortality Rates

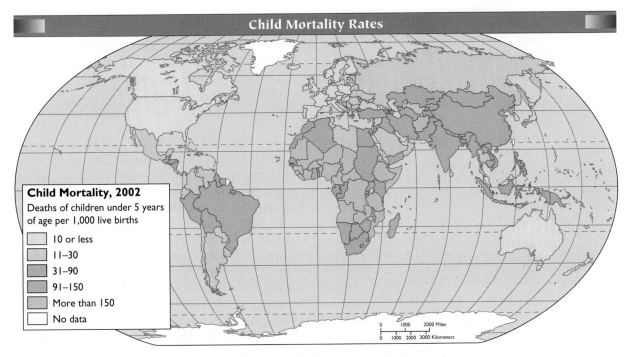

Child Mortality, 2002

Deaths of children under 5 years of age per 1,000 live births

- 10 or less
- 11–30
- 31–90
- 91–150
- More than 150
- No data

If children have a prescriptive right to enough health care to give them a reasonable chance of surviving to age five, then children in many countries, particularly the poorest ones, are being denied their rights. This map shows the global distribution of child mortality rates, the probability that a child will die before reaching age five. In the poorest countries, children are at least 15 times more likely to die before their fifth birthday than are children in the United States and other wealthy countries.

many hospital beds per capita in the EDCs as there are in the LLDCs. The health of people within these countries is an international concern for reasons beyond altruism. A healthy population is vital to economic growth because healthy people are economically productive and because unhealthy people often consume more of a society's resources than they produce.

The fate of children is one way to think about health care. In LLDCs, children under age five die at a rate that is 16 times higher than for children in the North. Compared to children in the EDCs, those in the LLDCs are more frequently exposed to disease because of poor sanitation and other factors, they are more vulnerable to disease because of malnutrition, and they more often succumb to disease because basic medical care is not available. Overall, an estimated 70% of the children under age five in the LDCs who die each year perish from infectious and parasitic diseases that are easily preventable and claim only 1% of the children in the EDCs. "No famine, no flood, no earthquake, no war has ever claimed the lives of this many children a year," the director of UNICEF once lamented.[33]

Adults also suffer from poor health conditions and lack of adequate health care. Nearly all births in the EDCs are attended by skilled health professionals; less than 40% of the births in LLDCs are. That is one reason that the maternal mortality rate in the LLDCs is 53 times the rate in the EDCs. Also, diseases once thought to be on the decline can reassert themselves catastrophically. Tuberculosis is one such disease. It has resurged in recent decades. Now over 40 million people have TB, 9 million new

Web Link

The beta version of the World Health Organization's World Health Chart, which contains graphical information on a range of health issues, is available at **www.whc.ki.se/index.php.**

cases occurred in 2004, and 1.7 million people died of the disease. TB is found everywhere, but the rate in the LLDCs is 13 times the rate in the EDCs. Plague is another old disease that refuses to die. The plague, or "Black Death," that killed one-third of Europe's population in the mid-1300s, still afflicts over 2,000 people a year, 99% of them in Africa. If strains resistant to antibiotics develop, as has happened with TB, plague could once again travel widely, as the Black Death did from Asia to Europe in 1347.

New problems add to these old worries. The worldwide AIDS epidemic, for one, is a global killer. At the beginning of 2005, one of every 161 humans, about 39 million people, worldwide were HIV-positive. That was a net annual increase of 2 million cases, a grim statistic derived from subtracting the 3 million people who died from AIDS-related causes from the 5 million new HIV-positive people. Some countries are truly devastated. More than 20% of the populations of seven sub-Saharan countries are HIV-positive, with Botswana having an especially disturbing 39% infection rate. Perhaps the most tragic victims are the 2.5 million children under age 15 who are HIV-positive. A half million of them died in 2004, and were sadly replaced by 650,000 new cases. Other children will fall victim to AIDS in a different way. In Botswana, about 40% of pregnant women were HIV-positive. The UN estimates that by the end of the decade well over 10 million children will lose their mothers to AIDS. These millions of orphans are a human tragedy, and they will also be an added economic burden on countries that are already struggling economically.

Yet other horrific emerging diseases lurk in the shadows and threaten to spread, as AIDS has, to a world with few or no natural or manufactured immunological defenses. SARS (severe acute respiratory syndrome) and West Nile virus are discussed in chapter 1. Neither of them is anywhere near as scary as the threat of avian influenza (avian flu, bird flu). In 2004 a flu outbreak in Southeast Asia was traced to a strain of avian flu that, unusually, had spread from domestic fowl to humans in Asia. Only 130 cases were confirmed in 2004 and 2005, but 51% of the sick died. WHO officials warn that if the disease spreads globally it might kill 50 million people within a year or two. Such numbers are not scare tactics: the great influenza pandemic of 1918–1919 caused an estimated 40 to 50 million deaths worldwide. In the United States, 28% of the population came down with the "Spanish flu," and 675,000 died from it. Possibly a strain of avian influenza, the disease spawned its own morbid child's verse used to skip rope:

SIMULATION
Threats to World Health

> I had a little bird,
> Its name was Enza.
> I opened the window,
> And in-flu-enza.

So far, preventive measures including the slaughter of more than 140 million chickens and other domestic fowl in Southeast Asia have kept bird flu in check. But flu vaccines used today do not work on the current strain, and WHO officials continue to warn that the threat of global contagion is real.

What makes these diseases even more of a world problem than they once were is the flow of humans and their products around the globe, which means that diseases can be spread very quickly from continent to continent. A person who contracts an

Through such organizations as UNAIDS, the United Nations is at the center of the international effort to combat the spread of the HIV virus and to ease the suffering of those with AIDS, their families, and their communities.

exotic disease in one place can board an airplane and, 12 hours later, be stifling a sneeze while sitting next to you in a restaurant.

Such diseases are more than just a threat to individual health; they are also a national security risk. For example, a U.S. Central Intelligence Agency report concludes that, "New and reemerging infectious diseases . . . pose a rising global health threat and . . . complicate U.S. and global security over the next 20 years" because they "endanger U.S. citizens at home and abroad, threaten U.S. armed forces deployed overseas, and exacerbate social and political instability in key countries and regions in which the United States has significant interests."[34]

International Response to Health Issues

Clearly, the greatest current threat to health globally is HIV and AIDS. Reflecting that, the most intense single international health initiative is coordinated by the Joint United Nations Programme on HIV/AIDS (UNAIDS), an alliance of ten UN agencies and other IGOs such as the World Bank. Founded in 1995 and with a budget of about $150 million, UNAIDS gathers information, works with national governments, and coordinates the international effort to slow and someday halt new HIV infections, to care for those already infected, and to ease the impact of the epidemic on the countries and families of the afflicted. The organization also works with other IGOs and NGOs, such as the Global Fund to Fight AIDS, Tuberculosis and Malaria, which is supported by national governments, IGOs, NGOs, and private donors, and spends about $1.8 billion annually. AIDS is proving nearly intractable, with the number of people infected each year still climbing. However, the various international efforts have reached many millions of people with AIDS prevention information and assistance and have provided some medical help to those who are HIV-positive or who have AIDS. It is probable that without such work, the disease rate would been even higher than it is today.

While combating AIDs is proving frustrating, much better progress is being made on other health fronts. Overall, health conditions and health care in the LLDCs has improved. A few decades ago only 5% of the children in LLDCs received any vaccinations; now 67% receive protection against diphtheria, whooping cough, tetanus, and polio. For this and other reasons, child mortality in the LLDCs is down from one in four children in 1960 to one in eight children now. Adults are also healthier in the

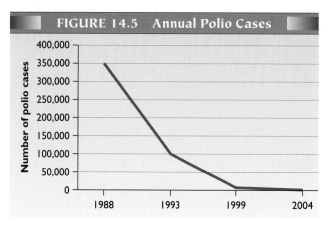

FIGURE 14.5 Annual Polio Cases

Global cooperation to provide better health wiped out smallpox and is on the verge of doing the same for polio. There were about 350,000 new cases of polio in 1988, the year that the World Health Organization resolved to eliminate the disease. With tens of millions of children being immunized each year, polio has become a rare disease. Overall, the number of countries where polio occurred dropped from 125 in 1988 to 18 in 2004.

Note: Cases for 1988, 1993, and 1999 approximate.
Data sources: Global Polio Education Initiative and UNICEF.

LLDCs. As discussed in chapter 13, their health prospects remain far below those in EDCs, but also like the children in the LLDCs, the adults are in better health and live longer than in previous decades.

Much of the credit for these advances goes to the **World Health Organization (WHO)**, headquartered in Geneva, Switzerland. The UN-affiliated WHO was created in 1946. It has 192 members and an annual budget of about $1 billion from member-countries and from other sources. The crusade against smallpox provides a heartening example of WHO's contributions. Smallpox was a scourge throughout human history. There were over 131,000 cases worldwide in 1967 when WHO began a 10-year campaign to eradicate the disease. It succeeded. The last case of smallpox, perhaps forever, occurred in Somalia in 1977. Polio is another disease whose death may be imminent. As Figure 14.5 shows, the annual global incidence has been cut by 99% since 1988. In 2004 WHO organized an all-out effort to eradicate polio within two years. One million health workers and volunteers began work in 23 countries to immunize 80 million children. The most resistant region to the vaccine and the one with the highest incidence of polio had been largely Muslim northern Nigeria. There, fundamentalist imams urged an immunization boycott, alleging that the polio vaccine was part of a U.S.-led plot to render Muslims infertile or infect them with the AIDS virus. However, parents' worries began to ease when vaccine made in Muslim countries was brought in and Nigeria's president and other top officials, including the governor of the northern province of Kano, appeared on television and personally placed drops of vaccine on the tongues of their young children or grandchildren. Perhaps when the next edition of this text is written, polio will have joined smallpox in the garbage can of history.

Basic Education

Education, like health, affects more than just the quality of life. Education is also a key to increased national and international productivity, population control, and other positive social goals.

Educational Needs

As with most other socioeconomic indicators, there is a vast gulf in the educational experience of children and young adults in the North and in the South. The LLDCs, the lowest-income countries, manage to annually spend only about $50 per student. The EDCs spend 110 times as much per student. Even factoring in purchasing power parity (see chapter 12) to account for the lower cost of living in LLDCs, the gap narrows to 23:1. The overall teacher-pupil ratio in EDC primary schools is 14:1; it is 43:1 in the LLDCs. About two-thirds of all students in EDCs go on to college or technical postsecondary training; only about 10% of students in the LLDCs do so. In our

Girls in many countries are still less likely to go to school or to remain in school than are boys. This gender disparity has decreased considerably, however, through the efforts of the United Nations Educational, Scientific, and Cultural Organization and other international agencies. The chances have improved that these girls in Hargeisa, Somalia, and other girls around the world will be able to play a fuller, more equal role in their societies than has been the case.

technological age, the lack of advanced training is a major impediment to development. In the North there are nearly 80 times as many scientists and technicians per capita as there are in the LLDCs.

The International Response to Education Issues

Promotion of education remains primarily a national function, but there are a number of international efforts. For one, the United Nations Educational, Scientific, and Cultural Organization (UNESCO) sponsors several programs. These national and international efforts are slowly paying off. In the 1950s less than 30% of all children in LLDCs ever attended any school; now almost all children begin the first grade and more than two-thirds complete primary school. This means that while the adult literacy rate in the LLDCs is still only 58%, the literacy rate for those ages 15 to 24 is now 71%. Data on secondary education is incomplete, but there are indications that there is progress at these levels also. Fairly typical of sub-Saharan Africa, only 8% of Malawi's high-school-age children were attending secondary school in 1990, now 33% are. Progress is also being made to narrow and eventually eliminate the gender gap in education. Among adults in LLDCs age 25 or older, men are 23% more likely to be literate than females. That gap is only 13% among people aged 15 to 24.

At the end of this section on prescriptive rights and the lengthier discussion of proscriptive rights, it is worthwhile to ask yourself how you feel about them. If a right is a justifiable claim, are these claims justified by whatever standard you believe should apply? Also, to the extent that you believe various rights exist, do the restraints of proscriptive rights and the obligations of prescriptive rights apply only in your own country or are they universal? To begin to answer these questions, consider the rights contained in the decision box, "Support a Global Bill of Rights?" Think about and debate them, as the box suggests. While doing that, particularly note which rights you believe are or should be prescriptive rights. If you believe that an obligation exists, does it end at national borders, or does it extend to humankind?

WRITE THE POLICY SCRIPT

Support a Global Bill of Rights?

It is easy to favor rights when ours are being violated. It is much harder to agree on what rights everyone, everywhere should have and which, therefore, we and our governments are obligated to respect and protect. There is also considerable controversy over whether rights are universal or culturally based and, even more, over whether prescriptive rights should be accorded the same support as the more familiar proscriptive rights.

The following list of rights are paraphrased from most of those contained in the Universal Declaration of Human Rights (1948). It arguably rejects culturally defined rights and favors universal rights in its preamble, which asserts the existence of "inalienable rights of all members of the human family." Many of them are very close to the proscriptive rights that most Americans and others are familiar with. For example, the language in the Universal Declaration and in clause 3 below is very much like the prohibition in the Eighth Amendment to the U.S. Constitution barring "cruel and unusual punishments." Other rights listed here are pre-scriptive. These obligate governments to assist people to achieve something, not to just protect people from being denied something. Clauses 23, 24, and 25 fall into that category; others may if you believe that they carry with them a positive obligation for societies and their governments to fulfill them.

What Do You Think?

In your class or with your friends, constitute yourselves as the World Constitutional Convention, debate the various clauses of the UNDHR, and decide whether to ratify or reject each one of them. You might also decide to open them up for amendment. For example, would you add "sexual orientation" to clause 11? You could even add a new clause, such as one that said, "The pronouns everyone and no one in this enumeration of rights include men and women without distinction." Also, note clause 27 and ponder whether it provides too much of an escape clause that potentially allows governments to violate rights. How say you to the propositions that:

1. Everyone has the right to life, liberty, and security of person.   Ratify _____   Reject _____

2. No one shall be held in slavery or servitude.   Ratify _____   Reject _____

3. No one shall be subjected to torture or to cruel, inhuman, or degrading treatment or punishment.   Ratify _____   Reject _____

4. Everyone is equal before the law and entitled to equal protection of the law.   Ratify _____   Reject _____

5. No one shall be subjected to arbitrary arrest, detention, or exile.   Ratify _____   Reject _____

6. Everyone charged with a crime shall be presumed innocent until proved guilty according to law in a public trial and shall be guaranteed the necessities for an adequate defense.   Ratify _____   Reject _____

7. Everyone has the right to freedom of movement and residence in their country.   Ratify _____   Reject _____

8. Everyone has the right to leave their country or any other and to return to their country whenever they wish.   Ratify _____   Reject _____

9. Everyone has the right to seek asylum in other countries to escape persecution.   Ratify _____   Reject _____

10. No one shall be arbitrarily deprived of their citizenship or the right to change it.   Ratify _____   Reject _____

11. Adults have the right to marry and have a family, without restrictions based on ethnicity, race, or religion. Both adults are entitled to equal rights both during marriage and at its dissolution.   Ratify _____   Reject _____

12. Everyone has the right to own property alone. No one shall be deprived of his property.

Ratify ____   Reject ____

13. Everyone has the right to freedom of thought, conscience, and religion and to express their beliefs in public and in private through teaching, practice, worship, and observance.

Ratify ____   Reject____

14. Everyone has the right to freedom of opinion and expression to seek, receive, and impart information and ideas through any media and regardless of frontiers.

Ratify ____   Reject ____

15. Everyone has the right to freedom of peaceful assembly and association.

Ratify ____   Reject ____

16. No one may be compelled to belong to an association.

Ratify ____   Reject ____

17. Everyone has the right to take part in their country's government, either directly or through freely chosen representatives.

Ratify ____   Reject ____

18. Everyone has the right to equal access to public services in his country.

Ratify ____   Reject ____

19. The will of the people shall be the basis of the authority of government; this will shall be expressed in periodic and genuine elections which shall be by universal and equal suffrage and shall be held by secret vote or by equivalent free voting procedures.

Ratify ____   Reject ____

20. Everyone has the right to work, to choose their work, to reasonable work conditions, and to protection against unemployment.

Ratify ____   Reject ____

21. Everyone has the right to equal pay for equal work.

Ratify ____   Reject ____

22. Everyone has the right to form and to join trade unions.

Ratify ____   Reject ____

23. Everyone has the right to an adequate standard of living, including food, clothing, housing, medical care, and other necessary social services regardless of age, health, or any other circumstance beyond their control.

Ratify ____   Reject ____

24. Mothers and children are entitled to special assistance and to equal help, regardless of marital or any other circumstance.

Ratify ____   Reject ____

25. Everyone has the right to education. It shall be compulsory and free, at least at the elementary level. Enrollment in more advanced levels shall be based on merit.

Ratify ____   Reject ____

26. Parents have a right to choose the kind of education given to their children.

Ratify ____   Reject ____

27. Everyone must uphold these rights, except as determined by law to be necessary to meet the just requirements of morality, public order, and the general welfare in a democratic society.

Ratify ____   Reject ____

Chapter Summary

The Nature of Human Rights

1. Rights can be divided between proscriptive rights, those that others cannot violate, and prescriptive rights, those that others are obligated to ensure everyone attains.
2. The universalist and relativist schools of thought have different approaches to the origin of rights.
3. Human rights abuses are widespread. They spring from intolerance, authoritarianism, societal biases, and other causes, and they are often rationalized by pseudoscientific theories, such as social Darwinism, and by repressive ideologies, such as fascism.

Proscriptive Human Rights

4. The discussion of proscriptive human rights, the abuses of them, and the efforts to ease them focuses on women, children, ethnic and racial groups, religious groups, indigenous peoples, and refugees and immigrants.
5. The area of human rights is one of the most difficult to work in because violations are usually politically based. Therefore, efforts to redress them are often resented and rejected by target countries. The greatest progress has been made in adopting a number of UN declarations, such as the Universal Declaration of Human Rights, and multilateral treaties that define basic human rights. The enforcement of human rights is much less well developed, but the rising level of awareness and of disapproval of violations on a global scale are having a positive impact. There are also many IGOs, such as the UN Human Rights Commission, and

NGOs, such as Amnesty International, that work to improve human rights.

Prescriptive Human Rights

6. The discussion of prescriptive human rights focuses on what some people claim are the rights to adequate nutrition, health prevention and care, and education.
7. Population growth, the underproduction of food, and the maldistribution of the food that is produced are factors contributing to food shortages and inadequate nutrition for many people in LDCs. International organizations, such as the Food and Agriculture Organization, attempt to provide short-term food relief and long-term agricultural assistance to countries facing nutritional shortages.
8. Many people in LDCs face disease and lack of medical care to degrees that boggle the minds of most people in EDCs. Some of the diseases, such as AIDS, can become a world health threat. The World Health Organization, other IGOs, and many NGOs are attempting to bring better health care to people globally.
9. The ability of individuals to achieve a higher quality of life and the ability of countries to develop economically depend in substantial part on education. More than 1 billion adults are still illiterate, many more have only the most rudimentary education, and the personal and societal productivity of these people is limited. The United Nations Educational, Scientific, and Cultural Organization is one of many international organizations working to improve education in the LDCs.

For simulations, debates, and other interactive activities, a chapter quiz, Web links, PowerWeb articles, and much more, visit **www.mhhe.com/rourke11/** and go to chapter 14. Or, while accessing the site, click on Course-Wide Content and view recent international relations articles in the *New York Times*.

Online *Learning*Center with POWERWEB

Key Terms

communitarianism
Convention on the Elimination of All Forms of Discrimination Against Women (CEDAW)
Convention on the Rights of the Child

cultural imperialism
individualism
International Convention on the Elimination of All Forms of Racial Discrimination

International Criminal Court (ICC)
prescriptive rights
proscriptive rights
relativists
Universal Declaration of Human Rights

universalists
World Conference on Women (WCW)
World Food Summit
World Health Organization (WHO)

CHAPTER 15

Preserving and Enhancing the Biosphere

Comfort's in heaven, and we are on the earth.
—William Shakespeare, *Richard II*

Dear earth, I do salute thee with my hand.
—William Shakespeare, *Richard II*

U.S. Senator John McCain (R-AZ) displays a blowup of the cover of the September 2004 issue of *National Geographic,* which warned of the dangers of global warming. McCain and others want the United States to reduce its emission of greenhouse gases, as most of the rest of the industrialized countries have agreed to do under the Kyoto Protocol. Others, including President George Bush, oppose major cutbacks as too costly and unnecessary. The issue in many ways epitomizes the debate between environmental pessimists and optimists, and a decision box at the end of this chapter asks which group's view you support.

THIS CHAPTER DEALS with the **biosphere:** the Earth's ecological system (ecosystem) that supports life—its land, water, air, and upper atmosphere—and the living organisms, including humans, that inhabit it. One certainty and two issues related to it are at the center of our discussion here. What is certain is that the well-being of each of us is connected to the ecological state of the world. Using medical analogies, one scientist refers to the biosphere as "the planet's life-support system." Another scientist calls it humankind's "umbilical cord," and adds, "Common sense . . . tells us that if we ruin the Earth, we will suffer grievously."[1]

Of the two related issues, the first is the state of the biosphere. Are there major problems and, if so, how threatening are they? If there are significant concerns, then the second issue is what to do. As you read this chapter you will see that most but not all scientific experts and political leaders believe that we face a range of ecological issues. Exactly what they are and how substantial they are is a bit more controversial. Subject to even more debate is what to do. One approach roughly coincides with the traditional path of world politics based on sovereign, self-interested states. Those who advocate this path resist the idea that their country should sacrifice short-term national economic gains in the interest of the long-term common ecological good. Those whom we might term ecological nationalists are especially averse to policies that restrain their country more than others. Ecological nationalists also oppose compromising their country's sovereignty by submitting to international regulation. By contrast, ecological internationalists, much like economic internationalists, believe that the interests of their country are inextricably bound up with the interests of all other countries. Therefore, ecological internationalists favor protecting the biosphere through a cooperative approach that includes international standards and regulations and, when necessary, making short-term sacrifices that will benefit their own and everyone else's long-term interests. In sum, ecology is about science, but it is also very much about politics.

The Ecological State of the World

Just as the U.S. president delivers an annual State of the Union address to Congress, each year the Worldwatch Institute assesses the ecological state of the world in a book, *The State of the World.*[2] We should follow its lead and regularly take stock of the Earth we all live on.

Green Accounting

A good place to start our survey of the state of the world is **green accounting.** This measures a country's strength by beginning with overall and per capita gross national product (GNP) and other traditional measures of national wealth and then adding two other factors. One is covered in chapter 8 and includes "human capital," the productive capacity of a country's population as determined by its education, health, and other factors. "Natural capital" is the second factor. It includes the quality and quantity, as appropriate, of land, air, water, and natural resources. Calculating human and natural capital is difficult, but the results are valuable. Nobel Prize–winning economist Robert M. Solow contends that green accounting is an advance over the traditional approach to measuring assets because "what we normally measure as capital is a small part of what it takes to sustain human welfare." Therefore, adds

SIMULATION
Worldwatch Issue Alerts

Web Link

For an interactive green accounting site, go to http://web.nmsu.edu/~dboje/ TDgreenaccounting.html.

another economist, green accounting "is a valuable thing to do even if it can only be done relatively crudely."[3]

Some parts of the ecological aspects of green accounting fall squarely within traditional measures of national power. For example, chapter 12 discusses the importance of petroleum and other natural resources and agricultural capacity. Other aspects of green accounting, such as giving economic value to clean air and water, are less standard. Nevertheless, the argument goes, they are also important determinants of national well-being because countries face a bleak future if they do not preserve and, when possible, replenish their natural capital. As one observer put it, "countries must be wary of pursuing short-term gains by selling off the family jewels."[4]

How much is the biosphere worth according to green accounting? One group of 13 scientists who set out to place a value on Earth's ecological systems assigned a dollar value to 17 different natural functions (such as water supply, soil formation, oxygen generation by plants) based on either the economic value they supply or what it would cost to replicate them artificially.[5] The estimates of the scientists ranged from $16 trillion to $54 trillion, with $33 trillion as a median figure. Adjusting for inflation to 2005, that is about $40 trillion, an amount slightly larger than the world's GNP that year. More importantly, whatever the exact value may be, it is clear that in sheer dollars and cents, the globe's ecological systems are extraordinarily valuable.

The Bottom Line

"How are we doing?" is the question that the bottom line of any accounting system seeks to answer. On this issue, there is agreement on the immense financial value of the biosphere and our dependence on it. Consensus ends, however, when we turn to the question of the current and future ecological state of the world. Here the range of opinions can be roughly divided into two camps: the environmental pessimists and the environmental optimists.

Environmental Pessimists

Those analysts who assess the state of the world and believe that humans are causing serious, even irreversible, damage to the environment are **environmental pessimists.** They further worry that the environmental damage will increasingly cause human suffering: severe and devastating storms due to global warming, skin cancer due to ozone layer depletion, warfare over scarce natural resources, and other problems. This school of thought charges that those who ignore the environmental degradation that is already occurring and hope that new energy supplies and other scientific and technological innovations will make strong conservation unnecessary are akin to the proverbial ostrich that keeps its head planted firmly in the sand so that it can avoid seeing trouble. Generally, environmental pessimists are also environmental internationalists, because they believe that only global cooperation can stem and hopefully reverse the damage they believe is being done to the biosphere.

caglecartoons.com/espanol

Emulating the annual publication, *The State of the World,* environmental pessimists give the biosphere a checkup, find it seriously ailing, and advocate strong measures to restore its health. Environmental optimists come to a different conclusion. They argue that any problems that do exist are not severe and that they can be addressed without taking dramatic measures.

Those who contribute to the annual *State of the World* volume are among the environmental pessimists group. The 2003 edition of the book warns that, "depending on the degree of misery and biological impoverishment that we [humans] are prepared to accept, we have only one or perhaps two generations [20 to 40 years] in which to reinvent ourselves" (p. 5). It is imperative to do so, the study warns, because, "by virtually every broad measure, our world is in a state of pervasive ecological decline." The analysis concedes that such "damage assessments have an air of unreality about them," but argues this is so because "few of us ever encounter the toxic waste, soil degradation, or unsustainable mining and logging to support our collective consumption," activities that are occurring yet constitute largely "invisible threats." Some pessimistic analysts even foresee "environmental scarcities" as the cause of future warfare among states desperate to sustain their economies and quality of life. According to one study, scarcities of renewable resources are already causing some conflict in the world, and there may be "an upsurge of violence in the coming decades . . . that is caused or aggravated by environmental change" (Homer-Dixon, 1998:342).

Environmental Optimists

Those who reject this gloomy view of the world environment and its future are termed **environmental optimists.** Some optimists believe that the pessimists resemble Chicken Little, the protagonist in a children's story who was hit on the head by a shingle that had fallen off the barn roof. Convinced that he had been struck by a piece of the sky, Chicken Little panicked and raced around the barnyard crying, "The sky is falling, the sky is falling," thereby creating unfounded pandemonium. Optimists tend to chastise the ecology movement for promoting "green guilt" by alarming people. "On average we overworry about the environmental areas," one such critic notes. That is not necessary, he continues, because "things are actually getting better and better, and they're likely to do so in the future." He concedes, "This does not mean that there are no problems," but reassuringly argues they "are getting smaller" (Lomborg, 2003:312). Just as most environmental pessimists are also environmental internationalists, most environmental optimists are also environmental nationalists. They believe that whatever problems exist are not worrisome enough to warrant countries either making economic and social sacrifices to overcome them, or surrendering any part of their sovereignty by submitting to international standards, monitoring, and enforcement.

Optimists say that the sky remains safely in its traditional location and that with reasonable prudence there is no need to fear for the future. They argue that we will be able to meet our needs and continue to grow economically through conservation, population restraints, and, most importantly, through technological innovation. They believe that new technology can find and develop additional oil fields. Synthetics can replace natural resources. Fertilizers, hybrid seeds, and mechanization can increase crop yields. Desalinization and weather control can meet water demands. Energy can be drawn from nuclear, solar, thermal, wind, and hydroelectric sources. In sum, according to one of the best-known optimists, economist Julian Simon (1994:297), not only do the scientific facts indicate that "the current gloom-and-doom about a 'crisis' of our environment is all wrong," but "almost every economic and social change or trend points in a positive direction." In fact Simon was so sure of his view that in 1980 he made a $1,000 bet with an equally convinced pessimist, biologist Paul Ehrlich, author of *The Population Bomb,* about the prices of five basic metal ores in 1990. Ehrlich wagered that population demands would drive the prices up; Simon bet they would not. A decade and nearly a billion people later, the prices were all down. Ehrlich sent Simon a check.

It is important to note that most optimists do not dismiss the problems that the world faces. "Progress does not come automatically," Simon wrote, "and my message is not complacency. In this I agree with the doomsayers—that our world needs the best efforts of all humanity to improve our lot." That effort will be provided, he continued, expressing his profound optimism, by our "ultimate resource . . . people— especially skilled, spirited, and hopeful young people . . . who will exert their wills and imaginations for their own benefit, and so inevitably they will benefit not only themselves but the rest of us as well" (p. 306).

Sustainable Development

Throughout most of history, the Earth has provided humans with the necessities of life, has absorbed what they have discarded, and has replenished itself. Now, the exploding human population and technology have changed this, and environmental pessimists warn that we are straining the Earth's **carrying capacity**: the largest number of humans that the planet can sustain indefinitely at current per capita rates of consumption of natural resources and discharges of pollution and other waste. Not only are there six times as many people as there were just a little more than 200 years ago, but our technological progress has multiplied our per capita resource consumption and our per capita waste and pollutant production. Technological wizardry may bring solutions, as the optimists predict, but such solutions are uncertain. Therefore, the environmental pessimists believe that the world faces a crisis of carrying capacity—the potential of no longer being able to sustain its population in an adequate manner or being able to absorb its waste. To put this as an equation:

Exploding population	$\times$	Spiraling per capita resource consumption	$\times$	Mounting waste and pollutant discharges	$=$	Potential catastrophe

If the environmental pessimists are correct in their equation, then a primary goal should be to ensure we do not reach or, for safety's sake, even approach full carrying capacity. That will not be easy, however, because another fundamental goal of humans has been and remains to increase their economic well-being and to reap the other benefits, such as better health, that come with prosperity. The world's economically developed countries (EDCs) have largely achieved that goal; the world's less developed countries (LDCs) are intent on also doing so. Industrialization and science are key elements of development, yet they are two-edged swords in their relationship to the environment and the quality of human life. On the positive side, industrialization has vastly expanded global wealth, especially for the EDCs. Science has created synthetic substances that enhance our lives; medicine has dramatically increased our chances of surviving infancy and has extended adult longevity. Yet, on the negative side, industry consumes natural resources and discharges pollutants into the air, ground, and water. Synthetic substances enter the food chain as carcinogens, refuse to degrade, and have other baleful effects. Similarly, decreased infant mortality rates and increased longevity are positive, yet they have also been major factors promoting the world's rapid population growth.

All these phenomena and trends, however, are part of modernization and are unlikely to be reversed. The dilemma is how to achieve **sustainable development**. That is, how can we protect the biosphere and, at the same time, advance human

Web Link

More information on sustainable development is available on the Web site of the Canada-based IGO, International Institute for Sustainable Development at www.iisd.org/.

socioeconomic development? This conundrum overarches specific issues such as population, habitat destruction, and pollution. Pessimists would certainly see this concern as immediate and critical, but even most optimists would concede that the challenge would be vastly compounded if you were to increase the industrial production and standard-of-living levels of the 5.3 billion people who live in LDCs in the South up to the levels enjoyed by the less than 1 billion people who reside in the North.

The Conundrum of Sustainable Development

Here is the problem you should ponder as you read the rest of this chapter: If the minority of the world's population who live in EDCs use most of the resources and create most of the pollution, how can the South develop economically without accelerating the ecological deterioration that already exists? Think about what consumption would be like if China were economically developed and the Chinese per capita consumption of petroleum and minerals and per capita CO_2 emissions were equal to that of Americans. Figure 2.5 on page 59 illustrates this. Given the fact that China's population is about 4.4 times that of the United States, a fully developed China with a per capita consumption equal to the current U.S. level would more than triple the two countries' combined CO_2 emissions. By the same standard, the two countries' petroleum consumption would increase more than 400%. Furthermore, if you were to bring the rest of the LDCs up to the U.S. level of resource use and emissions discharge, then you would hyperaccelerate the depletion of natural resources and the creation of pollution. Clearly, this is not acceptable. Less clear is what to do. Other than doing nothing, the options fall into two broad categories: restricting development and paying the price for environmentally sustainable development.

> **Did You Know That:**
>
> China's petroleum consumption was 6.5 million barrels a day (bbl/d) in 2004; the United States used 20.5 million bbl/d. If the Chinese consumed as much oil per capita as Americans do, China's 2004 total would have increased by 84.5 million bbl/d, about doubling the world's current consumption of 84 million bbl/d.

Option 1: Restrict Development

Preserving the environment by consuming less is one possibility. What is necessary, according to one analyst, is to institute "an integrated global program to set permissible levels" for consumption and emission, to mobilize huge financial resources for resource conservation and pollution control, and to create "effective international institutions with legally binding powers . . . to enforce [the] agreed-upon standards and financial obligations" (Johansen, 1994:381). Those who advocate stringent programs believe that even if they seem unpalatable to many people now, eventually we will be better off if we make the sacrifices necessary to restrain development and preserve the environment.

Objections to such solutions leap to mind. Are we, for instance, to suppress LDC development? If the Chinese do not acquire more cars, if Indians are kept in the fields instead of in factories, and if Africans continue to swelter in the summer's heat without air conditioners, then accelerated resource use and pollution discharges can be partly avoided. As we saw in chapter 12, however, the LDCs are demanding a global "New Deal," as UN Secretary-General Annan has called it, that will allow them to develop industrially and technologically.[6] The EDCs cannot "try to tell the people of Beijing that they can't buy a car or an air-conditioner" because they pollute, said one Chinese energy official. "It is just as hot in Beijing as it is in Washington."[7]

Another possible answer is for the people of the North to use dramatically fewer resources and to take the steps needed to reduce pollution drastically. Polls show that most people favor the theory of conservation and environmental protection. Yet practice indicates that, so far, most people are also unwilling to suffer a major reduction in their own conveniences or standards of living. Efforts to get more Americans

The economic leaps that China and some other less developed countries are making is captured by this recent photograph of a man in Beijing pushing a flatbed tricycle loaded with air conditioners. China and other LDCs are determined to continue their development, even though a negative by-product is rapidly increasing damage to the biosphere.

WEB POLL
Opportunity and Costs

to use mass transit, for example, have had very little success. Proposals to raise U.S. gasoline taxes (thereby reducing consumption and raising environmental protection revenue) have met with strong political opposition, and the steep increase in prices at the pump in recent years makes tax hikes almost inconceivable. Even before the gas prices went up, a 2003 poll that asked Americans if they would be willing to pay 50 cents extra a gallon to reduce pollution found only 18% willing to do so.[8] Laws could be passed mandating compact cars, but Americans would probably vote anyone out of office who threatened their SUVs and pickup trucks.

Option 2: Pay for Environmentally Sustainable Development

A second possibility is to pay the price to create and distribute technologies that will allow for a maximum balance between economic development and environmental protection. Without modern technology and the money to pay for it, China, for example, poses a serious environmental threat. China now stands second behind the United States in terms of national CO_2 emissions (Economy, 2004). A primary reason is that China generates most of its commercial power by burning coal, which is very polluting. In 2003, China consumed almost 1.4 billion tons of coal, about 27% of the world total. That, combined with the country's economic development, is a major reason why China's per capita CO_2 emissions rose 91% between 1980 and 2000, while the rest of the world's emissions went up 59%. Even on a per capita basis, China's emissions increased 53% during the period, compared to a 12% global per capita increase.

There are choices, but each has trade-offs. One option is to install pollution control equipment such as "stack scrubbers" to clean the emissions from burning coal. That would aid the environment, but it would be hugely expensive. For example, a recent proposal to retrofit a huge coal-fired generating plant in Bulgaria with stack scrubbers and other equipment, which would clean up its sulfur dioxide emissions by 95%, came with an estimated price tag of $650 million. Bulgaria had EU backing for the project, and China and other LDCs would need similar support to meet the costs of reducing the discharge of pollutants. Another approach China could take is to consume more oil to decrease the use of coal. Oil imports are vastly expensive, however, and act as a drag on the country's socioeconomic development. Increased oil consumption at the level China would need would also accelerate the depletion of the world's finite petroleum reserves. Moreover, the new oil fields that are being found often lie offshore, and drilling endangers the oceans.

A third possibility is using hydroelectricity to provide relatively nonpolluting energy. This requires the construction of dams that flood the surrounding country-side, displace its residents, and spoil the pristine beauty of the river valley downstream. China, for example, is trying to ease its energy crunch and simultaneously develop clean hydroelectric power by building the massive, $25 billion Three Gorges Dam and hydroelectric project on the Yangtze River. The project, which rivals the Great Wall of China in scope, will vastly increase the availability of clean power to rural provinces by generating 18,200 megawatts of electricity without burning highly polluting coal. The dam will also help stem floods that have often caused catastrophic damage and death downstream. To accomplish these benefits, however, the dam will create a 370-mile-long reservoir, inundating over 200 cities, towns, and villages, forcing 1.3 million people from their homes. The rising water will submerge numerous archeological sites and what many consider one of the most scenic natural areas in the world. Moreover, a collapse of the dam from structural failure, earthquake or other natural disaster, or military attack could cause a flood of unimaginable proportions. Critics also charge that as the reservoir covers some 1,500 factories, hospitals, dumps, and other sites containing human and industrial waste, the water will become contaminated as the pollutants seep into it. Thus, the Three Gorges project is an almost perfect illustration of the difficulty of sustainable development.

Although the project will ease some environmental problems (in this case, coal burning) it will also have an adverse impact on people and on the environment. Even if you can cut such Gordian knots, you will encounter other problems: the short-term costs of environmental protection in terms of taxes to pay for government programs; the high costs of products that are manufactured in an environmentally acceptable way and that are themselves environmentally safe; and the expense of disposing of waste in an ecologically responsible manner.

Moreover, since the LDCs are determined to develop economically, yet must struggle to pay the costs of environmentally sound progress, the North will have to extend significant aid to the South to help it develop in a relatively safe way. Money is needed to create nonpolluting energy resources, to install pollution control devices in factories, and to provide many other technologies. The costs will be huge, with some estimates exceeding $120 billion a year. Billions more are needed each year to help the LDCs stem their—and the world's—spiraling population.

Is the North willing to pay this price? Polls show that people in many countries are concerned about global warming, ozone layer destruction, deforestation, wildlife destruction, and acid rain. Cross-national polls also regularly find that a majority of respondents say that their governments should do more to protect their country's environment and also to be involved in the global environmental effort. Yet surveys additionally find that a majority of citizens think that their tax burdens are already too heavy and are reluctant to support large expenditures on environmental programs. One illustrative poll presented Americans with a range of options to protect the environment including more regulations of industry, tax breaks for energy saving, higher taxes to reduce consumption, and other choices. Only 2% of the respondents favored higher taxes, the choice with the most obvious and direct cost to

Web Link

An excellent informational and visual site, including film clips, on the Three Gorges Dam is associated with the PBS Great Wall Across the Yangtze program at **www.pbs.org/itvs/greatwall/ yangtze.html.**

them.[9] This resistance will work against any attempt to amass the funds that need to be spent internationally to help the LDCs simultaneously develop and protect the environment.

The Politics of Sustainable Development

There is not a great deal of debate over the fact that future development has to occur in a way that does not lay further waste to the biosphere. But what to do and who is responsible for doing it is a much more difficult question, and the lack of resolution of that issue has hampered efforts to fashion an overall global approach to achieving the goal of sustainable development. There are sections later in this chapter that address problems and programs associated with the atmosphere, water, land, and other elements of the biosphere, but before taking those up, it is appropriate to review the global approach to sustainable development and its politics at its broadest level.

The first step to dealing with any problem is recognizing that it exists. This has occurred with regard to sustainable development; an indication is the convening of two UN-sponsored "Earth Summits," one in 1992 and the other in 2002. However, both illustrate the limits to progress and the political disagreements that stand in the way.

Earth Summit I

The convening in 1992 of the **United Nations Conference on Environment and Development (UNCED)** meeting in Rio de Janeiro symbolized the growing concern with the environment and how to achieve sustainable development. Popularly dubbed Earth Summit I, the conference was attended by 178 countries and 115 heads of state. Additionally, 15,000 representatives of NGOs attended a nearby parallel conference. The official conference produced Agenda 21 (a 112-topic, nonbinding blueprint for sustainable development in the 21st century) and two treaties (the Biodiversity Convention and the Global Warming Convention).

Earth Summit I brought to the fore the often-divisive politics of environmental protection. In particular, the North and the South were at odds on many issues. First, the LDCs argued that the burden of sustainable development should fall substantially on the EDCs because they were responsible for most of the pollution and depletion of resources. Second, the LDCs also contended that they should be exempt wholly or in part from environmental restrictions because the EDCs had already developed and it was unfair to ask the LDCs not to achieve what the EDCs already had. Indeed, some in the LDCs suspect that EDC efforts to restrict their development may be part of a neocolonial effort to keep the LDCs poor, weak, and dependent. Third, the LDCs maintained that they were too poor to develop their considerable resources in an environmentally sustainable way and, therefore, that the EDCs should significantly increase aid to help the LDCs do so. For their part, most of the EDCs, especially the United States, disagreed with each of these LDC positions.

These divisions created what amounted to a stand-off. The EDCs averted efforts by the LDCs to force them to set binding timetables for reducing the use of fossil fuels and the emissions of CO_2 and other gases that contribute to global warming. The North also resisted making major financial commitments. "We do not have an open pocketbook," President George H. W. Bush observed.[10] Similarly, the South avoided restrictions, including those pertaining to forest resources. "Forests are clearly a sovereign resource. . . . We cannot allow forests to be taken up in global forums," Malaysia's chief negotiator asserted.[11] Given the various divisions, it was not surprising that neither the Biodiversity nor Global Warming Convention created legally binding mandates. It would be an overstatement to call the conference a failure, however, because important global initiatives normally gestate for an extended period and the two treaties, Agenda 21, and the attention the conference generated all helped firmly plant the environment on the world political agenda.

Earth Summit II

Agendas are not action, though, and insufficient progress persuaded the UN to convene Earth Summit II: the **World Summit on Sustainable Development (WSSD)** in 2002. Secretary-General Kofi Annan explained that the WSSD was needed because "There is a gap between the goals and the promises set out in Rio and the daily reality [of what has been accomplished]."[12] To address that gap, high-ranking delegates, including 104 heads of state, from almost all of the world's countries and representatives from some 8,000 NGOs gathered in Johannesburg, South Africa.

The political disputes there were similar to those that had bedeviled Earth Summit I. For their part the United States and some other EDCs were not willing to commit to providing the LDCs with substantially increased aid for sustainable development, to accepting restrictive energy, waste treatment, and other policies that did not also apply at least in some measure to the LDCs, or to creating mandatory international standards monitored and enforced by international agencies. Taking a distinctly environmental nationalist point of view, one U.S. official objected to creating "new global bureaucracies" and argued that the best approach to protecting the biosphere was for "both developing and developed nations" to agree to mandatory policies.[13] Taking the opposite view, Secretary-General Annan asserted, "The richest countries must lead the way. They have the wealth. They have the technology. And they contribute disproportionately to global environmental problems."[14]

As had occurred in 1992, the political divisions prevented significant substantive progress on fashioning a common global approach to the environment. The EDCs did announce some new funding commitments, including increased U.S. aid for economic development from $10 billion to $15 billion within three years. The conference also adopted some important new targets for reducing pollution, resource depletion, and other assaults on the biosphere, although these standards were once again voluntary. These modest steps disappointed many environmental internationalists. The *State of the World* 2003 declared itself "pessimistic about the world's ability to move forward" and lamented, "The severe North-South splits . . . seemed deeper than ever" (p. xvi). Seconding that view, an Indonesian diplomat portrayed the conference as "a battle, a conflict of interest between developed and developing countries."[15] Here again, though, as in 1992, it would be wrong to judge the conference a dismal failure. Kofi Annan provided a good perspective. "I think we have to be careful not to expect conferences like this to produce miracles," he advised. "It is not one isolated conference that is going to do this whole thing. What happens is the energy that we create here, the commitments that have been made, and what we do on the ground as individuals, as civil society, as community groups and as governments and private sector."[16]

We can gain further perspective on the problems facing Earth Summits I and II by examining some of the key issues regarding the biosphere and the possibility of achieving international cooperation toward sustainable development. We will first consider population. Then we will turn to concerns over such resources as minerals, forests, wildlife, and water. Last, the chapter will take up environmental issues, including pollution of the ground, water, air, and upper atmosphere.

Sustainable Development: Population Problems and Progress

On Tuesday, October 12, 1999, the world population passed the 6 billion mark. That is a stunning number. Humans in their modern form date back about 40,000 years, and their number did not reach 1 billion until 1804. It took only another 195 years, to 1999, to get to the 6 billion mark. The jump from 5 billion to 6 billion had only taken 12 years. The world is awash in humanity, with China alone having more people than had been on Earth in 1804. The upward spiral has begun to slow, but only slightly. Current UN projections, as depicted in Figure 15.1, show the world population continuing to grow to 9 billion by midcentury. Given a reasonably finite amount of resources and ability to absorb waste, this growing population presents a challenge to the Earth's carrying capacity. That will be an especially acute problem in some regions because their populations will continue to grow at a relatively rapid rate. Africa will be the most troubled, as the accompanying map shows. What differences in population mean is that between 2000 and 2050, Africa's population is projected to increase 126%, while the rest of the world's population will grow 35%.

Over the years, the population has grown at an increasing pace for several reasons. *High fertility rates* are one. As recently as 50 years ago, the average woman had five children. That overall rate has fallen considerably, but there are still regions where it is five. *Fewer deaths* is a second and increasingly important factor. Better health means that more infants survive to grow up and adults live longer. In 1960, 17 of every 1,000 people worldwide died, now only 9 of every 1,000 people die each year. A third factor causing population growth is the *population base multiplier effect*. This problem is one of mathematics. During the next decade, some 3 billion women will enter their childbearing years. At the current fertility rate, these women will have 7.8 billion children. When they grow up, most of them will also become parents, producing even more babies until the world fertility falls to 2.1, the approximate "replacement rate" at which each set of parents has two surviving children.

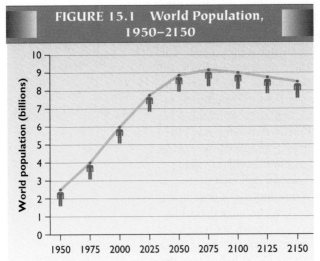

FIGURE 15.1   World Population, 1950–2150

The UN Population Division expects the world population to rise for about another 70 years to a peak of over 9 billion people, then to begin to gradually decline. Adding nearly 50% to the world's current population will strain the Earth's resources, especially given the increased use of resources and the generation of waste that is a by-product of economic development. Even the decrease shown here after 2075 will only be temporary. The UN expects the population to slowly rise again after 2150, once again reaching 9 billion in 2300.

Note: Data uses UN's "medium scenario."
Data source: UN Population Division, *World Population to 2003* (UN: New York, 2004).

Global Recognition of the Population Problem

The effort to control global population growth is led appropriately by the United Nations. There are a number of associated organizations and programs within the UN's purview. Of these, the United Nations Population Fund (UNFPA) is the largest. It began operations in 1969 and focuses on promoting family planning services and improving reproductive health in LDCs. During its history, UNFPA has provided over $6 billion to support population programs in the vast majority of the world's countries. In addition to its own programs, the agency helps

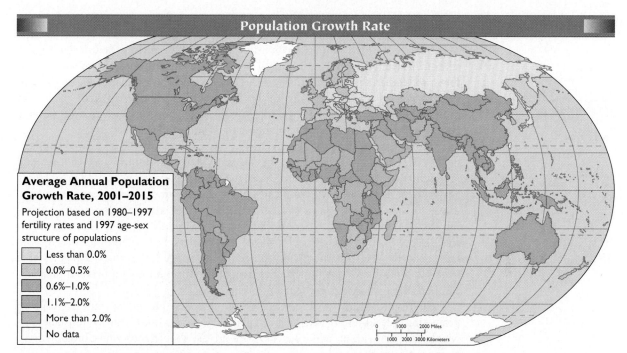

Population Growth Rate

Average Annual Population Growth Rate, 2001–2015

Projection based on 1980–1997 fertility rates and 1997 age-sex structure of populations

- Less than 0.0%
- 0.0%–0.5%
- 0.6%–1.0%
- 1.1%–2.0%
- More than 2.0%
- No data

The world's population approximately quadrupled during the 20th century. We continue to strain the Earth's resources by adding about 1 billion people every 13 years. Although Figure 15.1 and this map use slightly different data parameters, they are complementary. What you can see in this map is a graphic representation that the growth of population is not evenly spread around the globe. The fastest growth is in less developed countries of the South, which will struggle to house, educate, feed, and otherwise care for their burgeoning populations. At the same time, many of the economically developed countries of the North are near or even below the zero population growth rate. For these countries, an aging population will present a different set of challenges than face the LDCs with their massive number of children.

coordinate the programs of other related IGOs, NGOs, and national governments. Within the UN and its associated agencies, these include the United Nations Children's Fund (UNICEF) and the World Health Organization (WHO). UNFPA's efforts are further supplemented by and often coordinated with NGOs such as the International Planned Parenthood Federation (IPPF). This British-based organization, which was founded in 1952, operates its own international family planning programs and also links the individual planned parenthood organizations of about 150 countries.

In addition to these general responses, the need to control global population growth also led the UN to sponsor three world population conferences. The most recent of these was the 1994 **United Nations Conference on Population and Development (UNCPD)** in Cairo, Egypt. It brought together delegates from over 170 countries and a large number of NGOs and focused on population control and on reproductive health. Each year, for example, about 370,000 women (99% of whom live in LDCs) die from complications of pregnancy and childbirth.

Abortion was the most controversial issue at the conference. National laws governing abortion vary widely across the globe, with about one-third of the world's countries having some laws. These range from banning abortions or allowing them only to save a woman's life, having some restrictions based on a woman's motivation to seek an abortion, or having no restrictions other than limits to how long in the

MAP
Population Growth Rate

Web Link

You can watch the number of births, deaths, and other population data mount for the current day and other periods at **www.worldometers.info/**.

pregnancy an abortion is permitted. According to WHO, about 22% of all pregnancies are ended by induced abortions (those that occur for other than natural causes). Abortions performed in unsafe conditions, either in countries where it is illegal or severely restricted or in countries with an inadequate health care system, are a major threat to women's health. The World Health Organization estimates that of the millions of women who undergo unsafe abortions each year, about 68,000 die. There are estimates that in some countries, which both restrict abortions and are exceptionally poor, over half of all maternal mortality is the result of illegal abortions.

Controversy at the conference centered on how far it should go toward supporting abortion as a health measure or even as a population control approach. Several predominantly Muslim countries refused to attend the conference, and the Sudanese government charged that it would result in "the spread of immoral and irreligious ideas."[17] The Roman Catholic Church was also critical, with Pope John Paul II warning the conference not to "ignore the rights of the unborn."[18] Such stands drew sharp rebukes. For one, Prime Minister Gro Harlem Brundtland of Norway, who later headed WHO (1998–2003), charged that "morality becomes hypocrisy if it means accepting mothers' suffering or dying in connection with unwanted pregnancies and illegal abortions and unwanted children."[19]

The result of all this was a series of compromises. The document's language on promoting safe abortion was qualified by adding the phrase, "in circumstances in which abortion is legal," and it specified, "In no case should abortion be promoted as a method of family planning." The 1994 Cairo conference unanimously approved a "Program of Action" calling for spending $5.7 billion annually by the year 2000 on international programs to foster family planning. Funding never reached that goal, but the heightened awareness of the population problem and the closely associated issue of women's reproductive health and the postconference activity of the delegates and others did help to increase funding from $1.3 billion in 1993 to $2.2 billion in 2000.

Approaches to Reducing the Birthrate

There are two basic approaches to reducing the birthrate. *Social approaches* provide information about birth control and encouragement to practice it by making birth control devices and pills, sterilization, and, in some cases, abortion programs available. At the national level, many LDCs have made strong efforts, given their limited financial resources. In Thailand, for instance, 72% of all couples practice contraception (the contraceptive prevalence rate), a rate equal to most EDCs. These national efforts are supported by the UNFPA, other IGOs, and NGOs, and their combined efforts have had an impact. During the early 1960s, the contraceptive prevalence rate in the LDCs was only 9%. Now about half the couples in LDCs practice birth control. This contraceptive prevalence rate falls off drastically in the least developed countries (LLDCs), where it is only 23%. There are more than at least 15 countries in which the rate is a mere 10% or less.

Economic approaches to population growth can also be successful. There is a clear relationship between poverty and birthrates. In 2003, the birthrate per 1,000 population in the EDCs was 12. In the LLDCs it was 30, with sub-Saharan Africa at 39, more than triple the EDC rate. How does one explain the link between population and poverty? One view is that overpopulation causes poverty. This view reasons that with too many people, especially in already poor countries, there are too few resources, jobs, and other forms of wealth to go around. Perhaps, but that is only part of the problem, because it is also true that poverty *causes* overpopulation. The LLDCs tend to have the most labor-intensive economies, which means that children are economically valuable because they help their parents with farming or, when

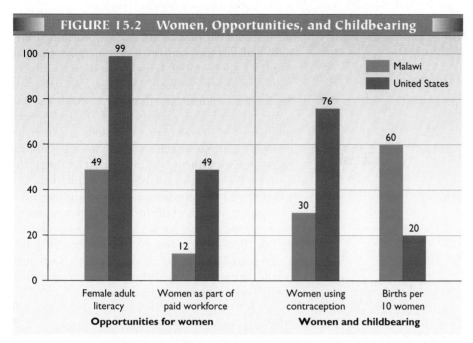

FIGURE 15.2   Women, Opportunities, and Childbearing

The greater the educational and economic opportunities that women have, the more likely they are to use contraception and the fewer babies they are likely to have. The two measures on the left show educational opportunities (the percentage of women who are literate) and economic opportunities (the percentage of the country's paid workers who are women). The two measures on the right show the likelihood that women are using contraception and how many children they have on average. Notice that American women have better educational and economic opportunities compared to women in Malawi and are also more likely to use contraception and less likely to have numerous children.

Notes: Workforce here excludes agricultural workers; contraception is percentage of women age 15–49 who have a sexual partner, one of whom uses contraception.
Data sources: World Bank (2005), UNDP (2005).

they are somewhat older, provide cheap labor in mining and manufacturing processes. As a result, cultural attitudes in many countries have come to reflect economic utility. Having a large family is also an asset in terms of social standing in many societies with limited economic opportunities.

Furthermore, women in LDCs have fewer opportunities to limit the number of children they bear. Artificial birth control methods and counseling services are less readily available in these countries. Another fact is that women in LDCs are less educated than are women in EDCs. It is therefore harder to convey birth control information, especially written information, to women in LDCs. Additionally, women in LDCs have fewer opportunities than do women in EDCs to gain paid employment and to develop status roles beyond that of motherhood. The lack of educational and economic opportunities are related to both the use of contraception and the fertility rate, as evident in Figure 15.2, which compares Malawi and the United States.

The evidence that poverty causes population increases has spurred efforts to advance the economic and educational opportunities available to women as an integral part of population control. This realization was one of the factors that led the UN to designate 1975 as International Women's Year and to kick off the Decade for Women. That year the UN also convened the first World Conference on Women (WCW). These initiatives were followed in 1976 by the establishment of the UN Development Fund for Women (UNIFEM, after its French acronym). The Fund

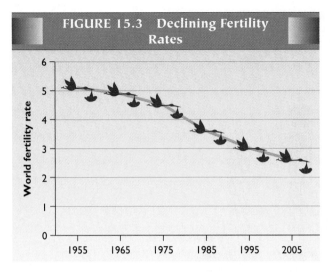

FIGURE 15.3   Declining Fertility Rates

The number of children the average woman bears (the fertility rate) has dropped by almost 50% over the last half-century. This welcome change is the result of numerous factors, including the work of international agencies to improve educational and economic opportunities for women and to provide information and other forms of assistance to women who wish to practice planned parenthood.

Data source: UN Population Division, *World Population to 2003* (UN: New York, 2004).

works through 10 regional offices to improve the living standards of women in LDCs by providing technical and financial support to advance the entry of women into business, scientific and technical careers, and other key areas. UNIFEM also strives to incorporate women into the international and national planning and administration of development programs and to ensure that the issues of particular concern to women such as food, security, human rights, and reproductive health are kept on the global agenda. The UN also established the International Research and Training Institute for the Advancement of Women with the task of carrying out research, training, and information activities related to women and the development process. Headquartered in the Dominican Republic, the institute conducts research on the barriers that impede the progress of women in social, economic, and political development.

The Impact of International Population Control Efforts

The effort to reduce global population growth is a success story. Part of this is due to the work of IGOs, NGOs, and national governments. Improved economic conditions in many LDCs and the slowly improving economic and educational status of women in many countries have also played a role. As a result, the average global fertility rate has declined dramatically, as evident in Figure 15.3. The goal is 2.1, which is about the stable replacement rate. The UN expects that standard to be reached by midcentury. Indeed, after that the UN expects the fertility rate to drop below the replacement rate, which will for a time at least decrease the world population late in this century. As recently as 1994, the population was expanding at 94 million a year, and the UN was estimating that it would reach 11.6 billion by 2150. Now the population is projected to peak at more than 2 billion people short of that. That is stellar news, but it merits two cautions. One is that population is hard to predict. There is a UN "worse-case scenario" that projects the population at 14 billion at the end of this century and peaking at 36 billion in 2300. Second, the slowdown does not mean that a substantial increase is not still looming. The difference in the old and new projections, according to one demographer, "is comparable to a tidal wave surging toward one of our coastal cities. Whether the tidal wave is 80 feet or 100 feet high, the impact will be similar."[20]

Sustainable Development: Resource Problems and Progress

Recent decades have witnessed increased warnings that we are using our resources too quickly. Most studies of the rates at which we are depleting energy, mineral, forest, land, wildlife, fishery, and water resources have expressed a level of concern ranging from caution to serious alarm.

Petroleum, Natural Gas, and Minerals

The supply of oil, gas, and mineral resources is one area of concern. At the forefront of these worries are the cost and supply of energy resources. World energy needs are skyrocketing. Global energy production increased roughly 48% between 1980 and 2002. Of the major sources, burning fossil fuels (coal, oil, gas) provides about three-fourths of the output; following in declining order are burning wood, crop residue, and other forms of biomass; then, nuclear energy. Only about 3% of energy is produced by such environmentally friendly sources as hydroelectric, solar, geothermal, and wind power. At one time the world had an estimated 2.3 trillion barrels of oil beneath its surface. Current known reserves are about half of that. At the rate that oil is being consumed—30 billion barrels in 2004—simple math would suggest that the world's oil wells will go dry in about 40 years. But projections are tricky because demand changes, because new sources of oil are sometimes discovered, and because new techniques such as deep sea drilling are developed to tap previously unusable oil deposits. The result is that the known reserves of petroleum actually increased from 1.01 trillion barrels in 1996 to 1.17 trillion barrels in 2005. Nevertheless, petroleum reserves are a concern because the supply is indisputably exhaustible and because new finds are smaller and less attractive to utilize (deeper, under the ocean, in environmentally sensitive land areas).

The story for natural gas is nearly the same. New discoveries, enhanced extraction methods, and other factors may have an impact on the timing, but the bottom line is that the supply is finite and at some point, perhaps within the lifetime of people being born today, it will be exhausted. Coal will last almost 500 years at current consumption rates, but it is a major pollutant if not controlled by expensive technology. The development of hydroelectric power is attractive in some ways, but it is expensive to develop, and damming rivers creates environmental and social problems. Nuclear power is yet another alternative, and some countries rely heavily on it. For one, France generates 80% of its electricity by nuclear power. However, only 30 countries generate nuclear power, and on average it amounts to only about 20% of their total commercial energy production. Additionally, there are high costs and obvious hazards to nuclear power. Some people advocate developing wind, solar, geothermal, and other such sources of power. So far, though, cost, production capacity, and other factors have limited the application of these energy sources and will continue to do so unless there are major technological breakthroughs.

Another factor in the supply and demand for energy is understanding use patterns. The vast majority of all energy is used by the EDCs. Most of the growing demand for energy, by contrast, is a result of increased needs by the countries of the South. During the period 1980–2002, the energy consumption of EDCs increased 32%, while the LDCs' energy use increased 67%. Most of the LDC increase was because of population growth rather than development. This is evident in the modest 9% per capita energy use increase by the LDCs during the period compared to the 17% increase in per capita energy consumption in the EDCs. These patterns indicate that the most immediate way to deal with energy consumption is to restrain per capita increases in the North and to reduce population growth in the South.

In addition to oil and natural gas, many other minerals are also being rapidly depleted. Based on world reserves and world use, some minerals that are in particularly short supply (and estimates of the year that the Earth's supply will be exhausted given known reserves) include copper (2056), lead (2041), mercury (2077), tin (2053), and zinc (2042). Certainly, discoveries of new sources or the decline of consumption based on conservation or the use of substitutes could extend those dates.

Did You Know That:

The world's first oil well was drilled in 1859 in Titusville, Pennsylvania. Sold as a lubricant, oil initially averaged $25 a barrel, compared to over $65 a barrel in August 2005. Adjusted for inflation, the 1859 price is equal to about $582 a barrel today.

JOIN THE DEBATE
Is a Government-Sponsored Clean Energy Program the Answer to Rising Oil Prices and Overall Economic and Environmental Security?

But it is also possible that the time interval to depletion could narrow if, for instance, extraction rates accelerate as LDCs develop.

The resource puzzle, as mentioned, is how to simultaneously (1) maintain the industrialized countries' economies and standards of living, (2) promote economic development in the South (which will consume increased energy and minerals), and (3) manage the problems of resource depletion and environmental damage involved in energy and mineral production and use. If, for instance, the South were to develop to the same economic level as the North, if the LDCs' energy-use patterns were the same as the North's currently are, and if the same energy resource patterns that now exist persisted, then petroleum reserves would almost certainly soon be dry. Natural gas and many other minerals probably would also quickly follow oil into the museum of geological history.

Forests and Land

For many who will read this book, the trees that surround them and the very land on which they stand will hardly seem like natural resources and will certainly not seem to be endangered. That is not the case. There are serious concerns about the depletion of the world's forests and the degradation of its land.

Forest Depletion

The depletion of forests and their resources concerns many analysts. Data compiled by the UN Food and Agriculture Organization (FAO) and other sources indicates that the increase in world population and, to a lesser degree, economic development are destroying the world's forests. Some 1 billion people depend on wood as an energy source, and many forests have disappeared because of such domestic needs as cooking and heating. Forests are also being cleared to make room for farms and grazing lands. Forests and woodland still cover about 30% of the Earth's land area. Once, however, they occupied 48% of the land area, and tree cover is declining by about 1% every five years. Logging is a major factor, but forests are also being drowned by hydroelectric projects and being strip-mined for minerals. Acid rain and other environmental attacks increase the toll on trees. Whatever the cause, the result is that some 35,000 square miles of forest are being lost every year. This is a loss roughly equivalent to clear-cutting Portugal.

WEB MAP
Hot Spots of Diversity

Forest loss is not spread evenly across the world. Through conservation, reforestation, and (less positively) importing forest products from the LDCs, the EDC forests are actually growing by 0.1% a year. By contrast 0.3% of the LDCs' forests are disappearing annually, and for the LLDCs the loss rate is 0.8%. Significant stretches of Brazil, China, East Africa, and Malaysia have been nearly denuded of their forests. The tropical forests, which account for over 80% of all forest losses, are of particular concern. Fifty years ago, 12% of the Earth's land surface was covered by tropical forest; now just 6% is. The Amazon River basin's tropical forest in Brazil and the surrounding countries is an especially critical issue. This ecosystem is by far the largest of its kind in the world, covering 2.7 million square miles, about the size of the 48 contiguous U.S. states. The expanding populations and economic needs of the region's countries have exerted great pressure on the forest. For example, the Amazon basin has recently been losing 9,000 square miles (an area about the size of Massachusetts) of forest every year.

LDCs recognize the problem, but there are powerful economic incentives for them to continue clearing forestland. Domestically, it helps open up farmland and economic development. Internationally, the annual global trade in wood and wood products (such as paper, pulp, and resins) is over $200 billion, and poor countries are cutting

The world's forests continue to disappear as they are cut down to provide lumber and to clear land for agriculture and human settlement. The damage to the Amazon basin rain forest is evident in this aerial view contrasting recently cleared land in the state of Mato Grosso, Brazil, with its scrub growth being burned off with the lush rain forest adjoining it.

their trees and exporting the wood to earn capital to pay off their international debt and to finance economic development. It is easy to blame the LDCs for allowing their forests to be overcut, but many in those countries ask what alternative they have. "Anyone . . . who comes in and tells us not to cut the forest has to give us another way to live," says an official of Suriname. "And so far they haven't done that." Instead, what occurs, charges the country's president, is "eco-colonialism" by international environmental organizations trying to prevent Suriname from using its resources.[21]

Deforestation has numerous negative consequences. One is global warming, which we will discuss in a later section. Another ill effect of forest depletion is that wood in many areas has become so scarce and so expensive that poor urban dwellers have to spend up to a third of their meager incomes to heat their homes and cook. Poor people in rural areas have to devote the entire time of a family member to gather wood for home use. The devastation of the forests is also driving many forms of life into extinction. A typical 4-square-mile section of the Amazon basin rain forest contains some 750 species of trees, 125 kinds of mammals, 400 types of birds, 160 different kinds of reptiles and amphibians, and perhaps 300,000 insect species. The loss of biodiversity has an obvious aesthetic impact, and there are also pragmatic implications. Some 25% of all modern pharmaceutical products are "green medicines" that contain ingredients originally found in plants. Extracts from Madagascar's rosy periwinkle, for example, are used in drugs to treat children's leukemia and Hodgkin's disease. Taxol is a drug derived from the Pacific yew for use in cancer chemotherapy, and a soil fungus is the source of the anticholesterol drug Mevacor. Many plants also contain natural pesticides that could provide the basis for the development of ecologically safe commercial pesticides to replace the environmental horrors (such as DDT) of the past.

Land Degradation

Not only are the forests in trouble, so too is the land. Deforestation is one of the many causes of soil erosion and other forms of damage to the land. Tropical forests rest on thin topsoil. This land is especially unsuited for agriculture, and it becomes exhausted quickly once the forest is cut down and crops are planted or grazing takes

Did You Know That:

Eating less meat has environmental benefits. Producing one pound of beef requires 7 pounds of grain, which use 7,000 gallons of water to grow. For each resulting pound of meat, cattle discharge 12 pounds of manure and other organic pollutants and copious amounts of ozone layer–depleting methane. Of all U.S. grain produced, 70% goes to feed livestock.

place. With no trees to hold soil in place, runoff occurs, and silt clogs rivers and bedevils hydroelectric projects. Unchecked runoff can also significantly increase the chances of down-river floods, resulting in loss of life and economic damage, and deadly mudslides down barren slopes with no trees to hold the dirt in place. More than once in recent years, for instance, Central America has been slammed by a hurricane and devastated. After one such storm, "Nightmarish mudslides obliterated entire villages, half the population of Honduras was displaced, and the country lost 95% of its agricultural production. And in the chaos and filth of [the hurricane's] wake, there followed tens of thousands of additional cases of malaria, cholera, and dengue fever" (Bright, 2000:23).

According to the United Nations Environmental Programme (UNEP), 3.5 million square miles (about the size of China or the United States) of land are moderately degraded, 1.4 million square miles (about equal to Argentina) are strongly degraded, and 347,000 square miles (about the same as Egypt) are extremely degraded (beyond repair). At its worst, *desertification* occurs. More of the world's surface is becoming desertlike because of water scarcity, timber cutting, overgrazing, and overplanting. The desertification of land is increasing at an estimated rate of 30,600 square miles a year, turning an area the size of Austria into barren desert. Moreover, that rate of degradation could worsen, based on UNEP's estimate that 8 billion acres are in jeopardy.

Forest and Land Protection

Because almost all of the world's land lies within the boundaries of a sovereign state, international programs have been few. Desertification is one area in which there has been international action. Almost all countries are party to the Convention on Desertification (1994), which set up a structure to monitor the problem and to assist countries in devising remedial programs to reclaim barren land. There have also been some advances at the regional level. Most European countries abide by a 1979 treaty to reduce acid rain, and addressing that issue was the main goal of the Canada-U.S. Air Quality Agreement (1991). More recently, and addressing another problem, leaders of seven central African countries agreed in 2005 to a treaty to protect their region's rain forest, which is second in size to the one in the Amazon basin.

Progress is also being made at the national level in the preservation of forest and land resources, as well as on other resource and environmental concerns. Membership in environmental groups has grown dramatically. In several European countries and in the European Union, "green parties" have become viable political forces. For example, they have 34 (6%) of the seats in the European Parliament and Germany's Green Party has 55 seats (9%) in the Bundestag. The growing interest in flora and fauna is also increasing the so-called ecotourism trade, which some sources estimate makes up as much as a third of the nearly $500 billion annual tourism industry. For this reason, many countries are beginning to realize that they can derive more economic benefit from tourists than from loggers wielding chain saws.

Wildlife

World wildlife is amazingly diverse. These life forms (and the approximate number of known species for each) include mammals (4,300), reptiles (6,800), birds (9,700), fish (28,000), mollusks (80,000), insects (+1,000,000), and arachnids (44,000).

Global Pressure on Wildlife

The march of humankind has driven almost all the other creatures into retreat and, in some cases, into extinction. Deforestation, land clearing for settlement and farming, water diversion and depletion, and pollution are but a few of modernization's byproducts that destroy wildlife habitat. There are pragmatic, as well as aesthetic, costs. The blood-pressure drug Capoten is derived from the venom of the Brazilian pit viper, and vampire bat saliva is the basis of an anti–blood-clotting drug being tested to prevent heart attacks and stroke.

While some species are the unintended victims of development, others are threatened because they have economic value. The estimated $20 billion annual illegal trade in feathers, pelts, ivory, and other wildlife products is leading to the capture and sale or slaughter of numerous species, including many that are endangered. A snow leopard pelt fetches $1,000 in Afghanistan, and Komodo dragons and orangutans bring $30,000 on the black market in Indonesia. Other animals are killed for parts of their bodies, which are thought to have medicinal value. For example, poachers illegally kill more than 40,000 bears each year in the United States in part to harvest their gall bladders. These supposedly relieve a range of ailments (including convulsions, fever, and hemorrhoids) and sell for up to $3,000 when smuggled abroad.

It should be noted that on the issue of wildlife, like many other matters discussed in this chapter, there are optimists who believe that the problem is being grossly overstated. According to Julian Simon, "a fair reading of the available data suggests a rate of extinction not even one–one-thousandth as great as the one the doomsayers scare us with." Simon was careful to say that he was not suggesting "that we should ignore possible dangers to species." He contended, though, "we should strive for a clear and unbiased view of species' assets so as to make sound judgments about how much time and money to spend on guarding them."[22] Other analysts have agreed with that assessment (Lomborg, 2001).

Protecting Wildlife

Although the world's list of endangered species is still growing, these threatened species are also now gaining some relief through the Convention on the International Trade in Endangered Species (CITES, 1975) and the 167 countries that are party to it. Elephants were added in 1989 to the CITES list of endangered species, and the legal ivory trade has dropped from 473 tons in 1985 to zero. About 500 elephants a year are still being killed for their ivory by poachers, but that is far better than the annual toll of 70,000 elephants during the last decade before they were protected under CITES. Wild cats, reptiles, and other types of wildlife have also found greater refuge, and the international sale of their skins has declined drastically. The global trade in live primates, birds, and reptiles has seen similar decreases. Individual countries have also acted to suppress poaching and punish those engaged in the illegal sales of wildlife. In 2003, for example, Chinese officials impounded 1,276 illegal pelts from 32 tigers, 579 leopards, and 665 otters that had been smuggled into the

The Convention on the International Trade in Endangered Species has provided some relief to many endangered species by banning the international sale of live wildlife or wildlife products, such as skins. This picture shows the confiscated pelts of a tiger and leopard being burned by customs officials at Mumbai's (Bombay) international airport. The blaze was meant to send out a signal to those engaged in the illegal wildlife trade that India's government is serious about protecting endangered wildlife. Still, saving the tiger and other species is difficult because of their monetary value to poachers. A tiger skin can fetch $900, a canine tooth goes for $125, and each claw brings $10. Other parts of the big cat are used in traditional medicines. Men hoping to improve their virility pay $800 for a potion made from a tiger penis, and tiger bones, which are said to relieve rheumatism, sell for $180 a pound.

country. It was the largest seizure in China's history, and a particularly helpful sign from a region that is the destination of a great deal of the illegal trade in wildlife, especially in parts used in traditional medicine. Penalties, it should be noted, are especially stringent for such activity in China, which has executed at least 28 wildlife smugglers since 1990.

Freshwater

"Water, water everywhere, Nor any drop to drink," cries out an adrift seaman in Samuel Taylor Coleridge's *Rime of the Ancient Mariner* (1798). That cannot quite be said of the world's freshwater, but there is less of it than you might think. Yes, 71% of the Earth's surface is covered by water, but 97% of it is salt water and another 2% is frozen in the polar ice caps. This leaves only 1% readily available for drinking, watering livestock, and irrigating crops. Moreover, some of the freshwater supply that exists is being depleted or being tainted by pollution. Freshwater use, after tripling between 1940 and 1975, has slowed its growth rate to about 2% to 3% a year. Much of this is due to population stabilization and conservation measures in the EDCs. Still, because the world population is growing and rainfall is a constant, the world needs to use an additional 7.1 trillion gallons each year just to grow the extra grain needed to feed the expanding population.

Complicating matters even more, many countries, especially LDCs, have low per capita supplies of water, as you can see in the accompanying map. The world per capita availability is 6,895 cubic meters (1 m^3 = 264.2 gallons), but it is unevenly distributed. Indeed, about 20% of all countries have an annual availability of less than 1,000 cubic meters of water per person. Given the fact that Americans annually use 1,677 cubic meters of water per capita, the inadequacy of less than 1,000 cubic meters is readily apparent.

To make matters worse, the water usage in the LDCs will increase as they develop their economies. These increases will either create greater pressure on the water supply or will limit a country's growth possibilities. Globally, most freshwater is used for either agriculture (70%) or industry (20%), with only 10% for domestic (personal) use. Industrialized countries, however, use greater percentages for industry and more water per capita overall than LDCs. It follows then, that as the LDCs industrialize, their water needs will rise rapidly. China provides an example: Water use for industry, which was 46 billion cubic meters in 1980, has increased 107% to 95 billion cubic meters. Adding to the problem in many countries, a great deal of the water needed for drinking is being contaminated by fertilizer leaching, industrial pollution, human and animal wastes, and other discharges.

Compounding the demands on the water supply even further, global population growth means that the water supply worldwide will decline by one-third by 2050, leaving 7 billion people in 60 countries facing a water shortage. "Of all the social and natural crises we humans face, the water crisis is the one that lies at the heart of our survival and that of our planet Earth," the director-general of the United Nations Educational, Scientific, and Cultural Organization (UNESCO) has commented.[23] Such a projection coming to pass could lead to a competition for water and to international tensions. There are, for example, 19 countries that get 20% or more of their freshwater from rivers that originate outside their borders. The security of these countries would be threatened if upstream countries diverted that water for their own purposes or threatened to limit it as a political sanction. Such possibilities have led some analysts to suggest that in the not-too-distant future the access to water supplies could send "thirsty" countries over the brink of war.

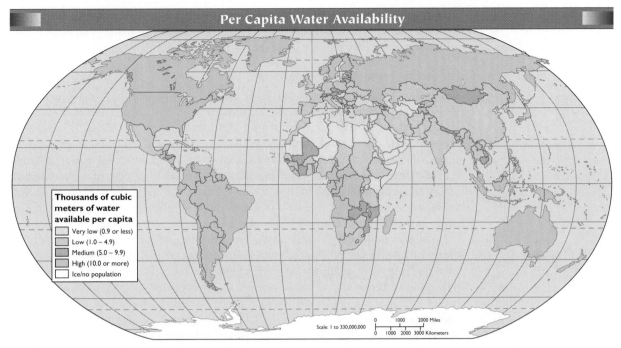

Per Capita Water Availability

Thousands of cubic meters of water available per capita
- Very low (0.9 or less)
- Low (1.0 – 4.9)
- Medium (5.0 – 9.9)
- High (10.0 or more)
- Ice/no population

Scale: 1 to 330,000,000

0   1000   2000 Miles
0 1000 2000 3000 Kilometers

A report by the United Nations Commission on Sustainable Development warns that 1.2 billion people live in countries facing "medium-high to high water stress."

Data source: World Resources Institute, 2005.

Such concerns are not new. The first known water treaty was negotiated 4,500 years ago by two Sumerian city-states to end their dispute over water in the Tigris River. Just since 1820, according to the UN, more than 400 treaties have been concluded relating to water as a limited and consumable resource. Nevertheless, old disputes reemerge and new ones break out. Such disputes recently moved the head of UNEP to contend that there is an "urgent need" for IGOs to "act as the water equivalent of marriage counselors, amicably resolving differences between countries . . . [that] may be straying apart."[24]

The Seas and Fisheries

The saltwater oceans and seas cover about two-thirds of the Earth's surface. The water may not be useful for drinking or irrigation, but the seas are immensely valuable resources. Their fish and the food they provide are covered in this section; marine pollution is taken up later in this chapter under environmental concerns.

Pressures on the Seas and Fisheries

Human food requirements put increasing pressure on the ocean's fish, mollusks, and crustaceans. The importance of marine life as a source of food plus the demands of a growing world population increased the marine (saltwater) catch from 19 million tons in 1950 to a plateau averaging 110 million tons during the past several years. Given an estimate by the Food and Agriculture Organization (FAO) that the sustainable annual yield of Earth's oceans is no more than 96 million tons, it is clear that a critical point has been reached. Among other concerns, damage to the world's fisheries, which supply 16% of the animal protein humans consume, poses a health threat to countries that rely on fish for vital protein supplies. Especially imperiled would be Asia and Africa, where fish contribute over 25% of the often inadequate animal protein in the diet of the regions' inhabitants.

Protecting Fisheries

One major step at the international level came in 1994 when the UN's convention on the Law of the Sea went into effect. Agreed to by 148 countries, not including the United States, the treaty gives countries full sovereignty over the seas within 12 miles of their shores and control over fishing rights and oil and gas exploration rights within 200 miles of their shores. That should improve conservation in these coastal zones. Additionally, an International Seabed Authority, headquartered in Jamaica, has been established. It will help regulate mining of the seabed in international waters and will receive royalties from those mining operations to help finance ocean-protection programs.

National and international efforts are also being made in other areas. A huge decline in demersal fish (such as cod, flounder, and haddock) in the northwest Atlantic prompted Canada and the United States to severely limit catches in rich fishing grounds such as the Grand Banks and the Georges Bank off their North Atlantic coasts. On an even broader scale, 99 countries, including all the major fishing countries, agreed in 1995 to an international treaty that will regulate the catch of all the species of fish (such as cod, pollock, tuna, and swordfish) that migrate between national and international waters. As evident in Figure 15.4, the treaty was part of the rapidly growing number of international pacts to regulate the marine catch that have made fishing, as one diplomat put it, "no longer a free-for-all situation."[25]

Despite its relatively minor economic impact, there is no issue of marine regulation that sparks more emotion than the control of whaling. At the center of the controversy is the International Whaling Commission (IWC), which was established in 1946. With whale populations plummeting and some species nearing extinction, the IWC banned commercial whaling in 1986. That did not end whaling, however. In 2004, Japan took over 700 whales, and Iceland took another 25 under the pretext of scientific study, which is permitted under IWC rules. The meat is sold commercially to supposedly pay for the research. St Vincent and The Grenadines was allowed 20 whales for food, and permits were given to indigenous people in Alaska and elsewhere to take about 500 whales. Norway rejects the IWC's rules and took almost 800 more whales. About 80% of all whales taken each year are minke whales, but more than a half dozen other types, including sperm and humpback whales, are also harpooned.

The controversy over whaling has occasioned strong clashes at each year's IWC meeting. Many countries, including the United States, strongly resist increased permits for Japan and Iceland, much less a resumption of commercial whaling. But other countries support Norway's view that the ban on whaling is based more on emotion than science. Estimates of the minke population run from 300,000 to 1,000,000, but advocates argue that even the lower number will support limited commercial whaling. New countries are joining Japan and the Scandinavian

Web Link

For a pro-whaling point of view, visit the Web site of the Japan Whaling Association at **www.whaling.jp/english/.** Whale-Watch has one of the numerous anti-whaling sites at **www.whalewatch.org.**

FIGURE 15.4 Treaties to Regulate International Fisheries

The world's marine fisheries are in danger of being exhausted. International recognition of this fact is evident in the rapid growth in the number of treaties regulating fishing, whaling, crabbing, and other forms of wildlife harvests in international waters.

Data source: Internet Guide to International Fisheries Law at www.intfish.net/.

countries in that view. During the 2005 IWC meeting, delegates from some Caribbean and African countries argued for a resumption of commercial whaling. "We would welcome the lifting of the moratorium," an official from Dominica said. "This is a creature like all others that people depend upon for food, and therefore because of its abundance we think that we can take a limited amount and make some money out of it."[26]

Whatever one's view of whaling, it is important to note that the overall numbers of most whale species and other marine wildlife are recovering. For one, the number of eastern north Pacific gray whales, once nearly extinct, has rebounded to 20,000 since the species was protected by the IWC. However, other species, such as the right whale, with only 400 surviving animals, remain at the edge of extinction. And while Galápagos fur seals, once at the edge of extinction, now have a viable population, a marine oil spill off the Galápagos Islands in 2000 wiped out 60% of the marine iguanas that live there and nowhere else. Thus, what has been accomplished is the beginning, rather than the culmination, of conservation efforts.

One of the themes of this book is the role that you as an individual can play on the world stage, and the protection of marine mammals provides one more opportunity for that. If governments cannot save whales, maybe consumers can. Younger Japanese shun whale meat and favor conservation. As a result, and despite a $5 million campaign by Japan's government to encourage whale meat consumption, about 20% of the whale meat taken by Japanese whalers in 2004 had to be frozen because it did not sell. Moreover, the fall in demand had dropped the price of whale meat by 20% in recent years. In another example, public pressure, which the industry refers to as the "Flipper" factor (after the 1960s TV series), forced U.S. tuna canners to demand that suppliers use dolphin-safe methods of netting to save dolphins. That was followed in 1990 by a U.S. law banning the importation of tuna caught without dolphin-safe methods. Other governments have followed suit. In 2002, concern over an increase in the number of dolphins dying as a result of fishing by European fleets led the European Union to station observers on suspect fishing boats. Other IGOs and NGOs are also involved. The Inter-American Tropical Tuna Commission sponsors a program that stations a monitor onboard all large tuna vessels. The result is that the number of dolphins killed annually has dropped from over 200,000 before 1990 to an estimated 3,000 in 2002.

> **Did You Know That:**
> In 2004, whale meat was selling for about $11 a pound in Japan.

Faced with adverse public opinion and economic boycotts, known in the tuna canning industry as the "Flipper factor," Starkist and all other major U.S. tuna canners now display logos, such as this one, to assure their consumers that the tuna are not taken using nets that kill dolphins.

Sustainable Development: The Environment

In the environmental equation on p. 490, the ever-growing world population and its increasing consumption of resources are only part of the problem. The third part of that equation is the mounting waste and pollutant production that comes from the excretions of over 6 billion people and the untold billions of domestic animals they keep for food or companionship and from the discharges of polluting gases, chemicals, and other types of waste into the water, air, and ground by industry, governments, and individuals.

The state of the biosphere is related to many of the economic and resource issues we have been examining. Like the concerns over those issues, international awareness and activity are relatively recent and are still in their early stages. Several concerns that have an environmental impact, such as desertification, deforestation, and biodiversity loss, have already been discussed. The next sections will look at threats to the quality of the ground we walk on, the water we drink, the air we breathe, and to the dangers posed by global warming and ozone layer depletion.

Among those promoting the cause of sustainable development is 2004 Nobel Peace Prize–recipient Wangari Maathai. She is framed here by one of the many small trees planted in Africa by the Green Belt Movement, which she leads in her country. Maathai was honored for fighting poverty by trying to save the continent's shrinking forests and was the first environmentalist and the first African woman to be awarded the prestigious prize.

Ground Quality

It seems almost comical to observe that there are serious concerns about the dirt getting dirty. Ground quality is no joke, however. Industrial waste and other discharges have polluted large tracts of land, some of the largest construction projects engineered by mankind are garbage dumps (euphemistically called landfills), and destructive farming techniques have depleted the soil of its nutrients in many areas.

International Ground Quality Issues

The pollution of the land is a significant problem, but the territorial dominance of states renders this issue primarily domestic and, therefore, outside the realm of international action. Exporting solid waste for disposal does, however, have an international impact. With their disposal sites brimming and frequently dangerous, EDCs annually ship millions of tons of hazardous wastes to LDCs. Financial considerations have persuaded some countries to accept these toxic deliveries. Sending old tires, batteries, and other refuse to the LDCs has now been joined by so-called e-dumping, which involves moving millions of computers that have been discarded overseas for disposal. One news story about such dumping in China described one site there with a "huge mound of computer circuit boards, broken cathode ray tubes and burning plastic components that leak toxic acids and heavy metals into stagnant water systems." Often, to avoid bans on exporting waste, the computers are supposedly exported for recycling. What occurs, though, is that small amounts of valuable minerals (gold, platinum, silver, copper, and palladium) found on some mother-boards are sometimes extracted, and the rest of the unit is dumped, where it adds to ground and water pollution and also poses a health threat to the throngs of poor who scavenge in the dumps for anything they might sell. In the view of one NGO report, "The export of e-waste remains a dirty little secret of the high-tech revolution."[27]

Although this practice—in essence, using LDCs as disposal sites—is widely condemned and illegal in some shipping and receiving countries, the UN reports that "the volume of transboundary movements of toxic wastes has not diminished." Even more alarmingly, the report went on to warn, "The wastes are sent to poor countries lacking the infrastructure for appropriate treatment. They are usually dumped in overpopulated areas in poor regions or near towns, posing great risks to the environment and to the life and health of the poorest populations and those least able to protect themselves."[28] A closely associated international aspect of ground pollution is that it is often caused by waste disposal by multinational corporations (MNCs), which may set up operations in LDCs because they have fewer environmental regulations.

International Efforts to Protect Ground Quality

There has been progress on international dumping. The 1992 Convention on the Control of Transboundary Movements of Hazardous Wastes and Their Disposal (the

Basel Convention), which was signed by 105 countries in Switzerland, limits such activity. It has been ratified by 165 countries. There have also been several regional agreements including the Bamako Convention (1998), which includes almost all African states and bans the transboundary trade in hazardous wastes on their continent, and the Waigani Convention (2001), which takes the same measures for its parties in the South Pacific. The limits in the Basel Convention were stiffened further in reaction to the continued export of hazardous wastes under the guise of declaring that the materials were meant for recycling or as foreign aid in the form of recoverable materials. At one time Great Britain alone annually exported up to 105,000 tons of such toxic foreign aid to LDCs, a practice that one British opposition leader called the "immoral . . . dumping of our environmental problems in someone else's backyard."[29] Now all such shipments for recycling and recovery purposes are banned.

Water Quality

There are two water environments: the marine (saltwater) environment and the freshwater environment. The quality of both is important.

International Water Quality Issues

Marine pollution has multiple sources. Spillage from shipping, ocean waste dumping, offshore mining, and oil and gas drilling activity taken together account for a significant part of the pollutants that are introduced into the oceans, seas, and other international waterways. Petroleum is a particular danger. Spills from tankers, pipelines, and other parts of the transportation system during the 1990s dumped an annual average of 110,000 tons of oil into the water, and discharges from offshore drilling account for another 20,000 tons. The flow of oil from seepage and dumpsites on land or oil discharge into inland waters making their way to the ocean is yet another large man-made source, with these sources annually adding about 41,000 tons of oil to the marine environment. Some spills are spectacular, such as the August 2003 grounding on Pakistan's coast of the Greek oil tanker *Tasman Spirit,* which spilled 28,000 tons (7.5 million gallons), but less noticed are the many smaller spills that add to the damage.

Another major part of the marine pollution is carried by the rivers, which serve as highways that carry human sewage, industrial waste, pesticide and fertilizer runoff, petroleum spillage, and other pollutants into the seas. One of the worst sources are fertilizers, and their global use has grown from about 40 million metric tons a year in 1960 to some 156 million metric tons annually in the late 1990s. Another major source is the exploding world population, which creates ever more intestinal waste. Many coastal cities are not served by sewage treatment facilities. Sewage is the major polluter of the Mediterranean and Caribbean seas and the ocean regions off East Africa and Southeast Asia. Industrial waste is also common. Late in 2005, for example, a chemical plant in Jilin, China, accidentally dumped 100 tons of carcinogenic benzene into the Songhua River. Its waters, after flowing into Siberia in Russia, empty into the northern Pacific Ocean.

Of these pollutants, the influx of excess nitrogen into the marine system is especially damaging. Human activities, such as using fertilizers and burning fossil fuels, add about 210 million metric tons to the 140 million metric tons generated by natural processes. Excess nitrogen stimulates eutrophication, the rapid growth of algae and other aquatic plants. When these plants die in their natural cycle, the decay process strips the water of its dissolved oxygen, thereby making it less and less inhabitable for aquatic plants, fish, and other marine life. To make matters worse, some algae

This photograph almost looks like a boat moving through pure white snow. Instead, it shows the foam from industrial and domestic pollution on the River Yamuna in New Delhi, India. Over 870 million gallons of untreated wastewater are discharged daily into the river from the city and its surrounding region.

blooms are toxic and take a heavy toll on fish, birds, and marine mammals. The Baltic Sea, Black Sea, the Caribbean, Mediterranean Sea, and other partly enclosed seas have been heavily afflicted with eutrophication, and even ocean areas such as the northeast and northwest coasts of the United States have seen a significant increase in the number of algae blooms in the last quarter century. Inasmuch as 99% of all commercial fishing is done within 200 miles of continental coasts, such pollution is especially damaging to fishing grounds.

Freshwater pollution of lakes and rivers is an international as well as a domestic issue. The discharge of pollutants into lakes and rivers that form international boundaries (the Great Lakes, the Rio Grande) or that flow between countries (the Rhine River) is a source of discord. Additionally, millions of tons of organic material and other pollutants that are dumped into the inland rivers around the world eventually find their way to the ocean. Freshwater pollution is also caused by acid rain and other contaminants that drift across borders.

International Efforts to Protect Water Quality

Marine pollution has also been on the international agenda for some time, and progress has been made. One of the first multilateral efforts was the International Maritime Organization, founded in 1958 in part to promote the control of pollution from ships. Increased flows of oil and spills led to the International Convention for the Prevention of Pollution from Ships (1973). More recently, 43 countries, including the world's largest industrial countries, agreed to a global ban effective in 1995 on dumping industrial wastes in the oceans. The countries also agreed not to dispose of nuclear waste in the oceans. These efforts have made a dramatic difference for marine oil spills as Figure 15.5 demonstrates. During the 1970s, the average year saw 314,000 tons of oil spew into the oceans and seas; that spillage was down to 29,000 tons a year during 2000–2004. National governments are also taking valuable enforcement steps, with, for instance, the U.S. Justice Department fining 10 cruise lines a total of $48.5 million between 1993 and 2002.

On another front, 122 countries agreed to the Stockholm Convention on Persistent Organic Pollutants (2001), a treaty that will eventually ban 12 so-called dirty dozen pollutants, such as various insecticides, PCBs, and dioxins, which have been linked to birth defects and other genetic abnormalities. These pollutants contaminate water either directly, through seepage from the land, or from rainfall and eventually enter the food chain. Some also cause other forms of destruction. DDT, for example, has attacked eagle and other populations by significantly reducing the chances that eggs will hatch.

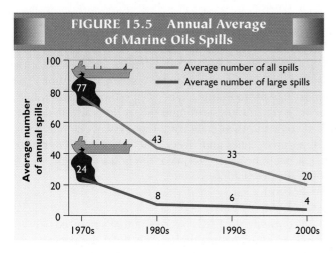

FIGURE 15.5   Annual Average of Marine Oils Spills

While the control of some areas of environmental concern, such as greenhouse gases, has been frustratingly slow, other areas have shown much better progress. Preventing oil spills in the oceans and seas is one such bright spot, with overall incidents in the early 2000s down 74% from the 1970s and large spills down 83% during the period.

Note: All spills are those reported over 7 tons. Large spills are those over 700 tons. 2000s is through 2004.
Data source: International Tanker Owners Pollution Federation, "Oil Tanker Spill Statistics," at www. itopf.com/statistics.html.

Air Quality

Air is the most fundamental necessity of the biosphere. It sustains life, but it can also contain pollutants that can befoul lungs as well as the land and water. Moreover, the world's air currents ignore national boundaries, making air quality a major international concern.

International Air Quality Issues

The quality of the air we breathe has deteriorated dramatically since the beginning of the industrial revolution. Now, air pollution from sulfur dioxide (SO_2), nitrogen dioxide (NO_x), and suspended particles (such as dust and soot) cause about 500,000 deaths a year, according to WHO. The majority of those are in Asia, where most of the major cities exceed WHO guidelines for suspended particles. For example, compared to New York City, Beijing's SO_2 concentration is 346% higher, its NO_x level is 154% higher, and its suspended particles measure is 406% higher. Beijing's pollution exceeds the WHO safety standard for SO_2 by 80% and for NO_x by 205%. There are no accepted standards for the safe level of suspended particulates, but anyone who has ever traveled to Beijing would tell you that its air feels almost "gritty."

Using SO_2 as an illustration, we can dig a bit deeper in air quality issues. Sulfur is common in raw materials such as petroleum, coal, and many metal ores. SO_2 is emitted when such material are burned for fuel or during such industrial processes as petroleum refining, cement manufacturing, and metal processing. SO_2 has numerous deleterious effects. It can cause or aggravate respiratory problems, especially in the very young and the elderly. The sulfurous gas in the atmosphere forms an acid when combined with water, and the resulting acid rain contaminates water resources and attacks forests. The damage done by acid

Industrialization and other aspects of development have led to serious air quality problems in many countries, such as China. Many of the cities with the most polluted air in the world are in that country, a condition illustrated by the photograph of Beijing's imposing Qianmen Gate to Tiananmen Square, which is barely visible through the haze and pollution.

rain has followed development. The United States, Canada, and Europe were the first to suffer. Especially in the northern part of the United States and in Canada there has been extensive damage to trees, and many lakes have become so acidified that most of the fish have been killed. Europe has also suffered extensive damage. About a quarter of the continent's trees have sustained moderate to severe defoliation. The annual value of the lost lumber harvest to Europe alone is an estimated $23 billion. The ecotourism industry in once-verdant forests around the world is also in danger, imperiling jobs. The death of trees and their stabilizing root systems increases soil erosion, resulting in the silting-up of lakes and rivers. The list of negative consequences could go on, but that is not necessary to make the point that acid rain is environmentally and economically devastating.

Protecting Air Quality

On the positive side, pollution control in the EDCs has substantially reduced new air pollution. Annual EDC emissions of air pollutants have declined dramatically. As one example, U.S. emissions between 1940 and 2004 dropped 51% for SO_2, 30% for NO_x, and 80% for particulate matter. Unfortunately, the improvement in the EDCs is being more than offset by spiraling levels of air pollution in the LDCs. This is particularly true in Asia. There, rapid industrialization combined with the financial inability to spend the tens of billions of dollars needed to control SO_2 emissions is expected to more than triple annual SO_2 emissions from 34 million tons in 1990 to about 115 million tons in 2020. Even now, according to the World Bank, China has 16 of the 20 most polluted cities globally. Among the ill effects, China's Ministry of Science and Technology estimates that air pollution annually kills 50,000 newborn babies.

There have also been several international efforts to address air quality. Some regional agreements, such as the 1985 Helsinki Protocol for reducing SO_2 emissions in Europe, have been followed by improved air quality (Ringquist & Kostadinova, 2005). Various international agencies, such as UNEP and WHO work to warn against the danger of air pollution and help countries reduce it. Some funding is also available. For example, about 6% of the loans the World Bank made in 2004 were for environmental improvement programs.

The Ozone Layer

Atmospheric ozone (O_3) absorbs ultraviolet (UV) rays from the sun. About 90% of all O_3 is found within the ozone layer, which rings the Earth 10 to 30 miles above the planet. Without it, human life could not exist.

Ozone Layer Depletion

There is little doubt that the ozone layer has been thinned or that the consequences are perilous. The ozone layer is being attacked by emissions of chlorofluorocarbons (CFCs), a chemical group used in refrigerators, air-conditioners, products such as Styrofoam, many spray can propellants, fire extinguishers, and industrial solvents. The chemical effect of the CFCs is to deplete the ozone by turning it into atmospheric oxygen (O_2), which does not block ultraviolet rays. This thinning of the ozone layer increases the penetration through the atmosphere of ultraviolet-B (UV-B) rays, which cause cancers and other mutations in life forms below. The impact of this on Americans was noted in chapter 1. Australia and New Zealand have measured temporary increases of as much as 20% in UV-B radiation, and light-skinned Australians have the world's highest skin cancer rate. Another possible deleterious effect

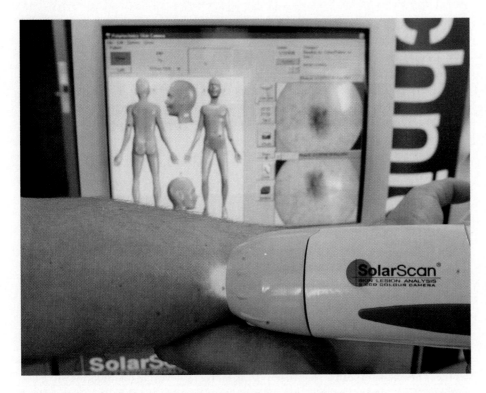

The depletion of the protective ozone layer has led to an increase in the incidence of skin cancer worldwide. The SolaScan device, shown here being introduced in Australia, detects skin cancer by capturing an image of a patient's skin spots, then comparing it to images of melanomas, the deadliest form of skin cancer, in a database. One of every 65 Americans will eventually be afflicted by melanoma, a 2,000% increase since 1930. The rate is six times higher in Australia. Mortality ranges from 15% in wealthier countries to 40% in poorer ones.

of increased UV-B bombardment came to light during a study of the water surrounding Antarctica. Over the area, a hole 3.86 million square miles in size—about the size of Europe and with as much as a 70% depletion of atmospheric O_3—occurs annually. There scientists found evidence of a 6% to 12% decline in plankton organisms during the period of the annual ozone hole. Such losses at the bottom of the food chain could restrict the nutrition and health of fish and eventually of humans farther up the food chain. Ozone levels over the rest of the world have declined less than over the South Pole, but they are still down about 10% since the 1950s.

Protecting the Ozone Layer

Among its other accomplishments, the UNEP sponsored a 1987 conference in Montreal to discuss protection of the ozone layer. There, 46 countries agreed to reduce their CFC production and consumption by 50% before the end of the century. Subsequent amendments to the Montreal Convention were negotiated at quadrennial conferences, the last of which was held in Nairobi, Kenya, in 2003. The major issue was a U.S. move to increase its permitted use of methyl bromide, a pest control. The effort was rejected.

Overall, there is relatively good news on ozone depletion. The annual buildup of CFC concentrations reversed itself from 5% in the 1980s to a slight decline beginning in 1994, only seven years after the Montreal Convention. Somewhat modifying this good news is the fact that the CFC buildup had increased so rapidly in the years before 1987 that, in the estimate of one scientist, "We might be back to 1979 [CFC concentration] levels sometime around 2050 or so."[30]

The scientist might have added "If we are lucky" to that prediction because there are uncertainties. The most important of these has to do with sustainable development and the economic advancement of the LDCs. The substitutes for CFCs in refrigerants and other products are expensive, and the estimates of phasing out CFCs worldwide range up to $40 billion. Therefore LDCs will be hard-pressed to industrialize and provide their citizens with a better standard of living while simultaneously abandoning the production and use of CFCs. For example, refrigerators, which not long ago were rare in China, are becoming more and more commonplace. China has pledged to end CFC production by 2010, but it still has 27 CFC plants operating, and ending production with outside help now would be better than ending it (hopefully) alone later.

Global Warming

ANALYZE THE ISSUE
Global Warming

Many scientists believe—and some disagree—that the Earth is experiencing a gradual pattern of global warming. The cause is said to be the accumulation of carbon dioxide (CO_2) and other gases, especially methane and chlorofluorocarbons (CFCs), in the upper atmosphere. This creates a blanket effect, trapping heat and preventing the nightly cooling of the Earth. Reduced cooling means warmer days, producing what is known as the **greenhouse effect** based on the way an agricultural greenhouse builds up heat by permitting incoming solar radiation but hindering the outward flow of heat.

Global Warming: What We Know

Three things are clear. First, global emissions of greenhouse gases have risen significantly. The primary cause has been a huge increase in the emissions of CO_2, methane, CFC, and other greenhouse gases from burning fossil fuels—the result of the industrial revolution and the need of the growing world population to warm itself and cook its food. Discharges have also increased steeply. For example, annual global CO_2 emissions more than quadrupled between 1950 and 2000. This connection between industrialization and CO_2 emissions is evident in Figure 15.6.

Deforestation accelerates the build up of CO_2 in the atmosphere because it destroys trees needed to convert CO_2 into oxygen by the process of photosynthesis. One way to calculate this is to compare the CO_2 impacts of an SUV and a big tree. With each gallon of gasoline burned emitting about 20 pounds of CO_2 into the atmosphere, an SUV driven 12,000 miles a year and getting 15 miles per gallon annually emits 16,000 pounds of CO_2. A large tree can absorb about 48 pounds of CO_2 each year. Therefore, it takes 333 trees to absorb the CO_2 emitted by each SUV.

A second certainty is that atmospheric CO_2 concentrations have risen. The greenhouse gases emitted into the atmosphere linger there for up to 200 years before dissipating. As a result, CO_2 concentrations have increased 34% since the beginning of the industrial revolution in the mid-1700s. The increase was slow at first, then rapid in the second half of the 20th century. Of the overall increase in the 250 years between 1750 and 2004, 60% of the buildup occurred after 1949.

Third, the global temperature is rising. Scientists estimate that over the last century the Earth's average temperature has risen 0.6°C/1.1°F. In fact, 9 of the 10 warmest years since records were first kept in 1856 occurred between 1995 and 2004. The warmest year on record was 1998; 2004 was fourth; and the first 10 years of the 21st century are projected to replace the last decade of the 1900s as history's hottest decade.

Did You Know That:

The first warning about global warming was issued in 1896 by Swedish chemist Svante Arrhenius, who wrote, "We are evaporating our coal mines into the air."

Global Warming: What Is in Dispute

Two things about global warming are controversial. One is whether global warming is caused by humans or is a natural phenomenon. As one atmospheric scientist accu-

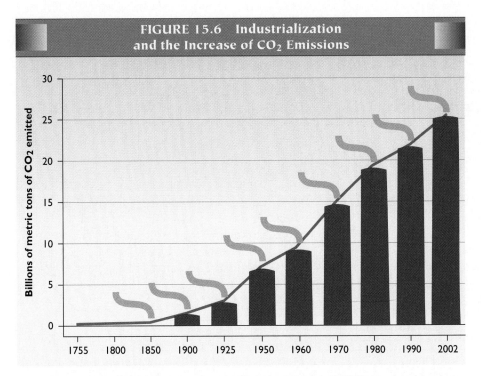

FIGURE 15.6 Industrialization and the Increase of CO₂ Emissions

Since the industrial revolution began in the mid-1700s, the discharge of CO_2 into the air by the industrial burning of coal, gas, oil, and other fossil fuels has rapidly increased. The majority of scientists who study this believe that these emissions are creating a global warming effect that is significantly altering the Earth's climate.

Note: The measure used here follows the World Bank reporting of mass of carbon weight, which is calculated by multiplying the carbon element weight used by the CDIAC by 3.664.
Data source: http://cdiac.esd.ornl.gov/trends/emis/tre_glob.htm.

rately notes, "I don't think we're arguing over whether there's any global warming. The question is, What is the cause of it?"[31] The second issue is whether global warming will have dire consequences or is an impact that will in some cases be beneficial and in other cases can be addressed using modern technology.

The Environmental Pessimists' View   *Environmental pessimists* contend that humans are causing dangerous global warming. The most recent report (2001) of the UN-sponsored Intergovernmental Panel on Climatic Change (IPCC) notes that probably "the present CO_2 concentration has not been exceeded during the past . . . 20 million years," making it reasonable to conclude that the rapid increase in greenhouse gases since the advent of the industrial revolution are not a natural event. Most importantly, the IPCC report concluded that "emissions of greenhouse gases . . . due to human activities continue to alter the atmosphere in ways that are expected to affect the climate."[32]

Environmental pessimists also worry about the impact of global warming. The IPCC estimates that global warming could increase the world's average temperature up to 3.2°C/5.8°F by the year 2100. That may not sound like much, but it is, given that the temperature increase since the last ice age is estimated to be, at most, about the same amount. Potential global temperature changes are shown in the map on page 518. The pessimists believe this change has already altered rainfall, wind currents,

Potential Global Temperature Change

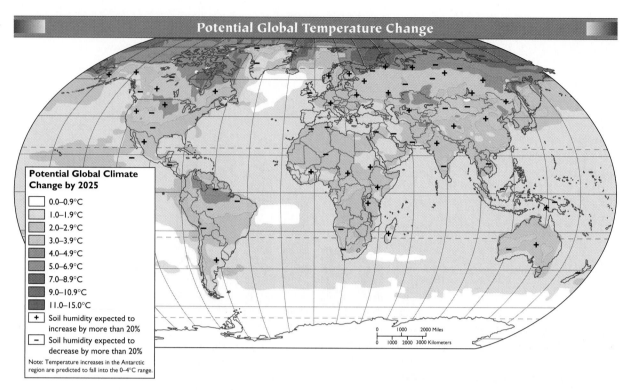

Potential Global Climate Change by 2025

- ☐ 0.0–0.9°C
- ☐ 1.0–1.9°C
- ☐ 2.0–2.9°C
- ☐ 3.0–3.9°C
- ☐ 4.0–4.9°C
- ☐ 5.0–6.9°C
- ☐ 7.0–8.9°C
- ☐ 9.0–10.9°C
- ☐ 11.0–15.0°C
- [+] Soil humidity expected to increase by more than 20%
- [−] Soil humidity expected to decrease by more than 20%

Note: Temperature increases in the Antarctic region are predicted to fall into the 0–4°C range.

If the estimates of potential increases in temperature and changes in precipitation (measured by soil humidity) shown on this map are correct, it is clear that climatic shifts will range from extensive to slight. It is normal to look first at the changes for the area in which you live, but it would be an error to assume that you can breathe a sigh of relief if you live in a low-change area or even welcome global warming if you live in a cold area that will get warmer or a dry area that will get wetter. Shifts in one part of the world can have impacts far away. For example, if those scientists who suspect that warmer ocean temperatures increase the "fuel" on which hurricanes thrive are correct, then there may be more and stronger hurricanes, such as Katrina in 2005, that are "born" in the equatorial waters off Africa and travel to strike the United States, Mexico, and the countries of the Caribbean Sea and Central America.

and other climatic patterns, and that the deleterious effects, such as the melting of the polar ice caps and the rise of sea levels, will escalate during the coming century as temperatures continue to rise. For example, a 2004 study by scientists entitled "Arctic Climate Impact Assessment" found that in the previous 30 years the area of the Arctic ice had shrunk by 8% (the equivalent of Norway, Sweden, and Denmark disappearing) and that the average thickness of the ice had declined 10% to 15%. According to IPCC, such melting could cause sea levels in different regions to rise between 3.5 inches and 37 inches, with the floods displacing well over 100 million people during this century. Particularly at risk are island countries, 42 of which have formed the Alliance of Small Island States. The question, as the president of the Maldives, an Indian Ocean island country, put it during the UN Millennium Summit in 2000, is, "When the UN meets [in 2100] to usher in yet another century, will the Maldives and other low-lying nations be represented here?"[33]

Destructive weather changes are yet another possible peril because global warming affects ocean temperatures and currents and upper atmosphere wind patterns, which, in turn, control rainfall, temperature, and other climatic variables. Droughts could occur in some places; other areas could see much heavier precipitation including periods of torrential rainfall. As discussed in chapter 1, El Niño/La Niña (un-

Web Link

The Arctic Climate Impact Assessment, which has great maps, photographs, and data presentations, is available at http://amap.no/acia/.

usual warming/cooling) conditions are occurring both more commonly and more strongly than in the past. These have been cited as at least one cause of, among other things, alternating periods of very wet and very dry weather along the U.S. West Coast. In May 2003, the head of the U.S. Bureau of Land Management's weather program predicted a busy wildfire season for the year and added, "We see increasing fire problems because of global warming, we know that drier conditions will exist over the next 10 to 20 years, and we have to figure out what actions to take."[34] He turned out to be unsettlingly correct. Five months later, Southern California was assailed by 13 simultaneous wildfires that charred 750,000 acres, incinerated at least 3,600 houses and other buildings, and killed 22 people. Estimated costs to fight the fires, assist the displaced, and rebuild were about $2 billion. El Niño appeared once again during the winter of 2004–2005, but it was one of the milder ones in recent years and caused only minor weather changes.

Some scientists also suspect that the warming oceans could spawn more and more intense hurricanes and other storms. Most scientists believe that more evidence is needed, but the impact of Katrina and other storms on the United States in 2005 led *Time* to ask on its October 3, 2005, cover, "Are We Making Hurricanes Worse?"

The IPCC projects many other negative impacts of global warming, but detailing them is not as important as the panel's primary point: Global warming is disruptive. The panel concedes that there have been and will be some benefits. For example, some areas that were once very dry or extremely cold are becoming more agriculturally productive. Overall, though, it concludes that the positive results "are expected to diminish as the magnitude of climate change increases. In contrast many identified adverse effects are expected to increase in both extent and severity with the degree of climate change. When considered by region, adverse effects are projected to predominate for much of the world, particularly in the tropics and subtropics."

The Environmental Optimists' View   *Environmental optimists* treat the pessimists as alarmists. In a recent op-ed piece, a former U.S. secretary of energy rejected the "political alarmism over global warming" and argued the "cold, hard facts take the heat out of global warming."[35] One counterargument that the optimists make is to point out that Earth has natural warming and cooling trends, and they attribute a good part of the current global warming to this natural cycle, rather than human activity. They note that the Earth cooled somewhat in the 1950s and 1960s, and some predict that the cooling trend will resume over the next few decades. Other environmental optimists do not believe that increases will be huge, either because they will not occur in any significant way or because offsetting factors, such as increased cloudiness, will ease the effect. According to one such scientist, "The prospects for having a modest climate impact instead of a disastrous one are quite good."[36]

Optimists also downplay the damage from global warming. "It should be pretty clear," says one, "that warming to date didn't demonstrably dent health and welfare very much." There is no reason, he added, "to expect a sudden [greater danger] in the next 50 years."[37] Moreover, the optimists predict that some areas could benefit and most could adapt to the changes brought on by global warming. Drought in some regions would damage their present agricultural areas, but new arable areas would be created and would prosper in other regions. Farmers in colder regions might have their growing seasons and bounty increased. Moreover, optimists contend that the world can use its technological and financial resources to deal with whatever climate change does occur. Danish scientist Bjørn Lomborg argues, for example, that while global warming is important, it "is not a problem that in any way will damage our future dramatically."[38] Lomborg calculates that the damage from global warming will come to between $5 trillion and $8 trillion. He concedes that

Web Link

The Public Broadcasting System has an excellent El Niño site at www.pbs.org/wgbh/nova/elnino/#.

Did You Know That:

La Niña is marked by unusually cold water in the mid-Pacific; El Niño is marked by unusually warm water in the same region. The term *El Niño* originated with South American fishermen who noticed that unexpectedly warm water would appear some years near Christmas. This led to the name, which means "little boy" and refers to the Christ child. Since La Niña is the opposite of El Niño, that name soon came into use.

Web Link

A global warming site representing the environmental optimists' point of view is that of the Cooler Heads Coalition at **www.globalwarming.org/**. The environmental pessimists' perspective is presented by a coalition of environmentalist groups at **www.climatehotmap.org/**.

this is "not a trivial amount," but points out that it is not overwhelming. Taking the 2000 world GNP of $31.4 trillion, and projecting it out over 50 years ($1.57 quadrillion), $8 trillion would come to 0.05% of that total.

The International Response to Global Warming

Partly because of the controversy about the origins and impact of global warming, progress on dealing with it has been more limited than with ozone layer depletion. However, a growing and widespread sense that there is a need to act prompted a UNEP-sponsored World Climate Conference, which convened in Geneva in 1990, with the CO_2 problem as a major focus. At that meeting of 130 countries, most EDCs pledged to stabilize or reduce greenhouse gas emissions by the year 2000. The United States, however, declined to join in because of concern about the cost and the negative domestic economic impact. The global effort to reduce greenhouse gas emissions was reconfirmed in the Global Warming Convention (more formally, the United Nations Framework Convention on Climate Change, UNFCC) signed at the 1992 Earth Summit. Virtually all countries, including the United States, have ratified the convention, thereby agreeing to take steps domestically to ease pressure on the climate and to work toward an international approach to address the problem. The convention also agreed that the parties would meet annually to discuss policy.

During the 1997 round of these discussions being held in Kyoto, Japan, conferees drafted a protocol (supplement) to the UNFCCC called the Kyoto Protocol. This agreement came after intense negotiations, often divided along familiar North–South lines. The South backed proposals to have the EDCs cut emissions by 12–15% by 2012, a standard many EDCs found unacceptable. The LDCs also wanted massive aid to help them stem pollution; the EDCs were reluctant to make specific commitments. The EDCs did not expect the LDCs to meet the same stringent targets, but they did want some upper limits on future emissions. To this, an LDC spokesman, Mark Mwandosya of Tanzania, who headed the LDC caucus in Kyoto, rejoined, "Very many of us are struggling to attain a decent standard of living for our people. And yet we are constantly told that we must share in the effort to reduce emissions so that industrialized countries can continue to enjoy the benefits of their wasteful lifestyle."[39]

The final agreement requires the EDCs to reduce greenhouse gas emissions by about 7% below their 1990 levels by 2012. The protocol also allows the EDCs to trade emissions quotas among themselves. If, say, the United States fails to meet its goal, it can buy emissions quota units from another EDC that has exceeded its goal. The pact relies on good conscience; there are no sanctions for failure to meet the standards. EDCs can also earn credits for excess emissions by funding projects in LDCs that reduce the emission of greenhouse gases or otherwise promote sustainable development. As for the LDCs, the protocol encourages them to do what they can but exempts them from specific targets for reducing emissions. The negotiators decided that the agreement would go into effect when ratified by at least 55 countries representing at least 55% of the world's emissions of greenhouse gases at that point. Those two standards were met and surpassed, and the protocol went into effect in February 2005. By August of that year, 152 countries emitting 62% of the greenhouse gases were parties to the protocol.

As illustrated in this Bulgarian cartoon, critics of the U.S. policy of rejecting the Kyoto Protocol argue that President Bush is a captive of U.S. industry and that his policies endanger the biosphere. Others praise the president for not pursuing an agenda that is unnecessary and that would be costly to Americans. Who do you think is right?

WRITE THE POLICY SCRIPT

Ratify the Kyoto Protocol?

To a substantial degree, the fate of the Kyoto Protocol in the United States rested on which party was in power. When the pact was negotiated in 1997, the Democrats controlled the White House, Vice President Al Gore had been the chief U.S. negotiator in Kyoto, and he signed it on behalf of the United States. However, the Republicans had a majority in both houses of Congress. Their Senate leader declared that Congress "will not ratify a flawed treaty," and the Speaker of the House called it an "outrage" that would cripple the U.S. economy.[1] Knowing that ratification faced sure defeat, President Bill Clinton did not submit the protocol to Congress.

Perhaps the protocol would have moved forward had Gore been elected president in 2000 and had the Democrats taken control of Congress. But neither happened. Republican George W. Bush became president and the Republicans remained in control of Congress. Another "might have been" came with the 2004 presidential election. Soon after the protocol had been signed, the 2004 Democratic candidate, Senator John Kerry (D-MA), had chastised opponents of the agreement for using "Chicken Little" scare tactics and for being "the very same people who spent millions of dollars opposing the Clean Air Act, the very same people who told America that that would be the end of our economy, that [the U.S. automobile industry] would shut down."[2] Bush, however, triumphed once again, and he strongly opposes the Kyoto Protocol. One reason he cites is the lack of requirements for the LDCs. "I oppose [it]," he told reporters. "It is ineffective, inadequate, and unfair to America because it exempts 80% of the world, including major population centers such as China and India, from compliance."[3] President Bush also objects to the emission reduction standards the protocol would require the United States to meet. "The Kyoto treaty would severely damage the United States' economy, and I don't accept that," he commented. Placing himself squarely in the camp of environmental optimists, he argued, "We can grow our economy and, at the same time, through technologies, improve our environment."[4]

The U.S. debate over whether to ratify the treaty rests on the relative costs of doing so and not doing so and on the LDC participation issue. If the United States ratifies the protocol, it would pledge itself to reducing its emission by 2012 to 7% below what they were in 1990. Using CO_2 as a rough guide, U.S. emissions in 1990 were 4.8 billion tons; they were 5.9 billion tons in 2004. So the target 7% below the 1990 level would be about 4.5 billion tons, a reduction of 24% from U.S. emissions in 2004. Other countries do not face such a challenge. Western Europe's emissions and those of Japan have grown little since 1990.

Predictions about the net costs of complying with the Kyoto Protocol range from astronomical to inconsequential. Neither extreme is probably correct. It is safe to assume that the costs would be substantial, but not impossibly high and would cut both ways. For instance, cutting fuel consumption would save billions annually from the huge bill for imported oil. But there would also be significant spending required to clean emissions, develop alternative energy sources, enhance mass transportation, offset losses to companies and workers harmed by restrictions on energy consumption and emissions, and otherwise pay for all that needs to be done. Citizens would bear these costs through higher taxes and higher costs for the products they consume. Lifestyle is another factor. To reverse global warming, people will not have to revert to living in unheated caves, eating raw meat, and walking everywhere. But the day of the SUV could go the way of the mastodon, and people will have to make other adjustments to how they travel and how they live (sweater, anyone?).

Then there is the issue of the LDCs. On the one hand, reducing EDC emissions without cutting LDC emissions would be like shutting one window in a two-window room to keep out the cold. On the other hand, the LDCs correctly point out that they are only a tiny part of the historical problems and are still only a small part of current emissions calculated on a per capita basis. Moreover, the LDCs claim that they cannot afford the costs of significantly improving emissions. So aid from the EDCs might be required to help the LDCs meet standards, thus further increasing the costs for the EDCs. Finally, there is the "so what" issue about the impact of global warming. Weather patterns will change, but that will only be bad for some regions. Others will benefit from milder winters and other positive shifts.

Amid all these disputes over economic and social costs, it is certain that neither option, ratifying the Kyoto Protocol and doing something significant about global warming, or not doing so, is risk free or cost free. Yet policy decisions have to be made, and if the choice is to do little or nothing, then it is better to take that option consciously than by inert default. Given the stakes and the theme of this entire book that you should be involved in global politics, it should hardly be a surprise that the last segment of the last chapter wants to know:

What Do You Think?

Assume that you are a U.S. senator and that the president has submitted the Kyoto Protocol for ratification. What is your vote, senator? Yea or nay?

Whatever the legal status of the Kyoto Protocol may be, its practical status remain uncertain because it is not recognized by the United States, which is both the world's dominant country and also its greatest source of greenhouse gas emissions (25% in 2000). This is not a case of the United States leading the North in resisting unreasonable demands by the South. Virtually all of the EDCs including Canada, France, Germany, Great Britain, Italy, and Japan have ratified the Kyoto Protocol (Fisher, 2004). The issue, then, is whether the United States should ratify the agreement. This is a question for you to consider in the decision box, "Ratify the Kyoto Protocol?" on page 521.

Chapter Summary

The Ecological State of the World

1. This chapter deals with international ecological concerns and cooperation. Self-interest—some people would say self-survival—compels us to attend to issues concerning the world's expanding population, the depletion of natural resources, the increase of chemical discharges into the environment, and the impact of these trends on the global biosphere.

2. A key concept and goal is sustainable development. The question is how to continue to develop industrially and otherwise while simultaneously protecting the environment. Given the justifiable determination of the LDCs to develop economically, the potential for accelerated resource depletion and pollution production is very high.

3. There is a wide range of views about how great the threats to the biosphere are and what can and should be done to address them.

Sustainable Development: Population Problems and Progress

4. Population is a significant problem facing the world, with the global population surpassing the 6 billion mark. The 1994 UN Conference on Population and Development in Cairo marked the latest step in the effort to control population and the associated attempts to improve women's reproductive and other rights. There are also numerous international organizations, such as the United Nations Population Fund, working in the area. The most effective way to control population is to improve the educational and economic status of women and to make contraceptive services widely available.

Sustainable Development: Resource Problems and Progress

5. Increasing population and industrialization have rapidly increased the use of a wide range of natural resources. It is possible, using known resources and current use rates, to project that petroleum, natural gas, and a variety of minerals will be totally depleted within the present century. The world's forests, its supply of freshwater, and its wildlife are also under population and industrialization pressure. There are many international governmental and nongovernmental organizations and efforts, symbolized by the 1992 Earth Summit, to address these problems.

Sustainable Development: The Environment

6. Population growth and industrialization are also responsible for mounting ground pollution, water pollution, air pollution, global warming, and ozone layer depletion due to atmospheric pollution. Work in other areas, such as reducing CO_2 emissions, has only just begun and is difficult because of the high costs.

7. The efforts at international cooperation in the areas discussed in this chapter return us to the question of standards of judgment. It is easy to view the vast extent of the problems facing the globe, to measure the limited effort being made to resolve them, and to dismiss the entire subject of international cooperation as superficial. It is true that not nearly enough is being done. But it is also true that only a very few decades ago nothing was being done. From that zero base, the progress made since World War II is encouraging. The only question is whether or not we will continue to expand our efforts and whether or not we will do enough, soon enough.

For simulations, debates, and other interactive activities, a chapter quiz, Web links, PowerWeb articles, and much more, visit **www.mhhe.com/rourke11/** and go to chapter 15. Or, while accessing the site, click on Course-Wide Content and view recent international relations articles in the *New York Times*.

Key Terms

biosphere
carrying capacity
environmental optimists
environmental pessimists
green accounting

greenhouse effect
sustainable development
UN Conference on Environment and Development (UNCED)

UN Conference on Population and Development (UNCPD)

World Summit on Sustainable Development (WSSD)

An Epilogue to the Text/
A Prologue to the Future

Where I did begin, there shall I end.
—William Shakespeare, *Julius Caesar*

S O HERE IT is some months later, and we are at the end of this book and this course. Finals await, and then, praise be, vacation. That well-deserved break from your academic labors brings you to an implicit point of decision about what to do with this text, the other course readings, and the knowledge you have gained from your instructor. One option is to sell what books you can back to the bookstore and forget the rest. I can remember from my undergraduate days how attractive an idea that sometimes seemed.

But then, is that really the best option? Probably not. We began our semester's journey with the idea that we are all inescapably part of the world drama. There may be times when we want to shout, "Stop the world, I want to get off," but we cannot. We have also seen that we are both audience and actors in the global play's progress. At the very least, we are all touched by the action in ways that range from the foreign designer jeans that we wear to, potentially, our atomized end.

We can leave it at that, shrug our shoulders, and complain and mumble at the forces that buffet us. But we also can do more than that. We do not have to be just passive victims. We can, if we want and if we try, help write the script. The plot is ongoing and improvisational. The final scene is yet unwritten. We are not even sure when it will occur. It could be well into the far distant future—or it could be tomorrow. This, more than any particular point of information, is the most important message. You are not helpless, and you owe it to yourself and your fellow humans to take an active role in your life and in the world's tomorrows.

The world is beset by great problems. War continues to kill without cessation. The specter of terrorism increasingly haunts many people as they go about their daily lives. A billion-dollar diet industry prospers in many countries of the North due to the fact that many of its citizens are overweight, while in the South, infants and the elderly starve to death in the dry dust. As if localized malnutrition were too slow and selective, we globally attack our environment with the waste products of our progress, and the human population tide threatens to overwhelm the Earth's ability to sustain the people who live on it. Of even more immediate peril, an expanse of nuclear mushroom clouds could instantly terminate our biosphere's more evolutionary decay.

To face these problems, we have, at best, a primitive political system. Sovereignty strengthens nationalities but divides the world. Frontier justice is the rule. As in a grade-B western, most of the actors carry guns on their hips and sometimes shoot it out. The law is weak, and the marshals have more authority in theory than in practice.

There are few anymore who really try to defend the system of assertive sovereignty as adequate for the future. Clearly, it is not. What is less certain is what to do next and how to do it. Cooperation, humanitarianism, enlightenment, and other such words provide easy answers, but they are vague goals. Real answers are difficult to come by. They may involve tough choices; we may be asked to give up some things now so that they will not be taken later, to curb our lifestyle, to risk arms control in the hope of avoiding nuclear war, and to think of the world in terms of "we."

At every step there will be those who urge caution, who counsel self-preservation first, who see the world as a lifeboat. Maybe they will be right—but probably not. We *have* begun to move toward a more rational order. Many chapters clearly show this. But they also show how limited and fragile this progress has been. This is where you come in. Your job is to work to make the world the place you want it to be. It is your job to consider the problems, to ponder possible solutions, to reach informed opinions, and to act on your convictions. Think? Yes, of course. But also DO!! That is what is really important.

We began this study with the thought from Shakespeare's *Henry V* that "the world [is] familiar to us and [yet] unknown." My hope is that this text and the course you have just about completed have made the world more familiar, less unknown to you. What you do with what you have learned is now the issue. Will you treat this moment as an end? Or is it a beginning? Heed, if you will, the counsel of Shakespeare's King Lear:

Be governed by your knowledge and proceed.

Endnotes

CHAPTER 1

1. *New York Times,* December 28, 1997.
2. National Geographic Society, "National Geographic—Roper 2002 Global Geographic Literacy Survey," November 2002.
3. *Hartford Courant,* February 8, 2005.
4. Former Assistant Secretary of Defense Lawrence J. Korb, quoted in the *New York Times,* January 22, 1996.
5. *USA Today,* October 29, 2004.
6. CNS News, October 26, 2004.
7. *New York Times,* August 28, 2002.
8. Paul Epstein, associate director of the Center for Health and Global Environment at Harvard University's medical school, quoted in the *Hartford Courant,* May 4, 2003.
9. Gallup Poll, January 4, 2002.
10. *Christian Science Monitor,* December 9, 2004.
11. *New York Times,* November 28, 1995.
12. *Washington Post,* February 2, 2005
13. *New York Times,* August 14, 1992.
14. *New York Times,* July 29, 1996.
15. *Washington Post,* February 3, 2005.
16. *Washington Post,* January 21, 2001.
17. John J. Mearsheimer and Stephen M. Walt, "Keeping Saddam Hussein in a Box," *New York Times,* February 2, 2003.
18. *New York Times,* October 6, 1995.

Play a Part in Your World box, "Supporting or Opposing the War in Iraq" p. 20

1. Quoted in Mina Hamilton, "In Memory of Abbie Hoffman," *Dissident Voice,* May 16, 2003, on the Web at http://www.Dissidentvoice.org/Articles4/Hamilton_Hoffman.htm.
2. ABC News/*Washington Post,* March 17, 2003. Data supplied by the Roper Center for Public Opinion Research, University of Connecticut. The question was straightforward: "Would you support or oppose the United States going to war with Iraq?"
3. Dan Reiter and Erick R. Tillman, "Public, Legislative, and Executive Constraints on the Democratic Initiation of Conflict," *The Journal of Politics* 64 (2002): 810–827.
4. Quoted in Alfred M. Lilienthal, "J. William Fulbright: A Giant Passes," *Washington Report on Middle East Affairs,* April/May 1995, p. 50.

CHAPTER 2

1. French foreign minister Hubert Védrine, quoted by Joseph Nye (2002) in *The Economist,* October 23, 1999.
2. *New York Times,* February 8, 2005.
3. Putin was quoted in the *Moscow Times,* May 28, 2003; Vajpayee was quoted in the *Hartford Courant,* May 29, 2003.
4. *Hartford Courant,* September 5, 1995.
5. U.S. Government, White House, "A National Security Strategy for a New Century," released January 5, 2000.
6. *Time,* June 1, 1992.
7. U.S. Government, White House, "A New Security Strategy for a New Century," released January 5, 2000.
8. *Time,* June 1, 1992.

Write the Policy Script box, "Is Preemptive War Good Policy?" p. 55

1. *Hartford Courant,* March 20, 2003
2. *New York Times,* September 24, 2003.

CHAPTER 3

1. The interview was with Dan Rather and aired on CBS News, February 26, 2003.
2. *Washington Post,* February 12, 2002.
3. *Washington Post,* October 30, 2002.
4. *Washington Post,* January 27, 2002.
5. *New York Times,* September 21, 2001.
6. Fareed Zakaria in *Newsweek,* October 15, 2001, on the Web at http://www.msnbc.com/news/639057.asp.
7. Gallup Poll Web site at http://www.gallup.com/poll/summits/islam.asp.
8. *New York Times,* June 1, 1998.
9. *Hartford Courant,* June 18, 1998.
10. The adviser was Arthur Goldberg, and the quote is from Robert B. Dallek, *Flawed Giant: Lyndon Johnson and His Times, 1961–1973* (New York: Oxford University Press, 1998), as quoted in Sean Wilentz, "Lone Star Setting," *New York Times Book Review,* April 12, 1998, p. 6.
11. *Washington Post,* March 4, 2003.
12. Pew Research Center, "Views of a Changing World: War with Iraq Further Divides Global Publics," June 3, 2003.
13. *New York Times,* October 12, 2001.
14. Pew Research Center, "Views of a Changing World: War with Iraq Further Divides Global Publics," June 3, 2003.
15. *Washington Post,* January 27, 2002.
16. Interview of retired Marine General Joseph P. Hoar, televised February 15, 2005 on *Frontline.* Transcript at http://www.pbs.org/wgbh/pages/frontline/.
17. Charles Duelfer, "Comprehensive Report of the Special Advisor to the DCI on Iraq's WMD," September 30, 2004.
18. *New York Times,* October 2, 1993.

19. *Washington Post,* February 3, 2002.
20. Charles Duelfer, "Comprehensive Report of the Special Advisor to the DCI on Iraq's WMD," September 30, 2004.
21. *New York Times,* June 17, 1991.
22. Interview of former U.S. Deputy Secretary of State Strobe Talbot, May 30, 2002, Salon.com at http://www.salon.com/books/.
23. Bush's remarks were made during an interview with Linda Douglas of KNBC, Jim Lampley of KCBS, and Paul Moyer of KABC in Los Angeles, California, June 15, 1991.
24. Doug Wead, "Bush Completes Father's Unfinished Business," op-ed piece, *USA Today,* June 15, 2003. Wead was an aide to George H. W. Bush.
25. *Albany Times-Union,* November 10, 2002.
26. Richard Brookhiser, "The Mind of George W. Bush," *Atlantic Monthly,* April 2003, pp. 55–69.
27. *Guardian Unlimited,* April 15, 2003.
28. *Investor's Business Daily, Christian Science Monitor* poll, 2002. Data provided by The Roper Center for Public Opinion Research, University of Connecticut.
29. "Letter from the President to the Speaker of the House of Representatives and the President Pro Tempore of the Senate," October 9, 2001, State Department Web site at http://usinfo.state.gov.
30. Transcript of joint press conference, October 21, 2001, on the White House Web site at http://www.whitehouse.gov.
31. *New York Times,* September 17, 1995.
32. Fox News, July 11, 2004.
33. *Washington Post,* July 23, 2003. The official was Stephen J. Hadley.
34. All quotes in this paragraph are from the *Washington Post,* July 25, 2003.
35. *New York Times,* October 12, 2003.
36. Representative James Leach, quoted in the *New York Times,* September 26, 2003.
37. *New York Times,* February 20, 2005.
38. *Washington Post,* February 1, 2002.
39. Press release, Department of Foreign Affairs and International Trade of Canada, May 9, 2003.
40. BBC News, December 12, 1999.
41. *Washington Post,* April 30, 2003.
42. *New York Times,* May 5, 1994.
43. CBS News, November 15, 2002.
44. Robert Dreyfuss, "The Thirty-Year Itch," *Mother Jones,* March/April 2003, online.
45. Michael Klare, professor of peace and world security studies at Hampshire College, quoted in Dreyfuss, "The Thirty-Year Itch."
46. Michael Lynch, managing director, Strategic Energy and Economic Resources, quoted in Faye Bowers, "Driving Forces in War-Weary Nations," *The Nation,* February 25, 2003, online.
47. *Investor's Business Daily, Christian Science Monitor* poll, April 2003. Data provided by The Roper Center for Public Opinion Research, University of Connecticut.

Write the Policy Script box, "Who Should Decide on War?" p. 80

1. "Letter from the President to the Speaker of the House of Representatives and the President Pro Tempore of the Senate," October 9, 2001, State Department Web site at http://usinfo.state.gov.

CHAPTER 4

1. Gallup/CNN/*USA Today* poll, June 2003. Data provided by The Roper Center for Public Opinion Research, University of Connecticut.
2. *Toronto Star,* August 31, 2001.
3. *Hartford Courant,* April 8, 1994.
4. *New York Times,* May 11, 1998.
5. Masoud Barzani, head of the Kurdistan Democratic Party, quoted in the *New York Times,* February 18, 2005.
6. *New York Times,* February 13, 2005.
7. Martha Brill Olcott of the Carnegie Endowment for International Peace, quoted in *The Kansas City Star,* November 26, 2001.
8. Quoted on the Web site of Consortiumnews.com, February 7, 2000.
9. *Washington Times,* March 14, 2005.
10. *New York Times,* October 6, 1995.
11. *New York Times,* June 8, 1994.
12. Henry J. Kaiser Family Foundation, Harvard School of Public Health survey, February 2002. Data provided by The Roper Center for Public Opinion Research, University of Connecticut.
13. Chicago Council on Foreign Relations, German Marshall Fund. Methodology survey, June 2002. Data provided by The Roper Center for Public Opinion Research, University of Connecticut.
14. From "Patrie" in *Dictionaire Philosophique,* 1764.
15. Comment by anthropologist Eugene Hammel in the *New York Times,* August 2, 1994.
16. *New York Times,* April 10, 1994.
17. Statement in "Report of the Secretary-General on the Work of the Organization," quoted in the *Hartford Courant,* September 9, 1999.
18. *Time,* March 12, 1990.
19. Irakli Gogava, chairman of the Georgian parliamentarian subcommittee on CIS issues, quoted in the *Hartford Courant,* July 17, 2001.
20. James's comment was in a letter, "The Philippine Tangle," to the editor of the *Boston Evening Transcript,* March 1, 1899, in reference to the desire for independence of the Filipinos.
21. Wilson's speech to Congress was on February 11, 1918.
22. Political scientist Rupert Emerson of Harvard University, quoted in Wiebe (2001), p. 2.
23. *Washington Post,* September 23, 1996.

CHAPTER 5

1. Thomas L. Friedman, "It's a Flat World, After All," *Sunday Magazine, New York Times,* April 3, 2005.
2. *Time,* June 15, 1996.
3. BBC News, January 30, 2004.
4. *Washington Post,* January 29, 2000.
5. The Pew Research Center for People and the Press, "Views of a Changing World," June 2003.
6. "The Yao Ming Dynasty," *China Economic Review,* March 28, 2005.
7. *Hartford Courant,* September 19, 1999.
8. *Hartford Courant,* March 7, 1996.

9. Pauline Maier, "No Sunshine Patriot," a review of *Tom Paine: A Political Life* (Boston: Little Brown, 1995) in the *New York Times Book Review,* March 12, 1995, 1–et. seq.

10. A good deal of this discussion of postmodernism relies on the contributions of Rosemary Shinko, Stamford Campus, University of Connecticut.

11. *Washington Post,* March 25, 2005.

12. The diplomat was Thomas Switzer, communications director for the American Foreign Service Association, quoted in *The Washington Diplomat,* June 2001.

13. The former diplomat was Jonathan Clarke, president of the American Journalism Foundation, quoted in *The Washington Diplomat,* June 2001.

14. All data on attitudes toward European and national political identification in this section are drawn from *Eurobarometer 59,* Spring 2003.

15. Richard M. Nixon, *Beyond Peace* (New York: Random House, 1994), excerpted in *Time,* May 2, 1994.

16. The Pew Research Center for People and the Press, "Views of a Changing World," June 2003.

17. The Reverend J. Bryan Hehir of Harvard University, quoted in the *New York Times,* August 24, 1994.

18. Quoted in *Time,* April 11, 2005.

19. *New York Times,* February 16, 1998.

20. *New York Times,* May 16, 1998.

21. *New York Times,* June 9, 1996.

22. *New York Times,* January 25, 2004.

23. BBC, March 22, 2002.

24. The Pew Research Center for People and the Press, "What the World Thinks in 2002."

25. Former Syrian prime minister Maaruf al-Dawalibi, quoted in the *New York Times,* June 2, 1993.

26. *New York Times,* February 27, 1998.

27. Gallup Poll Web site at http://www.gallup.com/poll/releases/pr020308.asp.

28. *Washington Post,* October 7, 2002. The poll was conducted in 2002.

29. *USA Today*-CNN-Gallup poll, reported in the *Arizona Republic,* March 5, 2002.

30. Sheik Abdalah bin Biyah, a member of the Supreme Council of Mosques and a professor of theology at King Abdul Aziz University in Jeddah, Saudi Arabia, quoted in the *New York Times,* June 2, 1993.

31. *New York Times,* April 14, 1996.

32. The Pew Research Center for People and the Press, "Views of a Changing World," June 2003.

33. *Hartford Courant,* July 10, 1992.

34. Survey in the *New York Times,* June 7, 2000.

35. *New York Times,* September 16, 1995.

36. *New York Times,* April 10, 1995.

37. *New York Times,* April 10, 1995.

38. David Shenk of the Columbia University Freedom Forum Media Studies Center, quoted in the *New York Times,* April 14, 1996.

CHAPTER 6

1. *New York Times,* February 26, 1992.

2. U.S. Department of State press release, April 6, 2005.

3. From Woodrow Wilson's *The State; Elements of Historical and Practical Politics* (1911), quoted on the Web site of the Woodrow Wilson International Center for Scholars at wwics.si.edu/.

4. Maurice Glele-Ahanhanzo, UN Special Rapporteur of the Commission on Human Rights. InterPress Service World News, September 20, 1998.

5. *Le Monde,* May 8, 1998.

6. *Chicago Tribune,* September 28, 2001 for the first two statements; *Deutsche Welle,* September 12, 2003, for the third.

7. The Pew Research Center for People and the Press, "Views of a Changing World," June 2003.

8. The Pew Research Center for People and the Press, "Views of a Changing World," June 2003.

9. Radio Free Europe, April 25, 2005.

10. The Pew Research Center for People and the Press, "Views of a Changing World," June 2003.

11. *New York Times,* January 28, 1998.

12. CNN.com, April 20, 2000.

13. *Washington Post,* October 2, 2004.

14. *Hartford Courant,* April 2, 2005.

15. *Hartford Courant,* April 4, 2005.

16. Kenneth Roth, executive director of Human Rights Watch, in the *New York Times,* July 1, 2001.

17. Representative Ron Paul, *Congressional Record,* July 17, 2001, p. H4022.

18. Shigeru Omi, director of WHO's Western Pacific regional office, quoted in a Reuters dispatch, November 30, 2004.

19. CNN.com, April 30, 2000.

20. Opening statement by Han Seung-soo, president of the General Assembly of the UN, at the International Conference on Financing for Development, Monterrey, Mexico, March 21, 2002.

21. CNN.com, January 24, 2003.

22. *Hartford Courant,* February 25, 1994.

CHAPTER 7

1. Group of 77, Declaration of the Twenty-Seventh Annual Ministerial Conference, United Nations headquarters, New York City, September 25, 2003.

2. Senator Richard Lugar (R-IN), quoted on CNN.com, April 12, 2005.

3. BBC News, February 11, 2003.

4. Valery Fyodorov, director of the Center for Political Trends in Moscow, quoted in the *Christian Science Monitor,* February 11, 2003.

5. BBC News, August 22, 2003.

6. Churchill made the widely quoted statement on June 26, 1954, while visiting the United States.

7. Address to the General Assembly, July 16, 1997, UN Document SG/SM/6284/Rev.2.

8. The Web site of the World Federalist Movement is at www.wfm.org/.

9. Jacques Santer, president of the European Commission (1995–1999), quoted in the *Manchester Guardian Weekly,* July 27, 1997.

10. BBC, October 21, 2004.

11. Eurobarometer *Special Report 214,* March 2005.

12. Reuters, June 16, 2005.

13. *Christian Science Monitor,* December 12, 2003.

14. Address to the Council on Foreign Relations, New York, April 22, 1997, UN document SG/SM/6218.
15. President Frederick J. T. Chiluba of Zambia, quoted in the *New York Times,* October 23, 1995.
16. Permanent Mission of Germany to the United Nations at http://www.germany-info.org/UN/ un_reform.htm.
17. Both quotes from United Press International, April 14, 2005.
18. UN press release GA/9692, December 20, 1999.
19. UN press release SG/SM/8965, October 27, 2003.
20. Fifty-Sixth General Assembly, November 1, 2001.
21. *New York Times,* March 6, 1995.
22. Address at commencement at the Massachusetts Institute of Technology, Cambridge, June 5, 1997, UN Document SG/SM/6247.
23. CNN.com, March 11, 2003.
24. Associated Press wire, October 4, 2003.
25. CNN.com, September 23, 2003.
26. BBC, March 29, 2005.
27. Fox News, March 29, 2005.
28. U.S. Deputy Assistant Secretary of State Mark Lagon, quoted on ABC News, April 21, 2005.
29. Address to the Council on Foreign Relations, New York, January 19, 1999, UN Document SG/SM/6865.
30. James Traub, "Kofi Annan's Next Test," *New York Times Magazine,* March 29, 1998.
31. UN, Secretary-General, "Renewing the United Nations: A Programme for Reform," Report to the General Assembly, Document A/51/950, July 14, 1997.
32. U.S. General Accounting Office, "United Nations Reforms Progressing, but Comprehensive Assessments Needed to Measure Impact," Report GAO-04-399, February 2004.
33. U.S. General Accounting Office, "United Nations Reforms Progressing, but Comprehensive Assessments Needed to Measure Impact," Report GAO-04-399, February 2004.
34. *New York Times,* September 12, 1995.
35. Address to "Empower America," Washington, D.C., October 16, 1998, UN Document SG/SM/6754.
36. *Time,* October 30, 1995.
37. *New York Times,* July 17, 1997.
38. *New York Times,* October 4, 2002.
39. Address at Princeton University, November 24, 1997, UN Document SG/SM/6404.
40 *Washington Post,* April 12, 2005.
41. *New York Times,* January 8, 1997.
42. *New York Times,* September 18, 1994.
43. Kofi Annan, "The Unpaid Bill that's Crippling the UN," an op-ed piece, *New York Times,* March 9, 1998.
44. BBC, April 6, 2005.

Writing the Policy Script box, "Santa or Scrooge? The United States and the UN Budget," p. 221

1. Worldview 2002 survey, June 2002. Data provided by The Roper Center for Public Opinion Research, University of Connecticut.
2. Gallup/CNN/*USA Today* poll, August, 2003. Data provided by The Roper Center for Public Opinion Research, University of Connecticut.
3. Gallup Poll, February 2003. Data provided by The Roper Center for Public Opinion Research, University of Connecticut.

CHAPTER 8

1. Churchill told this story in a speech on October 24, 1928, and it can be found, among other places, in Robert Rhodes James, ed., *Winston S. Churchill: His Complete Speeches 1897–1963, Vol. 5* (London: Chelsea House/Bowker, 1974), p. 5421.
2. *New York Times,* March 7, 1996.
3. George W. Bush, "The National Security Strategy of the United States of America," a report to Congress, September 19, 2002.
4. CNN and BBC, April 15, 2005.
5. From Henry A. Kissinger, *Diplomacy* (1994), quoted in *Newsweek,* April 11, 1994.
6. Both quotes from George W. Bush, "The National Security Strategy of the United States of America," a report to Congress, September 19, 2002.
7. *New York Times,* February 24, 1998.
8. Ambassador Howard H. Baker Jr, and Foreign Minister Nobutaka Machimura quoted in the *Washington Post,* November 7, 2004.
9. National Center for Education Statistics, *Comparative Indicators of Education in the United States and other G-8 Countries, 2002.* The study looked at 8th grade students.
10. Andrei Memin, president of the Public Health Association, quoted in the *Hartford Courant,* November 24, 1995.
11. Vladimir I. Simanenkov, St. Petersburg Medical Academy, quoted in the *Hartford Courant,* February 13, 2005.
12. *New York Times,* June 8, 1997.
13. Commission on the Intelligence Capabilities of the United States Regarding Weapons of Mass Destruction. Report to the President of the United States, March 31, 2005.
14. Sun Tzu, *The Art of War* (circa 500 B.C.), chapter 12.
15. CNN.com, December 9, 2003.
16. *Time,* October 31, 1994.
17. *New York Times,* June 15, 2000.
18. *New York Times,* February 19, 2001.
19. *Time,* April 9, 1990.
20. CBS News, September 29, 2003.
21. *New York Times,* February 3, 1996.
22. All quotes from the *Prague Post,* November 22, 2002.
23. Hans-Ulrich Klose, head of the foreign affairs committee in the German parliament, quoted by the Associated Press, May 18, 2003.
24. BBC, May 28, 2002. The reporter was BBC's Nick Bryant.
25. Ambassador J. Stapleton Roy's recollection of what President Jiang Zemin said. *New York Times,* July 3, 1995.
26. *New York Times,* March 7, 1996.
27. *New York Times,* February 27, 2000.
28. BBC News, February 24, 2003.
29. *Los Angeles Times,* February 25, 2003.
30. Associated Press, March 17, 2003.
31. *Washington Post,* January 28, 2002.
32. *New York Times,* March 3, 1998.
33. CBS News, January 16, 2003.
34. *Washington Post,* February 1, 2002.
35. *USA Today,* March 18, 2003.
36. *Washington Post,* February 2, 2002.
37. Michael E. O'Hanlon and Mike Mochizuki, "What North Korea Wants: Rescue Its Economy," op-ed piece in the *New York Times,* August 6, 2003.

38. Ambassador Robert Gallucci quoted in the *Hartford Courant,* October 14, 1994.
39. *Washington Post,* March 22, 2005.
40. *New York Times,* April 12, 2005.
41. *BusinessWeek,* April 29, 2005.
42. *Hartford Courant,* May 7, 2005.
43. *Rocky Mountain News,* April 25, 2005.
44. *Washington Post,* January 9, 2003.
45. *Washington Post,* January 12, 2003.
46. CNN, April 25, 2003.
47. Statement by Han Sung Joo in the *Washington Post,* January 12, 2003.
48. Joel Wit of the Center for Strategic and International Studies, quoted in the *Washington Post,* January 10, 2003.
49. *Washington Post,* December 29, 2002.
50. *Washington Post,* January 9, 2003.
51. *Hartford Courant,* May 2, 2005.
52. KnightRidder News Service, October 19, 2003.
53. *New York Times,* February 27, 2000.
54. *New York Times,* March 6, 2000.
55. *Washington Post,* April 1, 2000.
56. *Washington Post,* November 6, 2003.
57. Vice Admiral Archie Ray Clemins, quoted in the *New York Times,* March 17, 1996.
58. *Washington Post,* September 4, 2002.
59. *Washington Post,* January 14, 2003.
60. Acting Assistant Secretary of State Michael G. Kozak quoted in the *Washington Post,* March 29, 2005.
61. Assistant Secretary of Defense Joseph Nye, quoted in the *New York Times,* October 4, 1994.
62. *Washington Post,* March 14, 2005.
63. *Washington Post,* January 9, 2003.
64. *Washington Post,* March 22, 2005.
65. *New York Times,* April 30, 1988.
66. *Washington Post,* December 28, 2002.
67. *Washington Post,* October 3, 2003.
68. Assistant to the President for National Security Affairs Stephen Hadley, quoted in the *Hartford Courant,* May 9, 2005.
69. *Hartford Courant,* May 8, 2004.
70. *New York Times,* March 18, 1996.
71. *New York Times,* September 13, 2002.
72. Kurt Campbell of the Center for Strategic and International Studies, quoted in the *Washington Post,* December 29, 2002.

Write the Policy Script box, "Is Immigration a Solution to Demographic Graying?" p. 244

1. NBC News, *Wall Street Journal* poll, April 2005. Data provided by The Roper Center for Public Opinion Research, University of Connecticut.
2. Gallup Poll, June 2004. Data provided by The Roper Center for Public Opinion Research, University of Connecticut.

CHAPTER 9

1. UN Web site at http://www.un.org/icty/glance/milosevic.htm.
2. European Court of Justice Case C-285/98, January 11, 2000, paragraph 29.
3. *New York Times,* August 4, 1998.
4. *Washington Post,* March 29, 2005.
5. *New York Times,* July 9, 1996.
6. ICJ, *Legal Consequences of the Construction of a Wall in the Occupied Palestinian Territory,* July 9, 2004 at: http://www.icj-cij.org/icjwww/idecisions.htm.
7. Both quotes are from the BBC, July 9, 2004.
8. Address at Ditchley Park, United Kingdom, June 26, 1998, UN Document SG/SM/6313.
9. All quotes from President George W. Bush are from his address to the nation, March 17, 2003.
10. CNN.com, February 24, 2003.
11. *New York Times,* March 11, 2003.
12. Quoted on the Web at http://www.why-war.com/news/2002/10/12/iraqwarn.html.
13. Phyllis Bennis of the Institute for Policy Studies, quoted in Margot Patterson, "Beyond Baghdad: Iraq Seen as First Step to Extend U.S. Hegemony," *National Catholic Reporter,* December 12, 2002.
14. Radio Free Europe release, April 9, 2003.
15. Taken from the Web at http://worldnews.miningo.com/msub.12.htm.
16. BBC.com, July 4, 2001.
17. CNN.com, June 1, 2000.
18. Remarks by President Bill Clinton, University of Connecticut, October 15, 1995.
19. *New York Times,* June 16, 1998.
20. *New York Times,* August 13, 1997.
21. *New York Times,* June 15, 1998.
22. *Washington Post,* April 12, 2002.
23. Letter from Undersecretary of State for Arms Control and International Security John Bolton to Secretary-General Kofi Annan. *Hartford Courant,* May 6, 2002.
24. Interview of April 29, 2002, in Judicial Diplomacy on the Web at http://www.diplomatiejudiciaire.com/UK/ICCUK7.htm.
25. Statement of the Islamic Resistance Movement, Hamas-Palestine, issued December 17, 2001, in reaction to the speech of President Arafat, on the Web at http://www.jmcc.org/new/01/dec/hamasstate.htm.
26. Pew Research Center survey, March 2005. Data provided by The Roper Center for Public Opinion Research, University of Connecticut; 4% were unsure.
27. Kennedy's remark on June 24, 1963, can be found in the *Public Papers of the President of the United States: John F. Kennedy, 1963.*

CHAPTER 10

1. *Newsweek,* July 13, 1998.
2. *Boston Globe,* May 9, 2003.
3. *Washington Post,* July 20, 2003.
4. *Newsweek,* November 26, 1994.
5. *Time,* October 1, 1990.
6. *Washington Post,* January 11, 2002.
7. ABC News/Washington Post poll, December 2004. Data provided by The Roper Center for Public Opinion Research, University of Connecticut.
8. Jacob Heilbrunn and Michael Lind, "The Third American Empire," an op-ed piece in the *New York Times,* January 2, 1996.
9. Charles H. Thomas II, former U.S. envoy to Bosnia, quoted in the *New York Times,* November 29, 1995.

10. *Washington Post,* April 13, 2001.
11. Elements for success are from Alexander L. George, David K. Hall, and William R. Simons, *The Limits of Coercive Diplomacy* (Boston: Little Brown, 1971) and include (1) strong determination, (2) a less determined opponent, (3) clear goals, (4) a sense of urgency to accomplish these goals, (5) adequate domestic political support, (6) usable military options, (7) fear of escalation by the opponent, and (8) clarity concerning terms of the peaceful settlement. Other elements of success are from Barry Blechman and Stephen Kaplan, *Force without War: U.S. Armed Forces as a Political Instrument* (Washington, DC: Brookings, 1978) and include (1) opponent finds the threat credible, (2) opponent is not yet fully committed to a course of action, (3) goal is maintaining the authority of a particular regime abroad, (4) force is used to offset force by an opponent, (5) goal is to have an opponent continue current behavior, that is, to deter a change in behavior, (6) action is consistent with prior policy, (7) there has been previous U.S. action in the area, (8) involvement begins early in the crisis, (9) military action is taken rather than threatened, and (10) strategic forces become involved, thus signaling seriousness of purpose. Secretary of Defense Caspar Weinberger's six criteria included (1) vital interests at stake, (2) a clear intention of winning, (3) clear political and military objectives, (4) sufficient military force to succeed employed, (5) reasonable congressional and public support, and (6) combat as a last resort. General Colin Powell basically subscribed to the Weinberger Doctrine, as evident in the *New York Times,* September 29, 1992.
12. Gary W. Gallagher, "At War with Himself," a review of Michael Fellman, *Citizen Sherman: A Life of William Tecumseh Sherman* (New York: Random House, 1995) in the *New York Times Review of Books,* October 22, 1995.
13. *Global Views 2004: American Public Opinion and Foreign Policy,* The Chicago Council on Foreign Relations.
14. Interpress Service World News, November 29, 2001.
15. *Hartford Courant,* May 19, 2005.
16. *Washington Post,* April 24, 2002.
17. *Washington Post,* April 24, 2002.
18. World Islamic Front Statement, "Jihad Against Jews and Crusaders," February 23, 1998, on the Web site of the Federation of American Scientists at http://www.fas.org/irp/world/para/docs/980223-fatwa.htm.
19. *Washington Post,* January 11, 2002.
20. John Pike, director of the Global Security Organization, testifying before the U.S. Senate Committee on Foreign Relations, quoted in an ABC News report, March 6, 2002.
21. *World Press Review,* September 1996.
22. Associated Press, November 15, 2003.
23. Amy Smithson testifying before the U.S. House Committee on Energy and Commerce, October 10, 2001, at http://energycommerce.house.gov/107/hearings/10102001Hearing390/Smithson622.htm.
24. BBC News, March 22, 2002.
25. Paul Wilkenson, "The Strategic Implications of Terrorism," on the Web site of the Center for the Study of Terrorism and Political Violence at http://www.stand.ac.uk/academic/intrel/research/cstpv/publications1d.htm.
26. Senator Pat Robert of Kansas, quoted in the *Washington Post National Weekly Edition,* October 1–7, 2001.
27. U.S. Department of State, *Patterns of Global Terrorism 2002,* p. iii.
28. Bill Christison, a retired CIA official, writing "Why the War on Terror Won't Work," *Counterpunch,* March 4, 2002. On the Web at http://www.counterpunch.org/christison1.html.
29. BBC, March 26, 2005.
30. Under Secretary for Political Affairs R. Nicholas Burns, Testimony before the House Committee on International Relations and the House Armed Services Committee Washington, DC, April 14, 2005, at http://www.state.gov/p/2005/45146.htm.
31. BBC, February 22, 2005.
32. Elizabeth A. Fenn, "Biological Warfare, Circa 1750," an op-ed piece in the *New York Times,* April 11, 1998.
33. *New York Times,* February 25, 1996.
34. *New York Times,* February 14, 2003.
35. Fox News, May 5, 2005.
36. *Time,* May 19, 1997.
37. *Washington Post,* April 28, 2005.
38. Senator Dianne Feinstein (D-CA), quoted in the *Washington Post,* April 28, 2005.

CHAPTER 11

1. *Labor,* September 6, 1947.
2. U.S. Department of State Web site at http://www.state.gov/www/global/arms/np/mtcr/mtcr96.html.
3. *Time,* September 18, 1995.
4. *Pravda,* December 16, 2003.
5. The Chicago Council on Foreign Relations, *Global Views 2004: American Public Opinion and Foreign Policy.*
6. *New York Times,* May 12, 1996.
7. *Washington Post,* February 10, 2005.
8. BBC News, May 3, 2005.
9. *Los Angeles Times,* May 25, 2005.
10. United Nations Foundation, UN Wire, July 14, 2003, at http://www.unwire.org/News/328_426_6550.asp.
11. *New York Times,* May 16, 1998.
12. *New York Times,* May 29, 1998.
13. Statement as Prepared for Delivery by Secretary of Defense Donald H. Rumsfeld to the Senate Appropriations Committee, Washington, DC, Wednesday, April 27, 2005, www.defense.ink.mil.
14. Majority Leader Trent Lott in the *Congressional Record,* October 13, 1999, p. S12549.
15. *New York Times,* September 12, 1996.
16. *Newsweek,* May 25, 1998.
17. *New York Times,* May 31, 1998.
18. *Washington Post,* March 11, 2003.
19. High-Level Panel on Threats, Challenges, and Change, 2004, "A More Secure World: Our Shared Responsibility," a report commissioned by the Secretary-General of the United Nations, Anand Panyarachun, former prime minister of Thailand, chair (December 2, 2004).
20. Ambassador John Negroponte, quoted on Radio Free Europe, July 1, 2002.
21. Report of the Panel on United Nations Peace Operations, 2000, at http://www.un.org/peace/reports/peace_operations/.
22. J. Stephen Morrison, the director of Africa programs at the Center for Strategic and International Studies in Washington, quoted in the *New York Times,* May 10, 2000.

23. Report of the Panel on United Nations Peace Operations, 2002.
24. *New York Times,* January 6, 1995.
25. BBC News, December 17, 2003.
26. *New York Times,* May 4, 1997.
27. *New York Times,* October 3, 1999.
28. German Marshall Fund of the United States poll, June 2003. Data provided by The Roper Center for Public Opinion Research, University of Connecticut.
29. NBC News/*Wall Street Journal* poll, April 2003. Data provided by The Roper Center for Public Opinion Research, University of Connecticut.

Play a Part in Your World box, "Adopt a Minefield," p. 354

1. *New York Times,* May 1, 1996.
2. CNN, June 18, 1997.

Write the Policy Script box, "Is Zero-Nukes a Good Goal?" p. 358

1. *Time,* April 27, 1987.
2. C. Paul Robinson, president and director, Sandia National Laboratories, "A White Paper: Pursuing a Nuclear Weapons Policy for the 21st Century," March 22, 2001.
3. Attributed to Churchill by Prime Minister Margaret Thatcher in an address to a joint session of the U.S. Congress, February 20, 1985.

CHAPTER 12

1. Michael Ranneberger, testifying at U.S. Congress, House of Representatives, Hearings Before the Subcommittee on Trade of the Committee on Ways and Means, May 7, 1998.
2. Chicago Council on Foreign Relations, *Global Views 2004: American Public Opinion and Foreign Policy.*
3. *Hartford Courant,* April 14, 2005.
4. The Doha Declaration is available at www.g77.org/southsummit2/en/intro.html.
5. President Bush's comments were to the International Conference on Financing for Development in Monterrey Mexico, as quoted in the *Hartford Courant,* March 23, 2002.
6. Pew Research Center, "Views of a Changing World," *2003.*
7. Gallup Poll, February 2004. Data provided by The Roper Center for Public Opinion Research, University of Connecticut.
8. Associate Press dispatch, July 25, 2005.
9. BBC, June 25, 2005.
10. Productivity Commission, Government of Australia, "Measures of Restrictions on Trade in Services Database," Canberra, March 8, 2005.
11. Under Secretary of Commerce for Industry and Security Peter Lichtenbaum, Department of Commerce press release, June 28, 2005.
12. *Washington Post,* December 20, 2003.
13. *New York Times,* October 23, 1995.
14. *New York Times,* November 21, 2003.
15. *New York Times,* February 1, 1999.
16. Address to the World Economic Forum, January 28, 2001, at http://www.weforum.org/.
17. Klaus Schwab, director of the Davos Forum, quoted in Thomas L. Friedman, "The Revolt of the Wannabes," a column in the *New York Times,* February 7, 1996.

Write the Policy Script box, "Sanctions on China?," p. 396

1. BBC, May 18, 2005.
2. Senator Charles Schumer (D-NY), quoted in the *Wall Street Journal,* July 22, 2005.
3. CNN, May 5, 2005.

CHAPTER 13

1. *New York Times,* March 2, 1997.
2. *Hartford Courant,* March 12, 1995.
3. Reuters, July 6, 2005.
4. *Washington Post,* September 15, 2003.
5. *Guardian Unlimited,* September 5, 2003.
6. WTO press release, July 8, 2005. Supachai Panitchpakdi was still WTO director general.
7. Inter Press Service News Agency, April 17, 2002.
8. President Eduardo Duhalde of Argentina (2002–2003), quoted in the *Washington Post,* January 15, 2002.
9. Jeffrey D. Sachs, "IMF 'Cure' Is Adding to Crisis in Argentina," op-ed piece in the *Irish Times,* May 4, 2002.
10. Artemio Lopez, chief economist for Equis Research, quoted in the *Washington Post,* May 3, 2002.
11. President Nestor Kirchner, quoted by BBC News, May 26, 2003.
12. *Washington Post,* April 30, 2002.
13. BBC News, September 11, 2003.
14. BBC, March 21, 2005.
15. Comments in a speech, January 22, 1999, on the Web at http://www.oneworld.net/guides/imf_wb/front.shtml.
16. Professor John Kirton of the University of Toronto G-8 Information Centre, quoted by the BBC, July 12, 2005.
17. Nicholas Bayne, "Impressions of the Evian Summit, 1–3 June 2003," 2003 Evian Summit: Analytical Studies, G-8 Information Center, University of Toronto, http://www.g7.utoronto.ca/evaluations.
18. *Rolling Stone,* July 11, 2005.
19. Reuters, July 13, 2005.
20. Gary Hufbauer of the Institute for International Economics, quoted in the *Virginian-Pilot,* January 14, 2004.
21. *BusinessWeek,* December 22, 2003.
22. Address on January 13, 2004, on the White House Web site at http://www.whitehouse.gov/.
23. *Guardian Unlimited,* January 14, 2000.
24. *Miami Herald,* September 13, 2003.
25. *Miami Herald,* September 13, 2003.
26. *New Zealand Herald,* January 14, 2004.
27. U.S. Federal Reserve Bank of Dallas, *2002 Annual Report,* W. Michael Cox and Richard Alm, *The Fruits of Free Trade.*
28. BBC, March 22, 2002.
29. Associated Press, February 5, 2002.
30. *New York Times,* November 2, 1996.
31. Representative Joseph Gaydos in the *Congressional Record,* April 13, 1988.
32. Frank J. Gaffney Jr., "China's Charge," *National Review,* June 28, 2005.
33. Quoted in Charles R. Smith, "Rand Report Warns of Conflict with China," June 20, 2001, on the NewsMax Web site at http://www.newsmax.com/.
34. White House press release, May 20, 2002.

CHAPTER 14

1. U.S. State Department, Bureau of Democracy, Human Rights, and Labor, Country Reports on Human Rights Practices, 2002, released March 31, 2003.
2. *New York Times,* March 5, 1997.
3. The Pew Research Center for People and the Press, "Views of a Changing World," June 2003.
4. Gallup Poll, May 2005. Data provided by The Roper Center for Public Opinion Research, University of Connecticut.
5. Thomas Riggins, "Why Humanists Should Reject the Social Contract," March 20, 2001, Corliss Lamont Chapter of the American Humanist Association Web site at http://www.corliss-lamont.org/hsmny/contract.htm. Professor Riggins teaches the history of philosophy at the New School for Social Research and at New York University.
6. Address at the University of Tehran on Human Rights Day, December 10, 1997, UN Document SG/SM/6419.
7. *New York Times,* May 5, 1994.
8. *Washington Post,* March 4, 2005.
9. *Washington Post,* March 4, 2005.
10. Survey by Fox News, December 2002. Data provided by The Roper Center for Public Opinion Research, University of Connecticut.
11. *Hartford Courant,* January 26, 2004.
12. UN Population Fund (UNFPA), *Missing: Mapping the Inverse Child Sex Ratio in India,* June 2003, p. 1.
13. International Labor Organization, *The Sex Sector: The Economic and Social Bases of Prostitution in Southeast Asia,* 1998.
14. MADRE press release, April 12, 2002, on the Web at http://www.madre.org/criminalcourt.html.
15. *Hartford Courant,* December 12, 1996.
16. *Washington Post,* March 2, 2005.
17. Report on the World Congress Against Commercial Sexual Exploitation of Children, taken in December 1996 from the UNICEF Web site at http://www.childhub.ch/webpub/.
18. International Labour Organization, Juan Somavia, director-general, *Eliminating Child Labor: A Moral Cause and a Development Challenge,* May 2005.
19. European Union, Council of Europe press release 397a, July 12, 2005.
20. *The Telegraph,* January 26, 2005.
21. *Guardian Unlimited,* September 1, 2001.
22. Draft resolution presented to the conference, quoted in the *Guardian Unlimited,* September 3, 2001.
23. Secretary of State Powell on the State Department Web site at http://www.state.gov/p/io/uncnf/wcar/.
24. *Hartford Courant,* September 8, 2001.
25. The first commentator was Laura Silber, a senior policy adviser at the Open Society Institute, an NGO; the second was Elena Marushiakova, a Roma historian. They were quoted in the *New York Times,* February 5, 2005.
26. *New York Times,* March 31, 1996.
27. UN High Commissioner for Human Rights press release, May 12, 2002.
28. *New York Times,* March 31, 1996.
29. The Pew Research Center for People and the Press, "Views of a Changing World," June 2003.
30. Final document of the World Food Summit, November 17, 1996.
31. Final document of the World Food Summit, November 17, 1996.
32. United Nations *Chronicle,* 2001, Issue 3.
33. *Hartford Courant,* December 17, 1992.
34. Central Intelligence Agency, "The Global Infectious Disease Threat and Its Implications for the United States" (2000).

CHAPTER 15

1. *New York Times,* May 20, 1997.
2. The *State of the World* series is an annually published project of the Worldwatch Institute, with articles by a group of analysts on a variable agenda of issues related to the environment. The series is published by W.W. Norton, New York.
3. Both quotes, the second by Robert Repetto of the World Resources Institute, are from the *New York Times,* September 19, 1995.
4. Paul Portney of Resources for the Future, quoted in the *New York Times,* September 19, 1995.
5. *New York Times,* May 20, 1997.
6. *New York Times,* January 21, 2004.
7. *New York Times,* November 29, 1995.
8. CBS Poll, September 2003. Data provided by The Roper Center for Public Opinion Research, University of Connecticut.
9. CBS Poll, September 2003. Data provided by The Roper Center for Public Opinion Research, University of Connecticut.
10. *Hartford Courant,* June 8, 1992.
11. *Hartford Courant,* June 6, 1992.
12. September 2, 2003, on the WSSD site at http://www.un.org/events/wssd/statements/.
13. Under Secretary of State for Global Affairs Paula Dobriansky, on the Web site of the U.S. Embassy in Indonesia at http://www.usembassyjakarta.org/press_rel/wssd_bali4.html.
14. September 2, 2003, on the WSSD site at http://www.un.org/events/wssd/statements/.
15. Reuters wire story, June 7, 2002.
16. September 4, 2003, on the WSSD site at http://www.un.org/events/wssd/pressconf/.
17. *New York Times,* August 31, 1994.
18. *L'Observatore Romano,* n.d.
19. *New York Times,* September 6, 1994.
20. *New York Times,* December 31, 1997.
21. *New York Times,* September 4, 1995.
22. Julian Simon, "Environmentalists May Cause the Truth to Become Extinct," an op-ed piece in the *Hartford Courant,* June 15, 1992.
23. *Washington Post,* March 5, 2003.
24. *Arizona Republic,* March 23, 2003.
25. Satya Nandan of Fiji, chairman of the conference that in 1995 concluded the Agreement for the Implementation of the Law of the Sea Convention Relating to the Conservation and Management of Straddling Fish Stocks and Highly Migratory Fish Stocks; quoted in the *Hartford Courant,* August 4, 1995.
26. BBC, June 22, 2005.

27. Both quotes are from the *Asia Times,* August 8, 2003. The NGOs that issued the report were the Basel Action Network and the Silicon Valley Toxics Coalition.

28. UN Human Rights Commission, UN Document E/CN.4/1998/10, "Adverse Effects of the Illicit Movement and Dumping of Toxic and Dangerous Products and Wastes on the Enjoyment of Human Rights," January 20, 1998.

29. *Manchester Guardian Weekly,* March 20, 1994.

30. NASA's Marshall Space Flight Center, *Science@NASA* article, September 17, 2001, at http://www.southpole.com/headlines/y2001/ast17sep1.htm. The scientist was Paul Newman of the Goddard Space Flight Center.

31. *New York Times,* February 29, 2000.

32. International Panel on Climate Change, *Climate Change 2001,* at http://www.ipcc.ch/.

33. *New York Times,* September 6, 2000.

34. CNN.com, May 31, 2003.

35. James Schlesinger, an op-ed piece in the *Hartford Courant,* January 27, 2004.

36. *New York Times,* August 19, 2000.

37. *New York Times,* February 29, 2000.

38. Bjørn Lomborg, "Debating 'the Skeptical Environmentalist,'" a debate held at the Graduate Center of the City University of New York, April 2, 2002.

39. Mark Mwandosya of Tanzania, head of the LDC caucus in Kyoto quoted in the *New York Times,* November 20, 1997.

Write the Policy Script box, "Ratify the Kyoto Protocol?" p. 521

1. The quotes are from the *New York Times,* December 12 and 13, 1997.

2. CNN.com, December 14, 1997.

3. *New York Times,* December 13, 1997. Bush's remark was made while still a presidential hopeful.

4. *Washington Post,* June 5, 2002.

Glossary

Absolute power   An element of power, such as nuclear weapons, that indisputably exists and can be potentially used irrespective of other considerations.   236

Adjudication   The legal process of deciding an issue through the courts.   276

Amorality   The philosophy that altruistic acts are unwise and even dangerous, or that morality should never be the absolute guide of human actions, particularly in regard to international law.   293

Anarchical political system   An anarchical system is one in which there is no central authority to make rules, to enforce rules, or to resolve disputes about the actors in the political system. Many people believe that a system without central authority is inevitably one either of chaos or one in which the powerful prey on the weak. There is, however, an anarchist political philosophy that contends that the natural tendency of people to cooperate has been corrupted by artificial political, economic, or social institutions. Therefore, anarchists believe that the end of these institutions will lead to a cooperative society. Marxism, insofar as it foresees the collapse of the state once capitalism is destroyed and workers live in proletariat harmony, has elements of anarchism.   38

Anti-Ballistic Missile Treaty (ABM)   A treaty signed by the United States and the Soviet Union (now Russia) in 1972 that barred the two countries from developing and deploying a system to shoot down ballistic missiles. The United States withdrew from the treaty in 2001 in order to pursue the development and deployment of a national missile defense system.   346

Anti-Personnel Mine Treaty (APM)   A treaty signed in 1997 and effective in 1999 that commits its adherents not to produce, stockpile, or transfer antipersonnel land mines, to destroy any current inventory of mines, and to remove all mines they have planted. The United States is among the handful of countries that has not agreed to the treaty.   353

Appeasement policy   A policy advocated by the British and French toward the Germans following World War I. The hope was to maintain peace by allowing Hitler to annex the Sudentenland region of Czechoslovakia.   43

Arms control   A variety of approaches to the limitation of weapons. Arms control ranges from restricting the future growth in the number, types, or deployment of weapons; through the reduction of weapons; to the elimination of some types of (or even all) weapons on a global or regional basis.   343

Asia-Pacific Economic Cooperation (APEC)   A regional trade organization founded in 1989 that now includes 21 countries.   434

Association of Southeast Asian Nations (ASEAN)   A regional organization that emphasizes trade relations, established in 1967; now includes Brunei, Cambodia, Indonesia, Laos, Malaysia, Myanmar (Burma), the Philippines, Singapore, Thailand, and Vietnam.   433

Asymmetrical warfare   A strategy by which a national military or other armed force, including a terrorist organization, that is relatively small and lightly equipped attacks a militarily stronger opponent by using unconventional means, such as terrorism, or with limited unconventional weapons, such as nuclear explosives and material, biological agents, or chemical agents.   53

Authoritarian government   A political system that allows little or no participation in decision making by individuals and groups outside the upper reaches of the government.   76, 171

Authoritarianism   A type of restrictive governmental system where people are under the rule of an individual, such as a dictator or king, or a group, such as a party or military junta.   171

Balance of payments   A figure that represents the net flow of money into and out of a country due to trade, tourist expenditures, sale of services (such as consulting), foreign aid, profits, and so forth.   388

Balance of power   A concept that describes the degree of equilibrium (balance) or disequilibrium (imbalance) of power in the global or regional system.   40

Balance-of-power politics theory   The notion that countries seek to conserve and amass power, that some countries seek to become powerful enough to dominate their region or even the international system, and that other countries will seek to counter a hegemonic drive by further increasing their own power or cooperating with other powers in preventing any country or block from achieving dominance.   232

Beijing + 5 Conference   A meeting held at the UN in New York City in 2000 to review the progress made since the fourth World Conference on Women held in 1995.   160

Bilateral diplomacy   Negotiations between two countries.   251

Bilateral (foreign) aid   Foreign aid given by one country directly to another.   415

Biological Weapons Convention   A multilateral treaty concluded in 1972. The parties to the treaty agree not to develop, produce, stockpile, or acquire biological agents or toxins of types and in quantities that have no justification for prophylactic, protective, and other peaceful purposes and to destroy any such material that they might have.   346

Biopolitics   This theory examines the relationship between the physical nature and political behavior of humans.   66

Biosphere   The Earth's ecological system (ecosystem) that supports life—its land, water, air, and upper atmosphere—and the living organisms, including humans, that inhabit it.   487

Bipolar system   A type of international system with two roughly equal actors or coalitions of actors that divide the international system into two poles.   43

Bureaucracy   The bulk of the state's administrative structure that continues even when leaders change.   81

Capitalism   An economic system based on the private ownership of the means of production and distribution of goods, competition, and profit incentives.   376

Carrying capacity   The number of people that an environment, such as Earth, can feed, provide water for, and otherwise sustain.   490

Cartel   An international agreement among producers of a commodity that attempts to control the production and pricing of that commodity.   402

Chemical Weapons Convention (CWC)   A treaty that was signed and became effective in 1995 under which signatories pledge to eliminate all chemical weapons by the year 2005; to submit to rigorous inspection; to never develop, produce, stockpile, or use chemical weapons; and to never transfer chemical weapons to another country or assist another country to acquire such weapons.   350

Civil society   The voluntary and private (not controlled by the government) economic, cultural, and other interactions and associations of individuals.   131

Clash of civilizations   Samuel P. Huntington's thesis (1996, 1993) that the source of future conflict will be cultural.   147

Codify   To write down a law in formal language.   273

Coercive diplomacy   The use of threats or force as a diplomatic tactic.   262

Cognitive decision making   Making choices within the limits of what you consciously know.   63

Cold war   The confrontation that emerged following World War II between the bipolar superpowers, the Soviet Union and the United States. Although no direct conflict took place between these countries, it was an era of great tensions and global division.   43

Collective security   The original theory behind UN peacekeeping. It holds that aggression against one state is aggression against every member and should be defeated by the collective action of all.   360

Communism   An ideology that originated in the works of Friedrich Engels and Karl Marx that is essentially an economic theory. As such, it is the idea that an oppressed proletariat class of workers would eventually organize and revolt against those who owned the means of production, the bourgeoisie; a political system of government applied in China, and elsewhere, wherein the state owns the means of production as a system to expedite Engels and Marx's economic theory.   172

Communitarianism   The concept that the welfare of the collective must be valued over any individual rights or liberties.   452

Comprehensive Test Ban Treaty (CTBT)   A treaty that bans all testing of nuclear weapons. The treaty was signed in 1996 but will not go into force until ratified by the major nuclear weapons powers. The U.S. Senate rejected ratification in 2001.   349

Conditionality   A term that refers to the policy of the International Monetary Fund, the World Bank, and some other international financial agencies to attach conditions to their loans and grants. These conditions may require recipient countries to devalue their currencies, to lift controls on prices, to cut their budgets, and to reduce barriers to trade and capital flows. Such conditions are often politically unpopular, may cause at least short-term economic pain, and are construed by critics as interference in recipient countries' sovereignty.   423

Confederation   A group of states that willingly enter into an alliance to form a political unit for a common purpose, such as economic security or defense; it is highly interdependent, but has a weak directorate organization, thus allowing the individual states to maintain a fairly high degree of sovereignty.   199

Constructivism   An approach to analysis based on the notion that our understanding of the world and our relationship to it is based on our individual norms, experiences, and other factors that shape our perceptions.   140

Containment doctrine   U.S. policy that sought to contain communism during the cold war.   44

Convention on the Elimination of All Forms of Discrimination Against Women (CEDAW)   Adopted by the UN General Assembly in 1979 and subsequently adhered to by over 90% of all countries, the treaty defines what constitutes discrimination against women and sets forth an agenda for national action to end it.   460

Convention on the Rights of the Child   Adopted unanimously by the UN General Assembly in 1989, with sufficient ratifications to go into effect in 1990, the convention outlines a wide range of collective and individual rights for all persons under the age of 18.   463

Conventional Forces in Europe Treaty (CFE)   A treaty negotiated between the countries in NATO and the (now-defunct) Soviet-led Warsaw Pact that placed numerical limits on a range of conventional "heavy" weapons, including tanks and other armored combat vehicles, artillery, and fixed-wing and rotary combat aircraft permitted in the so-called Atlantic-to-the-Urals Zone (ATTU) region.   353

Conventional warfare   The application of force by uniformed military units usually against other uniformed military units or other clearly military targets using weapons other than biological, chemical, or nuclear weapons.   326

Council of the European Union   The most important decision-making body on the EU. The Council represents the member-states through each member's representatives, which can range from the head of state to specialized ministers (such as agriculture). Also known as the Council of Ministers.   204

Court of Auditors   An oversight institution within the EU. It is staffed by one individual from each member-country and monitors the implementation of EU budgets and policies.   205

Court of Justice   The most important court in the European Union.   206

Crisis situation   A circumstance or event that is a surprise to decision makers, that evokes a sense of threat (particularly physical peril), and that must be responded to within a limited amount of time.   77

Cultural imperialism   The attempt to impose your own value system on others, including judging others by how closely they conform to your norms.   452

Current dollars   The value of the dollar in the year for which it is being reported. Sometimes called inflated dollars. Any currency can be expressed in current value. *See also* Real dollars.   373

Debt service   The total amount of money due on principal and interest payments for loan repayment.   413

Decision-making process   The manner by which humans choose which policy to pursue and which actions to take in support of policy goals. The study of decision making seeks to identify patterns in the way that humans make decisions. This includes gathering information, analyzing information, and making choices. Decision making is a complex process that relates to personality and other human traits, to the sociopolitical setting in which decision makers function, and to the organizational structures involved.   63

Democracy/democratic government   The most basic concept describes the ideology of a body governed by and for the people; also the type of governmental system a country has in terms of free and fair elections and levels of participation.   76, 171

Democratic peace theory   The assertion that as more countries become democratic, the likelihood that they will enter into conflict with one another decreases.   178

Democratized diplomacy   The current trend in diplomacy where diplomats are drawn from a wider segment of society, making them more representative of their nations.   255

Demographic graying   The aging of a population, with the median age and the percentage of people who reach retirement age increasing.   242

Dependency theory   The belief that the industrialized North has created a neocolonial relationship with the South in which the less developed countries are dependent on and disadvantaged by their economic relations with the capitalist industrial countries.   376

Détente   A cold war policy involving the United States, the Soviet Union, and China, which sought to open relations among the countries and ease tensions.   45

Deterrence   Persuading an opponent not to attack by having enough forces to disable the attack and/or launch a punishing counterattack.   332

Development Assistance Committee (DAC)   The 22 member-countries of the Organization for Economic Cooperation and Development that give official development aid.   415

Development capital   Monies and resources needed by less developed countries to increase their economic growth and diversify their economies.   412

Direct democracy   Policy making through a variety of processes, including referendums, by which citizens directly cast ballots on policy issues.   22

Doha Round   The ninth and latest round of GATT negotiations to reduce barriers to international free economic interchange. The round is named after the 2001 WTO ministerial meeting in Doha, Qatar, where agreement to try to negotiate a new round of reductions in barriers by 2005 was reached.   421

Dual-use technology   Technology that has peaceful uses but also has military applications.   353

East-West axis   A term used to describe the ideological division between hemispheres following World War II. The East was associated with communism, while the West was associated with democracy.   44

Economic Community of West African States (ECOWAS)   A regional group of 15 countries founded in 1975. Its mission is to promote economic integration, and it has also taken on some peacekeeping activities through its nonpermanent function called Economic Community's African States Monitoring Group (ECOMOG).   360

Economic interdependence   See *Interdependence*.   54

Economic internationalism   The belief that international economic relations should and can be conducted cooperatively because the international economy is a non-zero-sum game in which prosperity is available to all.   375

Economic nationalism   The belief that the state should use its economic strength to further national interests, and that a state should use its power to build its economic strength.   374

Economic sanctions   Economic measures imposed by a country or international governmental organization on one or more countries to change their behavior. These sanctions include such tools as refusing to purchase another country's product, refusing to sell it something that it needs, freezing its accounts in your country, or imposing punitive tariffs and quotas on its products.   403

Economic structuralism   The belief that economic structure determines politics, as the conduct of world politics is based on the way that the world is organized economically. A radical restructuring of the economic system is required to end the uneven distribution of wealth and power.   376

Economically developed country (EDC)   An industrialized country mainly found in the Northern Hemisphere.   56, 374

Environmental optimists   Those analysts who predict that the world population will meet its needs while continuing to grow economically through conservation, population restraints, and technological innovation.   489

Environmental pessimists   Those analysts who predict environmental and ecological problems, based on current trends in ecology and population pressure.   488

Escalation   Increasing the level of fighting.   327

Ethnonational group   An ethnic group in which a significant percentage of its members favor national self-determination and the establishment of a nation-state dominated by the group.   51, 100

Ethology   The comparison of animal and human behavior.   66

European Commission   A 20-member commission that serves as the bureaucratic organ of the European Union.   204

European Communities   (EC) Established in 1967, the EC was a single unit whose plural name (Communities) reflects the fact that it united the European Coal and Steel Community, the European Economic Community, and the European Atomic Energy Community under one organizational structure. The EC evolved into the European Union beginning in 1993.   202

European Economic Community (EEC)   The regional trade and economic organization established in Western Europe by the Treaty of Rome in 1958; also known as the Common Market.   202

European Ombudsman   An official of the European Union appointed by the European Parliament to investigate EU citizens' complaints about maladministration in the activities of EU bodies, excluding the Court of Justice and the Court of First Instance.   205

European Parliament (EP)   The 626-member legislative branch of the European Union. Representation is determined by population of member-countries and is based on five-year terms.   206

European Union (EU)   The Western European regional organization established in 1983 when the Maastricht Treaty went into effect. The EU encompasses the still legally existing European Community (EC). When the EC was formed in 1967, it in turn encompassed three still legally existing regional organizations formed in the 1950s: the European Coal and Steel Community (ECSC), the European Economic Community (EEC), and the European Atomic Energy Community (EURATOM).   202

Eurowhites   A term to distinguish the whites of Europe and of Australia, Canada, New Zealand, the United States, and other countries whose cultures were founded on or converted to European culture from other races and ethnic groups, including Caucasian peoples in Latin America, the Middle East, South Asia, and elsewhere.   40

Exceptionalism   The belief by some that their nation or other group is better than others.   116

Exchange rate   The values of two currencies relative to each other—for example, how many yen equal a dollar or how many lira equal a pound.   382

Extreme poverty   A World Bank term for the condition of those living on less than $1 per day.   384

Failed states   Countries in which all or most of the citizens give their primary political loyalty to an ethnic group, a religious group, or some other source of political identity. Such states are so fragmented that no one political group can govern effectively and, thus, these states are more legal entities than functioning governments.   110

Fascism   An ideology that advocates extreme nationalism, with a heightened sense of national belonging or ethnic identity.   172

Federation   Also called a federal government, this power-sharing governance structure is one in which the central authority and the member units each have substantial authority.   199

Feminism   The theory of, and the struggle for, equality for women.   140

Feudal system   Medieval political system of smaller units, such as principalities, dukedoms, and baronies, ruled by minor royalty.   36

First-use option   The possibility of a nuclear country using its nuclear weapons first in a war with another nuclear country or using its nuclear weapons against a non-nuclear country.   333

Fiscal year (FY)   A budget year, which may or may not be the same as the calendar year. The U.S. fiscal year runs from October 1 through September 30 and is referred to by its ending date. Thus, FY2005 ran from October 1, 2004, through September 30, 2005.   11

Foreign direct investment (FDI)   Buying stock, real estate, and other assets in another country with the aim of gaining a controlling interest in foreign economic enterprises. Different from portfolio investment, which involves investment solely to gain capital appreciation through market fluctuations.   380

Foreign policy–making actors   The political actors within a state—including political executives, bureaucracies, legislatures, political opponents, interest groups, and the people—who influence the foreign policy process.   79

Foreign policy process   A concept that includes the influences and activities within a country that cause its government to decide to adopt one or another foreign policy.   63

Foreign portfolio investment (FPI)   Investment in the stocks and the public and private debt instruments (such as bonds) of another country below the level where the stock or bondholder can exercise control over the policies of the stock-issuing company or the bond-issuing debtor.   380

Formal powers   Authority to act or to exert influence that is granted by statutory law or by the constitution to a political executive or to another element of government.   79

Fourth World Conference on Women (WCW)   The largest and most widely noted in a series of UN conferences on the status of women. This international meeting took place in Beijing, China, in 1995.   160, 460

Free Trade Area of the Americas (FTAA)   The tentative name given by the 34 countries that met in December 1994 at the Summit of the Americas to a proposed Western Hemisphere free trade zone.   431

Frustration-aggression theory   A psychologically based theory that frustrated societies sometimes become collectively aggressive.   65

Functional relations   Relations that include interaction in such usually nonpolitical areas as communication, travel, trade, and finances.   271

Functionalism   International cooperation in specific areas such as communications, trade, travel, health, or environmental protection activity. Often symbolized by the specialized agencies, such as the World Health Organization, associated with the United Nations.   194

Fundamentalism   Religious traditionalism and values incorporated into secular political activities.   150

Gender opinion gap   The difference between males and females along any one of a number of dimensions, including foreign policy preferences.   67

General Agreement on Tariffs and Trade (GATT)   The world's primary organization promoting the expansion of free trade. Established in 1947, it has grown to a membership of over 100.   419

General and complete disarmament (GCD)   The total absence of armaments.   368

Globalization   A multifaceted concept that represents the increasing integration of economics, communications, and culture across national boundaries.   126, 378

Green accounting   An approach to measuring the comprehensive wealth of countries by calculating "human capital" (such as education, health, and equality) and "natural capital" (the quality and quantity of air, land, water, and natural resources), as well as such traditional economic measures as gross national product.   487

Greenhouse effect   The process by which the accumulation of carbon dioxide and other gases in the Earth's upper atmosphere arguably cause an increase in temperature by creating a thermal blanket effect; this prevents some of the cooling that occurs at night as the Earth radiates heat.   516

Gross domestic product (GDP)   A measure of income within a country that excludes foreign earnings.   11, 373

Gross national product (GNP)   A measure of the sum of all goods and services produced by a country's nationals, whether they are in the country or abroad.   56, 373

Group of Eight (G-8)   The seven economically largest free market countries: Canada, France, Germany, Great Britain, Italy, Japan, and the United States, plus Russia (a member on political issues since 1998).   426

Group of 77 (G-77)   The group of 77 countries of the South that cosponsored the Joint Declaration of Developing Countries in 1963 calling for greater equity in North-South trade. This group has come to include about 133 members and represents the interests of the less developed countries of the South.   419

Groupthink   How an individual's membership in an organization/decision-making group influences his or her thinking and actions. In particular there are tendencies within a group to think alike, to avoid discordance, and to ignore ideas or information that threaten to disrupt the consensus.   70

Hague system   Name given to the peace conferences held in the Netherlands in 1899 and 1907. This serves as the first example of an international attempt to improve the condition of humanity.   191

Hard currency   Currencies, such as dollars, euros, pounds, and yen, that are acceptable in private channels of international economics.   412

Hard power   Assets that can be used negatively as a threat or a sanction, or positively as an inducement by one country to shape the behavior of another country.   234

Head of government   The ranking official in the executive branch who is politically and constitutionally invested with the preponderance of authority to administer the government and execute its laws and policies. 79

Hegemonic power A single country or alliance that is so dominant in the international system that it plays the key role in determining the rules and norms by which the system operates. As the dominant power in the system, it has a central position in both making and enforcing the norms and modes of behavior. Hegemon is a synonym for a hegemonic power. 47, 90

Heuristic devices A range of psychological strategies that allow individuals to simplify complex decisions. Such devices include evaluating people and events in terms of how well they coincide with your own belief system ("I am anticommunist; therefore all communists are dangerous"), stereotypes ("all Muslims are fanatics"), or analogies ("appeasing Hitler was wrong; therefore all compromise with aggressors is wrong"). 64

Holy Roman Empire The domination and unification of a political territory in Western and Central Europe that lasted from its inception with Charlemagne in 800 to the renunciation of the imperial title by Francis II in 1806. 35

Horizontal authority structure A system in which authority is fragmented. The international system has a mostly horizontal authority structure. 88

Ideological/theological school of law A set of related ideas in secular or religious thought, usually founded on identifiable thinkers and their works, that offers a more or less comprehensive picture of reality. 272

Ideology Interconnected theological or secular ideas that establish values about what is good and what is not, and that indicate a course of action, create perceptual links among adherents, and perceptually distinguish those who adhere to a given ideology from those who do not. 100

Idiosyncratic analysis An individual-level analysis approach to decision making that assumes that individuals make foreign policy decisions and that different individuals are likely to make different decisions. 70

Imperial overstretch thesis The idea that attempting to maintain global order through leadership as a hegemon, especially through military power, is detrimental to the hegemon's existence. 308

Imperialism A term synonymous with colonization, meaning domination by Northern Eurowhites over Southern nonwhites as a means to tap resources to further their own development. 40

Individualism The concept that rights and liberties of the individual are paramount within a society. 452

Individual-level analysis An analytical approach that emphasizes the role of individuals as either distinct personalities or biological/psychological beings. 63

Industrial revolution The development of mechanical and industrial production of goods that began in Great Britain in the mid-1700s and then spread through Europe and North America. 40

Informal powers Authority to act or to exert influence that is derived from custom or from the prestige within a political system of either an individual leader or an institution. 81

Instrumental theory of government The notion that the purpose of political units and their governments is to benefit the people who established them and that the continued legitimate existence of these organizations rests on whether and how well they perform their tasks. 170

Interdependence The close interrelationship and mutual dependence of two or more domestic economies on each other. 378, 411

Interest group A private (nongovernmental) association of people who have similar policy views and who pressure the government to adopt those views as policy. 84

Intergovernmental organizations (IGOs) International/transnational actors that are composed of member-countries. 2, 191

Intermediate-Range Nuclear Forces Treaty (INF) A treaty between the United States and Soviet Union signed in 1987 that pledged the two countries to destroy all their ground-launched ballistic and cruise missiles with ranges of between 500 and 5,500 kilometers. 346

Intermestic The merger of *inter*national and do*mestic* concerns and decisions. 9, 77

International Conference on Financing for Development (ICFD) A UN-sponsored conference on development programs for the South that met in Monterrey, Mexico, during March 2002. Fifty heads of state or government, as well as over 200 government cabinet ministers, leaders from NGOs, and leaders from the major IGOs attended the conference. 418

International Convention on the Elimination of All Forms of Racial Discrimination Adopted in 1965 and in effect in 1969, the treaty defines and condemns racial discrimination and commits the states that are party to it to "pursue by all appropriate means and without delay a policy of eliminating racial discrimination in all its forms and promoting understanding among all races." 466

International Court of Justice (ICJ) The world court, which sits in The Hague, the Netherlands, with 15 judges and is associated with the United Nations. 277

International Criminal Court (ICC) The permanent criminal court with jurisdiction over genocide and other crimes against humanity. The court, seated in The Hague, the Netherlands, began its operations in 2003. 461

International Monetary Fund (IMF) The world's primary organization devoted to maintaining monetary stability by helping countries to fund balance-of-payment deficits. Established in 1947, it now has 170 members. 422

International political economy (IPE) An approach to the study of international relations that is concerned with the political determinants of international economic relations and also with the economic determinants of international political relations.   373

International system   An abstract concept that encompasses global actors, the interactions (especially patterns of interaction) among those actors, and the factors that cause those interactions. The international system is the largest of a vast number of overlapping political systems that extend downward in size to micropolitical systems at the local level. *See also* System-level analysis.   34

Iron triangle   An alliance between interest groups, bureaucracies, and legislators that forms a military-industrial-congressional complex.   359

Irredentism   A minority population's demand to join its motherland (often an adjoining state), or when the motherland claims the area in which the minority lives.   107

Issue areas   Substantive categories of policy that must be considered when evaluating national interest.   77

Jus ad bellum   The Western concept meaning "just cause of war," which provides a moral and legal basis governing causes for war.   283

Jus in bello   The Western concept meaning "just conduct of war," which provides a moral and legal basis governing conduct of war.   284

Leader-citizen opinion gap   Differences of opinion between leaders and public, which may have an impact on foreign policy in a democratic country.   86

League of Nations   The first, true general international organization. It existed between the end of World War I and the beginning of World War II and was the immediate predecessor of the United Nations.   192

Least developed countries (LLDCs)   Those countries in the poorest of economic circumstances. In this book, this includes those countries with a per capita GNP of less than $400 in 1985 dollars.   383

Less developed countries (LDCs)   Countries, located mainly in Africa, Asia, and Latin America, with economies that rely heavily on the production of agriculture and raw materials and whose per capita GDP and standard of living are substantially below Western standards.   56, 374

Levels of analysis   Different perspectives (system, state, individual) from which international politics can be analyzed.   63

Liberals   Analysts who reject power politics and argue that people are capable of finding mutual interests and cooperating to achieve them.   26

Limited membership council   A representative organization body of the UN that grants special status to members who have a greater stake, responsibility, or capacity in a particular area of concern. The UN Security Council is an example.   211

Limited unipolar system   A configuration of the international system in which there is one power center that plays something less than a fully dominant role because of a range of external and/or internal restraints on its power.   48

Maastricht Treaty   The most significant agreement in the recent history of the European Union (EU). The Maastricht Treaty was signed by leaders of the EU's 12 member-countries in December 1991 and outlined steps toward further political-economic integration.   203

MAD (mutual assured destruction)   A situation in which each nuclear superpower has the capability of launching a devastating nuclear second strike even after an enemy has attacked it. The belief that a MAD capacity prevents nuclear war is the basis of deterrence by punishment theory.   332

Majority voting   A system used to determine how votes should count. The theory of majoritarianism springs from the concept of sovereign equality and the democratic notion that the will of the majority should prevail. This system has two main components: (1) each member casts one equal vote, and (2) the issue is carried by either a simple majority (50 percent plus one vote) or, in some cases, an extraordinary majority (commonly two-thirds).   213

Manufactured goods   Items that required substantial processing or assembly to become usable. Distinct from primary products, such as agricultural and forestry products, that need little or no processing.   377

Marxist theory   The philosophy of Karl Marx that the economic (material) order determines political and social relationships. Thus, history, the current situation, and the future are determined by the economic struggle, termed dialectical materialism.   376

McWorld   This concept describes the merging of states into an integrated world. Benjamin Barber coined this term to describe how states are becoming more globalized, especially with the growth of economic interdependence.   51

Merchandise trade   The import and export of tangible manufactured goods and raw materials.   378

Microstate   A country with a small population that cannot survive economically without outside aid or that is inherently so militarily weak that it is an inviting target for foreign intervention.   119

Mirror-image perception   The tendency of two countries or individuals to see each other in similar ways, whether positive or negative.   69

Missile Technology Control Regime (MTCR)   A series of understandings that commits most of the countries capable of producing extended-range missiles to a ban on the export of ballistic missiles and related technology and that also pledges MTCR adherents to bring economic and diplomatic pressure to bear on countries that export missile-applicable technology.   346

Monarchism A political system that is organized, governed, and defined by the idea of the divine right of kings, or the notion that because a person is born into royalty, he or she is meant to rule. 172

Monetary relations The entire scope of international money issues, such as exchange rates, interest rates, loan policies, balance of payments, and regulating institutions (for example, the International Monetary Fund). 381

Moral absolutism A philosophy based on the notion that the ends never justify the means, or that morality should be the absolute guide of human actions, particularly in regard to international law. 292

Moral pragmatism The idea that there is a middle ground between amorality and moral absolutism that acts as a guide to human actions, particularly in regard to international law. 294

Moral relativism A philosophy that human actions must be placed in context as a means to inform international law. 293

Multilateral diplomacy Negotiations among three or more countries. 251

Multilateral (foreign) aid Foreign aid distributed by international organizations such as the United Nations. 415

Multinational corporations (MNCs) Private enterprises that have production subsidiaries or branches in more than one country. 381

Multinational states Countries in which there are two or more significant nationalities. 105

Multipolar system A world political system in which power is primarily held by four or more international actors. 40

Multistate nation A nation that has substantial numbers of its people living in more than one state. 106

Munich analogy A belief among post–World War II leaders, particularly Americans, that aggression must always be met firmly and that appeasement will only encourage an aggressor. Named for the concessions made to Hitler by Great Britain and France at Munich during the 1938 Czechoslovakian crisis. 65

Munich Conference A meeting between France, Germany, Great Britain, and Italy in 1938, during which France and Great Britain, unwilling to confront Hitler, acquiesced with Germany's decision to annex the Sudetenland (part of Czechoslovakia). This appeasement of Germany became synonymous with a lack of political will. 43

Nation A group of culturally and historically similar people who feel a communal bond and who feel they should govern themselves to at least some degree. 99

National interest A term that is often loosely applied to mean the interests of a country or its government as defined subjectively by those in power in the country, but which more accurately means the interests of the country's nation, its people. 184

National technical means (NTM) An arms control verification technique that involves using satellites, seismic measuring devices, and other equipment to identify, locate, and monitor the manufacturing, testing, or deployment of weapons or delivery vehicles, or other aspects of treaty compliance. 357

Nationalism The belief that the nation is the ultimate basis of political loyalty and that nations should have self-governing states. *See also* Nation-state. 42, 100

Nation-state A politically organized territory that recognizes no higher law, and whose population politically identifies with that entity. *See also* State. 101

Naturalist school of law Those who believe that law springs from the rights and obligations that humans have by nature. 272

Neocolonialism The notion that EDCs continue to control and exploit LDCs through indirect means, such as economic dominance and co-opting the local elite. 374

Neofunctionalism The top-down approach to solving world problems. 194

Neoliberals Analysts who believe the conflict and other ills that result from the anarchical international system can be eased by building global and regional organizations and processes that will allow people, groups, countries, and other international actors to cooperate for their mutual benefit. 26

Neorealists Analysts who believe that the distribution across and shifting of power among states in the anarchical international system is a causal factor that determines the actions of states and, thus, the dynamics of world politics. 24

Net trade The difference between exports and imports, either overall or for specific commodities. For example, if a state exports $10 billion in agricultural products and imports $8 billion dollars in agricultural products, that country has a net agricultural trade surplus of $2 billion. 389

New International Economic Order (NIEO) A term that refers to the goals and demands of the South for basic reforms in the international economic system. 394

Newly industrializing countries (NICs) Less developed countries whose economies and whose trade now include significant amounts of manufactured products. As a result, these countries have a per capita GDP significantly higher than the average per capita GDP for less developed countries. 56, 383

Nongovernmental organizations (NGOs) International (transnational) organizations with private memberships. 2, 143

Non-Proliferation Treaty (NPT) A multilateral treaty concluded in 1968, then renewed and made permanent in 1995. The parties to the treaty agree not to transfer nuclear weapons or in any way to "assist, encourage, or induce any nonnuclear state to manufacture or otherwise acquire nuclear weapons." Nonnuclear signatories of the NPT also agree not to build or accept nuclear weapons.   345

Nontariff barrier (NTB)   A nonmonetary restriction on trade, such as quotas, technical specifications, or unnecessarily lengthy quarantine and inspection procedures.   399

North   The economically developed countries (EDCs) including those of Western Europe, the United States and Canada in North America, Japan in Asia, and Australia and New Zealand in Oceania.   56, 383

North American Free Trade Agreement (NAFTA)   An economic agreement among Canada, Mexico, and the United States that went into effect on January 1, 1994. It will eliminate most trade barriers by 2009 and will also eliminate or reduce restrictions on foreign investments and other financial transactions among the NAFTA countries.   429

North Atlantic Treaty Organization (NATO)   An alliance of 26 member-countries, established in 1949 by Canada, the United States, and most of the countries of Western Europe to defend its members from outside, presumably Soviet-led, attack. In the era after the cold war, NATO has begun to admit members from Eastern Europe and has also expanded its mission to include peacekeeping.   44, 359

NUT (Nuclear Utilization Theory)   The belief that because nuclear war might occur, countries must be ready to fight, survive, and win a nuclear war. NUT advocates believe this posture will limit the damage if nuclear war occurs and also make nuclear war less likely by creating retaliatory options that are more credible than massive retaliation.   332

Objective power   Assets a country objectively possesses and has the will and capacity to use.   238

On-site inspection (OSI)   An arms control verification technique that involves stationing your or a neutral country's personnel in another country to monitor weapons or delivery vehicle manufacturing, testing, deployment, or other aspects of treaty compliance.   357

Open diplomacy   The public conduct of negotiations and the publication of agreements.   256

Operational code   A perceptual phenomenon that describes how an individual acts and responds when faced with specific types of situations.   74

Operational reality   The process by which what is perceived, whether that perception is accurate or not, assumes a level of reality in the mind of the beholder and becomes the basis for making an operational decision (a decision about what to do).   74

Organization for Economic Cooperation and Development (OECD)   An organization that has existed since 1948 (and since 1960 under its present name) to facilitate the exchange of information and otherwise to promote cooperation among the economically developed countries. In recent years, the OECD has started accepting a few newly industrializing and former communist countries in transition as members.   426

Organization for Security and Cooperation in Europe (OSCE)   Series of conferences among 34 NATO, former Soviet bloc, and neutral European countries that led to permanent organization. Established by the 1976 Helsinki Accords.   360

Pacificism   A bottom-up approach to avoidance of war based on the belief that it is wrong to kill.   368

Pacta sunt servanda   Translates as "treaties are to be served/carried out" and means that agreements between states are binding.   273

Parliamentary diplomacy   Debate and voting in international organizations to settle diplomatic issues.   255

Peace enforcement   The restoration of peace or the prevention of a breach of the peace by, if necessary, the assertive use of military force to compel one or more of the sides involved in a conflict to cease their violent actions.   364

Peacekeeping   The use of military means by an international organization such as the United Nations to prevent fighting, usually by acting as a buffer between combatants. The international force is neutral between the combatants and must have been invited to be present by at least one of the combatants. *See also* Collective security.   362

Perceptions   The factors that create a decision maker's images of reality.   68

Plenary representative body   An assembly, such as the UN's General Assembly, that consists of all members of the main organization.   211

Poliheuristic theory   A view of decision making that holds it occurs in two stages. During the first stage, nonrational considerations such as how an issue and the response to it will affect a decision maker's political or professional future are applied to narrow the range of choices. Then in the second stage decision makers use strategic considerations and other rational criteria to make a final policy choice.   75

Political culture   A concept that refers to a society's general, long-held, and fundamental practices and attitudes. These are based on a country's historical experience and on the values (norms) of its citizens. These attitudes are often an important part of the internal setting in which national leaders make foreign policy.   78

Political executives   Those officials, usually but not always in the executive branch of a government, who are at the center of foreign policy–making and whose tenures are variable and dependent on the political contest for power.   79

Political identity   The perceived connection between an individual and a political community (a group that has political interest and goals) and among individuals of a political community. Nationalism is the dominant political identity of most people, but others, such as religion, do exist as a primary political identity and are becoming more common. 98, 136

Popular sovereignty A political doctrine that holds that sovereign political authority resides with the citizens of a state. According to this doctrine, the citizenry grant a certain amount of authority to the state, its government, and, especially, its specific political leaders (such as monarchs, presidents, and prime ministers), but do not surrender ultimate sovereignty. 39, 102

Positivist school of law Those who believe that law reflects society and the way that people want the society to operate. 272

Postmodernism This theory holds that reality does not exist as such. Rather, reality is created by how we think and our discourse (writing, talking). As applied to world politics, postmodernism is the belief that we have become trapped by stale ways of conceiving of how we organize and conduct ourselves. Postmodernists wish, therefore, to "deconstruct" discourse. 138

Power The totality of a country's international capabilities. Power is based on multiple resources, which alone or in concert allow one country to have its interests prevail in the international system. Power is especially important in enabling one state to achieve its goals when it clashes with the goals and wills of other international actors. 232

Power capacity The sum of a country's power assets that determine its potential for exercising international power. 237

Power elite A relatively small group of people with similar backgrounds, values, and policy preferences who occupy most of the leadership positions in government, business, media, social, and other societal institutions and move back and forth among leadership positions in those institutions. 184

Power pole An actor in the international system that has enough military, economic, and/or diplomatic strength to often have an important role in determining the rules and operation of the system. Power poles, or simply poles, have generally been either (1) a single country or empire or (2) a group of countries that constitute an alliance or bloc. 40, 90

Power to defeat The ability to overcome in a traditional military sense—that is, to overcome enemy armies and capture and hold territory. 311

Power to hurt The ability to inflict pain outside the immediate battle area; sometimes called coercive violence. It is often used against civilians and is a particular hallmark of terrorism and nuclear warfare. 314

Prescriptive rights Obligations on a society and its government to try to provide a certain qualitative standard of life that, at a minimum, meets basic needs and perhaps does not differ radically from the quality of life enjoyed by others in the society. These rights are usually expressed in such terms as "the government shall . . ." 449

President of the Commission Comparable to being president of the European Union (EU), this person is the director of the 25-member European Commission, the policy-making bureaucratic organ of the EU. 204

Primary products Agricultural products and raw materials, such as minerals. 377

Procedural democracy A form of democracy that is defined by whether or not particular procedures are followed, such as free and fair elections or following a set of laws or a constitution. 174

Proscriptive rights Prohibitions to having something done to an individual or a group. These rights are usually expressed in such terms as "the government may not . . ." 449

Protectionism Using tariffs or nontariff barriers such as quotas or subsidies to protect a domestic economic sector from competition from imported goods or services. 398

Protestant Reformation The religious movement initiated by Martin Luther in Germany in 1517 that rejected the Catholic Church as the necessary intermediary between people and God. 37

Public diplomacy A process of creating an overall international image that enhances your ability to achieve diplomatic success. 256

Purchasing Power Parity (PPP) A measure of the relative purchasing power of different currencies. It is measured by the price of the same goods in different countries, translated by the exchange rate of that country's currency against a "base currency," usually the U.S. dollar. 11, 373

Rally effect The tendency during a crisis of political and other leaders, legislators, and the public to give strong support to a chief executive and the policy that leader has adopted in response to the crisis. 77

Real dollars The value of dollars expressed in terms of a base year. This is determined by taking current value and subtracting the amount of inflation between the base year and the year being reported. Sometimes called uninflated dollars. Any currency can be valued in real terms. *See also* Current dollars. 373

Realists Analysts who believe that countries operate in their own self-interests and that politics is a struggle for power. 24

Realpolitik Operating according to the belief that politics is based on the pursuit, possession, and application of power. 42

Regime A complex of norms, treaties, international organizations, and transnational activity that orders an area of activity such as the environment or oceans. 197

Regional government A possible middle level of governance between the prevalent national governments of today and the world government that some people favor. The regional structure that comes closest to (but still well short of) a regional government is the European Union. 199

Regional trade organization (RTO) An agreement and the organization to administer it between three or more countries in a geographical region to cooperate to reduce trade barriers and often to advance other areas of economic cooperation and integration. RTO is not synonymous with regional trade agreement, a broader term used by the World Trade Organization to define bilateral and cross-regional agreements as well as multilateral regional ones. 428

Relative power Power measured in comparison with the power of other international actors. 236

Relativists A group of people who subscribe to the belief that human rights are the product of cultures. 451

Renaissance A period of cultural and intellectual rebirth and reform following the Dark Ages from approximately 1350 to 1650. 37

Role How an individual's position influences his or her thinking and actions. 69

Secretariat The administrative organ of the United Nations, headed by the secretary-general. In general, the administrative element of any IGO, headed by a secretary-general. 215

Self-determination The concept that a people should have the opportunity to map their own destiny. 102

Services trade Trade based on the purchase (import) from or sale (export) to another country of intangibles such as architectural fees; insurance premiums; royalties on movies, books, patents, and other intellectual properties; shipping services; advertising fees; and educational programs. 378

Situational power The power that can be applied, and is reasonable, in a given situation. Not all elements of power can be applied to every situation. 239

Social contract The implicit understanding agreed to by those who merged into a society and created a government. The social contract details the proper functions of and prohibitions on government. 170

Social overstretch thesis The idea that spending money on altruistic social welfare programs to support the least productive people in society financially drains that economy. 308

Soft power Traits of a country that attract other countries to emulate it or otherwise follow its lead through the power of example. 234

South The economically less developed countries (LDCs), primarily located in Africa, Asia, and Latin America. 56, 383

Southern Common Market (Mercosur) A regional organization that emphasizes trade relations, established in 1995 among Argentina, Brazil, Paraguay, and Uruguay, with Bolivia, Chile, Peru, and Venezuela as associate members. 432

Sovereignty The most essential characteristic of an international state. The term strongly implies political independence from any higher authority and also suggests at least theoretical equality. 34, 165

Special drawing rights (SDRs) Reserves held by the International Monetary Fund that the central banks of member-countries can draw on to help manage the values of their currencies. SDR value is based on a "market-basket" of currencies, and SDRs are acceptable in transactions between central banks. 422

Special operations The overt or covert use of relatively small units of troops or paramilitary forces, which conduct commando/guerrilla operations, gather intelligence, and perform other specialized roles. Special operations forces in the U.S. military include such units as the U.S. Green Berets, Seals, and Delta Force; Great Britain's Special Air Services (SAS); and Russia's Special Purpose Force (SPETSNAZ). 325

State A political actor that has sovereignty and a number of characteristics, including territory, population, organization, and recognition. 38

State building The process of creating both a government and other legal structures of a country and the political identification of the inhabitants of the country with the state and their sense of loyalty to it. 103

State of nature A theoretical time in human history when people lived independently or in family groups and there were no societies of nonrelated individuals or governments. 169

State terrorism Terrorism carried out directly by, or encouraged and funded by, an established government of a state (country). 317

State-centric system A system describing the current world system wherein states are the principal actors. 88

State-level analysis An analytical approach that emphasizes the actions of states and the internal (domestic) causes of their policies. 76

Stateless nation A nation that does not exercise political control over any state. 107

Strategic Arms Limitation Talks Treaty (SALT I) The Strategic Arms Limitation Talks Treaty signed in 1972. 346

Strategic Arms Limitation Talks Treaty (SALT II) The Strategic Arms Limitation Talks Treaty signed in 1979 but withdrawn by President Carter from the U.S. Senate before ratification in response to the Soviet invasion of Afghanistan. 346

Strategic Arms Reduction Talks Treaty I (START I) A nuclear weapons treaty signed by the Soviet Union and the

United States in 1991 and later re-signed with Belarus, Kazakhstan, Russia, and Ukraine that will limit Russia and the United States to 1,600 delivery vehicles and 6,000 strategic explosive nuclear devices each, with the other three countries destroying their nuclear weapons or transferring them to Russia.   346

Strategic Arms Reduction Talks Treaty II (START II)   A nuclear weapons treaty signed by the Soviet Union and the United States in 1993, which established nuclear warhead and bomb ceilings of 3,500 for the United States and 2,997 for Russia by the year 2003 and that also eliminated some types of weapons systems. As of February 1997 the treaty had not been ratified by the Russian parliament and, therefore, the treaty is not legally in effect.   347

Strategic-range delivery vehicle   A missile or bomber capable of delivering weapons at a distance of more than 5,500 kilometers (3,416.8 miles).   330

Subjective power   A country's power based on other countries' perception of its current or potential power.   239

Substantive democracy   A form of democracy that is defined by whether qualities of democracy, such as equality, justice, or self-rule, are evident.   174

Summit meetings   High-level meetings for diplomatic negotiations between national political leaders.   252

Supermajority voting   A voting formula that requires a two-thirds vote or some other fraction or combination of fractions for passage of a measure.   213

Superpower   A term used to describe the leader of a system pole in a bipolar system. During the cold war, the Soviet Union and the United States were each leaders of a bipolar system pole.   43

Supranational organization   An organization that is founded and operates, at least in part, on the idea that international organizations can or should have authority higher than individual states and that those states should be subordinate to the supranational organization.   199

Sustainable development   The ability to continue to improve the quality of life of those in the industrialized countries and, particularly, those in the less developed countries while simultaneously protecting the Earth's biosphere.   58, 490

System-level analysis   An analytical approach that emphasizes the importance of the impact of world conditions (economics, technology, power relationships, and so forth) on the actions of states and other international actors.   88

Tariff   A tax, usually based on percentage of value, that importers must pay on items purchased abroad; also known as an import tax or import duty.   398

Terrorism   A form of political violence conducted by individuals, groups, or clandestine government agents that attempts to manipulate politics by attacking noncombatants and nonmilitary targets in order to create a climate of fear.   316

Theocracy   A political system that is organized, governed, and defined by spiritual leaders and their religious beliefs.   171

Third World   A term once commonly used to designate the countries of Asia, Africa, Latin America, and elsewhere that were economically less developed. The phrase is attributed to French analyst Alfred Sauvy, who in 1952 used *tiers monde* to describe neutral countries in the cold war. By inference, the U.S.-led Western bloc and the Soviet-led Eastern bloc were the other two worlds. But since most of the neutral countries were also relatively poor, the phrase had a double meaning. Sauvy used the older *tiers*, instead of the more modern *troisième*, to allude to the pre-Revolutionary (1789) third estate (*tiers état*), that is, the underprivileged class, the commoners. The nobility and the clergy were the first and second estates. Based on this second meaning, Third World came most commonly to designate the less developed countries of the world, whatever their political orientation. The phrase is less often used since the end of the cold war, although some analysts continue to employ it to designate the less developed countries.   44

Transnational advocacy networks (TANs)   IGOs, NGOs, and national organizations that are based on shared values or common interests and exchange information and services.   145

Transnational terrorism   Terrorism carried out either across national borders or by groups that operate in more than one country.   317

Transnationalism   Extension beyond the borders of a single country; applies to a political movement, issue, organization, or other phenomena.   126

Treaty of Amsterdam (1997)   The most recent agreement in a series of treaties that has further integrated the economic and political sectors of the European Union.   203

Treaty of Moscow   A treaty signed in 2002 by President George W. Bush and President Vladimir Putin. Under the treaty's provisions, the United States and Russia agree to reduce their nuclear arsenals of nuclear warheads and bombs to no more than 2,200 by 2012. When presidents Bill Clinton and Boris Yeltsin had earlier committed to the general levels established in the treaty, they had referred to the potential accord as the third Strategic Arms Reduction Treaty (START III), but that name was abandoned by Bush and Putin.   347

Treaty of Westphalia   The treaty that ended the Thirty Years' War (1618–1648). The treaty signals the birth of the modern state system and the end of the theoretical subordination of the monarchies of Europe, especially those that had adopted Protestantism, to the Roman Catholic Church and the Holy Roman Empire. While the date of 1648 marked an important change, the state as a sovereign entity had begun to emerge earlier and continues to evolve.   37

Tribalism   A term used by scholar Benjamin Barber to describe the internal pressure on countries that can lead to their fragmentation and even to their collapse.   51

Two-level game theory   The concept that in order to arrive at satisfactory international agreements, a country's diplomats actually have to deal with (at one level) the other country's negotiators and (at the second level) legislators, interest groups, and other domestic forces at home.   81, 255

UN Conference on Environment and Development (UNCED)   Often called Earth Summit I or the Rio Conference, this gathering in 1992 was the first to bring together most of the world's countries, a majority of which were represented by their head of state or government, to address the range of issues associated with sustainable development.   494

UN Conference on Population and Development (UNCPD)   A UN-sponsored conference that met in Cairo, Egypt, in September 1994 and was attended by delegates from more than 170 countries. The conference called for a program of action to include spending $17 billion annually by the year 2000 on international, national, and local programs to foster family planning and to improve the access of women in such areas as education.   497

UN Conference on Trade and Development (UNCTAD)   A UN organization established in 1964 and currently consisting of all UN members plus the Holy See, Switzerland, and Tonga, which holds quadrennial meetings aimed at promoting international trade and economic development.   419

UN Development Programme (UNDP)   An agency of the UN established in 1965 to provide technical assistance to stimulate economic and social development in the economically less developed countries. The UNDP has 48 members selected on a rotating basis from the world's regions.   419

UN General Assembly (UNGA)   The main representative body of the United Nations, composed of all 191 member-states.   211

UN Security Council   The main peacekeeping organ of the United Nations. The Security Council has 15 members, including 5 permanent members.   211

Unanimity voting   A system used to determine how votes should count. In this system, in order for a vote to be valid, all members must agree to the proposed measure. Abstention from a vote may or may not block an agreement.   214

Unconventional force   The application of force using the techniques of guerrilla warfare, covert operations, and terrorism conducted by military special forces or by para-

military groups. Such groups frequently rely on external sources for funds and weapons. Unconventional warfare is sometimes waged against nonmilitary targets and may use conventional weapons or weapons of mass destruction.   323

Unipolar system   A type of international system that describes a single country with complete global hegemony.   90

United Nations (UN)   An international body created with the intention to maintain peace through the cooperation of its member-states. As part of its mission, it addresses human welfare issues such as the environment, human rights, population, and health. Its headquarters are located in New York City, and it was established following World War II to supersede the League of Nations.   192

Universal Declaration of Human Rights   Adopted by the UN General Assembly, it is the most fundamental internationally proclaimed statement of human rights in existence.   455

Universalists   A group of people who subscribe to the belief that human rights are derived from sources external to society, such as from a theological, ideological, or natural rights basis.   450

Uruguay Round   The eighth round of GATT negotiations to reduce tariffs and nontariff barriers to trade. The eighth round was convened in Punta del Este, Uruguay, in 1986 and its resulting agreements were signed in Marrakesh, Morocco, in April 1994.   420

Vertical authority structure   A system in which subordinate units answer to higher levels of authority.   88

Veto   A negative vote cast in the UN Security Council by one of the five permanent members; has the effect of defeating the issue being voted on.   214

Weapons of mass destruction (WMDs)   Generally deemed to be nuclear weapons with a tremendous capability to destroy a population and the planet, but also include some exceptionally devastating conventional arms, such as fuel-air explosives, as well as biological, and chemical weapons. Weapons of mass destruction warfare refers to the application of force between countries using biological, chemical, and nuclear weapons.   53, 328

Weighted voting   A system used to determine how votes should count. In this system, particular votes count more or less depending on what criterion is deemed to be most significant. For instance, population or wealth might be the important defining criterion for a particular vote. In the case of population, a country would receive a particular number of votes based on its population, thus a country with a large population would have more votes than a less-populated country.   214

West   Historically, Europe and those countries and regions whose cultures were founded on or converted to European culture. Such countries would include Australia, Canada, New Zealand, and the United States. The majority of the populations in these countries are also "white," in the European, not the larger Caucasian, sense. After World War II, the term West took on two somewhat different but related meanings. One referred to the countries allied with the United States and opposed to the Soviet Union and its allies, called the East. The West also came to mean the industrial democracies, including Japan. *See also* Eurowhites.   39

Westernization of the international system   A number of factors, including scientific and technological advances, contributed to the domination of the West over the international system that was essentially created by the Treaty of Westphalia (1648).   40

Will to power   The willingness of a country to use its power capacity to influence global events.   237

World Bank Group   Four associated agencies that grant loans to LDCs for economic development and other financial needs. Two of the agencies, the International Bank for Reconstruction and Development (IBRD) and the International Development Association (IDA), are collectively referred to as the World Bank. The other two agencies are the International Finance Corporation (IFC) and the Multilateral Investment Guarantee Agency (MIGA).   425

World Conference(s) on Women (WCW)   A series of UN-sponsored global conferences on the status of women. Of these, the most recent was the fourth WCW held in Beijing in 1995.   160, 460

World Food Summit   Specifically, a 1996 meeting in Rome attended by almost all the world's countries and dedicated to addressing both the short-term and long-term food needs of less developed countries. More generically,

world food summit refers to any of a number of global meetings held on the topic.   476

World government   The concept of a supranational world authority to which current countries would surrender some or all of their sovereign authority.   199

World Health Organization (WHO)   A UN-affiliated organization created in 1946 to address world health issues.   480

World Summit on Sustainable Development (WSSD)   Often called Earth Summit II, this conference was held in Johannesburg in 2002. It was attended by almost all countries and by some 8,000 NGOs, and it established a series of calls for action and timetables for ameliorating various problems.   495

World systems theory   Based on Marxist constructs, this perspective emphasizes the interrelationships among all actors and forces within the capitalist world economic system and demonstrates how the structure of that system conditions outcomes.   377

World Trade Organization (WTO)   The organization that replaced the General Agreement on Tariffs and Trade (GATT) organization as the body that implements GATT, the treaty.   419

Xenophobia   Fear of others, "they-groups."   116

Zero-sum game   A contest in which gains by one player can only be achieved by equal losses for other players. A non-zero-sum game is a situation in which one or more players, even all players, can gain without offsetting losses for any other player or players.   236

Zionism   The belief that Jews are a nation and that they should have an independent homeland.   109

References

Abbott, Kenneth W., and Duncan Snidal. 1998. "Why States Act Through Formal International Organizations." *Journal of Conflict Organization,* 42:3–32.

Ajin, Choi. 2004. "Democratic Synergy and Victory in War, 1816–1992." *International Studies Quarterly,* 48/3:663–681.

Alulis, Joseph, and Vickie Sullivan, eds. 1996. *Shakespeare's Political Pageant: Essays in Politics and Literature.* Boulder, CO: Rowman & Littlefield.

Amstutz, Mark R. 2005. *International Ethics: Concepts, Theories, and Cases in Global Politics.* Lanham, MD: Rowman & Littlefield.

Anderson, Benedict. 1991. *Imagined Communities: Reflections on the Origin and Spread of Nationalism,* rev. ed. New York: Verso Books.

Andrade, Lydia M. 2003. "Presidential Diversionary Attempts: A Peaceful Perspective." *Congress & the Presidency,* 30:55–79.

Annan, Kofi. 2002. "Foreword." In *State of the World 2002.* Christopher Flavin, Hilary French, Gary Gardner et al. New York: W. W. Norton.

Antrobus, Peggy. 2004. *The Global Women's Movement: Issues and Strategies for the New Century.* New York: Palgrave Macmillan.

Archer, Clive. 1983. *International Organizations.* London: Allen & Unwin.

Arnold, Samantha. 2004. "'May He Guide Us Now:' Religious Discourse and America's War on Terror." Paper presented at the annual convention of the International Studies Association, Montreal.

Art, Robert J., and Kenneth W. Waltz. 2003. *The Use of Force: Military Power and International Politics,* 6th ed. Lanham, MD: Rowman & Littlefield.

Ashley, Richard K. 1989. "Living on Border Lines: Man, Poststructuralism, and War." In *International/Intertextual Relations,* eds. James Der Derian and Michael J. Shapiro. New York: Lexington Books.

Asmus, Ronald D. 2003. "Rebuilding the Atlantic Alliance." *Foreign Affairs,* 82/5:20–31.

Avant, Deborah. 2000. "From Mercenaries to Citizen Armies: Explaining Change in the Practice of War." *International Organization,* 54:41–73.

Axtmann, Roland. 2004. "The State of the State: The Model of the Modern State and Its Contemporary Transformation." *International Political Science Review,* 25/3: 259–279.

Baker William D., and John R. O'Neal. 2001. "Patriotism or Opinion Leadership? The Nature and Origins of the 'Rally 'round the Flag' Effect." *Journal of Conflict Resolution,* 45:661–688.

Balaam, David N., and Michael Veseth. 1996. *Introduction to International Political Economy.* Upper Saddle River, NJ: Prentice Hall.

Baldwin, David A. 2000. "The Sanctions Debate and the Logic of Choice." *International Security,* 24/3:80–107.

Baradat, Leon P. 2003. *Political Ideologies.* 8th ed. Englewood Cliffs, NJ: Prentice-Hall.

Barber, Benjamin R. 1995. *Jihad vs. McWorld.* New York: Times Books/Random House.

Barber, Benjamin R. 1996. *Jihad vs. McWorld: How Globalism and Tribalism Are Reshaping the World.* New York: Ballantine Books, Inc.

Barber, James D. 1985. *Presidential Character,* 3rd ed. Englewood Cliffs, NJ: Prentice Hall.

Barnett, Michael, and Martha Finnemore. 2004. *Rules for the World: International Organizations in Global Politics.* Ithaca: Cornell University Press.

Beer, Francis A. 1990. "The Reduction of War and the Creation of Peace." In *A Reader in Peace Studies,* ed. Paul Smoker, Ruth Davies, and Barbara Munske. New York: Pergamon.

Beiner, Ronald, ed. 1999. *Theorizing Nationalism.* Albany: State University of New York Press.

Belgrad, Eric A., and Nitza Nachmias. 1997. *The Politics of International Humanitarian Aid Operations.* Westport, CT: Praeger.

Bender, Peter. 2003. "America: The New Roman Empire?" *Orbis,* 47:145–159.

Benn, David Wedgwood. 2004. "Neo-Conservatives and Their American Critics." *International Affairs,* 80/5:963–969.

Bennett, Scott and Allan C. Stam. 2004. *The Behavioral Origins of War.* Ann Arbor: University of Michigan Press.

Beres, Louis Rene. 2004. "Israel and the Bomb." *International Security,* 29/1:175–180.

Berton, Peter, Hiroshi Kimura, and I. William Zartman. 1999. *International Negotiation: Actors Structure/Process, Values.* New York: St. Martin's.

Betsill, Michele M. and Harriet Bulkeley. 2004. "Transnational Networks and Global Environmental Governance: The Cities for Climate Protection Program." *International Studies Quarterly,* 48/2:471–487.

Betts, Richard K. 1998. "The New Threat of Mass Destruction." *Foreign Affairs,* 77/1:26–45.

Bhagwati, Jagdish. 2002. "Trading for Development: The Poor's Best Hope." *The Economist,* June 22, 25–28.

Bhagwati, Jagdish. 2004. *In Defense of Globalization.* Oxford, U.K.: Oxford University Press.

Biddle, Stephen, and Stephen Long. 2004. "Democracy and Military Effectiveness: A Deeper Look." *Journal of Conflict Resolution,* 48/4:525–546.

Blanton, Shannon Lindsey. 2000. "Promoting Human Rights and Democracy in the Developing World: U.S. Rhetoric versus U.S. Arms Exports." *American Journal of Political Science,* 44:123–133.

Bloomfield, Lincoln P., and Allen Moulton. 1997. *Managing International Conflict: From Theory to Policy.* New York: St. Martin's Press.

Bobrow, Davis B, and Mark A. Boyer. 1998. "International System Stability and American Decline: A Case for Muted Optimism." *International Journal,* 53: 285–305.

Boesche, Roger. 2002. *The First Great Realist: Kautilya and His Arthashastra.* Lanham, MD: Lexington Books.

Bond, Doug. 1992. "Introduction." In *Transforming Struggle: Strategy and the Global Experience of Nonviolent Direct Action.* Cambridge, MA: Program on Nonviolent Sanction in Conflict and Defense, Center for International Affairs, Harvard University.

Brandes, Lisa C. O. 1994. "The Liberal Feminist State and War." Presented at the annual meeting of the American Political Science Association, New York.

Braun, Chaim and Christopher F. Chyba. 2004. "Proliferation Rings: New Challenges to the Nuclear Nonproliferation Regime." *International Security,* 29/2:5–49.

Brecher, Jeremy. 1993. "Global Village or Global Pillage." *The Nation,* December 6.

Brecher, Michael, and Jonathan Wilkenfeld. 1997. *A Study of Crisis.* Ann Arbor: University of Michigan Press.

Breuning, Marijke. 2003. "The Role of Analogies and Abstract Reasoning in Decision-Making: Evidence from the Debate over Truman's Proposal for Development Assistance." *International Studies Quarterly,* 47:229–245.

Brewer. Paul R., Kimberly Gross, Sean Aday, and Lars Willnat. 2004. "International Trust and Public Opinion about World Affairs." *American Journal of Political Science,* 48/1: 93–116.

Bright, Chris. 2000. "Anticipating Environmental 'Surprise.'" In *State of the World 2000,* ed. Lester R. Brown, et al. New York: W. W. Norton.

Brooks, Stephen G. 1997. "Dueling Realisms." *International Organization,* 51:445–478.

Broomhall, Bruce. 2004. *International Justice and the International Criminal Court: Between Sovereignty and the Rule of Law.* Oxford, U.K.: Oxford University Press.

Brown, Michael E., ed. 2003. *Grave New World: Security Challenges in the 21st Century.* Washington, DC: Georgetown University Press.

Brown, Seyom. 1992. *International Relations in a Changing Global System.* Boulder, CO: Westview.

Brulé, David J. 2005. "Explaining and Forecasting Leaders' Decisions: A Poliheuristic Analysis of the Iran Hostage Rescue Decision." *International Studies Perspectives,* 6/1:99–113.

Brysk, Alison, ed. 2002. *Globalization and Human Rights.* Berkeley, CA: University of California Press.

Brzezinski, Zbigniew. 2004. "Hegemonic Quicksand." *The National Interest,* 74 (Winter 2003–2004):5–16.

Bueno de Mesquita, Bruce. 2002. "Domestic Politics and International Relations." *International Studies Quarterly,* 46:1–10.

Bueno de Mesquita, Bruce J., and James D. Morrow. 1999. "Sorting through the Wealth of Nations." *International Security,* 24/2:56–73.

Bugajski, Janusz. 2004. *Cold Peace: Russia's New Imperialism.* Westport, CT: Praeger.

Bunch, Charlotte, and Roxana Carillo. 1998. "Global Violence against Women: The Challenge to Human Rights and Development." In *World Security: Challenges for a New Century,* 3rd ed., ed. Michael T. Klare and Yogesh Chandran. New York: St. Martin's.

Bureau of the Census. *See* (U.S.) Bureau of the Census.

Burstein, Paul. 2003. "The Impact of Public Opinion on Public Policy: A Review and an Agenda." *Political Research Quarterly,* 56:29–40.

Butler, Michael J. 2003. "U.S. Military Intervention in Crisis, 1945–1994." *Journal of Conflict Resolution,* 47:226–248.

Byman, Daniel L., and Kenneth M. Pollack. 2001. "Let Us Now Praise Great Men." *International Security,* 25/4: 107–146.

Calleo, David P. 2003. *Rethinking Europe's Future.* Princeton, NJ: Princeton University Press.

Cameron, Gavin. 1999. *Nuclear Terrorism: A Threat Assessment for the Twenty-First Century.* New York: St. Martin's.

Campbell, Tom, Jeffrey Goldsworthy, and Adrienne Stone, eds. 2003. *Protecting Human Rights: Instruments and Institutions.* Oxford, U.K.: Oxford University Press.

Caplow, Theodore, and Louis Hicks. 2002. *Systems of War and Peace.* Lanham, MD: University Press of America.

Caprioli, Mary. 2000. "The Myth of Women's Pacifism." In *Taking Sides: Clashing Views on Controversial Issues in World Politics,* 9th ed., ed. John T. Rourke. Guilford, CT: McGraw-Hill/Dushkin.

Caprioli, Mary. 2004. "Feminist IR Theory and Quantitative Methodology: A Critical Analysis." *International Studies Review,* 6/2:253–269.

Caprioli, Mary, and Mark Boyer. 2001. "Gender, Violence and International Crisis." *Journal of Conflict Resolution,* 45:503–518.

Cardenas, Sonia, 2004. "Norm Collision: Explaining the Effects of International Human Rights Pressure on State Behavior." *International Studies Review,* 6/2:213–242.

Carrington, William J., and Enrica Detragiache. 1999. "How Extensive Is the Brain Drain?" *Finance & Development*, 36/2:108.

Carter, Ralph G. 2003. "Leadership at Risk: The Perils of Unilateralism." *PS: Political Science & Politics,* 36/1: 17–22.

Cashman, Greg. 1999. *What Causes War? An Introduction to Theories of International Conflict.* Lanham, MD: Lexington Books.

Cha, Victor D. and David C. Kang. 2004. "The Debate over North Korea." *Political Science Quarterly,* 119/2:229–254.

Chan, Steve, 2004. "Influence of International Organizations on Great-Power War Involvement: A Preliminary Analysis." *International Politics,* 41: 27–143.

Chernoff, Fred. 2004. "The Study of Democratic Peace and Progress in International Relations." *International Studies Review,* 6/1:49–65.

Chicago Council on Foreign Affairs. 2004. *Global Views 2004: American Public Opinion and Foreign Policy.* Chicago Council on Foreign Relations.

Chittick, William O., and Lee Ann Pingel. 2002. *American Foreign Policy: History, Substance and Process.* New York: Seven Bridges Press.

CIA. *See* U.S. (CIA).

Cimbala, Stephen J. 2002. *Military Persuasion in War and Policy: The Power of Soft.* Westport, CT: Praeger.

Cimballa, Stephen J. 2003. *Shield of Dreams: Missile Defenses and Nuclear Strategy.* Westport, CT: Praeger.

Cioffi-Revilla, Claudio. 2000. "Ancient Warfare: Origins and Systems." In *Handbook of War Studies II,* ed. Manus I. Midlarsky. Ann Arbor, MI: University of Michigan Press.

Clapham, Christopher. 1999. "Sovereignty and the Third World State." *Political Studies,* 47:522–537.

Cline, William. 2004. *Trade Policy and Global Poverty.* Washington, D.C.: Institute for International Economics.

Coate, Roger, and Jacques Fomerand. 2004. "The United Nations and International Norms: A Sunset Institution?" Paper presented at the annual meeting of the International Studies Association , Montreal, March 2004.

Coates, Neal. 2005. "The United Nations Convention on the Law of the Sea, the United States, and International Relations" Paper presented at the annual meeting of the International Studies Association, Honolulu, March 2005.

Cockburn, Alexander and Jeffrey St. Clair. 2004. *Imperial Crusades: Iraq, Afghanistan and Yugoslavia.* New York: Verso.

Cockburn, Cynthia. 1999. "Gender, Armed Conflict and Political Violence: A Background Paper." Washington, DC: World Bank.

Cohen, Raymond. 1987. *Theater of Power: The Art of Diplomatic Signaling.* Essex, U.K.: Longman.

Cohen, Raymond. 1996. "Reflection on the New Global Diplomacy." Paper presented at the annual meeting of the International Studies Association, San Diego, March 1996.

Cohen, Stephen D. 2000. *The Making of United States International Economic Policy,* 5th ed. Westport, CT: Praeger.

Coker, Christopher. 2002. *Waging War without Warriors? The Changing Culture of Military Conflict.* Boulder, CO: Lynne Rienner.

Colaresi, Michael. 2001. "Great Power Rivalry and the Leadership Long Cycle." *Journal of Conflict Resolution,* 45: 569–584.

Conversi, Daniel. 2002. *Ethnonationalism in the Contemporary World: Walker Connor and the Study of Nationalism.* London: Routledge.

Conversi, Daniele, ed. 2004. *Ethnonationalism in the Contemporary World.* Oxford, U.K.: Routledge.

Conway, David. 2004. *In Defense of the Realm: The Place of Nations in Classical Liberalism.* Aldershot, U.K.: Ashgate.

Cortright, David, and George A. Lopez. 2000. *The Sanctions Decade: Assessing UN Strategies in the 1990s.* Boulder, CO: Lynne Rienner.

Cortright, David, and George A. Lopez, eds. 2002. *Smart Sanctions: Targeting Economic Statecraft.* Lanham, MD: Rowman & Littlefield.

Cowles, Maria Green, and Desmond Dinan. 2004. *Development in the European Union.* Houndsmills, U.K.: Palgrave-McMillan.

Cox, Dan G. 2002. "Making Sense of Poll Results: Ambiguity in the Interpretation of Foreign Policy Questions Regarding the United Nations." *International Journal of Public Opinion Research,* 14:218–219.

Cozette, Murielle. 2004. "Realistic Realism? American Political Realism, Clausewitz and Raymond Aron on the Problem of Means and Ends in International Politics." *Journal of Strategic Studies,* 23/3:428–453.

Craig, Gordon A., and Alexander L. George. 1995. *Force and Statecraft: Diplomatic Problems of Our Time,* 3rd ed. New York: Oxford University Press.

Croucher, Sheila, L. 2003. "Perpetual Imagining: Nationhood in a Global Era." *International Studies Review,* 5:1–24.

Croucher, Sheila, L. 2003a. *Globalization and Belonging: The Politics of Identity in a Changing World.* Lanham, MD: Rowman & Littlefield.

Daalder, Ivo H., and James M. Lindsay. 2003. "The Bush Revolution: The Remaking of America's Foreign Policy." Paper presented at the conference on The Bush Presidency: An Early Assessment, Woodrow Wilson School, Princeton University, Princeton, NJ.

Dacey, Raymond and Lisa J. Carlson. 2004. "Traditional Decision Analysis and the Poliheuristic Theory of Foreign Policy Decision Making." *Journal of Conflict Resolution,* 48:38–55.

Dahbour, Omar. 2003. *The Illusion of the Peoples: A Critique of National Self-Determination.* Lanham, MD: Lexington Books.

Dalton, Russell J., Wilhelm Burklin, and Andrew Drummond. 2001. "Public Opinion and Direct Democracy." *Data Journal of Democracy,* 12/4:141–154.

Danspeckgruber, Wolfgang. 2002. *The Self-Determination of Peoples: Community, Nation, and State in an Interdependent World.* Boulder, CO: Lynne Rienner.

Davenport, Christian. 2004. "The Promise of Democratic Pacification: An Empirical Assessment." *International Studies Quarterly,* 48/3:539–561.

De Bary, William Theodore. 2004. *Nobility and Civility: Asian Ideals of Leadership and the Common Good.* Cambridge: Harvard University Press.

de la Garza, Rodolfo, and Harry Pinchon, eds. 2000. *Latinos and U.S. Foreign Policy: Representing the "Homeland"?* Lanham, MD: Rowman & Littlefield.

DeCamp, William T. 2000. "The Big Picture: A Moral Analysis of Allied Force in Kosovo." *Marine Corps Gazette,* 84/2:42–44.

Der Derian, James. 1988. "Introducing Philosophical Traditions in International Relations." *Millennium,* 17: 189–193.

DeRouen, Jr., Karl and Christopher Sprecher. 2004. "Initial Crisis Reaction and Poliheuristic Theory." *Journal of Conflict Resolution,* 48:56–68.

Destler, I. M., Leslie H. Gelb, and Anthony Lake. 1984. *Our Own Worst Enemy: The Unmaking of American Foreign Policy.* New York: Simon & Schuster.

Diamond, Larry. 2003. "Universal Democracy?" *Policy Review,* 119:3–26.

Diehl, Paul F. 2001. *The Politics of Global Governance: International Organizations in an Interdependent World.* Boulder, CO: Lynne Rienner.

DiIulio, John J. 2003. "Inside the Bush Presidency: Reflections of an Academic Interloper." Paper presented at the conference on The Bush Presidency: An Early Assessment, Woodrow Wilson School, Princeton University, Princeton, NJ.

Dinan, Desmond. 2004. *Europe Recast: A History of European Union.* Boulder, CO: Lynne Rienner Press.

Dollar, David, and Aart Kraay. 2001. "Trade, Growth and Poverty." *Finance & Development,* 38/3. Web edition at: http://www.imf.org/external/pubind.htm.

Dollar, David, and Aart Kraay. 2002. "Spreading the Wealth." *Foreign Affairs,* 81/1:1–18.

Donnelly, Jack. 2000. *Realism and International Relations.* New York: Cambridge University Press.

Donnelly, Jack. 2003. *Universal Human Rights in Theory and Practice.* Ithaca, NY: Cornell University Press.

Drainville, André C. 2004. *Contesting Globalization: Space and Place in the World Economy.* Oxford, U.K.: Routledge.

Drezner, Daniel W. 1998. "Conflict Expectations and the Paradox of Economic Coercion." *International Studies Quarterly,* 42:709–732.

Drezner, Daniel W. 2000. "Bargaining, Enforcement, and Multilateral Sanctions: When Is Cooperation Counterproductive?" *International Organization,* 54:73–102.

Druckman, Daniel. 1994. "Nationalism, Patriotism and Group Loyalty: A Social Psychological Perspective." *Mer-*

shon International Studies Review, supplement to *International Studies Quarterly,* 38:43–68.

Dunn, John. 1995. "Introduction: Crisis of the Nation State." In *Contemporary Crisis of the Nation State,* ed. John Dunn. Oxford, U.K.: Blackwell.

Economy, Elizabeth C. 2004. *The River Runs Black: The Environmental Challenge to China's Future.* Ithaca, NY: Cornell University Press.

Eichengreen, Barry. 1998. "Geography as Destiny." *Foreign Affairs,* 77/2:128–139.

Eland, Ivan. 2002. "The Empire Strikes Out: The 'New Imperialism': and Its Fatal Flaws." *Policy Analysis,* #469. Washington, DC: Cato Institute.

Elleiner, Eric and Andreas Pickel, eds. 2005. *Economic Nationalism in a Globalizing World.* Ithaca, NY: Cornell University Press.

Elliott, Kimberly Ann, and Barbara L. Oegg. 2002. "Economic Sanctions Reconsidered—Again." Paper presented at International Studies Association Convention, New Orleans, LA, March 23–26, 2002.

Enders, Walter and Todd Sandler. 2005. "After 9/11: Is It All Different Now?" *Journal of Conflict Resolution,* 49/2: 259–277.

Ensalaco, Mark and Linda C. Majka, eds. 2005. *Children's Human Rights: Progress and Challenges to Children Worldwide.* Lanham, MD: Rowman & Littlefield.

Eriksson, Mikael and Peter Wallensteen. 2004. "Armed Conflict, 1989–2003." *Journal of Peace Research,* 41: 625–636.

Erskine, Toni, ed. 2003. *Can Institutions Have Responsibilities: Collective Moral Agency and International Relations.* New York: Palgrave Macmillan.

Esposito, John. 2002. *Unholy War: Terror in the Name of Islam.* New York: Oxford University Press.

Etheredge, Lloyd S. 2001. "Will the Bush Administration Unravel?" Paper on the Web site of the Government Learning Project, http://www.policyscience.net/.

Etzioni, Amitai. 1993. "The Evils of Self-Determination." *Foreign Policy,* 89:21–35.

Etzioni, Amitai. 2004. A Self-Restrained Approach to Nation-Building by Foreign Powers." *International Affairs,* 80/1:1–17.

Everts, Philip, and Pierangelo Isernia, eds. 2001. *Public Opinion and the Use of Force.* London: Routledge.

Falk, Richard. 1999. "World Prisms: The Future of Sovereign States and International Order." *Harvard International Review,* 21/3:30–35.

(FAO) Food and Agricultural Organization. 1995. "Forest Resources Assessment 1990: Global Synthesis." *FAO Forestry Paper 124.* Rome: FAO.

Farer, Tom J. 2003. "The Ethics of Interventions in Self-Determination Struggles." *Human Rights Quarterly,* 25: 382–406.

Farrell, Robert.1998. *The Dying President: Franklin D. Roosevelt, 1944–1945.* Columbia: University of Missouri Press.

Fearon, James D., and David D. Laitin. 2003. "Ethnicity, Insurgency, and Civil War." *American Political Science Review,* 97:75–90.

Fearon, James D. and David D. Laitin. 2004. "Neotrusteeship and the Problem of Weak States."*International Security,* 28/4:5–43.

Feld, Werner J. 1979. *International Relations: A Transnational Approach.* New York: Alfred Publishing.

Feldstein, Martin. 1998. "Refocusing the IMF." *Foreign Affairs,* 77/2:46–71.

Ferguson, Niall. 2004. "A World without Power." *Foreign Policy* 143 (July/August):32–40.

Filson, Darren and Suzanne Werner. 2004. "Bargaining and Fighting: The Impact of Regime Type on War Onset, Duration, and Outcomes." *American Journal of Political Science,* 48/2:296–317.

Finnenmore, Martha. 2004. *The Purpose of Intervention: Changing Beliefs about the Use of Force.* Ithaca, NY: Cornell University Press.

Fisher, Dana R. 2004. *National Governance and the Global Climate Change Regime.* Lanham, MD: Rowman & Littlefield.

Fitzsimons, David M. 1995. "Thomas Paine's New World Order: Idealistic Internationalism in the Ideology of Early American Foreign Relations." *Diplomatic History,* 19: 569–582.

Florea, Natalie, Mark A. Boyer, Michael J. Butler, Magnolia Hernandez, Kimberly Weir, Scott W. Brown, Paula R. Johnson, Ling Meng, Haley J. Mayall, and Clarisse Lima. 2003. "Negotiating from Mars to Venus: Some Findings on Gender's Impact in Simulated International Negotiations." Paper presented at the International Studies Association, Northeast Convention, Providence, RI.

Foot, Rosemary, S. Neil MacFarlane, and Michael Mastanudo, eds. 2003. *U.S. Hegemony and International Organizations.* New York: Oxford University Press.

Fordham, Benjamin O. 2002. "Domestic Politics, International Pressure, and the Allocation of American Cold War Military Spending." *Journal of Politics,* 64:63–89.

Fordham, Benjamin O. 2004. "A Very Sharp Sword: The Influence of Military Capabilities on American Decisions to Use Force." *Journal of Conflict Resolution,* 48/5:632–656.

Fortna, Virginia Page. 2004. "Does Peacekeeping Keep Peace? International Intervention and the Duration of Peace after Civil War." *International Studies Quarterly,* 48/2:269–297.

Fowler, Michael Ross, and Julie Marie Bunck. 1995. *Law, Power, and the Sovereign States: The Evolution and Application of the Concept of Sovereignty.* University Park: University of Pennsylvania Press.

Fox, Jonathan. 2004. "The Rise of Religious Nationalism and Conflict: Ethnic Conflict and Revolutionary Wars, 1945–2001." *Journal of Peace Research,* 41:715–731.

Fox, Jonathan and Shmeul Sandler. 2004. *Bringing Religion into International Relations.* New York: Palgrave Macmillan.

Foyle, Douglas C. 1997. "Public Opinion and Foreign Policy: Elite Beliefs as a Mediating Variable." *International Studies Quarterly,* 41:141–170.

Foyle, Douglas C. 2004. "Leading the Public to War? The Influence of American Public Opinion on the Bush Administration's Decision to Go to War in Iraq." *International Journal of Public Opinion Research* 16/3:269–294.

Franck, Thomas M. 1997. "Is Personal Freedom a Western Value?" *American Journal of International Law,* 91:593–627.

Fraser, Arvonne S. 1999. "Becoming Human: The Origins and Development of Women's Human Rights." *Human Rights Quarterly* 21:853–906.

Freedom House. 1997. *Freedom in the World: The Annual Survey of Political Rights & Civil Liberties, 1996–1997.* New Brunswick, NJ: Transaction.

Fukuyama, Francis. 1989. "The End of History?" *National Interest,* 16:3–18.

Fukuyama, Francis. 1998. "Women and the Evolution of Politics." *Foreign Affairs,* 77/5:24–40.

Fukuyama, Francis. 2004. *State-Building: Governance and World Order in the 21st Century.* Ithaca, NY: Cornell University Press.

Fuller, Graham E., and Rend Rahim Francke. 2000. *The Arab Shi'a: The Forgotten Muslims.* New York: St. Martin's.

Gaenslen, Fritz. 1997. "Advancing Cultural Explanations." In *Culture and Foreign Policy,* ed. Valerie M. Hudson. Boulder, CO: Lynne Rienner.

Galtung, Johan. 1994. *Human Rights in Another Key.* Cambridge, U.K.: Polity Press.

Gartner, Scott Sigmund, and Randolph M. Siverson. 1996. "War Expansion and War Outcome." *Journal of Conflict Resolution,* 40:4–15.

Gartzke, Erik, Quan Li, and Charles Boehmer. 2001. "Investing in the Peace: Economic Interdependence and International Conflict." *International Organization,* 55: 391–438.

Gaus, Gerald F. 2000. *Political Concepts and Political Theories.* Boulder, CO: Westview.

Geisler, Michael, ed. 2005. *National Symbols, Fractured Identities.* Hanover, NH: University Press of New England.

Gelpi, Christopher, and Peter D. Feaver. 2002. "Speak Softly and Carry a Big Stick? Veterans in the Political Elite and the American Use of Force." *American Political Science Review,* 96:779–793.

Ghobara, Hazem, Adam, Paul Huth, and Bruce Russett. 2004. "Comparative Public Health: The Political Economy of Human Misery and Well-Being." *International Studies Quarterly,* 48/1:73–101.

Gibbs, David N. 1995. "Secrecy and International Relations." *Journal of Peace Research,* 32:213–238.

Gibler, Douglas M., Toby J. Rider, and Marc L. Hutchison. 2005. "Taking Arms against a Sea of Troubles: Conventional

Arms Races during Periods of Rivalry." *Journal of Peace Research,* 42:131–147.

Gibler, Douglas M., and John A. Vasquez. 1998. "Uncovering the Dangerous Alliances, 1495–1980." *International Studies Quarterly,* 42:785–810.

Gijsberts, Mérove, Louk Hagendoorn, and Peer Scheepers. 2004. *Nationalism and Exclusion of Immigrants: Cross-National Comparisons.* Aldershot, U.K.: Ashcroft.

Gilbert, Mark F. 2003. *Surpassing Realism: The Politics of European Integration since 1945.* Lanham, MD: Rowman & Littlefield.

Gilbert, Mark F. 2004. "A Fiasco but Not a Disaster: Europe's Search for a Constitution." *World Policy Journal,* 2 (Spring): 50–59.

Gilpin, Robert. 1981. *War and Change in World Politics.* Cambridge, U.K.: Cambridge University Press.

Gitlin, Todd. "America's Age of Empire." *Mother Jones* (January/February 2003): online.

Goddard, C. Roe, Patrick Cronin, and Kishore C. Dash, eds. 2003. *International Political Economy,* 2nd ed. Boulder, CO: Lynne Rienner.

Goddard, Stacie E. and Daniel H. Nexon. 2005. "Paradigm Lost? Reassessing Theory of International Politics." *European Journal of International Relations,* 11/1:9–61.

Goff, Patricia M. 2000. "Invisible Borders: Economic Liberalization and National Identity." *International Studies Quarterly,* 44:533–62.

Goldsmith, Jack L. and Eric A. Posner. 2005. *The Limits of International Law.* New York: Oxford University Press.

Goldsmith, Jack, and Stephen D. Krasner. 2003. "The Limits of Idealism." *Daedalus,* 132:47–63.

Graebner, Norman, ed. 1964. *Ideas and Diplomacy.* New York: Oxford University Press.

Gray, Colin S. 1994. "Force, Order, and Justice: The Ethics of Realism in Statecraft." *Global Affairs,* 14:1–17.

Green, Michael. 1996. *Arming Japan: Defense Production, Alliance Politics, and the Post-War Search for Autonomy.* Baltimore: Johns Hopkins University Press.

Greenfeld, Liah. 1992. *Nationalism: Five Roads to Modernity.* Cambridge, MA: Harvard University Press.

Greenstein, Fred I. 2003. "The Leadership Style of George W. Bush." Paper presented at the conference on The Bush Presidency: An Early Assessment, Woodrow Wilson School, Princeton University, Princeton, NJ.

Greider, William. 1997. *The Manic Logic of Global Capitalism.* New York: Simon & Schuster.

Grossman, Gene M. and Elhanan Helpma. 2002. *Interest Groups and Trade Policy.* Princeton, NJ: Princeton University Press.

Guibernau, Montserrat. 1996. *Nationalisms: The Nation-State and Nationalism in the Twentieth Century.* Cambridge, U.K.: Polity Press.

Gurr, Nadine, and Benjamin Cole. 2000. *The New Face of Terrorism: Threats from Weapons of Mass Destruction.* New York: St. Martin's.

Gurr, Ted Robert, Monty G. Marshall, and Deepa Khosla. 2001. *Peace and Conflict 2001: Armed Conflicts, Self-Determination Movements, and Democracy.* College Park Maryland: Integrated Network for Societal Conflict Research at the University of Maryland. Available on the Web at http://www.bsos.umd.edu/cidcm/peace.htm.

Haass, Richard N. 1997. *The Reluctant Sheriff: The United States after the Cold War.* New York: Council on Foreign Relations.

Hafez, Mohammmed. 2004. *Why Muslims Rebel: Repression and Resistance in the Islamic World.* Boulder, CO: Lynne Rienner.

Haftel, Yoram Z. 2004. "From the Outside Looking In: The Effect of Trading Blocs on Trade Disputes in the GATT/WTO." *International Studies Quarterly,* 48/1:121–149.

Hagen, Joe D. 2001. "Does Decision Making Matter: Systemic Assumptions vs. Historical Reality in International Theory." *International Studies Review,* 3:2 (summer): 5–46.

Hall, John. 1995. "Nationalism, Classified and Explained." In *Notions of Nationalism,* ed. Sukumar Periwal. Budapest: Central European University Press.

Hall, Rodney Bruce. 1999. *National Collective Identity: Social Constructs and International Systems.* New York: Columbia University Press.

Halperin, Morton H., Joseph T. Siegle, and Michael M. Weinstein. 2004. *The Democracy Advantage: How Democracies Promote Prosperity and Peace.* Oxford, U.K.: Routledge.

Handelman, Don. 2004. *Nationalism and the Jewish State.* Cambridge: Houndsmills, U.K.: Palgrave Macmillan.

Harnisch, Sebastian. 2001. "The Hegemon and the Demon: U.S. Nuclear Learning vis-à-vis North Korea." Unpublished paper on the Web at http://www.uni-trier.de/uni/fb3/politik/liba/harnisch/Pubs/Hegemon-Demon-Final.pdf.

Hasseler, Stephen. 2004. *Super-State: The New Europe and Its Challenge to America.* New York: Palgrave Macmillan.

Hawkins, Darren. 1999. "Transnational Activists as Motors for Change." *International Studies Review,* I/1:119–122.

Hawkins, Darren. 2004. "Explaining Costly International Institutions: Persuasion and Enforceable Human Rights Norms." *International Studies Quarterly,* 48/4:779–806.

Hayden, Deborah. 2003. *Pox: Genius, Madness, and the Mysteries of Syphilis.* New York: Perseus.

Heasley, James E., III. 2003. *Organization Global Governance: International Regimes and the Process of Collective Hegemony.* Lanham, MD: Lexington Books.

Heater, Derek. 2004. *Citizenship: The Civic Ideal in World History, Politics, and Education.* Houndsmills, U.K.: Palgrave Macmillan.

Hechter, Michael. 2000. *Containing Nationalism.* Oxford, U.K.: York: Oxford University Press.

Heith, Diane J. 2003. "One for All: Using Focus Groups and Opinion Polls in the George H. W. Bush White House." *Congress & the Presidency,* 30:81–94.

Helco, Hugh. 2003. "The Bush Political Ethos." Paper presented at the conference on The Bush Presidency: An Early Assessment, Woodrow Wilson School, Princeton University, Princeton, NJ.

Henderson, Earl Anthony. 1999. "The Democratic Peace through the Lens of Culture, 1820–1989." *International Studies Quarterly,* 42/3:461–484.

Henderson, Errol A. 2002. *Democracy and War: The End of an Illusion?* Boulder, CO: Lynne Rienner.

Henderson, Errol A. 2004. "Mistaken Identity: Testing the Clash of Civilizations Thesis in Light of Democratic Peace Claims."*British Journal of Political Science,* 34/3:539–554.

Henry, Charles P., ed. 2000. *Foreign Policy and the Black (Inter) National Interest.* Albany: State University of New York Press.

Hermann, Margaret G. 2001. "How Decision Units Shape Foreign Policy: A Theoretical Framework." *International Studies Review,* Special Issue, "Leaders, Groups, and Coalitions: Understanding the People and Processes in Foreign Policy Making," 47–82.

Hermann, Margaret G., and Joe D. Hagan. 1998. "International Decision Making: Leadership Matters." *Foreign Policy,* No. 110 (Spring):124–137.

Hermann, Margaret B., Thomas Preston, Baghat Korany, and Timothy M. Shaw. 2001. "Who Leads Matters: The Effects of Powerful Individuals." *International Studies Review,* Special Issue, "Leaders, Groups, and Coalitions: Understanding the People and Processes in Foreign Policy Making," 83–132.

Herrmann, Richard K. and Jonathan W. Keller. 2004. "Beliefs, Values, and Strategic Choice: U.S. Leaders' Decisions to Engage, Contain, and Use Force in an Era of Globalization." *Journal of Politics,* 66/2:557–575.

Hermann, Richard K., Thomas Risse, and Marilynn B. Brewer. 2004. *Transnational Identities: Becoming European in the EU.* Lanham, MD: Roman & Littlefield.

Herspring, Dale R., ed. 2004. *Putin's Russia: Past Imperfect, Future Uncertain.* Lanham, MD: Rowman & Littlefield.

Hetherington, Marc J., and Michael Nelson. 2003. "Anatomy of a Rally Effect: George W. Bush and the War on Terrorism." *Political Science and Politics,* 36:37–42.

Heymann, Philip B. 2002. "Dealing with Terrorism: An Overview." *International Security,* 26/3:24–38.

Hobbes, Heidi H., ed. 2000. *Pondering Postinternationalism: A Paradigm for the Twenty-First Century.* Albany, NY: State University of New York Press.

Hobsbawm, Eric J. 1990. *Nations and Nationalism since 1780: Programme, Myth, Reality.* Cambridge, U.K.: Cambridge University Press.

Hobsbawm, Eric J. 2001. "Democracy Can Be Bad for You." *New Statesman* 14/626 (March 5, 2001): 25–28.

Hobson, John M. 2005. "The Enduring Place of Hierarchy in World Politics: Tracing the Social Logics of Hierarchy and Political Change." *European Journal of International Relations,* 11/1:63–98.

Hoffmann, Stanley. 1995. "The Crisis of Liberal Internationalism." *Foreign Policy,* 98:159–179.

Hoffman, Stanley. 2003. "World Governance: Beyond Utopia." *Daedalus,* 132:27–35.

Holsti, K. J. 2004. *Taming the Sovereigns: Institutional Change in International Politics.* New York: Cambridge University Press.

Holsti, Ole R. 1997. *Public Opinion and American Foreign Policy.* Ann Arbor: University of Michigan Press.

Homer-Dixon, Thomas. 1998. "Environmental Scarcity and Intergroup Conflict." In *World Security: Challenges for a New Century,* 3rd ed., ed. Michael T. Klare and Yogesh Chandran. New York: St. Martin's.

Hopmann, P. Terrence. 1999. *Building Security in Post–Cold War Eurasia: The OSCE and U.S. Foreign Policy.* Washington, DC: United States Institute of Peace.

Horne, John. 2002. "Civilian Populations and Wartime Violence: Toward an Historical Analysis." *International Social Science Journal,* 26:426–435.

Hossay, Patrick. 2002. *Contentions of Nationhood: Nationalist Movements, Political Conflict and Social Change in Flanders, Scotland, and French Canada.* Lanham, MD: Lexington Books.

Howard, Peter. 2004. "Why Not Invade North Korea? Threats, Language Games, and U.S. Foreign Policy." *International Studies Quarterly,* 48/4:805–827.

Howell, William G. and Jon C. Pevehouse. 2005. "Presidents, Congress, and the Use of Force." *International Organization,* 59/1:209–232.

Hufbauer, Cary Clyde, and Barbara Oegg. 2003. "The Impact of Economic Sanctions on U.S. Trade: Andrew Rose's Gravity Model." *International Economics Policy Briefs,* Number PB03-4, April 2003. Washington DC: Institute for International Economics.

Hughes, Donna M. 2000. "The 'Natasha' Trade: The Transnational Shadow Market of Trafficking in Women." *Journal of International Affairs,* 53:625–652.

Huntington, Samuel. 1993. "The Clash of Civilizations." *Foreign Affairs,* 72(3):56–73.

Huntington, Samuel P. 1996. *The Clash of Civilizations and the Remaking of World Order.* New York: Simon & Schuster.

Huntington, Samuel P. 1999. "The Lonely Superpower." *Foreign Affairs,* 78/2 (March/April 1999):35–49.

Huth, Paul K. 1996. *Standing Your Ground: Territorial Disputes and International Conflict.* Ann Arbor: University of Michigan Press.

Ignazi, Piero and Mark Kesselman. 2004. "Extreme Right Parties in Western Europe." *Political Science Quarterly,* 119/2:369–371.

Ikenberry, G. John. 2001. "Getting Hegemony Right." *The National Interest,* (Spring) 63:17–24.

Ikenberry, G. John, ed. 2002. *America Unrivaled: The Future of the Balance of Power.* Ithaca, NY: Cornell University Press.

Ikenberry, G. John. 2004. "Liberalism and Empire: Logics of Order in the American Unipolar Age." *Review of International Studies,* 30:609–630.

Inglehart, Ronald. 2003. "How Solid Is Mass Support for Democracy—And How Can We Measure It?" *PS, Political Science and Politics,* 36/1:51–57.

Inglehart, Ronald, and Pippa Norris. 2003. "The True Clash of Civilizations." *Foreign Policy,* 136:63–70.

Isaak, Robert A. 2000. *Managing World Economic Change: International Political Economy,* 3rd ed. Upper Saddle River, NJ: Prentice-Hall.

Isernia, Pierangelo, Zoltan Juhasz, and Hans Rattinger. 2002. "Foreign Policy and the Rational Public in Comparative Perspective." *Journal of Conflict Resolution,* 46: 201–225.

Iyer, Pico. 1996. "The Global Village Finally Arrives." In *Annual Editions: Global Issues 96/97.* Guilford, CT: Dushkin/McGraw-Hill.

Jackson, Robert. 1999. "TI Sovereignty in World Politics: A Glance at the Conceptual and Historical Landscape." *Political Studies,* 47:431–56.

Jackson, Robert, and Georg Sørensen. 2003. *Introduction to International Relations: Theories and Approaches,* 2nd ed. Oxford, U.K.: Oxford University Press.

Jacobsen, John Kurt. 2003. "Dueling Constructivisms: A Post-Mortem on the Ideas Debated in Mainstream IR/IPE." *Review of International Studies,* 29:39–60.

James, Patrick. 2002. *International Relations and Scientific Progress: Structural Realism Reconsidered.* Columbus: Ohio State University Press.

Jaquette, Jane S. 1997. "Women in Power: From Tokenism to Critical Mass." *Foreign Policy,* 108:23–97.

Jayawickrama, Nihal. 2003. *The Judicial Application of Human Rights Law: National, Regional and International Jurisprudence.* Cambridge, U.K.: Cambridge University Press.

Jett, Dennis C. 2000. *Why Peacekeeping Fails.* New York: St. Martin's.

Johansen, Robert C. 1994. "Building World Security: The Need for Strengthened International Institutions." In *World Security: Challenges for a New Century,* ed. Michael T. Klare and Daniel C. Thomas. New York: St. Martin's.

Johnson, Dominic D. P. 2004. *Overconfidence and War: The Havoc and Glory of Positive Illusions.* Cambridge, MA: Harvard University Press.

Johnston, Douglas, ed. 2003. *Faith-Based Diplomacy: Trumping Realpolitik.* New York: Oxford University Press.

Joyner, Christopher C. 2000. "The Reality and Relevance of International Law in the Twenty-First Century." In *The Global Agenda: Issues and Perspectives,* ed. Charles W. Kegley, Jr., and Eugene R. Wittkopf. Boston: McGraw-Hill.

Joyner, Christopher C. 2005. *International Law in the 21st Century: Rules for Global Governance.* Lanham, MD: Rowman & Littlefield.

Jung, Hwa Yol. 2002. *Comparative Political Culture in the Age of Globalization.* Lanham, MD: Lexington Books.

Jusdanis, Gregory. 2004. *The Necessary Nation.* Princeton, NJ: Princeton University Press.

Jutta, Joachim. 2003. "Framing Issues and Seizing Opportunities: The UN, NGOs, and Women's Rights." *International Studies Quarterly,* 47:247–274.

Kaltenthaler, Karl C., Ronald D. Gelleny, and Stephen J. Ceccoli. 2004. "Explaining Citizen Support for Trade Liberalization." *International Studies Quarterly,* 48/4:829–851.

Kaplan, Lawrence F. 2004. "Springtime for Realism." *New Republic* (June 1, 2004): online.

Kaplan, Robert D. 1999. "Was Democracy Just a Moment?" In *Stand: Contending Issue and Opinion, World Politics,* ed., Marc Genest. Boulder, CO: Coursewise Publishing.

Karl, Terry Lynn. 1999. "The Perils of the Petro-State: Reflections on the Paradox of Plenty." *Journal of International Affairs,* 53:31–51.

Katada, Saori N., and Timothy J. McKeown. 1998. "Aid Politics and Electoral Politics: Japan, 1970–1992." *International Studies Quarterly,* 42:591–600.

Kateb, George. 2000. "Is Patriotism a Mistake?" *Social Research,* 67:901–923.

Keane, John. 1994. "Nations, Nationalism, and Citizens in Europe." *International Social Science Journal,* 140:169–184.

Kegley, Charles W., Jr., and Gregory A. Raymond. 1999. *How Nations Make Peace.* New York: St. Martin's.

Kennan, George F. 1986. "Morality and Foreign Policy." *Foreign Affairs,* 64 (Winter):205–218.

Kennedy, Paul. 1988. *The Rise and Fall of the Great Powers.* New York: Random House.

Kent, Ann. 1999. *China, the United Nations, and Human Rights: The Limits of Compliance.* Philadelphia: University of Pennsylvania Press.

Kent, George. 2002. "Food Trade and Food Rights." *United Nations Chronicle,* 39/1. Online edition at http://www.un.org/Pubs/chronicle/2002/issue1/0102p27.html.

Keohane, Robert O. 1998. "International Institutions: Can Interdependence Work?" *Foreign Policy,* 110:82–96.

Keohane, Robert O., and Lisa L. Martin. 1995. "The Promise of Institutionalist Theory." *International Security,* 20/1: 39–51.

Keohane, Robert O., and Joseph S. Nye, Jr. 1999. "Globalization: What's New? What's Not? (And So What?)." *Foreign Policy,* 114:104–119.

Kerr, Joanna, Ellen Spenger, and Alison Symington, eds. 2004. *The Future of Women's Rights: Global Visions and Strategies.* New York: Palgrave Macmillan.

Kerr, Rachel. 2004. *The International Criminal Tribunal for the Former Yugoslavia.* Oxford, U.K.: Oxford University Press.

Keshk, Omar M. G., Brian M. Pollins, and Rafael Reuveny. 2004. "Trade Still Follows the Flag: The Primacy of Politics in a Simultaneous Model of Interdependence and Armed Conflict." *Journal of Politics,* 66/4:1155–1182.

Keylor, William. 1996. *The Twentieth Century World.* New York: Oxford University Press.

Kille, Kent J., and Roger M. Scully. 2003. "Executive Heads and the Role of Intergovernmental Organizations: Expansionist Leadership in the United Nations and the European Union." *Political Psychology,* 24:175–190.

Kim, Samuel S. 1997. "China as a Great Power." *Current History,* 96:246–251.

Kimura, Masato, and David A. Welch. 1998. "Specifying 'Interests': Japan's Claim to the Northern Territories and Its Implications for International Relations Theory." *International Studies Quarterly,* 42:213–244.

Kinne, Brandon J. 2005. "Decision Making in Autocratic Regimes: A Poliheuristic Perspective." *International Studies Perspectives,* 6/1:114–128.

Kinsella, David, and Bruce Russett. 2002. "Conflict Emergence and Escalation in Interactive International Dyads." *Journal of Politics,* 64:1045–1069.

Kissinger, Henry A. 1970. "The Just and the Possible." In *Negotiation and Statecraft: A Selection of Readings,* U.S. Congress, Senate Committee on Government Operations, 91st Cong., 2nd sess.

Kissinger, Henry A. 1979. *The White House Years.* Boston: Little, Brown.

Kissinger, Henry A. 1982. *Years of Upheaval.* Boston: Little, Brown.

Kissinger, Henry A. 1994. *Diplomacy.* New York: Simon & Schuster.

Klare, Michael T., and Yogesh Chandrani, eds. 1998. *World Security: Challenges for a New Century,* 3rd ed. New York: St. Martin's.

Klare, Michael T., and Lora Lumpe. 2000. "Fanning the Flames of War: Conventional Arms Transfers in the 1990s." In *World Security: Challenges for a New Century,* 3rd ed., eds. Michael T. Klare and Yogesh Chandrani. New York: St. Martin's.

Kline, Scott. 2004. "The Culture War Goes Global: 'Family Values' and the Shape of U.S. Foreign Policy." Paper presented at the annual convention of the International Studies Association, Montreal.

Koehn, Peter H., and Olatunde J. B. Ojo. 1999. *Making Aid Work: Innovative Approaches for Africa at the Turn of the Century.* Lanham, MD: University Press of America.

Korbin, Stephen. 1996. "The Architecture of Globalization: State Sovereignty in a Networked Global Economy." In *Globalization, Governments and Competition.* Oxford, U.K.: Oxford University Press.

Koubi, Vally. 1999. "Military Technology Races." *International Organization,* 53:537–565.

Krasner, Stephen D. 1999. *Sovereignty: Organized Hypocrisy.* Princeton, NJ: Princeton University Press.

Krasno, Jean, Bradd C. Hayes, and Donald C. F. Daniel, eds. 2003. *Leveraging for Success in United Nations Peacekeeping Operations.* Westport, CT: Praeger.

Krause, Keith, and W. Andy Knight, eds. 1995. *State, Society, and the UN System: Perspectives on Multilateralism.* Tokyo: United Nations University Press.

Krauthammer, Charles. 1991. "The Unipolar Moment." *Foreign Affairs, America and the World, 1990/91,* 23–33.

Krauthammer, Charles. 2004. "In Defense of Democratic Realism." *The National Interest* (Fall 2004), online.

Kuttner, Robert. 1998. "Globalism Bites Back." *American Prospect,* 37 (March-April):6–8.

Kydd, Andrew. 2000. "Arms Races and Arms Control: Modeling the Hawk Perspective." *American Journal of Political Science,* 44:228–244.

Lackey, Douglas. 1989. *The Ethics of War and Peace.* Englewood Cliffs, NJ: Prentice Hall.

Lacy, Dean and Emerson M. S. Niou. 2004. "A Theory of Economic Sanctions and Issue Linkage: The Roles of Preferences, Information, and Threats." *Journal of Politics,* 66.1:25–54.

Lake, Daniel. 2005. "Why Play Hardball? The Political Incentives for Employing Coercive Statecraft." Paper presented at the annual convention of the International Studies Association, Honolulu.

Lal, Deepak. 2004. *In Praise of Empires: Globalization and Order.* New York: Palgrave Macmillan.

Lang, Anthony F., Jr., ed. 2003. *Just Intervention.* Washington, DC: Georgetown University Press.

Laqueur, Walter. 2004. *No End to War: Terrorism in the Twenty-First Century.* New York: Continuum International.

Larémont, Ricardo Réne. 2005. *Borders, Nationalism, and the African State.* Boulder, CO: Lynne Rienner.

Lebovic, James H. 2004. "Uniting for Peace? Democracies and United Nations Peace Operations after the Cold War." *Journal of Conflict Resolution,* 48/6:910–936.

Legro, Jeffrey W. 1996. "Culture and Preferences in the International Cooperation Two-Step." *American Political Science Review,* 90:118–137.

Legro, Jeffrey W. 1997. "Which Norms Matter: Revisiting the 'Failure' of Internationalism." *International Organization,* 51:31–63.

Lensu, Maria, and Jan-Sefan Fritz, eds. 1999. *Value Pluralism, Normative Theory, and International Relations.* New York: St. Martin's.

Lentner, Howard. 2004. *Power and Politics in Globalization: The Indispensable State.* Oxford, U.K.: Routledge.

Leogrande, William M. 2002. "Tug of War: How Real Is the Rivalry between Congress and the President over Foreign Policy?" *Congress & the Presidency,* 29:113–118.

Levey, David H. and Stuart S. Brown. 2005. "The Overstretch Myth." *Foreign Affairs,* 84/3 (March/April 2005): online.

Li, Quan, and Rafael Reuveny. 2003. "Economic Globalization and Democracy: An Empirical Analysis." *British Journal of Political Science,* 33:29–54.

Li, Quan and Drew Schaub. 2004. "Economic Globalization and Transnational Terrorism: A Pooled Time-Series Analysis." *Journal of Conflict Resolution,* 48/2:230–258.

Lieven, Anatol. 2004. *America Right or Wrong: An Anatomy of American Nationalism.* New York: Oxford University Press.

Lind, Michael. 1994. "In Defense of Liberal Nationalism." *Foreign Affairs,* 73(3):87–99.

Lindsay, James M. 1994. "Congress, Foreign Policy, and the New Institutionalism." *International Studies Quarterly,* 38:281–304.

Litfin, Karen T. 1994. *Ozone Discourses: Science and Politics in Global Environmental Cooperation.* New York: Columbia University Press.

Lobell, Steven E. 2004. "Historical Lessons to Extend America's Great Power Tenure." *World Affairs* (Spring 2004): online.

Locher, Birgit and Elizabeth Prügl. 2001. "Feminism and Constructivism: World Apart or Sharing the Middle Ground?" *International Studies Quarterly,* 45:111–129.

Lomborg, Bjørn, 2001. *The Skeptical Environmentalist: Measuring the Real State of the World.* New York: Cambridge University Press.

Lomborg, Bjørn. 2003. "Debating the Skeptical Environmentalist." In *Taking Sides: Clashing View on Controversial Issues in World Politics,* 11th ed., ed. John T. Rourke. Guilford, CT: McGraw-Hill/Dushkin.

Longman, Phillip. 2004. *The Empty Cradle: How Falling Birthrates Threaten World Prosperity and What to Do about It.* New York: Basic Books.

Lopez, George A., Jackie G. Smith, and Ron Pagnucco. 1995. "The Global Tide." *Bulletin of the Atomic Scientists,* 51/6 (July/August):33–39.

Luttwak, Edward. 2000. "Kofi's Rule: Humanitarian Intervention and Neocolonialism." *The National Interest* 58 (Winter): 57–62.

Macridis, Roy C., and Mark L. Hulliung. 1996. *Contemporary Political Ideologies.* New York: Harper-Collins.

Mahmud, Sakah S. 2004. "Contesting Hegemony? The Islamic Nation as a Dominant Actor in International Relations." Paper presented at the annual convention of the International Studies Association, Montreal.

Maley, Willy. 2003. *Nation, State, and Empire in English Renaissance Literature: Shakespeare to Milton.* New York: Palgrave Macmillan.

Malone, David M., and Yuen Foong Khong, eds. 2003. *Unilateralism and U.S. Foreign Policy: International Perspectives.* Boulder, CO: Lynne Rienner.

Mandaville, Peter G. 2000. "Territory and Translocality: Discrepant Idioms of Political Identity." Paper presented at the International Studies Association Convention, Los Angeles, CA.

Mann, Michael. 2004. *The Dark Side of Democracy: Explaining Ethnic Cleansing.* New York: Cambridge University Press.

Mann, Michael. 2004a. "The First Failed Empire of the 21st Century." *Review of International Studies,* 30:631–653.

Mansbach, Richard W. 1996. "Neo-This and Neo-That: Or, 'Play It Sam' (Again and Again)." *Mershon International Studies Review,* 40:90–95.

Mansfield, Edward D., and. Brian M. Pollins. 2001. "The Study of Interdependence and Conflict: Recent Advances, Open Questions, and Directions for Future Research." *Journal of Conflict Resolution,* 45:834–860.

Marshall, Bryan W., and Brandon C. Prins. 2002. "The Pendulum of Congressional Power: Agenda Change, Partisanship, and the Demise of the Post–World War II Foreign Policy Consensus." *Congress & the Presidency,* 29:195–212.

Marshall, Monty G., and Ted Robert Gurr. 2002. *Peace and Conflict, 2003: A Global Survey of Armed Conflicts, Self-Determination Movements, and Democracy.* College Park, MD: Center for International Development and Conflict Management.

Martin, Andrew and George Ross, eds. 2004. *Euros and Europeans: Monetary Integration and the European Model of Society.* Cambridge, UK: Cambridge University Press.

Marx, Anthony W. 2003. *Faith in Nation: Exclusionary Origins of Nationalism.* New York: Oxford University Press.

Maurer, Andreas. 2003. "The Legislative Powers and Impact of the European Parliament." *Journal of Common Market Studies,* 41:227–248.

Mayall, James. 1999. "Sovereignty, Nationalism, and Self-Determination." *Political Studies,* 47/3:474–502.

Maynes, Charles William. 1998. "The Perils of (and for) an Imperial America." *Foreign Policy,* 111:503–521.

McDonald, Patrick J. 2004. "Peace through Trade or Free Trade?" *Journal of Conflict Resolution,* 48/4:547–572.

McDowall, David. 2004. *The Modern History of the Kurds,* 3rd ed. Houndsmills, U.K.: Palgrave Macmillan.

McGinnis, Michael Dean, and John T. Williams. 2001. *Compound Dilemmas: Democracy, Collective Action, and Superpower Rivalry.* Ann Arbor: University of Michigan Press.

McKay, David. 1999. "The Political Sustainability of European Monetary Union." *British Journal of Political Science,* 29:463–486.

McKeown, Timothy J. 2001. "Plans and Routines, Bureaucratic Bargaining, and the Cuban Missile Crisis." *Journal of Politics,* 63:1163–1191.

Mearsheimer, John J., and Stephen Walt. 2003. "An Unnecessary War." *Foreign Policy,* 134:50–59.

Meernik, James and Michael Ault. 2005. "The Diverted President: The Domestic Agenda and Foreign Policy." Paper presented at the annual convention of the International Studies Association, Honolulu.

Melander, Erik. 2005. "Political Gender Equality and State Human Rights Abuse." *Journal of Peace Research,* 42: 149–166.

Mercer, Jonathan C. 1996. *Reputation and International Politics.* Ithaca, NY: Cornell University Press.

Meunier, Sophie. 2000. "What Single Voice? European Institutions and EU-US Trade Negotiations." *International Organization,* 54/2:103–135.

Midlarsky, Manus. 1999. "Democracy and Islam: Implications for Civilizational Conflict and the Democratic Peace." *International Studies Quarterly,* 42:485–512.

Migdal, Joel S. 2004. "State-Building and the Non-Nation-State." *Journal of International Affairs*, 58/1:17–47.

Milner, Helen V. and Benjamin Judkins. 2004. "Partisanship, Trade Policy, and Globalization: Is There a Left-Right Divide on Trade Policy?" *International Studies Quarterly*, 48/1:95–114.

Mindich, David T. Z. 2004. *Tuned Out: Why Americans Under 40 Don't Follow the News*. New York: Oxford University Press.

Mintz, Alex. 2004. "How Do Leaders Make Decisions? A Poliheuristic Perspective." *Journal of Conflict Resolution*, 48/1:3–13.

Mitchell, Sara McLaughlin and Brandon C. Prins. 2004. "Rivalry and Diversionary Uses of Force." *Journal of Conflict Resolution*, 48/6:937–961.

Moaz, Zeev. 2004. "The Mixed Blessing of Israel's Nuclear Policy." *International Security*, 28/2:44–77.

Monshipouri, Mahmood. 2004. "The Road to Globalization Runs through Women's Struggle: Iran and the Impact of the Nobel Peace Prize." *World Affairs*, 167/1:3–14.

Monshipouri, Mahmood, Neil Englehart, Andrew J. Nathan, and Kavita Philip, eds. 2003. *Constructing Human Rights in the Age of Globalization*. Armonk, NY: M. E. Sharpe.

Moore, Gale. 1998. *Climate of Fear: Why We Shouldn't Worry about Global Warming*. Washington, DC: Cato Institute.

Moore, Rebecca R. 2001. "China's Fledgling Civil Society." *World Policy Journal*, 18/1:56–66.

Moore, Will H., and David J. Lanoue. 2003. "Domestic Politics and U.S. Foreign Policy: A Study of Cold War Conflict Behavior." *Journal of Politics*, 65:376–397.

Moravcsik, Andrew. 2000. "The Origin of Human Rights Regimes: Democratic Delegation in Postwar Europe." *International Organization*, 54:217–252.

Morefield, Jeanne. 2004. *Covenants without Swords: Idealist Liberalism and the Spirit of Empire*. Princeton, NJ: Princeton University Press.

Morgan, T. Clifton. 2005. "When Threats Succeed: A Formal Model of the Threat and Use of Economic Sanctions." Paper presented at the annual convention of the International Studies Association, Honolulu.

Morgan, T. Clifton, and Glenn Palmer. 2003. "To Protect and Serve: Alliances and Foreign Policy Portfolios." *Journal of Conflict Resolution*, 47:180–203.

Morgenthau, Hans W. 1973, 1986. *Politics among Nations*. New York: Knopf. Morgenthau's text was first published in 1948 and periodically thereafter. Two sources are used herein. One is the fifth edition, published in 1973. The second is an edited abstract drawn from pp. 3–4, 10–12, 14, 27–29, and 31–35 of the third edition, published in 1960. The abstract appears in Vasquez 1986:37–41. Pages cited for Morgenthau 1986 refer to Vasquez's, not Morgenthau's, book.

Morse, Edward L. 1999. "A New Political Economy of Oil?" *Journal of International Affairs*, 53:1–30.

Mortimer, Edward, and Robert Fine. 1999. *People, Nation, and State: The Meaning of Ethnicity and Nationalism*. New York: St. Martin's.

Mueller, John. 2004. *The Remnants of War*. Ithaca, NY: Cornell University Press.

Muldoon, James P., Jr. 2003. *The Architecture of Global Governance*. Boulder, CO: Westview.

Murphy, John. 2004. *The United States and the Rule of Law in International Affairs*. New York: Cambridge University Press.

Nabulsi, Karma. 2004. "The Peace Process and the Palestinians: A Road Map to Mars." *International Affairs*, 80/2: 221–231.

Namkung, Gon. 1998. *Japanese Images of the United States and Other Nations: A Comparative Study of Public Opinion and Foreign Policy*. Doctoral dissertation. Storrs, CT: University of Connecticut.

Nathan, James A. 2002. *Soldiers, Statecraft, and History: Coercive Diplomacy and the International Order*. Westport, CT: Praeger.

Navaretti, Giorgio Barba and Anthony J. Venables. 2004. *Multinational Firms in the World Economy*. Princeton: Princeton University Press.

Neack, Laura. 1995. "UN Peace-Keeping: In the Interest of Community or Self?" *Journal of Peace Research*, 32: 181–196.

Nelsen, Brent F. and James L. Guth. 2003. "Roman Catholicism and the Founding of Europe: How Catholics Shaped the European Communities." Paper presented at the annual meeting of the American Political Science Association, Philadelphia, August 2003.

Nogee, Joseph L., and John Spanier. 1988. *Peace Impossible—War Unlikely: The Cold War between the United States and the Soviet Union*. Glenville, IL: Scott, Foresman.

Norris, Pippa and Ronald Inglehart. 2004. *Sacred and Secular: Religion and Politics Worldwide*. New York: Cambridge University Press.

Nye, Joseph. 2000. *Understanding International Conflicts*, 3rd ed. New York: Longman.

Nye, Joseph S., Jr. 2002. "Limits of American Power." *Political Science Quarterly*, 117:545–559.

Nye, Joseph S., Jr. 2004. *Soft Power: The Means to Success in World Politics*. New York: Public Affairs.

Nye, Joseph S., Jr. 2004a. "The Decline of America's Soft Power." *Foreign Affairs*, 83/3 (May/June 2004):16–21.

O'Leary, Brendan. 1997. "On the Nature of Nationalism: An Appraisal of Ernest Gellner's Writings on Nationalism." *British Journal of Political Science*, 27:191–222.

Oneal, John R., and Bruce M. Russett. 1997. "The Classical Liberals Were Right: Democracy, Interdependence, and Conflict, 1950–1985." *International Studies Quarterly*, 41:267–294.

O'Neill, Kate. 2004. "Transnational Protest: States, Circuses, and Conflict at the Frontline of Global Politics." *International Studies Review,* 6/2:233–249.

Opello, Walter C., Jr., and Stephen Rosow. 1999. *The Nation-State and Global Order: A Historical Introduction to Contemporary Politics.* Boulder, CO: Lynne Rienner.

Opello, Walter C., Jr. and Stephen J. Rosow. 2004. *The Nation-State and Global Order: A Historical Introduction to Contemporary Politics.* Boulder, CO: Lynne Rienner.

Orford, Anne. 2003. *Reading Humanitarian Intervention: Human Rights and the Use of Force in International Law.* Cambridge, U.K.: Cambridge University Press.

Orme, John. 1998. "The Utility of Force in a World of Scarcity." *International Security,* 22/3:138–167.

Owen, John M., IV. 2001. "Transnational Liberalism and U.S. Primacy." *International Security,* 26:117–153.

Owen, John M. 2004. "Democratic Peace Research: Whence and Whither?" *International Politics,* 41:605–617.

Paquette, Laura. 2003. *Analyzing National and International Policy: Theory, Method, and Case Studies.* Lanham, MD: Lexington Books.

Park, Bert Edward. 1994. *Ailing, Aging, Addicted: Studies of Compromised Leadership.* Lexington, KY: University Press of Kentucky.

Paterson, Thomas G. J., Garry Clifford, and Kenneth J. Hagen. 2000. *American Foreign Relations: A History, Vol. II: Since 1945,* 5th ed. Boston: Houghton Mifflin.

Patrick, Stewart, and Shepard Forman, eds. 2002. *Multilateralism and U.S. Foreign Policy: Ambivalent Engagement.* Boulder, CO: Lynne Rienner.

Patterson, Thomas E. 2005. *Young Voters and the 2004 Election.* Cambridge, MA: Joan Shorenstein Center on the Press, Politics, and Public Policy, John F. Kennedy School of Government, Harvard University.

Paul, T. V., G. John Ikenberry, and John A. Hall. 2004. *The Nation-State in Question.* Princeton, NJ: Princeton University Press.

Peterson, Peter G. 2001. "A Graying World: The Dangers of Global Aging." *Harvard International Review,* 23/3:1–4 (online).

Pevehouse, Jon C. 2004. "Interdependence Theory and the Measurement of International Conflict." *Journal of Politics,* 66/1:247–272.

Pew Research Center for the People and the Press. 2002. *Pew Global Attitudes Project 44-Nation Major Survey.* Washington, D.C.: Pew Research Center for the People and the Press.

Pew Research Center for the People and the Press. 2003. *Views of a Changing World, 2003.* Washington, DC: Pew Research Center for the People and the Press.

Phelps, Edward, 2004. "Young Citizens and Changing Electoral Turnout, 1964–2001." *Political Quarterly,* 75: 238–248.

Pickering, Jeffrey and Emizet F. Kisangani. 2005. "Democracy and Diversionary Military Intervention: Reassessing Regime Type and the Diversionary Hypothesis." *International Studies Quarterly,* 49/1:23–46.

Pierre, Andrew J., ed. 1997. *Cascade of Arms: Managing Conventional Weapons Proliferation.* Washington, DC: Brookings Institution.

Pilch, Frances. 2005. "Developing Human Rights Standards in United Nations Peacekeeping Operations." Paper presented at the annual meeting of the International Studies Association, Honolulu, March 2005.

Poole, Peter A., and Michael Baun. 2004. "Europe Unites: The EUs Eastern Enlargement." *Political Science Quarterly,* 119/2 368–369.

Porter, Bruce D. 1994. *War and the Rise of the State.* New York: Free Press.

Post, Jerrold M. 2004. *Leaders and Their Followers in a Dangerous World: The Psychology of Political Behavior.* Ithaca, NY: Cornell University Press.

Price, Richard M. and Mark W. Zacher, eds. 2004. *The United Nations and Global Security.* New York: Palgrave Macmillan.

Qvortrup, Mads. 2002. *A Comparative Study of Referendums: Government by the People.* Manchester, U.K.: Manchester University Press.

Rabkin, Jeremy. 1994. "Threats to U.S. Sovereignty." *Commentary,* 97(3):41–47.

Ralph, Jason. 2005. "International Society, the International Criminal Court, and American Foreign Policy." *Review of International Studies,* 31/1:27–44.

Ramet, Sabrina P. 2000. "The So-Called Right of National Self-Determination and Other Myths." *Human Rights Review,* 2:84–103.

Ratner, Steven R. 1998. "International Law: The Trials of Global Norms." *Foreign Policy,* 110:65–81.

Razavi, Shahra. 1999. "Seeing Poverty through a Gender Lens." *International Social Science Journal,* 51:473–483.

Reardon, Betty A. 1990. "Feminist Concepts of Peace and Security." In *A Reader in Peace Studies,* ed. Paul Smoker, Ruth Davies, and Barbara Munske. Oxford, U.K.: Pergamon Press.

Redd, Steven B. 2005. "The Influence of Advisers and Decision Strategies on Foreign Policy Choices: President Clinton's Decision to Use Force in Kosovo." *International Studies Perspectives* 6/1:129–144.

Reed, Thomas C. 2004. *At the Abyss: An Insider's History of the Cold War.* New York: Ballantine.

Reiter, Dan, and Allan C. Stam. 2002. *Democracies at War.* Princeton, NJ: Princeton University Press.

Reiter, Dan, and Erik R. Tillman. 2002. "Public, Legislative, and Executive Constraints on the Democratic Initiation of Conflict." *Journal of Politics,* 64:810–837.

Renan, Ernest. 1995. "Qu'est-ce Qu'une Nation?" In *Nationalism*, ed. John Hutchinson and Anthony D. Smith. New York: Oxford University Press.

Rengger, Nicholas. 2002. "On the Just War Tradition in the Twenty-First Century." *International Affairs*, 78:353–363.

Renshon, Stanley A. 1995. "Character, Judgment, and Political Leadership: Promise, Problems, and Prospects of the Clinton Presidency." In *The Clinton Presidency: Campaigning, Governing, and the Psychology of Leadership*, ed. Stanley Renshon. Boulder, CO: Westview.

Renshon, Stanley A., and Deborah Welch Larson, eds. 2002. *Good Judgment in Foreign Policy: Theory and Application*. Lanham, MD: Rowman & Littlefield.

Reynolds, Andrew. 1999. "Women in the Legislatures and Executives of the World: Knocking at the Highest Glass Ceiling." *World Politics*, 514:547–569.

Rhein, Wendy. 1998. "The Feminization of Poverty: Unemployment in Russia." *Journal of International Affairs*, 52:351–367.

Rhodes, Edward. 2003. "The Imperial Logic of Bush's Liberal Agenda." *Survival*, 45:131–154.

Ringquist, Evan J. and Tatiana Kostadinova. 2005. "Assessing the Effectiveness of International Environmental Agreements: The Case of the 1985 Helsinki Protocol." *American Journal of Political Science*, 49/1:86–114.

Rodin, David. 2005. *War and Self-Defense*. New York: Oxford University Press.

Romano, Cesare P. R., André Nollkaemper, and Jann K. Kleffner. 2005. *Internationalized Criminal Courts: Sierra Leone, East Timor, Kosovo, and Cambodia*. Oxford, U.K.: Oxford University Press.

Rosen, Stephen Peter. 2004. *War and Human Nature*. Princeton: Princeton University Press.

Rosenau, James N. 1998. "The Dynamism of a Turbulent World." In *World Security: Challenges for a New Century*, 3rd ed., ed. Michael T. Klare and Yogesh Chandran. New York: St. Martin's.

Rossiter, Clinton. 1960. *The American Presidency*, 2nd ed. New York: Harcourt Brace Jovanovich.

Rostow, Walt W. 1978. *The World Economy*. Austin: University of Texas Press.

Rothgeb, John M., Jr. 1993. *Defining Power: Influence and Force in the Contemporary International System*. New York: St. Martin's.

Rothkopf, David J. 1998. "Cyberpolitik: The Changing Nature of Power in the Information Age." *Journal of International Affairs*. 51:325–360.

Rourke, John T. 1983. *Congress and the Presidency in U.S. Foreign Policy Making: A Study of Interaction and Influence, 1945–1982*. Boulder, CO: Westview.

Rourke, John T. 1993. *Presidential Wars and American Democracy: Rally 'Round the Chief*. New York: Paragon.

Rourke, John T., Richard P. Hiskes, and Cyrus Ernesto Zirakzadeh. 1992. *Direct Democracy and International Politics*. Boulder, CO: Lynne Rienner.

Ruggie, John Gerard. 1998. "What Makes the World Hang Together? Neo-Utilitarianism and the Social Constructivist Challenge." *International Organization*, 52: 855–885.

Rummel, R. J. 1995. "Democracy, Power, Genocide, and Mass Murder." *Journal of Conflict Resolution*, 39:3–26.

Rusk, Dean, as told to Richard Rusk. 1990. *As I Saw It*. New York: W. W. Norton.

Russett, Bruce. 2000. "How Democracy, Interdependence, and International Organizations Create a System for Peace." In *The Global Agenda: Issues and Perspectives*, ed. Charles W. Kegley, Jr., and Eugene R. Wittkopf. Boston: McGraw-Hill.

Ryan, Stephen. 2000. *The United Nations and International Politics*. New York: St. Martin's.

Saideman, Stephen M. 2001. *The Ties that Divide: Ethnic Politics, Foreign Policy, and International Conflict*. New York: Columbia University Press.

Saunders, Robert M. 1994. "History, Health and Herons: The Historiography of Woodrow Wilson's Personality and Decision-Making." *Presidential Studies Quarterly*, 24: 57–77.

Sayer, Andrew. 2000. *Realism and Social Science*. Thousand Oaks, CA: Sage

Schafer, Mark, and Scott Crichlow. 2002. "The Process-Outcome Connection in Foreign Policy Decision Making: A Quantitative Study Building on Groupthink." *International Studies Quarterly*, 46:45–68.

Schell, Jonathan. 2003. *The Unconquerable World: Power, Nonviolence, and the Will of the People*. New York: Metropolitan Books.

Schmidt, Brian C. 1997. *The Political Discourse of Anarchy*. Albany: State University of New York Press.

Schmidt, Brian C. 2004. "Realism as Tragedy." *Review of International Studies*, 30:427–441.

Schmitz, Hans Peter. 2004. "Domestic and Transnational Perspectives on Democratization." *International Studies Review*, 6/3:403–421.

Schneider, Gerald, Katherine Barbieri, and Nils Petter Gleditsch, eds. 2003. *Globalization and Armed Conflict*. Lanham, MD: Rowman & Littlefield.

Schultz, Kathryn R., and David Isenberg. 1997. "Arms Control and Disarmament." In *A Global Agenda: Issues before the 52nd General Assembly of the United Nations*, ed. John Tessitore and Susan Woolfson. Lanham, MD: Rowman & Littlefield.

Schultze, Charles L. 2004. *Offshoring, Import Competition, and the Jobless Recovery*. Policy Brief 136. Washington, D.C.: Brookings Institution.

Schulzinger, Robert D. 1989. *Henry Kissinger: Doctor of Diplomacy*. New York: Columbia University Press.

Schweller, Randall L. 2004. "Unanswered Threats: A Neoclassical Realist Theory of Underbalancing." *International Security*, 29/2:159–201.

Scott, James M., and Ralph G. Carter. 2002. "Acting on the Hill: Congressional Assertiveness in U.S. Foreign Policy." *Congress & the Presidency,* 29:151–170.

Scully, Roger, and David M. Farrell. 2003. "MEPs as Representatives: Individual and Institutional Roles." *Journal of Common Market Studies,* 41:269–288.

Seligson, Mitchell A. and John T. Passé-Smith, eds. 2003. *Development and Underdevelopment: The Political Economy of Global Inequality.* Boulder, CO: Lynne Rienner.

Sen, Amartya. 1999. *Development as Freedom.* New York: Alfred A. Knopf.

Setala, Maija. 1999. *Referendums and Democratic Government.* New York: St. Martin's.

Seymour, Michel. 2000 "Quebec and Canada at the Crossroads: A Nation within a Nation." *Nations and Nationalism,* 6:227–256.

Shaheed, Farida. 1999. "Constructing Identities: Culture, Women's Agency and the Muslim World." *International Social Science Journal,* 51:61–75.

Shambaugh, George E. 2000. *States, Firms, and Power: Successful Sanctions in United States Foreign Policy.* Albany, NY: State University of New York Press.

Shambaugh, George E. 2004. "The Power of Money: Global Capital and Policy Choices in Developing Countries." *American Journal of Political Science,* 48/2:281–311.

Sharp, Paul. 1999. "For Diplomacy: Representation and the Study of International Relations." *International Studies Review,* 1:33–58.

Sharp, Paul. 2001. "Making Sense of Citizen Diplomats: The People of Duluth, Minnesota, as International Actors." *International Studies Perspective,* 2:131–150.

Sherman, Dennis, and Joyce Salisbury. 2004. *The West in the World,* 2nd ed. Boston: McGraw-Hill.

Shinko, Rosemary. 2004 (forthcoming). "Postmodernism: A Genealogy of Humanitarian Intervention." In *Making Sense of IR Theory,* ed. Jennifer Sterling-Folker. Boulder, CO: Lynne Rienner.

Silverman, Adam L. 2002. "Just War, Jihad, and Terrorism: A Comparison of Western and Islamic Norms for the Use of Political Violence." *Journal of Church and State,* 44: 73–92.

Simon, Craig. 1998. "Internet Governance Goes Global." In *International Relations in a Constructed World,* eds. Vendulka Kubalkova, Nicholas Onuf, and Paul Kowert. Armonk, NY: M. E. Sharpe.

Simon, Julian L. 1994. "More People, Greater Wealth, More Resources, Healthier Environment." In *Taking Sides: Clashing Views on Controversial Issues in World Politics,* 6th ed., ed. John T. Rourke. Guilford, CT: Dushkin.

Sinclair, Andrew. 2004. *An Anatomy of Terror: A History of Terrorism.* New York: Palgrave Macmillan.

Singh, Sonali and Christopher R. Way. 2004. "The Correlates of Nuclear Proliferation: A Quantitative Test." *Journal of Conflict Resolution,* 48/6:859–885.

(SIPRI) Stockholm International Peace Research Institute. Annual Editions. *SIPRI Yearbook.* Oxford, U.K.: Oxford University Press.

Slantchev, Branislav. L. 2003. "The Power to Hurt: Costly Conflict with Completely Informed States." *American Political Science Review,* 97:123–133.

Slaughter, Anne-Marie. 2003. "The Global Community of Courts." *Harvard International Law Journal,* 44:217–219.

Smith, Anthony D. 2004. *Chosen Peoples: Sacred Sources of National Identity.* Oxford, U.K.: Oxford University Press.

Smith, Anthony D. 2005. *The Antiquity of Nations.* Cambridge, U.K.: Polity.

Smith, Tom W. and Lars Jarkko. 1998. "National Pride: A Cross-National Analysis." CGS Cross-National Report No. 19. National Opinion Research, University of Chicago.

Snyder, Jack. 2002. "Myths of Empire, Then and Now." Morton-Kenney Public Affairs Lecture Series. Department of Political Science, Southern Illinois University, Carbondale, IL.

Sobel, Richard. 2001. *The Impact of Public Opinion on U.S. Foreign Policy Since Vietnam—Constraining the Colossus.* Oxford, U.K.: Oxford University Press.

Sørensen, Georg. 1999. "Sovereignty: Change and Continuity in a Fundamental Institution." *Political Studies,* 47: 590–609.

Sørensen, Georg. 2001. *Changes in Statehood: The Transformation of International Relations.* London: Palgrave.

Sørensen, Georg. 2004. *The Transformation of the State: Beyond the Myth of Retreat.* New York: Palgrave Macmillan.

Spegele, Roger D. 1996. *Political Realism in International Theory.* Cambridge, U.K.: Cambridge University Press.

Spruyt, Hendrik. 1994. *The Sovereign State and Its Competitors: An Analysis of Systems Change.* Princeton, NJ: Princeton University Press.

Stansfield, Gareth. 2005. "The Kurds: Nation without a State." Paper presented at the annual meeting of the International Studies Association, Honolulu.

Starkey, Brigid, Mark A. Boyer, and Jonathan Wilkenfeld. 2005. *Negotiating a Complex World: An Introduction to International Negotiation,* 2nd ed. Lanham, MD: Rowman & Littlefield.

Steger, Manfred B., ed. 2003. *Rethinking Globalism.* Lanham, MD: Rowman & Littlefield.

Steinbruner, John. 2003. "Confusing Ends and Means: The Doctrine of Coercive Pre-emption." *Arms Control Today,* 33/1 (January/February). On the Web at http://www.armscontrol.org/.

Steiner, Barry H. 2004. "Diplomacy and International Theory." *Review of International Studies,* 30:493–509.

Sterling-Folker, Jennifer. 1997. "Realist Environment, Liberal Process, and Domestic-Level Variables." *International Studies Quarterly,* 41:1–26.

Sterling-Folker, Jennifer. 2002. *Theories of International Cooperation and the Primacy of Anarchy: Explaining U.S.*

International Monetary Policy-Making after Bretton Woods. Albany: State University of New York Press.

Stoessinger, John G. 1998. *Why Nations Go to War,* 7th ed. New York: St. Martin's.

Sutterlin, James. 2003. *The United Nations and the Maintenance of International Security,* 2nd ed. Westport, CT: Praeger.

Sylvester, Caroline. 1994. "A Review of J. Ann Tickner's *Gender in International Relations.*" *American Political Science Review,* 87:823–824.

Tabb, William K. 2004. *Economic Governance in the Age of Globalization.* New York: Columbia University Press.

Taber, Charles S. 1989. "Power Capability Indexes in the Third World." In *Power in World Politics,* ed. Richard J. Stoll and Michael D. Ward. Boulder, CO: Lynne Rienner.

Talbott, Strobe. 2000. "Self-Determination in an Interdependent World." *Foreign Policy,* 118 (Spring 2000):152–163.

Tamir, Yael. 1995. "The Enigma of Nationalism." *World Politics,* 47:418–440.

Tammen, Ronald L., et al. 2002. *Power Transitions: Strategies for the Twenty-First Century.* New York: Chatham House/Seven Bridges Press.

Taras, Ray, and Rajat Ganguly. 1998. *Understanding Ethnic Conflict: The International Dimension.* New York: Longman.

Tarzi, Shah M. 2005. "Coercive Diplomacy and an 'Irrational' Regime: Understanding the American Confrontation with the Taliban." *International Studies,* 42/1:21–41.

Tehranian, Majid. 1999. *Global Communication and World Politics: Domination, Development, and Discourse.* Boulder, CO: Lynne Rienner.

Telhami, Shibley and Michael Barnett, eds. 2002. *Identity and Foreign Policy in the Middle East.* Ithaca, NY: Cornell University Press.

Tessman, Brock F. and Steve Chan. 2004. "Power Cycles, Risk Propensity, and Great-Power Deterrence." *Journal of Conflict Resolution,* 48/2:131–153.

Thies, Wallace J. 1998. "Deliberate and Inadvertent War in the Post–Cold War World." In *Annual Editions, American Foreign Policy 98/99,* ed. Glenn P. Hastedt. Guilford, CT: Dushkin/McGraw-Hill.

Thompson, Kenneth W. 1995. *Fathers of International Thought: The Legacy of Political Theory.* Baton Rouge: Louisiana State University Press.

Thompson, William R., and Richard Tucker. 1997. "A Tale of Two Democratic Peace Critiques." *Journal of Conflict Resolution,* 41:428–454.

Tickner, J. Ann. 2005. "What Is Your Research Program? Some Feminist Answers to International Relations Methodological Questions." *International Studies Quarterly,* 49/1:1–14.

Tomuschat, Christian. 2004. *Human Rights: Between Idealism and Realism.* Oxford, U.K.: Oxford University Press.

Travis, Rick, and Nikolaos Zahariadis. 2002. "A Multiple Stream Model of U.S. Foreign Aid Policy." *Policy Studies Journal,* 30:495–514.

Trumbore, Peter F. 1998. "Public Opinion as a Domestic Constraint in International Negotiations: Two-Level Games in the Anglo-Irish Peace Process." *International Studies Quarterly,* 42:545–565.

Trumbore, Peter F. 2003. "Victims or Aggressors? Ethno-Political Rebellion and Use of Force in Militarized Interstate Disputes." *International Studies Quarterly,* 47:183–201.

Tsang, Steve, ed. 2004. *Peace and Security across the Taiwan Strait.* New York: Palgrave Macmillan.

Tsygankov, Andrei P. 2003. "The Irony of Western Ideas in a Multicultural World: Russia's Intellectual Engagement with the 'End of History' and 'Clash of Civilizations.'" *International Studies Review,* 5:53–76.

Tucker, Jonathan B. 2000. *Toxic Terror: Assessing Terrorist Use of Chemical and Biological Weapons.* Cambridge, MA: MIT Press.

Tucker, Nancy Bernkopf, ed. 2005. *Dangerous Strait: The U.S.-Taiwan-China Crisis.* New York: Columbia University Press.

Turner, Frederick C., and Alejandro L. Corbacho. 2000. "New Roles for the State." *International Social Science Journal,* 163:109–120.

UN, Department of Economic and Social Affairs, Population Division. 2004. At http://www.undp.org/.

(UNDP) United Nations Development Programme. Annual editions. *Human Development Report.* New York: Oxford University Press.

(UN, UNICEF) United Nations Children's Fund. Annual editions. *State of the World's Children.* New York: Oxford University Press.

United Nations. *See* (UN).

(U.S.) Bureau of the Census. Annual editions. *Statistical Abstract of the United States.* Washington, DC.

U.S. (CIA) Central Intelligence Agency. Annual editions. *World FactBook.* Washington, DC: GPO.

Vandenbroucke, Lucien. 1991. *Perilous Options: Special Operations in U.S. Foreign Policy.* Unpublished dissertation, University of Connecticut. A manuscript based on Vandenbroucke's revised dissertation was published in 1993 under the same title by Oxford University Press.

Vasquez, John A., ed. 1986. *Classics of International Relations.* Englewood Cliffs, NJ: Prentice Hall.

Vasquez, John, and Marie T. Henehan. 2001. "Territorial Disputes and the Probability of War, 1816–1992." *Journal of Peace Research* 38/2:123–138.

Vertzberger, Yaakov Y. I. 1994. "Collective Risk Taking: The Decisionmaking Group and Organization." Presented at the annual meeting of the International Studies Association, Washington, DC.

Vlahos, Michael. 1998. "Entering the Infosphere." *Journal of International Affairs,* 51:497–526.

Voeten, Erik. 2000. "Clashes in the Assembly." *International Organization,* 54:185–216.

Voeten, Erik. 2004. "Resisting the Lonely Superpower: Responses of States in the UN to U.S. Dominance." *The Journal of Politics,* 66: 729–754.

Walker, Stephen G., Mark Schafer, and Michael D. Young. 1998. "Systematic Procedures for Operational Code Analysis: Measuring and Modeling Jimmy Carter's Operational Code." *International Studies Quarterly,* 42: 175–189.

Walt, Stephen M. 1996. "Alliances: Balancing and Bandwagoning." In *International Politics,* 4th ed., ed. Robert J. Art and Robert Jervis. New York: HarperCollins.

Walzer, Michael. 2004. *Arguing about War.* New Haven, CT: Yale University Press.

Wang, Kevin H., and James Lee Ray. 1994. "Beginnings and Winners: The Fate of Initiators of Interstate Wars Involving Great Powers since 1495." *International Studies Quarterly,* 38:139–154.

Watkins, Kevin. 2002. "Making Globalization Work for the Poor." *Finance & Development,* 39/1. Web edition at http://www.imf.org/external/pubind.htm.

Watson, James L. 2000. "China's Big Mac Attack." *Foreign Affairs,* 79/3:120–142.

Wead, Douglas. 2003. *All the President's Children: Triumph and Tragedy in the Lives of America's First Families.* New York: Atria.

Weisband, Edward. 2000. "Discursive Multilateralism: Global Benchmarks, Shame, and Learning in the ILO Labor Standards Monitoring Regime." *International Studies Quarterly,* 44:643–666.

Weiss, Linda. 1998. *The Myth of the Powerless State.* Ithaca, NY: Cornell University Press.

Welsh, Jennifer M., ed. 2004. *Humanitarian Intervention and International Relations.* Oxford, U.K.: Oxford University Press.

Wendt, Alexander. 2004. "The State as Person in International Theory." *Review of International Studies,* 30: 289–316.

Wiebe, Robert H. 2002. *Who We Are: A History of Popular Nationalism.* Princeton, NJ: Princeton University Press.

Wilkinson, David. 2004. Analytical and Empirical Issues in the Study of Power-Polarity Configuration Sequences." Paper presented at a Conference of a Working Group on Analyzing Complex Macrosystems as Dynamic Networks, Santa Fe Institute, Santa Fe.

Williams, Michael C. 2004. "Why Ideas Matter in International Relations: Hans Morgenthau, Classical Realism, and the Moral Construction of Power Politics." *International Organization,* 58/4:633–665.

Williams, Michael C. 2005. *The Realist Tradition and the Limits of International Relations.* New York: Cambridge University Press.

Williams, Jr., Rob M. 2003. *The Wars Within: People and States in Conflict.* Ithaca, NY: Cornell University Press.

Wimmer, Andreas. 2002. *Nationalist Exclusion and Ethnic Conflict.* Cambridge, U.K.: Cambridge University Press.

Witko, Christopher. 2003. "Cold War Belligerence and U.S. Public Opinion toward Defense Spending." *American Politics Research,* 31:379–392.

Wohlforth, William C. 1999. "The Stability of a Unipolar World." *International Security,* 24/1:5–41.

Woodwell, Douglas. 2004. "Unwelcome Neighbors: Shared Ethnicity and International Conflict during the Cold War." *International Studies Quarterly,* 48/1:197–216.

World Almanac and Book of Facts. Annual editions. New York: Funk & Wagnalls.

World Bank. 2004. *World Development Indicators 2004.* Washington, DC: World Bank.

World Bank. Annual editions. *World Development Report.* New York: Oxford University Press.

World Resources Institute. Annual editions. *World Resources.* New York: Oxford University Press.

Zakaria, Fareed. 1993. "Is Realism Finished?" *National Interest,* 32:21–32.

Zakaria, Fareed. 1996. "Speak Softly, Carry a Veiled Threat." *New York Times Magazine,* February 18.

Zehfuss, Maja. 2002. *Constructivism in International Relations: The Politics of Reality.* New York: Cambridge University Press.

Zunes, Stephen. 2004. "U.S. Christian Right's Grip on Middle East Policy." *Foreign Policy in Focus,* Internet edition, June 28, 2004.

Zunes, Stephen. 2005. "The Two Faces of American Policy as a Generator of Anti-American Attitudes in the Middle East and North Africa." Paper presented at the annual convention of the International Studies Association, Honolulu.

Index

Photo Credits

U.S.

CANADA

NORTH
PACIFIC
OCEAN

UNITED STATES

NORTH
ATLANTIC
OCEAN

Tropic of Cancer

U.S.

MEXICO

GUYANA
SURINA
FF
G
(F

COLOMBIA

Equator

ECUADOR   VENEZUELA

PERU

BRAZ

WESTERN
SAMOA

TONGA

BOLIVIA

PARAGUAY

Tropic of Capricorn

CHILE

ARGENTINA

U
U

SOUTH
PACIFIC
OCEAN

Antarctic Circle

THE
BAHAMAS

0   300 Miles

0   300 Kilometers

U.S.

CUBA

MEXICO

DOMINICAN
REPUBLIC
PUERTO RICO

JAMAICA   HAITI

BELIZE

ST. KITTS AND NEVIS
ANTIGUA AND BARBUDA
DOMINICA

GUATEMALA   HONDURAS

CARIBBEAN
SEA

MARTINIQUE

ST. LUCIA

EL
SALVADOR   NICARAGUA

ST. VINCENT AND THE GRENADINES

BARBADOS
GRENADA

COSTA RICA

PANAMA

COLOMBIA

TRINIDAD AND TOBAGO

VENEZUELA

Scale: 1 to 125,000,000

0   1000   2000 M

0   1000   2000   3000 Kilo